Ius Comparatum – Global Studies in Comparative Law

Volume 26

More information about this series at http://www.springer.com/series/11943

Académie Internationale de Droit Comparé
International Academy of Comparative Law

Yuko Nishitani
Editor

Treatment of Foreign Law - Dynamics towards Convergence?

Springer

Editor
Yuko Nishitani
Graduate School of Law
Kyoto University
Kyoto, Japan

ISSN 2214-6881 ISSN 2214-689X (electronic)
Ius Comparatum – Global Studies in Comparative Law
ISBN 978-3-319-56572-9 ISBN 978-3-319-56574-3 (eBook)
DOI 10.1007/978-3-319-56574-3

Library of Congress Control Number: 2017943337

Printed on acid-free paper

This Springer imprint is published by Springer Nature
The registered company is Springer International Publishing AG
The registered company address is: Gewerbestrasse 11, 6330 Cham, Switzerland

Preface

The treatment of foreign law is a crucial issue for the functioning of private international law. If the relevant conflicts rule or the applicable foreign law is not applied in court proceedings, the designation of foreign law as the law governing the international legal relationship remains superfluous and purely theoretical. Thus, in cross-border cases, we primarily need to examine whether the application of conflicts rules of the forum state is mandatory or facultative and whether and how far judges are obliged to apply and ascertain foreign law ex officio or the extent to which parties are held to plead and prove foreign law. Further, we ought to consider and develop effective means of obtaining information on foreign law, subject to the limitations of the civil procedure rules of the forum state.

The methods of applying and ascertaining foreign law differ among jurisdictions. Conflicts lawyers used to separate two distinctive features: Civil law jurisdictions characterize foreign law as "law" and provide for the ex officio application and ascertainment of foreign law by the judge. Common law jurisdictions consider foreign law as "fact" and request that parties plead and prove foreign law. Nowadays, however, the "law-fact" dichotomy no longer seems to duly reflect reality.

A closer look reveals more differentiated features with their own nuances even among civil law jurisdictions. Some civil law countries restrict the mandatory application of conflicts rules to a certain category of rights or issues. Due to the judges' limited resources and expertise on foreign law, parties may be asked to provide assistance in ascertaining foreign law. Some civil law countries even place the onus of proving foreign law upon the party. Unlike domestic law, the judicial review of foreign law may be excluded or subject to particular restrictions. In common law jurisdictions, on the other hand, the judge may exceptionally be obliged or entitled to take judicial notice of foreign law in certain cases. Unlike usual facts, the absence of evidence on foreign law does not result in the dismissal of the claim, but generally leads to the application of the lex fori. The court's previous findings on the point of foreign law can also be referred to in subsequent cases as evidence of that foreign law, and the application of foreign law is appealable. Thus, foreign law may better be classified as a "question of fact of a peculiar kind" or "tertium genus" in common law jurisdictions. As a consequence, the difference between the conventional civil law approach and the common law approach is not as large as it appears at the outset.

The underlying volume examines different and multifaceted characteristics of applying and ascertaining foreign law and the methods of accessing foreign law in various jurisdictions. While extensive research already exists on these issues, this book is unique in comparatively scrutinizing the treatment of foreign law in different countries and regions worldwide, which extend from Europe over North and South America to the Asia-Pacific Area and Africa. Furthermore, this volume explores existing mechanisms and the possibility of establishing a new scheme for obtaining information on foreign law, in particular through administrative and judicial cooperation. It remains to be seen whether and how far legal systems around the world will integrate and converge in their treatment of foreign law.

This volume includes one general report and 29 national reports. The Hague Conference on Private International Law also provided a report on the state and progress of its envisaged project on the treatment of foreign law. The general report, as well as most of the individual reports, was prepared for the Vienna Conference of the International Academy of Comparative Law in the summer of 2014 and subsequently updated in the autumn of 2016. Spanish and Tunisian reports were submitted for publication. The questionnaire prepared for national reports is included at the end of this volume.

It is a great pleasure and honor that so many experts in private international law and civil procedure law from various jurisdictions have contributed to this volume. Special thanks go to Prof. Katharina Boele-Woelki, Prof. Diego P. Fernández Arroyo, Prof. George A. Bermann and Prof. Jürgen Basedow, the present and former President and Secretary General of the International Academy of Comparative Law, for their kind support and recommendations and also for including this volume in the honorable *Ius Comparatum* series. The editor would also like to sincerely thank Prof. Béligh Elbalti for his assistance in the editing work. Last but not least, the editor expresses her gratitude to Mr. Neil Olivier and Ms. Diana Nijnhuijzen at Springer for their patience and warm encouragement in completing this volume.

Kyoto, Japan
June 2017

Yuko Nishitani

Contents

Part I General Report

Treatment of Foreign Law: Dynamics Towards Convergence? — General Report ... 3
Yuko Nishitani

Part II National Reports I – Europe

Belgium: Foreign Law in Belgian Courts – From Theory to Practice ... 63
Patrick Wautelet

Croatia: Foreign Law Before Croatian Authorities – At the Crossroads? ... 93
Mirela Župan

Czech Republic – Treatment of Foreign Law in the Czech Republic ... 113
Monika Pauknerová

Denmark: Foreign Law in Danish Civil Litigation: A Pragmatic Approach ... 131
Clement Salung Petersen

Estonia: Applying Foreign Law in Estonia – The Perspective of an e-State ... 145
Maarja Torga

France – The Evolving Balance Between the Judge and the Parties in France ... 157
Sabine Corneloup

Germany: Proof of and Information About Foreign Law – Duty to Investigate, Expert Opinions and a Proposal for Europe ... 183
Oliver Remien

Greece: Foreign Law in the Greek Private International Law: Positive Solutions and Future Perspectives ... 221
Chryssapho Tsouca

Hungary: Inconsistencies Between Theory and Practice in the Treatment of Foreign Law in Hungary ... 239
László Burián and Sarolta Szabó

Italy: Proof and Information about Foreign Law in Italy ... 255
Nerina Boschiero and Benedetta Ubertazzi

Poland: Proof and Information About Foreign Law – Theory and Reality ... 289
Michal Wojewoda

Portugal: Proof of and Information About Foreign Law in Portugal ... 309
Rui Manuel Moura Ramos

Romania: Proof of and Information About Foreign Law in Romania ... 323
Flavius George Păncescu

Spain: The Application of Foreign Laws in Spain – Critical Analysis of the Legal Novelties of 2015 ... 329
Carmen Azcárraga Monzonís

Sweden: Proof of and Information About Foreign Law in Civil and Commercial Matters – Swedish Perspectives ... 347
Ulf Maunsbach

United Kingdom: The Traditional Approach to Foreign Law in Civil Litigation in the Legal Systems of the United Kingdom ... 361
Verónica Ruiz Abou-Nigm

Switzerland: The Principle *Iura Aliena Novit Curia* and the Role of Foreign Law Advisory Services in Swiss Judicial Practice ... 375
Ilaria Pretelli and Shaheeza Lalani

Part III National Reports II – North and South America

The United States: The Use and Determination of Foreign Law in Civil Litigation in the United States ... 397
Peter Hay

Canada: The Status and the Proof of Foreign Law in Québec ... 429
Gérald Goldstein

Argentina: The Changing Character of Foreign Law in Argentinian Legal System ... 453
Diego P. Fernández Arroyo and Paula María All

Uruguay: Proof of and Information About Foreign Law in Uruguay 473
Cecilia Fresnedo de Aguirre

Venezuela: Finding Foreign Law in Venezuela. General Overview 487
Eugenio Hernández-Bretón and Claudia Madrid Martínez

Part IV National Reports III – Asia-Pacific Region and Africa

Australia: Foreign Law in Australian International Litigation: Developing the Common Law 503
Mary Keyes

Japan: Proof of and Information About Foreign Law in Japan 529
Shunichiro Nakano

Macau: Proof and Information About Foreign Law in Macau 541
Guangjian Tu

Turkey: The Treatment of Foreign Law in Turkey 549
Zeynep Derya Tarman

Israel: Proof of and Information About Foreign Law in Israel 563
Talia Einhorn

Tunisia: Treatment of Foreign Law in Tunisia 583
Lotfi Chedly and Béligh Elbalti

Commonwealth Africa: Foreign Law in Commonwealth African Courts 601
Richard Frimpong Oppong

Part V Hague Conference on Private International Law

The Evolution of Work on Access to Foreign Law at the Hague Conference on Private International Law 615
Philippe Lortie and Maja Groff

Questionnaire on Proof of and Information About Foreign Law 639

Contributors

Veronica Ruiz Abou-Nigm Senior Lecturer in International Private Law, Edinburgh Law School, University of Edinburgh, Edinburgh, UK

Paula María All Professor, Faculty of Law and Social Sciences, National University of Littoral, Santa Fe, Argentina

Carmen Azcárraga Monzonís Assistant Professor, Faculty of Law, University of Valencia, Valencia, Spain

Nerina Boschiero Professor, School of Law, University of Milan, Milan, Italy

László Burián Professor, Faculty of Law and Political Sciences, Pázmány Péter Catholic University, Budapest, Hungary

Lotfi Chedly Professor, Faculty of Legal, Political and Social Sciences, The University of Carthage, Tunis, Tunisia

Sabine Corneloup Professor, University of Paris II (Panthéon-Assas), Paris, France

Talia Einhorn Professor, Department of Economics and Business Administration, Ariel University, Ariel, Israel

Visiting Senior Research Fellow, Faculty of Management, Tel-Aviv University, Ramat-Aviv, Tel-Aviv, Israel

Béligh Elbalti Associate Professor, Graduate School of Law and Politics, Osaka University, Osaka, Japan

Diego P. Fernández Arroyo Professor, Sciences Po Law School, Paris, France

Cecilia Fresnedo de Aguirre Professor, University of the Republic, Montevideo, Uruguay

Gérald Goldstein Professor, Faculté de Droit, Université de Montréal, Pavillon Maximilien-Caron, Montréal, QC, Canada

Maja Groff Senior Legal Officer, Permanent Bureau of the Hague Conference on Private International Law, The Hague, The Netherlands

Peter Hay Professor, Emory University School of Law, Atlanta, GA, USA

Eugenio Hernández-Bretón Professor, School of Law, University of Monteávila, Caracas, Venezuela

Mary Keyes Professor, Griffith Law School at Griffith University, Nathan, QLD, Australia

Shaheeza Lalani Senior Researcher, University of Paris 1 – Panthéon-Sorbonne, Paris, France

Philippe Lortie First Secretary, Permanent Bureau of the Hague Conference on Private International Law, The Hague, The Netherlands

Claudia Madrid Martínez Professor, School of Law, Central University of Venezuela, Caracas, Venezuela

Andrés Bello Catholic University, Caracas, Venezuela

Ulf Maunsbach Associate Professor, Faculty of Law, University of Lund, Lund, Sweden

Rui Manuel Moura Ramos Professor, Faculty of Law, University of Coimbra, Coimbra, Portugal

Shunichiro Nakano Professor, Graduate School of Law, Kobe University, Kobe, Japan

Yuko Nishitani Professor, Graduate School of Law, Kyoto University, Kyoto, Japan

Richard Frimpong Oppong Associate Professor, Faculty of Law, Thompson Rivers University, Kamloops, BC, Canada

Flavius George Păncescu Dr. Romanian Ministry of Justice, Bucureşti, Romania

Romanian Academy, Bucureşti, Romania

Monika Pauknerová Professor, Institute of State and Law, Academy of Sciences of the Czech Republic, Prague, Czech Republic

Clement Salung Petersen Associate Professor, Faculty of Law, University of Copenhagen, Copenhagen, Denmark

Ilaria Pretelli Legal Adviser, Swiss Institute of Comparative Law, Lausanne, Switzerland

Oliver Remien Professor, Faculty of Law, Julius-Maximilians-University of Würzburg, Würzburg, Germany

Sarolta Szabó Associate Professor, Faculty of Law and Political Sciences, Pázmány Péter Catholic University, Budapest, Hungary

Zeynep Derya Tarman Associate Professor, Department of Private International Law, Koc University Law School, Sariyer/Istanbul, Turkey

Maarja Torga Lecturer, University of Tartu, Tartu, Estonia

Chryssapho Tsouca Associate Professor, Law School, National and Kapodistrian University of Athens, Athens, Greece

Guangjian Tu Professor, Faculty of Law (FLL), University of Macau, Taipa, Macau, China

Benedetta Ubertazzi Full Tenured Aggregate Professor, University of Milan-Bicocca, Milan, Italy

Patrick Wautelet Professor, School of Law, University of Liège, Liège, Belgium

Michal Wojewoda Associate Professor, Faculty of Law and Administration University of Lodz, Lodz, Poland

Mirela Župan Associate Professor, Faculty of Law, Josip Juraj Strossmayer University of Osijek, Osijek, Croatia

Part I
General Report

Treatment of Foreign Law: Dynamics Towards Convergence? — General Report

Yuko Nishitani

Abstract This general report conducts a comparative study mainly on the following three points. First, the report examines comparatively the question of whether the application of conflict of laws is mandatory or facultative. Second, the report analyses the nature of foreign law and distinctive features of its treatment, particularly in relation to the mandatory and the facultative application of foreign law, the ascertainment of foreign law and the review of foreign law by appeal courts. Although the starting point on how to treat foreign law differs in civil law and common law jurisdictions, the practical outcome is more similar than would appear at first, even though unification of the treatment of foreign law is still a long way off. Third, the report critically scrutinizes the existing methods for obtaining information on foreign law in the light of administrative and judicial cooperation and analyses possibilities for improving access to foreign law.

Abbreviations

CC	Civil Code
CJEU	Court of Justice of the European Union
CPC	Civil Procedure Code
EC	European Community
EU	European Union
HCCH	Hague Conference on Private International Law
PIL	Private International Law
TEC	Treaty establishing the European Community ([consolidated version 2006] *O.J.* 29.12.2006, C 321E/37)
TFEU	Treaty on the Functioning of the European Union ([consolidated version 2016] *O.J.* 7.6.2016, C 202/47)

Y. Nishitani (✉)
Professor, Graduate School of Law, Kyoto University, Yoshida-Honmachi, Sakyoku, Kyoto 606-8501, Japan
e-mail: nishitani@law.kyoto-u.ac.jp

Y. Nishitani (ed.), *Treatment of Foreign Law - Dynamics towards Convergence?*,
Ius Comparatum – Global Studies in Comparative Law 26,
DOI 10.1007/978-3-319-56574-3_1

I. Introduction

Globalization is intensifying cross-border movements of people, goods, services and information. This results in more international legal relationships—not only for large enterprises in business transactions but also for individuals in everyday life such as through consumer contracts, family relations and succession planning. Private international law (conflict of laws or choice of law) assumes an important role in determining the applicable law and regulating international legal relationships. Once a cross-border case is governed by foreign law, it is crucial to know whether and to what extent conflicts rules are applied ex officio, and how foreign law is ascertained and applied.

Foreign law is obviously distinct from domestic law. This is because it emanates from a foreign sovereign with its own prescriptive and judicial jurisdiction. Judges do not have the power to modify the content of foreign law; they can only accept or refuse its application. Moreover, while judges are obliged to conduct court proceedings and render a judgment pursuant to domestic law, they do not necessarily afford the same status to foreign law.[1] In fact, although most civil law jurisdictions provide for the ex officio application of foreign law by judges, the ascertainment and review of foreign law may be subject to certain restrictions, which do not apply to domestic law. Common law jurisdictions even require the parties to plead or invoke and prove the content of foreign law. Furthermore, a crucial issue arises as to how to obtain information on foreign law, since access to foreign law is generally limited not only for courts but also for parties, lawyers, notaries, arbitrators and other stakeholders.

This general report conducts a comparative study mainly on the following three points. First, the report analyses the treatment of conflict of laws in court proceedings in various jurisdictions. This concerns the question of whether the application of conflict of laws is mandatory or facultative. Second, the report analyses the nature of foreign law and examines distinctive features of the treatment of foreign law in different jurisdictions, particularly in relation to the mandatory and the facultative application of foreign law, the ascertainment of foreign law and the review of foreign law by appeal courts. The report also pays special attention to the divergent treatment of foreign law among various jurisdictions when uniform conflicts rules in international treaties[2] or EU Regulations[3] ought to be applied. Third, the report

[1] Pierre Mayer/Vincent Heuzé, *Droit international privé*, 11th ed. (Paris 2014), p. 140.

[2] *See* the conventions adopted by the Hague Conference on Private International Law (http://www.hcch.net/) and the Organization of American States (http://www.oas.org/).

[3] Regulation (EC) No 593/2008 of the European Parliament and of the Council of 17 June 2008 on the law applicable to contractual obligations (Rome I), *O.J.* 2008, L 177/6; Regulation (EC) No 864/2007 of the European Parliament and of the Council of 11 July 2007 on the law applicable to non-contractual obligations (Rome II), *O.J.* 2007, L 199/40; Council Regulation (EC) No 4/2009 of 18 December 2008 on jurisdiction, applicable law, recognition and enforcement of decisions and cooperation in matters relating to maintenance obligations, *O.J.* 2009, L 7/1 (*hereinafter* "Maintenance Regulation"); Council Regulation (EU) No 1259/2010 of 20 December 2010 implementing enhanced cooperation in the area of the law applicable to divorce and legal separation, *O.J.* 2010, L 343/10 (*hereinafter* "Rome III Regulation"); Regulation (EU) No 650/2012 of the

critically scrutinizes the mechanism and functionality of existing methods for obtaining information on foreign law in light of administrative and judicial cooperation. The relevant international instruments are, in particular, the London Convention (1968),[4] the Montevideo Convention (1979)[5] and the Minsk Convention (1993).[6] The report then analyses the possibility of improving access to foreign law and scrutinizes several expedient methods to this end.

Extensive research already exists on these issues—consider, in particular, the work prepared by the Hague Conference on Private International Law (HCCH),[7] the European Judicial Network in Civil and Commercial Matters (EJN)[8] and the research projects subsidized by the European Union (EU)[9]. Although this general report considers these existing works, it takes an alternative approach by comparatively examining the treatment and application of foreign law in various jurisdictions worldwide. This study also considers the feasibility of establishing a common framework for collecting information on foreign law.

European Parliament and of the Council of 4 July 2012 on jurisdiction, applicable law, recognition and enforcement of decisions and acceptance and enforcement of authentic instruments in matters of succession and on the creation of a European Certificate of Succession, *O.J.* 2012, L 201/107 (*hereinafter* "Succession Regulation"); Council Regulation (EU) 2016/1103 of 24 June 2016 implementing enhanced cooperation in the area of jurisdiction, applicable law and the recognition and enforcement of decisions in matters of matrimonial property regimes, *O.J.* 2016, L 183/1 (*hereinafter* "Matrimonial Property Regimes Regulation"); Council Regulation (EU) 2016/1104 of 24 June 2016 implementing enhanced cooperation in the area of jurisdiction, applicable law and the recognition and enforcement of decisions in matters of the property consequences of registered partnerships, *O.J.* 2016, L 183/30 (*hereinafter* "Partnership Regulation").

[4] European Convention of 7 June 1968 on Information on Foreign Law; Additional Protocol of 15 March 1978 to the European Convention on Information on Foreign Law.

[5] Inter-American Convention of 8 May 1979 on Proof of and Information on Foreign Law.

[6] Convention of 22 January 1993 on Legal Aid and Legal Relations in Civil, Family and Criminal Matters, amended on 28 March 1997.

[7] Various preliminary documents are available on the HCCH website (http://www.hcch.net/) under "Work in Progress" then "General Affairs; *also* Conclusions and Recommendations of the Joint Conference of the *European Commission and Hague Conference on Private International Law on* "Access to Foreign Law in Civil and Commercial Matters" (Brussels, 15–17 February 2012) (available at: http://www.hcch.net/index_en.php?act=events.details&year=2012&varevent=248).

[8] http://ec.europa.eu/civiljustice/index_en.htm; for an overview of conflicts rules and the treatment of foreign law in the EU Member States, *see* http://ec.europa.eu/civiljustice/applicable_law/applicable_law_gen_en.htm.

[9] Swiss Institute of Comparative Law, *The Application of Foreign Law in Civil Matters in the EU Member States and its Perspectives for the Future* (*hereinafter* "SICL Report") (JLS/2009/JCIV/PR/0005/E4), Part I: Legal Analysis; Part II: Empirical Analysis; Synthesis Report with Recommendations (2011) (available at: http://ec.europa.eu/); Carlos Esplugues/José Luis Iglesias/Guillermo Paolo (eds.), *Application of Foreign Law* (Munich 2011) (it includes "Principles for a Future EU Regulation on the Application of Foreign Law" ["Madrid Principles"]); *see also* Carlos Esplugues Mota, "Harmonization of Private International Law in Europe and Application of Foreign Law: The 'Madrid Principles' of 2010", *Yearbook of Private International Law* 13 (2011), pp. 273 ff.

This general report has greatly benefitted from 32 national reports submitted for the 2014 Vienna Conference[10] and two national reports submitted subsequently[11] by experts in private international law and civil procedure law from various jurisdictions in Europe, North and South America, Asia-Pacific Area and Africa. The Hague Conference on Private International Law also provided a report on the state and progress of its envisaged project on the treatment of foreign law.[12] The aim of this general report is to provide fresh insights into the status quo in the treatment of and access to foreign law in different countries and possibly pave the way for further developments in the future.[13]

II. Conflict of Laws

A. General Remarks

The application of foreign law comes into consideration when the conflict of laws rules of the forum state designate foreign law as applicable to the cross-border legal relationship concerned. The content of the conflicts rules and the connecting factors that are employed determine the frequency of the application of foreign law.[14]

Notably, the applicable foreign law is not limited to the substantive law of the foreign state. Rather, foreign law may include foreign conflicts rules when the court solves conflicts of laws within the foreign legal system in a Multi-Unit state or exceptionally determines a renvoi. This is also the case when the court applies the conventional "vested rights theory" in the U.S.[15] or the "principle of recognition" in the EU.[16] Furthermore, foreign procedural law could also be considered when the court

[10] Argentina, Australia, Belgium, Commonwealth African Countries, Croatia, Czech Republic, Denmark, Estonia, Finland, France, Georgia, Germany, Greece, Hungary, Israel, Ireland, Italy, Japan, Macau/China, Malta, Poland, Portugal, Quebec/Canada, Romania, Sweden, Switzerland, Tunisia, U.K., Uruguay, Turkey, U.S. and Venezuela. The questionnaire prepared for the 2014 Vienna Conference is included at the end of this volume.

[11] Spain and Tunisia (as revised).

[12] Report of the Hague Conference on Private International Law (hereinafter "HCCH report"); *see also* Philippe Lortie/Maja Groff, "The Missing Link between Determining the Law Applicable and the Application of Foreign Law: Building on the Results of the Joint Conference on Access to Foreign Law in Civil and Commercial Matters (Brussels, 15–17 February 2012)", in: *A Commitment to Private International Law. Essays in honour of Hans van Loon* (Cambridge *et al.* 2013), pp. 325 ff.

[13] The original, slightly shorter version of this general report will be published as "Proof of and Information about Foreign Law", in: Schauer/Verschraegen (eds.), *General Reports of the XIXth Congress of the International Academy of Comparative Law (forthcoming 2017)*.

[14] *See* Maarit Jänterä-Jareborg, "Foreign Law in National Courts: A Comparative Perspective", *Recueil des cours* 304 (2003), pp. 202 ff.

[15] *See infra* note 32.

[16] Art. 18 and 21 TFEU (ex-Art. 12 and 18 TEC): *see, in particular,* CJEU, 2.10.2003, Case C-148/02 [*Garcia Avello*], Rep. 2003, I-11613; CJEU, 14.10.2008, Case C-353/06 [*Grunkin Paul*], Rep. 2008, I-7639; CJEU, 22.12.2010, Case C-208/09 [*Sayn-Wittgenstein*], Rep. 2010, I-13693;

determines the international jurisdiction to adjudicate,[17] the recognition of foreign judgments[18] or the opening of insolvency proceedings and its effects on the debtor's assets.[19] The relevant court proceedings are not limited to civil litigation, but include *exequatur*, insolvency and any other disputes before courts. Nevertheless, since the treatment of conflicts rules and foreign law in civil litigation principally applies to other types of court proceedings, this study concentrates on civil litigation.

B. Designation of Foreign Law

1. Conflict of Laws Rules

The majority of jurisdictions considered in this report[20] principally follow the conflict of laws method that goes back to Savigny in the mid-nineteenth century.[21] This method consists in designating the law that has the closest connection with the category of the legal relationship concerned, presupposing the equality and interchangeability of domestic law and foreign law. The conflicts rules are formulated in the form of bilateral conflicts rules that designate domestic law and foreign law under the same conditions ("internationalist approach").[22]

Depending on the content of conflicts rules, there are differences in how frequently there is reference to foreign law. In most jurisdictions in the world, party autonomy in contracts is an established principle, allowing the parties to designate

---

CJEU, 12.5.2011, Case C-391/09 [*Runevič-Vardyn*], Rep. 2011, I-3787; CJEU, 2.6.2016, Case C-438/14 [*Bogendorff von Wolffersdorff*] (not yet reported); *see* Michael Grünberger, "Alles Obsolet? Anerkennungsprinzip vs. klassisches IPR", in: Leible/Unberath (ed.), *Brauchen wir eine Rom 0-Verordnung?* (Sipplingen 2013), pp. 81 ff.; Paul Lagarde (ed.), *La reconnaissance des situations en droit international privé* (Paris 2013); Matthias Lehmann, "Recognition as a Substitute for Conflict of Laws?", in: Leible (ed.), *General Principles of European Private International Law* (Aphen aan den Rijn 2016), pp. 11 ff.; Heinz-Peter Mansel, "Anerkennung als Grundprinzip des Europäischen Rechtsraums. Zur Herausbildung eines europäischen Anerkennungs-Kollisionsrechts: Anerkennung statt Verweisung als neues Strukturprinzip des Europäischen internationalen Privatrechts?", *RabelsZ* 70 (2006), pp. 651 ff., 705 ff.

[17] For example, § 98 (1) No. 4 FamFG (divorce jurisdiction depends on the recognition of German judgments in the spouses' country of origin).

[18] For example, § 328 (1) No. 5 ZPO and § 109 (4) FamFG; Art. 118 No. 4 Japanese CPC (reciprocity requirement).

[19] *See* Art. 3 (4)(a) and Art. 5-14 of the EU Insolvency Regulation (Council Regulation (EC) No 1346/2000 of 29 May 2000 on insolvency proceedings, *O.J.* 2000, L 160/1); Art. 3 (4)(a) and Art. 8-17 of the EU Insolvency Regulation Recast (Regulation (EU) 2015/848 of the European Parliament and of the Council of 20 May 2015 on insolvency proceedings (recast), *O.J.* 2015, L 141/19).

[20] Argentina; Australia; Croatia; France; Georgia; Greece; Israel; Italy; Japan; Poland; Portugal; Quebec; Turkey; Uruguay; Venezuela.

[21] Friedrich Karl von Savigny, *System des heutigen römischen Rechts,* Vol. 8 (Berlin 1849), pp. 2 ff.

[22] *Cf.* 1989 Santiago de Compostela Resolution of the Institute of International Law: "Equality of Treatment of the Law of the Forum and of Foreign Law" (http://www.idi-iil.org/idiE/resolutionsE/1989_comp_02_en.PDF).

the applicable law without restricting the range of eligible laws from which the choice can be made.[23] This renders the application of foreign law more likely, subject to the parties' choice of law.

In family and succession law, the principle of nationality that traditionally prevailed in civil law jurisdictions often led to the application of foreign law. This is arguably also the case with the "alternative connecting factors" method, which aims to achieve a certain substantive law policy at the level of private international law (e.g., "favor filiationis" or "favor testamenti"). Since the 1970s, with a view to achieving gender equality, civil law countries have abolished conflicts rules that solely refer to the law of nationality of the husband and have introduced in their place the "cascading connecting factors" method ("Anknüpfungsleiter") to seek common elements between the spouses. By restricting the designation of the law of nationality to the case where spouses share a common nationality, the applicability of foreign law has been considerably reduced. Moreover, the recent tendency of European countries to facilitate the acquisition of nationality and accept dual nationalities to enhance the integration of immigrants[24] will lead to greater application of the lex fori. Furthermore, the Hague Conventions,[25] as well as recent EU regulations[26] and various recent domestic legislation,[27] are gradually shifting from the principle of nationality to the principle of habitual residence when determining the applicable law. The conflicts rules that point to the law of habitual residence regularly result in the application of the lex fori due to coincidence with the jurisdiction rules.[28] Some specific conflicts rules, such as party autonomy under the EU regula-

---

[23] Only some Latin American and Arab states still exclude or limit party autonomy. In the U.S., the eligible laws that can be chosen by the parties are generally limited to those that have a close relationship with the contract. *See* Jürgen Basedow, "The Law of Open Societies: Private Ordering and Public Regulation of International Relations", *Recueil des cours* 360 (2013), pp. 164 ff.; Yuko Nishitani, "Party Autonomy in Contemporary Private International Law — The Hague Principles on Choice of Law and East Asia —", *Japanese Yearbook of International Law* 59 (2016), pp. 300 ff.

[24] Randall Hansen/Patrick Weil, "Citizenship, Immigration and Nationality: Towards a Convergence in Europe?", in: Hansen/Weil (eds.), *Towards a European Nationality. Citizenship, Immigration and Nationality Law in the EU* (Hampshire/New York 2001), pp. 5 ff.; Olivier W. Vonk, *Dual Nationality in the European Union* (Leiden 2012), pp. 47 ff.

[25] *See, inter alia,* Art. 3 of the Convention of 25 October 1980 on the Civil Aspects of International Child Abduction (*hereinafter* "Child Abduction Convention"); Art. 4-5 of the Convention of 29 May 1993 on Protection of Children and Co-operation in Respect of Intercountry Adoption; Art. 15-17 of the Convention of 19 October 1996 on Jurisdiction, Applicable Law, Recognition, Enforcement and Co-operation in Respect of Parental Responsibility and Measures for the Protection of Children; Art. 13-16 of the Convention of 13 January 2000 on the International Protection of Adults; Art. 3-6 of the Protocol of 23 November 2007 on the Law Applicable to Maintenance Obligations (*hereinafter* "Hague Protocol") (available at: http://www.hcch.net/).

[26] *See* Art. 15 Maintenance Regulation (Art. 3-6 of the 2007 Hague Protocol); Art. 8 Rome III; Art. 21 Succession Regulation.

[27] Belgium (2004 PIL Act); Czech Republic (2012 PIL Act); Switzerland (1987 PIL Act); *also* Finland.

[28] Brigitta Lurger, "Die Verortung natürlicher Personen im europäischen IPR und IZVR: Wohnsitz, gewöhnlicher Aufenthalt, Staatsangehörigkeit", in: Hein/Rühl (eds.), *Kohärenz im Internationalen Privat- und Verfahrensrecht der Europäischen Union* (Tübingen 2016), pp. 217 f.; Heinz-Peter

tions that gives the parties an option to refer to the lex fori[29] or conflicts rules that protect weaker parties like maintenance creditors,[30] also favour the application of the lex fori.

On the other hand, the law governing family relations and succession in the U.K., Australia, the U.S. and other common law jurisdictions is generally the lex fori as a matter of course, or the law of habitual residence or domicile of the person which usually corresponds to the lex fori.[31] Foreign law is, therefore, rarely applied to family relations and succession in common law jurisdictions.

Furthermore, the modern approaches of conflict of laws in proprietary issues prevail over the traditional method of referring to fixed connecting factors grounded in the vested rights theory in most states of the U.S.[32] The modern approaches derive from the so-called U.S. "conflicts revolution" beginning in the 1960s.[33] They rely on, in particular, the "most significant relationship",[34] "governmental interests",[35] the "better law" approach[36] or the "lex fori" approach[37]. These "revolutionary" methods leave a wide leeway for U.S. courts in assessing the closest connection, governmental interests or other substantive interests to determine the applicable law. As a result, U.S. cases generally show a strong "homeward" trend of preferring the lex fori. Indeed, foreign law has seldom been applied before federal or state courts in the U.S., except for in specific commercial centres, such as New York. This tendency may intensify in light of recent developments surrounding bans on Shari'a law and foreign law.[38]

Mansel, "Die kulturelle Identität im Internationalen Privatrecht", *BerDGesVO* 43 (2008), p. 171; Marc-Philippe Weller/Bettina Rentsch, "'Habitual Residence': A Plea for 'Settled Intention'", in: Leible (ed.), *General Principles of European Private International Law* (Aphen aan den Rijn 2016), p. 175.

[29] Art. 3 Rome I; Art. 14 Rome II; Art. 5 Rome III; Art. 15 Maintenance Regulation (Art. 7 and 8 of the 2007 Hague Protocol); Art. 22 Succession Regulation; Art. 22 Matrimonial Property Regimes Regulation; Art. 22 Partnership Regulation (*supra* note 3).

[30] Art. 15 Maintenance Regulation (Art. 4 (2)(3) of the 2007 Hague Protocol).

[31] *See, e.g.*, Dicey, Morris & Collins, *The Conflict of Laws*, 15th ed., vol. 2 (London 2012), para. 17R-001 ff. (marriage: Rule 73–75), 18R-032 ff. (divorce and separation: Rule 85), 19R-001 ff. (parental responsibility: Rule 104–105), 20R-009 ff. (parentage: Rule 113–118), 27R-010 ff. (succession: Rule 149–164) and 28 R-001 ff. (the effect of marriage on property: Rule 165–167); Peter Hay/Patrick J. Borchers/Symeon C. Symeonides, *Conflict of Laws*, 5th ed. (St. Paul, MN 2010), pp. 614 ff., 1285 ff.

[32] Joseph Henry Beale, *A Treatise on the Conflict of Laws*, vol. 1 (New York 1935), pp. 53 ff.; also Restatement (First) Conflict of Laws (1934).

[33] Hay/Borchers/Symeonides, *supra* note 31, pp. 27 ff.; Symeon C. Symeonides, *The American choice-of-law revolution: past, present and future* (Leiden 2006), pp. 9 ff.

[34] Restatement (Second) Conflict of Laws (1971).

[35] Brainerd Currie, "The Constitution and the Choice of Law: Governmental Interests and the Judicial Function", in: *Selected Essays on the Conflict of Laws* (Durham/NC 1963), pp. 188 ff.

[36] Robert Allen Leflar, *American Conflicts Law*, 3rd ed., (Indianapolis/NY *et al.* 1977), pp. 212 ff.

[37] Albert Armin Ehrenzweig, *Private International Law. A Comparative Treatise on American International Conflicts Law*, vol. 1: General Part (Leyden/NY 1967), pp. 91 ff.

[38] U.S. District Court for the Western District of Oklahoma, 15 August 2013 [Awad v. Ziriax], 966

Some other factors are also likely to reduce the number of cases where foreign law is referred to as the applicable law. First, the application of foreign law can be excluded if it would contravene public policy, particularly when foreign law relies on values that are fundamentally different from the values of the forum state. Second, the so-called "blocking statutes" in the U.S.[39] or the overriding mandatory rules of the forum state in civil law countries may lead to the exclusion of the application of foreign law. Third, in cross-border business transactions, the frequent use of arbitration, instead of litigation, could mean courts more rarely apply foreign law. Fourth, allowing a simple renvoi, which consists of applying the domestic law pursuant to the foreign conflicts rules that refer back to the law of the forum, will result in excluding the application of the foreign substantive law.[40] Yet a simple renvoi does not fully exempt the court from applying foreign law, as the court needs to apply foreign conflicts rules to determine the renvoi. Finally, courts in the U.S., U.K. or Australia may dismiss the action or stay proceedings due to the court being a "forum non conveniens", on the ground that foreign law is applicable to the case at hand. A Japanese judge may also declare lack of international jurisdiction on account of special circumstances (Art. 3-9 CCP), owing to the fact that foreign law cannot be properly established or applied in Japan. Although foreign law will then no longer govern the subject matter of the dispute, a number of court proceedings invariably discuss the applicability of foreign law in precisely these circumstances (*infra* VII.A).[41]

2. Frequently Designated Sources of Foreign Law

Which foreign laws are applied vary considerably depending on the jurisdiction and area of law. First, due to geographic closeness and frequent movements of persons and goods, many jurisdictions regularly apply the foreign laws from neighbouring countries.[42] In the EU, the freedom of movement of persons, goods, services and capital—that is, the freedom of establishment within the internal market—increases the applicability of laws of other Member States. Further, the special connection

F. Supp. 2d 1198; *see* Peter Hay, "Section II.B: Private International Law: The Use and Determination of Foreign Law in Civil Litigation", *Am. J. Comp. L.* 62 (2014), pp. 217 ff.

[39] Hay, *supra* note 38, pp. 233 ff.

[40] *See* Jürgen Basedow, "The Application of Foreign Law—Comparative Remarks on the Practical Side of Private International Law", in: Basedow/Pißler (eds.), *Private International Law in Mainland China, Taiwan and Europe* (Tübingen 2014), p. 91.

[41] U.K. (Richard Fentiman, *International Commercial Litigation,* 2nd ed. (Oxford 2015), para. 20.03 f.); *also* Australia; U.S. (Hay, *supra* note 38, p. 232); for Japan, *see* Tokyo District Court, 22 February 2013 (Westlaw Japan Case No. 2013WLJPCA02226001); for Japanese jurisdiction rules, *see* Yuko Nishitani, "International Jurisdiction of Japanese Courts in Comparative Perspective", *Netherlands International Law Review* 60 (2013), pp. 270 ff.

[42] Croatia (German, Austrian, Italian, Hungarian and Swiss laws; laws of former Yugoslavian countries); Czech Republic (Slovakian, German, Polish and Austrian law); Georgia (Russian, Turkish or Ukrainian laws); Germany (Dutch law and laws of other EU Member States); Hungary (Austrian, German and Romanian laws); Tunisia (laws of Arab countries and certain European countries).

between former colonial powers and their colonies,[43] among Commonwealth countries,[44] and among states who share a common language or cultural background[45] often leads to the reciprocal application of the laws. In Multi-Unit states such as the U.K., Australia, Canada, the U.S. and Nigeria, the law of other political units, such as states, regions or provinces is also considered to be foreign law and often applied in interregional or interstate conflict of laws cases.

Second, the presence of immigrants or ethnic minorities within a jurisdiction may often lead to the application of foreign law when the principle of nationality governs their family relations.[46] In Japan, with immigrants from North and South Korea, China and Taiwan, as well as from the Philippines, Vietnam and Brazil, courts often apply the laws of these jurisdictions, including those of North Korea and Taiwan which Japan does not recognize as statehood.[47]

Third, foreign law is frequently applied by way of the parties' choice of law in contracts, reflecting case-specific commercial considerations as well as the general need for efficiency in cross-border business transactions. The laws that are frequently chosen by the parties are, in particular, New York, English, French, German and Swiss.

C. Application of Conflict of Laws

1. General Remarks

A question that arises in the application of conflict of laws rules is whether and to what extent conflicts rules ought to be applied ex officio once the internationality or foreign elements of the case have been ascertained.[48] This question turns on what role the parties should play in civil procedure, so that conflicts rules are applied by the judge. This is a matter of task-sharing between the judge and the parties. In fact, various factors influence the practical implementation of conflicts rules, particularly the civil procedural rules of the relevant jurisdiction. A general distinction can be drawn between the civil law approach and common law approach, even though there are exceptions and considerable variations within these categories.[49]

---

[43] Portugal and Brazil or Cape Verde.

[44] U.K., Australia.

[45] Nordic countries (Sweden, Norway, Finland); Latin American countries (Argentina, Uruguay, Venezuela).

[46] *See, e.g.,* Czech Republic (Vietnamese, Ukrainian and Russian law); Germany (Turkish and Iranian law); Italy (Moroccan, Egyptian and Tunisian law).

[47] Yayohi Satoh, "Law Applicable to Personal Status of Korean and Chinese Nationals before Japanese Courts", *Japanese Yearbook of International Law* 55 (2012), pp. 323 ff.

[48] For the ascertainment of the internationality or foreign elements of the case in civil procedure, *see infra* II.C.2.

[49] *See* Esplugues *et al.* (eds.), *supra* note 9, pp. 18 ff.; Sofie Geeroms, *Foreign Law in Civil Litigation: A Comparative and Functional Analysis* (Oxford 2004), para. In 11 ff.

In the following study, the term "mandatory" application of conflicts rules is used to indicate that the judge is obliged to apply conflicts rules ex officio. This is distinguishable from conflicts rules being "binding", which means that neither the court nor the parties may modify or deviate from the content of conflicts rules.

2. Mandatory Application of Conflicts Rules

a) Uniform Approach

The majority of the civil law jurisdictions considered in this report provide for the mandatory application of conflicts rules for all categories of legal relationships.[50] Under this system, the judge must apply conflicts rules suo moto without the parties' invocation. In these countries, the conflicts rules constitute a part of the domestic legal system, independently of whether their legal sources are domestic law, international treaties or EU regulations. Because the conflicts rules are legitimate sources of law in the forum state that are currently in force, they are regarded as binding upon the judge and the parties. Thus, the judge applies conflicts rules ex officio pursuant to the principle of "iura novit curia", in the same manner as the substantive domestic law, once the court confirms the internationality of the case.

Some academics in these civil law countries have argued in favour of deviating from the ex officio application of conflict of laws. In particular, Flessner advocated the theory of the "facultative conflict of laws" in 1970 in Germany, according to which conflicts rules are applicable only when at least one party invokes them. This meant giving the parties control over whether conflicts rules are applied, on the ground that the quality of the administration of justice cannot be guaranteed when foreign law is always applied ex officio.[51] Yet the scholarly consensus was then against this position, because it could hamper legal certainty and thwart the integrity of the domestic legal system by allowing the parties to circumvent the application of domestic mandatory rules. In addition, there was a concern that the theory of the facultative conflict of laws would frustrate legal certainty and international harmony of decisions, which is the primary goal of conflict of laws.[52] Currently, however, the

---

[50] Argentina; Austria; Macau; Croatia; Czech Republic; Denmark; Estonia; Georgia; Germany; Italy; Greece; Japan; Poland; Portugal; Quebec; Romania; Switzerland; Tunisia; Turkey; Uruguay; Venezuela. *See* Hague Conference on Private International Law, "Summary Tables on the Status of and Access to Foreign Law in a Sample of Jurisdictions", Information Document B of February 2007 (*hereinafter* "Summary Tables").

[51] Axel Flessner, "Fakultatives Kollisionsrecht", *RabelsZ* 34 (1970), pp. 547 ff.; *also* idem, "Das Parteiinteresse an der Lex Fori nach europäischem Kollisionsrecht", in: Verbeke *et al.* (eds.), *Liber Amicorum Walter Pintens* (Cambridge *et al.* 2012), pp. 593 ff.; idem, "Das ausländische Recht im Zivilprozess—die europäischen Anforderungen", in: Reichelt (ed.), *30 Jahre österreichisches IPR-Gesetz—Europäische Perspektiven*—(Wien 2009), pp. 35 ff.

[52] *See, inter alia,* Rudolf Hübner, *Ausländisches Recht vor deutschen Gerichten* (Tübingen 2014), pp. 190 ff.; Oliver Remien, "Proof of and Information about Foreign Law", in: Schmid-Kessel (ed.), *German National Reports on the 19th International Congress of Comparative Law* (Tübingen 2014), p. 224; Jänterä-Jareborg, *supra* note 14, pp. 197 ff.

facultative application of conflict of laws, at least in attenuated form, is gaining support in the process of seeking to harmonize the treatment of uniform conflicts rules in the EU (*infra* VII.B.2).

b) Distinctive Approach

Some other civil law jurisdictions take a distinctive approach to the treatment of conflicts rules, depending on the nature of the subject matter at stake. France in particular classifies the subject matter into two types, depending on whether the parties can dispose of the rights concerned: "non-disposable rights" (droits indisponibles) and "disposable rights" (droits disponibles).[53] This corresponds to the distinction between "indispositive" ("mandatory") issues and "dispositive" ("non-mandatory") issues in Sweden and Finland.[54]

Pursuant to French case law which has developed since the 1959 Bisbal decision[55] with several fluctuations,[56] the application of conflicts rules is mandatory in relation to "non-disposable rights". The non-disposable rights generally concern status issues, such as capacity, divorce, nullity of marriage and parentage. On the other hand, the application of conflicts rules is facultative for "disposable rights", which in particular relate to civil and commercial contracts, non-contractual obligations and succession. The application of conflicts rules for disposable rights becomes mandatory for the judge once a party invokes the applicable foreign law. Otherwise, the judge has discretion as to whether or not to apply conflicts rules and foreign law suo moto. However, once the parties enter a "procedural agreement" to preclude the application of conflicts rules, the judge is bound to refer to the lex fori.[57]

Arguably, the distinctive approach in France and other countries seeks to strike a fair balance between legal certainty and flexibility, that is, the "iura novit curia" principle and the adversarial principle of civil procedure. On the other hand, as the French reporter points out, it is difficult to draw a clear line between "non-disposable rights" and "disposable rights" or other comparable bifurcated categories of rights or issues pursuant to the lex fori. Today, rights arising out of contractual or non-contractual obligations are not necessarily regarded as disposable, since they are increasingly governed by mandatory rules to protect employees and consumers, regulate the market, or enhance competition. Nor do legal relationships grounded in non-disposable rights strictly exclude the parties' disposition in conflict of laws but allow party

[53] For France, *see, e.g.*, Sabine Corneloup, "Rechtsermittlung im Internationalen Privatrecht der EU: Überlegungen aus Frankreich", *RabelsZ* 78 (2014), pp. 845 ff.; idem, "L'application de la loi étrangère", *Rev. int. dr. comp.* 2014, pp. 363 ff.; Bénédicte Fauvarque-Cosson, "Foreign Law before the French Court: The Conflicts of Law Perspective", in: Cavinet *et al.* (eds.), *Comparative Law before the Courts* (London 2004), pp. 3 ff.

[54] For Scandinavian countries, *see* Jänterä-Jareborg, *supra* note 14, pp. 277 ff.

[55] Cour de cassation, 12.5.1959, *Rev. crit. dr. int. pr.* 1960, 62.

[56] Cour de cassation, 4.12.1990, *Rev. crit. dr. int. pr.* 1991, 558; Cour de cassation, 26.5.1999, *Rev. crit. dr. int. pr.* 1999, 707; Cour de cassation, 28.6.2005, *Rev. crit. dr. int. pr.* 2005, 645.

[57] Corneloup, *supra* note 53, *RabelsZ* 2014, pp. 845 ff.

autonomy to some extent nowadays, as in the case of divorce under Art. 5 of the Rome III Regulation. The facultative approach in conflict of laws does not always correspond to the existence of the parties' freedom of disposition in substantive law. In light of this, some French academics advocate abolishing the conventional dichotomy between "non-disposable rights" and "disposable rights" de lege ferenda.[58]

c) Procedural Agreement

France, Sweden and several other countries allow the parties to enter into a procedural agreement ("accord procédural"),[59] with the effect of excluding the application of conflicts rules. The procedural agreement is characterized as an agreement to waive any cross-border elements of a case and render it a domestic case to be governed by definition by the lex fori. The judge is bound once the parties enter a procedural agreement explicitly or tacitly. While some of the countries considered accept procedural agreements only in relation to disposable rights or matters not related to public policy,[60] others extend its scope to all categories of legal relationships.[61] The procedural agreement is justified in light of procedural economy and flexibility to circumvent inappropriate conflicts rules or foreign law, with the argument that there is no need to apply foreign law when the parties are not interested in it. This argument particularly applies to cases where the parties are allowed to subject their legal relationship to the lex fori by means of choice of law and dispose of their substantive rights.

d) General Limitations

In addition to these methods of attenuating the mandatory application of conflict of laws, there are other relevant factual limitations. First, even among civil law jurisdictions, the mandatory application of conflicts rules may be restricted due to the adversarial principle in civil procedure law ("Verhandlungsmaxime" or "principe dispositive"). The majority of civil law countries,[62] except Austria and Italy, require the parties to invoke the facts constituting the cross-border elements of the case (e.g., nationality, habitual residence or place of performance). Exceptions are only granted in some countries for status and family matters, or matters concerning public policy, in which case foreign elements are ascertained ex officio[63] or on grounds

[58] Corneloup, *supra* note 53, *Rev. int. dr. comp.* 2014, pp. 365 ff.

[59] *Also* Belgium, Denmark, Hungary and Tunisia; for procedural agreement, *see, inter alia,* Bénédicte Fauvarque Cosson, *Libre disponibilité des droits et conflits de lois* (Paris 1996), pp. 241 ff.; *see infra* II.C.2.

[60] France; Sweden; Belgium; Tunisia.

[61] Denmark; Hungary.

[62] Germany; Italy; Japan; Sweden; Tunisia; for further detail, *see* SICL Report, *supra* note 9, pp. 10 ff.

[63] Belgium (*see* François Rigaux/Marc Fallon, *Droit international privé,* 3rd ed. (Bruxelles 2005), para. 6.52).

of inquisitional procedural rules.[64] Otherwise, the internationality of the case depends on the party's conduct in court proceedings. The court may be entitled[65] or obliged[66] to invite the parties to provide factual explanations on foreign elements of the case, but cannot examine them ex officio. This may, de facto, render the application of conflicts rules facultative or optional.

Second, in some jurisdictions like Spain and Tunisia, the judge takes a markedly passive position concerning the proof of foreign law. The parties need to provide the judge with sufficiently specific information on the content of foreign law to have it applied, otherwise the lex fori will come into play.[67] Again, the parties are given the opportunity to refrain from proving the content of foreign law in order to prevent the application of foreign law.

Third, some reporters have pointed out cases where the court has seemingly ignored the international aspects of a case or has provided a questionable interpretation of the relevant conflicts rules, with a view to circumventing the application of foreign law. These cases may result from insufficient legal education on conflict of laws. It is even reported from Italy that judges intentionally avoid applying foreign law as much as possible by discouraging the parties from requesting it, although the ex officio application of conflicts rules is taken for granted. This "homeward trend" in favour of the application of the lex fori can be observed throughout various jurisdictions.[68]

3. Facultative Application of Conflicts Rules

Mainly in jurisdictions grounded in or influenced by the common law,[69] the application of conflicts rules depends on the parties' pleading or invocation of foreign law. Due to the adversarial principle in civil procedure, the courts cannot intervene unless at least one party pleads the internationality of the case and the applicability of foreign law. In the absence of such pleadings, conflict of laws does not come into play and the matter is treated as a domestic case. Furthermore, in Australia, the parties can strategically circumvent the application of conflicts rules by accumulating actions and choosing a claim among them that is governed by the lex fori.

However, once a party pleads foreign law the judge has an obligation to apply conflicts rules, because conflicts rules constitute a part of the forum state's legal system. By pleading foreign law, a party can render the application of conflicts rules mandatory and binding, and it is the judge's task to find out the content of those conflicts rules. Once the court decides that foreign law is applicable, the content of that law needs to be proven by the party in principle. Yet some common law jurisdic-

[64] Germany (Art. 26 FamFG); Japan (Art. 20 Personal Matters Procedure Act and Art. 56 (1) Family Procedure Act).

[65] Quebec; Sweden.

[66] France.

[67] *See* Esplugues *et al.* (eds.), *supra* note 9, p. 20.

[68] Argentina; Croatia; Georgia; Germany; Tunisia.

[69] Australia; Commonwealth African countries; Israel; Ireland; U.K.; U.S.; *also* Malta; Quebec; Luxemburg.

tions are becoming more responsive to the idea of judges taking judicial notice of foreign law. In this respect, although the starting points of civil law jurisdictions and common law jurisdictions deviate from each other, the practical outcome will come closer than it appears at the outset (*infra* III).

4. Legal Sources of Conflicts Rules

The divergent approaches delineated so far raise the question of whether the source of conflicts rules necessarily determines how the conflicts rules are deployed. Domestic conflicts rules directly address the court in the forum state, so that it is a simple matter to define the operation of these domestic conflicts rules. On the other hand, conflicts rules deriving from international treaties or EU regulations are grounded in international law or EU law, which the forum state is obliged to abide by. For this reason, the majority of authors in Germany, Italy and Hungary assume specific obligations on the part of the forum state to apply conflicts rules grounded in international law or EU law ex officio.

Other countries do not seem to distinguish between the sources of conflicts rules. While this still results in the mandatory application of conflicts rules in the majority of civil law countries, it leads to a distinctive approach in France, although the previous case law had accepted a constant mandatory application of conflicts rules emanating from international treaties. Consequently, the application of the Rome I and the Rome II Regulations as conflicts rules relating to "disposable rights" are not mandatory in France, but subject to the parties' invocation and procedural agreements.[70] Further, the legal systems of the U.K. treat the application of foreign law as a matter of "evidence and procedure", which is outside the scope of Rome I (Art. 1 (3)) and Rome II (Art. 1 (3)). U.K. judges, therefore, are not obliged to apply foreign law, but the question depends on the parties' pleadings and proof of foreign law.[71]

This situation may well undermine the functioning of the uniform conflicts rules and hamper international harmony of decisions among Member States of the EU or Contracting States of international treaties. Particularly in the EU, this could eventually frustrate the purpose of adopting uniform conflicts rules to guarantee the free movement of persons, goods and capital, as well as the free circulation of judgments for the sake of an internal market (*infra* VII.B).

---

[70] Corneloup, *supra* note 53, *Rev. int. dr. comp.* 2014, pp. 372 f. This point is disputed in Hungary.

[71] Dicey, Morris & Collins, *supra* note 31, vol. 1, para. 9-011; Trevor C. Hartley, "Pleading and Proof of Foreign Law: The Major European Systems Compared", *Int'l & Comp.L.Q.* 45 (1996), pp. 282 ff. However, a deviating opinion emphasizes the mandatory character of the conflicts rules of the EU regulations and conventions, and the resulting application of foreign law. Richard Fentiman, *Foreign Law in English Courts. Pleading, Proof and Choice of Law* (Oxford 1998), pp. 92 ff.; *also* idem, *supra* note 41, para. 5.07.

III. Nature of Foreign Law

A. General Remarks

The nature of foreign law concerns the question of whether to characterize foreign law as "law" or "fact". The characterization of foreign law as "law" would equate foreign law with domestic law and presuppose the mandatory application of foreign law by the judge. The characterization of foreign law as "fact" would result in the facultative application of foreign law based on the parties' pleadings and proof, like other facts. Although the characterization of foreign law may directly influence the way foreign law is introduced, ascertained and applied in the court proceedings, this classification does not apply in its genuine form. A comparative study on the treatment of foreign law reveals multi-faceted features as to the division of tasks between the parties and the court in civil procedure.

B. Classification

1. Foreign Law as "Law"

Foreign law is considered "law" in almost all civil law jurisdictions.[72] France, Sweden and other civil law countries which take a distinctive approach as to the mandatory or facultative application of conflicts rules, depending on the rights or issues at hand, regard foreign law as "law".[73] Germany and Greece do too, even in the area of public law. Equating foreign law with domestic law generally results in the mandatory judicial ascertainment and application of foreign law ("iura novit curia"). Once designated by conflicts rules, foreign law ought to be applied to achieve international harmony of decisions; this is the primary goal of conflict of laws. Therefore, in the majority of civil law jurisdictions, an erroneous application of foreign law is appealable to higher courts—including the Supreme Court—under the same conditions as domestic law (*infra* V.B).

However, the treatment of foreign law is in fact differentiated from that of domestic law in several aspects. First, it is commonly assumed that the judge cannot always know the content of foreign law. With a view to alleviating the duty of courts to ascertain and apply foreign law, the parties may be required to provide information on foreign law in all the civil law jurisdictions considered. In Germany and Switzerland, the parties incur the obligation ("Mitwirkungspflicht"; "Obliegenheit") to cooperate with the court.[74] In Tunisia, it is even incumbent upon the parties to

[72] Argentina; Croatia; Czech Republic; Estonia; Finland; Georgia; Germany; Greece; Hungary; Italy; Japan; Poland; Portugal; Romania; Tunisia; Turkey; Uruguay; Venezuela.

[73] *Also* Denmark.

[74] For further detail, Hübner, *supra* note 52, pp. 274 ff.; *also* Max Keller/Daniel Girsberger, "Art. 16 IPRG", in: *Zürcher Kommentar zum IPRG*, 2nd ed. (Zürich 2004), para. 20 ff.; Monica Mächler-

prove the content of foreign law, whereas the judge is permitted, not obliged, to ascertain foreign law suo moto in principle. Thus the "iura novit curia" principle does not apply as a matter of course, and the task division between the court and the parties is effected in a manner different from domestic law (*infra* IV.B).

Second, even when foreign law is classified as "law", some countries deny or restrict appeals regarding its interpretation and application to the highest court, unlike in the case of domestic law. This is so in France, Germany and the Netherlands (*infra* V.B). For this reason, some Dutch authors characterize foreign law as neither law nor fact, but as a kind of "tertium genus".[75] In Belgium and Tunisia, foreign law has been confirmed as legal since the Supreme Court sanctioned the review of lower courts' errors in applying foreign law.

2. Foreign Law as "Fact"

The jurisdictions grounded in or influenced by common law consider foreign law to be "fact".[76] They deny the legal nature of law originating from a foreign state. Foreign law needs to be pleaded and proven with sufficient specificity by the parties so that the judge can apply it. The judge is assumed not to have any knowledge of foreign law and, in principle, is not allowed to take judicial notice of foreign law (*infra* IV.B.3).

In reality, the classification of foreign law as "fact" is not implemented consistently. While the existence, the nature and the scope of foreign law is a matter of fact, the application of foreign law is a matter of law. Thus there are some distinctive features of the treatment of foreign law that do not fit squarely within the "fact" doctrine.

First, questions of foreign law are no longer submitted to the jury, but are determined by judges in the U.K., Australia and the U.S.[77] Second, judges are obliged or entitled to take judicial notice of foreign law in certain cases. U.K. criminal courts hearing bigamy charges determine the validity of the first marriage celebrated abroad ex officio, referring to the applicable foreign law. English judges may also apply foreign law sua sponte for a declaration of status, summary judgment or the application of foreign law under international obligations (e.g., Art. 8 (2)(b) of the IMF Agreement).[78] Third, in the case of usual facts, the absence of evidence results in the dismissal of the claim of the party who bears the onus of proof, whereas in the case of foreign law, a default rule may be provided to refer to the lex fori. Fourth, the interpretation and application of foreign law is appealable. Appellate courts may reconsider foreign law in an analogous manner as an issue of law, accept new evidence, and reverse the findings of the trial judge on the foreign law. In the U.K., Australia and Malta, foreign law can even be reviewed by the highest judiciary in

---

Erne/Susanne Wolf-Mettier, in: Honsell *et al.* (eds.), Basler Kommentar: Internationales Privatrecht, 3rd ed. (Basel 2013), Art. 16 IPRG, para. 9 ff.

[75] Esplugues *et al.* (eds.), *supra* note 9, p. 17.

[76] U.K.; Australia; Commonwealth African countries; Ireland; Israel; *also* Malta; Quebec.

[77] *See* Dicey, Morris & Collins, *supra* note 31, vol. 1, para. 9-012.

[78] Hartley, *supra* note 71, pp. 285 ff.

limited circumstances. Fifth, unlike usual facts, the court's previous findings on the same point of foreign law can be referred to as evidence of the content of that foreign law if the judgment is available in a citable form. Such findings are presumed to be correct unless rebutted by contrary evidence.[79] In light of these characteristics, foreign law is considered as "a question of fact of a peculiar kind" in the jurisdictions that follow the common law approach.[80]

On the other hand, there are some civil law countries that classify foreign law as "fact". This is the case, in particular, with Luxemburg. In Luxemburg, judges are exempt from the obligation to apply conflicts rules or foreign law, although judges are allowed to apply foreign law sua sponte. Once a party invokes foreign law, the party needs to prove it in principle.[81]

3. "Tertium Genus"

There are several hybrid characterizations of foreign law among certain jurisdictions. In almost all states in the U.S., foreign law is considered to be "law". Although the parties still need to invoke foreign law both in state courts and federal courts, formal pleading is no longer required. The determination of foreign law is incumbent on the judge, not the jury. State courts may take judicial notice of foreign law, provided that the parties make sufficient information available. Under Rule 44.1. of the U.S. Federal Rules of Civil Procedure, federal courts are entitled to go beyond the evidence submitted by the parties and use other sources and materials. As a ruling on "law", the court's decision on foreign law is appealable, but generally lacks in precedential value (*infra* IV.B.3). In light of these characteristics, foreign law is generally considered to be "law" of a peculiar nature, *i.e.*, "tertium genus" in the U.S.[82]

In Spain, following the mandatory application of conflicts rules, judges proceed to apply foreign law, irrespective of the parties' pleading or invoking of foreign law. Yet the principle "iura novit curia" does not apply for the ascertainment of foreign law, as the parties have the primary duty to prove foreign law, even though they can rely on the assistance of the court. For this reason, foreign law is characterized as "tertium genus" or of "hybrid nature" in Spain.[83] Similarly in Macau, foreign law is characterized as having a hybrid nature, lying somewhere between "law" and "fact", even though the legal nature is given greater emphasis.

---

[79] In England, Civil Evidence Act 1972, s. 4 (2); J.J. Spigelman, "Proof of Foreign Law by Reference to the Foreign Court", *Law Quarterly Review* 127 (2011), pp. 208 f.

[80] High Court of Justice, Probate, Divorce and Admiralty Division (England & Wales), *Parkasho v Singh* [1968] P 233; Court of Appeal, Civil Division (England & Wales), *Dalmia Dairy Industries Ltd v National Bank of Pakistan* [1978] 2 Lloyd's Rep. 223; Court of Appeal, Civil Division (England & Wales), *Bumper Development Corp Ltd v Comr of Police* [1991] 1 WLR 1362; for further detail, *see* Fentiman, *supra* note 41, para. 20.131 ff.; idem, *supra* note 71, pp. 77 ff., 286 ff.; Trevor Hartley, *International Commercial Litigation*, 2nd ed. (2015), pp. 576 ff.

[81] Gilles Cuniberti/Isabella Rueda, "Luxemburg", in: Esplugues *et al.* (eds.), *supra* note 9, pp. 256 ff.

[82] Hay, *supra* note 38, pp. 227, 234.

[83] José Luis Iglesias *et al.*, "Spain", in: Esplugues *et al.* (eds.), *supra* note 9, pp. 357 f.

The Netherlands primarily considers foreign law as "law" because conflicts rules are applied ex officio.[84] However, given that foreign law cannot be reviewed by the Supreme Court ("Hoge Raad"), some authors characterize foreign law as "tertium genus".[85] In Finland, while the majority of academics presuppose the legal nature of foreign law, others assert that debates on the nature of foreign law have little consequence for the treatment of foreign law in civil procedure.

C. Reflections

A comparative overview of the nature of foreign law shows the distinctive treatment of foreign law in various jurisdictions. Even in civil law jurisdictions that depart from the premise that foreign law is "law", the "iura novit curia" principle is relativized by allowing the judge to seek the parties' assistance in ascertaining foreign law or by limiting appeals on questions of foreign law. Nor does the "fact" doctrine, which is the conventional common law principle, apply in its genuine form. Foreign law is treated distinctly from the usual types of facts and provided, to a certain extent, with effects comparable to domestic law. The existence of jurisdictions that consider foreign law to be "tertium genus" or of a hybrid nature indicates the difficulty of categorically determining the nature of foreign law.

Given these conditions, the question of how to characterize foreign law does not appear to yield fruitful, conclusive results.[86] Instead of upholding the conventional "law-fact" dichotomy, a tailored analysis of the treatment of foreign law ought to be conducted for the respective jurisdiction, although some classifications make sense in order to understand the general framework and point out features that are characteristic of certain legal systems. In fact, every jurisdiction makes its own decision on how to ascertain and apply foreign law, considering the functioning of conflict of laws, as well as the civil procedure and evidence rules, the available court resources, and the effective administration of justice. This is because the treatment of foreign law is a question of how best to divide the tasks between the court and the parties. Bearing this in mind, the relevant issues are further examined in detail in the following study.

---

[84] Art. 10:2 CC; *see* A. (Teun) V. M. Struycken, "The Codification of Dutch Private International Law: A Brief Introduction to Book 10 BW", *RabelsZ* 78 (2014), p. 607.

[85] *See supra* n. 75.

[86] Esplugues *et al.* (eds.), *supra* note 9, pp. 17 f.; Hartley, *supra* note 71, p. 272.

IV. Foreign Law Before Judicial Authorities

A. *Introducing and Applying Foreign Law*

1. Mandatory Application of Foreign Law

The majority of civil law jurisdictions considered in this report which provide for the mandatory application of conflicts rules generally presuppose the mandatory application of foreign law.[87] Insofar as a judge has an obligation to apply conflicts rules on his or her own motion and determines the relevant conflicts rule that designates foreign law as the governing law, the judge should also ascertain and apply foreign law ex officio. Hence, the parties do not need to plead or prove the content of foreign law, but solely take a passive position in introducing and applying foreign law in court proceedings.

In Austria, the ex officio application of foreign law is expressly provided for.[88] The same rule applies in Italy and several other countries, although the statutes solely stipulate the mandatory ascertainment of foreign law.[89] Despite the distinctive approach of France and some other countries as to the application of conflicts rules (*supra* II.C.2), foreign law is always applied ex officio, once the court establishes that foreign law is applicable.[90] § 293 ZPO of Germany provides that contents of foreign law ought to be proven "only insofar as the court is not aware of them." Despite its ambiguity, this provision is generally construed as ordering the court to apply foreign law ex officio.[91] While the Inter-American Convention on General Rules of Private International Law[92] provides for the mandatory application of foreign law by the judge, the parties are allowed to take the initiative to plead and prove foreign law (Art. 2). The same principle had already been adopted in the 1928 Bustamante Code (Art. 408-411).[93]

There are a few notable exceptions where the treatment of conflicts rules does not correspond with the mandatory or facultative application and ascertainment of foreign law. Luxemburg, for example, provides for the facultative application of

---

[87] Argentina; Croatia; Czech Republic; Estonia; Finland; Georgia; Germany; Greece; Hungary; Italy; Japan; Netherlands; Poland; Portugal; Romania; Switzerland; Turkey; Uruguay; Venezuela.

[88] Austria (§§ 3 and 4 PIL Act).

[89] Belgium (Art. 15 PIL Act); Croatia (Art. 13 (1) PIL Act); Italy (Art. 14 (1) PIL Act); Switzerland (Art. 16 (1) PIL Act).

[90] Belgium; Denmark; France; Sweden.

[91] Remien, *supra* note 52, pp. 229 ff.

[92] Inter-American Convention on General Rules of Private International Law, signed at Montevideo on 8 May 1979. It is in force in Argentina, Brazil, Colombia, Ecuador, Guatemala, Mexico, Paraguay, Peru, Uruguay and Venezuela (for the status table, *see* http://www.oas.org/juridico/english/sigs/b-45.html).

[93] Convention on Private International Law (Bustamante Code), signed at Havana on 20 February 1928, ratified by Bolivia, Brazil, Chile, Costa Rica, Cuba, Dominican Republic, Ecuador, El Salvador, Guatemala, Haiti, Honduras, Nicaragua, Panama, Peru and Venezuela (for the status table, *see* http://www.oas.org/juridico/english/sigs/a-31.html).

conflicts rules as a general principle, but courts apply foreign law sua sponte in certain cases.[94] In Spain, the judge has an obligation to apply conflicts rules ex officio to determine whether foreign law governs the case at hand (Art. 12 (6) CC). For the foreign law to be applied, however, the parties are required to prove its content, possibly with the assistance of the court.[95] Romania seems to follow a similar principle.

2. Facultative Application of Foreign Law

In the jurisdictions grounded in or influenced by common law, foreign law generally needs to be pleaded by at least one party to be introduced in court proceedings. Unless a party raises the issue of the application of foreign law, the case is treated as a domestic case. The party who pleads foreign law further needs to prove it with sufficient specificity, so that the judge can apply it. In the U.S., the formal pleading of foreign law is no longer required in state courts and federal courts and substituted by mere invocation of foreign law.[96]

A party is likely to plead foreign law when it offers far greater advantages than the lex fori, or provides claims or defences that are not available in the lex fori.[97] The limited applicability of foreign law has practical advantages in that the judge is exempt from the duty to ascertain and apply foreign law. Parties may also avoid the application of foreign law by refraining from pleading or invoking it, and have their dispute decided by the lex fori. This rule in common law jurisdictions guarantees effective and expeditious administration of justice.[98]

B. Ascertainment of Foreign Law

1. General Remarks

Depending on whether foreign law is applied ex officio or through a party pleading foreign law, the task of ascertaining foreign law is conferred either on the judge or on the parties. The following separately examines the methods of and the means for ascertaining foreign law.

---

[94] Cuniberti/Rueda, *supra* note 81, pp. 256 ff.

[95] Esplugues *et al.* (eds.), *supra* note 9, pp. 20, 28; similarly also in Tunisia.

[96] Hay, *supra* note 38, pp. 223 ff.

[97] Fentiman, *supra* note 41, para. 20.01.

[98] Dicey, Morris & Collins, *supra* note 31, vol. 1, para. 9-002.

2. Regimes Under the Mandatory Application of Foreign Law

a) Duty of the Judge

Countries requiring the mandatory application of foreign law generally make it incumbent on the judge to ascertain foreign law. The ascertainment of foreign law is not subject to the general rules of evidence in court proceedings, but the courts have a duty to use all means available to find sufficient information on foreign law.[99] In Switzerland, "the corroboration of the content of foreign law may be burdened on the parties in the case of patrimonial matters" (Art. 16 (1) PIL Act). This provision is understood not as imposing the burden of proof on the parties, but simply as facilitating the judge's duty by means of the parties' corroboration.[100] In light of the right to be heard, the parties ought to be given an opportunity to take a position on the content of foreign law in Switzerland.[101] Similarly, as a matter of the finding of law, a German court is required to refer to how it has proceeded to ascertain foreign law in its decisions.[102]

b) Means for the Ascertainment of Foreign Law

aa) Developments and Internet Sources

To ascertain foreign law, the most accessible and useful resources for the judge are documents and Internet sources from the relevant jurisdiction.[103] These include foreign statutes, commentaries, textbooks, and other publications. In different countries, the government, the courts or other institutions provide information on their own legal system on the Internet for foreign stakeholders. The EU has developed, in cooperation with the notariat and academia, a number of Internet databases on specific areas of private law, in particular marriage and succession.[104]

In France, Belgium and Tunisia, courts mostly rely on "certificats de coutumes" (affidavits of law and customs).[105] These certificates are drawn up either by public authorities such as consulates, or by lawyers, notaries or academics. Certificates prepared by private persons, however, are subject to the risk that they are party-

---

[99] Provided for in: Croatia (Art. 13 (1) PIL Act); Czech Republic (Sec. 23 (1)(2) PIL Act); Italy (Art. 14 (1) PIL Act).

[100] Keller/Girsberger, *supra* note 74, Art. 16 IPRG, para. 18 ff.; Mächler-Erne/Wolf-Mettier, *supra* note 74, Art. 16 IPRG, para. 13 f.

[101] *See* BGE 124 I 49; *also* BGE 119 II 93.

[102] Remien, *supra* note 52, pp. 230 ff.

[103] Argentina; Belgium; Croatia; Czech Republic; Estonia; France; Germany; Greece; Hungary; Italy; Japan; Macau; Poland; Portugal; Romania; Spain; Sweden; Switzerland; Tunisia; Venezuela.

[104] *See* http://www.couplesineurope.eu/ and http://www.successions-europe.eu; *cf.* "European Legislation Identifier" (ELI) and "European Case Law Identifier" (ECLI) (*see* http://www.hcch.net/upload/wop/gap2014pd14en.pdf).

[105] *See* Mayer/Heuzé, *supra* note 1, p. 145.

biased. Courts have to use other verification methods when referring to other documents (statutes, case law etc.), as courts cannot order a hearing or cross-examination of the authors of such certificates.

bb) Inquiry to Domestic Authorities

The courts in a number of jurisdictions also make inquiries of domestic authorities, such as a Ministry of Justice, a Ministry of Foreign Affairs, and embassies and consulates abroad. Japanese Family Courts frequently make inquiry to the General Secretariat of the Supreme Court in family and personal status matters, where the Family Courts' proceedings are governed by the inquisitional procedural rules.

cc) Inquiry to Foreign Authorities

Inquiry via diplomatic channels, through the intermediation of embassies or consulates located in the forum state, may also be employed in a number of jurisdictions.[106] However, this is not frequently used, presumably because it is time-consuming and an abstract answer on foreign law is generally not sufficient for courts to apply foreign law.[107] Nor is the judicial assistance pursuant to the London Convention (1968), the Montevideo Convention (1979) or the Minsk Convention (1993) frequently used (*infra* VIII.A).

dd) Experts or Expert Institutes

In some jurisdictions, such as Germany, Greece, Austria, Switzerland, Italy and the Netherlands, courts often appoint an expert to obtain information on foreign law. Unlike party-appointed experts, courts can readily rely on court-appointed experts to be neutral and objective. Courts may entrust an expert opinion to individual academics or practitioners, as well as to universities and independent research institutions, such as the Max Planck Institute in Hamburg (MPI) and other university institutes in Cologne, Heidelberg and Munich in Germany,[108] the Swiss Institute in Lausanne (SICL),[109] the International Legal Institute in The Hague (IJI)[110] and the Hellenic Institute in Athens (HIIFL).[111] The inquiry to experts or expert institutes is regularly effected at a party's request, not on the judge's own motion. The experts

---

[106] Belgium; Georgia; Germany; Greece; Italy; Japan.

[107] *See* Hilmar Krüger, "Zur Ermittlung ausländischen Rechts in Deutschland: Ein Bericht aus der Praxis", in: *Ergin Nomer'e Armağan* (Istanbul 2002), pp. 372 f.

[108] Max Planck Institute for Comparative and International Private Law (MPI) in Hamburg, Germany; for other institutions in Germany, *see* Oliver Remien, "Die Anwendung und Ermittlung ausländischen Rechts im System des Europäischen Internationalen Privatrechts", *ZVglRWiss* 115 (2016), pp. 575 f.

[109] Swiss Institute of Comparative Law (SICL) in Lausanne, Switzerland.

[110] International Legal Institute (*Internationaal Juridisch Instituut*) (IJI) in The Hague, Netherlands.

[111] Hellenic Institute of International and Foreign Law (HIIFL) in Athens, Greece.

are seldom summoned to courts as a witness, because their written statements are usually specific and clear enough for the court to determine foreign law.

In Venezuela, expert witnesses are reportedly becoming the most important method of ascertaining foreign law. In other countries, court-appointed experts are available but rarely used, presumably due to difficulties in finding suitable experts.[112] Most jurisdictions do not seem to require any specific qualifications for experts. It is generally considered sufficient that the experts have expertise in the relevant foreign law either on the basis of their legal training, or professional experience as an academic or practitioner or both.

ee) Assistance by the Parties

In civil law countries, the courts are generally allowed to seek assistance from the parties.[113] This principle is stipulated in the Inter-American Convention on General Rules of Private International Law (Art. 2), which further authorizes the parties to prove foreign law of their own motion. The party relying on foreign law is often advised to submit evidence in Venezuela.[114] In Japan, the judge often asks the parties for assistance in business disputes, where the parties usually have the resources to obtain evidence on foreign law.[115] In Germany and Switzerland, despite the mandatory application of foreign law, the parties even incur the obligation to cooperate with the court when asked to assist ascertain foreign law.[116]

The parties will submit (translated) foreign statutes, court decisions, opinions of party-appointed experts (e.g., academics or foreign law firms), and any other documents (e.g., textbooks or relevant publications). The parties may be interested in assisting the courts, with a view to clarifying the foreign rules, accelerating court proceedings and possibly inducing a favourable decision by the court. Yet, as a corollary of the mandatory application of foreign law, the information on foreign law submitted by the parties is neither binding on the judge, nor does it discharge the judge from the duty of ascertaining foreign law. The court is entitled and obliged to verify ex officio the evidence tendered by the parties. The court is not restricted to considering the evidence submitted by the parties, but will conduct its own examinations by using additional means where necessary. Hence, the parties' submission on the content of foreign law remains without legal effect in civil law jurisdictions.

---

[112] Argentina; Georgia; Hungary; Japan; Poland.

[113] Belgium; Croatia; Czech Republic; Denmark; Estonia; Finland; France; Georgia; Hungary; Italy; Portugal; Romania; Sweden; Tunisia; Turkey.

[114] In Venezuela, the court may issue a non-binding procedural order to request the party to submit sufficient information on foreign law, without imposing on the party an obligation to do so.

[115] Ex-Art. 219 CPC of Japan (Law No. 29 of 1890) which was modelled on § 293 ZPO of Germany was abolished in 1926, allegedly because the underlying principle was self-evident. Some authors still assert that the parties incur the obligation to cooperate with the courts in ascertaining foreign law, as in Germany.

[116] Germany (§ 293 CPC); Switzerland (Art. 16 PIL Act). The effects of breaching such an obligation are uncertain. Ivo Bach/Urs Peter Gruber, "Austria and Germany", in: Esplugues *et al.* (ed.), *supra* note 9, p. 105.

ff) Other Methods

In Germany, some courts have established divisions or chambers that specialize in foreign law. The Regional Court (Landgericht) of Hamburg as well as the Higher Regional Courts (Oberlandesgericht) of Bamberg and Stuttgart currently have such a specific civil chamber, the same as the Senat that existed at the Court of Appeal (Kammergericht) of Berlin in the 1930s.[117] Creating a division specialising in foreign law is certainly reasonable, because it will enable judges to be trained specifically for conflicts cases and obtain experience and expertise. The same advantages are derived by concentrating the subject-matter jurisdiction for return proceedings in the implementation of the 1980 Hague Child Abduction Convention.[118]

In other countries, such as the Czech Republic, informal cooperation between judges within the Internal Judicial Network has played an important role. This mechanism enabled judges to exchange information with respect to foreign law or share their experience concerning the service of documents in different states.

c) Effects of Obtaining Information

Information obtained with respect to foreign law is not binding in most jurisdictions.[119] This ensures leeway for the judge. In fact, there is generally no mechanism to check the reliability of information provided by domestic or foreign authorities, or the court-appointed or party-appointed experts.[120] The judge needs to examine the quality of the obtained information in court proceedings, possibly by using additional materials. In light of this, it is sensible policy to exclude the binding force of any information provided in relation to foreign law. Although the inability to independently verify foreign law is a drawback, this can be remedied by developing various mechanisms to facilitate access to foreign law and improving the quality of information on foreign law.

In a number of jurisdictions, the costs of judicially ascertaining foreign law is a cost of litigation and is split between the parties like other litigation costs. The costs of party-appointed experts are borne by the respective party.[121] However, in some other jurisdictions, the costs are generally borne by the state. Due to the court's obligation to apply foreign law ex officio, these countries do not classify these costs as "litigation costs". The costs can only be incurred by a party in specific circumstances, where the party has requested the ascertainment of foreign law.[122]

---

[117] Remien, *supra* note 52, pp. 213 f.; *also* Remien, *supra* note 108, p. 574.

[118] *See* Yuko Nishitani, "Internationale Kindesentführung in Japan—Auf dem Weg zur Ratifikation des HKÜ? —", in: *Festschrift Bernd von Hoffmann* (Bielefeld 2011), pp. 319 ff.; idem, "Aktuelle Entwicklungen im internationalen Familienrecht Japans", *ZJapanR/J. Jap. L.* 43 (2017), p. 37.

[119] Argentina; Belgium; Czech Republic; Estonia; Germany; Greece; Portugal; Venezuela. As an exception, information on foreign law is said to be binding in Macau.

[120] For example, Uruguay.

[121] Belgium; Denmark; Estonia; Finland; Germany; Greece; Japan; Sweden.

[122] Argentina; Czech Republic; Hungary; Uruguay; Venezuela.

3. Regimes Under the Facultative Application of Foreign Law

a) Proof of Foreign Law

Pursuant to the traditional common law principle established or taken as a model in various jurisdictions,[123] the application of foreign law invariably depends on the parties' pleading or invocation of foreign law. Further, the parties are required to prove foreign law with sufficient specificity so that the judge is able to apply it. This is because issues of foreign law are treated as issues of fact, and the proof of foreign law as a matter of evidence (*supra* III.B.2).[124] The courts are presumed not to have any knowledge of foreign law. Thus, the courts are neither obliged to ascertain and apply foreign law, nor allowed to take judicial notice of foreign law as a rule. This conventional common law principle, however, is subject to some exceptions.

First, where the content of a particular foreign law is a "notorious" fact, the court is entitled to take judicial notice of it. In the U.K., as in Ireland, the fact that roulette is not unlawful in Monte Carlo has been accepted as a notorious fact.[125]

Second, foreign law need not be pleaded and proved if statutory rules or international instruments explicitly permit judicial notice.[126] Notably, Article 14 of the 1980 Hague Child Abduction Convention stipulates that the law of the country in which the child habitually resides may be amenable to judicial notice to determine whether there was a wrongful removal or retention of the child (Art. 3). Pursuant to the Trans-Tasman agreement,[127] proof of New Zealand law is not necessary before Australian courts, or vice versa Australian law before New Zealand courts. The court is allowed to inform itself in any adequate way.

Third, in Multi-Unit states, the law of other internal political units enjoys special treatment. In the U.S., sister-state law is generally amenable to judicial notice.[128] In Nigeria, courts are invariably compelled to take judicial notice of laws of states within the federation. In Israel, courts can apply without proof the law of all recognized religious communities as an integral part of Israeli law.[129] The U.K. courts have applied colonial laws, in some cases even foreign-country laws (e.g., German law

---

[123] U.K.; Ireland; Australia; U.S.; Commonwealth African countries. A similar rule has been adopted in Malta, Quebec and Israel.

[124] Fentiman, *supra* note 41, para. 20.06 ff.

[125] Court of Appeal, *Saxby v Fulton* [1909] 2 K.B. 208; for further detail, *see* Dicey, Morris & Collins, *supra* note 31, vol. 1, para. 9-005; *also* Fentiman, *supra* note 71, pp. 244 ff.

[126] U.K. (Maintenance Orders Act 1950, s. 22 (2); Civil Evidence Act 1972, s. 4 (2)); *also* Australia.

[127] 2008 Agreement between the Government of Australia and the Government of New Zealand on Trans-Tasman Court Proceedings and Regulatory Enforcement (entry into force in 2013); sec. 97 (1)(2) of the Trans-Tasman Proceedings Act (An Act relating to proceedings in Australian and New Zealand courts and tribunals, and for related purposes) 2010 (Cth).

[128] The Uniform Judicial Notice of Foreign Law Act (1936) and Uniform Interstate and International Procedure Act (1962) were withdrawn in 1977 for being obsolete. Hay/Borchers/Symeonides, *supra* note 31, p. 605; Hay, *supra* note 38, pp. 221 ff.

[129] However, the court may also ask the parties to prove the religious laws and appoint an expert in family matters.

on simultaneous death and eligibility to succession),[130] with no evidence submitted by the parties. Furthermore, an appeal court that has jurisdiction to hear appeals from the court of several political units takes judicial notice of any of those units. Thus where the U.K. Supreme Court hears an appeal from England or Northern Ireland, it takes judicial notice of Scots law; vice versa, where it hears an appeal from Scotland, the Court takes judicial notice of English or Northern Irish law.[131]

Fourth, some jurisdictions have distanced themselves from the common law tradition. Most U.S. states allow the courts to take judicial notice of foreign law in general, although this does not free parties of the task of assisting the court by providing references to foreign-country legislation or case law, or by adducing expert testimony. Under Rule 44.1., U.S. federal courts may also establish foreign law based on their own research. Empirically, U.S. state and federal courts often judicially notice the law of England or other common law jurisdictions.[132] Among Commonwealth African countries, the position is divided as to whether judicial notice of foreign law is permissible (in the affirmative in South Africa and Lesotho).

Finally, foreign law need not be proved when the parties expressly or tacitly admit it.[133] The courts will presume agreement on the content of foreign law when the parties admit or do not dispute allegations made in pleadings, or agree that the presumption of similarity ought to apply. However, although courts generally respect such an agreement under the adversarial principle in civil procedure, they may disregard the agreement if the parties' common allegation of the similarity with the lex fori appears unlikely.[134]

b) Means for the Ascertainment of Foreign Law

aa) Expert Evidence

At common law, it is an established principle that foreign law must be proved by expert evidence. It is not sufficient to solely submit the text of foreign legislation or cite foreign decisions or books of authority. Such materials have to be brought before the court as part of the evidence of an expert witness so that the judge can evaluate or interpret them.[135] This conventional common law principle still applies in the U.K., Ireland and Commonwealth African countries. In Australia and the U.S., parties are exceptionally allowed to submit written documents as evidence

---

[130] High Court of Justice, Chancery Division (England & Wales), *Re Cohn* [1945] Ch. 5.

[131] Dicey, Morris & Collins, *supra* note 31, vol. 1, para. 9-006 ff.

[132] Hay/Borchers/Symeonides, *supra* note 31, pp. 605 ff.; Hay, *supra* note 38, pp. 221 ff.

[133] Dicey, Morris & Collins, *supra* note 31, vol. 1, para. 9-008.

[134] New South Wales Court of Appeal, *Damberg v Damberg* (2001) 52 NSWLR 492, 519; [2001] NSWCA 87 [154] (the parties' agreement that German law is similar to Australian law was not accepted).

[135] Dicey, Morris & Collins, *supra* note 31, vol. 1, para. 9-013.

without the documents being proven by the expert witness, although expert evidence is still most commonly used. Comparable rules apply in Israel and Quebec.

Expert evidence can be submitted as a witness statement or affidavit, or as oral evidence, including cross-examination of the expert. There is no special qualification required to be eligible as a competent expert in all these jurisdictions. Any suitable persons, such as current or former judges, lawyers, academics and even non-jurists (e.g., traders or officers) who are familiar with the foreign legal system qualify themselves as an expert witness. It is no longer required that the expert has practiced, or at least is entitled to practice in the foreign jurisdiction.[136] The expert evidence can be tested and challenged by the opposing party in cross-examination or by calling a different expert. If the evidence of the expert witness is uncontradicted or each party's expert witness agrees on the meaning and effect of the foreign law, the court will accept such evidence unless it is clearly false or evidently inconsistent. If the evidence of several expert witnesses conflicts as to the effect of foreign sources, the court has a duty to look at those sources to decide between the conflicting testimonies.[137]

Failing judicial notice of foreign law, English courts are not entitled to conduct their own research into foreign law, but limited to the evidence tendered by the parties. Only if an expert refers to foreign statutes, decisions or books, may the court look at these materials as part of the evidence.[138] On the other hand, Australian courts are allowed to consider the primary sources of foreign law (statutes, cases or treaties) under the rules of evidence. The Supreme Court of New South Wales also has the power to appoint a referee for the question of foreign law, similarly to Maltese courts. Pursuant to Rule 44.1., U.S. federal courts may go beyond the materials submitted by the parties and engage in their own research on foreign law without being bound by the formal rules of evidence. In Israel, the Supreme Court may take advantage of foreign clerks in ascertaining foreign law.

In the U.K., the U.S. and Australia, expert testimony is increasingly criticized given that experts are often expensive, unhelpful, incompetent and party-biased. Moreover, experts of equal qualification and persuasiveness may well deliver conflicting opinions on the same issue of foreign law. Thus courts no longer accept expert testimony blindly, but turn it down where appropriate and possibly undertake independent research into foreign law.[139] Judge Posner of the U.S. Court of Appeals for the Seventh Circuit asserts that judges conduct their own research on the basis of relevant published English-language materials,[140] although some other judges have

---

[136] U.K. (Civil Evidence Act 1972, s. 4 (1)); Australia; Commonwealth African countries; Ireland; *also* Malta; Quebec; Israel.

[137] U.K. (Dicey, Morris & Collins, *supra* note 31, vol. 1, para. 9-015 ff.; Fentiman, *supra* note 41, para. 20.48 ff.); Australia; Ireland; *also* Malta.

[138] *See, e.g., Bumper, supra* note 80. Fentiman, however, contends that English courts are empowered in principle to appoint their own expert instead of those of the parties. Fentiman, *supra* note 41, para. 20.07.

[139] *See* Fentiman, *supra* note 41, para. 20.38, 20.48 ff.; Hay, *supra* note 38, pp. 228 ff.

[140] *Sunstar, Inc. v. Alberto-Culver Co.*, U.S. Court of Appeals for the Seventh Circuit, 586 F.3d 487

cautioned against the loss of original meaning in translation.[141] As an alternative, courts are entitled to appoint experts or use "special masters" to decide the case on the basis of accurate information on foreign law, but this method is seldom used. The trial court's decision on the acceptance of expert opinion can be reviewed by appellate courts.[142]

bb) Documents

Departing from the conventional common law principle, Australia, Israel, Quebec and the U.S. exceptionally permit documentary evidence of foreign law without expert witness. Hence, foreign statutes, cases, treaties and acts of state, as well as books, pamphlets and other publications may be referred to by the court. In Quebec, certificate of a "jurisconsult" drawn by a lawyer or anybody having knowledge on the specific foreign law is also used as written proof.

cc) Inquiry to Domestic or Foreign Authorities

Because the ascertainment of foreign law depends on the parties' pleading and proof at common law, courts generally do not make inquiries to domestic or foreign authorities to obtain information on foreign law. Notably the British Law Ascertainment Act 1859 has enabled courts in any part of the "British Dominion" to seek the view of courts in any other part of the "British Dominion" as to the law governing the case at hand. The court inquired of has complete discretion as to whether or not to state a case. The Act continues to be in force in many Commonwealth countries, except Australia. This procedure, however, has seldom been implemented, as it is costly and time-consuming.[143] Nor have international instruments for access to foreign law, such as the London Convention (1968) and bilateral treaties been applied. In this respect, judicial cooperation with foreign courts may be more useful in common law jurisdictions (*infra* VIII).

c) Effects of Obtaining Information

The effects of the information on foreign law provided by expert witnesses, documents submitted by the parties or any other means is not binding on the judge. The costs of ascertaining foreign law are generally borne by each party at the time of litigation. However, the costs may be partly recovered by the successful party at the conclusion of the case.

(28 Oct. 2009); also *Bodum USA, Inc. v. La Cafetiere,* Ibid., 621 F.3d 624 (2 Sept. 2010).

141 Opinion of *Judge Wood* in *Bodum, supra* note 140.

142 Hay, *supra* note 38, pp. 229 ff.; *Jinro America Inc. v. Secure Investments, Inc.,* U.S. Court of Appeals for the Ninth Circuit, 266 F.3d 993 (14 Sept. 2001).

143 Dicey, Morris & Collins, *supra* note 31, vol. 1, para. 9-023.

C. Interpretation and Application of Foreign Law

1. General Rule

In the majority of jurisdictions considered, including both common law and civil law jurisdictions,[144] it is generally accepted that foreign law ought to be interpreted and applied in accordance with the rules of interpretation established in the country of origin. This principle is explicitly provided for in the Inter-American Convention on General Rules of Private International Law (Art. 2). In fact, this principle conforms to the purpose and significance of conflict of laws. Where conflicts rules designate foreign law as the applicable law, it ought to be interpreted and applied correctly—in the same manner that a judge in that country would—to achieve international harmony and respect the parties' interests.

As a corollary of this principle, gaps in foreign law are generally filled pursuant to the criteria in the country of origin to ensure the coherence of the foreign legal system.[145] Belgium has adopted and Swedish authors are responsive to the alternative approach of pointing to another foreign law that belongs to the same legal system and is likely to have similar content to the applicable foreign law. While German courts are hesitant to adopt innovative means to interpret foreign law ("Rechtsfortbildung"),[146] Georgia is responsive to this idea so long as the interpretation accords with the foreign legal system.

2. Other Features

Some jurisdictions deviate from the prevailing method of interpretation and gap-filling of foreign law. In the U.K., foreign law is interpreted on the basis of the evidence adduced by the expert witness. When there is no evidence as to the interpretation of the foreign law, the court is allowed to construe the relevant foreign provisions as it would construe its domestic law.[147] Australian courts interpret and apply foreign law according to Australian law, by reference to the law of the country of origin, as has been ruled in the Neilson case in relation to Chinese law (2005).[148] As a general framework, (i) the general interpretation of foreign law is distinguished from (ii) the application of the foreign law to the facts of the case at hand. Evidence

---

[144] Austria; Belgium; Croatia; Czech Republic; Denmark; Estonia; Finland; France; Georgia; Germany; Greece; Hungary; Israel; Italy; Japan; Macau; Poland; Portugal; Romania; Sweden; Switzerland; Tunisia; Turkey.

[145] Belgium; Czech Republic; Estonia; Finland; Georgia; Germany; Hungary; Italy; Poland; Uruguay.

[146] BGH, 4 July 2013, NJW 2013, 3656.

[147] Dicey, Morris & Collins, *supra* note 31, vol. 1, para. 9-018 f.; Fentiman, *supra* note 41, para. 20.138 ff.

[148] High Court of Australia, *Neilson v Overseas Projects Corporation of Victoria Ltd.* (2005) 223 CLR 331; [2005] HCA 54.

is only admissible in relation to (i), since (ii) is always decided by Australian courts. If the evidence as to the foreign principles of statutory construction is not sufficient, Australian courts may apply Australian principles of interpretation. By the same token, gaps in the proof of foreign law are filled by the lex fori.

D. Failure to Establish Foreign Law

1. General Remarks

Foreign law cannot be applied when the judge fails to ascertain the content of foreign law ex officio or the party incurring the onus of proving foreign law fails to fulfil that task. This problem commonly occurs. Different solutions have been adopted throughout various jurisdictions.

2. Different Methods

a) "Presumption of Similarity"

At common law, the parties need to plead and prove foreign law to the court's satisfaction. Where a party pleads foreign law but fails to adduce sufficient evidence of the foreign law or refrains from proving the foreign law, courts traditionally applied the lex fori pursuant to the "presumption of similarity" (or "presumption of identity"). A rebuttable presumption was accepted that foreign law is the same as the lex fori. This approach used to prevail throughout jurisdictions grounded in or influenced by the common law tradition,[149] and in some civil law jurisdictions as well.[150]

However, the fictitious character of the presumption of similarity gradually came to light in the U.K., Australia and other common law jurisdictions, as well as in Israel. Pursuant to this rule, an Australian judge accepted in Tisand that Liberian law on ship registration and ownership was essentially the same as Australian law.[151] The High Court of Australia also applied Australian law in Neilson due to a lack of proof that the canons of statutory construction of Chinese law were different from those of Australian law.[152] Yet in Damberg, the judge refused to presume that German tax law was identical to Australian law, dismissing the party's claim for having

---

[149] U.K.; Australia; Commonwealth African countries (codified by statute in Ghana); *also* Malta and Quebec.

[150] Until 1966, Switzerland also placed the burden of proving foreign law upon the parties (Bundesgericht 11 May 1966, BGE 92 II 111) and applied in its absence Swiss law, assuming that the content of foreign law corresponds to the lex fori.

[151] Federal Court of Australia, *Tisand Pty Ltd v Owners of the Ship MV Cape Morton* (2005) 219 A.L.R. 48.

[152] *Neilson, supra* note 148; *see* Dicey, Morris & Collins, *supra* note 31, vol. 1, para. 9-026.

failed to discharge his onus to prove German law.[153] Similarly in the U.K., the Court of Appeal in Shaker refused to assume that the applicable Pennsylvanian company law was identical to the English company law, as the latter incorporated the Second Directive as a harmonized measure of the EU and provided for the prudential principle only in relation to public companies and not to private companies.[154]

Without yielding a consistent result, case law in Australia and the U.K. increasingly declines the presumption of similarity where it is obvious that the foreign law is unlikely to be the same as the lex fori. U.S. and Israeli courts have also gradually abandoned the presumption of similarity whenever the foreign law evidently belonged to an entirely different legal system. Such recent developments reflect "concern in the courts and the literature about the desirability of the presumption".[155] Arguably, insofar as the particular foreign law belongs to the same legal system and has comparable rules as the law of the forum state, the presumption of similarity makes sense in the absence of proof of foreign law. However, this could only be accepted in limited circumstances.

b) Dismissal of the Claim

Instead of the "presumption of similarity" doctrine, courts in the U.K., Australia and other common law jurisdictions have occasionally decided against the party who bears the onus of proving foreign law. This is for failing to state sufficient grounds on the merit.[156] The courts simply dismiss the claim allegedly governed by foreign law due to the absence of proof of foreign law. This position has been supported by some leading English authors on the ground that the default application of the lex fori—particularly statutory rules—would be artificial where the dispute is obviously governed by a foreign law. Nor could appropriate, tailor-made substantive law rules be developed for the individual case at hand.[157] Nevertheless, the dismissal of the party's claim would in effect result in denial of justice. It is also a delicate question of whether the task sharing between the court and the parties as to the proof of foreign law could contravene the party's right to be heard in court proceedings. To alleviate this problem, Israeli courts encourage the party to amend their pleadings and adduce subsequent expert evidence.

---

[153] *Damberg, supra* note 134.

[154] Court of Appeal, Civil Division (England & Wales), *Shaker v Al-Bedrawi* [2002] EWCA Civ 1452, [2003] Ch. 350; *also* Court of Appeal, Civil Division (England & Wales), *Fourie et al v Le Roux et al* [2005] EWCA Civ 204 (South African law on set-off in the course of insolvency); idem, *MA (Ethiopia) v Secretary of State for the Home Department* [2009] EWCA Civ 289 (Ethiopian nationality law).

[155] Fentiman, *supra* note 41, para. 20.94; *see also* Talia Einhorn, *Private International Law in Israel,* 2nd ed. (Alphen aan den Rijn 2012), pp. 411 ff.

[156] *Neilson, supra* note 148.

[157] Dicey, Morris & Collins, *supra* note 31, vol. 1, para. 9-025 ff.

In the U.S., some courts used to dismiss claims in the absence of proof of foreign law, holding that the foreign state was "uncivilized" and did not have law that could have been applied. Today, U.S. courts no longer accept this argument.[158]

c) Lex Fori Solution

In jurisdictions that request the parties to prove foreign law, courts nowadays prefer to simply refer to the lex fori in default of proof of foreign law without the interposition of the "presumption of similarity" or dismissing the action. The same solution is adopted in Quebec (Art. 2809 CC of Quebec). This is also the case with Spanish case law, although some previous decisions dismissed claims for lack of proof of foreign law. The reasoning is that courts have a duty to render justice and may not dismiss the claim solely because they do not know the content of foreign law. Since the law of the forum state is the only law of which the courts are presumed to have knowledge, it is only natural for the law of the lex fori to apply in the absence of proof of foreign law. However, not all common law courts follow this approach.

In civil law jurisdictions that presuppose the mandatory application of foreign law, the judge is obliged to ascertain the content of foreign law. If courts utilize all available means but fail to ascertain the content of foreign law within a reasonable timeframe, the lex fori may be applied as the last resort. However, it is generally understood that courts should not immediately apply the lex fori, but instead first make reasonable efforts to ascertain the foreign law before they can justifiably resort to the "default" or "substitute" application of the lex fori.[159] In this respect, it may be worth contemplating applying the following reasonableness tests prior to referring to the lex fori.

d) Reasonableness Tests

Prior to or instead of referring to the methods examined so far, some jurisdictions follow the reasonableness test. Two methods of applying this test can be distinguished: the conflict of laws method and the substantive law method.

The conflict of laws method for applying the reasonableness test has been statutorily adopted in Italy and Portugal. The rationale is to point to the 'second best' law in terms of conflict of laws to fill gaps in the applicable law. In Italy, when the applicable foreign law cannot be ascertained, the judge is required to look for other connecting factors when the relevant conflicts rules refer to cascading or alternative connecting factors. In the absence of such conflicts rules, the Italian judge will refer

[158] Hay, *supra* note 38, p. 220.

[159] Argentina; Belgium; Croatia; Czech Republic; Denmark; Estonia; Finland; Georgia; Germany (prevailing opinion); Greece; Hungary; Poland; Romania; Sweden; Switzerland; Tunisia; Turkey; Uruguay; Venezuela.

to the lex fori.[160] In Portugal, when the ascertainment of the applicable foreign law—that is, the law of the parties' nationality in status and family matters—has failed, the courts will have recourse to the subsidiary applicable law, which is the law of the parties' habitual residence.[161]

On the other hand, the substantive law method for applying the reasonableness test seeks to find out the presumed content of the foreign law. In particular, the majority of Japanese courts have sought to deduce rules that are apparently in force in the country of origin, in light of fundamental principles of the pertinent foreign law, envisaging a substantively appropriate solution. Some other Japanese courts have referred to different sources of foreign law presumed to be most similar to the applicable foreign law. To find out North Korean law, for example, the Japanese courts have referred to the general principles of socialism on divorce (1965),[162] or to the rules on post-mortem recognition of a child in the Soviet Union, Czechoslovakia and Poland at that time (1966).[163] Similarly, to find out Chinese adoption law, a Japanese court referred to the law of the Soviet Union, East Germany, Poland, Romania and Hungary at that time (1983).[164] This substantive reasonableness test aims to find out the apparently living law in the foreign country. This approach respects the significance and functioning of conflicts rules by seeking to apply the primarily applicable foreign law as far as possible and to avoid readily referring to the lex fori.

A comparable solution exists in Israel, Portugal and Switzerland.[165] Similarly, some German authors advocate a flexible approach to look for the probable rule under the applicable foreign law or the rule most closely related to it. The suggestion is that the judge ought to refer to general principles, uniform law or principles of contract law (UPICC[166] or PECL[167]). This position, however, has encountered criticism among German academics for being of limited use and causing uncertainty.[168]

[160] Italy (Art. 14 (2) PIL Act).

[161] Portugal (Art. 23 (2) and Art. 348 No. 3 CC). If this subsidiary applicable law cannot be ascertained either, the "common law" of Portugal will apply.

[162] Chiba District Court (Matsudo Branch), 11 August 1965, *Katei Saiban Geppô* 18-9, 53 (North Korea).

[163] Tokyo District Court, 19 March 1966, *Kaminshû* 27-1/4, 125 (North Korea).

[164] Nagoya Family Court, 30 November 1983, *Katei Saiban Geppô* 36-11, 138 (China).

[165] For Switzerland, *see* Kurt Siehr, *Das Internationale Privatrecht der Schweiz* (Zürich 2002), pp. 577 f.

[166] UNIDROIT Principles of International Commercial Contracts (UPICC).

[167] Principles of European Contract Law (PECL).

[168] *See* Remien, *supra* note 52, p. 249.

V. Judicial Review

A. *Conflict of Laws*

1. General Trends

The vast majority of the jurisdictions considered in this report, including both civil law and common law jurisdictions,[169] treat an erroneous application of conflicts rules as a question of law. An erroneous application of conflicts rules means that the judge points to the law of state B instead of the law of state A due to applying the wrong conflicts rule or wrongly interpreting a conflicts rule or connecting factor. Conflict of laws is a part of the legal system of the forum state, irrespective of whether the source of conflict of laws is domestic law, EU law or public international law. The conflicts rules ought to be respected and correctly applied by the judge. Thus the determination of applicable law under conflicts rules is appealable in most jurisdictions in the same way as domestic substantive law, subject to the usual conditions and constraints on appeals. In Switzerland, this principle is stipulated explicitly.[170]

With a view to correcting an erroneous application of conflicts rules, the appeal courts in most civil law jurisdictions only need to apply ex officio the law of state A that actually governs the case, substituting it for the law of state B that the lower applied in error. In jurisdictions grounded in or influenced by the common law tradition, however, the appeal court cannot apply ex officio the law of state A. The parties are required to plead or invoke and prove afresh the law of state A pursuant to the general rules of the treatment of foreign law.

2. Exceptional Features

France is the exception in the case of the judicial review of conflicts rules. An erroneous application of conflicts rules by the Court of Appeal can be reviewed by the Supreme Court ("Cour de cassation"). If the case apparently indicates foreign elements but the Court of Appeal has not applied conflicts rules at all, the parties may invoke conflicts rules in an appeal to the Supreme Court for the first time in relation to "non-disposable rights", but not in relation to "disposable rights". However, regardless of the category of rights, the Supreme Court may refuse to review a decision of the Court of Appeal on the basis of an "exception of

---

[169] Argentina; Australia; Belgium; Commonwealth African countries; Czech Republic; Denmark; Estonia; Finland; Georgia; Germany; Greece; Israel; Italy; Japan; Netherlands; Poland; Portugal; Quebec; Romania; Spain; Sweden; U.K.; Tunisia; Turkey; Uruguay; Venezuela.

[170] Art. 43a (1)(a) and Art. 68 (b)(c) OG; Art. 96 (a) BGG; Keller/Girsberger, *supra* note 74, Nach Art. 16 IPRG, para. 6 ff.

equivalence" insofar as the applied law and the law which would have been applicable are equivalent with respect to the legal consequences of the dispute.[171]

B. Foreign Law

1. Civil Law Approach

The majority of civil law countries, which provide for the mandatory application of foreign law, nowadays accept that errors in applying foreign law can be reviewed by higher courts including the Supreme Court, subject to the usual limitations on appeals.[172] This is a relatively recent development in Austria and Italy. In some countries, an appeal to the highest court is still subject to certain particular restrictions. The conditions under which an appeal may lie vary considerably among different countries.[173]

In Switzerland, an appeal on non-patrimonial matters lies to the Federal Supreme Court (Bundesgericht) under the same conditions as domestic law, including cases where the foreign law has been erroneously applied. In patrimonial matters, however, the revision of foreign law is only possible when the judge has wrongly and arbitrarily held the foreign law to be impossible to ascertain.[174] Under current Belgian case law, the Supreme Court can only review the application of foreign law if there is also an allegation of a breach of the relevant conflicts rules—except for EU conflicts rules. In addition, the scope of the review of questions concerning foreign law is restricted to verifying conformity with the interpretation prevailing in the foreign country. In particular, where there are several possible interpretations (e.g., as to the nature and scope of prescriptions in a foreign country),[175] the task of the highest court in Belgium is not to give an authoritative interpretation of the foreign law, but is limited to verifying that the lower court's decision accords with the interpretation upheld in the foreign country.[176]

Notably, some other civil law countries still restrict the review of the interpretation and application of foreign law by the highest court. In France, the interpretation and application of foreign law are not generally subject to review by the Supreme Court. Exceptions are only admitted in the following two cases: where the Court of Appeal has distorted the foreign law, i.e., committed a gross misinterpretation of

---

[171] Corneloup, *supra* note 53, *Rev. int. dr. comp.* 2014, pp. 383 f.

[172] Argentina; Austria; Croatia; Czech Republic; Denmark; Estonia; Finland; Georgia; Greece; Hungary; Italy; Japan; Poland; Portugal; Romania; Sweden; Tunisia; Turkey; Uruguay; Venezuela.

[173] In Spain, while academic opinions are still divided, courts have become responsive to the review of foreign law. Yet the determination of foreign law does not qualify as Spanish case law.

[174] Art. 43a (1)(2), Art. 68 (d) OG; Art. 96 (b) BGG; Keller/Girsberger, *supra* note 74, Nach Art. 16 IPRG, para. 4, 6 ff.

[175] Cour de cassation, 18 March 2013 (*La générale des carrières et des mines/R.L., Umicore*) (n° C.12.0031.F, available at: http://justice.belgium.be/fr/).

[176] Michael Traest, "Belgium", in: Esplugues *et al.* (eds.), *supra* note 9, pp. 130, 137 ff.

foreign law, or where the Court of Appeal has failed to state sufficient grounds on the application and interpretation of foreign law to justify its decision and did not fulfil formal requirements.[177] Similarly in Germany, the review of an erroneous application of foreign law by the highest court has generally been denied except in labour and criminal matters. However, where the appeal concerns an erroneous application of German procedural rules on the ascertainment of foreign law, the highest courts review the lower courts' decision for violating the duty to duly scrutinize foreign law (§ 293 ZPO). This position has not changed since the 2009 reform of procedural rules (§ 545 (1) ZPO and § 72 (1) FamFG) against the expectation of some authors.[178] In the 1991 Prendas Navalas case, the Federal Supreme Court (Bundesgerichtshof) reviewed and reversed the decision of the Higher Regional Court of Bremen, on the ground that the lower court judge had erroneously relied on an expert opinion delivered solely on the basis of "black-letter law", violating the obligation to ascertain foreign law.[179] In the Netherlands, appeals to the Supreme Court are procedurally excluded, although the mandatory application of foreign law has been explicitly provided for since 2012.[180] The Dutch highest court can only review foreign law indirectly following a plea of incorrect reasoning.[181]

2. Common Law Approach

In the U.K. and other jurisdictions where foreign law is traditionally deemed to be "fact" and the application of foreign law depends on the parties' pleadings and proof, parties are entitled to appeal the trial judge's decision. Unlike the usual types of facts, foreign law becomes appealable when the judge from a lower court fails to apply logically a foreign rule where the content of that rule has been clearly proven or where the judge has disregarded evidence. Although U.K. appellate courts tend to limit the scope of review to reassessing the evidence, they may proceed to interpret the foreign law themselves.[182] Granting appeals on points of foreign law aims to ensure protection for the parties, and has been followed in the U.K., Australia and Israel. In certain cases, an appeal to the highest court can even be admitted to consider points of foreign law.[183]

In the U.S., the trial court's determination of foreign law is regarded as a "question of law", and the appellate court may review it by considering the same, additional or other sources de novo. However, there is not yet case law regarding to what extent

[177] Corneloup, *supra* note 53, *Rev. int. dr. comp.* 2014, pp. 384 f.

[178] BGH, 4.7.2013, NJW 2013, 3656; BGH, 14.1.2014, NJW 2014, 1244; *see* Remien, *supra* note 108, pp. 577 f.

[179] BGH, 21.1.1991, NJW 1991, 1418; *see* Remien, *supra* note 52, pp. 250 ff.

[180] Art. 10:2 CC; Struycken, *supra* note 84, p. 607.

[181] Geeroms, *supra* note 49, para. 5.147 ff.

[182] Geeroms, *supra* note 49, para. 5.68 ff.

[183] For the U.K., *see* House of Lords, *Attorney General of New Zealand v. Ortiz* [1984] AC 1; [1984] 2 WLR 809; [1983] 2 All ER 93; *cf.* Hartley, *supra* note 71, p. 272.

review is allowed and whether the rejection of unrebutted expert testimony is admissible. No appeals have been approved to proceed to the U.S. Supreme Court.[184]

3. Reflections

The different positions on whether points of foreign law are appealable are primarily attributable to the role of the highest court in each legal system. The restrictive position in the Netherlands, France and Germany is because the highest court in a jurisdiction has the duty of guaranteeing a uniform interpretation of domestic law alone, and has no such duty regarding foreign law. It is not the task of the highest court to judicially confirm or develop foreign law. Further, even if the highest court did decide on the correct interpretation and application of foreign law, lower courts could not rely on that decision as such, since the lower courts would have to continuously examine the latest state of the foreign law. Such a passive attitude enables the highest court to maintain its authority and functionality—by avoiding the possibility that it would itself wrongly apply foreign law—and to limit its workload.

However, other jurisdictions permit the review of the interpretation and application of foreign law by the highest court. This is due to the following reasons: First, the equivalent treatment of foreign law and domestic law means that the highest court should be able to review foreign law just as it does domestic law. Second, the interpretation of a specific foreign law before domestic courts needs to be coherent. It is arguably contradictory to expect lower courts to ascertain and apply foreign law yet refuse any appeal to the highest court, given that the highest court is charged with ensuring the proper administration of justice in the respective legal system. Third, the significance of conflicts rules would be compromised if the designated foreign law was applied erroneously in a certain case but the highest court could not review it. Fourth, the highest court may be the legal institution best able to conduct its own research on foreign law, because it is generally better equipped with personnel and resources than lower courts.[185]

Therefore, there are good reasons why most jurisdictions allow judicial review of the interpretation and application of foreign law at the highest court. This also explains the academic criticisms of the more restrictive approach evident in French and German case law.[186]

---

[184] Geeroms, *supra* note 49, para. 5.88 ff.

[185] The Belgian, French, Japanese and Tunisian reporters in particular bring forward these arguments.

[186] *See, e.g.*, Corneloup, *supra* note 53, *Rev. int. dr. comp.* 2014, pp. 386 f.; Hübner, *supra* note 52, pp. 374 ff.; Matthias Jacobs/Tino Frieling, "Revisibilität ausländischen Rechts in den deutschen Verfahrensgesetzen—zugleich Besprechung des Beschlusses des Bundesgerichtshofs vom 4 Juli 2013", *ZZP* 2014, pp. 137 ff.

VI. Foreign Law in Other Instances

A. Administration

State authorities may be required to observe foreign law to carry out their administrative functions. In the majority of civil law countries, civil registry officers ascertain and observe foreign law ex officio to carry out marriage and other status acts or to change the name, as well as to recognize foreign judgments and status acts effected in a foreign country.[187] This is also the case where a legally valid family relationship is a prerequisite for family reunification in immigration matters, the acquisition of nationality, or the enjoyment of a tax exemption. The authorities may further refer to foreign law on child abduction and the protection of children, foreign contract law for transactions concerning immovable property, foreign tax law to examine tax exemption and imputed income, or foreign social welfare law to circumvent the double payment of child allowance. On the other hand, in Finland and France, civil registrars apply foreign law governing status issues ex officio, but the parties incur the obligation to prove its content. In default of the proof of the foreign law, the lex fori applies.[188]

Denmark has specific institutions for complaints against administrative acts, such as the Administrative Boards of Appeal and the Parliamentary Ombudsman. These institutions incur the obligation to apply foreign law ex officio. In Australia, foreign law is often relevant before administrative tribunals in immigration and tax matters. The invocation and proof of foreign law is incumbent on the parties as in civil litigation, even though the rules of evidence do not apply strictly to administrative tribunals.

B. Alternative Dispute Resolution

a) Arbitration

International arbitrations regularly relate to cross-border business transactions, so the arbitrators are often confronted with the application of foreign law.

In a number of jurisdictions, the treatment of foreign law in arbitration generally follows the procedural rules that govern the court proceedings at the situs of arbitration. Therefore, in common law jurisdictions, parties are required to plead and prove foreign law. Evidence on foreign law is provided by expert witnesses, and parties

[187] Czech Republic; France; Germany; Italy; Japan; Poland; Sweden; Tunisia; Uruguay; *also* U.K.

[188] Similarly also Belgium and Quebec.

may consent to the relevant aspects of the foreign law.[189] On the other hand, in most civil law countries, the ascertainment and application of foreign law is mostly incumbent on the arbitrators, as with judges in court proceedings.[190] However, given the specificities of arbitration as a means of private dispute resolution, the tribunal should arguably inform the parties of the applicable foreign law, ask the parties to provide materials for ascertaining foreign law and invite the parties to comment on its interpretation and application before rendering an arbitral award.[191] In any case, the task of determining foreign law is generally less demanding in arbitration than in court proceedings, as the parties usually appoint arbitrators who are knowledgeable regarding the relevant foreign legal norms and trade usages.

In some other countries like Estonia and Japan, the treatment of foreign law in arbitration is clearly different to that of court proceedings. There, arbitrators usually urge the parties to ascertain foreign law, possibly to obtain expert opinions, and the parties are allowed to enter submissions on the content of foreign law.

b) Mediation

Countries are establishing cross-border family mediation, especially the Contracting States of the 1980 Hague Child Abduction Convention. Mediation enables the left-behind parent and the taking parent to reach an amicable solution on visitation, accommodation, maintenance and other conditions. A voluntary agreement is likely to be observed by the parties and is generally suited to realizing the best interests of the child.[192] In cross-border child abduction, the mediators are not obliged but should have knowledge of the law of the child's habitual residence to find an appropriate solution in accordance with the Convention.

In some jurisdictions like Japan, where court-connected mediations are incorporated into the judicial system in family and inheritance matters, foreign law is applied ex officio by mediators.

---

[189] U.K.; Australia; *also* Malta; Israel.

[190] Argentina; Czech Republic; Denmark; Germany; Italy; Portugal; Uruguay; Venezuela.

[191] *Cf.* International Law Association, 2008 Rio de Janeiro Resolution: "Ascertaining the content of the applicable law in international commercial arbitration" (available at: http://www.ila-hq.org/en/committees/index.cfm/cid/19).

[192] *See, e.g.,* Hague Conference on Private International Law, *Guide to Good Practice under the Hague Convention of 25 October 1980 on the Civil Aspects of International Child Abduction: Mediation* (2012) (available at: http://www.hcch.net/upload/guide28mediation_en.pdf); Sybille Kiesewetter/Christoph C. Paul, *Cross-Border Family Mediation. International Parental Child Abduction, Custody and Access Cases*, 2nd ed. (Frankfurt am Main 2014); Sarah Vigers, *Mediating International Child Abduction Cases. The Hague Convention* (Oxford *et al.* 2011).

C. Advisory Work

a) Lawyers

Foreign law may be relevant in the advisory work of attorneys. Attorneys generally do not incur the obligation to ascertain the content of the applicable foreign law. In fact, attorneys are not qualified to advise clients on foreign law and could even be subject to professional liability by doing so. Large law firms have an established international network, so reliable information on foreign law for business transactions can be provided by foreign partner law firms. Otherwise, attorneys in Europe may refer to the European Judicial Network, but are not entitled to utilize the London Convention or bilateral treaties for judicial cooperation.

b) Notaries

In a number of jurisdictions, notaries play an important role in legal practice. Notaries often refer to foreign law in drafting documents such as contracts, testaments and prenuptial agreements, or when verifying the legal status of the client. Notaries in Belgium, France, Italy and some other countries have a duty to indicate any foreign elements of a case and ascertain foreign law ex officio, using documents or expert opinions, possibly with the parties' assistance.[193] In contrast, notaries in Germany and Portugal do not incur such a duty and only perform the act if they know the content of foreign law.[194] To obtain information on foreign law, notaries in some countries often seek assistance from their umbrella organization, such as the "Royal Federation of Notaries" in Belgium or the "Deutsches Notarinstitut" in Germany.

VII. Future Developments

A. Revision of Conflict of Laws

This study has shown that the application of foreign law is not an easy task for judges when applying foreign law ex officio, or for parties when seeking to plead and prove foreign law. The extent to which a case relies upon foreign law primarily depends on the relevant conflicts rules or connecting factors. It may therefore be worth contemplating the revision of conflicts rules of the forum state with a view to reducing the number of cases governed by foreign law.

---

[193] Belgium; France; Italy; *also* Quebec; Uruguay.

[194] Also in Poland and Japan.

Nevertheless, few national reporters advocate changing conflicts rules to privilege the lex fori. National reporters seem to consider that conflicts rules should reflect other superior ideas and policy considerations rather than simply increasing the frequency of applying the lex fori. In fact, conflict of laws in common law jurisdictions favour the application of the lex fori in family and succession matters by directly designating the lex fori or indirectly referring to habitual residence or domicile as the connecting factor. Furthermore, quite a few national reporters from civil law jurisdictions suggest empirically that the gradual shift from the principle of nationality to the principle of habitual residence in family and succession matters through Hague Conventions, EU Regulations or national legislation has considerably reduced the number of cases governed by foreign law. The existing EU regulations also provide for party autonomy, which regularly gives the parties an option to refer to the lex fori and avoid the application of foreign law.[195] Other conflicts mechanisms like renvoi, the reference to public policy or blocking statutes may also lead to the application of the lex fori (*supra* II.B.1). Consequently, national reporters rarely see the need to change the existing conflicts rules in the interest of avoiding the application of foreign law.

Instead of conflict of laws solutions, the Australian and some other national reporters suggest restricting and improving the rules on international jurisdiction so that cases governed by foreign law are more appropriately determined by foreign courts. For the sake of effective remedies and proper administration of justice, coordination between international jurisdiction and applicable law is desirable.

B. Treatment of Conflicts Rules and Foreign Law

1. Lack of Harmonisation

The treatment of conflicts rules and foreign law in court proceedings differ considerably among jurisdictions, even though the dichotomy of characterizing foreign law as "law" or "fact" no longer strictly applies and the practical outcome may not lie as far apart as it seems at first sight (*supra* III and IV.A). The divergent approaches to the mandatory or facultative application of conflicts rules and the ascertainment and application of foreign law may well affect the operation of uniform conflict of laws rules that exist in form of EU regulations or international treaties.

To take an example, suppose an English company (through its main establishment in London) and a Japanese service provider (through its main establishment in Tokyo) conclude a service contract without designating the applicable law. In the absence of choice of law, the contract is governed by Japanese law as the law of the service provider's habitual residence pursuant to Article 4 (1)(b) Rome I. Provided

[195] *See supra* note 29; for the *status quo*, *see* Eva-Maria Kieninger, "Ascertaining and Applying Foreign Law", in: Leible (ed.), *General Principles of European Private International Law* (Alphen aan den Rijn 2016), pp. 359 ff., 363 ff.

that international judicial jurisdiction is affirmed, a German judge sitting in Berlin will decide the case on the merits by applying Japanese law as the law governing the contract under Rome I ex officio, as in the majority of other EU Member States. However, an English judge sitting in London will apply English law, insofar as the parties do not plead and prove Japanese law. For a French judge sitting in Paris, contractual obligations relate to "disposable rights". Unless a party invokes Japanese law, the French judge is not obliged to refer to Rome I. However, once the parties enter a procedural agreement to exclude conflicts rules, the judge is bound to apply French law.

Despite uniform conflicts rules in the EU, international harmony of decisions cannot be achieved due to the divergent treatment of conflicts rules and foreign law among EU Member States.[196] This may fall short of the objective of unifying conflicts rules for the sake of market integration and judicial cooperation in civil matters in the EU (Art. 81 TFEU). The same problems inhere in international treaties that contain elaborate uniform conflicts rules, such as the 1971 Hague Convention on the Law Applicable to Traffic Accidents or the 1973 Hague Convention on the Law Applicable to Products Liability.[197]

2. Solutions

To guarantee the operation of uniform conflicts rules, several solutions may be envisaged de lege ferenda. Particularly in the EU, it may be worth contemplating the elaboration of an EU instrument unifying the treatment of conflicts rules in all Member States, as several national reporters have suggested.

The first solution advocated in the EU consists in introducing a specific instrument to provide for the mandatory application of conflicts rules and foreign law. The so-called "Madrid Principles" are one such proposal,[198] with support among some in the academic community.[199] Given the primacy of EU law over Member State national law, it may be justifiable to order the mandatory application of EU conflicts rules. The argument is that legal relationships governed by substantive mandatory rules (e.g., consumer and employee protection, anti-trust or maintenance obligations) should be regulated by the mandatory application of conflicts rules.[200] Even Fentiman, a prominent English lawyer, maintains in a comparable way that some

[196] *See, inter alia,* Remien, *supra* note 108, pp. 571 ff.; Clemens Trautmann, *Europäisches Kollisionsrecht und ausländisches Recht im nationalen Zivilverfahren* (Tübingen 2011), pp. 17 ff.

[197] Available at: http://www.hcch.net/

[198] *See* Principle IV of the Madrid Principles at: Esplugues *et al.* (eds.), *supra* note 9, p. 95.

[199] Hans Jürgen Sonnenberger, "Randbemerkungen zum Allgemeinen Teil eines europäisierten IPR", in: *Festschrift Jan Kropholler* (Tübingen 2008), pp. 245 ff.; Andreas Spickhoff, "Die Rechtswahl und ihre Grenzen unter der Rom I-VO", in: Kieninger/Remien (ed.), *Europäische Kollisionsrechtsvereinheitlichung* (Baden-Baden 2012), pp. 119 ff.; Trautmann, *supra* note 196, pp. 415 ff.

[200] Trautmann, *supra* note 196, pp. 418 ff.

EU conflicts rules require the introduction and application of foreign law (e.g., for consumer and employee protection).[201] From a practical viewpoint, however, this solution would inevitably alter division of responsibilities between the judge and the parties in applying and ascertaining foreign law. This would arguably necessitate a fundamental revision of substantive and procedural rules in the Member States that entirely or partly presuppose the facultative application of conflicts rules or foreign law, such as the U.K., Ireland and Malta, as well as France, Finland and Sweden. Furthermore, by solely targeting EU law, this solution would lead to a discrepancy between the mandatory application of EU conflicts rules and the facultative application of national conflicts rules within the same Member State.[202] Although this solution would be best suitable to achieve international harmony of decisions which is the objective of uniform conflicts rules, it certainly requires a careful analysis of feasibility and practicality throughout various Member States.

The second solution, also envisaging a specific EU instrument, involves introducing a "procedural agreement" in civil law jurisdictions that provide for the mandatory application of conflicts rules and foreign law at present. The procedural agreement allows parties to exclude conflicts rules and have the lex fori applied instead of foreign law in certain cases. Unlike the "facultative conflict of laws" theory advocated by Flessner,[203] this solution presupposes the facultativity of conflicts rules not for all, but solely for a specific category of legal relationships. This solution seeks to strike a fair balance between the international harmony of decisions and the proper administration of justice. In identifying the category of legal relationships for which parties can enter a procedural agreement, the French or Swedish approach of distinguishing between "disposable rights" and "non-disposable rights" has not been followed due to the difficulty and uncertainty in classifying the bifurcated categories of rights or issues (*supra* II.C.2). A tentative proposal of Lagarde employs the notion of "patrimonial matters" for which a procedural agreement should be admissible,[204] but the same difficulty of characterization arguably inheres in this proposal.[205] Alternatively, Kieninger advocates allowing a procedural agreement for those legal relationships for which the EU conflicts rules authorize parties to enter a subsequent choice of law during the court proceedings. This accords with the existing EU Regulations that generally provide for party autonomy.[206] Certainly, party autonomy enabling the parties to designate the

[201] Fentiman, *supra* note 71, pp. 66 ff., 87 ff. (*e.g.,* Art. 5 and 6 of the 1980 Rome Convention on the law applicable to contractual obligations, *O.J.* 1980, L 266/1).

[202] Stefania Bariatti/Étienne Pataut, "Codification et théorie générale du droit international privé", in: Fallon *et al.* (eds.), *Quelle architecture pour un code européen de droit international privé?* (Bruxelles *et al.* 2011), pp. 343 ff.

[203] *Supra* note 51.

[204] Art. 133 (2) of the "Embryon de règlement portant code européen de droit international privé", in: Fallon *et al.* (eds.), *Quelle architecture pour un code européen de droit international privé?* (Bruxelles *et al.* 2011), p. 373.

[205] *See* Corneloup, *supra* note 53, *RabelsZ* 2014, pp. 856 f.

[206] *See supra* note 29 and 195.

applicable substantive law has different functions from procedural agreement. Yet Kieninger convincingly argues that it is consistent to allow parties to opt out of conflicts rules and have the lex fori govern the case at hand, insofar as parties are already entitled to designate the lex fori as the applicable law before the court.[207] By adopting this compromise solution that favours the reference to the lex fori, an enhanced harmonization of the treatment of foreign law can be reached among the EU Member States which take a different position as to the mandatory or facultative application of conflicts rules and foreign law, even though the law actually applied to the case depends on the forum and the parties' procedural conduct.

The third possible solution that could be contemplated is to authorize the judges in common law jurisdictions to take judicial notice of foreign law. This solution does not touch upon the conventional principle that the party incurs the onus of pleading and proving foreign law. The party who intends to rely on foreign law needs to invoke foreign law. Judicial notice solely deals with the manner of determining the content of foreign law, providing the court with the authority to do so. Common law jurisdictions are becoming more responsive to the idea of taking judicial notice of foreign law (*supra* IV.B.3). Particularly in the U.K., allowing judicial notice of foreign law has the advantage of enabling the courts to refer to foreign legal materials in the absence of expert testimony and to deploy their own knowledge and expertise in establishing foreign law.[208] Notably, Article 14 of the Hague Child Abduction Convention, which has so far attracted 97 Contracting States,[209] entitles the judge in return proceedings to examine the illegality of a removal or retention of the child under the law of the child's habitual residence sua sponte. The relevant foreign law is considered to have the same effect as domestic law.[210] The possibility of judicially noticing foreign law may well facilitate implementing uniform conflicts rules in international treaties or EU regulations without disturbing the existing methods for the treatment of foreign law in common law jurisdictions.[211]

Adopting uniform or harmonized solutions on the treatment of conflicts rules and foreign law is a long way off. It is already a challenging task and requires painstaking efforts at the regional level as in the EU, let alone at the global level. Although some national reporters have been in favour of adopting an instrument to unify the treatment of foreign law, it is a delicate matter to touch upon substantive and procedural rules of various countries grounded in divergent legal institutions and traditions.[212] While the unification or harmonization of the methods of introducing, ascertaining and applying foreign law can be set as ultimate goals, a swifter way to

[207] It is suggested that the scope of procedural agreements should be limited to the subject-matter before the court and third parties' rights ought to be reserved. Kieninger, *supra* note 195, pp. 370 ff.; *also* Corneloup, *supra* note 53, *RabelsZ* 2014, pp. 854 ff.

[208] Fentiman, *supra* note 41, para. 20.144 ff.

[209] As of 17 April 2017 (*see* the Website of the HCCH at http://www.hcch.net/).

[210] Australia, Israel and Quebec.

[211] A proper definition of judicial notice will be required. For the conceptual ambiguity of judicial notice, *see* Fentiman, *supra* note 71, pp. 314 f.

[212] For example, Finland and U.K.

guarantee the operation of uniform conflicts rules may lie in developing mechanisms to enhance access to foreign law. This point is examined under the next section.

VIII. Improving Access to Foreign Law

A. *Status Quo*

Most accept that ascertaining the content of foreign law is challenging. While many jurisdictions provide information on their own statutes and case law on the Internet, the crucial question is how to obtain verifiable, up-to-date and reliable information on foreign law swiftly and efficiently that serves to decide the case at hand. This is not sufficiently addressed by the various means different jurisdictions utilize to obtain information on foreign law (*supra* IV.B). To explore an alternative solution, this section critically examines the existing methods of administrative and judicial cooperation to access foreign law before developing ideas on how to improve the existing mechanisms and contemplate new methods to facilitate access to foreign law.

1. Administrative Cooperation

a) Multilateral Treaties

aa) Mechanism of Judicial Assistance

International instruments grounded in administrative cooperation to facilitate access to foreign law include, in particular, the London Convention (1968) and its Additional Protocol (1978), the Montevideo Convention (1979) and the Minsk Convention (1993).[213]

The London Convention (1968) and its Additional Protocol (1978) adopted by the Council of Europe (COE) have established a system of judicial assistance to obtain information on foreign law (Preamble). Contracting States deliver to each other requested information via the "receiving agency" (Art. 2 (1)). Requests may

[213] There is also the Convention on Information in Legal Matters with respect to Law in Force and its Application signed on 22 September 1972 in Brasilia. Argentina and Portugal are party to this treaty. In addition, the Riyadh Arab Agreement for Judicial Cooperation was adopted by the League of Arab States (signed on 6 April 1983), which serves to exchange "the texts of legislations in force, legal and judicial publications, pamphlets and studies, and journals containing legal statutes and judgments, as well as information pertaining to judicial regulations" (Art. 1 (1)) (unofficial English translation available at: http://www.refworld.org/docid/3ae6b38d8.html [accessed 30 December 2016]). According to the Tunisian national reporters, this instrument has not frequently been employed.

be sent by one or more "transmitting agencies" or directly by courts (Art. 2 (2)).[214] Requests for information ought to emanate from a judicial authority (Art. 3 (1)). This includes arbitral tribunals if it is permissible under the domestic law,[215] and states can extend the scope to authorities other than judicial authorities (Art. 3 (3)). The receiving agency may draw up the reply itself or delegate the task to another state or official body, a private body or qualified lawyer (Art. 6 (1)(2)). The service is generally free, but a private body or lawyer can charge the requesting state on the basis of its consent (Art. 6 (3); Art. 15 (1)(2)). The information given in the reply is not binding on the requesting body (Art. 8).

The London Convention has attracted 46 Contracting States, including non-Member States of the Council of Europe (Art. 18), such as Costa Rica, Mexico and Morocco.[216] In implementing the Convention, Austria, Italy, Sweden and Switzerland designated the (Federal) Ministry of Justice as both the receiving and the transmitting agency. In Belgium, the Ministry of Justice acts as the receiving agency and the Ministry of Foreign Affairs as the transmitting agency. Due to its federal system, Germany has designated the Federal Ministry of Justice as the receiving agency, whereas the Justice Department of each Land acts as the transmitting agency.[217] Greece has appointed the HIIFL as both the receiving and the transmitting agency to rely on its expertise.[218]

The Montevideo Convention adopted by the Organization of American States (OAS) largely follows the mechanism of the London Convention. The receiving authority is the Central Authority designated by each Contracting State, while requests for information can either be directly sent by courts or through the Central Authority (Art. 7). The Montevideo Convention has attracted 12 Contracting States, including Spain as a non-American state. While Colombia, Ecuador and Mexico have appointed the Ministry of Foreign Affairs as the Central Authority, Brazil and Spain have chosen the Ministry of Justice. In Guatemala and Peru, the Supreme Court of Justice acts as the Central Authority.[219]

The Minsk Convention on legal assistance in civil, family and criminal matters (inter alia, service of documents, taking of evidence, recognition and enforcement of foreign judgments and extradition) was adopted by the Commonwealth of Independent States (CIS). The Minsk Convention, in particular, establishes a mech-

---

[214] Explanatory Report, para. 13 (available at: http://conventions.coe.int/Treaty/en/Reports/Html/062.htm). Art. 4 (1) of the Additional Protocol, however, requires that Contracting States designate one or more bodies to act as transmitting agency.

[215] Explanatory Report, *supra* note 214, para. 20.

[216] For status table, *see* http://conventions.coe.int/

[217] §§ 1 ff. of the Gesetz zur Ausführung des Europäischen Übereinkommens betreffend Auskünfte über ausländisches Recht und seines Zusatzprotokolls (AuRAG) of 5.7.1974 (BGBl. I S. 1433); § 72 (1) of the Rechtshilfeordnung für Zivilsachen (ZRHO) of 28.10.2011.

[218] *See* Raphael Perl, "European Convention on Information on Foreign Law", *IJLL* 8 (1980), pp. 151 f.

[219] For status table and declarations, *see* http://www.oas.org/juridico/english/sigs/b-43.html

anism comparable to the London Convention and the Montevideo Convention for the authorities of Contracting States to mutually provide information on their law (Art. 15). The Minsk Convention has been signed by the following CIS Member States: Armenia, Belarus, Kazakhstan, Kyrgyzstan, Moldova, Russia, Tajikistan, Turkmenistan, Uzbekistan and Ukraine. States outside the CIS, such as Azerbaijan and Georgia, also acceded to the Convention in 1996 (Art. 86).[220]

bb) Assessments

The national reports and several empirical studies conducted so far indicate that the London Convention has not been successful in practice. The reasons for this are fourfold.[221]

First, a number of judges, attorneys and other practitioners are simply not aware of the Convention. Second, a lack of efficiency seems to discourage the use of the Convention mechanism. The absence of a clear timeframe for replies (Art. 12) and the requirement to translate the inquiry into the vernacular language (Art. 14 (1)) risk causing delays and costs. Third, the inquiry is often not detailed or precise enough (Art. 4), and the reply is limited to brief, abstract information on foreign law (Art. 7). Inquiries with complex questions tailored to the case at hand are gradually increasing, but are held to exceed the framework of the Convention. This is precisely the problem, because abstract information on foreign law is generally not sufficient to determine a case. Some even claim that an Internet search for a foreign statutory text produces similar results to a formal reply provided under the Convention. Fourth, the inquiry needs to emanate from judicial or other authorities, to the exclusion of parties, attorneys and other individual stakeholders (Art. 3 (1)). Presumably for this reason, in the U.K., as in Malta, where the parties need to plead and prove foreign law and the evidence is to be adduced by expert witnesses, the judicial authority does not employ the Convention mechanism, although the U.K. receives about 15 inquiries from abroad every year.[222]

To date, there have not been any comprehensive assessments on the functioning of the Montevideo Convention or the Minsk Convention, but some national reporters indicate that the same drawbacks as the London Convention inhere in the

---

[220] *See* Hague Conference on Private International Law, "The Convention on Legal Assistance and Legal Relations in Civil, Family and Criminal Matters" (submitted by the Delegation of the Russian Federation: Information Document No 1 of April 2005 for the attention of the 20th Session of June 2005 on Jurisdiction, Recognition and Enforcement of Foreign Judgments in Civil and Commercial Matters [available at: http://www.supremecourt.ge/files/upload-file/pdf/act20.pdf]).

[221] *See, inter alia,* Eberhard Desch, "Best Practices Survey of the European Convention on Information on Foreign Law (ETS No. 62, London, 7 June 1968)", *CDCJ* (2002) 15 (cdcj/doc2002/cdcj15e2002); individual responses to the HCCH questionnaire on the treatment of foreign law (http://www.hcch.net/upload/wop/genaff_resp_pd09.html); SICL Report, Part II, *supra* note 9, pp. 17 f.; *cf.* Hübner, *supra* note 52, pp. 250 ff.; Krüger, *supra* note 107, pp. 360, 387 ff.; Trautmann, *supra* note 196, pp. 177 f.

[222] Reply of the U.K. to the HCCH questionnaire, *see supra* note 221.

Montevideo Convention. In respect of the Minsk Convention, the Russian authority points out that the coordination between the Central Authority and the Supreme Courts that draw up the reply is not yet sufficient.[223]

b) Bilateral Treaties

Various countries have signed bilateral treaties on judicial assistance and access to foreign law. This is particularly the case with (former) socialist countries (inter alia, East European countries, Russia, China, Georgia, Cuba and Vietnam). There are also bilateral treaties on judicial assistance between Germany and Morocco (1985),[224] as well as between Australia and the Republic of Thailand (1997)[225] and between Australia and the Republic of Korea (1999)[226]. While in Australia these bilateral treaties are not often used, the Trans-Tasman Treaty between Australia and New Zealand, which permits the court to take judicial notice of the law of the other state using any means,[227] is referred to from time to time and seems to be a useful tool.

2. Judicial Cooperation

a) Judicial Network

The Hague Conference on Private International Law has established the Hague Judicial Network to enable direct communications between liaison judges or between a judge and another authority sitting in different countries. The Hague Judicial Network, which is operative in over 90 jurisdictions as of April 2017,[228] has proven to be particularly efficient and helpful in implementing the 1980 Hague Child Abduction Convention to ensure a safe return of the child and the taking parent. Indeed, the liaison judge sitting in the country where the child habitually resided prior to the abduction can inform his or her counterpart of whether, for example, the removal of the child was illegal, protective measures are available, undertakings can

---

[223] Reply of Russia to the HCCH questionnaire, *see supra* note 221.

[224] Vertrag zwischen der Bundesrepublik Deutschland und dem Königreich Marokko über die Rechtshilfe und Rechtsauskunft in Zivil- und Handelssachen of 14 April 1958 (BGBl. 1959 II S. 118).

[225] Agreement on Judicial Assistance in Civil and Commercial Matters and Co-operation in Arbitration between Australia and the Kingdom of Thailand, done at Canberra on 2 October 1997, [1998] ATS 18.

[226] Treaty on Judicial Assistance in Civil and Commercial Matters between Australia and the Republic of Korea, done at Canberra on 17 September 1999, [2000] ATS 5.

[227] *Supra* note 127.

[228] Among other countries, Argentina, Australia, Canada, Denmark, Germany, Hong Kong, Israel, Japan, Malta, the Netherlands, New Zealand, the U.K., Uruguay and the U.S. participate in the Hague Judicial Network. *See* https://assets.hcch.net/docs/18eb8d6c-593b-4996-9c5c-19e4590ac66d.pdf (accessed 17 April 2017).

be enforced or a mirror order can be issued pursuant to the law of his or her jurisdiction. The communications may take place in writing or orally via telephone or videoconference.[229] This mechanism of direct judicial communications could also be useful to obtain information on foreign law in other family matters, as well as civil and commercial matters. Arguably, this mechanism to directly refer to judges sitting in a foreign court will appear expedient and advantageous when the judge in charge of a case in a civil law jurisdiction incurs the obligation to ascertain and apply foreign law ex officio, or when the judge in a common law jurisdiction is entitled to refer to the primary source of the foreign authority in conducting his or her own research into foreign law.

At a regional level, the EU has successfully established the European Judicial Network.[230] The European Judicial Network aims to ensure effective administration of justice to create a uniform area of justice. The European Judicial Network serves, among other purposes, to obtain information on the national law of other Member States via the website or direct judicial communications. Meetings and training programs of liaison judges are regularly organized by the European Commission; this enables the liaison judges to develop mutual trust and close cooperation.

Comparable judicial networks exist under the "Ibero-American Network of Judicial Cooperation in Civil and Criminal Matters"[231] and the "UNCITRAL Model Law of Cross-Border Insolvency"[232]. Yet these networks have not been used frequently, possibly due to a lack of awareness among practitioners.

b) Memorandum of Understanding

In 2010, the Supreme Court of New South Wales (NSW), Australia, and the Supreme Court of Singapore (SG) signed a Memorandum of Understanding (MOU) on "References of Questions of Law".[233] The NSW/SG-MOU has introduced an innovative procedure for referring questions of foreign law from one court to the other.

---

[229] *See, e.g.,* Hague Conference on Private International Law, *Direct Judicial Communications* (available at: https://www.hcch.net/en/publications-and-studies/details4/?pid=6024&dtid=3) (accessed 17 April 2017), p. 12; *also* Philippe Lortie, *Report on Judicial Communications in Relation to International Child Protection* (Preliminary Document No. 8 of October 2006 for the attention of the 5th meeting of the Special Commission to review the operation of the Hague Convention of 25 October 1980 on the Civil Aspects of International Child Abduction), pp. 5 ff.

[230] *Supra* note 8.

[231] Red Iberoamericana de Cooperación Jurídica Internacional (Iber-RED). This network has gained 22 Member States, which comprise Portugal, Spain and Latin American countries. *See* https://www.iberred.org/

[232] Art. 25 (2) of the UNCITRAL Model Law on Cross-Border Insolvency (1997) (available at: http://www.uncitral.org/).

[233] Memorandum of Understanding between the Supreme Court of Singapore and the Supreme Court of New South Wales on References of Questions of Law 2010; UCPR 2005 (NSW), r 6.44 (1).

Pursuant to this MOU, where the judge in charge of a case finds that the case is governed by the law of the other jurisdiction, the judge is to give consideration to directing the parties in the proceedings, instead of acting sua sponte, to take steps to have any contested issue of law determined by the other court, subject to the relevant procedural rules (Art. 1).

A comparable MOU was also entered into in the same year by the Chief Justice of New South Wales, Australia, and the Chief Judge of the State of New York (NY), U.S.[234] However, the U.S. has constitutional problems both on the state and federal levels, since answering a reference from a foreign country could be understood as providing an advisory opinion. Thus the NSW/NY-MOU was, unlike the NSW/SG-MOU, signed in the names of the representing judges. The answering body in New York is a panel of referees consisting of five volunteer judges, specifically a member of the Court of Appeals of New York and a member of each of the four appellate divisions, who act solely in an unofficial capacity.[235]

The method adopted in both MOUs to obtain information on foreign law may be more expensive than using expert evidence, but it has been supported for yielding more accurate, certain and authoritative results emanating from judiciary in the eyes of common lawyers. This is particularly the case when the foreign law has significant uncertainties and its determination on the basis of conflicting evidence adduced by expert witnesses carries the risk of being "speculative".[236] Despite their advantages, however, both MOUs have scarcely been utilized. To date, there has only been one case reported from New South Wales where the referral of a question of law was actually employed under the NSW/NY-MOU.[237] According to the Australian reporter, both MOUs require that separate proceedings be conducted in the foreign system, which carries undesirable cost implications and undermines the parties' expectation of litigating before the Australian court. In 2014, the NSW Court of Appeal held that the system envisaged in the MOU, which requires that the Chief Justice of the foreign court appoint the referees, is incompatible with the NSW rules of court, under which the NSW court must appoint the referees. Thus it is uncertain whether and how far the MOU system can still be employed.

---

[234] Memorandum of Understanding between the Chief Justice of New South Wales and the Chief Judge of the State of New York on References of Questions of Law 2010; UCPR 2005 (NSW), r 6.44 (2).

[235] Hay, *supra* note 38, p. 223; Chris Finn, "The first of its kind—questions of foreign law referred to New York—Marshall v Fleming" (19 July 2013: available at http://www.kennedys-law.com/article/MOU/ [reproduced from *Australian Civil Liability*]) (accessed 17 April 2017). The NSW/NY-MOU allows the judge to act sua sponte to send inquiries to the other courts (Art. 1).

[236] Spigelman, *supra* note 79, p. 213.

[237] *Marshall v Fleming* [2013] NSWSC 566.

c) Certification of Law

A specific mechanism of certification of foreign law within the Multi-Unit state has been developed in the U.K. and the U.S. As mentioned above, the British Law Ascertainment Act 1859 has enabled courts in any part of the "British Dominion" to seek the view of courts in any other part of the "British Dominion" as to the law governing the case at hand (*supra* IV.B).

In the U.S., there was an obvious need for federal courts to obtain information on state law, after Erie (1938)[238] required the federal courts to apply and interpret state law in nonfederal matters rather than relying on general common law. In intrastate cases, likewise, state courts encountered the challenging task of determining sister-state law. Lack of expertise frequently resulted in inappropriate references to old case law or lower court decisions without authority in the controlling State. This situation jeopardized the uniformity of application and construction of state law within the U.S., which opened the way for undesirable "forum shopping". Thus, the use of certification of state law via judicial cooperation was encouraged by the Supreme Court.[239] Further, the Uniform Law Commission adopted the Uniform Certification of Questions of Law Act (UCQLA) in 1967, which was last amended in 1995.[240] Pursuant to the UCQLA, federal courts and state appellate courts can efficiently obtain reliable answers to questions of law from the highest court of the relevant State. This certification system is considered to be advantageous not only in terms of the rendering court and the parties to save time and resources, but also in terms of States acquiring additional opportunities to preserve their control over state-law questions and state policy decisions. This is particularly the case with Delaware in relation to its corporate law. Delaware accepts inquiries from other states' highest courts and federal courts including bankruptcy courts in the U.S., and even from the U.S. Securities and Exchange Commission (SEC).[241] Between 1985 and 2013, however, the number of certified questions that the Delaware Supreme Court received was limited to 26, and only 38% of them came from outside of Delaware or, in the case of federal appeals courts, outside of the Third Circuit. This indicates the general reluctance of courts to refer questions of law to other courts across borders.[242]

---

[238] *Erie Railroad. Co. v. Tompkins,* 304 U.S. 64 (1938). Further, *Railroad Commission of Texas v. Pullman Co.*, 312 U.S. 496 (1941) decided that a federal court may abstain from applying state law while parties seek a decision on state law issues in state court.

[239] U.S. Supreme Court, *Clay v. Sun Insurance Office,* 363 U.S. 207 (1960); *Lehman Bros. v. Schein,* 416 U.S. 386 (1974); *Bellotti v. Baird,* 428 U.S. 132 (1976); *Houston v. Hill*, 482 U.S. 451 (1987); for further reference, *see* Rebecca Cochran, "Federal Court Certification of Questions of State Law to State Courts: A Theoretical and Empirical Study", *Journal of Legislation* 29 (2003), pp. 157 ff.; Verity Winship, "Cooperative Interbranch Federalism: Certification of State-Law Questions by Federal Agencies", *Vand. L. Rev.* 63 (2010), pp. 185 ff.

[240] Uniform Certification of Questions of Law Act [Rule] (1995) (available at the website of the Uniform Law Commission: http://www.uniformlaws.org/shared/docs/certification_of_questions_of_law/ucqla_final_95.pdf [accessed 30 December 2016]).

[241] Winship, *supra* note 239, pp. 191 ff.; idem, "Delaware invites Certified Questions from Bankruptcy Courts", *Del. J. Corp. L.* 39 (2014), pp. 429 ff.

[242] Winship, *supra* note 241, pp. 434 f.

B. Further Developments

1. Need to Access Foreign Law

In light of the limited means and instruments that are currently available, national reporters from civil law jurisdictions almost unanimously affirm the need to improve access to foreign law, taking the mandatory application of foreign law for granted. Some national reporters from jurisdictions with common law tradition also advocate enhancing access to foreign law, considering current limitations of expert evidence when it comes to proving foreign law.[243]

Given the mandatory application of foreign law, the primary stakeholders in enhancing access to foreign law are judges from civil law jurisdictions. National reporters, however, generally indicate that parties also necessitate assistance in obtaining information on foreign law, particularly those parties with limited resources, such as persons involved in family and succession matters, consumers or employees. While large-scale business transactions are catered for by well-resourced law firms which have their own networks to obtain information on foreign law, commercial parties involved in small or medium-scale transactions or originating from jurisdictions that do not have developed facilities or institutions to access foreign law may be in need of obtaining accurate and reliable information on foreign law. In addition to judicial settings, the majority of national reporters point out that advising attorneys and notaries, as well as arbitrators and mediators, are also stakeholders. To ensure and facilitate access to foreign law across different sectors, several possible methods of cooperation should be envisaged, not on an exclusive but rather on a complementary basis, as has been recommended by the Hague Conference on Private International Law.[244]

---

[243] Australia; Commonwealth Africa; *also* Israel and Quebec.

[244] HCCH report; Lortie/Groff, *supra* note 12, pp. 329 ff.; *see also* Shaheeza Lalani, "A Proposed Model to Facilitate Access to Foreign Law", *Yearbook of Private International Law* 13 (2011), pp. 299; Permanent Bureau, "Report of the Meeting of Experts on Global Co-operation on the Provision of Online Legal Information on National Laws (19–21 October 2008)", Prel. Doc. No 11 B of March 2009 for the attention of the Council of March / April 2009 on General Affairs and Policy of the Conference (available at: http://www.hcch.net/upload/wop/genaff_pd11b2009e.pdf). According to the Conclusions and Recommendations of the 2012 Joint Conference (*supra* note 7), any "future instrument should contemplate a range of mechanisms to cater to the needs of various actors of different means and resources who are seeking access to foreign law, including judges, legal practitioners, notaries, government officials and the general public, in a variety of circumstances, and should be operational in different legal systems and traditions, and address language barriers. Circumstances may include cross-border litigation and non-contentious matters such as contractual negotiations, estate planning, and family arrangements." (para. 6).

2. Developing New Mechanisms

a) Administrative Cooperation

A number of national reporters from civil law jurisdictions support instruments of administrative cooperation in obtaining information on foreign law,[245] although some have expressed scepticism.[246] Despite the party-oriented treatment of foreign law, Australia and Canadian reporters also see advantages to administrative cooperation in alleviating the burden on parties with limited financial means when it comes to proving foreign law. This will also prevent insufficient, conflicting or party-biased expert evidence.[247] In fact, Fentiman points out that litigants in the U.K. could rely on the 1968 London Convention by way of the court's inherent powers in evidential matters. In his view, the real reason why U.K. courts do not refer to the Convention mechanism includes the delays in receiving replies and the limited value of the obtained abstract information.[248] In this respect, administrative cooperation could be an expedient way of accessing foreign law both in civil law and common law jurisdictions. However, given the drawbacks of the existing instruments discussed above (*supra* VIII.A.1), several improvements will be desirable as regards the envisaging of a new instrument on administrative cooperation.

First, as a number of national reporters indicate, the entitlement to request information on foreign law should no longer be limited to the judicial authority, but should extend to attorneys, arbitrators, mediators and notaries, as well as to parties in my eyes. While opinion is divided among national reporters as to the eligibility of the parties, the parties may well have legitimate interests in utilizing the instrument when they are involved in small or medium-sized pecuniary claims or family or succession matters and cannot afford to refer to other means to obtain information on foreign law. Yet in order to filter out unnecessary requests, the transmission of requests should be between the authorities (also Art. 2 London Convention), although some national reporters advocate allowing direct submission of requests to the answering body.

Second, abstract information on foreign black-letter rules is often insufficient for the case at hand. It is submitted that judges and other stakeholders should be allowed to include detailed questions in the request and, where necessary, subsequently contact the answering body with additional questions to obtain information tailored to the case. To avoid excessive workloads, however, the requested state should further be allowed to delegate the task of answering the request to expert institutions or individual experts (also Art. 6 London Convention).

Third, to ensure swift management of inquiries, it would make sense to set a clear time frame. In addition, to alleviate language barriers and reduce processing

---

[245] Argentina; Croatia; Czech Republic; Estonia; Finland; Greece; Hungary; Italy; Japan; Macau; Portugal; Romania; Spain; Tunisia; Uruguay; Venezuela.

[246] Germany.

[247] Australia; Commonwealth Africa; *also* Quebec.

[248] Fentiman, *supra* note 71, pp. 239 ff.

time, my view is that English ought to be used as a lingua franca instead of translating inquiries and replies into the vernacular language. While quite a number of national reporters support remunerating the task so that such new instrument yield high quality information and function expeditiously,[249] other national reporters prefer services to be free as a general principle, as is the case under the London Convention (Art. 15 (1)).

Finally, the large majority of national reporters argue that the reply should not be binding upon the judge (also Art. 8 London Convention), although this is not a unanimous view. In my eyes too, the reply ought to remain non-binding to allow the judge to examine the reliability and accuracy of the provided information and, if it is imprecise or incorrect, conduct further research into the content of foreign law by referring to other sources.

b) Access to Legal Professionals and Experts

For complex issues on foreign law, parties, attorneys, arbitrators or mediators may prefer to contact directly expert institutions, individual experts, law firms or other institutions in the foreign country to obtain detailed information promptly, instead of relying on administrative cooperation. For this purpose, a number of national reporters support a system to identify such institutions or experts (e.g., by creating a list of experts) and encourage the establishment of networks of practitioners through associations (particularly lawyers and notaries),[250] as has been proposed by the Hague Conference on Private International Law.[251] In particular, the Australian reporter supports this idea, with a view to enhancing access to foreign law and avoiding problems of insufficient, incomplete or conflicting evidence adduced by the parties.

c) Judicial Cooperation

The usefulness and effectiveness of judicial cooperation, particularly as implemented by the Hague Judicial Network and the European Judicial Network, is widely acknowledged among national reporters both from civil law and common law jurisdictions.[252] Some Family Court judges in Australia are reported to have

---

[249] *See also* Conclusions and Recommendations of the 2012 Joint Conference (*supra* note 7), para. 14.

[250] Croatia; Czech Republic; Finland; Hungary; Italy; Japan; Portugal; Quebec; Spain; Sweden; Switzerland; Uruguay; Venezuela.

[251] Conclusions and Recommendations of the 2012 Joint Conference (*supra* note 7), para. 12 f.; Lortie/Groff, *supra* note 12, p. 334.

[252] Australia; Croatia; Czech Republic; Estonia; Italy; Japan; Macau; Portugal; Quebec; Sweden; Uruguay; Venezuela. As an exception, Turkey refrained from taking part in the European Judicial Network due to concerns regarding the additional workload.

initially resisted engaging in direct judicial communication, on the ground that the parties should bear the onus of proving foreign law. Yet once the Family Court judges used the mechanism, they were convinced of its utility. This seems to be the case not only in Australia, but also in Israel and other countries. The method of direct judicial communications, which has particularly been successful in implementing the 1980 Hague Child Abduction Convention, may well be useful in enhancing access to foreign law in other cases too. However, caution will be required regarding whether and how far foreign judges are able to deliver an opinion tailored to the detailed facts of the case at hand and whether they might possibly encounter constitutional limitations when answering a question.[253]

The above-mentioned NSW/SG-MOU and NSW/NY-MOU establish a unique scheme of cooperation between two courts from common law jurisdictions. Although this method currently encounters procedural restrictions and difficulties of implementation, enabling referral to the foreign court is an innovative idea which is worth further exploring. Also, the certification of questions of law established by the British Law Ascertainment Act 1859 in the U.K. or the UCQLA within the U.S. may be a useful way of obtaining accurate information on foreign law. Along the same lines, Remien has advocated introducing a kind of preliminary reference among the EU Member State courts, adopting the structure of the preliminary ruling of the European Court of Justice (Art. 267 TFEU).[254] Pursuant to this model, any EU Member State court, including the Supreme Court, is entitled to request a preliminary ruling at the court of the same rank in another EU Member State whose law governs the case at hand. The requested court will then be asked to provide information on foreign law tailored to the concrete case. If this innovative mechanism is implemented one day, the Member State court in charge of a case will be able to obtain precise and tailored information on foreign law, relying on the expertise and experience of the counterpart court in another Member State. In the long run, this would enhance cooperation and improve the quality of the administration of justice in the EU Member States.

Jänterä-Jareborg goes further and suggests that the EU Member State courts be allowed discretion to transfer the case to another EU Member State whose law governs the case, when the forum state is not able to properly ascertain the relevant foreign law.[255] This model amounts to adopting a European version of forum non conveniens doctrine. Introducing the possibility of a discretionary dismissal to avoid applying foreign law largely runs counter to the existing EU jurisdiction

[253] Spigelman, *supra* note 79, p. 216.

[254] Remien, *supra* note 108, pp. 582 f.; idem, "Illusion und Realität eines europäischen Privatrechts", *Juristenzeitung* 1992, p. 282; idem, "European Private International Law, the European Community and its Emergng Area of Freedom, Security and Justice", *Common Market Law Review* 38 (2001), pp. 78 f.; idem, "Iura novit curia und die Ermittlung fremden Rechts im europäischen Rechtsraum der Artt. 61 ff. EGV—für ein neues Vorabentscheidungsverfahren bei mitgliedstaatlichen Gerichten", in: *Aufbruch nach Europa: 75 Jahre Max-Planck-Institut für Privatrecht* (Tübingen 2001), p. 627.

[255] Jänterä-Jareborg, *supra* note 14, p. 323.

system in light of the jurisdiction rules in civil and commercial matters,[256] divorce,[257] maintenance obligations,[258] succession,[259] as well as matrimonial property regimes and the property consequences of registered partnerships.[260] Under the current state of the law, however, a limited mechanism for transfer of the case is already provided for in relation to child protection (Art. 15 Brussels II*bis*), which corresponds to Article 8 of the 1996 Hague Child Protection Convention. While the child protection cases are generally governed by the lex fori (Art. 15 (1) Child Protection Convention), a comparable scheme to transfer to a court better placed to hear the case could possibly be developed for other settings. This would enable the judge facing insurmountable difficulties in applying foreign law to request a judge in the other relevant state to take over the task.

Notably, the Uniform Law Conference of Canada adopted a corresponding reference mechanism by the 1994 Uniform Court Jurisdiction and Proceedings Transfer Act.[261] This Act introduced the possibility for the superior courts of Canada to transfer all or part of proceedings to a more appropriate forum concerning a question of interpretation or application of foreign law. Pursuant to this Act, the superior courts of Canada may even ask courts outside Canada to take up the litigation if the receiving court accepts such a transfer.[262]

3. Result

The innovative settings discussed above for administrative and judicial cooperation are not easy to implement. Yet, they certainly deserve attention in improving access to foreign law. The feasibility of such mechanisms depends on how much workload might be incurred by the participating authorities, the time and costs the

[256] Art. 4 ff. of the Regulations (EU) No 1215/2012 of the European Parliament and of the Council of 12 December 2012 on jurisdiction and the recognition and enforcement of judgments in civil and commercial matters (recast), *O.J.* 2012, L 351/1 ("Brussels I*bis*"); *see* CJEU, 1.3.2005, Case C-281/02 [*Owusu*], Rep. 2005, I-1383; *see* criticism at Trautmann, *supra* note 196, p. 410.

[257] Art. 3 ff. of the Council Regulation (EC) No 2201/2003 of 27 November 2003 concerning jurisdiction and the recognition and enforcement of judgments in matrimonial matters and the matters of parental responsibility, repealing Regulation (EC) No 1347/2000, *O.J.* 2003, L 338/1 ("Brussels II*bis*").

[258] Art. 3 ff. Maintenance Regulation.

[259] Art. 5 ff. Succession Regulation.

[260] Art. 4 ff. Matrimonial Property Regimes Regulation; Art. 4 ff. Partnership Regulation.

[261] Sec. 13 ff. of the 1994 Uniform Court Jurisdiction and Proceedings Transfer Act (UCJPTA) (available at: http://ulcc.ca/en/home-en-gb-1/183-josetta-1-en-gb/uniform-actsa/court-jurisdiction-and-proceedings-transfer-act/1092-court-jurisdiction-proceedings-transfer-act).

[262] Introductory Comments to the UCJPTA (*supra* note 261); for further detail, *see* Vaughan Black/Stephen Pitel/Michael Sobkin, *Statutory Jurisdiction: An Analysis of the Court Jurisdiction and Proceedings Transfer Act* (Toronto 2012), pp. 214–249 (the author sincerely thanks Prof. Richard Oppong for providing this citation).

mechanisms will trigger, and how far judges and other stakeholders will be inclined to utilize such instruments.

Another arguably crucial factor to improve access to foreign law is proper legal education and training of judges, attorneys, government officers and other practitioners, as several national reporters point out.[263] In fact, the scarcity of references to the London Convention or other existing means of administrative or judicial cooperation is partly attributable to lack of knowledge. The functioning of conflicts rules and the application of foreign law can only be guaranteed by decent expertise and proper experience of judges, attorneys and other practitioners.

IX. Conclusions

This comparative study on the treatment of foreign law has focused on the following three points: (i) conflict of laws and its impact on the application of foreign law, (ii) the distinctive features of the treatment of foreign law in different jurisdictions, and (iii) the need for and possibility of improving access to foreign law.

First, the underlying study has shown that the mandatory or non-mandatory nature of conflicts rules affects their functioning and the application of foreign law. In fact, the application of foreign law is often avoided due to the treatment of conflicts rules, the connecting factors or general principles of private international law, and other practical reasons that favour the application of the lex fori.

Second, this study has analysed the nature of foreign law and examined different features of introducing, ascertaining and applying foreign law in various jurisdictions comparatively. Civil law jurisdictions used to characterize foreign law as "law" and provide for the ex officio ascertainment and application of foreign law, whereas common law jurisdictions regarded foreign law as "fact" which ought to be pleaded and proven by the parties so that the judge can apply it. However, in light of the distinctive features of the treatment of foreign law in various jurisdictions, this study has demonstrated that the two-tier characterization of foreign law as "law" or "fact" no longer yields fruitful or conclusive results. Instead of upholding the conventional "law-fact" dichotomy, a tailored characterization of the treatment of foreign law ought to be elaborated in light of the procedural rules and the task division between the court and the parties. In fact, while judges in civil law jurisdictions often request parties to assist in ascertaining foreign law, some common law jurisdictions are becoming more responsive to the idea of judges taking judicial notice of foreign law. Although the starting point on how foreign law is treated differs in civil law and common law jurisdictions, the practical outcome comes closer than would appear at the outset. Nonetheless, unifying the treatment of foreign law at the global or regional level is still a long way off, even if this would be desirable in guaranteeing the functioning of uniform conflicts rules adopted in EU regulations or international treaties.

---

[263] Greece, Hungary; Ireland; Israel; Poland.

Third, after confirming that the existing methods of obtaining information on foreign law are not sufficiently effective, this study has proposed several possible mechanisms for enhancing administrative and judicial cooperation. In March 2015, the Council on General Affairs and Policy of the Hague Conference on Private International Law decided to remove from the Agenda of the Hague Conference the topic of developing mechanisms for access to foreign law for the time being, providing that this topic may be re-introduced at a later stage.[264] Member States of the Hague Conference were not yet ready to fully engage in this project, due to the higher priority of other legislative projects currently on a very full work Agenda of the Conference and the limited resources of the organisation's Secretariat; and also perhaps due to scepticism of a few States about the usefulness of new instruments or fear about national workload implications in providing information on their own law. However, this does not diminish the existing need to access foreign law in practice. In the long run, more institutionalized and sophisticated administrative or judicial cooperation may appear feasible and desirable. There are ample opportunities for further developments in the future in this field.

[264] Conclusions and Recommendations adopted by the Council on General Affairs and Policy of the Conference, held from 24 till 26 March 2015 (available at: http://www.hcch.net/upload/wop/gap2015concl_en.pdf).

Part II
National Reports I – Europe

Belgium: Foreign Law in Belgian Courts – From Theory to Practice

Patrick Wautelet

Abstract The present contribution attempts to critically describe the status of foreign law in Belgian courts. Because this status is intrinsically linked to that of conflict of laws rules, the position of the latter is also taken into consideration. An attempt is made to go beyond the mere description of principles to explain how the rules are applied in practice by courts and practitioners. The main lesson to be learned from this overview is that the status of foreign law in Belgian courts is subject to contradictory policies: on the one hand, courts and the legislator have adopted a highly ambitious policy whereby the position of foreign law is aligned with that of local law, with the consequence that it falls upon courts to determine the content of foreign law and that courts should strive to read and construe foreign law as it would be applied by foreign courts. On the other hand, Belgium has failed to adopt any mechanism to assist courts coping with this ambitious principle. This great divide between theory and practice casts a long shadow over the viability of the whole system.

I. Introduction

The status of foreign law is a classic topic which has already attracted much attention.[1] Exploring this topic anew remains, however, useful. This is in the first place because the attitude of courts towards foreign law is not static. Over the years,

[1] See among other, the following contributions: M. Traest, "Belgium", in *Application of Foreign Law*, C. Esplugues, J.-L. Iglesias and G. Palao (eds.), Sellier, 2011, pp. 129–143 (hereinafter 'Traest'); H. Storme, "Vreemd recht voor Belgische rechter", *Nieuw Juridisch Weekblad*, 2005, at pp. 1154–1166 (hereinafter Storme); S. Geeroms, *Foreign law in Civil litigation. A comparative and functional analysis*, OUP, 2004 (hereinafter Geeroms); M. Traest & V. Vanovermeire, "Over vreemd nationaal recht voor de nationale rechter en de Unierechter", in *Liber spei et amicitiae Ivan Verougstraete*, Larcier, 2011, 437–449; M. Traest, "Bedenkingen over de verantwoordelijkheid van de rechter bij het vaststellen van de inhoud en de toepassing van het vreemde recht", in *Verantwoordelijkheid en recht*, Kluwer, 2008, 168–183 and W. Pintens, "L'établissement du contenu du droit étranger en Belgique" in *Application du droit étranger par le juge national. Allemagne, France, Belgique et Suisse*, C. Witz (ed.), Société de législation comparée, 2014, pp. 37–46.

P. Wautelet (✉)
Professor, School of Law, University of Liège, Quartier Agora - Place des Orateurs, 3, Bât. B 31, Liège B 4000, Belgium
e-mail: patrick.wautelet@ulg.ac.be

Y. Nishitani (ed.), *Treatment of Foreign Law - Dynamics towards Convergence?*, Ius Comparatum – Global Studies in Comparative Law 26,
DOI 10.1007/978-3-319-56574-3_2

changes may occur in the way courts deal with the application of foreign law. These changes may in turn be prompted by technological developments, making it easier to uncover the content and scope of foreign law. The changes may also result from a codification of Belgian private international law, particularly the Code of Private International Law (CPIL) in 2004.[2] While this Code merely stipulated existing laws and practices to a large extent, it did bring a number of changes which may have had a direct or indirect impact on the status of foreign law. Now that more than ten years have passed after the Code entered into force, it is useful to take stock of the existing practice. Finally, the significant development of European private international law, with its emphasis on close cooperation among Member States, may bring about some changes in the role of courts and parties in dealing with foreign law.

In the following paper, an attempt will be made to clarify the position of foreign law under Belgian law, with a focus on the practice of courts.[3] This specific focus is justified, as experience has shown that there may be some distance between the rules and the practice in relation to the application of and proof of foreign law. In the first part, the status of conflict of laws rules will be explored. The next part will focus on the application of foreign law by judicial authorities. The possibility for higher courts to review the application of foreign law will be analysed in a separate part. In the last part, the status of foreign law before other authorities than judicial authorities will be examined.

II. Conflict of Laws Rules Under Belgian Private International Law

Foreign law does not come in as such in proceedings before Belgian courts. It can only be taken into account when the conflict of laws rules designate foreign law as applicable to the case at hand. The status of conflict of laws rules is therefore a key question when analyzing the role played by foreign law in Belgian court practice. In other words, one should determine whether a court or any other authority is required to apply conflict of laws rules, possibly on its own motion, or whether the application of these rules is left to the discretion of parties.

---

[2] Act of 16 July 2004, which entered into force on 1st of October 2004. See *e.g.* A. Fiorini, "The codification of private international law. The Belgian Experience", *I.C.L.Q.*, 205, 499–519; M. Fallon, "Le droit international privé belge dans les traces de la loi italienne dix ans après", *R.D.I.P.P.*, 2005, 315–338; M. Fallon, "Le droit international privé en 2004, entre *ius commune*, codification et droit privé européen", in *Le Code civil entre ius commune et droit privé européen*, A. Wijffels (ed.), Bruylant, 2005, 225–267; S. Francq, "Das Belgische IPR – Gesetzbuch", *RabelsZ*, 2006, 235 – 278 and M. Pertegás Sender, "The Belgian Code on Private International Law : a tour d'horizon", *IPRax*, 2006, 53–61.

[3] The following text is based on a questionnaire prepared by Prof. Yuko Nishitani, general reporter for the topic 'Proof of and information about foreign law' at the 19th International Congress of Comparative Law (Vienna, 2014).

The starting point under current Belgian private international law is that conflict of laws rules should be treated as any other legal rules – this explains why the CPIL does not include a general rule on the position or status of its conflict of laws rules.[4] As a general rule, courts and other authorities have an *obligation* to apply the law to the facts of the case, as the legal aspects of a case belong to the scope of the *ex officio* determination by the judge. This also applies to conflict of laws rules. As a consequence, the judge has the duty to identify the relevant conflicts rules. If parties have neglected to assert the relevant conflict of laws rules, the judge ought to proceed to identify these rules on his or her own motion. The judge should also consider the fact pattern presented by parties and the judge may recharacterize it, *i.e.* select a characterization which leads to the application of another conflict of laws rule than the one suggested by the parties. The court should not, in other words, rely on the parties to select and apply the relevant conflict of laws rules.

However, this starting point is subject to a number of important nuances. First, the court is bound by the so-called '*Verhandlungsmaxime*', *i.e.* it may not modify or add to the facts presented by parties. This principle rests on the idea that it is for the parties to take the initiative in a civil suit. The court is able to act on its own motion only in exceptional cases, where the public interest requires its intervention. The court must, in other words, only adjudicate within the factual boundaries drawn by parties. If parties have skilfully presented their case by erasing all cross-border elements or are not aware of the cross-border dimension of their case, the court may not on its own motion attempt to uncover the cross-border dimension of the case. The court will in this situation be bound to apply local law, except if the dispute concerns public policy.

Second, a distinction should be made depending on the *nature of the rights* at stake. Not all conflict of laws rules are subject to the same treatment. According to the prevailing view, when the underlying dispute does not in any way touch upon public policy, parties may prevent the application of conflict of laws rules.[5] The agreement between parties is in this hypothesis binding upon the judge, who may not disregard the agreement to rely on a conflict of laws rule which parties had agreed to exclude. The boundaries of this nuance are difficult to draw, in the first place because the demarcation between matters which are of public policy and other matters, is not always easily identifiable. It seems at least that reference should not be made to the concept of public policy which is specific to private international law, but rather to the general notion of public policy. Further, in matters which do not concern public policy, the conflict of laws rules may themselves grant parties the freedom to select the applicable law. The distinction between facultative conflict of

[4] Some authors read, however, in Article 15 of the Code of Private International Law, an implied reference to the mandatory nature of conflict of laws rules, see *e.g.* J. Erauw and H. Storme, *Internationaal privaatrecht*, Kluwer, 2009, p. 359, § 284.

[5] This was stated by Advocate General Krings in its opinion in the seminal *Babcok* case (opinion published in *Pasicrisie*, 1981, I, at p. 167).

laws rules and a choice of law rule allowing parties to choose the applicable law, is not always understood in practice.[6]

If parties have argued their case without making any reference to the cross-border nature of the case and without commenting on the conflict of laws rules that are possibly applicable, the court should in the first place verify whether the dispute calls for the application of a conflict rule allowing the parties to make a choice of law.[7] If this rule enables the parties to make a tacit choice of law, the court should verify whether the attitude of parties reveals that they indeed intended to select the law of the forum. If the matter in dispute calls for the application of a conflict rule which does not allow parties to choose the applicable law (or allows only an express choice of law and no tacit choice of law), the court should verify whether the silence of parties may not be interpreted as indicating that they dispense with the application of the conflict of laws rules. Such a waiver, however, cannot be accepted in all cases. It may in particular be questioned whether such a waiver is possible in matters where the conflict of laws rules do not grant parties the freedom to choose the law.

Third, when the question of the application of a conflict rule has been raised in the course of judicial proceedings, the court is required to guarantee that the parties have the possibility to *debate the applicability* and application of the conflict rules. In other words, when a court raises a rule *ex officio*, it should do so in a manner which allows parties the opportunity to react.[8] When parties have, however, based their case on foreign law, without going into detailed arguments as to the proper interpretation of the relevant provisions of that foreign law, the court may go further and undertake to examine how to apply these provisions without allowing parties to comment further on this application.[9] In the same line, a court should also provide explanations as to why it selected a particular conflict of laws rule. All judgments must be reasoned and this requirement also applies to the selection and application by the court of conflict of laws rules.

Finally, account should be taken of the fact that a great deal of the conflict of laws rules applied by courts in Belgium either derives from international treaties (such as the Conventions adopted within the framework of the Hague Conference for Private International Law) or European Union (EU) Regulations. The question is whether

---

[6] For more details, see H. Storme, at pp. 1156–1157, § 5.

[7] In her groundbreaking research (Jinske Verhellen, *Het Belgisch IPR-Wetboek in familiezaken. Wetgevende doelstellingen getoetst aan de praktijk*, Die Keure, 2012, at pp. 100–102, § 174 – hereinafter referred to as 'Verhellen'), Verhellen indicates that practitioners are not very keen to see foreign law applied. She adds that many practitioners present their cases without mentioning the cross-border dimension, thereby hoping that the court would apply local law. Drawing on interviews with judges, Verhellen shows that some judges take their duty seriously and raise *ex officio* the application of conflict of laws rules.

[8] Supreme Court (Court of cassation), 22 October 1982, *Pasicrisie*, 1983, I, 254; Supreme Court (Court of cassation), 18 February 1985, *Pasicrisie*, 1985 I, 741. And more recently Supreme Court (Court of cassation), 4 September 1992, *Pasicrisie*, 1992, I, 993 (the Supreme Court quashes a decision issued by the Court of Appeal of Antwerp because the Court of Appeal had applied Dutch law without giving parties the possibility to comment on the application of this law).

[9] Supreme Court (Court of cassation), 7 October 2004, Tijdschrift@ipr.be, 2005/2, at p. 32.

the international origin of a conflict of laws rules modifies the position of these rules. As far as EU conflict rules are concerned, it should be admitted that they be afforded the same treatment as national conflict rules. This follows from the long standing position of the ECJ that if it is for the domestic legal system of each Member State to lay down the *detailed procedural rules governing actions for safeguarding rights which individuals derive from the direct effect of European Union law, such rules must not be less favourable than those governing similar domestic actions nor render virtually impossible or excessively difficult the exercise of rights conferred by European Union law.*[10]

For conflict of laws rules in international treaties, the obligation for courts to apply them *ex officio* can also be justified by the supremacy of international law. Under Belgian court practice, international conventional law is indeed deemed to enjoy priority over domestic law. Hence, it should be applied by taking precedence over the provisions of domestic law. In addition, conflict rules incorporated in a treaty become a part of domestic law, as soon as the treaty enters into force in Belgium. Hence, these rules should enjoy the same treatment as domestic conflict rules.[11] Along the same lines, the application of uniform rules depend on the weight given to the instrument in which they are incorporated. Uniform rules incorporated in an international treaty, such as the rules of the 1980 Vienna Sales Convention, enjoy the same treatment as international treaties. They are therefore directly applicable and have priority over national law.

III. Foreign Law Before Judicial Authorities

Conflict of laws rules in force in Belgium may lead to the application of foreign law. Before reviewing the status of foreign law when applied by courts, it is worthwhile to note that it is quite difficult to provide a detailed assessment of the frequency and nature of application of foreign law in Belgian court practice. There has indeed not been any systematic and comprehensive research on the application of foreign law by Belgian courts.[12,13]

[10] As exemplified by the ruling in the *van Schijndel* case: ECJ, 14 December 1995, *Jeroen van Schijndel and Johannes van Veen v. Stichting Pensioenfonds voor Fysiotherapeuten*, cases C-430/93 and 431/93, Rep. 1995, I-4705.

[11] See F. Rigaux and M. Fallon, *Droit international privé*, 3rd ed., Larcier, 2005, p. 265, § 6.53.

[12] While very useful, the empirical report prepared by the Swiss Institute of Comparative Law does not offer a comprehensive study of the application of foreign law by Belgian courts and practitioners. The study is based on a very limited number of responses (by seven persons) which cannot be sufficient to draw general conclusions (see Swiss Institute of Comparative Law, The Application of Foreign Law in Civil Matters in the EU Member States and its Perspectives for the Future, Part II – Empirical Analysis (JLS/2009/JCIV/PR/005/E4), 2011, at p. 32).

[13] The lack of precise statistical data on the application of foreign law by Belgian courts can be explained by the reasons which were mentioned in the introduction to the Empirical Analysis conducted by the Swiss Institute of Comparative Law (Swiss Institute of Comparative Law, The Application of Foreign Law in Civil Matters in the EU Member States and its Perspectives for the Future, Part II – Empirical Analysis (JLS/2009/JCIV/PR/005/E4), 2011, pp. 3–4).

One can, however, safely assume that there have been less occasions to apply foreign law in recent years in Belgium. This is because of the decisions made by the legislator when adopting the CPIL. The Code indeed grants a very significant role to the *habitual residence* in determining the applicable law. In personal and family matters, application of the law of the habitual residence of the persons concerned has become the rule – except for selected issues such as access to marriage (Art. 46), the name and surname (Art. 37) and issues of parentage (Art. 62). As courts are more frequently seized of disputes concerning persons residing in Belgium, they will presumably apply more often local law as the law of the habitual residence of the persons concerned. The issue of matrimonial property provides a good example: all spouses who settle in Belgium directly after their marriage (whether they lived in Belgium or not before their marriage) will, by virtue of Article 51 CPIL, be subject to Belgian law if they have not selected another law. The same cannot be said, however, of disputes in civil and commercial matters, where application of foreign law continues to occur more frequently.

There is one field where the application of foreign law has been studied in detail: in her very innovative study, Jinske Verhellen undertook to examine the application by courts, administrations and other official instances of the conflict rules relating to parentage.[14] She reviewed about 100 court cases and many more files where issues of parentage had arisen and interviewed judges and magistrates. Her review shows first of all that courts and official authorities in Belgium frequently have to apply foreign law on the basis of Article 62. Foreign law was applied in almost 50% of the court cases she reviewed. The analysis also shows that courts and other instances have applied the laws of many different countries, ranging from other EU Member States to very distant countries such as Afghanistan and Sierra Leone.

Since it is difficult, if not impossible, to provide details on the actual application of foreign law by courts in Belgium, it is obviously also quite difficult to determine with precision which foreign laws are most commonly applied before courts in Belgium. No comprehensive research has been conducted which would allow to answer this question with precision. One may, however, rely on the figures provided by the '*Point d'appui en droit international privé*' [Helpdesk Private International Law], a specialized desk set up in 2005 to provide legal advice in matters of international family law to practitioners (lawyers, civil servants) and individuals. According to the figures published by the 'Point d'appui' for the years 2005–2010, the country which received the most attention was by far Morocco. In Europe, the following countries were prime targets of cases opened: France, Italy, Romania, Turkey, Spain, Portugal, Poland, Russia and Sweden, with France and Turkey drawing the biggest share of cases. In Africa, the Democratic Republic of Congo took the lion's share, which may be explained by the historic ties with Belgium. The following countries were also frequently mentioned: Algeria, Ivory Coast, Senegal, Togo, Cameroon, Rwanda, Burkina Faso, Guinea, Tunisia, Burundi and Madagascar. As

[14] J. Verhellen, at pp. 90–120. Ms Verhellen conveniently summarized her research in the following paper: J. Verhellen, "Access to foreign law in practice: easier said than done", *J. Priv. Intl. L.*, 2016, at pp. 281–300.

far as Asia is concerned, China, India and Pakistan were the most frequently encountered cases. Many requests for assistance also came from Brazil. While this list only concerns matters of family law and does not indicate that the law of these countries was in fact applied, it gives a good indication of the potential geographic spreading when it comes to foreign law in Belgium.

With this background information in mind, one may start exploring the legal framework developed to deal with the application of foreign law in Belgium. The first question which needs to be addressed is that of the nature of foreign law. Once some light has been shed on this difficult issue, the analysis will turn to the classic questions of application, ascertainment and interpretation of foreign law.

A. *Nature of Foreign Law: Fact, Law or Tertium Genus?*

While it is generally considered that the distinction between foreign law as 'law' or 'fact' is not the most appropriate to describe the treatment afforded to foreign law,[15] this distinction remains useful as a starting point for the discussion. If one considers the various aspects of the regime of foreign law in Belgium, the position of foreign law resembles closely that given to local law. In that sense, foreign law is much closer to law than it is to fact.[16] There are, however, nuances to this general statement. The main one is that courts applying foreign law will react differently when faced with a *lacuna* or a difficult issue of interpretation of the existing rules. When such issue of interpretation arises in relation to local law, courts in Belgium will use all relevant methods of interpretation to come to what they deem to be the most appropriate solution - even though courts are required to narrow the scope of their judgments to the facts of the case they are seized with and they cannot enter judgments with precedent value. When a court is required to apply a foreign law and it comes to the conclusion that the relevant provision of foreign law raises a question of interpretation or when no relevant provision seem to exist, the court will act with utmost precaution. It will not claim the authority to interpret foreign law as it would with local law (see below).

The question of the nature of foreign law has given rise to a lively, if purely semantic discussion in relation to Article 608 of the Code of Civil Procedure (CCP). This provision defines the main mission of the Supreme Court (*Cour de cassation/ Hof van cassatie*). According to Article 608 CCP, the Court has jurisdiction to review rulings issued by lower courts and may quash them if it finds that the ruling contains a "violation of the law" ("... *contravention à la loi*"/"*overtreding van de wet*"). Early on, the question arose whether the Court also had jurisdiction when it

[15] And beyond. See the convincing demonstration by S. Lalani, "Establishing the Content of Foreign Law: a Comparative Study", *MJ*, 2013, 75–112 – the author shows that the 'fact-law' distinction is a fallacy and does not help in understanding how jurisdiction deal with foreign law.

[16] Traest goes further and indicates that foreign law is "generally considered as 'law' and not as a fact" (M. Traest, at p. 129).

was alleged that a lower court had misapplied a provision of foreign law. Until 1980, the Court steadfastly refused to review the application of foreign law by lower courts (see below). It was not until an important decision was rendered in October 1980 that the Court started to accept that its mission also included verifying the application of foreign law by lower courts. The question therefore arose whether this meant that foreign law also constituted 'law' within the meaning of Article 608 CCP. This discussion was tied with the nature of the review exercised by the Supreme Court on the application of foreign law by lower courts: if the Supreme Court exercised a full review, this was taken to mean that foreign law should fully considered to be law in the meaning of Article 608 CCP.[17] Those advocating a more limited role for the Supreme Court in the review of the application by lower courts of foreign law, also argued that foreign law was not completely law within the meaning of that provision.[18] The matter has now been settled, the Supreme Court having it made clear that it will only verify the conformity of the lower court ruling with the interpretation prevailing in the country of origin.[19]

B. Application of Foreign Law: What Is the Role of Courts and Parties?

It is one thing to know that foreign law may in general be said to be closer to law than fact. It is another thing to explore when and under which conditions foreign law is applied before judicial authorities in Belgium.

Whenever a court comes to the conclusion that a matter is governed by foreign law, the court has the obligation to apply foreign law *ex officio*. This is not stated with so many words in Article 15 CPIL. It has not either been mentioned by the Supreme Court.[20] However, it follows from the general system adopted by the legislator: since a court is required to apply on its own motion conflict rules and it should also ascertain the content of foreign law, it should also apply foreign law *ex officio*.[21] In several cases, courts have applied foreign law on their own motion, although parties had presented their arguments on the basis of Belgian law.[22]

---

[17] See *e.g.* L. Simont, "La Cour de cassation et la loi étrangère. Quelques réflexions", in *Imperat Lex. Liber amicorum Pierre Marchal*, Larcier, 2003, 189–207, at p. 197.

[18] According to Traest, "foreign law can probably no longer be considered 'law' witing the meaning of Article 608 of the Belgian CPC" (M. Traest, at p. 130).

[19] On this basis, it has been suggested that the concept of 'law' of Article 608 should be read to mean 'foreign law as it is interpreted in the country of origin': Pierre Lecroart (clerk to Supreme Court Justice Parmentier), in *Annual Report of the Court of Cassation*, 2006, at p. 254.

[20] The Supreme Court (Court of cassation) did not rule on this question in its milestone *Babcock* case. However, in its advisory opinion in this case Ernest Krings, who was at that time advocate general, pleaded for an ex officio application of foreign law by courts (opinion published in *Pasicrisie*, 1981, I, at p. 167).

[21] See *e.g.* H. Storme, at pp. 1157, § 6; S. Geeroms, at pp. 55–56, § 2.37 and M. Traest, at p. 131.

[22] See the various cases referred to by S. Geeroms, at pp. 56–57, § 2.38.

Although Belgium is a founding member of the EU that has grown to become a union based on the rule of law, no preferential treatment is granted to the law of fellow EU Member States. The laws of these States is afforded the same treatment as the law of other countries. The only difference lies in the existence of specific means to ascertain the content of the laws of other EU Member States. Indeed, as a Member of the EU, Belgium offers its courts access to the European Judicial Network (EJN). This network is fully operational in Belgium. It is, however, difficult to ascertain whether courts effectively make use of the possibility to directly communicate with foreign judges in order to obtain legal information. What may be said is that the EJN is not yet well known among practitioners.[23]

C. Ascertainment of Foreign Law

A key question when analyzing the status of foreign law relates to the division of labor in ascertaining the content of foreign law. It should be made clear whether the '*iura novit curia*' principle applies or whether parties have to prove the content of foreign law. It is obvious that the discrepancy between theory and practice is the sharpest with regard to this question. Hence, attention will first be paid to the principles before exploring how these principles are (mis-)applied in practice. In a separate section, the various tools used by practitioners and courts to discover the content of foreign law, will be reviewed.

1. The Principles

In theory, the situation in Belgium is very clear: the task of ascertaining the content of the rules of foreign law falls onto the judicial authorities. This principle has been affirmed in a milestone case decided in 1981 by the Supreme Court. In this landmark ruling, the Court was required to rule on the question of the interpretation of Article 1645 of the French Civil Code.[24] After indicating that the content of that provision should be determined in accordance with the interpretation given by French courts, the Supreme Court held that "*s'agissant de normes juridiques relevant d'un droit étranger*" ("as far as legal norms are concerned which belong to a foreign law"), the court has an obligation "*de rechercher et de déterminer le contenu de ce droit*" ("to seek and determine the content of that law").

In the CPIL of 2004, the principle has again been confirmed. Article 15 CPIL indeed provides that "The content of foreign law declared applicable by the present Statute is ascertained by the court".[25] By entrusting this mission to the court itself, the legislator has confirmed that the rules of evidence do not apply to the ascertain-

[23] As noted by J. Verhellen, at p. 112, § 184.

[24] Supreme Court, 9 October 1980, *Pasicrisie*, 1981, I, 159.

[25] "*Le contenu du droit étranger désigné par la présente loi est établi par le juge*"/"*De inhoud van het door deze wet aangewezen buitenlands recht wordt door de rechter vastgelegd*".

ing of the content of foreign law.[26] The legislator has also been careful to provide an alternative solution for cases in which a court cannot ascertain the content of foreign law. According to Article 15 (2), the court may in this situation "request the cooperation of parties".[27]

2. The Practice

The principle *iura curit novia* fails, however, to capture how courts deal with foreign law in Belgium.[28] In the first place, it may be underlined that both the ascertaining and the application of foreign law differ in some aspects from the equivalent mission of the court when domestic law applies (see below). More importantly, practice reveals that a completely different division of labour is put in place when it comes to ascertaining the content of foreign law. While Article 15 puts the *primary* responsibility on courts, which may only require the cooperation of parties in case they cannot ascertain the content of foreign law, courts rarely make use of this alternative possibility. This is not because courts excel in the fine art of ascertaining the content of foreign law and do not need to be assisted in this respect by parties. On the contrary, parties involved in disputes bear most of the burden of determining the content of foreign law. Courts do not frequently engage in this exercise because they may in most cases rely on the efforts undertaken by parties. Parties to the proceedings have indeed a direct interest in providing the court with information on the content of foreign law. Hence, parties will spontaneously attempt to uncover the content of foreign law and provide relevant information in that respect. In the vast majority of cases, courts will rely on that information and not undertake efforts on their own to ascertain the content of foreign law.[29] By doing so, courts do not violate the legal principle which entrust them with the task

[26] See Supreme Court, 3 December 1990, *Pasicrisie*, 1991, I, 329 : one should not submit "*la recherche et la détermination du contenu et de la portée de la loi applicable aux règles relatives à la charge de la preuve, lesquelles ne s'appliquent qu'aux faits de la cause*" – "the search and determination of the content and scope of the applicable law to the rules of evidence, which only apply to the facts of the case").

[27] Article 15 par. 2 provides that "*Wanneer de rechter die inhoud niet kan vaststellen, kan hij een beroep doen op de hulp van de partijen*"/"*Lorsque le juge ne peut pas établir ce contenu, il peut requérir la collaboration des parties.*". Traest seems to read this provision as allowing courts to request the cooperation of parties without first attempting on its own to ascertain the content of foreign law – M. Traest, at pp. 132–133.

[28] Some scholars have argued that the *iura novit curia* principle cannot apply when a case is governed by foreign law, as Belgian judges and magistrates cannot be required to have a knowledge of foreign legal systems (see *e.g.* J. Erauw, *Beginselen van internationaal privaatrecht*, Story scientia, 1985, at p. 107). This opinion rests upon a literal reading of the principle, which does not require that judges possess a personal knowledge of the law, but only that they undertake to find out what the law provides.

[29] In one case, the Labour Court of Appeal of Brussels had to decide a case applying the labour laws of the Democratic Republic of Congo. In its ruling it indicated that "to its knowledge and that of the parties" ["*A la connaissance de la Cour … et des parties*"], there was no precedent under the law of DRC for a specific issue, implying that it itself had undertaken some efforts to discover the content of the applicable foreign law – Labor Court of Appeal of Brussels, 29 October 2003, as quoted in Supreme Court (Cour de cassation), 18 April 2005, *Nieuw Juridisch Weekblad*, 2005, at p. 1167.

of ascertaining the content of foreign law.[30] Courts may indeed deem that the information obtained from parties allows them to settle the dispute without need for an additional investigation.[31] Recent research has even suggested that courts may in practice go further and directly request that parties provide information on the relevant foreign law, although no mention of this will be made in court decisions.[32]

At the same time, when a court relies on the information provided *sua sponte* by parties, it does not apply the alternative solution provided in Article 15 (2) CPIL. When parties have not provided sufficient explanations on the content and meaning of the applicable foreign law, the court should in theory undertake to find out by its own means the content of that law. In practice, it is not uncommon for courts in this situation to stay the proceedings and allow parties to file additional briefs with comments on the content of foreign law.[33] *Prima facie*, the court, by doing so, makes it possible for parties to debate the content of the foreign law, thereby satisfying the general principle that parties should be afforded the possibility to debate the rules which the court intends to apply. In practice, this may, however, hide a request by the court that parties provide information on the applicable foreign law, without that the court satisfies its primary obligation to attempt by itself to ascertain the content of the applicable foreign law.[34]

---

[30] Although it has been noted that this practice leads to a reversal in the division of labor between parties and courts when compared to what is contemplated by Article 15: J. Verhellen (ed.), *Loi et pratique en droit international privé familial. Compte rendu des tables rondes printemps 2013*, La Charte, 2013, at p. 25.

[31] This is precisely what happened in a recent case decided by the Supreme Court (Supreme Court (Court of cassation) of 7 December 2012 (*Rechtspraak Brussel, Antwerpen, Gent*, 2013, at p. 1267): in that case, English law applied to determine whether a claim was barred by the statute of limitations. One of the parties requested a legal opinion from an English lawyer on section 5 of the 1980 Limitation Act, while the other party did not produce any information on the content of English law. The Court of appeal noted that the legal opinion was coherent and sufficiently clear. The Court explained that it was convinced by the opinion and based its ruling on the content thereof. The other party challenged this ruling before the Supreme Court, arguing that by basing its ruling solely on the legal opinion, the Court of appeal had failed to discharge its mission to ascertain the content of the relevant foreign law. The Supreme Court refused to quash this ruling, noting that the Court of Appeal had undertaken its own review of the legal opinion. According to the Supreme Court, this constituted a sufficient effort by the Court of appeal. In another case, a court of appeal noted that parties had filed an affidavit issued by a Ukrainian lawyer, commenting on the family law consequences of surrogacy agreements under Ukrainian law. The opposing party had challenged the affidavit on the ground that it had been produced upon request by one party. The court held, however, that it could be used in court, since the opposing party had been in a position to produce information on Ukrainian law but had neglected to do so (Court of Appeal of Brussels, 31 July 2013, D & R v. Belgian State).

[32] See the information provided by J. Verhellen, at pp. 100–101, § 174 – on the basis of interviews with judges and magistrates.

[33] See *e.g.* the ruling of the Court of First Instance of Neufchateau, 2 July 2008, *Journal des Tribunaux*, 2008, at p. 573: the court orders that the debate be reopened so that parties can produce information on the relevant US legislation pertaining to issues of parentage. See also Court of Appeal of Liège, 10 July 2008, *Journal des Tribunaux*, 2009, at p. 538.

[34] See *e.g.* Court of Appeal of Mons, 6 November 2006, *Jurisprudence de Liège, Mons et Bruxelles*, 2007/20, at p. 829 (the Court finds out that Luxemburg law applies to the case. It notes that parties have not presented any argument as to the content of that law and reopens the case to make it possible for parties to comment on the content of the applicable law); Justice of Peace of Oudenaarde-Kruishoutem, 16 July 2009, *Tijdschrift voor Vrederechters*, 2011, at p. 109, with comments by M. Traest (the justice of peace reopens the case after having heard the parties in order to allow parties to demonstrate whether the claim should be upheld on the basis of Dutch law. The court even notes that parties should produce copies of the relevant statutory texts and provide comment on these texts).

3. The Tools

Courts have always heavily relied on parties to uncover the content of foreign law. There is, however, no standard method used by practitioners to ascertain foreign law. Experience indeed shows that practitioners use a variety of methods.[35] The practice is not only difficult to trace, it is also most probably very fragmented. One may assume that practitioners and courts rely first and foremost on online sources when attempting to determine the content of foreign law.[36] No specific training is available in Belgian law schools to teach future practitioners how to locate foreign law using online resources. While students in law school generally must attend a course on legal research, which helps them understand how to find legal sources, this course usually does not pay attention to the sources of foreign law. Likewise, most courses on comparative law will not specifically devote attention to the methodology of finding foreign law. Some university libraries offer on line guides to locate legal resources, which may include access to (a limited number of) foreign law.[37]

Next to online resources, it is quite certain that practitioners involved in disputes governed by foreign law, also call upon *experts*. These may be foreigner practitioners qualified in the jurisdiction whose law is applicable or university professors holding a chair in that jurisdiction.[38] Traditionally, the expert opinion submitted on foreign law will be called a '*certificat de coutume*' (*i.e.* a 'certificate of customary law'). No specific rule exist which would provide a legal framework for such certificate.[39] University professors working at Belgian universities will not infrequently be contacted by practicing attorneys seeking information on a specific foreign law. It does not seem to be customary for practitioners to seek information from foreign research institutions, such as the *Max Planck Institute for Comparative and International Private Law* in Germany or the *Internationaal Juridisch Instituut* in The Hague.

As in practice, it is parties who undertake the largest part of the efforts to ascertain the content of foreign law, they bear the cost of finding out about foreign law. Likewise, if a party files documentary evidence in relation to the content of foreign law, it bears the costs of producing a translation of these documents in the language of the court proceedings.

---

[35] As noted by Verhellen, it is often difficult, if not impossible, to determine on the basis of the court opinion how foreign law was ascertained. The court opinion will not include detailed information on the process whereby foreign law was ascertained – J. Verhellen, at p. 99, § 173.

[36] On the basis of interviews she conducted with judges, Verhellen notes that judges also mainly rely on online resources to ascertain the content of foreign law : J. Verhellen, at p. 108, § 181.

[37] See *e.g.* www.rechtslinks.be

[38] See *e.g.* recently the ruling of the Supreme Court (Court of cassation) of 7 December 2012 (*Rechtspraak Brussel, Antwerpen, Gent*, 2013, at p. 1267) : it appears from the ruling that one of the parties requested a legal opinion from an English lawyer on section 5 of the 1980 Limitation Act. The opinion was submitted as a 'witness statement'.

[39] For more details see Nadine Watté, 'Certificat de coutume', in *Répertoire pratique de droit belge*, Additional Vol. VII, 1990, at pp. 119–124, in particular §§ 13–44.

There is no special mechanism allowing a party who has borne the cost of ascertaining foreign law to recover this expense from the other party when the former wins the case. Rather, the party who has won the case, may obtain a flat fee covering court costs.[40] This fee may be used to cover part of the expenses incurred in ascertaining the content of foreign law. The fee scale which is binding on the court, does not, however, include a specific item for cases involving the application of foreign law. Hence, expenses incurred in ascertaining the content of foreign law will need to be compensated using the general fee. It may also be possible to file a new claim requesting compensation of all costs incurred in ascertaining the content of foreign law. However, this has not yet been attempted.

A party who benefits from judicial assistance (under Art. 664 CCP) will not by this fact only, obtain assistance in ascertaining the content of foreign law. Attorneys appointed under the system of judicial assistance do not have access to a special mechanism helping them to uncover the content of foreign law.

Parties bear the largest burden when it comes to discover the content of foreign law. Courts may not, however, simply take for granted whatever information is presented by parties. It is indeed up to the court to take a decision on the dispute of which it is seized. When doing so, the court is not bound by the information provided by parties. Even if expert witnesses provide information on the relevant foreign law or an affidavit is provided, courts retain the final word and may decide whether they grant any weight, and if yes, which weight they grant to the information provided by parties or experts.[41]

Hence, even if courts rely heavily on parties to collect information on the content of foreign law, courts will occasionally tread on the path leading to foreign law, if only to verify the information provided by parties. It is not easy to determine how courts go about their mission when they attempt themselves to determine the content of foreign law, either because parties have neglected to inform them on such content or because the court would like to verify the information provided by parties.

Some means of finding information on foreign law may be excluded at the outset. Direct communication between judges for example is never used in order to obtain information on the content of relevant foreign law. Such direct communication is not part of the judicial tradition in Belgium. It is even felt that such communication would run against the need for courts to decide independently. In any case, without a proper legal basis for such communication, courts are very unlikely to attempt to engage in any type of dialogue with foreign courts.[42] Likewise, a court in Belgium cannot call upon the assistance of a specialized institution whose mission it is to provide information on foreign law. Although plans have been made from

[40] In application of Article 1017-6° and 1022 of the Code of Civil Procedure.

[41] See Nadine Watté, 'Certificat de coutume', at p. 124, § 39.

[42] See, however, the observation by one judge in J. Verhellen (ed.), *Loi et pratique en droit international privé familial...*, at p. 27 – the judge notes that the network of judges set up by the Hague Conference could encourage direct communication between courts. This would, however, require that courts abandon their reluctance to use information which is not provided by the parties.

time to time to set up a government financed institute providing expert opinion on foreign law, such plans have never materialized. It is unlikely that such an institution will be created in the near future.[43] This may also help explaining why no qualifications have been developed which would be applicable to institutions or individuals providing advice on the content of foreign law. It is felt that if parties or courts call upon the assistance of an individual in order to obtain information on foreign law, they will do so after having examined the credentials of the individual in order to ensure the quality of the performance.

What are then the means used by courts when attempting to collect and/or verify information on foreign law? It is likely that the court will rely first and foremost on *documentary resources* – either those available in law libraries or online.[44] Most (university) law libraries offer a more than decent access to foreign legal resources, in particular those of other European countries. From time to time, a court may attempt to obtain information from a domestic non judicial authority. In particular, courts may seek assistance from the Ministry of Foreign Affairs, which houses a library holding resources on foreign law.[45] It is, however, not easy to determine the extent of the collections of the library.[46]

A court may from time to time also attempt to obtain information through a Belgian embassy or consulate operating in the country whose law is applicable.[47] Although the CCP provides detailed rules on the appointment of experts in order to assist court, courts will not appoint experts in order to ascertain the content of foreign law. The principle is indeed that experts cannot be entrusted with the mission

---

[43] In a parallel development, one may note that the authorities in Belgium only make available limited information about Belgian law. The federal government has set up a repository of legislation, which is freely accessible (www.juridat.be). However, such repository is only available in the three official languages of the Kingdom (Dutch, French and Germany), and not in English. Further, the on line repository does not always offer a codified version of the existing legislation. The same repository also offers access to court opinions. Most opinions of the Supreme Court are published. This is not the case for opinions of lowers courts (first instance and appellate courts) : only selected opinions are published. Regional authorities also operate on line repositories offering free access to their legislations. These repositories are usually comprehensive – see *e.g.* for the Flemish Region the 'Vlaamse Codex' (http://codex.vlaanderen.be/) and for the Walloon Region the 'Wallex' (http://wallex.wallonie.be/).

[44] It appears that some judges, who are frequently faced with the task of applying foreign laws, attempt to compile existing sources on relevant foreign legal systems so as to be able to rely on these private collection in later cases – see the observation to this effect by J. Verhellen (ed.), *Loi et pratique en droit international privé familial...*, at p. 25.

[45] See *e.g.* Supreme Court, 4 November 1993, *Pasicrisie*, 1993, I, at p. 921 – in this case, the dispute concerned the possibility for two Belgian spouses to adopt a US citizen. The question arose which law would be applied by US courts to the adoption. The Court noted in its ruling that a note had been prepared by the Ministry of Foreign Affairs on the conflict of laws rule in force in the United States. Verhellen indicates that the library received 257 requests for information in 2011, coming from judges, notaries but also practicing attorneys (J. Verhellen, at p. 113, § 185).

[46] For more details, see http://diplomatie.belgium.be/en/documentation/libraries/practical_information

[47] See *e.g.* Court of Appeal of Brussels, 30 June 1981, *Journal des Tribunaux*, 1981, 723 (in that case, the Court was faced with the mission of applying the law of Sudan to decide whether the recognition of a child by a person of Sudanese nationality, could be challenged by the mother of the child. The court first noted that parties had undertaken extensive efforts to uncover the content of the law of Sudan. The court then mentioned a note communicated by the Belgian embassy in Sudan, provding some information on the content of the law of Sudan).

of ascertaining the law. Their mission should be limited to provide information on factual matters (Art. 962 CCP).

Occasionally, a court will request informal advice from a (local) university professor to confirm a finding.

In all these instances, courts will not be able to employ a mechanism to examine the reliability of the information on foreign law. Courts will rather rely on their own impression and finding to assess the reliability of the information provided by parties. If the information provided by both parties goes in the same direction, it is likely that the court will accept to rely on that information without more. If the information provided by parties diverge, the court's mission is more difficult.[48] The court will likely rely on information obtained from official sources (such as an official collection of statutory provisions or official publication of court reports) rather than on a private source.[49]

In some cases, parties and courts attempt to obtain information from foreign official channels. To that end, questions are usually put to the embassy or consulate of the foreign country, with a view to obtain a copy of the relevant legislation. So it is that in a case where the law of Sierra Leone was applicable to determine whether a person was the father of a child, a lower court twice requested the assistance of the Consulate of Sierra Leone to obtain information on the applicable principles.[50] Experience has shown, however, that this provides limited result: when a request is answered, it mostly only contains a copy of the relevant legislation, without any further explanation as to the application of the statutory provisions.

Courts may also attempt to use the various international instruments which have been concluded in order to provide assistance in collecting information on foreign law. Belgium is party to the European Convention of 7 June 1968 on Information on Foreign Law. The 'London' Convention was signed January 1972, ratified in

---

[48] If only one party has provided information on foreign law and the other one failed to do so, while challenging the accuracy of the information provided by the other one, the court will in all likelihood proceed to a *prima facie* review of the information put forward by one party. It may also take into account the fact that the other party failed to provide information on foreign law, while it had the possibility to do so. This is what happened in a case concerning the consequences of a surrogacy agreement concluded between two Belgian spouses and a Ukrainian woman. The court of appeal noted that the parents had filed an affidavit issued by a Ukrainian lawyer, commenting on the family law consequences of surrogacy agreements under Ukrainian law. This affidavit had been challenged by the Belgian State, which opposed the parents' claim. The court held, however, that the affidavit could be used in court, since the opposing party had been in a position to produce information on Ukrainian law but had neglected to do so (Court of Appeal of Brussels, 31 July 2013, *D & R v. Belgian State*).

[49] See *e.g.* Commercial Court of Hasselt, 21 September 2001, *Revue de droit commercial belge*, 2002, p. 78 : the court relied on an outprint of a section of the US Code of Federal Regulation, which one of the parties had found online. The other party challenged the use of an internet outprint. The court found, however, that there was no good reason to doubt the authenticity of the legislation. It is interesting to note that some online repositories of national legislation operated by official authorities explicitly provide that they constitute an "official" source – see e.g. the online version of the Civil Code of Quebec available at http://www2.publicationsduquebec.gouv.qc.ca/dynamicSearch/telecharge.php?type=2&file=/CCQ_1991/CCQ1991.html

[50] Court of First Instance of Liège, 11 January 2008, *Revue du droit des* étrangers, 2009, 712.

October 1973 and came into force for Belgium in January 1974. Belgium did not make any reservation when ratifying the Convention. Two different authorities have been appointed by Belgium as national liaison bodies: the Ministry of Foreign Affairs has been appointed as transmitting agency, while the Ministry of Justice has been appointed as receiving agency. Belgium has also concluded a limited number of bilateral treaties which make it possible to request information from a foreign authority on the content and application of its local law. There is *e.g.* a Convention signed in April 1981 with the Kingdom of Morocco.[51] Article 18 to 26 of this Convention set up a mechanism whereby courts of one State may request information on the law of the other State. The request must be transmitted through the respective ministries of justice. It bears close resemblance to the mechanism provided in the London Convention. The Convention does not seem to be applied frequently.[52] A convention signed between Belgium and Hungary in 1983 also provides for a detailed mechanism enabling mutual assistance in order to ascertain the content of the law of the two contracting states.[53] Another Convention concluded with Romania only provides a basic mechanism for cooperation between the Ministries of Justice in order to obtain information on each other's law.[54]

There is no comprehensive data available on the application of the 1968 London Convention, nor of the other bilateral conventions. It is, however, generally accepted that these Conventions are only infrequently applied by courts. This is confirmed by the data collected by the Swiss Institute of Comparative Law.[55] The Ministry of Justice has received only 10 requests for information during the first eight years of application of the London Convention.[56] In a recent case, the Supreme Court refused to quash a ruling by a lower court which had not requested application of the London Convention. The Court of Appeal was seized of a dispute governed by English law. One of the parties had submitted a witness statement written by an English practi-

[51] Convention of 30 April 1981 between Belgium and Morocco on judicial assistance in civil, administrative and commercial matters and in relation to exchange of legal information, published in the *Official Gazette* of 10 January 1984.

[52] See for one case where the Convention could have been applied, but was neglected by the court : CFI Brussels, 22 November 1988, *Revue trimestrielle de droit familial*, 1990, at p. 256.

[53] Convention between Belgium and Hungary in relation to legal information, signed in Budapest on 5 September 1983.

[54] Article 16 of the Convention between Belgium and Romania concerning mutual judicial assistance in civil and commercial matters signed in Bucarest on 3 October 1975. Other Conventions were also concluded with the former Yugoslavia (Convention of 24 September 1971), with the former Eastern Germany (Convention of 29 November 1982) and with the former Czechoslovakia (Convention of 15 October 1984). These Conventions are no longer in force.

[55] In its Empirical Study, the Institute indicates that the London Convention is „never or rarely used" : Swiss Institute of Comparative Law, The Application of Foreign Law in Civil Matters in the EU Member States and its Perspectives for the Future, Part II – Empirical Analysis (JLS/2009/JCIV/PR/005/E4), 2011, at pp. 40–41. Although this is based on a limited number of answers, the answers converge and are therefore interesting.

[56] Swiss Institute of Comparative Law, The Application of Foreign Law in Civil Matters in the EU Member States and its Perspectives for the Future, Part II – Empirical Analysis (JLS/2009/JCIV/PR/005/E4), 2011, at p. 68.

tioner, outlining how English law should be applied in the particular case. The Court of Appeal deemed that it had been sufficiently informed by this witness statement. Hence, it did not request information from England on the basis of the London Convention. Before the Supreme Court, the plaintiff alleged that by not using the mechanism put in place by the London Convention, the Court of Appeal had breached its treaty obligation. The Supreme Court rejected this argument, holding that the London Convention did not require that a court should always seek information on foreign law through the Convention mechanism when it is required to apply foreign law.[57]

The poor track record of application of the London Convention may be traced back to the fact that the Convention is not well known among practitioners – judges and attorneys alike.[58] Further, it is also felt that the mechanism set up by the London Convention is too time consuming.[59]

When information on foreign law is provided by a foreign authority, the relevant treaty provisions usually provide that the information does not bind the authority which requested the information.[60]

D. Interpretation and Application of Foreign Law

When looking at the status of foreign law in Belgian courts, a last question should be addressed: that of the methods and rules which the guide the process of interpretation of foreign law. This question must be examined together with the pathological case in which a court finds out that the applicable foreign law lacks a rule for the question raised.

The principle is that foreign law should be applied as it is applied in the country of origin. This has been affirmed by the Supreme Court in the *Babcok-Smulders* case: in this landmark ruling,[61] the court was required to rule on the question of the interpretation of Article 1645 of the Civil Code. This provision is identical in both the French and the Belgian Civil Code. It provides that the seller is liable for hidden defects affecting goods which it has sold. In both countries, the professional seller

---

[57] Supreme Court (Court of cassation), 7 December 2012, *Rechtspraak Brussel, Antwerpen, Gent*, 2013, at p. 1267.

[58] This is stated by J. Verhellen (ed.), *Loi et pratique en droit international privé familial...* at p. 25. See also J. Verhellen, at p. 113, § 185.

[59] The excessive length of time was mentioned in the empirical study of the Swiss Institute of Comparative Law as the main reason for the lack of use of the London Convention (Swiss Institute of Comparative Law, The Application of Foreign Law in Civil Matters in the EU Member States and its Perspectives for the Future, Part II – Empirical Analysis (JLS/2009/JCIV/PR/005/E4), 2011, at p. 42). See also J. Verhellen, at p. 113, § 185.

[60] See *e.g.* Article 8 of the 1968 London Convention and Article 23 of the Convention of 30 April 1981 between Belgium and Morocco on judicial assistance in civil, administrative and commercial matters and in relation to exchange of legal information.

[61] Supreme Court, 9 October 1980, *Pasicrisie*, 1981, I, 159.

is deemed to have known the hidden defects of the goods he sells. However, while courts in Belgium had held that the professional seller may rebut this presumption, French courts held at that time that the presumption could not be overturned. In the case at hand, a French company had sold some goods to a Belgian buyer, which proved to be defective. It was unchallenged that the contract was governed by French law. However, the lower courts had held that the French seller could not have known about the defects. The ruling was quashed by the Supreme Court on the ground that the lower court had applied Article 1645 of the Civil Code taking into account the interpretation given to this provision under Belgian law. The Supreme Court held that account should have been taken of the French provision and of the interpretation given in France to that provision. The Court held that:

> *Attendu que, bien que rédigés en termes identique et ayant une origine commune, les articles 1645 du Code civil belge et 1645 du Code civil français ont cessé de constituer une même loi et ne comportent pas la même interprétation; que, d'après ladite disposition de la loi française, suivant l'interprétation qu'elle reçoit en France et dont le juge devait tenir compte, le vendeur professionnel est présumé de manière irréfragable, avoir conu le vice de la chose qu'il a livrée.*[62]

It is worth noting that in its opinion in this case, the Advocate-General explicitly referred to the two decisions issued by the Permanent International Court of Justice in the Serbian and Brazilian loan cases, in which the PICJ held that foreign law should be applied taking into account foreign case law.[63]

Article 15 CPIL has confirmed the principle outlined in *Babcok*. It explicitly provides that foreign law should be applied "according to the interpretation received abroad".[64]

It is accepted that under Article 15 CPIL, courts should not only apply foreign legal provisions as they are interpreted in the jurisdiction of origin, but also take into account methods of interpretation used in the jurisdiction of origin of the rules. Advocate General Krings explained in the seminal *Babcok* case that courts should take into account what is the weight of judicial precedents in the foreign legal system and what role can be granted to custom as a source of law.[65]

The position under Belgian law is therefore highly ambitious: courts should strive to read and construe foreign law as it would be applied by foreign courts. It is worth asking how courts cope with this ambitious goal. Experience has revealed that in most cases, courts will not go further than looking at the relevant statutory

---

[62] "Considering that articles 1645 Belgian Civil Code and 1645 French Civil Code, although formulated in identical terms and having a common origin, have cease to constitute the same statute and do not bear the same interpretation; that according to the French provision, following the interpretation it receives in France and which the judge should take into account, the professional salesman is irrebutably presumed to know any defect in the product he has delivered" (translation taken over from Geeroms, at p. 302, note 109).

[63] Opinion of Advocate general Krings, published in *Pasicrisie*, 1981, I, at pp. 163–164.

[64] "*Het buitenlands recht wordt toegepast volgens de in het buitenland gevolgde interpretatie*"/"*Le droit étranger est appliqué selon l'interprétation reçue à l'étranger*".

[65] Opinion of Advocate general Krings, published in *Pasicrisie*, 1981, I, at p. 165.

provisions of foreign law. Only in a few cases, reference will also be made to case law in order to discover how the relevant provisions are applied.[66]

In some instances, courts will engage in a more detailed review of the applicable foreign law, using thereto available court cases and scholarly comments.[67] One area where courts in Belgium have gone to some length in determining the content of foreign law concerns the dismissal of employees under the law of the Democratic Republic of Congo (DRC).[68] Due to historical ties between the two countries, a significant number of Belgian citizens have been working in the DRC – some of them for companies incorporated in Belgium but most of them for companies incorporated in the DRC. Following the very weak performance of the DRC economy over the last decades, many of these employees have been dismissed. Some of these dismissals have been challenged before courts in Belgium. This has given rise to a substantial number of rulings where courts had to apply the labour law of DRC. A number of cases were decided by the Supreme Court.[69] In order to decide these cases, which raised delicate questions of interpretation of foreign law, courts have examined with due care not only the existing statutory provisions, but also the interpretation given to these norms by local courts and scholars.[70]

In general, courts feel very insecure when applying foreign law, as they rely on limited resources. Courts have the impression that they may be making mistakes in ascertaining the content of the relevant foreign law, but that it is difficult, if not impossible for them to verify whether this is the case.[71]

Linked to the question of the interpretation of foreign law, one should also investigate how courts in Belgium deal with so-called 'gaps' in foreign law. Before addressing this question, it is worth underlining that it is not always easy to determine with precision that a given foreign law does not provide an answer for the specific legal question at stake. It may be that the relevant foreign law is not easily

[66] As noted by J. Verhellen, at p. 106, § 180 – see the cases listed in footnote 351.

[67] See the various cases discussed by J. Verhellen, at pp. 104–105, § 179.

[68] In another case, a Court of Appeal engaged in an extensive discussion of the application of one provision of Dutch labour law, in order to determine whether this provision, which made it impossible to file an appeal against a first instance ruling, was part of Dutch civil procedure or Dutch labour law – see Labor Court of Appeal of Antwerpen, 21 October 2008, *Rechtskundig Weekblad*, 2009–2010, at p. 541. The Court reviewed took into account the opinion of Dutch courts and Dutch scholars.

[69] See Supreme Court (Court of cassation), 3 June 1985, *Pasicrisie*, 1985, I, 1241, n° 597; Supreme Court (Court of cassation), 9 December 1991, *Pasicrisie*, 1992, I, 271, n° 190; Supreme Court (Court of cassation), 13 May 1996, *Pasiscrisie*, 1996, I, 455, n° 170; Supreme Court (Court of cassation), 17 January 1994, *Pasicrisie*, 1994, I, 46; Supreme Court (Court of cassation, 14 February 2005, *J.T.T.*, 2005, 621 and Supreme Court (Court of cassation), 18 April 2005, *N.J.W.*, 2005, 1168.

[70] See *e.g.* Labor Court of Brussels, 15 July 2002, *Journal des Tribunaux du Travail*, 2003 at p. 48 (the court makes reference to a number rulings of courts in DRC and also to scholarly comments written by DRC scholars).

[71] This is the conclusion drawn by Verhellen on the basis of interviews conducted with judges – see J. Verhellen, at p. 107–109, § 181.

accessible, that its sources are vague, etc. Courts in Belgium have not yet developed a comprehensive method to determine whether such a gap exists.

If it has indeed been ascertained that there is a gap, courts in Belgium will look to the general principles of interpretation of the relevant foreign law in order to solve it. In other words, courts will not resort to the gap filling methods available under Belgian law, but attempt to apply those methods in force under the relevant foreign law. This is again an example of the ambitious policy set by Belgian courts when faced with foreign law.

A recent case turning on the application of the labour law of the Democratic Republic of Congo illustrates this method. As has been explained, in a number of cases, employees have challenged their dismissal by their DRC employers before courts in Belgium. The difficulty is that in most of these cases, the DRC employers had not formally terminated the contract of employment. Rather, in view of the dire economic condition of the DRC during most of the 1990's and early 2000, employers have resorted to *suspend* the contract of employment for an indefinite period of time. As explained by employers, this allowed employees to seek other employment while having the possibility to keep the employment contract in place. A number of Belgian employees have challenged this suspension before courts in Belgium, alleging that it constituted a case of constructive dismissal. The question which arose in this respect was whether the rules of the DRC Labour Code in relation to termination of employment contracts could be deemed to exhaustively list all possible modes of termination: if the answer was positive, courts would not have been able to look beyond the suspension and analyse it as a case of constructive dismissal.

Courts have first established that the rules of the Labour Code left some room to take into account other modes of termination of employment contracts. It then became necessary to examine whether courts could also avail themselves of a mode of termination not expressly foreseen in the DRC Labour Code, i.e. termination by courts. After reviewing the available sources, one Labour Court has held that this termination method was not excluded by the law of the DRC and could therefore be applied.[72] One should recognize that it is difficult to assess whether the Court's ruling was in any way the right one to take: first, because the court came to the conclusion that the law of the DRC showed a gap only because it did not include a rule known under Belgian law and second because the solution adopted by the Court was only thinly motivated.

A court could also attempt to fill a gap in a foreign law by trying to determine what solution would be given to the question by laws of countries which belong to the same legal tradition as the country whose law is applicable.[73]

Once a court has determined that a given foreign law is applicable, the rules currently applicable do not make it possible for the court to step aside from this result

[72] Labour Court, 15 July 2002, *Journal des Tribunaux du Travail*, 2003, at p. 48.

[73] The Labor Court of Brussels has alluded to this solution in its ruling of 2002 (Labour Court, 15 July 2002, *Journal des Tribunaux du Travail*, 2003, at p. 48). In order to substantiate its analysis, the Court referred to the fact that the solution it adopted, could also be found in several legal systems belonging to the same „family" as the one whose law was applicable.

and apply another conflict of laws rule if it finds that the applicable foreign law does not provide a solution for the question at hand. A court may, however, sometimes be able to avoid finding a solution for the gap it finds in the applicable foreign law, by using a general mechanism of private international law, such as the public policy exception.[74]

E. Failure to Establish Foreign Law

A last question must be addressed when considering the application of foreign law by courts in Belgium: what mechanism do these courts use when the content of foreign law cannot be ascertained?

According to Article 15 CPIL, application may be made of Belgian law. This possibility only exists when it is "manifestly impossible" to determine the content of foreign law.[75] Presumably, the court should therefore explain in its decision the efforts it has undertaken in order to ascertain the content of the relevant foreign law before it resorts to the default solution provided in Article 15.[76] The main rationale to the default solution provided in Article 15 CPIL is that justice must be done. If a question is governed by foreign law and it appears impossible to determine the content of the relevant foreign law, this should not prevent the court from adjudicating the dispute. The court cannot refuse to grant the relief sought merely because it is impossible to identify the content of the relevant foreign law.[77]

This default solution has in the past already been used by the Supreme Court. In one case involving an issue of parental responsibility, a lower court had awarded the mother custody of the child, finding that the father, who also requested custody of the child, had failed to demonstrate that under the law or Iran, which according to the father was applicable, children should be entrusted to their fathers. The Supreme Court refused to follow the father's plea to quash the lower court ruling. The father

[74] See *e.g.* Court of Appeal of Brussels, 30 June 1981, *Journal des Tribunaux*, 1981, 723 (in that case, the Court was faced with the mission of applying the law of Sudan to decide whether the recognition of a child by a Sudanese national could be challenged. The court struggled to ascertain the exact content of the law of Sudan. It found that it was most likely that the law of Sudan did not make it possible for the Sudanese national to recognize the child, as the person was not married with the mother of the child. On this basis, the Court concluded that the application of the law of Sudan would violate Belgian public policy, as it made a distinction between children born in and outside marriage. Hence the court did not feel it needed to pursue its quest for Sudanese law.

[75] "*Wanneer het kennelijk onmogelijk is de inhoud van buitenlands recht tijdig vast te stellen, wordt Belgisch recht toegepast*"/"*Lorsqu'il est manifestement impossible d'établir le contenu du droit étranger en temps utile, il est fait application du droit belge*".

[76] According to Traest, the mechanism provided in Art. 15 can only be resorted to if "strict proof of the manifest impossibility to ascertain the content of foreign law in time" has been produced: M. Traest, at p. 135.

[77] This solution was, however, advocated by some scholars, see *e.g.* R. Vander Elst, note under Supreme Court, 9 October 1980, *Journal des Tribunaux*, 1981, at p. 76.

had argued that the lower court had incorrectly applied the laws of Iran. The Supreme Court answered that given the particular nature of the proceedings, which were conducted in summary proceedings, the lower court had not erred by applying Belgian law as a substitute to the relevant foreign law.[78]

Although it would go too far to read in this ruling a general rule that Belgian law may always be used as a substitute to the relevant foreign law when the content of the latter cannot be ascertained,[79] it remains that Article 15 CPIL has clearly accepted that the law of the forum can be used as a subsidiary to the applicable foreign law when the latter cannot be ascertained.

Practice has shown that courts tend to accept rather quickly that it is impossible to determine the content of foreign law. In a recent case, a lower court applied Article 15 and resorted to the application of the law of the forum after stating that it had failed to obtain an answer from the foreign authorities, to whom it had send a request to obtain information on the applicable statutory provisions in relation to the establishment of a parentage link. The Court had twice requested the assistance of the Consulate of Sierra Leone to obtain information on the applicable principles.[80] The court noted that in matters concerning children, one could not wait for the "uncertain outcome of a sophisticated attempt" to discover the content of foreign law. It is submitted that this ruling significantly and unreasonably lowers the threshold to resort to the law of the forum as substitute law.

IV. Judicial Review

When discussing the status of foreign law, one should take full account of the position of foreign law before higher courts. These courts indeed are called upon to review the decisions issued by lower courts. When doing so, they may call into question the position of conflict of laws rules and of foreign law. In order to obtain a complete picture of the position of foreign law, it is therefore necessary to pay attention to the practice of higher courts. This will be done first for conflict of laws rules, after which the position of foreign law before higher courts will be discussed.[81]

---

[78] Supreme Court, 12 December 1985, *Pasicrisie*, 1986, I, 479.

[79] See the analysis by Geeroms, at p. 208–209, § 2.475–2.476.

[80] Court of First Instance of Liège, 11 January 2008, *Revue du droit des étrangers*, 2009, 712.

[81] See in general, W. Pintens, "Le contrôle de l'application du droit étranger par la Cour de cassation de Belgique" in *Application du droit étranger par le juge national. Allemagne, France, Belgique et Suisse*, C. Witz (ed.), Société de législation comparée, 2014, pp. 135–142.

A. Conflict of Laws Rules

The status of conflicts of laws rules in appellate proceedings follows naturally from the position held by these rules in first instance proceedings. As already indicated, conflict of laws rules are afforded the same treatment and status as other rules of law. If a court has erroneously applied a conflict of laws rule, this may be therefore challenged before a higher court. The only limitations to such review are those applicable to all other rules of law. So it is that in some cases, no direct appeal may be brought against a provisional decision, but that instead, one should wait until the court has issued a decision on the merits of the case. Further, the jurisdiction of the Supreme Court is limited to issues of law, and may not be extended to issues of fact. Provided these limitations are taken into account, mistakes in the application of conflict of laws rules may be reviewed in full by a higher court.

B. Foreign Law

When foreign law has been erroneously applied, one should enquire whether parties may appeal to higher courts to challenge this application. The position in this respect in Belgium is quite clear: as courts have an obligation to ascertain *sua sponte* the content of and apply provisions of foreign law declared applicable by the relevant conflict of laws rules, it is also accepted that the application by courts of foreign law may be reviewed by higher courts. Appellate courts may therefore be called upon to review the application of foreign law by lower courts. They will face, however, the same difficulties in ascertaining the content of foreign law.

The Supreme Court (*Cour de cassation/Hof van cassatie*) also has jurisdiction to review the application by a lower court of a provision of foreign law. This is a rather recent development. Until 1981, the Supreme Court refused to consider an appeal based on the allegedly incorrect application of foreign law.[82] In a landmark case decided in 1981, the Court decided that it could review the application by a lower court of the applicable foreign law. This was a logical development of the court's ruling that lower courts should apply foreign law as it is applied in the country of origin. The Supreme Court was of the opinion that it could only impose such obligation on lower courts if it accepted the possibility to review the application by lower courts of foreign law. The main rationale for the position of the Supreme Court is the need to keep the system coherent: if lower courts have a duty to ascertain the content of foreign law on their own motion, there must be a possibility for the Supreme Court to review this application. Otherwise, the duty risks becoming dead letter.

For a long time, it has, however, remained unclear whether the Supreme Court would adopt the same standard of review when examining a court decision having made application of foreign law than when reviewing a decision where local law

[82] See for a detailed review, Geeroms, pp. 296–300, §§5.38 – 5.45.

was applied. This question is in particular relevant when it appears that the relevant provision of foreign law is amenable to several different interpretations, none of which have yet prevailed, or when the exact meaning of a provision of foreign law is unclear. In those cases, it must be ascertained whether the Supreme Court will engage in a *full review*, thereby accepting to engage in the construction of foreign rules. The majority of scholars advised against such ambitious review, arguing that it is not for the Supreme Court of Belgium to decide whether a given interpretation of foreign law is indeed well founded.[83]

The question was tied to a technical issue, that of the legal ground which must be raised before the Supreme Court in order to challenge the application made by a lower court of a provision of foreign law. The Supreme Court (*'Cour de cassation'/'Hof van cassatie'*) is a jurisdiction of last resort. It does not engage in a review of the facts of the case. Its mission is limited to examining whether the lower courts have correctly applied the law. A recourse to the Supreme Court must clearly indicate which provisions of law have been incorrectly applied by the lower court. When the challenge concerns the application by a lower court of a provision of foreign law, one may hesitate between indicating the provision of foreign law which has been incorrectly applied or the conflict of laws rule which led to the application of the foreign law. If a lower court has incorrectly applied the relevant foreign law, it has been argued that it has also breached the conflict of laws rule prescribing the application of the foreign law. Hence it was submitted that a challenge before the Supreme Court should not only indicate which provisions of the relevant foreign law had been incorrectly applied, but also which conflict of law rules. At the same time, tying up of the conflict of laws rule with the relevant provisions of foreign law seemed to indicate that the Supreme Court would only engage in a limited review of the decision, the application by the lower court of the provisions of foreign law being 'protected' by the conflict of laws rules.[84]

For some years, the position of the Supreme Court was unclear. In a ruling of 1993, the Supreme Court quashed a decision whereby a provision of Dutch law had been incorrectly applied. In doing so, the Supreme Court only referred to the rele-

[83] See *e.g.* E. Krings, "Aspects de la contribution de la Cour de cassation à l'édification du droit", 109 *Journal des Tribunaux* 545 (1990); L. Simont, "La Cour de cassation et la loi étrangère. Quelques réflexions", in *Liber amicorum Pierre Marchal*, Larcier, 2003, (189–207), at pp. 197–198; Ph. Gerard, J.-F. van Drooghenbroeck and H. Boularbah, *Pourvoi en cassation en matière civile*, RPDB, Bruylant, 2012, at p. 287, par. 595. See also the position taken by Pierre Lecroart, clerk to Supreme Court Justice Parmentier, in *Annual Report of the Court of Cassation*, 2006, at pp. 251–254. According to M. Lecroart, "... It is logical that the Supreme Court exercises a limited control over the application of foreign law by the lower courts. One of the essential missions of the Court is indeed to 'say the law', which includes guaranteeing the uniformity of interpretation of the law and also filling in gaps which may appear in the law. Obviously the Court cannot assume this role in respect of the law of a foreign State, because it would otherwise breach the sovereignty of that State". *Compare* with P. Wautelet, "Aux confins de la norme : quelques réflexions sur le statut du droit étranger en droit international privé belge", in *Liber amicorum Paul Martens. L'humanisme dans la résolution des conflits. Utopie ou réalité?*, M. Pâques et al (eds.), Larcier, 2006, 637–649.

[84] See *e.g.* M. Traest, at p. 130, footnote 8.

vant provision of Dutch law, without indicating the applicable conflict of laws rule. This suggested that the Court was prepared to examine directly the application of the provision of foreign law, without any 'cushion'.[85] In a later ruling, the Supreme Court on the contrary refused to examine whether the lower court had made any mistake in applying foreign law, because the appeal had not made any mention of the relevant conflict of laws rule.[86] According to the Court, it is only seized "par le truchement de la règle de conflit" [through the intermediation of the conflict of laws rule].[87]

In a recent development, the Court has made it clear that it will *not* apply the same standard of review when examining a lower court ruling applying foreign law than when it reviews a lower court ruling applying Belgian law.[88] The question arose in yet another case involving the application of the laws of the DR of Congo. A dispute arose between a DRC company and a former employee who had been dismissed, in relation to the payment of arrears of remuneration. The company alleged that the claim should be dismissed because the statute of limitations had lapsed. A discussion ensued on the precise nature of the statute of limitations under the law of the DRCongo. In order to conclude that the claim was not barred by the statute of limitations, the Court of Appeal reviewed recent cases decided by courts in DRC. It also noted that scholars in the DRC were divided on the nature and exact scope of the statute of limitations. The Court of Appeal took side with one of the possible interpretations of the relevant statutory provisions, after noting that this interpretation was more in line with the reading adopted by the expert working group which had prepared the relevant statute.

This ruling was challenged before the Supreme Court. The plaintiff alleged that the Court of Appeal had wrongly applied the relevant provisions of DRC law, by neglecting to take into account some recent court cases and granting too much weight to the comments of DRC scholars. The Supreme Court refused to overrule the Court of Appeal. It held that its mission was to "verify that the lower court's

---

[85] Supreme Court, 18 June 1993, *Revue générale des assurances et responsabilités*, 1994, nr. 12366, with comments by M. Fallon.

[86] Supreme Court, 14 February 2005, *Arresten Cassatie*, 2005, N) 89. See also in the same line, Supreme Court, 18 April 2005, *Nieuw Juridisch Weekblad*, 2005, at p. 1168 and Supreme Court, 4 November 2010, *Rechtskundig Weekblad*, 2011–2012, at p. 824, with comments by M. Traest. This later ruling was issued *en banc* by the entire bench, giving the ruling additional weight. This opinion had been criticized. See *e.g.* J. Kirkpatrick, "Dans les moyens de cassation en matière civile, doivent seules être indiquées les dispositions légales dont la violation est invoquée", *Liber amicorum Bernard Glandsorff*, Bruylant, 2008, at pp. 335–344, specially at p. 344.

[87] See for the question whether the obligation to refer not only to the provision of foreign law, but also to the conflict of laws rules which has led to the application of foreign law, takes formalism too far and could therefore be in violation with Article 6 Eur. Convention Human Rights, the comments by M. Traest, "Over het vreemd recht en het cassatiecontrole hierop", *Rechtskundig Weekblad*, 2011–2012, at pp. 827–828.

[88] Supreme Court (Cour de cassation, 3rd Chamber), 18 March 2013, *La générale des carrières et des mines/R.L., Umicore, Journal des tribunaux du travail*, 2013, at p. 271; *Rechtspraak Antwerpen, Gent en Brussel*, 2013, at p. 1263, with comments by M. Baetens-Spetschinsky; Revue@dipr.be 2013/2, at p. 11).

decision is in conformity with the interpretation" upheld in the country of origin. After noting that the precise scope and meaning of the relevant statutory provision were subject to debate in the DRC, the Court explained that its review of the Court of Appeal's ruling "did not reveal that the Court of Appeal had adopted an interpretation [of the relevant statutory provisions] which could manifestly not be held to be in conformity with the interpretation given to these provisions in the DRC".[89]

In other words, the Supreme Court made it clear that when a provision of foreign law is vague or subject to various interpretations, its role is not to settle once and for all the interpretation question, but rather to verify whether the interpretation adopted by the lower court can reasonably be accepted.[90]

The review by the Supreme Court of the application by lower courts of foreign law, remains constrained due to the limited jurisdiction exercised by the Supreme Court. The Supreme Court cannot engage in a factual assessment of the case. Its jurisdiction is limited to examining whether a lower court ruling is in conformity with the law. When doing so, the Court has developed a number of highly sophisticated techniques. This limits the review by the Court of the application of foreign law. This can be illustrated by a ruling of 1984 in a case involving a Spanish divorce: two Spanish nationals were involved in a dispute before the courts in Belgium. One of the spouses had requested that the court issues a decree of legal separation. It was not challenged that Spanish law was applicable. Before the Supreme Court, one of the parties alleged, however, that the Court of Appeal had incorrectly applied Spanish law, in that it had not taken into account the interpretation given by the Spanish Supreme Court (*Tribunal Supremo*) to the relevant provisions of Spanish law. This was a new argument, which had not been presented before the lower courts. The Supreme Court refused to take it into account, holding that since not of the parties had made mention of this interpretation before the lower courts, the Court of Appeal was not required to specifically review it. This should not be taken to mean that courts only have to take into account the interpretation of foreign law when parties have expressly drawn the court's attention to it. In fact the Supreme Court also noted that the Court of appeal had indeed taken note of all requirements for a decree of legal separation under Spanish law.[91]

When foreign law is applied on the basis of a conflict of laws rule found in a European regulation, it may be that the picture is different. It has been argued that because of the supremacy enjoyed by European law, a violation of foreign law may be relied on as such, without alleging as well the breach by the lower court of the conflict of law rule which led to the application of foreign law.[92]

---

[89] It is, however, unclear whether it is still necessary to invoke the breach of the conflict of laws provision on the basis of which foreign law was applied.

[90] For a more ambitious perspective on the role of the Supreme Court, see Storme, at pp. 1164.

[91] Supreme Court, 23 February 1984, *Pasicrisie*, 1984, I, nr. 353, p. 728.

[92] See M. Traest, at p. 130.

V. Foreign Law in Other Instances

There are undoubtedly a great number of cases where administrative and other non-judicial authorities must apply foreign law.[93] This is *e.g.* the case each time a person, who does not possess Belgian nationality, wishes to recognize a child in Belgium. Such recognition is indeed subject to the national law of the person wishing to recognize the child (Art. 62 CPIL). Further, the establishment of the name of a child is also often governed by foreign law, as it is subject to the national law of the child.[94]

No explicit provision determines how foreign law should be ascertained and applied in such case. In particular it is unclear whether Article 15 CPIL should also be applied in such situation. According to its wording, Article 15 only targets the application of foreign law by courts. It could therefore be argued that this provision does not apply when the question of the application of foreign law occurs not before a court, but before an administrative authority, such as *e.g.* the civil status registrar (*'officier d'état civil'/'ambtenaar van burgerlijke stand'*).

According to Mr Erauw, the absence of reference to non-judicial authorities in Article 15 can be explained by the fact that these authorities are bound by a strict duty to apply the law. This duty would also cover the application of foreign law.[95] Ms Verhellen has argued that Article 15 CPIL should be amended to include a reference to non-judicial authorities, in particular registrars.[96]

There is one legal provision which clarifies the role of non-judicial authorities in respect of the application of foreign law. Article 64 of the Civil Code provides that when a foreigner wishes to marry in Belgium, he or she may be requested to produce a document outlining the requirements for such marriage under his/her national law. In this particular case, the duty to ascertain and demonstrate the content of foreign law therefore does not lie on the authority, but rather on the citizens. In practice, many registrars do not require such a certificate when the purported marriage concerns spouses who possess a nationality which frequently occurs in Belgium. The registrar will in that case rely on information collected in previous instances.

There is no information available on the process whereby foreign law is ascertained in arbitration or mediation proceedings. As these proceedings are by essence

[93] It has been argued that non-judicial authorities do not 'apply' foreign law but only 'take it into account' (M. Traest, at p. 140). The distinction does not seem to be convincing: when a registrar applies Article 62 of the Code of Private International Law and concludes that French law is relevant to determine whether a person may recognize a child, the registrar goes further than merely taking into account French law. It is difficult to operate a distinction between what the registrar does and what a court would do in the same situation.

[94] Verhellen provides a vivid overview of the many instances where registrars are faced with the application of foreign law. She draws in large part from the experience of the 'Helpdesk Private International Family Law' to show that registrars are faced with difficulties when trying to ascertain the content of foreign law – J. Verhellen, at pp. 118–120, §§ 189–192).

[95] See the position explained in J. Verhellen (ed.), *Loi et pratique en droit international privé familial. Compte rendu des tables rondes printemps 2013*, La Charte, 2013, at p. 32, § 104.

[96] J. Verhellen, at p. 477, § 733.

confidential, it is difficult to obtain information. It may be presumed that in arbitration proceedings, which by and large concern commercial disputes, parties will bear most of the burden of demonstrating the content of foreign law.[97] It may also be presumed that foreign law will not play an important role in mediation.

Attorneys do not have a statutory duty to ascertain the content of the relevant foreign law. However, such duty could indirectly arise as a consequence of the professional obligation that attorneys undertake all possible efforts to advise their clients as best as they can. Attorneys may also be subject to professional liability rules going in the same direction. In practice, attorneys will rely on various methods to ascertain the content of foreign law: next to the attempt to locate the content of foreign law using online resources, attorneys may also contact a professional of the country concerned in order to obtain the required information.

Notaries (*'notaire'/'notaris'*) play an important role in many private transactions – such as the sale and transfer of immovables, divorce, succession or matters concerning children. It is not uncommon for notaries to come to the conclusion that a given question which they must solve, is governed by foreign law. A notary is required to have knowledge of the conflict of laws rules applicable in Belgium. This duty is the consequence of the professional liability which notaries may incur when advising their clients.[98] In some cases, notaries will act upon being instructed to do so by courts. This will be the case when a notary is requested to manage the estate of a deceased. In such a case, the duty of the notary to know and apply the relevant conflict of laws rules will follow from the mission entrusted to him by the court.

It follows logically from the previous, that the notary is also required to know and apply the relevant foreign law. A notary could be held liable if it appears that he erroneously applied a rule of foreign law. However, it is argued that the obligation resting on notaries is an obligation of means and not an obligation of result. In practice, this means that the notary is not deemed to have an absolute knowledge of all possible rules of the relevant foreign law. Rather, in order to escape liability, the notary will have to demonstrate that he used his best efforts to uncover the content of the relevant foreign law. If he failed to do so notwithstanding good faith efforts, he may be able to escape liability.

It may be presumed that in order to ascertain the content of foreign law, the notary will avail itself of the same means used by courts and attorneys. Notaries may also call upon the expertise of a 'Knowledge Centre' ('*Centre de consultation*') which operates within the Royal Federation of Notaries. This centre provides advice on difficult issues of law. Although the experts working in the centre are all lawyers trained in Belgian law, they regularly assist notaries in ascertaining the content of the relevant foreign law.

---

[97] See for more details, F. de Ly, L. Radicati di Brozolo & M. Friedman, "Ascertaining the contents of the applicable law in international commercial arbitration. Report of the International Arbitration Committee of the International Law Association". *Arbitration International*, 2010 (26), pp. 191–220.

[98] See N. Watté, „Introduction au droit international privé notarial", in *Les relations contractuelles internationales. Le rôle du notaire*, Maklu uitgevers, 1995, at p. 43, § 61.

VI. Conclusion

The position of foreign law in Belgian courts has undergone a tremendous evolution in the past decades: while for a long time, ascertaining and pleading foreign law was treated as falling solely within the ambit of parties, it gradually became part of the courts' own duty to uncover and apply provisions of foreign law. As a consequences, there is today almost no difference between foreign law and local law from the perspective of the courts. This evolution can for the largest part be traced to the ambition of the Supreme Court to improve the standing of foreign law before Belgian courts. Step by step, the Court has built a coherent framework in which the various elements nicely fit each other. This framework, which has been codified in 2004, has in general been warmly received, with very few voices questioning its relevance or usefulness.

A closer look reveals, however, a great tension between the general framework and its application in practice: while courts have in principle the duty to ascertain the content of foreign law, much of the weight rests in practice on the parties and their counsels. To a very large extent, courts rely on the efforts undertaken by parties to discover the content of foreign law. At the same time, experience shows that courts tend to approach foreign law in a superficial manner: only in rare cases will courts go beyond the simple, mechanic application of provisions of foreign statutory law and effectively consider how these provisions are applied by foreign courts. Finally, the analysis reveals that courts tend to take a rather broad view of the escape clause which allows them to resort to Belgian law when the content of the relevant foreign law cannot be ascertained.

In view of this tension, one may wonder whether the position adopted by the Supreme Court should not be reconsidered. Is it truly realistic to require from courts that they undertake to ascertain the content of foreign law and to apply foreign law as it is applied in the country of origin? If this position is to be confirmed, one should at the very least expect that courts receive the necessary assistance in order to help them in this exacting mission. However, the very ambitious starting point on which Belgian law is currently based, has not yet resulted in the adoption of any tool designed to help the courts. Scholars have long ago made clear that courts should receive proper assistance if they are to ascertain the content of foreign law.[99] Nothing has, however, been undertaken to ease up the courts' mission. This explains why courts are not inclined to take the matter of foreign law in their own hands and prefer to rely on the efforts of parties. This in turn creates the risk that the party with more means and better finances, will have easier access to foreign law. At the same time, courts may be placed in a difficult situation if both parties come up with different versions of the applicable foreign law.

Requesting from courts in Belgium that they extend their law finding mission to foreign law is an ambition which cannot be sustained without some investment by

---

[99] See notably J. Erauw, *De bron van het vreemde recht vloeit overvloedig*, Story-Scientia, 1984, 43 p., in particular at pp. 12–13.

public authorities in tools and mechanisms providing courts the necessary assistance in this perilous task. Over the past decades, many voices have called for such investment.[100] The debate has made it clear that if one leaves aside the old dream to set up an institute which would compile all existing laws,[101] there is room for more flexible solutions: one could for example attempt to provide courts in Belgium with privileged access to the existing institutes working in neighboring countries. Such access may be limited to certain matters, such as family disputes.

Given the current budgetary constraints, it is, however not realistic to expect any investment, even limited, by public authorities. Courts will therefore remain stuck in a delicate situation: formally they should take up the task of finding foreign law but they lack the means to do so. One can therefore expect the current situation to continue, in which courts are *nominally* in charge of finding foreign law, but rely in the vast majority of cases on parties to carry out the necessary investigations. Such a wide gap between theory and practice is not a fertile ground for a stable legal framework. This even smacks of hypocrisy: the law pretends that courts are in charge of ascertaining the content of the relevant foreign law while in practice, this task is delegated to parties.

If everything else fails, it is submitted that one should accept to modify the existing principles and acknowledge the substantial role played by parties. This would entail modifying Article 15 CPIL to provide that parties have the primary duty to find the relevant foreign law. Courts would work primarily on the basis of information collected and presented by parties. This change would not affect the court's obligation to apply foreign law. Nor would it modify the obligation for courts to identify and apply the relevant conflict of laws rules. Scaling down the ambition may not solve all problems. It would at least ensure that law in the books reflects more closely law in action.

---

[100] See the recent examination by M. Traest, "Vloeit de bron van het vreemde recht niet te overvloedig?", in *Liber amicorum Johan Erauw*, Intersentia, 2014, 207–217.

[101] This was a project of the International Law Institute, expressed in a Resolution adopted at its session in Brussels in 1885. The Institute adopted a "*Proposition pour un accord international aux fins de l'institution d'un Comité international permanent pour faciliter aux gouvernements et aux citoyens de chaque pays la connaissance des lois actuellement en vigueur*".

Croatia: Foreign Law Before Croatian Authorities – At the Crossroads?

Mirela Župan

Abstract Mandatory application of conflict of law rules seems undisputable in the Croatian legal system. Principle of iura novit curia is embodied in relevant legal sources (Constitution, PIL Act, sectoral laws), confirmed by legal writings and rulings of Supreme Court and Constitutional Court. Despite the compulsory character of the choice of law rules, first instance courts are rather reluctant in application of choice of law rules. Foreign law is considered a "law", whereas court is obliged to ascertain the content of foreign law ex officio. Establishing the content of foreign law is most often done through the Ministry of Justice. Case law however confirms that parties can play an active and supporting role in judge's efforts to establish foreign law as well. It is conceived that establishing foreign law can endanger procedural efficiency, as it is time consuming and costly (due to translations). Data on application of bilateral or multilateral regimes (EJN, HIJN) that provide framework for direct judicial cooperation in establishing the content of foreign law have not been reported yet. Non-application of foreign law may be justified on the grounds of public policy. Future PIL Act provides additional devices for departure of foreign law application: lois de application immediate and general escape clause. If the content of foreign law is not established, lex fori is applied.

I. Conflict of Law Rules

In Croatian legal system application of conflict of law rules is mandatory. The mandatory character derives first of all from the principle of *iura novit curia* embodied in Article 118(3) of the Croatian Constitution stating that "Courts shall administer justice according to the Constitution, international treaties and other valid sources of law."[1] It follows from the clear wording of the Law on Resolution of Conflict of

[1] Ustav Republike Hrvatske, (Constitution of the Republic of Croatia, consolidated text), Croatian Official Gazette (Narodne novine) no. 56/90, 135/97, 8/98, 113/00, 124/00, 28/01, 41/01, 55/01, 76/10, 85/10.

M. Župan (✉)
Associate Professor, Faculty of Law, Josip Juraj Strossmayer University of Osijek,
S. Radića,13, 31 000, Osijek, Croatia
e-mail: mzupan@pravos.hr

Y. Nishitani (ed.), *Treatment of Foreign Law - Dynamics towards Convergence?*,
Ius Comparatum – Global Studies in Comparative Law 26,
DOI 10.1007/978-3-319-56574-3_3

Laws with Regulations of Other Countries (hereinafter: Croatian PIL Act, Act),[2] stating that court is obliged to apply the Act and its choice of law rules whenever the situation fulfils the scope of application of the Act prescribed by its Article: status, family and pecuniary relations, as well as other substantive legal relations with an international element.[3] Mandatory nature of conflict of law rules is retained with the Draft Private International Law Act of 2016 (hereinafter: Draft PIL Act).[4] However, mandatory application of choice of law rules is not restricted to legal relations listed in the PIL Act/Draft PIL Act of 2016. Considering the structure of internal legal sources of private international law in Croatia, besides provisions of Croatian PIL Act, particular legal relations are regulated in *lege specialis*. The Croatian PIL Act gives precedence to such rules due to the principle of *lex specialis derogat legi generali*,[5] yet the basic principles, as well as legal lacunas are complemented with rules of the PIL Act.[6] Therefore, compulsory application of the choice of law rules extends to the special acts as well,[7] namely the Bill of Exchange Act,[8] the Cheque Act,[9] and the Arbitration Act.[10] Besides internal legal sources, Croatian legal system entails numerous choice of law rules deriving from international conventions[11] and European Union instruments.[12] They do not address the issue of nature of choice of

---

[2] Croatian PIL act dates back to 1983, when it was enacted in former Yugoslavia. It was adopted to Croatian system in 1991 The Law on Resolution of Conflict of Laws with Regulations of Other Countries, (Službeni list SFRJ No. 43 of 23 July 1982 with corrigenda in No. 72/82, adopted in Croatian Official Gazette (Narodne novine) No. 51/91.

[3] Article 1 (1) of Croatian PIL Act: "This law contains rules for determination of the applicable law with respect to status, family and pecuniary relations, as well as other substantive legal relations with an international element."

[4] Article 8 Draft PIL Act (https://esavjetovanja.gov.hr/ECon/MainScreen?entityId=3787).

[5] Article 3 of Croatian PIL Act states: "The provisions of this law shall not apply to relations mentioned under Article 1 of this law if these relations are regulated by another law or international treaty."

[6] Article 2 of the Croatian PIL Act, as well as Article 7 of the Draft PIL Act of 2016.

[7] Some of them were fully superseeded by EU regulations, such as The Obligations and *In Rem* Relations in Air Traffic Act Croatian Official Gazette (Narodne novine) No. 132/98; Maritime Code Croatian Official Gazette (Narodne novine) No. 118/204, 76/2007. The Consumer Protection Act (Croatian Official Gazette (Narodne novine) No. 79/07, 125/07, 79/09, 89/09, 133/09, 78/12, 56/13.)

[8] Croatian Official Gazette (Narodne novine) No. 74/94.

[9] Croatian Official Gazette (Narodne novine) No. 74/94.

[10] Croatian Official Gazette (Narodne novine) No. 88/2001.

[11] See Vesna Tomljenović and Ivana Kunda „"Conflict of Laws Conventions and their Reception in National Legal Systems: The Croatian National Report", in: Jorge Sánchez Córdero (eds)., *The Impact of Uniform Law on National Law. Limits and Possibilities/L'incidence du droit uniforme sur le droit national. Limites et possibilités*(Mexico City, Instituto de investigationes Juridicas, 2010) p. 1024–1069.

[12] Ivana Kunda/Carlos Manuel Goncalves de Mel Marinho, *Practical Handbook on European Private International Law* (2010) (http://ec.europa.eu/justice/civil/files/practical_handbook_eu_international_law_en.pdf); Vilim Bouček, *Evropsko međunarodno privatno pravo u eurointegracijskom procesu i harmonizacija hrvatskog međunarodnog privatnog prava* (Zagreb, 2009).

law rules, but it is conceived that nature of choice of law rules as prescribed by the national PIL Act determines the nature of application of these legal sources as well.[13]

Such clear standing of the choice of law rules as *ius cogens* has been supported by legal writing, dating back to the first Croatian private international law scholars: Eisner,[14] Katičić[15] and Matić[16]to contemporary Croatian private international law scholars: Babić[17] Bouček,[18] Klasiček,[19] Kunda,[20] Medić,[21] Sajko,[22] Sikirić,[23] Šarčević,[24] Tomljenović[25] and Župan.[26] Conflict of law rules of Croatian PIL Act is in vast majority by its nature multilateral, so they point under the same conditions to domestic or foreign law.[27] It follows that opportunities for application of foreign law are plentiful. At the moment, application of foreign law happens more often in contracts and tort than in family, status or inheritance matters. Regarding contracts and torts, connecting factors of characteristic performance and *lex loci delicti commissi* often lead to application of foreign law.[28] On the contrary, reason for rare

[13]Vesna Tomljenović, „Tumačenje kolizijskih pravila međunarodnih konvencija – primjer tumačenja kolizijskih odredbi Haške konvencije o prometnim nezgodama"*Zbornik Pravnog fakulteta u Zagrebu*, Vol. 62 No.1–2/2012, p. 103.

[14]Eisner Bertold, *Međunarodno privatno pravo* (Zagreb 1953).

[15]Natko Katičić, *Ogledi o međunarodnom privatnom pravu* (Zagreb 1971) p. 404.

[16]Željko Matić, "The Yugoslav act concerning private international law", *Netherlands international law review*, vol. 30 (1983), p. 220–239.

[17]Davor Babić, "Izbor stranog prava za ugovor bez međunarodnog obilježja", *Pravo u gospodarstvu* 42(2003)2, p. 18–31.

[18]Krešimir Sajko, Hrvoje Sikirić, Vilim Bouček, Davor Babić, Nina Tepeš, "Teze za hrvatski zakon o međunarodnom privatnom pravu", in: Krešimir Sajko, et al. *Izvori hrvatskog i europskog međunarodnog privatnog prava* (Zagreb 2001)

[19]Damir Klasiček, "Primjena stranog prava: kako i kada?", *Pravo u gospodarstvu* 40(2001)4, p. 231–233; Damir Klasiček, „Primjena stranog prava", *Zbornik Pravnog fakulteta u Zagrebu*, 51(2001) 3/4, p. 535–555, at. p. 539–540.

[20]Tomljenović/Kunda, *supra* note 12, p. 1024–1069.

[21]Ines Medić Musa, "Dokazivanje u međunarodnom privatnom pravu", *Zbornik radova Pravnog fakulteta u Splitu* 1–2 (2004), p. 139–150.

[22]Krešimir Sajko, „Kako i kada primjenjivati strano pravo", *Pravo i porezi* 11(2002)1, p. 27–33.

[23]Hrvoje Sikirić, "Primjena kolizijskih pravila i stranog prava u sudskom postupku", *Zbornik Pravnog fakulteta u Zagrebu*, 56 (2006), 2/3, p. 617–686, at. p. 619.

[24]Petar Šarčević, "The Modernization of private international law after World War II", in: C. Von Bar (ed.), *Perspektiven des Internationalen Privatrechts nach dem Ende der Spaltung Europas* (Carl Heymanns Verlag, Köln etc. 1992) p. 21.

[25]Tomljenović/Kunda, supra note 12, p. 1047.

[26]Mirela Župan, "Dijete u međunarodnom privatnom pravu", in Branka Rešetar (ed.), *Dijete i pravo* (Osijek, 2009) p. 223–255, at. p. 223–224.

[27]Krešimir Sajko, *Međunarodno privatno pravo* (Zagreb 2009) p. 92.

[28]Courts are eager to application of Hague convention on traffic accidents. Recent ruling of Supreme Court on that matter states that application of foregn law deriving from application of Conventional coice of law rules, is obligatory. Rev. x 470/14–2, Croatian Supreme Court of 1.4.2015.(available at: www.iusinfo.hr).

application of foreign law in status, family and inheritance matters lies with the connecting factors applied in the current Croatian PIL Act, where nationality and domicile are dominant. Due to the types of migrations that take place on the Croatian territory for the past decades, most situations with the foreign element were related to Croatian nationals living abroad, but which tended to settle their legal issues of divorce, maintenance, inheritance etc. before the Croatian authorities. In these types of cases, connecting factors of nationality and domicile have not often led to the application of foreign law; they mainly led to the application of Croatian substantive law. Over the last few years these connecting factors have for various family and inheritance matters been replaced by habitual residence as a result of accession to several conventions of the Hague Conference of Private International Law (hereinafter: HCCH) and EU choice of law regulations. In respect to some matters, changes would be introduced to the new Croatian PIL Act.[29] Such course of development is most welcome, having in mind contemporary conditions of mobility and intense migration across borders. If Croatia would have to face modern types of migrations with more foreign nationals living on its territory under the old legislative approach based on nationality, that would lead to application of foreign law in increasing number of cases.[30]

Straight wording of the PIL Act regarding the mandatory nature of the choice of law rules clearly signals that court may not escape its application; moreover, it is an obligation of a judge to apply the choice of law rules even when the parties do not plead for it. In other words, the application of the choice of law rules in Croatian system does not depend on the attitude of the parties.[31] "Legal rules, abstract legal imperative on the question how to regulate legal relations, the court has to acquaint… procedural legal dispositions of the parties cannot prevail over the court obliged *ex officio* and by its consciousness, to apply the relevant applicable legal norm.".[32]

Despite the compulsory character of the choice of law rules, courts are rather reluctant to apply them.[33] Examination of available case law reveals that in number of cases neither the judge applies nor the parties plead for application of the choice of law rules at the first instance of the trial.[34] However, as a rule, the misapplication of the law is relied on in the appeal: omission to apply the choice of law rules and/or foreign law is invoked at the second instance by the party unsatisfied with the first instance decision. Despite silence at the firt instance, non-application of the choice

[29] See more *infra*.

[30] Mirela Župan/Senija Ledić "Cross-border family matters – Croatian experience prior EU accession and future expectations", *Pravni vjesnik* 30(2014) 3/4, p. 49–76.

[31] Sajko, *supra* note 28, p. 229.

[32] Siniša Triva/Mihajlo Dika, *Građansko parnično procesno pravo* (Zagreb 2004) p. 183.

[33] Tomljenović/Kunda, *supra* note 12, p. 1047.

[34] Exceptionally it may happen even before the second instance court. In audit procedure, after complex elaboration of several Croatian substantive law provisions disputed before the first and second instance courts, The Supreme Court warned:"… due to the fact that loan contract was concluded in Germany it should have been questioned weather to this case Croatian or foreign legislation is applicable." Supreme Court of Republic of Croatia, No. VSRH Rev. 2981/1993–2, judgement of 26 March 1997. (available at: http://www.iusinfo.hr).

of law rules and subsequently foreign law seems to be an important reason for parties to raise an appeal.[35] In many second instance court judgements, one may find the same wording indicating the failure of a trial court to obey *ius cogens* nature of the choice of law rules.[36] Omission to apply the choice of law rules is sanctioned by the rulings of the Supreme Court of the Republic of Croatia as well.[37]

Various arguments have been placed by trial courts justifying the non-application of the choice of law rules. For example, jurisdiction of Croatian courts was conceived as clear indication to application of the Croatian substantive law.[38] Such standing was abandoned in subsequent decisions of the same High Commercial Court stating: "…there is no doubt that Croatian authority is competent to act … since the harmful consequence occurred in Croatia. This, however, does not automatically entails the application of the Croatian law to a dispute".[39]Another example is a case where the court calculated that the application of the choice of law rules would interfere with procedural economy, and directly applied domestic law.[40]

---

[35] High Commercial Court No. Pž 5292/02–3, judgement of 4 May 2005(available at: .http://www.iusinfo.hr).

[36] "Because the trial court failed to establish the material facts relevant to the application of relevant substantive law, the impugned judgment can not be questioned because it is incomprehensible and does not contain reasons concerning the decisive facts, which yielded absolutely essential violation of civil procedure described in Article 354 Paragraph 2 Item 13 CAP. "High Commercial Court, judgement of 9 July 2005., "File data reveals that in this case we face a dispute with an international element, and the trial court failed to establish the material facts decisive in the dispute with an international element for proper application of substantive law."– judgements of High Commercial Court: No. Pž-254/03–3, judgement of 15 February 2006; No. Pž 632/03–3, judgement of 19 July 2005; No. Pž 2039/03–3, judgement of 4 November 2006 (available at: http://www.iusinfo.hr). For many examples see Mirela Župan, *Pravo najbliže veze u hrvatskom i europskom međunarodnom privatnom ugovornom pravu* (Rijeka, 2006), p. 190–199

[37] "First of all, this Supreme Court founds that this was a dispute which has international elements, as the plaintiff is a foreign person domiciled abroad, and the assessment regarding the misapplication of substantive law poses the first question, whether the lower courts found that such relevant substantial law has to apply to this dispute. Lower courts haven't made any statement to this issues, but it is apparent they went from the perspective that *lex fori* applies, therefore Croatian substantive law; moreover, as in their decisions application of foreign law was not invoked. According to the provisions of Article 356 CAP misapplication of substantive law exists when the court failed to apply the provisions of substantive law that should have been applied, or when such a provision was not correctly applied. As lower courts did not discuss and determine which substantive law was to be applied in this dispute with an international element, for that reason this audit court could not assess whether the substantive law was correctly applied to the dispute.

"…. "For these reasons, by reference to the provision of Article 395 (2) Civil Procedure Act, audit has been accepted, both lower-instance decisions have been abolished and the case returned to the court of first instance for retrial …." Supreme Court of Republic of Croatia, No. VSRH, II Rev.-61/99–2, judgement of 12 March 2003 (available at: http://www.iusinfo.hr).

[38] High Commercial Court, No. Pž. 3473/2001, judgement of 10 March 2003, in Župan, *supra* note 37, p. 202.

[39] High Commercial Court, No. Pž 385/03–3, judgement of 8 March 2006 (available at: http://www.iusinfo.hr).

[40] "Part of the decision on the defendant's objection on statute of limitation is incomprehensible, since the court for reasons of judicial economy decided not to obtain the content of foreign law in

Sometimes the lack of knowledge of the comparative law leads to improper handling of the case with foreign element.[41]

In many cases, courts fail to recognise situations with foreign element.[42] Interestingly, recognition of foreign element occurs more often in commercial matters than in family, status or inheritance matters. Some examples from the case law indicate that if one of the parties is a foreign firm, case is easily declared to have an international element.[43] On the other hand, family law cases that relate to Croatian nationals, often with a formal domicile in Croatia, but where parties have been undoubtedly living abroad for years, is not so easily recognized as a situation with foreign element entailing application of the choice of law rules.[44]

Croatian doctrine is rather scarce on the issues of the scope of application of the choice of law rules.[45] If it is acknowledged that the choice of law rules apply whenever the factual situation of a case has an international element, one may still question whether such statement encompasses "foreign domestic cases"[46] as well. The case law signals that choice of law method is applied only if facts of the case bear strong foreign element. Such practice is undesired because it deprives the strength of *ius cogens* nature of the choice of law rules. As previously stated, in many past and pending cases with the foreign element brought before Croatian judicial authorities, connecting factors on the Croatian PIL Act lead to the application of the Croatian substantive law. Regardless of that, cases of application of foreign law before the Croatian authorities are not at all rare.[47] Since there is a lack of relevant

order to assess the merits of the complaint (because it found that the plaintiff did not prove that the defendant caused him harm). However, the plaintiff submitted the content of foreign law for statutory limitation, which the trial court did not take into account nor was it valued in accordance with the provisions of Article 13th Croatian PIL Act. "High Commercial Court, No. Pž-5414/04, judgement of 4 July 2007 (available at: http://www.iusinfo.hr).

[41] Commercial court simply accepted the argument that a claim fell within the statute of limitation of timeline prescribed by the Croatian law and ended the trial. High Commercial Court corrects the fault and explains that statute of limitations is defined with different timeframes in various legal systems. If a case contains foreign element, the court must first establish which substantive law is applicable to a disputed question on statute of limitations, and it is only then that the court can take a position weather that period has expired or not. PŽ 3979/99–2, judgement of 16.11.1999., High Commercial Court (available at: www.iusinfo.hr).

[42] Ivo Grbin, „Hrvatska sudska praksa u sporovima s međunarodnim obilježjem", *Zbornik Pravnog fakulteta u Zagrebu*, Vol.62 No.1–2 / 2012, p. 154.

[43] For example see High commercial court, No. Pž 2957/06–4, judgement of 3 February 2009 (http://www.iusinfo.hr).

[44] For particular case law elaboration see: Župan/Ledić, *supra* note 31; also more recent cross-border family cases are uploaded on database of the project 'Planning the future of cross-border families: a path through coordination' (EUFam's) (http://www.eufams.unimi.it/category/database/).

[45] Some considerations are given in Sikirić, *supra* note 24, p. 618; Župan, *supra* note 27, p. 223.

[46] Ted De Boer, "Facultative choice of law: the procedural status of choice of law rules and foreign law", in *Recueil des cours*, 257(1996), p. 223–427, at. p. 244–245.

[47] For example, parties to a distribution agreement made a choice of Swiss law in accordance with art. 19 of the Croatian PIL Act. The court made efforts to establish and apply its content. High Commercial Court, No. Pž 5292/02–3, judgement of 4 May 2005 (http://www.iusinfo.hr). For many examples see Župan, *supra* note 37, p. 202 et seq.

statistical data it is not possible to identify the states whose substantive laws are most frequently applied. Yet, due to the intense migrations and traditional tendency of close relations with several central, mid and western European countries, as well as neighbouring countries of the region, most frequently applied foreign substantive laws would be of Germany, Austria, Italy, Hungary and Switzerland, and following the dissolution of Yugoslavia, of Bosnia and Herzegovina, Serbia, Slovenia, Macedonia or Montenegro.

II. Foreign Law Before Judicial Authorities

A. Nature of Foreign Law

Foreign law is considered a "law", not a fact.[48] Yet, foreign law is not a part of domestic legal order, but it is applied only if domestic choice of law rules provide so. It is often emphasised that the principle placing domestic and foreign law on equal footing is a heritage of Savignyan doctrine that all of the legal systems of the world are equal.[49] Following this theory, a judge is required to "know" foreign law just as he knows the domestic one.

B. Application of Loreign Law

According to the Croatian PIL Act, the court has to apply foreign law *ex officio*: "The court or another competent authority shall at its own motion establish the content of foreign law that is applicable."[50] Consequently, even if parties do not claim or reject its application,[51] the court has to place foreign law on equal footing with domestic law. Case law additionally confirmed that a court cannot be excused for non-application of foreign law due to inactivity of the party to a case.[52]

---

[48] Sajko, supra note 28, p. 231.

[49] Friedrich Carl von Savigny, *Systems Des Heutigen Romischen Rechts* (1894) p. 24–28.

[50] Article 13 of PIL Act, Article 8 Draft PIL Act.

[51] Doctrine questioned if the court could accept party agreement where parties waive the right of application of foreign law? Extensive interpretation would bear that parties are free to dispose in the domain that is in dispositive sphere. Yet, such standing would not stand the fact that Croatian choice of law rules are *ius cogens*. Sajko, supra note 27, p. 232.

[52] "The fact that the plaintiff did not plead on the basis of which legislation he had paid out transitional compensation to the person insured by him, cannot be a reason for rejecting that part of the claim of the plaintiff, because the court was bound by the law to determine the content of the applicable foreign law." County Court of Varaždin, No. Gžx.144/11–2, of 25 January 2012. (http://www.iusinfo.hr).

Pursuant to the provisions of the Croatian PIL Act,[53] deviations could be justified on the grounds of public policy exemption.[54] However, doctrine firmly defends restrictive application of public policy clause. One can read arguments that direction of the choice of law rules towards the law of the state whose legal and political system significantly departs from the Croatian one, would not justify an application of the public policy clause. Moreover, application of the law of the state that is not internationally recognized is advocated as well.[55] Practice of the High Commercial Court,[56] as well as the Supreme Court[57] and the Constitutional Court[58] confirms the attitude towards restricted application of public policy exception.

Besides public policy exemption, the *lois de application immediate* could present an obstacle to application of foreign law, as it is elaborated by doctrine.[59] At the moment, there is no general provision on *lois de application immediate* in the Croatian PIL Act, but, according to the doctrine, this does not prevent the court from enforcing its own overriding mandatory provisions.[60] The Draft PIL Act of 2016 provides for such a general provision in Article 13, entailing that application of Croatian law would prevail if such application is directed at protection of a public interest enshrined in the political, social or economic organisation. Delimitation of application of foreign law to this respect has been the subject of the case law, where distinction between mandatory rules and *lois de application immediate* has been

---

[53] Article 4 Croatian PIL Act, Article 12 Draft PIL Act.

[54] Article 4 of the Croatian PIL Act: "The law of a foreign State shall not be applied if its effect would be contrary to the basic principles of social organization laid down by the Croatian Constitution". Mihajlo Dika / Gašo Knežević / Srđan Stojanović, *Komentar zakona o međunarodnom privatnom pravu* (Beograd, 1991), p. 41.

[55] Krešimir Sajko, „Javni poredak – zaštita osnovnih pravnih načela domaćeg prava", *Pravo i porezi* 1 (2003), p. 3–11, at.p. 8.

[56] High Commercial Court, No. Pž 1574/04–6, judgement of 12. December 2006 (http://www.iusinfo.hr).

[57] Supreme Court, No. VSRH Gž 36/2012–2, judgement of 4 January 2013 (http://www.iusinfo.hr); Supreme Court, No.VSRH Revt 74/2007–2, judgement of 7 November 2009. (http://www.iusinfo.hr).

[58] In the reported case of the law of the Constitutional Court of Croatia plaintiffs alleged their right to property as well as their right on equality before the law (guaranteed by Croatian Constitution) which was violated when the Municipal Court applied foreign law which was less favourable to their claim then Croatian one. Plaintiffs claimed that foreign law should have been set aside by public policy clause, as they argued that its application deprived them from the above mentioned Constitutional rights. Constitutional court of Croatia rejected their claim sticking to restrictive application of public policy clause, and defending the obligatory nature of foreign law. Constitutional court of the Republic of Croatia, No. U-III / 987 / 2007, judgement of 9 July 2007. (http://sljeme.usud.hr/usud/praksaw.nsf/Ustav/C12570D30061CE53C1257395003F96B0?OpenDocument).

[59] Petar Šarčević, "Prisilni propisi i mjerodavno pravo s posebnim osvrtom na ograničenje autonomije stranaka", *Izvođenje investicijskih radova*, 2 (Zagreb 1987) p. 127. Damir Klasiček„„Prisilni propisi u međunarodnom pivatnom pravu", *Pravni vjesnik* 16 (2000) 3–4, p. 23–32.

[60] Petar Šarčević, "The New Yugoslav Private International Law Act", *AJCL* 33 (1985), at p. 131; Ivana Kunda, & Romana Matanovac Vučković, "Raspolaganje autorskim pravom na računalnom programu: materijalnopravni i kolizijskopravni aspekti", *Zbornik Pravnog fakulteta u Rijeci*. 31 (2010), at p. 126.

outlined.[61] The Draft PIL Act provides for general *escape clause* as well, which may be bases for derogation from the foreign law as well.[62]

C. Ascertainment of Foreign Law

Foundations of the Croatian PIL Act date back to 1973. Thesis launched by the *Institute for international law and international relations* advocated that "The competent authority should use all of the means at its disposal to establish the content of foreign law". Explanatory report referred particularly to those means prescribed by the procedural rules.[63] Doctrine clearly distinguished determining the factual situation in the legal proceedings from application of legal norms to it. In the first part of the court proceedings, the court has to determine the facts of a case, where parties actively participate in submitting the evidences. When it comes to applying the legal norm to the established facts, the task of the court is not to prove (*dokazati*) the content of the law but to establish (*utvrditi*) relevant legal norms. It follows that judge can properly administer the justice only if he or she is familiar with the relevant legal norm. Consequently, if he or she is not familiar with the content of the relevant legal norm, he or she has to establish it.[64] Even if the court had established the content of foreign law at the hearing, relying on certain means of proof, such procedure would neither correspond to taking of evidence, nor would foreign law have the character of a relevant fact.[65] Therefore, "content of abstract legal norms cannot be subject to proof in the proceedings".[66]

A judgement of the High Commercial Court clarifies that "determination of foreign law is a legal, not factual question of procedure". It meant to say that Article 13 relates only to establishing the legal norm of foreign law, not establishing the facts that should have been proved (by the interested parties) in accordance to some foreign law.[67] Consequently, a) the parties do not bear a burden of proving the content of foreign law; b) failure of the parties to assist the court in establishing the content

[61] Parties contested application of the foreign Austrian law which had been chosen among them to a part of an interest rate. Namely, as the amount of interest rate in Austrian law exceeded the maximum amount of the interest rate prescribed by the Croatian law, parties claimed foreign law was contrary to mandatory rules of the Republic of Croatia, and was therefore inapplicable. The County court of Varaždin, No. Gž 1246/2007–2, judgement of 28 December 2007 (http://www.iusinfo.hr).

[62] Article 11 Draft PIL Act of 2016.

[63] Natko Katičić / Željko Matić / Krešimir Sajko, „Teze za zakon o međunarodnom privatnom pravu", *Prinosi* (1973) 6, p. 14.

[64] Đuro Vuković / Eduard Kunštek, *Međunarodno građansko postupovno pravo* (Zagreb 2005), p. 209–210.

[65] For all see Sikirić, *supra* note 24, p. 675.

[66] Triva / Dika, *supra* note 33, p. 183.

[67] In particular case a party claimed that a judge was obliged by Article 13 to seek for a foreign decree on liquidation procedure, what is clearly a matter of fact which is up to the parties having intererst in establishing such facts to a claim. High Commercial Court, No. Pž 7676/08–3, judgement of 3 March 2009 (http://www.iusinfo.hr).

of foreign law cannot lead to conclusion that such foreign legal norm does not exist; c) parties can use legal remedies to overturn judgements where foreign law (substantive or the choice of law) was not applied properly.[68]

It has already been clarified that the court should establish the content of foreign law in line with *"iura novit curia"*. Doctrine is unanimous that even though the court should establish and apply foreign law on its own motion, the judge cannot possibly be familiar with all of the foreign legal systems.[69] If this fact is accompanied with practical reasons, competent authority must be given certain devices to enable easier finding of the content of foreign law.[70] To achieve this goal a legislator directs the court to cooperate with parties and/or other state organs. The authority is given legal aid, as it ".... may request information on foreign law from the authority competent in the field of justice."[71] Information received thereof should be attributed in merely informative and indicatory nature and does not oblige the court.[72] If the court is familiar with applicable foreign law, it is not obliged to pose a request on establishing the content of foreign law from the Ministry of Justice! Such standing has been confirmed in the practice of High Commercial Court.[73]

The judicial authorities often use the possibility to formally seek for the content of applicable law; moreover, they exclusively rely on this option in finding the content of foreign law! Judges feel confident only if they have received such official statement of content on foreign law. Yet, trial can get extremely extended once the court launches a request to establish foreign law via Ministry of Justice. Case law can indicate to this assumptions, as it may take approximately 2 years to receive a response on the content of foreign law![74]

The legislator provides additional device to support courts endeavours to ascertain the content of foreign law: party's activity.[75] The parties in the proceedings may give

---

[68] Triva / Dika, *supra* note 33, p. 184.

[69] Sajko, *supra* note 23, p. 28; Sikirić, supra *note* 24, p. 673; Triva / Dika, *supra* note 33, p. 183–184.

[70] Petar Šarčević, "The new Yugoslav Private International Law Act", *The American Journal of Comparative Law* 33(1985), p. 283–296, at. p. 288.

[71] Article 13(2) Croatian PIL Act.

[72] Dika et al., *supra* note 55, p. 50.

[73] High Commercial Court refused the review of a party contesting the first instance judgements objecting on the applicable material law. A plaintiff claimed the first instance court had failed to properly apply the law as in the proceedings of a case the court had refused the request of a plaintiff to pose an inquiry on the content of the Italian choice of law rules. Verdict of High Commercial Court confirmed that "In a case where the court is familiar with legal norms of foreign law, the court has no duty to seek for a notice of content of foreign law from the competent authority in the field of justice. High Commercial Court, No. Pž-1936/82, of 12 April 1983. Sajko et al., *supra* note 19, p. 144–145.

[74] Trial court launched the procedure to establish the content of foreign Austrian law on 3 February 2005. As no response was recieved in due time, court repeated the request on 23 November 2005; 17 February 2006 and 22 March 2007. The notice on foreign law was delivered to the court on 7 February 2007. Supreme Court of the Republic of Croatia, No. VSRH Gzp 1289/2008–3, judgement of 20 August 2009. (http://www.iusinfo.hr).

[75] Article 13 (2) of Croatian PIL Act, retained in Article 8(4) of the Draft PIL Act of 2016.

substantial aid to the court, as they are entitled to submit a public document (*certificate de coutume*) on the content of foreign law). Such document contains objective and uncommented information on positive legal source, interpretation deriving from relevant legal practice or positions of legal doctrine.[76] Legal nature of such public document on the content of foreign law is the same as the nature of any other public document: it is presumed to be authentic (issued by the organ stated in the document) and true (information of foreign law, practice or doctrinal standpoints are truthful and enable the court to form a certain conclusion on the content of foreign law.) Although old judicature took a stand that parties could not rebut validity of foreign public document on the content of foreign law, doctrine is unanimous that presumptions that are associated with public document are *premsumptio iuris*, and are therefore rebuttable![77] Consequently a party could object such finding of a court and in the course of the procedure contest its authenticity, truthfulness, fact that information on foreign law is incomplete, etc.[78] Any public document submitted by the party has to be translated to Croatian language by official translator.[79]

Case law confirms that parties can truly play an active and supporting role in judge's efforts to establish foreign law.[80] The case law also indicates that the parties' misuse of procedural dispositions by abusing the fact that foreign law has to be established is sanctioned![81] Proceedings with foreign element can be costly and

---

[76] Triva / Dika, *supra* note p. 33, p. 184.

[77] Dika et al., *supra* note 55, p. 50; Sikirić, *supra* note 24, p. 677; Triva / Dika, *supra* note 33, p. 184.

[78] Dika et al., *supra* note 55, op.cit. p. 50.

[79] Article 232 (2) of Civil Procedure Act, Zakon o parničnom postupku (Civil Procedure Act) Official Gazette (Narodne novne) No. 53/91, 91/92, 58/93, 112/99, 88/01, 117/03, 88/05, 02/07, 84/08, 123/08, 57/11, 148/11, 25/13

[80] A party warned the court that the case has an international element and therefore the choice of law rules should have been used to establish the applicable substantive law. The court has not taken such objections into account and proceeded in accordance with the Croatian law. Second instance court returned a judgement to retrial. High Commercial Court, No. PŽ 3904/04–3, judgement of 23 January 2007. A party made efforts to obtain the relevant foreign legal norm to the court, but the trial court ignored it. High Commercial Court, No. Pž-5414/04, judgement of 4 July 2007. (http://www.iusinfo.hr).

[81] High Commercial Court faced the same case with foreign element twice. In the first review procedure the High Commercial Court instructed the first instance court to have not properly established the amount of interest that was valid in specific period of time in Italy. To remedy this omission, the trial court was suggested to issue a formal diplomatic procedure towards Italy: Ministry of Economy and Finance of Italy should issue a confirmation of the interest rate that applied to the Republic of Italy on 5 March 1990 onwards. HCH further stated that in accordance to article 13 even the plaintiff could serve the court with that information. In the subsequent procedure a plaintiff delivered copies of the official newspaper of the Italian GAZZETA Ufficiale related to the amount of the default interest rate of 5 March in 1990 onwards translated into Croatian by a certified court interpreter. The defendant complained to the truthfulness of data delivered by the plaintiff as well as quality of its translation. Defendant actually lapsed to check truthfulness of delivered data and its translation but he objected merely to get an extension of a procedure – therefore the trial court judge punished the defendant for misuse of procedural dispositions! The plaintiff continued requiring a court to launch a diplomatic procedure to receive the relevant information

long. Yet, the fact that a case has a foreign element and requires establishment and application of foreign law does not justify that such trials are unreasonably long, as confirmed by the Croatian Supreme Court.[82]

Besides these two devices prescribed by Croatian PIL Act, doctrine advocates that the court could hear expert witnessing.[83] Even though it is not explicitly prescribed by the law, the Court could not practice hearing of witnesses or hearing of the parties in order to ascertain the content of foreign law.[84] Case law reveals an example where hearing of an attorney was conceived by the trial court as a public document on the content of foreign law; such standing was later overruled by the second instance court.[85]

Courts could use models established by bilateral agreements[86] but there are no reported cases. Croatia has recently joined European Union, so the European Judicial Network (hereinafter: EJN) mechanism is at disposal as well.[87] Obtaining information on the content of the applicable law is among many functions of the EJN. "In securing the content of the applicable law of another Member State the contract point may avail itself of the support of any of the other Network members in its Member State in order to supply the information requested. The information in reply to the request for judicial cooperation is not binding upon the contact point, the authorities consulted or the authority which made the request."[88]

Although Croatia is an active party to Hague conference on private international law, benefits of Hague International Judicial network (hereinafter: HIJN)[89] in find-

through the Ministry of Justice. Since the court rejected this claim and delivered the judgement, the defendant complained on proper application of foreign law. High Commercial Court (now dealing with the case for the second time) explained that article 13 does not oblige the court to launch diplomatic procedure if it is confident with the relevant information on foreign law. High Commercial Court, No. Pž 778/07–3, judgement of 7 May 2007. (http://www.iusinfo.hr).

[82] Particular sensibility of the Croatian Supreme Court for cases with application of foreign law was manifested in its ruling upon a request of a plaintiff to protect the right for a trial within reasonable time. The Supreme Court overturned the judgement of the County Court which had denied such a request. The Supreme Court clearly stated that circumstances such as obligation to apply foreign law cannot justify the procedure in inheritance matter to last more than 6 years and 8 months! The Supreme Court of the Republic of Croatia, No. Gžzp 212/07–2 of 20 December 2007,; The Supreme Court of the Republic of Croatia, No. Gzp 1289/2008–3, judgement of 20 August 2009 (http://sudskapraksa.vsrh.hr/supra/SearchResultsPublic.asp).

[83] Triva / Dika, *supra* note 33, p. 184.

[84] Such standing is supported with explicit wording of many PIL Acts that have been used as a role model in drafting our PIL Act. It is explicitely provided by Austrian, Italian and Swiss law, as stated by Sajko, *supra* note 23, p. 28.

[85] High Commercial Court, No. Pž-1136/07–4, judgment of 4 April 2007.

[86] See more *infra*.

[87] Croatia joined full membership of European Union on 1 June 2013.

[88] Kunda / Marinho, *supra* note Handbook on private international law, op.cit. p. 50.

[89] Philippe Lortie, "Direct Judicial Communications and the International Hague Network of Judges under the Hague 1980 Child Abduction Convention" in Mirela Župan (ed.) *Private International Law in the Jurisprudence of European Courts – Family at Focus* (Osijek, 2015) (available at: http://www.pravos.unios.hr/knjiznica/fakultetska-izdanja-25-04-2016) p. 147.

ing applicable law to child related matters haven't been recognized yet to domestic legal order. So far, no judge is appointed to the HIJN network. Direct judicial communication as a model of informal communication is unfamiliar to Croatian judiciary in its endeavours to ascertain foreign law.

The court can decide which of the tools it prefers to use, and should therefore elect ways to ascertain foreign law on its own.[90]

In cases where the content of foreign law is ensured via Ministry of Justice, further problems arise in relation to translation costs. Translation costs are rather high and courts do not have enough funds for them. However, if one states that the nature of foreign law is obligatory, it is clearly for the state to ensure the finding of its context including financial cost of it. Unreported case law witnesses that in practice in many cases such translation costs are borne by the parties.[91] However, peculiar attitude towards foreign non-translated legal sources has been detected with recent Rijeka Appellate Court ruling.[92]

D. Interpretation and Application of Foreign Law

Croatian court is directed with clear provision to apply the law of a foreign State according to its own sense and the terms that it contains.[93] It follows that Croatian competent authority is to act as if the authority of the relevant state would have, while applying its own law. This wording obliges competent authority to follow not merely the wording, but also the interpretation of that law, even if the meaning and interpretation is completely different that it would have been under the Croatian law and inherent interpretation.[94] Most prominent example is with the statute of limitations: even though it is from the Croatian legal standpoint conceived as a part of the

---

[90] Sajko, *supra* note 23, p. 28.

[91] Župan / Ledić, *supra* note Cross-border family matters – Croatian experience prior EU accession and future expectations, op.cit.

[92] Husband initiated a divorce lawsuit, whereas wife informed the court that there is a pending separation lawsuit in Italy. According to Regulation 2201/2003 "the court second seised shall of its own motion stay its proceedings until such time as the jurisdiction of the court first seised is established". First instance court received a document proving that the case is pending before Italian court. Document was in Italian language. Appellate court return the case to renew trial, as it found that the application of foreign legal document without official translation is contrary to Article 232(2) of Croatian Civil Procedure Act. As it is clear from the wording of the Regulation that move is done *ex officio* by the court, the judge that understands a respective foreign language (Italian here) should not be obliged to rely only upon official translation of relevant document. Rijeka Gž-3397/2014, of 17.11.2014. (http://www.eufams.unimi.it/category/database/).

[93] Croatian PIL Act states: "The law of a foreign State shall be applied according to its own sense and the terms that it contains." what is retained with Article 8(4) of Draft PIL Act of 2016.

[94] Dika et al. *supra* note 56, p. 41. Such standpoint is accepted in practice: The court explicitly states that whereas parties agreed on applicable English law, legal system should have been applied for its interpretation as well. High Commercial Court, No. Pž-5414/04, judgement of 4 July 2007. (www.ius-info.hr).

substantive law, the provisions on the statute of limitations in the USA law are to be interpreted as part of the procedural law.[95]

Since Croatian legal system acknowledges *renvoi* (Article 6), the wording of this provision extends to application of the foreign choice of law as well. The foreign choice of law should also be applied as if it would be applied in the relevant foreign state. There is a departure from this standing in the Draft PIL Act of 2016, where *renvoi* is in general abolished with exception of certain issues.[96] Regarding the time frame, the court has to apply foreign law that is in force at the moment of issuing a decision.[97]

E. Failure to Establish Foreign Law

Having used all of the available methods to establish the content of the applicable law, and having failed in its endeavours, court cannot dismiss the complaint as it would purport to denial of justice. Due to practical difficulties that arise in establishing the content of the foreign applicable law, foundations of Croatian PIL system in 1973 predicted a clause promoting ascertaining of foreign law: "Competent authority must use all of the means on its disposal", assuring "everything possible was done to ascertain and apply the appropriate foreign rules".[98] The provision further promoted alternative solution in a situation of failure to establish foreign law, as it enabled: a) application of the law that is most closely connected to the applicable law (similar legal system); b) the application of *lex fori* in cases of hardship or failure to establish foreign law. Nevertheless, that clause is omitted from the official Act with explanation that international relations should be promoted, and that such a clause referring to *lex fori* would undermine the purpose and significance of conflict rules.[99] Due to legal lacuna contemporary authors advocate the approach that *lex fori* should be used to substitute the missing foreign legal source. Such standing is supported with legal certainty, predictability and procedural economy, along with the fact that there must be some connection to our legal system by the mere fact that Croatian courts have international jurisdiction over a case.[100]

Despite logical and comparatively most common approach to a situation where foreign law was not established, application of *lex fori* solution can encounter problems in application of other provision of Croatian PIL Act where practical opportunity of this solution arises.[101]

---

[95] Dika et al. *supra* note 56, p. 33–34.

[96] *Renvoi* is retained for pure status issues, personal name, conclusion of marriage and adoption. See Article 9 in conjunction to Articles 14, 17, 18, 31 and 44 of Draft PIL Act.

[97] Sajko, *supra* note 28, p. 233.

[98] Petar Šarčević, "The new Yugoslav Private International Law Act", *The American Journal of Comparative Law;* vol. 33 (1985), p. 283–296, at. p. 289.

[99] Šarčević, op.cit., p. 289.

[100] Sikirić, *supra* note 24, p. 677–678.; Dika et al. *supra* note 55, p. 50; Sajko, *supra* note 28; p. 236–238.

[101] Sikirić, *supra* note 24, p. 679–681.

III. Judicial Review

Conflict of law rules are *ius cogens* and are therefore treated as any other legal rules in a situation of its non-application or misapplication. In such situations, judgement is subject to judicial review pursuant to Article 353(1)(3) of the Civil Procedure Act. Misapplication is manifested either in the fact that court erroneously interpreted the choice of law rule and applied foreign law where it should have applied domestic law or a different foreign law, and *vice versa*. Ordinary judicial review based on the appeal (*žalba*) is available against the first-instance decisions while the extraordinary review is available before the Supreme Court based on the review (*revizija*).[102] The same applies to erroneous application of foreign law. Underlying policy considerations steem from the approach that the choice of law rules are *ius cogens*, and foreign law is considered a law, not a fact.[103]

IV. Foreign Law in Other Instances

The Croatian PIL Act, as well as other legal sources, provides legal framework for both judicial and non-judicial authorities, using the expression "competent authority". Therefore, all of the above responses relate either to a court, an organ of public administration or any other agency, notary etc. that is competent, under the pertinent Croatian legislation, to adjudicate in specific matters. Statistics are not available so one cannot reliably state how often foreign law occurs in other instances.

Arbitration proceedings are regulated in the Croatian Arbitration Act. In international arbitration, the choice of the law rules enable application of the law chosen by the parties and, failing that, the los of the closest connection. Unlike the courts, arbitral tribunals may, under the explicit parties' direction, be obliged to apply "the rules of law", not necessarily "the law" of some state.[104] Parties may authorise a tribunal to proceed *ex aequo et bono* as well.[105]

---

[102] Civil Procedure Act, Article 385 (1) point 3.

[103] Sikirić, *supra* note 24, p. 682; Triva and Dika, *supra* note 33, p. 184; Dika et al. *supra* note 55, p. 50

[104] See Léna Gannagé, „Le contrat sans loi en droit international privé", *Electronic Journal of Comparative Law*, vol 11.3 (2007), (http://www.ejcl.org) p. 8.

[105] Hrvoje Sikirić, „Mjerodavno materijalno pravo za arbitražne sporove s međunaronim obilježjem", *Zbornik Pravnog fakulteta u Zagrebu*, 44(1994) 4, p. 341–362; Krešimir Sajko, „Mjerodavno materijalno pravo za arbitražne sporove s međunarodnim obilježjem", *Privreda i pravo*, 3(1994) 3/4, p. 234–244; Davor Bouček, „Određivanje mjerodavnog prava u praksi Stalnog izabranog sudišta pri Hrvatskoj gospodarskoj komori", *Hrvatska pravna revija*, 2(2002) 12, p. 153–162.

V. Access to Foreign Law: Status Quo

Croatian Official Gazette is freely accessible on line for over a two decade. Official websites of particular departments of the Government of the Republic of Croatia also provide information on positive legal sources, with updated versions of normative acts. These information are not provided in foreign languages, only in Croatian.[106] However, since Croatia has recently joined EU, many internal legal acts have been translated and made publicly available,[107] or their outline has been enabled public access through official website of relevant DG of European Commission.[108]

The European Judicial Network is available to Croatian authorities since its entry to EU. Due to a short period passed since the accession, there are no accessible data on intensity of its use to find the content of foreign law. It has already been stated that Croatia is not taking part in the HIJN, whereas legal writings have emphasized the added values of direct judicial communication and benefits for Croatian judicial system if it were to join the Malta Declaration and the HIJN.[109]

In their writings, scholars have also pointed long time ago to other international tools that aim at facilitating ascertainment of foreign law, the European Convention of 7 June 1968 on Information on foreign law ("London Convention") being of the utmost importance. It took two decades for Croatia to decide to take part in this Convention.[110] Convention is applicable as regards Croatia as of May 2014.[111]

Several surveys have been conducted on the issues of possible EU regulation on foreign law[112] one of which resulted in the Madrid Principles.[113] The initiative is currently only on doctrinal level, but if such piece of *acquis* were adopted, proof and application of foreign law among EU Member States would be significantly improved.[114]

---

[106] Croatian Ministry of Justice official website, http://www.mprh.hr/zakoni; Ministry of Social Policy and Jouth (http://www.mspm.hr/pravni_okvir).

[107] Ministry of European and International Relations, (http://www.mvep.hr/hr/hrvatska-i-europska-unija/hrvatska-i-europska-unija0/prijevodi-pravnih-propisa-republike-hrvatske/).

[108] https://e-justice.europa.eu/content_member_state_law-6-en.do

[109] Mirela Župan "European judicial cooperation in cross border family matters", in: Timea Drinoczi and Tamara Takacs (eds.) *Cross-border and EU legal issues: Hungary – Croatia* (Osijek-Pecs 2011) p. 621–647, at. p. 643.

[110] Zakon o potvrđivanju europske konvencije o obavijestima o stranom pravu, NN MU br. 13/2013.

[111] NN MU 2/2014.

[112] "The Application of Foreign Law by Judicial and Non –Judicial Authorities in Europe" and "Basic Principles for a Future EU Regulation on the Application of Foreign Law". (Project JLS/CJ/2007–1/03), (www.elra.eu/wp-content/uploads/file/Valencia.doc). The application of foreign law in civil matters in the EU member states and its perspectives for the future, Institute Suisse de droit comparé (project JLS/2009/JCIV/PR/0005/E4) (ec.europa.eu/justice/civil/.../foreign_law_iii_en.pdf).

[113] Carlos Esplugues, "Madrid prinicples", in: Espuluges et al.eds.*Application of Foreign Law* (Munich 2011).

[114] Carlos Esplugues, "Harmonization of Private International Law in Europe and Application of Foreign Law: The Madrid Principles of 2010", *Yearbook of Private International Law*, Vol. 13, 2011. pp. 273–297, at. p. 290 et. seq.

Available bilateral regimes with countries in the region and worldwide provide specific framework to establish foreign law as well.[115] They work through diplomatic channels, resulting in very formal and time-consuming procedure. There are no relevant statistical data indicating with what the frequency these instruments are used.

VI. Access to Foreign Law: Further Developments

Improving access to foreign law is the worldwide[116] and European focal interest,[117] and is certainly a policy worthy of future endeavours. Access to foreign law should be improved for the sake of all stakeholders, but most significantly, it could affect the proper administration of justice.

To the extent one may predict future, Croatian competent authorities will most probably have to deal with contracts of sale, lease and rent, tort in car accidents and injury, as well as status, family and inheritance matters. These matters may be subject to litigation, arbitration or special procedures, such as for execution of a will.

A. Conflict of Laws Solutions

The new Croatian PIL Act is currently being drafted, and, if adopted, some changes would be introduced in the sphere of application of foreign law as well. The first initiatives to draft a new Croatian PIL Act occurred in 2001 when a group of authors led by Prof. Sajko presented the Thesis for the New Croatian PIL Act.[118] In 2008, the group of scholars commenced continuous work on a new draft.[119] Formal legislative

---

[115] Standard provision on legal aid in foreign law matters is: "The Contracting States shall, on request, inform each other of the rules, which are valid and in force on its territory and will, if necessary, send the text of those provisions.

[116] For all of endeavour of HCCH see *Accessing the Content of Foreign Law And the Need For the Development of a Global Instrument in this Area – A Possible Way Ahead*, Permanent Bureau, Prel Doc. No. 11 A, March 2009. (http://www.hcch.net/upload/wop/genaff_pd11a2009e.pdf).

[117] See *supra*. Also see: Meeting report. Access to Foreign Law in Civil and Commercial Matters, European Commission and of the Hague Conference on Private International Law. (http://www.hcch.net/upload/xs2foreignlaw_rpt.pdf).

[118] Sajko / Sikirić / Bouček / Babić / Tepeš, *supra* note 19, p. 255–340.

[119] Scientific working group for new Croatian PIL Act consisted of scolars: Sajko Krešimir, Vesna Tomljenović, Hrvoje Sikirić, Vilim Bouček, Davor Babić, Vjeskoslav Puljko, Ivana Kunda, Ines Medić and Mirela Župan. Formal working group was formed by the Croatian Government in 2011. Several of these PIL professors were members of the formal working group. A draft of the Croatian PIL Act has been presented to public in July 2016, *supra* note.

procedure began in 2013, and is still ongoing. However, in summer the 2016 Draft PIL Act has been presented for public consultation.

Regarding the foreign law issue, the 2001 Thesis proposed introduction of the provision enabling the court to decide not to ascertain foreign law if that would take an unreasonably long time. Thesis no. 14 provided that "if the content of foreign law cannot be ascertained within reasonable time, Croatian law is applied".[120] Although such provision was discussed, it has not been inserted into the 2016 Draft PIL Act, which remains faithful to the old PIL Act regarding the obligation to establish foreign law. However, it widens the options for ascertaining its content, by allowing the court to request the information on the foreign law not only from the Ministry of Justice, but also other bodies, as well as experts and specialized institutions. Options for party engagement will be widened too. For instance, parties will have the right to submit a public or private document on the content of foreign law. However, if the content of foreign law cannot be ascertained using previously mentioned means, Croatian law would be applied.

At many points, the 2016 Draft PIL Act modifies the conflict of law rules with the result of reducing the number of cases in which a foreign law would have to be applied. It was previously explained that due to the current types of cases with foreign element which mostly relate to Croatian nationals, the conflict of law rules very often led to application of the Croatian substantive law. Yet, such approach is outdated, and wdoes not longer accommodate the social and economic circumstances. The Draft PIL Act retains the nationality connecting factor merely for issues of the personal status. For many family and inheritance matters, the EU regulations and the HCCH conventions have already introduced habitual residence instead of nationality and domicile. Along with jurisdictional rules that employ the same criterion of habitual residence, such approach results in the choice of law rules technically reaching the paradigm of the *lex fori in proprio foro*. Such outcome is beneficial and welcome both for practical reasons (certainty, simplicity, promptness), as well as because it serves our doctrinal preoccupation that each legal relation should be "situated" in the most closely connected legal system. In child-related matters, it serves the best interest of a child for prompt and efficient procedure.[121] This synergy of jurisdictional criteria and choice of law connecting factors has been widely used in modern European legislation.[122]

---

[120] Article 8 of the Draft of the PIL Act 2016.

[121] Mirela Župan "The best interest of the child – a guiding principle in administering cross-border child related matters?", in: T. Liefaard and J. Sloth-Nielsen (eds.) *The United Nations Convention on the Rights of the Child. Taking Stock after 25 Years and Looking Ahead.* (Brill | Nijhoff, 2017).

[122] Michael Bogdan, *Private International Law as Component of the Law of the Forum* (Hague Academy of International Law, AIL-POCKET, 2012), p. 100.

B. Methods of Facilitating Access to Foreign Law

Contemporary international and EU instruments rely on effective mechanism of administrative and judicial cooperation in exchanging information on participating States' law to facilitate access to foreign law. Model of administrative authorities that was effectively established first in the framework of the Hague Child Abduction Convention was copied to the subsequent Hague Conventions, as well as to recently enacted EU regulations.[123] Such a network is multiply beneficial for European countries: supranational nature of EU *acquis* drives its Member States to take particular care when draftingthe respective regulations and do their best to obey tight time limitations. Since both the HCCH and the EU are now acting as complementary organizations, one body performs functions of central authority for the Hague conventions and the EU regulations. Specialization and expertise, as well as further education of staff would contribute to the excellence, whereas central authority should perform a significant role in the sphere of ascertaining foreign law in matters that do fall under its jurisdiction (family matters) as well. Moreover, central authority system is a financial burden for the State budget, not the parties.

Enactment of the European convention of 1968 is beneficial. Possible enactment of the new European instrument on foreign law, which would complement the possible new HCCH convention, would be desirable as well. Yet, none of the legal norms will be truly effective if the courts or authorities are not properly trained. Creation of networks of professionals of particular branches (judges, notaries, attorneys) would facilitate better operation of legal norms. Because the cases requiring application and ascertaining of foreign law do not happen in everyday practice of every law office or judge chamber in Croatia as well as in many other countries, the future specialization for cases with foreign element within each of the branches of legal profession might be a desirable policy.

[123] Ian Curry-Summer, "Administrative Co-operation and Free Legal Aid in International Child Maintenance Recovery: what is the Added Value of the European Maintenance Regulation?" 3 *Nederlands Internationaal Privaatrecht*, vol. 28/2010, p. 611–621.

Czech Republic – Treatment of Foreign Law in the Czech Republic

Monika Pauknerová

Abstract Czech national report introduces the modern Czech legislation favouring application and treatment of foreign law in Czech courts and non-judicial authorities. Further, the author compares the position of the Hague Conference, European Commission and European Group for Private International Law towards the treatment of foreign law, in particular under the viewpoint of seeking feasible methods to facilitate access to foreign law. The author is personally rather sceptical of states' willingness to be subjected to unifying tendencies, regardless of how limited they may be and even if only aimed at simplification of access to their law. However, the requirement to apply foreign law corresponds with a classical concept of equality of legal orders which should be respected by all of us.

I. Conflict of Laws in the Czech Republic

Conflict-of-laws rules in the Czech Republic have had a long tradition instituted by, and derived from, the Vienna Draft of Private International Law of 1913, which became a model for the codification of private international law in many countries in Central Europe.[1] The Czech Republic has been a typical example of a country whose legal system stems from continental law. Czech law maintains that conflict-of-laws rules are binding on judges; if a conflict rule in a particular matter determines foreign law to be the governing law, a Czech judge is obliged to apply that law. Czech doctrine speaks about the obligatory or binding nature of conflict-of-laws rules. Their binding nature in this sense should be distinguished from another dichotomy, namely whether respective conflict rules are mandatory or dispositive, i.e. with no possibility to derogate from their wording, or allowing for derogation, respectively. The binding nature of conflict-of-laws rules, usually termed

[1] For the history of Czech private international law see Pauknerová, Monika. 2011. *Private International Law in the Czech Republic*. 13 et seq. The Netherlands: Kluwer Law International.

M. Pauknerová (✉)
Professor, Institute of State and Law, Academy of Sciences of the Czech Republic, Prague, Czech Republic
e-mail: paukneroprf.cuni.cz

Y. Nishitani (ed.), *Treatment of Foreign Law - Dynamics towards Convergence?*,
Ius Comparatum – Global Studies in Comparative Law 26,
DOI 10.1007/978-3-319-56574-3_4

"mandatory conflict-of-laws rules" (as opposed to the other type, called "facultative conflict-of-laws rules"), signifies different consequences: it indicates whether there is a duty for a judge to apply the rules.[2]

Conflict-of-laws rules within Czech law frequently lead to the application of foreign law, particularly in cases where the nationality is relevant as a connecting factor, i.e. in the fields of family law, succession law and the law of personal status. This approach has radically changed with the new Private International Law Act[3] which entered into force on 1 January 2014 and replaced the existing Act Concerning Private International Law and the Rules of Procedure Relating Thereto (hereinafter "1963 PIL Act").[4]

The new Private International Law Act (hereinafter "2012 PIL Act") replaces, in many respects, nationality as a connecting factor with habitual residence which may reasonably be expected to significantly reduce the necessity to apply foreign law. However, there will still be cases in which foreign law would have to be applied, not only in the field of family law, but also within obligations, rights *in rem*, etc. The law of neighbouring countries – Slovakia, Germany, Poland and Austria – is most frequently applied or invoked before courts in the Czech Republic. Due to ethnic and language minorities established in the Czech Republic, the application of Vietnamese, Ukrainian or Russian law has been expanded, primarily in family and succession law cases; in addition, relations with other countries have been growing and their law may also be applied, such as that of a certain states of the US. As far as the law chosen by parties to obligations is concerned, the most frequently selected governing law is that of Switzerland, Germany or England; the choice of law in such cases usually depends upon the country of origin of the foreign party which incorporates its law in initial contractual documents which constitute the basis for concluding the subsequent main contract.

II. Foreign Law Before Judicial Authorities

A. Introduction

The issue of treatment of foreign law is covered by special regulation within Czech law. The new 2012 PIL Act contains Section 23 entitled "Ascertainment and application of foreign law", which builds upon the application of foreign law as it is perceived by contemporary Czech jurisprudence.[5] The section reads as follows:

---

[2] Esplugues, Carlos, Iglesias, José Luis, Palao, Guillermo (Eds.). 2011. *Application of Foreign Law.* 18 et seq. Munich: Sellier. European Law Publishers.

[3] Act No. 91/2012 Coll. (Coll. – Collection of Laws of the Czech Republic), the Private International Law Act.

[4] Act No. 97/1963 Coll., Concerning Private International Law and the Rules of Procedure Relating to, as amended.

[5] Kučera, Zdeněk. 2009. *Mezinárodní právo soukromé* (Private International Law, in Czech). 186–189. Brno-Plzeň: Doplněk a Čeněk; Pauknerová, Monika. 2011. Treatment of foreign law in a comparative perspective. *Revue hellénique de droit international* 1:5–25; Pauknerová, Monika, Brodec, Jan. 2011. Czech Republic and Slovakia. In *Application of Foreign Law,* eds. Esplugues, Carlos, Iglesias, José Luis, Palao, Guillermo, 173–183. Munich: Sellier, European Law Publishers.

2012 PIL Act, Section 23 Ascertainment and Application of Foreign Law

1. Unless other provisions of this Act stipulate otherwise, the foreign law which is to be applicable under the provisions of this Act shall be applied also of own motion (*ex officio*) and in a manner in which it is applied in the territory to which it applies. Such provisions thereof shall be applied in the territory to which the law applies to the matter in question, regardless of their systematic classification or their public nature, provided they are not contrary to overriding mandatory rules of the Czech law.
2. Unless further stipulated otherwise, the content of the foreign law which is to be applied under the provisions of this Act shall be determined of own motion. The court or public authority deciding upon matters covered by this Act shall undertake all necessary measures for such a determination.
3. Should the content of the foreign law be unknown to the court or public authority deciding upon matters covered by this Act, it may request for its determination an opinion from the Ministry of Justice.
4. Should a legal order of a state with more than one legal system or with different provisions for individual groups of persons apply, the law of such state shall determine the application of relevant legal provisions.
5. If the foreign law is not determined within a reasonable time or if such determination is impossible, the Czech law shall apply.

B. Nature and Application of Foreign Law

Czech jurisprudence and practice rely on the premise that foreign law is treated as "law", not as a "question of fact" which should be proved. It is the very sense of private international law rules that, in particular cases, foreign law applies instead of the domestic law.

Continental legal systems generally maintain an assumption that where a conflict-of-laws rule refers to foreign law (including cases where foreign law has been chosen by the parties) a judge is obliged to apply the foreign law because it is ordered by the conflict rule. The judge applies foreign law *ex officio* irrespective of any reciprocity principle.[6] Such approach was reflected in the opinion of the Supreme Court of the Czechoslovak Republic R 26/87, under which a court primarily deals with the issue of its jurisdiction. If the qualifying requirements for proceedings and adjudication have been met from the perspective of Czechoslovak judicial authorities and jurisdiction has been established, then it is necessary to consider the question of which legal order and under which particular rules the case at issue should be considered.[7]

---

[6] Kučera, Zdeněk. 2009. *Mezinárodní právo soukromé* (Private International Law, in Czech). 187. Brno-Plzeň: Doplněk a Čeněk.

[7] R 26/87 – Collection of Judicial Decisions and Opinions of the Supreme Court of the Czechoslovak Republic No. 26/1987: On some questions of interpretation and application of rules regulating relations with a foreign element in international civil procedure, opinion approved by the Civil Law Division of the Supreme Court of the Czechoslovak Republic, August 27, 1987 (in Czech), 483.

The 2012 PIL Act explicitly provides that, unless another provision of the Act stipulates otherwise, foreign law applicable under this Act should be applied by a competent body of its own initiative and in such a way as is common in the territory of original application of that law [Sections 23 (1) and (2) 2012 PIL Act]. The Explanatory Report clarifies that both foreign conflict-of-laws rules and foreign law referred to by the conflict rules are applied by an adjudicating body of its own initiative (without a motion raised by parties).

C. Ascertainment of Foreign Law

1. The Principle of "Iura Novit Curia" Before Judicial Authorities

Although a Czech judge is obliged to ascertain the content of foreign law referred to by the respective conflict-of-laws rule, it is up to the court how it chooses to ascertain foreign law. The 2012 PIL Act provides that unless there is a clause in the Act stipulating otherwise, the content of foreign law to be applied under this provision is to be ascertained by an adjudicating body of its own initiative *ex officio*. A court, or a public body charged with adjudication in matters governed by the Act, will take all necessary measures to ascertain the content of foreign law. If a court or public body adjudicating a matter governed by the Act is unaware of the content of foreign law, it may request an opinion of the Ministry of Justice regarding the ascertainment [Sections 23(2) and (3) 2012 PIL Act]. Consequently, this is certain clarification if compared with the 1963 PIL Act, which regulated only acts of judicial authorities. Foreign law is applied not only by courts but also by administrative bodies adjudicating private relations with a foreign element; prior to the 2012 PIL Act, they had no direct legal grounds to apply foreign law and relied on the 1963 PIL Act, with necessary modifications. Under the new Act, a certain shift seems to have happened in that a judge may now choose the method of ascertaining foreign law: the judge may request an opinion (not just information) from the Ministry of Justice, but not as the first option, as has been the practice so far; the wording of Section 23 suggests that the request may be made after the judge has taken their own steps to become acquainted with the foreign law but has failed to sufficiently ascertain its content.

Considering the "*iura novit curia*" principle, a comparative study in the Valencia Report entitled *General Report on the Application of Foreign Law by Judicial and Non-Judicial Authorities in Europe*, in which the Czech Republic and the author of this Chapter as its representative took part, emphasizes that the European legal reality only rarely – if at all – directly reflects the theoretical classification of foreign law as *law* or as *fact*. Conflicts arise with respect to other issues, particularly to active cooperation in practice between parties and courts in ascertaining foreign law and the application of the *iura novit curia* principle.[8] Whilst the latter has tradition-

[8] Esplugues, Carlos, Iglesias, José Luis, Palao, Guillermo (Eds.). 2011. *Application of Foreign Law.* 30. Munich: Sellier. European Law Publishers.

ally been connected with the classification of foreign law as *law*, procedural systems and practice often reflect the reality that "knowledge of the law" of a foreign country may appear to be rather difficult for a judge and that in many legal systems the position of foreign law need not necessarily lead to the presumption of *iura novit curia* in relation to applicable foreign law.

This is the case in the Czech Republic. Although foreign law is considered *law* and a judge is obliged to apply it *ex officio*, these principles are, to a certain extent, softened by the wording of Section 23 of the 2012 PIL Act which implies that the *iura novit curia* principle is inapplicable to foreign law. A judge has a duty to use foreign law *ex officio,* but a judge has no duty to know that foreign law.[9] The Valencia Report on the Application of Foreign Law concludes that such cases which can be seen in many countries, imposing upon courts the duty to apply foreign law, but which result from the fact that a judge cannot be knowledgeable of all legal systems of the world, have a direct impact upon the effectiveness of the application of foreign law.[10]

This issue was explicitly considered in relation to the case before the Arbitration Court (attached to the Economic Chamber of the Czech Republic and the Agricultural Chamber of the Czech Republic) in case Rsp 78/92. Arbitrators stated that, essentially, they did not refuse to consider imperative regulations of foreign law; however, there is no duty on the part of arbitrators to know such regulations. Thus the principle *iura novit curia* is inapplicable as it applies only to national law.[11]

2. Means Used to Ascertain Foreign Law

The Explanatory Report attached to the 2012 PIL Act clarifies that a Czech court is not obliged to know foreign law but it is obliged to find out, i.e. to ascertain, the content of the foreign law to which a respective conflict-of-laws rule refers. A court itself should consider the means it is to use in ascertaining the foreign law. A court itself may find relevant foreign regulation should it have reliable documents at its disposal. It may request cooperation of the parties and their legal representatives to arrange for, if practicable, the competent bodies of a foreign state to issue a certificate of relevant legal regulations. A court may request that legal specialists from the relevant foreign country provide official information on the law applicable in that country. Even if all such means fail in achieving the objective, i.e. obtaining knowledge of the foreign law, a court, or any other adjudicating body, is not relieved from its duty to ascertain the content of the foreign law. The Act enables the body to apply to the Ministry of Justice for its opinion on the content of the foreign law. However, the opinion is not binding on the court as it may be possible, for example, that the

[9] *Ibidem*, p. 34 referring to Czech and Slovak law (Pauknerová, M. Brodec, J. *Czech Republic and Slovakia, National Report)*, p. 176.

[10] Esplugues, Carlos, Iglesias, José Luis, Palao, Guillermo (Eds.). 2011. *Application of Foreign Law.* 37. Munich: Sellier. European Law Publishers.

[11] The award was not published. In details see Pauknerová, Monika. 2010. Overriding Mandatory Rules and Czech Law. *Czech Yearbook of International Law*, 1: 81–94. New York: Juris Publishing, Inc.

Ministry's opinion could be based upon documents not reflecting all recent amendments of foreign legislation at issue.

The duty to ascertain foreign law cannot be delegated by the court to the parties to a respective case; however, it should not be interpreted in a way that a court, or any other adjudicating body, cannot ask the parties to substantiate the content of the foreign law or cannot rely in its decision making on instruments proving the content of foreign law that were submitted by the parties. Such procedure may be considered "necessary measures" taken by an adjudicating body in order to ascertain the content of foreign law under Section 23(2) of the 2012 PIL Act, which has also been confirmed by the Explanatory Report. Another method for a court or public body to ascertain the content of foreign law may be, for example, to rely on instruments at its disposal (such as those from older cases); however it is necessary in such instances to check the force and effect of the relevant foreign legislation. If a court or other adjudicating body is proficient in the relevant foreign language it may itself ascertain the content of foreign law through, for example, publicly accessible Internet databases or printed sources. However, the court or adjudicating body is fully responsible for the correctness and appropriateness of its conclusions regarding foreign law – not only in relation to a potential appellate review by a superior institution, but particularly with respect to the parties. This gives rise to the consequence that although a court or an adjudicating body knows foreign law and does not take steps to ascertain it further it is obliged to inform the parties to the proceedings of its content (the principle of predictability of a judicial decision) so that the parties may become acquainted with the foreign law and may procedurally react to the conclusions of the court or adjudicating body accordingly. This is why the file of the case should contain a material source of the wording of foreign law although the court may communicate the content of foreign law in any other way, such as during a hearing, where such communication is recorded in the case report.[12]

Czech courts cooperate with courts abroad - however, not directly but through the Ministry of Justice; cf. *infra* for the application of bilateral and multilateral treaties and utilization of international judicial networks. Informal cooperation between judges within the Internal Judicial Network has been significant: judges exchange information with respect to foreign law, share their experience regarding the service of documents to different states, etc. Another option has been to contact and engage a sworn expert, of whom a register is maintained by the Ministry of Justice, or to ask a specialist for an expert opinion who is not listed in the Ministry Register of sworn experts, but possesses relevant professional and educational background and knowledge and is competent to provide an opinion on the relevant foreign law (e.g. an attorney-at-law experienced in the respective foreign law). Opinions on foreign law can also be provided by certain private institutions abroad.

A classical principle, stemming also from treaties, has been maintained in the Czech Republic, namely that the provided legal information on the content of for-

[12] Zavadilová, Marta, 2013. Commentary on Sec. 23 PIL Act. In Pauknerová, Monika, Rozehnalová, Naděžda, Zavadilová, Marta. *Zákon o mezinárodním právu soukromém. Komentář* (Act on Private International Law. Commentary, in Czech), Prague: Wolters Kluwer. 171.

eign law is not binding upon judicial authorities; such information should be perceived only as one of the potential methods of ascertaining foreign law.

The costs of ascertaining foreign law are usually borne by the state. However, it is possible that, under certain circumstances, a court may call upon the party who has invoked the application of foreign law, which is not known to that court and the ascertainment of which would impose significant costs, to cooperate in the ascertainment and share in those costs.

D. Application and Interpretation of Foreign Law

Another highly demanding duty imposed upon a Czech judge is that foreign law should be applied in the way it would be applied by a judge of a respective foreign legal system. Mere knowledge of the text of a foreign legislation appears to be insufficient; what should be complemented is the context of relevant case law and/or relations with other legislation within the foreign legal system, including amendments. Czech judges are usually provided with the bare text of a foreign statute, as relevant foreign case law is not easily available. What may follow are expert opinions and reports including those issued by renowned foreign institutions; however, arranging for such documents is usually rather expensive. What may become a helpful source are foreign commentaries on, or annotations of, legislation and possibly textbooks, but with such resources, it is critical to determine their currency and whether they have been affected by developments in the foreign legal system, either through amendment or, in the case of common law systems, judicial interpretation.

The new 2012 PIL Act expressly provides for such a principle. As indicated above, Section 23(1) requires that foreign law referred to by a conflict-of-laws rule should be used in the same manner as it is applied in the territory of the respective foreign legal system. Such provisions are to be used which would be applied in adjudication of a case within that territory, irrespective of their systematic categorization or public nature, unless the foreign provisions are non-compliant with applicable mandatory Czech laws. The Explanatory Report notes that, should an order of the respective conflict-of-laws rule referring to foreign law be satisfied, it is necessary that the foreign law be applied to a respective case in the same way it is applied and interpreted in the country of its origin. Any other approach would not respect the order contained in the conflict rule and would lead not only to incorrect treatment of foreign law but also to the violation of a national conflict-of-laws rule.

The principle that foreign law should be applied in the way it applies in the country of its origin means that attaining just the text of a relevant law is insufficient in order to ascertain the content of the foreign law; where the content and method of application is not clearly ascertainable from the text itself, it should be complemented with information on its interpretation (commentaries, interpretative opinions, case law). A gap in foreign law should be filled under the same principles.

E. Failure to Establish Foreign Law

Czech jurisprudence maintained that, in the event provisions of an applicable foreign law could not be ascertained within a reasonable period of time, the *lex fori* principle should be applied.[13] This principle has been incorporated into Section 23 of the 2012 PIL Act: if the content of a foreign law which should be applied under a respective conflict-of-laws rule is not ascertained within a reasonable period of time, then Czech law applies. We would argue that "a reasonable period of time" should not be treated as a uniform time-limit since it is necessary to always consider the circumstances of a particular case. What would be decisive is the nature of the facts at issue and relating specialization of the legislation: for example, the ascertainment of the content of foreign law regarding divorce would be undoubtedly easier than ascertaining a particular legal institution within intellectual property law. In addition, the "distance" of foreign law from Czech law may be another decisive factor, whether it is a geographical, legal (e.g. continental vs. common law) or linguistic remoteness. An important aspect for considering "proportionality" may be whether the Czech Republic has a certain legal basis (international treaty) upon which an exchange of information on foreign law and experience in its recent application may be built. The reasonableness of the time period determined for ascertaining foreign law should be considered in the light of settled case law of international courts with respect to the right to a fair trial and relating reasonable lengths of judicial proceedings. Acts of a court aimed at ascertaining foreign law may take more time compared to other procedural acts of the court; however, if a court pursues rational acts aimed at attaining the desired objective, i.e. ascertaining foreign law, the time spent on such activity should not be a considered delay in proceedings. "Substitute" application of Czech law should be substantiated in the reasoning of a judgment; otherwise it would be considered a defect in judgment having a potential impact upon the correctness of the decision on the merits and would constitute grounds for successful appellate review, if requested.[14]

III. Judicial Review

A general premise has been that a judicial decision may be contested in an appeal by one of the parties, unless the law precludes it. If conflict-of-laws rules have been applied erroneously, or the foreign law has been applied incorrectly or insufficiently, the parties may file an appeal under standard conditions included in the Czech Code

[13] Kučera, Zdeněk. 2009. *Mezinárodní právo soukromé* (Private International Law, in Czech). 189. Brno-Plzeň: Doplněk a Čeněk.

[14] Zavadilová, Marta, 2013. Commentary on Sec. 23 PIL Act. In Pauknerová, Monika, Rozehnalová, Naděžda, Zavadilová, Marta. *Zákon o mezinárodním právu soukromém. Komentář* (Act on Private International Law. Commentary, in Czech), Prague: Wolters Kluwer. 171.

of Civil Procedure (hereinafter CCP).[15] Recourse on a point of law is admissible against the judgment of an appellate court.[16]

The appellate procedure is standard in accordance with the current conditions set forth in the CCP. An appeal may be filed within 15 days of service on the parties of the court's decision to be contested. The appeal should be filed with the court whose decision is challenged.[17]

This approach results from the assumption that there has been erroneous application of the conflict-of-laws within Czech proceedings, irrespective of whether the rule originated in Czech law or was a uniform conflict-of-laws rule contained in European or international legal instruments whose application is superior over national law. Erroneous application may generally be included in the cause of appeal under Section 205(2) g) CPP, i.e. the appeal against the first instance judgment is challenging the incorrect legal consideration of the matter by the first instance court. It is essentially possible (as an extraordinary remedy) to file an application for appellate review on a point of law with the Supreme Court of the Czech Republic, unless expressly stipulated grounds render such application inadmissible. Special restrictions existing in certain legal systems regarding appellate proceedings in the matter of application of foreign law are absent in Czech law.

IV. Foreign Law Before Non-judicial Authorities

It should be emphasized in the beginning that other instances, i.e. non-judicial adjudicating authorities, have to deal with foreign law only exceptionally. The necessity to apply foreign law mostly concerns agenda covered by registry offices. These authorities, in most cases, do not apply foreign law directly; for example, they have to determine from the perspective of foreign law whether the requirements for marriage have been met as they assess the capacity of a foreigner to enter into marriage, or evaluate conditions for the registration of changes in the name and surname of individuals in international cases.

The Czech Office for International Legal Protection of Children as well as the Ministry of Labour and Social Affairs may observe foreign rules on child abduction, maintenance obligations towards children, inter-country adoption, and the protection of children in general.[18] In addition, administrative proceedings before other Ministries and regional or district administrative authorities may include certain civil matters with a foreign element.

The issue of the application of foreign law by non-judicial authorities was not specially regulated before the 2012 PIL Act; these authorities usually cooperated

[15] Sec. 201 Act No. 99/1963 Coll., the Code of Civil Procedure (CCP).

[16] In details see Sec. 236 and 237 CCP.

[17] Sec. 204 CCP.

[18] See Act No. 359/1999 Coll., on Social and Legal Protection of Children and the respective Hague conventions.

with the Ministry of Justice and conditions for observing foreign law were the same as in cases determined by judicial authorities. With the entering into force of the 2012 PIL Act on 1 January 2014, there now is express regulation in Section 23(2) under which any adjudicating body, whether a court or a public body charged with adjudication in matters governed by the Act, will take all necessary measures to ascertain foreign law. A 'public body' is any authority entrusted with powers to adjudicate matters within the scope of the 2012 PIL Act, i.e. with respect to private relations and circumstances.

There is a need from time to time to ascertain and apply foreign law in arbitration, mediation and any other method of alternative dispute resolution. As a result, an arbitrator has a duty to ascertain the content of foreign law referred to by a conflict-of-laws rule as was explicitly stated in the above quoted award of the Arbitration Court Rsp 78/92.[19] Arbitrators may ascertain foreign law by themselves; many states provide sufficiently reliable information on their legislation on the Internet. Arbitrators may ask parties to submit relevant foreign laws; however, such documents would be acceptable only if submitted in a trustworthy format. Arbitrators may also ask a general court for cooperation under Section 20(2) of the Arbitration Act[20]; the requested court would then direct the question to the Ministry of Justice. However, it is not excluded, as has been shown in practice, that the Secretariat of the Arbitration Court attached to the Economic Chamber of the Czech Republic and the Agricultural Chamber of the Czech Republic address the Ministry of Justice directly to request cooperation. The Ministry is not obliged to satisfy such a request, but has done so in the past; what would undoubtedly be the determining factor is the complexity of the question raised.

V. Access to Foreign Law: Starting Points

The Czech Republic provides its legal information through its official Government website[21] in the Czech language; however, certain significant laws, such as the Czech Constitution, are also available in English.

Czech judges can make use of foreign Internet resources, such as the Hague Conference Judicial Network or the European Judicial Network; however they do so quite rarely and prefer obtaining information on foreign law directly from the Ministry of Justice.

The Czech Republic is party to the European Convention on Information on Foreign Law, London 1968, and to the Additional Protocol to this Convention of

[19] In details see Pauknerová, Monika. 2012. Aktuální otázky používání zahraničního práva v soudním a v rozhodčím řízení (Current issues of the treatment of foreign law in judicial and arbitration proceedings, in Czech with English summary). *Právník (The Lawyer)*, 12: 1265–1290.

[20] Act No. 216/1994 Coll., on Arbitral Proceedings and Enforcement of Arbitral Awards, the Arbitration Act.

[21] http://portal.gov.cz/app/zakony/?path=/portal/obcan/. Accessed 8 October 2016.

1978. Positive experiences with the European Convention on Information on Foreign Law have been reported, although a rather lengthy process of acquiring requested information appears to be a problematic aspect of the application of the Convention.

In addition, the Czech Republic has concluded some bilateral agreements on legal assistance, which permit the Czech Ministry of Justice to require information concerning foreign law from the respective foreign authority (usually the Ministry of Justice) of the other Contracting State. Some of these bilateral agreements were agreed upon by Czechoslovakia before its division into the Czech Republic and the Slovak Republic on 1 January 1993. For example, under Article 4 of the Agreement between the Government of Czechoslovakia and the Government of the French Republic on legal assistance, recognition and enforcement of decisions in civil, family and commercial matters of 1984,[22] the Ministries of Justice of both Contracting States should mutually provide, upon request, information on legislation which is, or was during the relevant time period, applicable in the territory of their States.

The Agreement between Czechoslovakia and Spain on legal assistance, recognition and enforcement of decisions in civil matters of 1987[23] states in Article 10 that central authorities of the Contracting Parties must provide, upon request and within the scope of that Agreement, information on legislation which is, or was, applicable in their territories along with the wording of these rules and information on the practice of judicial authorities. There are bilateral agreements on legal assistance in civil matters concluded by the former Czechoslovakia, or later by the Czech Republic, with states outside the EU, such as Cuba,[24] Vietnam,[25] the Russian Federation (formerly the Union of Soviet Socialist Republics)[26] and some states of the former USSR, which succeeded in the original bilateral agreement (e.g., Belarus,[27] Moldova[28]); while a new modern bilateral agreement has been concluded between the Czech Republic and Ukraine,[29] among others.[30] These instruments, in particular bilateral agreements on mutual legal assistance, are applied regularly.

When considering communication with foreign authorities, the linguistic aspect should be recognized, which under certain circumstances might amount to a language barrier, although foreign language proficiency of officers of the Czech Ministry of Justice is often above the usual standards. What appears to be most

---

[22] No. 83/1985 Coll.

[23] No. 6/1989 Coll.

[24] No. 80/1981 Coll.

[25] No. 98/1984 Coll.

[26] No. 95/1983 Coll.

[27] No. 79/2009 Coll. of International Treaties.

[28] No. 81/2009 Coll. of International Treaties.

[29] No. 123/2002 Coll. of International Treaties.

[30] Pauknerová, Monika, Brodec, Jan. 2011. Czech Republic and Slovakia. In *Application of Foreign Law,* eds. Esplugues, Carlos, Iglesias, José Luis, Palao, Guillermo, 177–178. Munich: Sellier, European Law Publishers.

significant in determining the ease of communication is which authority abroad is contacted; in addition, personal contacts between officers in different countries, as well as their individual approach to searching and providing information on foreign law play a significant role in whether the desired goal is achieved. In order to obtain the most relevant information about foreign law, practice has indicated that it is extremely important how the question is formulated when presented to foreign authorities. However, practice and experience in formulating the foreign law queries may differ among jurisdictions.

VI. Access to Foreign Law: Further Developments

A. *Practical Need*

The need to improve access to foreign law appears to objectively exist whether with respect to judicial authorities, administrative and other non-judicial authorities, arbitrators, attorneys, parties, especially those who cannot afford costly measures to be taken, and/or any other stakeholders.

These questions have been studied by a number of scholars and they have been a subject of interest debated at various forums for a long time, in particular at the Hague Conference on Private International Law and at the European Commission.

As far as the latter regional work in the EU is concerned, special attention should be drawn to two studies that were prepared on the basis of contracts awarded by the European Commission. The first study "Application of foreign law by judicial and non-judicial authorities in Europe" was conducted by the University of Valencia team (so called Valencia Report), which resulted in the publication of a book entitled "*Application of Foreign Law*".[31] The second study was conducted by the Swiss Institute of Comparative Law in Lausanne[32] and its published outcome was entitled "*Foreign Law and its Perspectives for the Future at the European Level*".

On the other hand, the Hague Conference has presented *inter alia* two important documents in recent years: "Accessing the content of foreign law and the need for the development of a global instrument in this area – a possible way ahead",[33] and "Guiding Principles to be considered in Developing a Future Instrument".[34] The Guiding Principles were also annexed to another important document called

[31] Esplugues, Carlos, Iglesias, José Luis, Palao, Guillermo (Eds.). 2011. *Application of Foreign Law.* 30. Munich: Sellier. European Law Publishers.

[32] This study was published by the EU Commission in 2012. http://ec.europa.eu/justice/civil/document/index_en.htm. Accessed 8 October 2016.

[33] Hague Conference on Private International Law, General Affairs and Policy, Prel. Doc. No. 11 A, March 2009.

[34] Principles developed by the experts who met in 2008 at the invitation of the Permanent Bureau of the Hague Conference on Private International Law as part of its feasibility study on the access to foreign law.

"Conclusions and Recommendations – Access to Foreign Law in Civil and Commercial Matters", adopted at a Brussels conference, organized jointly by the European Commission and the Hague Conference on Private International Law, held on 15–17 February 2012.[35] In April 2013, the Council of the Hague Conference invited the Permanent Bureau to continue to follow developments in accessing the content of foreign law and the need for the development of a global instrument in this area.[36] Unfortunately, no particular results can be noted and prospects in this direction seem to be rather unclear.

What should not be forgotten in this context is the activity of, and long-lasting debates within, GEDIP (*Groupe européen de droit international privé*), which resulted in a report entitled "*Reflexions on the application and proof of, and access to, foreign law*", Copenhagen 2010, Brussels 2011, The Hague 2012, and Lausanne 2013.[37] GEDIP terminated its activities in this area in 2013 with conclusions that, undoubtedly, a global instrument on improving access to foreign law would be useful, as has been repeatedly pointed out by the Hague Conference. For some time it appeared that, with respect to the various existing concepts of the treatment of foreign law, such a solution on a global level was the only realistic approach. However, the recent results within the Hague Conference show that the States are not yet ready to start particular activities (preparatory work) in this respect.

The 2012 Brussels Conference stressed that such a global instrument should focus on the effective *facilitation* of access to foreign law and should not attempt to harmonize the status of foreign law in national procedures. Specific features of the European Union, consisting of specific sources of law and close judicial cooperation in cross-border civil matters, together with the first proposals of specific rules on the treatment of foreign law, may indicate new starting points. It is evident that such rules cannot exist in a vacuum and they should be accompanied by certain guarantees that the access to the foreign law could be facilitated.[38]

A practical need to unify and simplify the access to foreign law arises in the Czech Republic as well. Due to its geographical position in Central Europe, members of different nationalities and ethnic origins meet, and often collide, in the Czech Republic, whether they are individuals or juridical persons, and the scope of regulation applicable to their matters range from family and succession law to the law of business transactions. The need to apply foreign law referred to by a conflict-of-

---

[35] The English and French texts of the Conclusions, the Conference Report and other documents are available at http://www.hcch.net/upload/hidden/2012/xs2foreignlaw.html. Accessed 8 October 2016.

[36] The Conclusions and Recommendations adopted by the Council (9–11 April 2013) can be retrieved at: http://www.hcch.net/upload/wop/gap2013concl_e.pdf. Accessed 8 October 2016.

[37] See Pauknerová, Monika, van Loon, Hans. 2010. Reflexions on the application and proof of, and access to, foreign law. European Group for Private International Law (GEDIP), Copenhagen meeting, available at < http://www.gedip-egpil.eu/reunionstravail/gedip-reunions-20-fr.htm>, refer also to Geneva meeting of the GEDIP Group in 1995. The next outputs are reported at the webpage of the GEDIP at http://www.gedip-egpil.eu/gedip_reunions.html – "*La condition du droit étranger selon le droit de l'Union*". Accessed 8 October 2016.

[38] GEDIP Report 2013, see http://www.gedip-egpil.eu/gedip_reunions.html. Accessed 8 October 2016.

laws rule arises in proceedings before courts, notaries, in rare situations before non-judicial authorities, and also before arbitrators and mediators. Since judgments and other adjudicating documents, including arbitral awards, are not published (with the exception of judgments of the Supreme Court and the Constitutional Court) it is difficult to provide a reliable number of cases in which foreign law has been applied.

B. Conflict of Laws Solutions

In general, when looking for solutions to the access to foreign laws issue, we may refer to the debates held within the framework of the GEDIP focusing on the possibility that parties would, in particular cases, simply agree on the application of *lex fori*. However, no compromise solution has been found yet.[39]

A trend in recent European Regulations can also be seen in recent Czech law, namely that an accord between *ius* and *forum* should be reached, i.e. an accord between the applicable law and the venue where a case is to be adjudicated. This objective can be reached, or at least approximated, by introducing the concept of *habitual residence* as the connecting factor in lieu of the traditional connecting factor of *nationality*. This has been incorporated in the 2012 PIL Act in new conflict-of-laws rules relating to matrimonial property relations (Section 49), succession (Section 76), or personal status of individuals (Section 29). In cases of contracts that are not covered by European law or an international treaty, the choice of law is usually permitted (Section 87); it depends upon parties to decide which law they choose and whether they subsequently alter their choice. However, a situation when only Czech law would apply before courts in the Czech Republic would never be reached. Foreign law should be respected not only if it has been chosen by the parties, but especially in cases where foreign law has been referred to by mandatory conflict-of-laws rules – typically within the protection of children and adoption (Sections 54, 61), capacity to marry (Section 48) or the area of rights *in rem* (Section 69). This trend has been apparent both in European law (Maintenance Regulation[40] and The Hague Protocol,[41] Succession Regulation[42]) and certain Hague conventions, such as the Convention of 19 October 1996 on Jurisdiction, Applicable Law, Recognition, Enforcement and Co-operation in Respect of Parental Responsibility and Measures for the Protection of Children. There are no doubts that the issue of the treatment of

[39] GEDIP Report 2013, *ibidem*.

[40] Regulation (EC) No. 4/2009 on jurisdiction, applicable law, recognition and enforcement of decisions and cooperation in matters relating to maintenance obligations (OJ L 7/1, 10.1.2009).

[41] Protocol of 23 November 2007 on the Law Applicable to Maintenance Obligations (OJ L 331/19, 16.12.2009).

[42] Regulation (EU) No. 650/2012 of the European Parliament and of the Council of 4 July 2012 on jurisdiction, applicable law, recognition and enforcement of decisions and acceptance and enforcement of authentic instruments in matters of succession and on the creation of a European Certificate of Succession (OJ L 201/107, 27.7.2012).

foreign law must be solved collectively at an international level or, in the beginning, at least at the European level. However, to harmonize ideas and goals of individual states representing civil law and common law respectively seems to be an unattainable task for the time being.

C. Methods of Facilitating Access to Foreign Law

The author of this Chapter is also a co-author of the GEDIP Reports on the treatment of foreign law, particularly of Part II entitled "*The practical means of improving the determination, by the authorities of EU Member States, of the content of the applicable foreign law*". Three ways to advance future work and mechanisms in this area might be outlined as basic starting points: (a) Information technology and its impact on ascertainment of foreign law; (b) Judicial and administrative cooperation; and (c) Networks of experts.[43]

1. International or Regional Instruments

There is no doubt, and it has already been emphasized, that the only way to effectively solve the issue of administrative and/or judicial cooperation in exchanging information on the law of participating States is the adoption of a uniform legal instrument incorporating the rules for such cooperation. As to the structure and mechanisms of such instrument, the European Judicial Network in Civil and Commercial Matters (EJN) seems to be a proper platform as it provides a wide range of information on EU law, as well as some information on national law of the Member States. Evidently, it may be difficult to assess the efficiency of this type of activity in general; it substantially depends on individual national contact points and their mutual relations and interaction. As is well known, administrative cooperation is connected with increased costs, which is one of the main challenges in the ascertainment of foreign law in general. International cooperation within the Hague Conference on Private International Law would obviously be a more appropriate forum because the issue of the treatment of foreign law cannot be reduced just to EU law; on the other hand, a decline in interest of the members of the Hague Conference in dealing with this issue has been recently quite evident and should be noted and taken into consideration.

Another problem deserving attention and emphasis in cooperation between authorities of different states has been the issue of translation of legal texts and case law. In countries whose official language is not one of the international languages, such as the Czech Republic using the Czech language, the requirement to provide accessible information on legal texts would require arranging for thorough and reliable translations of their legislation, with regular subsequent updates. Therefore,

[43] GEDIP Report 2013, see http://www.gedip-egpil.eu/gedip_reunions.html. Accessed 8 October 2016.

translation apparently represents another financial barrier in relation to facilitating access to foreign law.

Due to so many circumstances resulting in difficulties in attaining quality and reliable information on foreign law, a realistic approach should be taken regarding the access to services supplying legal information. Such services cannot be provided for free; they should be adequately appraised and a reasonable system of fees should be maintained.

Legal information supplied to courts cannot be binding because such an approach would, *inter alia*, intrude on the independence of judges and courts; moreover, it can never be excluded that such information may be imprecise or even incorrect. As a result, it is necessary that courts or any other adjudicating body preserve their discretion in considering and deciding the issue.

2. Other Feasible Methods of Facilitating Access to Foreign Law

Such methods naturally involve processes enhancing direct communication between judges; establishing networks for other legal professionals; identifying qualified experts whether individuals or juridical persons; and providing information on national legislation on the Internet.

Making all those methods work, however, is quite financially demanding. As suggested earlier in this Chapter, this applies particularly to countries whose official language is not international and globally used. The Czech Republic, with the Czech language as the official language of its national laws, finds itself in a much more complex situation than countries with English as the official or widely spoken language. This linguistic handicap can affect even the first above-mentioned option, namely establishing direct contacts between judges and other persons charged with the duty to ascertain and apply foreign law. A linguistic barrier, along with the workload of judges, indicates that this method is far from being a reality.

Networks among certain professional groups have existed: typically between lawyers and particularly within large groups of law firms. However, these are just internal relations of particular groups arranged to, *inter alia*, reduce time and financial costs relating to the networking. A certain solution may be the engagement of experts, whether individuals or institutions; but even in such cases, high costs and lengthy procedures have to be taken into account.

The Internet is still a relatively new phenomenon and as a result it has not yet been utilised to its fullest capacity to facilitate the sharing of information on foreign law. We have to bear in mind that much information on foreign law currently offered by way of the Internet may be provided on many websites and, as to its provenance, it is not necessarily reliable, up-to-date or transparent. Such information must often be verified and perhaps also authenticated by other sources. Moreover, finding and ascertaining the contents of foreign law using various Internet databases requires a person experienced in using such databases and familiar with the respective legal system. Usually, only the plain text of the applicable legislation is accessible, which may not be sufficient to understand the full contents and context of the law as it is applied in the foreign country. To understand the full contents and context, the language issue plays its role again: such information is mostly available only in the language of the respective state. Thus we return back to those basic and sensitive issues determining and/or limiting chances to attain information on foreign law: time demands, language barriers and particularly high financial expenditures.

D. Conclusions

There is an accord, more or less, as it has been indicated, that access to foreign law should be made more efficient, in particular in cases where foreign law is to be applied as a result of a unified conflict-of-laws rule. Opinions differ in the appropriate way in which the issue may be solved, and in determining the extent to which the coordination of efforts to find a uniform solution should be maintained.

It seems to be obvious that, irrespective of any potential unification of national procedural laws, it is necessary to arrange for the widest possible access to foreign law. This premise has been supported by all specialists, whether academics, scholars or practitioners, who have recently dealt with such an issue. Neither unification, nor harmonization of procedural provisions, should be blind.

I am personally sceptical of states' willingness to be subjected to unifying tendencies, regardless of how limited they may be and even if only aimed at simplification of access to their law. For most countries whose language is not an international language it would require them to arrange for and provide quality translation of their legislation. In addition, in some states legislation is not publicly available on the Internet and information on their law is provided primarily by specialized offices for a fee.

Another serious issue is the role of a judge who is to decide a case under foreign law. Even if the foreign law has been ascertained, which by itself is a rather demanding task, the judge would have to rely on the information acquired and to work with foreign law, which is again extremely demanding. My personal experience suggests that certain wider contexts of the relevant law may remain concealed, for example when the regulation of a related legal institution is contained in a law other than that for which a translation has been provided.

It should be noted in conclusion that the requirement to apply foreign law with all relating consequences, as it has been understood in the Czech Republic, corresponds with a classical concept of equality of legal orders which should be respected by all of us.

Denmark: Foreign Law in Danish Civil Litigation: A Pragmatic Approach

Clement Salung Petersen

Abstract This chapter concerns the treatment of foreign law in Danish civil litigation. It first highlights some essential features of Danish civil litigation that are generally relevant for the application of (any) law and the pragmatic Danish understanding of the "nature" of foreign law. On this background, it analyses the principles for application and ascertainment of foreign law as well as the consequences of failure to establish relevant foreign law.

1. Introduction

Danish law is part of the Nordic legal tradition, which among comparative law scholars is traditionally regarded as a distinct "legal family".[1] A distinct feature usually attributed to this legal family is a pragmatic approach to legal formalities, conceptualism and theory in favour of what is useful and necessary in practice.[2] Such pragmatism is also a key feature of the Danish approach to application and ascertainment of foreign law in civil litigation, which is the topic of this paper.[3] The paper will first highlight some essential features of Danish civil litigation that are generally relevant for the application of (any) law and the pragmatic Danish understanding of the "nature" of foreign law. On the basis of this general framework, the paper will analyse the principles for application and ascertainment of foreign law and the consequences of failure to establish relevant foreign law in Danish civil litigation.

---

[1] See, *e.g.*, K. Zweigert & H. Kötz (eds.), *Introduction to Comparative Law* (3rd Edition 1998), D. Tamm, The Nordic Legal Tradition in European Context, in: P Letto-Vanamo (ed.) *Nordisk Identitet – Nordisk rätt i europeisk gemenskap*, University of Helsinki 2011 (pp. 15–31), and U Bernitz, *What is Scandinavian law? Concept, characteristics, future.* Scandinavian Studies in Law (2007) 50:13–29.

[2] Zweigert & Kötz and Tamm, both mentioned *supra* note 1.

[3] This paper is based on my report to the XIXth International Congress of Comparative Law in Vienna 2014.

C.S. Petersen (✉)
Associate Professor, Faculty of Law, University of Copenhagen,
Karen Blixens Plads 16, DK-2300 Copenhagen S, Denmark
e-mail: clement.petersen@jur.ku.dk

Y. Nishitani (ed.), *Treatment of Foreign Law - Dynamics towards Convergence?*,
Ius Comparatum – Global Studies in Comparative Law 26,
DOI 10.1007/978-3-319-56574-3_5

2. Danish Civil Litigation

The ordinary Danish court system consists of a Supreme Court, two high courts and 24 district courts with general jurisdiction to hear both civil and criminal cases, as well as a few courts with special jurisdiction, including the Maritime and Commercial Court and the Land Registration Court.[4] Denmark has a single procedural code, the Danish Administration of Justice Act, which governs both the ordinary court system and its procedures.

All cases which are not criminal cases are heard under the rules of civil procedure. Danish civil litigation thus comprises not only cases between private parties but also all non-criminal cases between a private party and a public authority, including cases for judicial review and other administrative law cases.[5]

Danish civil procedure law is normally based on adversarial proceedings with a high degree of party autonomy (so-called *dispositive disputes*). However, there are also a number of special civil proceedings in which the court has a more investigative role (inquisitorial procedure) and party autonomy is more limited (so-called *non-dispositive disputes*). These non-dispositive disputes include, in particular, matrimonial cases and cases concerning custody, affiliation or guardianship, cases concerning review of detentions imposed by an administrative decision or decisions of adoption without consent, and procedures for obtaining judgments declaring a document null and void or judgments to determine ownership.[6]

Before looking at the procedural treatment of foreign law in Danish civil litigation, it is useful to first highlight some basic procedural rules in Danish civil procedure law which are generally relevant for the application of (any) law.[7]

2.1. Adversarial Proceedings and Party Autonomy

In civil litigation, it is normally for the parties to define their judicial controversy, *i.e.* the disputed issues which the court is requested to adjudicate, and to submit evidence to support their allegations.[8] The judicial controversy is defined by the claims ("*påstande*") and allegations ("*anbringender*") of the parties. It is a fundamental principle of Danish civil procedure law that a court cannot award a party

---

[4] The Court of the Faroe Islands and the courts of Greenland fall outside the scope of this paper.

[5] A few criminal offences are subject to private prosecution in civil proceedings, and certain civil claims filed and growing out of public prosecution of a criminal offence may also be decided by the court in such criminal proceedings ("*adhæsionsproces*").

[6] These special procedures are governed by the rules in chapters 42, 42 a, 43, 43 a, 43 b and 44 of the Danish Administration of Justice Act.

[7] The account in part 2.1–2.2 is based on C Salung Petersen, *Treaties in Domestic Civil Litigation: Jura Novit Curia?*, Nordic Journal of International Law 80 (2011) 369–402.

[8] This is referred to as *Forhandlingsmaksimen* (comparable to the German *Verhandlungsmaxime*).

something more than he has claimed, and that the court can base its decision only on the allegations made by the party or on allegations that cannot be waived.[9]

A *claim* consists of a concise statement of the preferred outcome of the case. The claimant may, *e.g.*, claim that the defendant has to pay a certain amount of money, whereas the defendant may claim rejection of the plaintiff's claim. *Allegations* consist of concise statements of fact which the party claims to be able to prove, and which – if proven – can justify the party's claim. In the allegations, a party must also explain the legal relevance of the facts to such an extent that it is clear for the other parties (and the court) how the alleged facts may legally justify his claim.[10] Traditionally, the allegations are not supposed to comprise the "pure" legal arguments of the parties. Since the recent reform of Danish civil procedure, the parties are required to also include statements of their legal arguments in the pleadings.[11] At the trial, the parties (their lawyers) argue their case based on the allegations which also include the "pure" legal arguments on which they rely.

The high degree of party autonomy in civil litigation (the dispositive principle), which reflects the general private law principle of party autonomy, is not without exceptions. In particular, if a claim is illegal under applicable mandatory law, including fundamental rules of public policy (*ordre public*), and the mandatory law cannot be waived by contract under any circumstances, a party is unable to waive an allegation that the claim of the counterparty is illegal under such mandatory law. Consequently, a court will normally always *ex officio* consider such mandatory law, provided that the facts of the case make it sufficiently clear that such law applies.[12]

Traditionally, Danish courts have no power over the choice of issues and evidence put forward by the parties. Danish courts thus have no general investigative powers or authority to order the production of evidence in civil litigation. However, Danish courts have formal control over the litigation process and may, to a certain extent, also seek to influence the substantive outcome of the proceedings through judicial guidance ("*materiel procesledelse*"). A court can thus, *e.g.*, call on a party to declare his position as regards questions of fact or questions of law, which are deemed potentially relevant, or call on a party to provide evidence of facts, which may otherwise be uncertain.[13] A Danish court is also entitled to disallow evidence that the court deems to be irrelevant.[14]

The high degree of party autonomy in ordinary civil litigation is not present in the *special civil proceedings* briefly mentioned *supra*. In those special proceedings, the parties are not as free to define their judicial controversy, and the court plays a (much) more active (inquisitorial) role.

---

[9] Section 338 of the Danish Administration of Justice Act.

[10] See, *e.g.*, P. Spleth, "Omkring den borgerlige retspleje", Juristen 1959, 321–349, at 344.

[11] See, *e.g.*, Section 348(2)(4) and section 351(2)(3) of the Danish Administration of Justice Act.

[12] Section 338 of the Danish Administration of Justice Act.

[13] Section 339 of the Danish Administration of Justice Act.

[14] Section 341 of the Danish Administration of Justice Act.

2.2. Application of Law (Iura Novit Curia)

When the claims and allegations of the parties are sufficiently clarified, it is for the court to render a judgment based on the relevant law.[15] In this regard, a Danish court is under an obligation to independently (*i.e.* regardless of the legal arguments of the parties) and *ex officio* consider which law is relevant and to apply this law correctly, also where the parties have not explicitly referred to the relevant law. These principles for the judicial application of law reflect the Latin adages *iura novit curia* and *da mihi factum, dabo tibi jus*.[16]

However, rules apply to specific facts. If the facts necessary to apply a rule are not sufficiently covered by the allegations of the parties, the court cannot apply that rule.[17] In this way, the allegations of the parties affect the rules applied by the courts in ordinary civil litigation.

Even though the court is not bound by the "pure" legal arguments of the parties, the obligation of courts to *ex officio* consider and apply the law is presumed to presuppose that the parties have "sufficiently clarified" their allegations, and that this required degree of clarification is generally higher in the high courts and the Supreme Court than in the district courts.[18] The court can thus apply a relevant rule only if *the decisive facts* (the factual circumstances which are necessary to apply the rule) are sufficiently addressed by at least one of the parties.[19] It is also assumed that the required degree of clarification may depend on the nature of the applicable rule: Whereas well-known rules should always be considered and applied (if applicable), a court may choose to consider and apply more specialised or controversial rules (*i.e.* where the content of the rule is legally uncertain) *only if* the allegations of the parties make it sufficiently clear that at least one of the parties wishes to invoke such rule. If it is unclear whether a specialised or controversial rule is applicable in a specific dispute, Danish courts have sometimes refrained from considering and applying the rule, if the question has not been addressed (or has only been superficially addressed) by the parties in their legal arguments.[20]

---

[15] See, *e.g.*, Section 64(1) of the Danish Constitution: "In the performance of their duties, the judges shall be governed solely by the law. [...]".

[16] See B Gomard and M Kistrup. "Civilprocessen" (Copenhagen: KarnovGroup, 6th Edition 2013), at p. 606, and E Werlauff and L Lindencrone Petersen. "Dansk retspleje" (Copenhagen: Thomson, 6th Edition 2007), at p. 299 et seq. See also Salung Petersen, *supra* note 7.

[17] A Danish court may instead call on the parties to consider making further allegations, see Section 339, ss. 1–3

[18] Gomard and Kistrup, *supra* note 16, at p. 606. In civil litigation before the district courts, a party not represented by counsel is also entitled to (some) guidance by the court, see Section 339(4) of the Danish Administration of Justice Act.

[19] See judgment of 31 March 1976 from the Danish Supreme Court, reported in the Danish Weekly Law Reports 1976, p. 385.

[20] See M Munch, "Jura novit curia", Ugeskrift for Retsvæsen 1972, B, 189–192, p. 189, and Gomard and Kistrup, *supra* note 16, at p. 606 et seq.

It is fair to say that these principles governing the judicial application of law leave a margin of discretion to the Danish courts in civil litigation and that the parties are able to influence the judicial application of law through their allegations and arguments, even though the "pure" legal arguments of the parties are not formally binding on the courts in relation to their interpretation and application of law *(iura novit curia)*.

2.3. Appeals

The Danish civil justice system is based on a general right to appeal once (often referred to as the *two-instance principle*).[21] An appellate court (a high court or the Supreme Court) can try the case in full based on a new full hearing of the case at which the parties can present new evidence and to some extent also include new claims and allegations.[22] Before an appellate court, a party may thus submit that the lower court has erroneously applied conflict of laws rules or foreign law. The appellate court can try this question in full. If the lower court has not even considered the choice of law, and the appellate court finds that this is relevant, the appellate court will normally remit the case to the lower court.[23]

A Danish court can make an interlocutory order concerning the choice of law applicable to the dispute. A leave to appeal is generally required to independently appeal such interlocutory order.[24]

3. Nature of Foreign Law

The Danish Administration of Justice Act has no specific rules governing the ascertainment and application of foreign law.[25] The distinction between "fact" and "law" serves the same purpose in the Danish civil justice system as in traditional civil law

---

[21] However, a leave to appeal is required if the appeal concerns a district court judgment, and the claim does not exceed DKK 20,000, see Section 368(1) of the Danish Administration of Justice Act.

[22] See Sections 380–384 of the Danish Administration of Justice Act.

[23] See decision of 20 December 2011 from the High Court of Eastern Denmark (reported in Fuldmægtigen 2012, p. 172), decision of 20 June 2012 from the High Court of Western Denmark (reported in Fuldmægtigen 2012, p. 266 and p. 298). See also Fogt, "International privatret", p. 488, and compare decision of 1 August 2007 from the High Court of Eastern Denmark (reported in Fuldmægtigen 1-2007-1,342,912).

[24] See, *e.g.*, Sections 389 and 392 of the Danish Administration of Justice Act, and U R Bang-Pedersen and L H Christensen, "Den Civile Retspleje" (Copenhagen: PEJUS, 3rd Edition 2015), at p. 354.

[25] Such as is known, *inter alia*, in Norway and Germany. The first preparatory works for the Danish Administration of Justice Act (from 1877) included a similar provision, see Gomard and Kistrup, *supra* note 16, at p. 618 in footnote 101.

countries, namely that of demarcating the power of the judge vis-à-vis the parties.[26] It is, therefore, no surprise that the classic question about the nature of foreign law, *i.e.* whether foreign law should be treated as "fact" (*fact doctrine*) or as "law", has also been discussed in Danish law.[27]

In Danish legal scholarship, there is today general agreement that foreign law, on the one hand, must be considered as "law" but that, on the other hand, this does not automatically entail that the procedural treatment of foreign law must be the same as other law in civil litigation.[28] It is thus widely accepted that even though foreign law is regarded as "law", the procedural rules governing ascertainment and application of foreign law must take into account the special circumstances related to foreign law, including (in particular) that judges cannot be expected to know foreign law.

From a Danish perspective, the issues related to the procedural treatment of foreign law are thus too complex to be regarded as merely a question of whether to treat foreign law as a question of "fact" or "law".[29] Even though foreign law is considered as "law", a pragmatic approach to the treatment of foreign law has been developed, which is analysed *infra* 4–6.

---

[26] For a comparative perspective, see S Geeroms, "Foreign law in civil litigation: A comparative and functional analysis" (Oxford University Press 2014), at pp. 13 et seq, and J A Jolowicz, "On civil procedure" (Cambridge University Press 2000), at pp. 185 et seq,

[27] See, in particular, A S Ørsted, "Eunomia 3. deel" (Copenhagen 1819), p. 560, P G Bang and J E Larsen, "Systematisk fremstilling af den danske procesmaade" (Copenhagen 1841), p. 111, J Nellemann, "Den ordinære civile procesmåde", p. 84 and 847, J H Deuntzer, "Den danske Civilproces fremstillet til Brug for de Studerende" (Copenhagen 1901), p. 133, H Munch-Petersen, "Den danske civilproces i hovedtræk" (Copenhagen 1906), p. 257, K F Hammerich, "Forhandlingsmaximen" (Copenhagen 1910), p. 65, O A Borum, "Domstolene og Anvendelsen af fremmed ret", Ugeskrift for Retsvæsen 1928, B, 201–209, H Munch-Petersen, "Den danske retspleje" (Copenhagen 1923), p. 259, A Philip, "Om domstolenes anvendelse af fremmed ret", Ugeskrift for Retsvæsen 1960, B, 149–166, O Lando, "Fremmed ret. for skandinaviske domstole", Juristen 1967:1–11, S Hurwitz and B Gomard, "Tvistemål" (1965), p. 121, H Zahle, "Udeblivelsesdomme" (Jurist- og Økonomforbundets Forlag 1983), pp. 193–195, E Siesby, "Lærebog i International Privatret" (Jurist- og Økonomforbundets Forlag 1983), p. 62, T S Schmidt, "International formueret"(Forlaget Thomson, Copenhagen, 2000), p. 40, P A Nielsen, "International privat- og procesret" (Jurist- og Økonomforbundets Forlag 1997), p. 49, Gomard and Kistrup, *supra* note 16, pp. 615–620.

[28] This view was recently followed by a Danish District Court in a decision of 25 September 2008, which is reported in TfS 2008, p. 1363, and SKM 2008, p. 814.

[29] Compare C Esplugues, J L Iglesias and Guillermo Palao (eds.). "*Application of foreign law*" (Munich: Sellier, 2011), pp. 8–10.

4. Application of Foreign Law

As described *supra* 2, the allegations of the parties indirectly affect which rules a court can apply, because the court can only apply a rule if the facts necessary to apply the rule are covered by the allegations of the parties.[30] This raises the question how *specific* the allegations need to be for a court to apply *foreign law*.

In an older appeal case, the Danish Supreme Court held that it could not apply foreign law to the dispute for the mere reason that none of the parties had made a claim in this regard.[31] It is not clear whether the Supreme Court presupposed that a party must explicitly plead the application of foreign law or that the factual circumstances relevant to apply foreign law must be (explicitly or separately) pleaded by a party for the court to take foreign law into consideration.[32]

Danish scholarship has, however, rejected that such requirements should exist. According to Danish scholarship, the parties are thus not required to *explicitly* emphasize those facts which make foreign law applicable in the allegations.[33] This seems to be in line with the general principles for applying Danish law, where a court can apply a relevant rule if the factual circumstances which are necessary to apply the rule are *covered by* the allegations and arguments of the parties.[34] It is further assumed that the parties are normally not required to make any explicit references to particular *rules* under foreign law.[35] In this regard, the courts also seem to treat foreign law as other applicable law, see *supra* 2.2.[36]

In conclusion, a Danish court is under an obligation to independently (*i.e.* regardless of the "pure" legal arguments of the parties) and *ex officio* consider which law is relevant, including foreign law, and to apply this law correctly, also where none of the parties have explicitly referred to the relevant law, as long as the relevant factual circumstances are covered by the allegations of the parties. These findings are especially important if one of the parties fails to appear in court and the court must give a default judgment: If the plaintiff's claim and allegations cover facts which make it relevant to consider and apply foreign law, the court must *ex officio* ascertain and apply the relevant foreign law.[37] How the court should ascertain the content of foreign law is discussed *infra* para. 5.

---

[30] See *supra* 2.2.

[31] Supreme Court judgment of 14 February 1918 reported in the Danish Weekly Law Reports 1918, p. 212.

[32] See, *in particular*, Philip, *supra* note 27, Gomard and Kistrup, *supra* note 16, p. 617.

[33] See Gomard and Kistrup, *supra* note 16, p. 617.

[34] See judgment of 31 March 1976 from the Danish Supreme Court, reported in the Danish Weekly Law Reports 1976, p. 385, also mentioned *supra* 2.2.

[35] See Gomard and Kistrup, *supra* note 16, p. 617.

[36] There is thus no procedural discrimination between Danish law and foreign law. Compare the findings in the Swiss Institute of Comparative Law, "The Application of Foreign Law in Civil Matters in the EU Member States and its Perspectives for the Future", p. 14, available at: http://ec.europa.eu/justice/civil/files/foreign_law_en.pdf

[37] See Philip, *supra* note 27, and Zahle, *supra* note 27, p. 195.

If a court finds that the factual circumstances of the case makes it relevant to consider the application of foreign law, but the parties have not clearly addressed this issue, it is assumed that the court should provide judicial guidance ("*materiel procesledelse*") and ask the parties to clarify their position in this regard.[38] The courts should probably do this regardless of the economic value of the dispute even though application of foreign law may increase the costs related to the case.[39] This obligation supports the efficiency of the conflict of laws rules but also respects the party autonomy of the parties to make a deliberate choice of law.[40]

The result of this may be that the parties declare that they wish the court to decide the case based on Danish law (*lex fori*). Under the general principle of party autonomy in civil litigation (the *dispositive principle*), the parties can thus normally make an agreement on the choice of law – before or in the course of civil litigation.[41] Such agreement must be respected by the courts, unless it is contrary to mandatory rules which the court must apply ex officio.[42]

The parties can often not enter into a binding agreement about the applicable laws in the *special civil proceedings* briefly mentioned *supra* para. 2. In such proceedings, the court must thus *ex officio* consider and apply any relevant foreign law.[43] The Danish High Court of Eastern Denmark seems to have followed this approach in an older decision from 1949.[44]

If a Danish court decides to apply foreign law, the Danish court must interpret and apply the foreign law in the same way as that law is interpreted and applied by courts in the country of origin.[45] It may be a challenging task to get sufficiently precise information about how courts in the country of origin interpret and apply the applicable foreign law for instance when the parties present divergent legal opinions.[46] Challenges related to the ascertainment of foreign law are analysed *infra* 5.

It is assumed that a Danish court should apply foreign law only if the court is convinced about the content of the applicable foreign law.[47] If the court is not

---

[38] See Gomard and Kistrup, *supra* note 16, p. 617, and Nielsen, *supra* note 27, p. 51.

[39] *Ibid.* However, Lando, *supra* note 27, p. 4, and Siesby, *supra* note 27, p. 48, argue that the court should not do this in disputes of little economic value. About costs, see *infra* 5.3.

[40] This seeks to address the discrepancy mentioned in Swiss Institute of International Law, *supra* note 36, p. 19.

[41] See P A Nielsen, *supra* note 27, p. 51, Gomard and Kistrup, *supra* note 16, p. 616.

[42] See Section 338 of the Danish Administration of Justice Act and *supra* para. 2.1.2.

[43] See, *inter alia*, Schmidt, *supra note 27*, p. 42, Nielsen, *supra* note 27, p. 50, P A Nielsen, "International handelsret" (Thomson 2006), p. 47, and M M Fogt, "International privatret" in: "Formueretlige emner" (Copenhagen: Jurist- og Økonomforbundets Forlag, 2013), 471–557, at 488.

[44] Reported in the Danish Weekly Law Reports 1949, p. 1049. This decision is discussed by Philip, *supra* note 27.

[45] Nielsen, *supra* note 27, p. 54.

[46] As an example, see the Danish Supreme Court judgment of 10 December 1969 (reported in the Danish Weekly Law Reports 1960, p. 104): In this case, the parties had obtained divergent legal opinions about relevant US laws ("Harter Act" and "Carriage of Goods by Sea Act").

[47] Nielsen, *supra* note 27, p. 54, Gomard and Kistrup, *supra* note 16, p. 619.

convinced, the court should either seek to obtain more precise information or, if the knowledge gap about foreign law seems impossible to rectify, decide the case based on *lex fori*.[48] The consequences of such failure to establish foreign law are discussed in detail *infra* para. 6.

5. Ascertainment of Foreign Law

Even though Danish judges are not expected to "know" foreign law, there are no rules in the Danish Administration of Justice Act about how they should ascertain foreign law.[49] Danish judges may ascertain foreign law on their own, but they may also ask the parties to assist them in doing this.

5.1. Court Investigations

In ordinary civil litigation, a Danish court is entitled – but has no obligation – to ascertain foreign law on its own. If a Danish court obtains knowledge on its own of relevant foreign law, the court must present this knowledge to the parties and invite the parties to comment on it before making a final decision in the case.[50] In those special proceedings where party autonomy is limited, see *supra* 2, it is assumed that Danish courts have an obligation to ascertain foreign law on their own.[51]

There are no formal requirements as regards the means a court may use to ascertain foreign law. Therefore, a Danish court is free to choose any relevant means. Denmark participates in the Hague Judicial Network, and Denmark has been a member of the Hague Conference since 1955.[52] Denmark has ratified the European Convention of 7 June 1968 on Information on Foreign Law ("London Convention") as well as its protocol of 15 March 1978. The Danish Ministry of Justice has issued guidelines (in Danish) about this convention.[53] There is no statistics available about the use of this convention, but the reported Danish case law shows that this convention is sometimes used by the Danish courts.[54] The convention is mentioned in all

---

[48] Nielsen, *supra* note 27, p. 54, Gomard and Kistrup, *supra* note 16, p. 619.

[49] The first preparatory works for the Danish Administration of Justice Act (from 1877) included a draft provision concerning this matter, but that provision was not part of the final legislative proposal which became the Administration of Justice Act, see Gomard and Kistrup, *supra* note 16, p. 618 in footnote 101

[50] Gomard and Kistrup, *supra* note 16, p. 618.

[51] Gomard and Kistrup, *supra* note 16, p. 618.

[52] For further information, see http://www.hcch.net/index_en.php?act=states.details&sid=25

[53] "Vejledning om tilvejebringelse af oplysninger om fremmed ret" of 15 June 1988 (72/1988).

[54] See, *e.g.*, the Supreme Court decision reported in the Danish Weekly Law Reports 2000, p. 631.

leading Danish text books on this topic, but there seems to be no knowledge about how well it works in facilitating access to information about foreign law.[55]

Denmark is a member state of the European Union, but Denmark has been granted certain opt-outs from the EU treaties, including from the area of freedom, security and justice, and Denmark thus only participates in the EU judicial cooperation at an intergovernmental level. As a consequence, Denmark does not currently participate in the European Judicial Network in civil and commercial matters.[56] However, Denmark does participate in the European e-justice Portal, which includes comprehensive information about the different legal systems of the European member states.[57]

5.2. Input from the Parties

In ordinary civil litigation, a Danish court may ask the parties to ascertain relevant foreign law.[58] The parties may draft a list of relevant legal questions and ask a legal expert of their choice (*e.g.* a professor, a practising lawyer or a relevant legal institution) to prepare a legal opinion. If the parties disagree about how to ascertain foreign law, information about foreign law should be obtained through the London Convention (if applicable) or in another reliable way.[59] The court may here play an active role in approving the questions asked and the procedure for consulting foreign legal expertise.

A party may also choose to obtain a legal opinion about foreign law on his own. If a party has obtained such legal opinion *before* legal proceedings are instituted, that party is normally allowed to submit the legal opinion to the court to support his legal arguments.[60] If, on the other hand, a party obtains a legal opinion on his own *after* legal proceedings are instituted, the party is normally allowed to submit such legal opinion *only if* none of the other parties object to this.[61] When legal

[55] According to L Ervo et al., "Scandinavian Countries", in: Esplugues, Iglesias, Palao (eds.), *supra* note 29, *at* 331–332, the convention "has not worked very well in practice".

[56] See, *inter alia*, Decision 470/2001/EC as amended by Decision 568/2009/EC establishing a European Judicial Network in civil and commercial matters.

[57] See http://e-justice.europa.eu

[58] This explicitly follows from certain Danish legislation, including the Danish Act on Cheques (Section 65) and the Danish Bills of Exchange Act (Section 87). See *e.g.* P A Nielsen, *supra* note 27, p. 52.

[59] See decision of 17 September 2008 from the District Court of Glostrup reported in the Danish Weekly Law Reports 2009, p. 2583, and decision of 25 September 2008 from the District Court of Svendborg (where the London Convention did not apply), reported in TfS 2008, p. 1364, and SKM 2008, p. 814. See also decision of 22 December 1999 from the Supreme Court, reported in the Danish Weekly Law Reports 2000, p. 631.

[60] See decision from the Danish Supreme Court of 11 October 2013, reported in the Danish Weekly Law Reports 2014, p. 138.

[61] See decision from the Danish Supreme Court of 11 November 2010, reported in the Danish Weekly Law Reports 2011, p. 479.

proceedings are instituted, the parties should thus usually cooperate to obtain a legal opinion as described above.

The court is under an obligation to interpret and apply the foreign law in the same way as any "local court" in the relevant foreign country would do. Input from the parties and input obtained from third parties about foreign law is not binding upon the court, but there is no formal mechanism to examine the reliability of the provided legal information about foreign law.

In ordinary civil proceedings, the high degree of party autonomy (*dispositive principle*) generally does not extend to the interpretation and application of "law".[62] However, if the court finds that the relevant foreign law is unclear and the parties agree on a specific interpretation of foreign law which is not (clearly) wrong, the court is likely to base its judgment on this common understanding.[63]

5.3. Costs

Costs related to ascertaining foreign law are regarded as part of the general costs related to civil litigation. Such costs are governed by the rules in chapter 30 of the Danish Administration of Justice Act. It follows from these rules that, as a starting point, each party must make a provisional payment of the costs related to procedural steps taken or requested by him in the course of litigation.[64] A party may, however, request the court to order other parties to make a provisional payment of part of the costs, if other parties have contributed significantly to increasing the costs.[65] The parties can also make an agreement about the provisional payment of the costs related to obtaining information about foreign law, *e.g.* from a legal expert.

If the court on its own initiative seeks to obtain information about foreign law in a way that incurs costs, *e.g.*, by requesting a legal opinion from a foreign legal expert, the court will direct the proportion in which the parties are to make a provisional payment of such costs.[66] A Danish court will usually only take such a procedural step in proceedings governed by the special procedural rules mentioned *supra* 2 where public policy requires the court to seek to ascertain foreign law on its own.

When deciding the case, the court will usually issue an order *ex officio* regarding distribution of costs, unless the parties have made an agreement about the distribution of costs.[67] If a party succeeds with his primary claim, the court will normally order the losing party to pay the costs of that winning party ("the English rule"), but

---

[62] See *supra* 2.2.

[63] Compare (as regards Danish law) Gomard and Kistrup, *supra* note 16, p. 624, and see also *supra* 2.2.

[64] Section 311(1) of the Danish Administration of Justice Act.

[65] Section 311(2) of the Danish Administration of Justice Act.

[66] Section 311(3) of the Danish Administration of Justice Act.

[67] Section 322 of the Danish Administration of Justice Act.

the court may also, in special cases, order the opposing party to pay only a part of these costs or decide that the opposing party shall not pay any costs to the winning party.[68] If no party succeeds with his primary claim, the court may order one party to pay (part of) the costs of the other party or decide that neither party is to pay any costs to the other party.[69] The court will distribute the costs related to ascertaining foreign law based on the *actual costs* incurred by the (substantially) winning party. Such costs are recoverable in full in so far as they have been necessary for the adequate conduct of the case.[70]

If a party has free legal aid ("*fri proces*"), this also covers necessary costs for ascertaining foreign law.

6. Failure to Establish Foreign Law

Different procedural solutions are available if a court is not convinced about the content of the applicable foreign law. If it is likely that foreign law may be sufficiently ascertained within a reasonable time, the court may *stay the proceedings* in order to obtain further information about foreign law through the procedural steps mentioned *supra* 5.[71] This is usually not relevant, if significant efforts to ascertain foreign law have already been made.[72]

If the court cannot ascertain foreign law, it is assumed that the court should normally give judgment based on Danish law (*lex fori*). An appeal case from 1923 provides an example of such situation: The court of first instance had applied Danish law, but before the Supreme Court one of the parties claimed that the court should decide the case according to Dutch law. The Supreme Court rejected this claim and applied Danish law. It is stated in an official footnote to this decision that Dutch law was probably applicable, but that the court of first instance had decided the case based on Danish law and that none of the parties had provided any information about the relevant Dutch law.[73]

A plaintiff's failure to establish the relevant foreign law on which he relies has also in a few older cases caused Danish courts to give judgment in favour of the defendant.[74] In the most recent of these cases (from 1960), the plaintiff had based

[68] For details, see Section 312(1) and (2) of the Danish Administration of Justice Act.

[69] See section 313 of the Danish Administration of Justice Act.

[70] See Section 316 of the Danish Administration of Justice Act.

[71] Under Section 345 of the Danish Administration of Justice Act, a court can stay proceedings if warranted by the situation.

[72] Gomard and Kistrup, *supra* note 16, p. 620, Philip, *supra* note 27, and Nielsen, *supra* note 27, p. 55.

[73] See the comments by A Philip, "Om søpant og pant i skib i den internationale privatret", Ugeskrift for Retsvæsen 1964, B, 121–127, at 123.

[74] See decision of the Danish Supreme Court of 10 December 1969, reported in the Danish Weekly Law Reports 1960, p. 104, and decision of the Maritime and Commercial Court reported in SHT 1923, p. 209.

his claim on a specific understanding of US federal law which was disputed between the parties. Divergent legal opinions showed that the question was controversial under US law and that the question had not been tried by the US Supreme Court. The Danish Supreme Court stated that the plaintiff had not established that the prerequisite for his claim was correct and decided to give judgment in favour of the defendant.[75] The court emphasized that this outcome was the result of the claims and allegations of the parties: The plaintiff had based his claim and allegations on his specific understanding of US law, so the Danish courts could hardly apply *lex fori* instead (which was not comparable).[76] This solution has been criticized by some Danish legal scholars.[77]

Some Danish scholars assume that a Danish court may, in (very) special circumstances, choose a secondary *lex causae* instead of applying *lex fori*.[78] In a case from 1959 concerning a ship collision in Polish waters, the content of the applicable foreign law (*lex loci delicti*, Polish law) could not be ascertained. Instead of applying *lex fori* (Danish law), the Danish Maritime and Commercial Court decided the case based on Finnish law, because it was a Finnish ship that caused the collision. However, the court also noted that the same result would follow from Danish law.[79]

Danish scholars agree that *dismissing the case* is usually not a desirable solution.[80] However, they assume that a Danish court may consider dismissing a case if the basis for jurisdiction in Denmark is vague and there is a more appropriate forum available to the parties (*forum conveniens*), or if a judgment based on Danish law (*lex fori*) will cause a significant loss of rights or result in setting aside significant mandatory rules.[81] Otherwise, the preferred solution is to apply Danish law (*lex fori*).

7. Concluding Remarks

The pragmatic approach to treatment of foreign law in Danish civil litigation analysed in this paper seems to be in line with generally accepted principles such as the Principles for a Future EU Regulation on the Application of Foreign law ("The Madrid Principles")[82] and the ALI/UNIDROIUT Principles of Transnational

---

[75] See decision of 10 December 1969, reported in the Danish Weekly Law Reports 1960, p. 104.

[76] See T Gjerulff, "8. Skibssammenstød – Søforsikring – Fremmed Ret", Tidsskrift for Rettsvitenskap (TfR) (Universitetsforlaget, Oslo, Norway, 1960), 231–237, at 234.

[77] See Schmidt, *supra* note 27, pp. 45–46, Lando, *supra* note 27, p. 10, and Siesby, *supra* note 27, p. 50. However, see also Gomard and Kistrup, *supra* note 16, p. 619.

[78] See Nielsen, *supra* note 27, p. 56, referring to Lando, *supra* note 27.

[79] See decision reported in the Danish Weekly Law Reports 1959, p. 419.

[80] See *e.g.* Nielsen, *supra* note 27, p. 53, Gomard and Kistrup, *supra* note 16, p. 620.

[81] Gomard and Kistrup, *supra* note 16, at 620.

[82] See Esplugues et al., *supra* note 29, at 95–97.

Civil Procedure (Principle 22.1).[83] It is important that the procedural treatment of foreign law in civil litigation also takes into account the specific principles and values of the relevant national procedural law, including the role of judges and party autonomy.[84]

Facilitating access to correct and sufficient information about relevant foreign law remains a significant challenge also in Denmark.[85] Nevertheless, the need to improve access to foreign law has attracted little public attention in Denmark and reported case law provides only few examples of (mainly old) cases where endeavors to establish foreign law have failed. Consequently, it is very difficult to assess the need for new international or regional instruments in this area. However, international instruments generally seem to be useful tools to facilitating access to foreign law and in this regard it is interesting to follow the work in the European Union as well as the work in the Hague Conference on Private International Law on a three-part Convention to Facilitate Access to Foreign Law.[86]

---

[83] Available at www.unidroit.org

[84] Compare S Geeroms, *supra* note 26, at 389–393. For a comparative analysis of the fundamental aims, principles and values of Nordic civil procedure law, see C Salung Petersen, "A Comparative Perspective on recent Nordic Reforms of Civil Justice: A Common Nordic Approach?" in: L Ervo and A Nylund (eds.), "The future of Civil Litigation", Springer 2014.

[85] It is indeed a global challenge, see *inter alia* Conclusions and Recommendations from the Joint Conference of the European Commission and the Hague Conference on Private International Law concerning Access to Foreign Law in Civil and Commercial Matters (held on 15–17 February 2012), available at: http://www.hcch.net/index_en.php?act=events.details&year=2012&varevent=248

[86] See Preliminary Document No 11 A of March 2009, available at: http://www.hcch.net/upload/wop/genaff_pd11a2009e.pdf

Estonia: Applying Foreign Law in Estonia – The Perspective of an e-State

Maarja Torga

Abstract Estonian courts do not often apply foreign law. However, it is to be expected that the introduction of the new Estonian e-residency program would bring along the rise in the cases involving foreign element. This development would lead to the Estonian judges needing to apply and establish the contents of foreign law more often. There are several tools, which the Estonian judges could use for that purpose, but these tools are unfortunately not perfect. Hopefully, the mechanisms of cooperation that could be taken on a European and international level in the future would enable Estonian judges to more efficiently establish the contents of foreign law. Ideally, such mechanisms should be in the form of an e-databases or online platforms enabling the judges to ask assistance from foreign judges or experts.

I. Conflict of Laws Rules

Conflict of laws rules are not contained in the Estonian Code of Civil Procedure (CCP),[1] but in various other instruments. However, conflict of laws rules are still regarded as a special type of procedural law in Estonia. This means that Estonian judge or another authority required to apply conflict of laws rules is bound to apply such rules *ex officio* whenever the conditions for the application of such rules are met. Since Estonian conflict of laws rules are perceived to have procedural nature, Estonian authorities would always apply their own conflict of laws rules, except when a particular conflict of laws rule applicable in Estonia expressly allows the application of a foreign conflict of laws rule. In addition, the obligation of a judge or other authority to apply conflict of laws rules does not depend on the parties pleading the application of such rules - the courts and other authorities have to apply Estonian conflict of laws rules on their own initiative.

---

[1] *Tsiviilkohtumenetluse seadustik*. (Code of Civil Procedure). 20.04.2005, RT I 2005, 26, 197.

M. Torga (✉)
Lecturer, University of Tartu, Tartu, Estonia
e-mail: maarja.torga@ut.ee

Y. Nishitani (ed.), *Treatment of Foreign Law - Dynamics towards Convergence?*,
Ius Comparatum – Global Studies in Comparative Law 26,
DOI 10.1007/978-3-319-56574-3_6

Since Estonian conflict of laws rules are contained in different types of instruments (international conventions, EU regulations and national law instruments),[2] it is not surprising that the main connecting factors used in such rules vary considerably. While the national rules and European rules mainly use a person's place of residence or habitual residence as the main connecting factors, Estonian international agreements, such as the broad legal assistance treaty concluded with the Russian Federation,[3] often refer to a person's nationality as the main connecting factor. Since there are currently very many Russian nationals living in Estonia,[4] the most commonly applied foreign law in Estonian courts is thus that of the Russian Federation. The second most often applied foreign law in Estonia is probably Finnish law, though this is just an estimation based on the fact, that Finland is the main destination of Estonian emigration[5] and hence the number of cases involving Finnish element has been on the rise since the restoration of Estonian independence in 1991. The number of cases where the foreign law would actually have been applied is, however, not very high. On one hand this is due to the smallness of Estonian population and the small number of courts,[6] but might also be caused by the Estonian authorities not being familiar with the relevant conflict of laws rules calling for the application of foreign law.

II. Foreign Law Before Judicial Authorities

A. Nature of Foreign Law

Estonian judge has a duty to apply foreign substantive law if, according to conflict of law rules, such application is designated. This obligation to apply foreign law *ex officio* comes from Art 2(1) of the Estonian Private International Law Act (PILA),[7] which can be regarded as a general part to all conflict of laws rules applicable in

[2] Conflict of laws rules applicable in Estonian courts and before the other Estonian authorities are allocated between various international conventions, European Union regulations and national laws. For a general overview on such instruments see: K. Sein and others. Private International Law Estonia. Kluwer Law International 2013, pp. 31–39.

[3] *Eesti Vabariigi ja Vene Föderatsiooni leping õigusabi ja õigussuhete kohta tsiviil-, perekonna- ja kriminaalasjades*. (Treaty between the Republic of Estonia and Russian Federation on legal assistance and legal relationships in civil, family and criminal matters). 12.05.1993. RT II 1993, 16, 27.

[4] According to 31.12.2011 poll there were 105,605 foreign nationals living in Estonia of whom 90,510 had Russian nationality. See: Database of the Statistical Office of Estonia, available at: http://pub.stat.ee/px-web.2001/Dialog/statfile2.asp (visited November 2014).

[5] Statistical Office of Estonia Press Release 28 May 2012, available at: http://www.stat.ee/57429/ (visited November 2014).

[6] Currently, there are only four courts of first instance dealing with civil and commercial matters for the whole Estonia (Harju County Court, Tartu County Court, Pärnu County Court and Viru County Court), two appellate courts (Tallinn Circuit Court and Tartu Circuit Court) and one court of cassation (the Supreme Court of the Republic of Estonia).

[7] *Rahvusvahelise eraõiguse seadus* (Private International Law Act). 27.03.2002. RT I 2002, 35, 217.

Estonian courts. Although a judge can ask parties to present evidence on the contents of foreign law (Art 4(1) of the PILA), the inability of the parties to present such evidence would not free Estonian judge from the obligation to apply foreign law. If the evidence on the content of foreign law has been presented, Estonian judge would not be bound by such evidence (Art 4(2) of the PILA). Similarly, the evidence or arguments presented by the parties on the content of Estonian own substantive law would not be binding on Estonian judge.[8] Thus, foreign law is considered as a 'law' in Estonia and has almost equal standing to Estonian own substantive law.

There is, however, one aspect where Estonian substantive law and foreign substantive law are given different treatment in Estonian courts. According to Art 4(4) of the PILA Estonian courts can refuse to apply designated foreign law if the content of such foreign law cannot be determined within a reasonable time despite all efforts taken by the court. In these situations Estonian courts would apply Estonian own substantive law instead of foreign substantive law. Thus, although foreign law is generally considered as 'law' which has equal standing to Estonian own substantive law, for practical considerations, Estonian courts could excuse themselves from applying foreign law if it is impossible for them to familiarize themselves with the content of foreign law – an excuse which they could never make in relation to Estonian own substantive law and which in Estonian case-law has only been referred to as a theoretical possibility.[9]

B. Application of Foreign Law

As a general rule, Estonian courts have a duty to apply foreign law *ex officio* regardless of whether the parties plead it (Art 2(1) of the PILA). This rule is, however, subject to one exception. Namely, in the cases where the conflict of laws rules allow parties to choose applicable law, Estonian courts would have to apply Estonian own substantive law, if both parties rely on Estonian substantive law during the proceedings instead of pleading foreign law which would be applicable in the absence of the choice of law. Such 'silent agreements' to disregard otherwise applicable foreign law and apply Estonian substantive law instead, are, however, allowed only in limited cases: most often in relation to contracts and non-contractual obligations and only rarely in family- and succession matters.[10] The, Estonian Supreme Court has

[8] This can be derived from Art 477(5) of the CCP and from the principle established by the Supreme Court that the courts are not bound by the arguments on the content of law presented by the parties. See for example: Order of the Civil Chamber of the Supreme Court of 7 June 2011 No 3-2-1-44-11, Judgment of the Civil Chamber of the Supreme Court of 22 February 2011 No 3-2-1-153-10.

[9] Order of the Civil Chamber of the Estonian Supreme Court of 15 November 2010 No 3-2-1-100-10, Judgment of the Civil Chamber of the Estonian Supreme Court of 9 December 2009 No 3-2-1-119-09, Judgment of the Estonian Civil Chamber of the Supreme Court of 29 September 2003 No 3-2-1-100-03.

[10] On the extent of party autonomy in Estonian private international law, see: M. Torga. *Kohalduva õiguse ja selle sisu kindlakstegemine rahvusvahelistes eraõiguslikes vaidlustes.* (Determining the Applicable Law and Its Contents in International Civil Cases). Juridica V 2014, pp. 406–408.

given effect to such 'silent agreements' only in contractual disputes[11] and disputes over certain non-contractual obligations.[12]

C. Ascertainment of Foreign Law

Since foreign law is deemed to have an equal standing to Estonian own substantive law, the principle of *iura novit curia* applies to the determination of the content of foreign law, just as it applies to the determination of the content of Estonian own substantive law.[13] Although Estonian judge can ask parties to present themselves with the evidence on foreign law (Art 4(1) of the PILA), the inability of the parties to do this would not change the judge's obligation to determine the contents of foreign law. In addition, Estonian courts would not be bound by the documents, which the parties present on the contents of foreign law (Art 4(2) of the PILA), but would have to determine the true meaning of foreign law by themselves. In order to do this, Estonian courts have a wide range of options that they can use.

1. Diplomatic Channels and Requests Under Broad Legal Assistance Treaties

The courts are entitled to turn to the Estonian Ministry of Justice and the Ministry of Foreign Affairs for help in order to determine the contents of foreign law (Art 4(3) of the PILA). It is presumed that the ministries would use their contacts and (in the case of Ministry of Foreign Affairs) diplomatic channels of the Republic of Estonia in order to fulfil such requests. The Ministry of Justice can also submit requests under the broad legal assistance treaties concluded by the Republic of Estonia with certain near-by states to establish the content of the law of those states.[14] Unfortunately

[11] Judgement of the Civil Chamber of the Estonian Supreme Court of 5 October 2010 No 3-2-1-52-10.

[12] Namely, in relation to a non-contractual obligation to compensate for unlawful damage and a non-contractual obligation to present a document. See respectively: Judgement of the Civil Chamber of the Estonian Supreme Court of 23 May 2012 No 3-2-1-53-12, Order of the Civil Chamber of the Supreme Court of 17 January 2011 No 3-2-1-108-10.

[13] This is established by the line of case-law of the Supreme Court, see for example: Order of the Civil Chamber of the Supreme Court of 7 June 2011 No 3-2-1-44-11, Judgment of the Civil Chamber of the Supreme Court of 22 February 2011 No 3-2-1-153-10.

[14] Currently, the Republic of Estonia has concluded four such treaties with Latvia, Lithuania, Poland, Russia and Ukraine. For the respective treaties see: *Eesti Vabariigi, Leedu Vabariigi ja Läti Vabariigi õigusabi ja õigussuhete leping*. - RT II 1993, 6, 5 (Treaty between the Republic of Estonia, Republic of Lithuania and the Republic of Latvia on legal assistance and legal relationships); *Eesti Vabariigi ja Poola Vabariigi vaheline leping õigusabi osutamise ja õigussuhete kohta tsiviil-, töö- ning kriminaalasjades*. - RT II 1999, 4, 22 (Treaty between the Republic of Estonia and the Republic of Poland on legal assistance and legal relationships in employment, civil and and criminal matters); *Eesti Vabariigi ja Vene Föderatsiooni leping õigusabi ja õigussuhete kohta tsiviil-, perekonna- ja kriminaalasjades*. - RT II 1993, 16, 27 (Treaty between the Republic of Estonia and Russian Federation on legal assistance and legal relationships in civil, family and criminal matters); *Eesti Vabariigi ja Ukraina leping õigusabi ja õigussuhete kohta tsiviil- ning kriminaalasjades*. - RT II 1995, 13/14, 63 (Treaty between the Republic of Estonia and Ukraine on legal assistance and legal relationships in civil and criminal matters).

these methods are often not very successful, as the Estonian ministries do not have sufficient funding and staff to determine the contents of foreign law themselves and since there are no mechanisms to force the authorities of other states to provide information on the content of their laws.

2. Expert Opinions

In addition to asking help from Estonian ministries, Estonian courts could use experts in order to determine the content of foreign law (Art 4(3) of the PILA). The law does not specify whether a court would have to hear the expert in person or whether a court could turn to foreign experts, but it can be presumed that these options are also possible, though not mandatory. Thus, Estonian courts could theoretically also turn to foreign experts or foreign institutes specialised on determining the contents of foreign law, as there are currently no expert institutes in Estonia, which would specifically deal with determining the contents of foreign law. According to Art 294(1) of the CCP an expert can be someone who has the necessary knowledge and experience in order to give expert opinion. This is the minimum qualification that a foreign expert should have according to Estonian law. The opinion of an expert would not be binding on the Estonian court asking for such opinion, as it would only be one among the other evidence on the content of foreign law, which the judge has to assess.

3. Other Methods

Besides appointing experts or asking help from the Estonian ministries, Estonian courts could use various other methods to try to establish the content of foreign law. As Art 234 of the CCP expressly states, a court can use 'other means' to obtain information on foreign law, though the exact meaning of such 'other means' has not been specified. For example, an Estonian judge could directly ask help from a foreign judge, provided that he trusts the information that the foreign judge provides. In addition, a judge could, in principle, look for a foreign legal acts in Internet, though it is generally believed that only the official gazettes of the other states should be used on the condition that the accuracy of such databases is not in question and they provide up-to-date information on foreign law. A helpful starting point in this respect could be the European n-lex database,[15] which provides information on the State Gazettes of the Member States of the European Union. However, there is yet no record, that Estonian courts have ever used this database in practice.

Depending on the method that is used in order to determine the content of foreign law, the parties might become responsible for bearing the costs for such determination. There are no detailed rules on who would have to bear the costs if a judge has asked for an assistance from the ministries or when a judge has searched something

[15] See: N-lex. A Common Gateway to National Law. Available: http://eur-lex.europa.eu/n-lex/ (visited November 2014).

in Internet – it is presumed that these actions should be done for free, or at least, that all possible expenses related to such actions should be borne by the state. However, the parties are responsible for procedural expenses, including the reasonable costs that the winning party has made in order to draw up the documents submitted to the courts. The expert fees are also considered to be part of the court fees, which are borne by the loosing party (Art 143(1) of the CCP).

D. Interpretation and Application of Foreign Law

Since foreign law has an equal standing to Estonian own substantive law, foreign case-law on the interpretation of foreign law should be taken into account when interpreting foreign law, such as Estonian case-law is taken into account when interpreting Estonian law. When applying foreign law, an Estonian judge therefore has to take into account the interpretations and practices applicable in the foreign state which law is to be applied by the Estonian court (Art 2(2) of the PILA). For example, if there is a gap in foreign law, the Estonian court would have to determine how this gap would be filled under the applicable foreign law. However, since under Estonian own substantive law a gap would be filled by analogy (Art 4 of the General Part to the Civil Code[16]), it is likely, that Estonian courts could be tempted to use this method to fill a gap in foreign law as well.

E. Failure to Establish Foreign Law

If the content of foreign law cannot be established within a reasonable time regardless of all the efforts of Estonian judge, then judge would apply Estonian own substantive law instead of the foreign law designated by conflict of laws rules (Art 4(4) of the PILA). However, this option should not be used lightly – a judge should use the methods prescribed by PILA and CCP for determining the content of foreign law before she can refuse to apply the designated foreign law.[17] Only if the parties have failed to provide evidence on foreign law and there are no competent experts to be found who could help the court to establish the content of foreign law and if the requests to the ministries have not been successful, can the court declare that it is impossible to determine the content of foreign law.

[16] *Tsiviilseadusiku üldosa seadus*. 27.03.2002, RT I 2002, 35, 216. (General Part of the Civil Code Act).

[17] Order of the Civil Chamber of the Estonian Supreme Court of 15 November 2010 No 3-2-1-100-10, Judgment of the Civil Chamber of the Estonian Supreme Court of 9 December 2009 No 3-2-1-119-09, Judgment of the Estonian Civil Chamber of the Supreme Court of 29 September 2003 No 3-2-1-100-03.

III. Judicial Review

In the cases where conflict of laws rules have been applied erroneously by Estonian lower courts, the parties can appeal to higher courts including the Estonia Supreme Court. The CCP generously provides for the review of lower courts' judgements for the cases where conflict of laws rules or foreign law has been applied incorrectly by the lower courts. For example, under Art 668(1) of the CCP the parties may appeal to the Supreme Court if the appellate court has substantially breached a procedural rule (including conflict of laws rules, which should be considered as procedural rules for the purpose of this provision)[18] or because the appellate court has wrongly applied substantive law rules (including the substantive law of a foreign state designated by the conflict of law rules).[19]

IV. Foreign Law in Other Instances

The rules applicable to courts on the application of foreign law are also binding on the other Estonian public authorities (Art 5 of the PILA), though these authorities do not necessarily have the same possible mechanisms available to them in order to determine the contents of foreign law as do the courts. For example, the procedure for appointing experts is reserved only to the courts as the rules on the appointment of experts are contained in the CCP, which covers only civil proceedings in courts. However, all the other public authorities could, similarly to the courts, ask assistance from the Ministry of Justice and the Ministry of Foreign Affairs or from the parties in order to determine the contents of the applicable foreign law.

The other Estonian public authorities, which might need to apply foreign law, are most often notaries and vital statistic offices. For example, notaries could be required to apply foreign law when issuing certificates on succession or deciding upon marriage or divorce.[20] Vital statistics offices might need to apply foreign law in divorce matters, though this rarely happens in practice as courts and not the vital statistics offices generally deal with international divorce cases.[21] Any arbitral tribunal, mediation body or other similar alternative dispute resolution body located in Estonia could also apply foreign law. However, since these bodies are not considered as public

---

[18] See: Judgment of the Civil Chamber of the Estonian Supreme Court of 16 January 2013 No 3-2-1179–12; Judgment of the Civil Chamber of the Estonian Supreme Court of 5 March 2014, No 3-2-1-187-13.

[19] Note, however, that so far Estonian higher courts have not overturned the lower court's judgments for the reasons relating to the way that foreign law has been interpreted or applied by the lower courts.

[20] As of 2010, Estonian notaries are competent to certify marriages or divorce spouses. See: Art 29(3)7 of the *Notariaadiseadus*. 06.12.2000, RT I 2000, 104, 684 (Notaries Act).

[21] According to Art 64 of the *Perekonnaseadus*. 18.11.2009, RT I 2009, 60, 396 (Family Law Act) a vital statistics office can divorce spouses only if the spouses live in Estonia.

authorities within the meaning of Art 5 of the PILA, the rules on the application of foreign law contained in the PILA are not applicable to such bodies and there is no data collected on how often these bodies actually apply foreign law. However, it can be assumed, that foreign law is not often applied in arbitral proceedings conducted in Estonia. This is so because, although arbitral tribunals situated in Estonian would always apply the law chosen by the parties (Art 742(1) of the CCP), if the parties have not agreed on the applicable law, Estonian law would be applied (Art 742(2) of the CCP) and it is unlikely that parties would choose to arbitrate in Estonia without choosing Estonian law as the applicable law. If the parties to arbitration have chosen to apply foreign law, the arbitrators would proceed from the evidence that the parties have submitted to the tribunal in order to determine the content of such foreign law. The arbitral tribunal could also appoint experts (Art 739 of the CCP) or ask help from the courts (Art 740 of the CCP) in order to establish the content of foreign law.

Estonian attorneys advising clients in international civil matters would probably try to collect information on foreign law through sources available in Internet, but they could also use various networks of contacts available to different law offices. But if foreign law is the core issue in a legal dispute, Estonian lawyers would probably refrain from giving advice on such matters and would instead refer their clients to their colleagues abroad, as they are generally not qualified to give advice on foreign law.

V. Access to Foreign Law: Status Quo

The Republic of Estonia is a party to the European Convention of 7 June 1968 on Information on Foreign Law (the London Convention).[22] In addition, the Republic of Estonia has concluded legal assistance treaties with Ukraine, Russian Federation Poland, Lithuania and Latvia.[23] All these treaties could be used in order to ask assistance from other states in order to determine the content of foreign laws. However, the requests to give information on foreign law are rarely made based on these treaties. Since the request procedure provided by the treaties could be criticized as being relatively time-consuming, it might be assumed that Estonian judges just find it more useful to use other mechanisms in order to determine the content of applicable foreign law.

Though Estonia is proud to be an e-State, which can boast with its highly advanced electronic databases on Estonian own legislation[24] and case-law,[25] no

[22] In Estonian: Välisriikide õigusinfo Euroopa konventsioon. 06.06.1968. RT II 1997, 7, 35.

[23] See footnote 15.

[24] The Estonian electronic state gazette (*Riigiteataja*, available at: www.riigiteataja.ee, visited November 2014) offers a very quick and simple search mechanism for finding any current or past Estonian legal acts (including laws, decrees of local governments or Estonian international agreements), their amendments or the versions of legal acts in force on any given date in the past.

[25] Case-law from all Estonian courts is daily published in the official gazette (*Riigiteataja*) where it can be accessed by anyone. Up-to-date publication is possible as most of the civil proceedings is conducted electronically. For example, Estonian judges are required by law to sign their judgments by using electronic and not manual signing (Art 441(1) of the CCP). Estonian Supreme Court's judgments are additionally published in the Supreme Court's own web-page: www.riigikohus.ee (visited November 2014).

sources on foreign laws are offered by the Estonian government. Estonian judges can, of course, access the European Judicial Network's e-Justice portal[26] and other similar web-pages which offer a gate-way to the laws of different states. However, not all Estonian judges might be aware of the existence of such pages though attention to them has been drawn in various judicial training programs. In addition, the Estonian judges might not be prone to trust the information provided by such web-pages as the information on Estonian own law is sometimes not as up-to-date on these pages as it should be and the judges might be tempted to assume the same about the information on the laws of the other Member States. In practice, the burden to research foreign law thus often lies on the parties. The judges can, however, also use their personal connections with the other state's judges in order to request the information on the content of the applicable foreign laws. Most such requests would be made in English as English is widely spoken in Estonia.

VI. Access to Foreign Law: Further Developments

A. Practical Need

There is definitely a need to improve access to foreign law in Estonia as more and more cases that reach the courts involve international element. International civil cases which currently reach Estonian courts can generally be divided into three types of cases: consumer disputes involving Estonians who have left Estonia and who are later sued in Estonian courts, employment disputes involving Estonians working in Finland and family- and succession disputes involving either Russian nationals living in Estonia or persons who have left Estonia within the last decade. In the first type of cases, the courts would often apply Estonian own consumer law or a very similar consumer regulation of the other Member States, so the need to establish the content of foreign law is not so pressing. In the second type of cases, the courts might need to apply foreign law, but due to the nature of such employment disputes, the parties usually provide the courts with the evidence on the content of foreign law. In the last type of cases, however, the disputes often involve parties who do not have good access to or knowledge on the content of foreign law. This means that the burden to establish the content on foreign law is put on the courts and other authorities required to apply foreign law.

The number of Estonian cases involving foreigners is expected to grow considerably in the future, taking into account the recent initiative of the Estonian government to introduce a so-called e-residency[27] plan. E-residency allows anyone from anywhere in the world to use Estonian governmental services and offers an opportunity to give digital signatures in an electronic environment which would be equal

[26] Available at: https://e-justice.europa.eu/home.do (visited November 2014).

[27] See further: https://e-estonia.com/e-residents/e-residency/ (visited November 2014).

to face-to-face identification and handwritten signatures in the European Union. In combination to the relative ease of an e-resident to set up a company in Estonia[28] this opportunity is expected to encourage foreigners even more to start doing business in Estonia or through Estonian companies.

B. Conflict of Laws Solutions

Conflict of laws rules contained in Estonian national law, in the EU regulations applicable in Estonia and in international conventions that the Republic of Estonia has joined generally point to the law that the parties could most likely have foreseen when entering into legal relationships or assuming rights and obligations. The same cannot, however, always be said about the conflict of laws rules contained in the broad legal assistance treaties concluded by the Republic of Estonia with its neighboring states.[29]

The conflict of laws rules contained in the broad legal assistance treaties that the Republic of Estonia has concluded with its neighboring states often use nationality of persons as the main connecting factor in family and succession matters. However, this is not always the best solution in terms of foreseeability and legal certainty. For example, applying the nationality principle in relation to Russian nationals living in Estonia might not be in the best interest of such people. Often, these people own property in Estonia, work in Estonia and have lived in Estonia for several decades. Applying Russian law to the family or succession disputes involving such people might not be foreseeable to such people as their ties to Estonian legal system are often much stronger than to Russian law - the legal system of the state of their nationality. Since the broad legal assistance treaties do not allow party autonomy in family and succession disputes, the parties and courts are burdened to establish the content of Russian law in the cases involving Russian nationals even if the parties would like to plead Estonian own substantive law in these types of cases. At the moment, there is a very large minority of Russian nationals living in Estonia,[30] which triggers a large number of legal disputes in courts. Hence, there is a practical need to try to renegotiate the conflict of laws rules contained in the broad legal assistance treaty concluded with the neighboring state of the Republic of Estonia, especially the one concluded with the Russian Federation.

[28] Currently, a private limited company can be set up electronically via the e-Business Register's Company Registration Portal if the person wishing to register a company, has an Estonian ID card, if the contribution of share capital is paid electronically via the same portal, all of the persons involved in establishing the company have a registered place of residence in Estonia and all of the founders, members of the management board and other persons related to the entry have an ID-card and can provide digital signatures. Such registration would take less than 30 min and would be available to the future Estonian e-residents. See further: https://www.eesti.ee/eng/topics (visited November 2014).

[29] For the list of these treaties, see footnote 15.

[30] According to the 2011 poll, out of 1,294,236 people living in Estonia, 89,913 were Russian nationals. See: http://www.stat.ee/64305 (visited November 2014).

Another way of avoiding practical problems which the obligation to apply foreign law may entail, could theoretically be the adoption of a rule in Estonian case law according to which a judge would apply the conflict of laws rules only when so pleaded by the parties. Although Estonian legislator has not expressly prohibited such practice, Estonian judges are used to think of foreign law as something 'equal' to Estonian law, which has to be applied *ex officio* by the court. The system where parties have to plead and prove foreign law in order for it to be applied would mean that foreign law would suddenly have a lower standing in Estonia than Estonian own law. This kind of legal thinking is alien to Estonian lawyers. Thus, instead of trying to change the current doctrine, the attention should rather be given to improving access to foreign law.

C. Methods of Facilitating Access to Foreign Law

Estonian judges are used to working with various e-resources. Thus, from an Estonian point of view, it would be very beneficial to have an electronic portal similar to eur-lex, which enables access to different national laws. Such database should be easily searchable, reliable and up-to-date and should contain (at least) English translation of various legislation. The further development of the n-lex[31] portal, which provides an access to national laws of the Member States of the European Union, would be a very welcomed initiative in this respect. Although international and regional instruments establishing administrative and/or judicial cooperation to exchange information on participating State's law would be very useful tools as well, individual judges might be reluctant to fulfil incoming requests based on such instruments and the question whether a foreign authority has provided Estonian judge with all the relevant information on foreign law might arise. In the end of the day, it is the responsibility of the judge solving the case to apply foreign law. Thus, the judge should himself also have an access to the whole system of foreign law and the judicial assistance and administrative cooperation should be used only for getting the requesting judge on the right track or for double-checking whether the understanding of foreign law that the judge has acquired by himself or with the help of the parties or experts has been correct. A judge should always have an opportunity to directly go to the sources of foreign law himself. For this purpose, it would be ideal if a common international, single-format and up-to-date database on foreign law combined with the possibility to request further assistance online from a foreign expert would exist.

[31] http://n-lex.europa.eu (visited November 2014).

France – The Evolving Balance Between the Judge and the Parties in France

Sabine Corneloup

Abstract Balancing between conflicting considerations of private international law justice on the one hand and procedural economy on the other, the *Cour de cassation* has over the past decades progressively strengthened the role of the judge. Today, the application of the conflict of laws rule is mandatory if the proceedings involve rights which the parties cannot freely dispose of or if, in the case of rights which the parties can freely dispose of, one party invokes the conflict of laws. However, as fundamental changes have affected both substantial and conflict of laws rules, the concept of 'rights which the parties can freely dispose of' has become inappropriate, and the position of the *Cour de cassation* is expected to evolve in the near future. The judge who has acknowledged that foreign law is applicable, either because he has applied ex officio the conflict of laws rule or because a party has pleaded foreign law, must ascertain its content, with the assistance of the parties and even personally if necessary.

S. Corneloup (✉)
Professor, University of Paris II (Panthéon-Assas), Paris, France
e-mail: sabine.corneloup@u-paris2.fr

Y. Nishitani (ed.), *Treatment of Foreign Law - Dynamics towards Convergence?*,
Ius Comparatum – Global Studies in Comparative Law 26,
DOI 10.1007/978-3-319-56574-3_7

I. Introduction

In France, the procedural status of conflict of laws rules and the application of foreign law is governed by case law. Since 1999,[1] the legal basis referred to by the *Cour de cassation* has been Art. 3 of the *Code civil*[2] which is the general provision of the *Code civil* on the applicable law.[3] As this provision contains no explicit solution, all principles have been forged by the *Cour de cassation.* The regime has evolved in depth during the last decades and even if it has acquired some stability since 2005,[4] it is not unlikely to change again in the near future. The hesitations of the *Cour de cassation* result from the opposition of two contradictory objectives that need to be reconciled. On the one hand, considerations of private international law justice require that the conflict of laws rule be applied *ex officio* by the judge who should also ascertain the content of foreign law himself, if the parties fail to provide sufficient proof. Indeed, conflict of laws rules serve specific purposes which are not compatible with a merely facultative applicability. On the other hand, considerations of procedural economy require a more pragmatic approach. The knowledge and interpretation of foreign law raise important difficulties that should not be underestimated. The risk of erroneous application of a foreign law is quite significant. Moreover, it implies additional costs for the parties and a delayed outcome of the proceedings. The *Cour de cassation* is particularly concerned that one party might raise the argument of the applicability of a foreign law only as a delaying tactic. Therefore a realistic solution advocates for not placing unnecessary burden upon the judge and the parties.[5] Balancing between these objectives, the *Cour de cassation* has progressively elaborated its position through a complex framework of

---

[1] 1e Civ., 26.5. 1999, *Soc. Mutuelle du Mans*, *Rev. crit. DIP* 1999. 707, comm. H. Muir Watt. Before this decision, the *Cour de cassation* referred to Art. 12 of the *Code de procédure civile*: "The judge settles the dispute in accordance with the rules of law applicable thereto. He must give or restore their proper legal definitions to the disputed facts and deeds notwithstanding the denominations given by the parties. However, he may not change the denomination or legal ground where the parties, pursuant to an express agreement and in the exercise of such rights that they may freely alienate, have bound him by legal definitions and legal arguments to which they intend to restrict the debate. Where a dispute has arisen, the parties may, under the same matters and conditions, confer upon the judge a mandate to determine a case as an amicable compounder subject to an appeal where the parties have not expressly abandoned their right of appeal". The change in the legal basis of the regime is interpreted as a shift from considerations of procedural economy to those of private international law: H. Muir Watt, "Loi étrangère", Répertoire de droit international, Dalloz, 2010, n° 5.

[2] Art. 3 states: "Statutes relating to public policy and safety are binding on all those living on the territory. Immovables are governed by French law even when owned by aliens. Statutes relating to the status and capacity of persons govern French persons, even those residing in foreign countries".

[3] B. Ancel, "Destinées de l'article 3 du Code civil", in Le droit international privé: esprit et méthodes, Mélanges en l'honneur de Paul Lagarde, 2005, Dalloz, p. 1.

[4] 1e Civ., 28. 6 .2005, *Aubin*, Com., 28. 6. 2005, *Itraco*, *Rev. crit. DIP* 2005. 645, comm. B. Ancel, H. Muir Watt.

[5] M.-L. Niboyet, G. de Geouffre de la Pradelle, *Droit international privé*, LGDJ, 2015, n° 669.

numerous decisions based on subtle shades of meaning. The general tendency in this evolution is the strengthening of the role of the judge. The current state of the compromise reached by the *Cour de cassation* can be summarized as follows: the application of the conflict of laws rule is mandatory if the proceedings involve rights which the parties cannot freely dispose of or if, in the case of rights which the parties can freely dispose of, one party invokes the conflict of laws. The judge who has acknowledged that foreign law is applicable, either because he has applied *ex officio* the conflict of laws rule or because a party has pleaded foreign law, must ascertain its content, with the assistance of the parties and even personally if necessary.

The topic will be addressed in the following developments through four specific issues: the procedural status of conflict of laws rules (II), the application of foreign law by judicial authorities (III), the judicial review of the application of conflict of laws rules and of foreign law (IV) and the application of foreign law by non-judicial authorities (V).

II. Conflict of Laws Rules

The *Cour de cassation* no longer applies the *Bisbal* ruling, according to which conflict of laws rules were for a long time considered in France to be facultative for the judge.[6] This ruling has been replaced by a distinction based upon the nature of the rights involved in the proceedings.[7] The criterion of the distinction is whether the parties have, or have not, free disposal of their rights (A). It determines the role of the judge (B) as well as the scope of party autonomy during the proceedings (C). *De lege ferenda*, an evolution is desirable, in order to take into account some fundamental reforms that have taken place in the past 15 years (D).

A. The Distinction Between Available and Unavailable Rights

The whole regime built by the *Cour de cassation* is based on the distinction between *droits indisponibles* and *droits disponibles*.[8] It has already been shown that several English translations of these expressions are conceivable but that none of them fits perfectly.[9] Literally, *droits disponibles* are rights the parties can freely dispose of. In other words, these rights are of such nature that the parties are free to resolve the

[6] 1e Civ., 12. 5. 1959, *Bisbal, Rev. crit. DIP* 1960. 62, comm. H. Batiffol, *JDI* 1960. 810, comm. J.-B. Sialelli.

[7] 1e Civ., 26. 5. 1999, *Soc. Mutuelle du Mans, Rev. crit. DIP* 1999. 707, comm. H. Muir Watt.

[8] On this distinction, see especially B. Fauvarque-Cosson, *Libre disponibilité des droits et conflits de lois*, LGDJ, 1996.

[9] S. Fulli-Lemaire, D. Rojas-Tamayo, "France", in C. Esplugues, J. L. Iglesias, G. Palao (ed.), *Application of Foreign Law*, Sellier, 2011, p. 187.

dispute by a settlement.[10] Parties can waive these rights. The distinction is sometimes translated by *available* and *unavailable rights* which seems to be a convenient solution.[11] The criterion was introduced for the first time by Henri Batiffol in order to reduce the negative effects of the *Bisbal* ruling.[12] The *Cour de cassation* has referred to it since 1984 (burden of proof of foreign law)[13] and 1990 (application of the conflict of laws rule),[14] but without giving any general definition.

It is necessary to determine according to which law a right is to be characterized as available or unavailable. French authors hesitated between the *lex causae* and the *lex fori*.[15] As the distinction governs the applicability of the conflict of laws rule of the forum, and as it raises a question of procedure, the characterization is to be operated according to the lex fori. Moreover it would have been puzzling to apply a foreign law in order to decide whether the judge must apply foreign law....[16] The rights are therefore characterized according to French law. However this does not resolve all issues. It is still to be determined what makes a right unavailable. The fact that mandatory rules govern the right is generally not considered to be sufficient, as the example of arbitration agreements demonstrates. According to Art. 2059 of the *Code civil,* all persons may make arbitration agreements relating to rights of which they have the free disposal; but at the same time subject matters which are governed by mandatory rules are clearly not excluded from arbitration. Moreover, mandatory rules increasingly exist in patrimonial matters, for example, to protect the weaker party in a contract, while party autonomy has been introduced in matters of personal status. Another approach has been proposed, which is also used for the waiver of rights and which depends on the – public or private – nature of the interest at stake.[17] If public interest dominates, the rights are unavailable. Art. 2060 of the *Code civil* mentions as rights of which the parties do not have free disposal – and therefore may not enter into arbitration agreement – matters of status and capacity of the persons as well as matters relating to divorce and judicial separation. More precisely, according to the *Cour de cassation,* this is the case, among

[10] M. Bogdan, "Private International Law as Component of the Law of the Forum: General Course on Private International Law", RCADI 2011, vol. 348, p. 100.

[11] S. Fulli-Lemaire, D. Rojas-Tamayo, *op. cit.*

[12] H. Batiffol, *Rev. crit. DIP* 1960. 62

[13] 1e Civ., 24. 1. 1984, *Thinet, Rev. crit. DIP* 1985. 89, comm. P. Lagarde, *JDI* 1984. 874, comm. J.-M. Bischoff.

[14] 1e Civ., 4. 12. 1990, *Coveco, Rev. crit. DIP* 1991. 558, comm. M.-L. Niboyet, *JDI* 1991. 371, comm. D. Bureau.

[15] B. Ancel, Y. Lequette, Les grands arrêts de la jurisprudence française de droit international privé, Dalloz, 2006, n° 84.11.

[16] P. Mayer, V. Heuzé, *Droit international privé*, Montchrestien, 2010, n° 147–1.

[17] B. Fauvarque-Cosson, Libre disponibilité des droits et conflits de lois, LGDJ, 1996, n° 192 f.

others, of rights relating to divorce,[18] nullity of marriage,[19] parentage,[20] and capacity.[21] On the contrary, rights relating for example to commercial and civil contracts,[22] non-contractual obligations,[23] successions,[24] or the legal personality of a company[25] are considered to be available.

In its prior decisions, the *Cour de cassation* focused on the subject matter (*matière*) of the proceedings, examining whether it is one of those in which the parties have free disposal of their rights.[26] In more recent decisions, the *Cour de cassation* has not mentioned the subject matter anymore. The analysis is to be conducted right by right. As a result of this approach, the *Cour de cassation* decided for example that divorce proceedings involve unavailable rights as far as the principle of divorce is concerned, but that proceedings relating to maintenance obligations between ex-spouses involve, on the contrary, available rights.[27] Between the first instance judge and the court of appeal, the status of the conflict of laws rule can therefore change, if the appeal relates only to the financial compensation between ex-spouses and does not question the principle of the divorce itself.

The criterion of the availability of a right determines whether the judge is under the duty of applying the conflict of laws rule or has only the discretion to do so (B), and whether the parties can conclude procedural agreements on the applicable law which are binding for the judge (C).

---

[18] The decisions are numerous. For example, 1e Civ., 4. 6. 2009, *Rev. crit. DIP* 2010. 353, comm. H. Muir Watt, *JDI* 2010. 485, comm. C. Legros; 1e Civ., 3. 3. 2010, *D.* 2010. 709, comm. I. Gallmeister; 1e Civ., 3. 3. 2011, *D.* 2011. 1374, comm. F. Jault-Seseke; 1e Civ., 23. 11. 2011, *D.* 2011. 2933.

[19] 1e Civ., 1. 6. 2011 (3 decisions), *Gaz. Pal.* 2011. somm. 1812, jur. 2176, concl. P. Chevalier, chron. 2425, comm. M. Eppler.

[20] 1e Civ., 26. 5. 1999, *Belaïd A., Rev. crit. DIP* 1999. 707, comm. H. Muir Watt.

[21] 1e Civ., 6. 1. 2010, *Rev. crit. DIP* 2010. 357, comm. P. Lagarde.

[22] For example, 1e Civ. 4. 6. 2009, *Rev. trim. dr. com.* 2010. 458, comm. Ph. Delebecque (contract of carriage); 1e Civ., 28. 11. 2006, n° 05–19838 (repayment of a loan).

[23] 1e Civ., 19. 4. 1988, *Roho, Rev. crit. DIP* 1989. 69, comm. H. Batiffol; 2e Civ., 17. 9. 2009, *Rev. gén. dr. ass.* 2010. 480, comm. V. Heuzé.

[24] 1e Civ., 20. 10. 2010, *Ettehadieh, Rev. crit. DIP* 2011. 55, comm. B. Ancel. *Contra* 1e Civ., 20. 6. 2006, *JDI* 2006.125, comm. H. Gaudemt-Tallon, *Rev. crit. DIP* 2007. 383, comm. B. Ancel, analyzing the transfer by succession of a right in immovable property as unavailable.

[25] Court of appeal Versailles, 26. 6. 2008, *Rev. trim. dr. com.* 2010. 205, comm. J.-L. Vallens.

[26] Civ., 4. 12. 1990, *Coveco, Rev. crit. DIP* 1991. 558, comm. M.-L. Niboyet, *JDI* 1991. 371, comm. D. Bureau.

[27] 1e Civ., 11. 3. 2009, *Rev. crit. DIP* 2010. 344, comm. P. Hammje.

B. The Role of the Judge: Mandatory Application of Conflict of Laws Rules

The application of conflict of laws rules is mandatory for the judge if unavailable rights are involved (1). On the contrary, conflict of laws rules are in principle facultative for the judge and at his sole discretion if the proceedings relate to available rights. However, the role of the judge depends then on the attitude of the parties. If at least one party pleads foreign law, the conflict of laws rule becomes mandatory for the judge, even though only available rights are involved (2).

1. Mandatory Application of the Conflict of Laws Rule When Unavailable Rights Are Involved

If the proceedings involve unavailable rights, the judge must apply *ex officio* the conflict of laws rule and determine the applicable law even though the parties pleaded only French law. Moreover, the conflict of laws rule is mandatory not only for the judge but also for the parties, who cannot agree on the application of another law. This has been a constant principle in French case law since the *Soc. Mutuelle du Mans* decision of 1999.[28]

However, this duty implies that the judge is aware of the existence of a conflict of laws. When all parties plead French law, the judge does not necessarily have knowledge of the cross-border element, because the relevant facts are not always mentioned by the parties.[29] The procedural status of the cross-border element of the case is therefore important. According to Art. 7 of the *Code de procédure civile*, the judge may not base his decision on facts absent from the debate. However, among all the facts mentioned in the debate, the judge may take into consideration even those which the parties have not expressly relied upon to support their claims. Art. 8 of the *Code de procédure civile* allows the judge to invite the parties to provide factual explanations that he deems necessary for the resolution of the dispute. In domestic matters, these provisions confer merely discretionary power on the judge, whereas in private international law they are interpreted as being mandatory.[30] The judge must use these powers in order to establish the cross-border element raising the conflict of laws. The *Cour de cassation* is very firm on this point. The judge must use all the elements he can find in the case file, including the document instituting the proceedings, the submissions of the parties and all evidence available. For example, the document instituting the proceedings generally indicates the nationality and the place of domicile which are relevant elements in particular in matters of personal status.[31] In parentage proceedings, if the case file mentions that the mother

[28] 1e Civ., 26. 5. 1999, *Soc. Mutuelle du Mans*, *Rev. crit. DIP* 1999. 707, comm. H. Muir Watt.

[29] J.-L. Elhoueiss, "L'élément d'extranéité préalable en droit international privé", *JDI* 2003. 39.

[30] D. Bureau, H. Muir Watt, *Droit international privé*, vol. 1, PUF, 2014, n° 377.

[31] 1e Civ., 18. 11. 1992, *Maklouf*, *Rev. crit. DIP* 1993. 276, comm. B. Ancel (capacity).

of the child holds a resident card, the cross-border element is mentioned in the debate and the judge must apply *ex officio* the conflict of laws rule.[32] The *Cour de cassation* even decided that regarding the international protection of an adult domiciled in France, the lower courts should have checked his/her nationality because the adult in question was born in Tunisia and therefore could be Tunisian, which would make the conflict of laws rule mandatory.[33] This solution has been criticized because unlike the possession of a resident card, the place of birth does not establish in itself a foreign nationality.[34]

2. Mandatory Application of the Conflict of Laws Rule When Available Rights Are Involved and One Party Pleads Foreign Law

Since the *Soc. Mutuelle du Mans* decision of 1999, when the proceedings have involved available rights, the role of the judge has depended on the attitude of the parties. In case none of them invoke a foreign law, the application of the conflict of laws rule is facultative for the judge, regardless of its source. No distinction is indeed made according to the national, European or international source of the conflict of laws rule.[35] Therefore, when no party pleads foreign law and the rights are available, the judge usually applies French law. The judge has nevertheless the discretionary power – at least in theory – to apply the conflict of laws rule *ex officio*,[36] provided that the parties have not concluded a procedural agreement on the applicable law.[37] If he does so, he must initiate a debate between the parties on the application of the conflict of laws rule, in order to comply with the adversarial principle laid down in Art. 16 of the *Code de procédure civile*.[38] However, the *Cour de cassation* sometimes considers the mutual silence of the parties regarding the applicability of foreign law as an implicit procedural agreement on the application

[32] 1e Civ., 26. 5. 1999, *Belaïd A., Rev. crit. DIP* 1999. 707, comm. H. Muir Watt.

[33] 1e Civ., 6. 1. 2010, *Rev. crit. DIP* 2010. 357, comm. P. Lagarde.

[34] P. Lagarde, *op. cit.*

[35] The *Cour de cassation* no longer devotes a specific regime to conflict of laws rules having their source in international conventions. From 1990 (Civ., 4. 12. 1990, *Coveco, Rev. crit. DIP* 1991. 558, comm. M.-L. Niboyet, *JDI* 1991. 371, comm. D. Bureau) until 1999 (1e Civ., 26.5. 1999, *Soc. Mutuelle du Mans, Rev. crit. DIP* 1999. 707, comm. H. Muir Watt), their application was considered to be mandatory for the judge even in the area of available rights, but this solution has been abandoned. The availability of the rights is considered to be more decisive than the source of the rule: H. Muir Watt, « Loi étrangère », Répertoire de droit international, Dalloz, 2010, n° 32.

[36] Civ., 2. 3. 1960, *Cie algérienne de credit et de banque, Rev. crit. DIP* 1960. 97, comm. H. Batiffol.

[37] On procedural agreements in general, see *infra*, II/C.

[38] 1e Civ., 6. 5. 2005, n° 03–10274 (application of the Hague Convention on the law applicable to international sales of goods). Art. 16 of *Code de procédure civile* states: "In all circumstances, the judge must supervise the respect of, and he must himself respect, the adversarial principle. In his decision, the judge may take into consideration grounds, explanations and documents relied upon or produced by the parties only if the parties had an opportunity to discuss them in an adversarial manner. He shall not base his decision on legal arguments that he has raised sua sponte without having first invited the parties to comment thereon".

of French law, which has binding effect on the judge and makes the *ex officio* application impossible. This solution was criticized because the procedural agreement should be clear and non-ambiguous, but as far as the *Cour de cassation* maintains this interpretation, there is no place in practice for an *ex officio* application of the conflict of laws rule.[39] Therefore, if the rights involved are available, a foreign law generally applies only when the parties invoke its applicability. This solution contrasts with the case law on the application of conventions on uniform substantive rules, as the Convention on Contracts for the International Sale of Goods, for example. Although these conventions deal with available rights, they are to be applied *ex officio* by the judge, regardless of the nature of the rights involved, whenever the situation fulfils the scope of application of such a convention.[40] The regime of these conventions thus differs clearly from the regime of conflict of laws rules. However, the Vienna Convention allows the parties to exclude its application (Art. 6) and the *Cour de cassation* accepts even implicit exclusions,[41] which limits the *ex officio* application of the convention, whereas the Convention on the Contract for the International Carriage of Goods by Road, for example, cannot be derogated by the parties (Art. 41).

In case at least one party pleads foreign law, the conflicts of laws rule becomes mandatory for the judge and the same regime will apply as in matters involving unavailable rights. As soon as the conflict of laws has been introduced into the debate by one party, the judge must apply the conflict of laws rule and determine the applicable law.[42] The exact meaning of "pleading foreign law" however is debated. Authors wonder whether the allegation (*allégation*) of foreign law by the parties must be "qualified" (*circonstanciée)*, which would mean that the party has to give some information about the content of foreign law, in order to show how the foreign law serves the submission, without requiring however from this party the complete proof of the foreign law.[43] In line with this interpretation, the *Cour de cassation* sometimes requires the foreign law to be invoked expressly and a real claim to be based on the allegation of that particular foreign law.[44] The purpose of these requirements is to tackle the use of the conflict of laws rule as a merely delaying tactic. In case the parties plead a foreign law which is not applicable according to the conflict of laws rule, the judge must replace their argumentation with the right reasoning.[45]

---

[39] Recently, the possibility of implicit procedural agreements has been reiterated: Com., 1, 10, 2013, n° 12–17067 and 12–17250.

[40] 1e Civ., 25. 10. 2005, *Rev. crit. DIP* 2006. 373, comm. D. Bureau, *D.* 2007. 530, comm. C. Witz. D. Bureau, H. Muir Watt, *Droit international privé*, vol. 1, PUF, 2014, n° 377.

[41] 1e Civ., 26. 6. 2001, *JDI* 2001. 1121, comm. A. Huet, *Rev. crit. DIP* 2002. 93, comm. H. Muir Watt.

[42] For some recent decisions, see for example: 1e Civ., 22. 3. 2012, n° 09–68067; 1e Civ., 7. 11. 2012, n° 11–25588; 1e Civ., 19. 12. 2012, n° 11–20421.

[43] H. Muir Watt, "Loi étrangère", Répertoire de droit international, Dalloz, 2010, n° 47 f.

[44] 1e Civ., 28. 1. 2003, *Rev. crit. DIP* 2003. 462, comm. B. Ancel.

[45] 1e Civ., 22. 1. 2008, n° 06–18822.

In particular, the judge must apply the right conflict of laws rule,[46] but here again the tackling of delaying tactics sometimes lessens the requirements.[47] If the conflict of laws rule contains an exception clause, as in Art. 4 para 3 Regulation n° 593/2008 Rome I or Art. 4 para 3 Regulation n° 864/2007 Rome II, the judge is only supposed to apply the general rule. He is not required to also apply the exception clause *ex officio*. Only if the parties claim that the contract is manifestly more closely connected with another country, the judge must analyze all the connecting factors of the case.[48]

C. Party Autonomy: Procedural Agreements on the Applicable Law

A procedural agreement on the applicable law is an agreement, concluded between the parties during the course of judicial proceedings, setting aside the conflict of laws rule for the pending proceedings. Unlike choice of law agreements, which rely on party autonomy granted by the conflict of laws rule itself, procedural agreements are not an application of the conflict of laws rule, but a means to elude its application.[49] Their lawfulness has been established, provided that the proceedings involve available rights, since the *Roho* decision of the *Cour de cassation* in 1988.[50] In its prior decisions, the *Cour de cassation* required an explicit agreement, but today implicit procedural agreements are possible.[51] In particular, if the submissions of the parties are based on a law which is not applicable according to the conflict of laws rule, the judge can interpret this attitude as an implicit procedural agreement. The effects of the agreement are limited to the current proceedings, and cannot affect rights of third parties.[52] It is subject to debate whether the parties can choose French law only or also foreign law. The dominant interpretation sees in these agreements

[46] 1e Civ., 9. 12. 2003, n° 00–12872; 1e Civ., 31. 5. 2005, *Rev. crit. DIP* 2005. 465, comm. P. Lagarde.

[47] 3e Civ., 16. 1. 2013, *Rev. crit. DIP 2013*. 620, comm. D. Bureau: the court of appeal applied the Hague Convention of 1955 on the sales of goods, invoked by one party, instead of the Hague Convention of 1973 on product liability. The *Cour de cassation* decided that the court of appeal was not expected to change the legal basis of the claims, thus contradicting the decisions quoted in the previous footnotes. The explanation therefore probably lays in the particular circumstances of the case.

[48] 1e Civ., 22. 5. 2007, *Rev. crit. DIP* 2007. 592, comm. P. Lagarde; P. Rémy-Corlay, "Mise en œuvre et régime procédural de la clause d'exception dans le conflit de lois", *Rev. crit. DIP* 2003. 37.

[49] P. Lagarde, *Rev. crit. DIP 1990. 316*; H. Muir Watt, "Loi étrangère", Répertoire de droit international, Dalloz, 2010, n° 54.

[50] 1e Civ., 19. 4. 1988, *Roho, Rev. crit. DIP* 1989. 69, comm. H. Batiffol.

[51] 1e Civ., 6. 5. 1997, *Rev. crit. DIP* 1997. 514, comm. B. Ancel, *JDI* 1997. 804, comm. D. Bureau; for a recent confirmation, see Com., 1, 10, 2013, n° 12–17067 and 12–17250.

[52] 1e Civ., 22. 2. 2005, *Rev. crit. DIP* 2005. 304, comm. P. Lagarde.

a waiver of the cross-border element of the case, transforming an international dispute into a domestic one.[53] A choice of foreign law should therefore not be possible according to this interpretation. The *Cour de cassation* also seems to limit the choice exclusively to French law.[54]

Procedural agreements are justified with two kinds of arguments. Firstly, they satisfy pragmatic considerations. The ascertainment of foreign law is generally time consuming and costly. A less expensive and faster resolution of the dispute often serves the interests of the parties and the proper administration of justice. Secondly, procedural agreements sometimes appear to be a convenient way to rectify inappropriate effects of the conflict of laws rule. If the conflict of laws rule is too rigid, procedural agreements introduce some flexibility, especially in subject matters where available rights are involved but no exception clause and no party autonomy is granted by the conflict of laws rule.[55] And if the conflict of laws rule designates a foreign law whose content violates the public policy of the forum, procedural agreements avoid its application in a diplomatic manner. For example, in disputes over financial compensation between ex-spouses involving a Maghreb country, a procedural choice of French law provides a solution avoiding any discrimination against women.

D. De Lege Ferenda

The existing regime has rightly been criticized by French authors (1). The treatment of the conflict of laws rule should therefore be modified *de lege ferenda* (2).

1. Criticisms of the Existing Solution

Criticisms can be summarized in two points. Firstly, the Europeanization of conflict of laws rules cannot be completely ignored. The shift from national to international and European rules must be taken into account when deciding on the mandatory nature of conflict of laws rules (a). Secondly, the distinction between available and unavailable rights has become inappropriate since fundamental changes have affected both substantial and conflict of laws rules (b).

---

[53] J.-M. Bischoff, "Les problèmes actuels posés par l'application des lois étrangères, Rapport introductif", *Trav. com. fr. DIP* 1990–1991. 19; H. Muir Watt, "Loi étrangère", Répertoire de droit international, Dalloz, 2010, n° 62; B. Audit, L. d'Avout, *Droit international privé*, Economica, 2013, n° 327 (these authors interpret the agreement as a waiver of the applicable law).

[54] 1e Civ., 6. 5. 1997, *Rev. crit. DIP* 1997. 514, comm. B. Fauvarque-Cosson: for rights of which the parties have free disposal, they can agree on the application of the French law of the forum, despite the existence of an international convention designating a different law.

[55] B. Fauvarque-Cosson, "L'accord procédural à l'épreuve du temps (retour sur une notion française controversée)", in *Le droit international privé: esprit et méthodes, Mélanges en l'honneur de Paul Lagarde*, 2005, Dalloz, p. 263 (278).

a) An Inappropriate Disregard of the Source of the Conflict of Laws Rule

Under the current framework of French case law, no distinction is made according to the source of the conflict of laws rule.[56] The *Cour de cassation* no longer considers conflict of laws rules which originate in international conventions as mandatory regardless of the nature of the rights involved (see *supra*), while European conflict of laws rules have never received any specific treatment in France. Therefore, as the majority of European conflict of laws rules are related to available rights, they are facultative if none of the parties invoke foreign law. French authors largely agree that this solution is compatible with the requirements of international law.[57] And it may also be compatible, at least until today, with the requirements of EU law, although several authors expect the European Court of Justice to impose one day an *ex officio* application of the rules aiming specifically at the protection of a weaker party.[58] Nevertheless, the current solution undermines the international and European process of unification of conflict of laws rules. Indeed, when the application of the conflict of laws rule is facultative, it is not granted that a certain case will be decided by the courts of any Member or Contracting State according to the same substantive law. The intended uniformity of results is not achieved. One may then wonder whether the effort of unification is really worth it. One may also wonder whether the *effet utile* (the effectiveness) of the EU regulations is really preserved. The only way to ensure the intended uniformity would be to elaborate a European instrument unifying the treatment of conflict of laws rules in all Member States.

b) An Inappropriate Distinction Between Available and Unavailable Rights

The distinction based on the criterion of the free disposal of the rights has always been elusive and difficult to apply. However, uncertainties have gotten worse in the past few years. On the one hand, traditional areas of available rights are increasingly regulated by mandatory rules. This is the case in contract law, for example, where mandatory rules aim at the protection of the weaker party. Today, this policy is not only targeted at consumers or employees, but also at professionals, such as

---

[56] The Cour de cassation no longer dedicates a specific regime to conflict of laws rules having their source in international conventions. From 1990 (Civ., 4. 12. 1990, *Coveco, Rev. crit. DIP* 1991. 558, comm. M.-L. Niboyet, *JDI* 1991. 371, comm. D. Bureau) until 1999 (1e Civ., 26.5. 1999, *Soc. Mutuelle du Mans, Rev. crit. DIP* 1999. 707, comm. H. Muir Watt), their application was considered to be mandatory for the judge even in the area of available rights, but this solution has been abandoned. The availability of the rights is considered to be more decisive than the source of the rule: H. Muir Watt, "Loi étrangère", Répertoire de droit international, Dalloz, 2010, n° 32.

[57] M.-L. Niboyet, G. de Geouffre de la Pradelle, *op. cit.*, n° 672; H. Muir Watt, *op. cit.*, n° 28 f.

[58] S. Clavel, "Les mutations de l'office du juge à l'aune du développement des règles du droit international privé supranationales", in *La coordination des justices étatiques*, Bibliothèque de l'Institut de recherche juridique André Tunc, vol. 43, p. 63; B. Audit, L. d'Avout, *op. cit.*, n° 325; M.-L. Niboyet, G. de Geouffre de la Pradelle, *op. cit.*, n° 673. Predicting more generally a strengthening of the role of the judge under the influence of EU law: H. Muir Watt, *op. cit.*, n° 7 f.

commercial agents for example.[59] Legislation in these areas thus carries public interests and the characterization as available rights does not reflect the complexity of the interests at stake. The same is also true for non-contractual obligations like product liability or non-contractual obligations arising out of violations of competition or financial markets law. At the international or European level, conflict of laws rules progressively reflect the mandatory nature of the objectives of these legislations. Authors have long agreed that conflict of laws rules cannot be seen as politically neutral anymore and that they can implement mandatory policies. Therefore, even though the subject matters involve patrimonial rights, their characterization as available rights – conferring on the conflict of laws rule a facultative nature – does not fit with the policies conducted. On the other hand, party autonomy has found its way into traditional areas of unavailable rights. The example of divorce is particularly striking. In French case law, divorce is the subject matter giving rise to the most frequent application of the regime for unavailable rights. However, its characterization as unavailable rights cannot be maintained anymore, since the regulation n° 1259/2010 Rome III has introduced party autonomy in the new European conflict of laws rule. An area subject to party autonomy necessarily involves available rights. This does not mean that the rules applicable to divorce are based on non-mandatory policies. In fact, the pursuit of mandatory policies is not incompatible with a certain dose of party autonomy. The example only demonstrates that the current distinction between available and unavailable rights is not appropriate anymore. As Horatia Muir Watt pointed out, it is necessary to rethink the criteria of the distinction between public and private interests on the basis of the values and policies conveyed by conflict of laws rules and on the basis of the changing purpose of these rules. The current distinction is no longer able to identify the situations where a societal interest requires not leaving the conflict of laws at the disposal of the parties.[60]

2. Proposal for the Future[61]

Regarding the mandatory or facultative nature of conflict of laws rules, a clear distinction should be made between the judge and the parties. Conflict of laws rules should always be applied *ex officio* by the judge.[62] In other words, their application should always be mandatory for him, being specified that the current solution of the *Cour de*

[59] See for example ECJ, 17. 10. 2013, *United Antwerp Maritime Agencies (Unamar)*, C-184/12.

[60] H. Muir Watt, "Loi étrangère", Répertoire de droit international, Dalloz, 2010, n° 6.

[61] From a European perspective, see A. Flessner, "Das Parteiinteresse an der *Lex fori* nach europäischem Kollisionsrecht", in *Liber Amicorum Walter Pintens*, Cambridge, 2012, p. 593; E.-M. Kieninger, "Ermittlung und Anwendung ausländischen Rechts", in *Brauchen wir eine Rom O-Verordnung?*, Jenaer Wissenschaftliche Verlagsgesellschaft, 2013, p. 479; S. Corneloup, "Rechtsermittlung im internationalen Privatrecht der EU: Überlegungen aus Frankreich", *RabelsZ* 2014, p. 844.

[62] This solution is also advocated, for example, by H. Muir Watt, *op. cit.*, n° 44, 59 and 67; H. J. Sonnenberger, "Randbemerkungen zum Allgemeinen Teil eines europäisierten IPR", in *Festschrift für Jan Kropholler*, Mohr Siebeck, 2008, p. 227; C. Esplugues, J. L. Iglesias, G. Palao (ed.), *Application of Foreign Law*, Sellier, 2011, "Madrid Principles", p. 95, principle IV.

cassation regarding the discovery of the cross-border element seems satisfactory and should be maintained. Each time the judge applies *ex officio* the conflict of laws rule, he should initiate a debate between the parties, making sure that they are aware of the applicability of foreign law and enabling them to make an informed choice. Indeed, for the parties on the contrary, the conflict of laws rule should not be mandatory in general. Procedural agreements should be admitted whenever party autonomy is admitted by the conflict of laws rule,[63] with the particularity however that in the course of the proceedings the choice should be restricted to the *lex fori* and limited to the current proceedings. Moreover, the procedural agreement should not affect third parties.

It might be useful to illustrate the results of this proposal with some examples. Procedural agreements should always be possible for contractual obligations. Even for contracts involving a weaker party, the solution finally seems to be acceptable, as far as the choice is limited to the *lex fori*, because jurisdictional rules generally take into account the need for protection of the weaker party. For instance, most consumer disputes are brought before the court of the consumer's domicile, while employment disputes are generally brought before the court of the place where the employee habitually carries out his work or where he is domiciled. Moreover, jurisdiction and applicable law are often governed by the same connecting factor, which leads- in practice anyway – to the application of the *lex fori*. For non-contractual obligations, a distinction must be made according to the subject matter. Although regulation n° 864/2007 Rome II contains a general provision on party autonomy, exceptions exist. Procedural agreements should thus not be possible in disputes relating to obligations arising out of violations of competition law or out of infringements of intellectual property rights, because party autonomy is not admitted there. In matters of divorce, procedural agreements should become possible,[64] whereas in matters of parental responsibility, they should not. For the latter, there is actually no need in practice for procedural agreements because the applicable law according to the Hague Convention of 1996 is the *lex fori*. The same is also true for the Hague Convention of 2000 on the protection of adults. Procedural agreements should be excluded, in general, in matters of personal status and marriage where party autonomy is not admitted. For maintenance obligations, the Hague Protocol of 2007

[63] This criterion seems preferable to the criterion based on the patrimonial nature of the rights involved, which has been suggested by P. Lagarde, "En guise de synthèse", in *Quelle architecture pour un code européen de droit international privé?*, P.I.E. Peter Lang, 2011, p. 365 (373). See also E.-M. Kieninger, *op. cit.* Of course, procedural agreements are different from choice of law agreements because their aim is to elude the application of the conflict of laws rule whereas choice of law agreements constitute an implementation of the conflict of laws rule. Nevertheless, the admission of party autonomy by the conflict of laws rule seems to be an appropriate criterion also for the lawfulness of procedural agreements. In any case, the decision on their lawfulness should be made within private international law, in order to guarantee that conflict of laws rules are not undermined by domestic rules in civil procedure which do not have the same purposes and objectives: H. J. Sonnenberger, *Münchener Kommentar zum Bürgerlichen Gesetzbuch*, C.H. Beck, 5th ed., Einl.IPR, n° 228.

[64] The possibility for the spouses to specify the applicable law during the course of the proceedings depends, according to Art. 5 para 3 regulation Rome III, on the law of the forum. Refusing this possibility would be quite inconsistent with the general acceptance of a certain dose of party autonomy by the regulation.

already contains a specific provision allowing procedural agreements. On the contrary, according to EU regulation n° 650/2012 on successions, a choice of law can only be made by the deceased himself, which inevitably means that the choice must be made before the death, excluding thereby any possibility of a procedural agreement.[65] Finally, as long as rights *in rem* are governed by the *lex rei sitae* and party autonomy is not admitted, procedural agreements should be excluded.

The form of procedural agreements should be express, but an implicit agreement could be accepted if it can be inferred with reasonable certainty from the attitude of the parties in the course of the proceedings. As the judge is supposed to initiate a debate between the parties when he applies *ex officio* the conflict of laws rule, this condition should rarely be an issue.

III. Foreign Law Before Judicial Authorities

Foreign law has been considered as law and not as fact by the *Cour de cassation* since the *Coucke* decision of 1993.[66] However, because of its foreign nature, foreign law is governed by a specific procedural regime, which differs from that of French law as well as from that of mere facts, and which is mainly determined by pragmatic considerations. In other words, the particularity of the regime of foreign law does not rely on its specific nature but only on its exteriority.[67] This hybrid status was explained by Batiffol on the basis of the distinction which must be made between the imperative element and the rational element of the law. Foreign law loses its imperative element in the forum, but it conserves its rational element as a rule effectively applied in some specific situation.[68]

Particularities in the regime of foreign law can be observed as to its ascertainment (A) and as to its application and interpretation (B).

A. Ascertainment of Foreign Law[69]

The *iura novit curia* principle, which presumes that the judge knows the law, does not apply to foreign law because of its exteriority. Such a presumption is deemed to be unrealistic in the case of foreign law.[70] After a long evolution,[71] it is today

[65] E.-M. Kieninger, *op. cit.*, p. 498.

[66] 1e Civ., 13. 1. 1993, *Rev. crit. DIP* 1994. 78, comm. B. Ancel.

[67] M.-L. Niboyet, G. de Geouffre de la Pradelle, *op. cit.*, n° 668; H. Muir Watt, "Loi étrangère", Répertoire de droit international, Dalloz, 2010, n° 77.

[68] H. Batiffol, *Aspects philosophiques du droit international privé*, Dalloz, 1956, p. 50 f. Contemporary authors contest this analysis: P. Mayer, V. Heuzé, *op. cit.*, n° 179.

[69] N. Nord, "L'établissement du contenu du droit étranger en France", in Cl. Witz (ed.), *Application du droit étranger par le juge national: Allemagne, France, Belgique, Suisse*, Société de législation comparée, 2014, p. 13.

[70] M.-L. Niboyet, G. de Geouffre de la Pradelle, *op. cit.*, n° 668.

[71] On the evolution of the position of the *Cour de cassation*, see H. Muir Watt, *op. cit.*, n° 83 f.

established that the judge has a duty to ascertain foreign law but that he can request the parties to cooperate with him (1). While the means of proof can be chosen freely, certificates are the most frequent means of proof used in practice (2), which is not completely satisfactory and should be improved *de lege ferenda* (4). If the establishment of foreign law fails, the judge applies the *lex fori* (3). No distinction is made at this stage according to the nature of the rights involved. Therefore, the ascertainment of foreign law is governed by one single regime, regardless whether unavailable or available rights are involved.

1. Burden of Proof

By two solemn decisions on the same day, the *Cour de cassation* ruled that the judge who has acknowledged that foreign law is applicable, either because he has applied *ex officio* the conflict of laws rule or because a party has pleaded foreign law, must ascertain its content, with the assistance of the parties and even personally if necessary.[72] In other words, each time the conflict of laws is in the debate and the judge concludes that a foreign law is applicable to the dispute, he must ascertain its content. Hence, the judge has an active role in the search of the content of the foreign law. He leads the investigation, but has the possibility to request the parties to assist him, especially by inviting them to collect every element at their disposal establishing the content of the foreign law.

2. Means of Proof

Foreign law can be proved by any means. The most important means of proof used by the parties are certificates drafted by experts called *certificats de coutume* (an affidavit of law and customs). These certificates are drawn up either by public authorities such as consulates, or by private persons, who can be practitioners like lawyers or notaries, or academics. Individuals or institutions that provide this kind of legal information do not have to fulfil specific qualifications. As the parties are free to choose the author of the certificate and as they have to pay for it, certificates of private origin often lack objectivity. While the certificates of public authorities are objective but generally very brief, certificates of lawyers are more detailed but generally support the point of view of the party at the request of whom they were established. The legal information provided by the document is subject to adversarial debate and it is not binding upon the judge who has to verify, among other things, the impartiality of the certificate. However, in France, courts cannot order a hearing or cross-examination of the authors of such certificates. They have to use other means of verification. The parties can also establish the content of foreign law

[72] Com., 28. 6. 2005, *Itraco* and 1e Civ., 28. 6. 2005, *Aubin*, *Rev. crit. DIP* 2005. 645, comm. B. Ancel and H. Muir Watt. For recent confirmations, see Com., 1. 10. 2013, n° 12–17067 and 12–17250; 1e Civ., 7. 11. 2012, n° 11–25588; 1e Civ., 1.6.2016, n° 15–13221.

by using other documents, such as pieces of legislation, court decisions, academic books, etc. Here again, verifications must be made by the judge in order to ascertain the applicability of the rule introduced by a party or the authenticity of a quotation of a legal source for example.

The judge can use the investigation methods provided for by the *Code de procédure civile*, in order to prove the facts.[73] For example, the judge can appoint an expert and commission him/her to draw up a report on the content of the foreign law. However, in practice, French judges make little use of this possibility.[74] In general, they request the parties to provide a *certificat de coutume* or any other document establishing the content of the foreign law. One original feature of the regime is the possibility for the judge to use his personal knowledge of the foreign law.[75] His knowledge may stem for example from frequent applications of certain foreign laws, such as the laws of the Maghreb countries in matters of divorce or child custody under the regime of *Kafala*. When the judge intends to base the decision on his personal knowledge of the foreign law, he must nevertheless respect the adversarial principle and submit the elements to the parties for debate. Unlike Germany or Switzerland, France has not an expert institute specialized in comparative law which might provide the courts with reports on the content of foreign law.

International judicial cooperation[76] is possible, first of all, on the basis of the European Convention on Information on Foreign Law.[77] However, this convention is rarely applied in practice.[78] The reasons for its limited use may be firstly that French judges are largely unfamiliar with this convention and secondly that its mechanism is rather complex, which raises the fear that such international cooperation might considerably delay the outcome of the dispute.[79] France has also ratified several bilateral agreements on mutual judicial assistance.[80] Within the European Union, the European Judicial Network offers the possibility of cooperation on the basis of national contact points whose role is, among others, to provide information in order to facilitate the application of the law of other Member States. On a global level, French judges can also use the information exchange mechanisms of the recent Hague Conventions promoting international cooperation through central authorities. Moreover, courts have the possibility to request the assistance of

[73] Art. 10 and 11 Code de procédure civile.

[74] For an example, see Civ., 19. 10. 1971, *JDI* 1972. 828, comm. Nisard, *Rev. crit. DIP* 1973. 70, comm. M. Simon-Depitre.

[75] Civ., 2. 3. 1960, *Cie algérienne de credit et de banque*, *Rev. crit. DIP* 1960. 97, comm. H. Batiffol; J. Chevallier, "Remarques sur l'utilisation par le juge de ses informations personnelles", *RTD civ.* 1962, p. 2.

[76] F. Mélin, "Les conventions internationales favorisant la connaissance des lois étrangères", in Cl. Witz (ed.), *Application du droit étranger par le juge national: Allemagne, France, Belgique, Suisse*, *op. cit.*, p. 63.

[77] Elaborated within the European Council and signed in London the 7. 6. 1968.

[78] According to P. Mayer and V. Heuzé, less than ten requests per year are made by French Courts: P. Mayer, V. Heuzé, *op. cit.*, n° 189.

[79] H. Muir Watt, *op. cit.*, n° 113; B. Audit, L. d'Avout, *op. cit.*, n° 334.

[80] They can be accessed at http://basedoc.diplomatie.gouv.fr/Traites/Accords_Traites.php

the International and European Affairs Department of the French Ministry of Justice, which works with a network of national correspondents.[81] This procedure has been described by French authors as practical and comfortable, but not always reliable.[82]

3. Failure of Proof

Since the parties no longer bear the burden of proof of foreign law and since the judge has to ascertain himself the content of the applicable law, the failure of proof cannot lead to a dismissal of the claim. Such a consequence would only be conceivable if the judge had a passive role in the ascertainment of foreign law. Therefore, when it is objectively impossible to establish the content of the foreign law, due to external circumstances, depending neither on insufficient effort of the parties and the judge, nor on the deficient nature of the foreign law itself, the judge applies the *lex fori*.[83] The judge must then explain precisely in the legal grounds of the decision the circumstances making the application of foreign law impossible. The subsidiary application of the *lex fori* is justified by the necessity to avoid a denial of justice,[84] by the abstract nature of legal rules conferring them a universal character and making it possible to apply them regardless the geographical localization of a situation,[85] and by the fact that the *lex fori* is in general subsidiarily applicable in the forum.[86]

4. *De Lege Ferenda*

The compromise reached by the *Cour de cassation* on the allocation of roles between the judge and the parties regarding the ascertainment of foreign law is fully satisfactory. The subsidiary application of the *lex fori*, when foreign law cannot be ascertained, should also be maintained.

On the contrary, the means of proof mainly used in French practice are unanimously criticized and need to be improved. As to the lack of impartiality of *certificats de coutume*, French authors see the best remedy in the Common Law practice of cross-examination but generally point out that this seems to be incompatible with the French judicial tradition.[87] Another way to improve the current system would be to create an expert institute like the Max Planck Institute for Comparative and

---

[81] 1e Civ., 21. 11. 2006, *Rev. crit. DIP* 2007. 575, comm. H. Muir Watt.

[82] P. Mayer, V. Heuzé, *op. cit.*, n° 189.

[83] For example, 1e Civ., 21. 11. 2006, *Rev. crit. DIP* 2007. 575, comm. H. Muir Watt: impossibility to establish the content of the law on parentage of Belarus, even though the court had requested the assistance of the International and European Affairs Department of the French Ministry of Justice.

[84] B. Audit, L. d'Avout, *op. cit.*, n° 336.

[85] P. Mayer, V. Heuzé, *op. cit.*, n° 184.

[86] H. Muir Watt, *op. cit.*, n° 99.

[87] P. Mayer, V. Heuzé, *op. cit.*, n° 188; M.-L. Niboyet, G. de Geouffre de la Pradelle, *op. cit.*, n° 687.

International Private Law or the Swiss Institute of Comparative Law.[88] But as the key solution, all authors call for a better use of international judicial cooperation. According to some, the mechanism of the European Convention on Information on Foreign Law should be considered as mandatory for the judge every time no better source of information is available.[89] Within the European Union, the European Judicial Network should become the main tool for a judge-to-judge dialogue, which would be the best way to establish the content of foreign law.[90] Several authors also underline the potential carried by electronic means, facilitating judicial cooperation as well as the creation of databases on foreign law.[91] France itself has an excellent official website on French law (www.legifrance.gouv.fr) which is accessible to everyone free of charge. It contains the complete collection of legal texts applicable in France, and also the main judicial decisions of the superior courts.[92] Of course, the website is in French, but an increasing number of legal documentation have been translated into foreign languages. Above all, the increasing number of English translations is making it an interesting tool for foreign courts.

B. Interpretation and Application of Foreign Law

The judge has to apply the foreign law exactly as it is applied in its country of origin. He must base his decision not only on the foreign legal texts but also on the existing foreign court decisions, and decide the case in the way a judge of the country of origin would have decided. Each time an interpretation of the foreign law is necessary, the judge must follow the interpretation given by the authorities of the State of origin. In other words, when an interpretation given by a foreign court exists, the judge of the forum is not supposed to give his own interpretation of a foreign text. However, if the question has not yet received an answer in the foreign country, or if different answers contradict each other, an interpretation by the judge of the forum cannot be avoided. A distinction is then to be made. As a basic principle, the judge should search for the right interpretation by reasoning in the way a foreign judge would do, applying the methods of interpretation generally practiced by the foreign judge. But this approach can only succeed if there are at least some elements guiding the interpretation, such as parliamentary debates, academic writings, etc., enabling to establish the content of the foreign law with reasonable certainty. Exceptionally, if there is no clear element guiding the interpretation, the judge should conclude that the content of foreign law cannot be ascertained and that French law applies instead.[93]

---

[88] B. Audit, L. d'Avout, *op. cit.*, n° 333.

[89] P. Mayer, V. Heuzé, *op. cit.*, n° 189.

[90] B. Audit, L. d'Avout, *op. cit.*, n° 335.

[91] H. Muir Watt, *op. cit.*, n° 114; B. Audit, L. d'Avout, *op. cit.*, n° 333.

[92] The collection is less comprehensive nevertheless regarding the decisions of lower courts.

[93] P. Mayer, V. Heuzé, *op. cit.*, n° 194; H. Muir Watt, *op. cit.*, 117.

IV. Judicial Review

Regarding the judicial review, a distinction is to be made between the review by courts of appeal and the review by the Supreme Court (*Cour de cassation*). All aspects, whether legal or factual, of a first instance decision are subject to review by the court of appeal. The parties can challenge without any restriction the application or non-application of the conflict of laws rule, which can be pleaded for the first time before the court of appeal.[94] Moreover, the court of appeal controls the application and interpretation of the foreign law by the lower court. On the contrary, decisions of courts of appeal are only subject to a limited review by the *Cour de cassation*. The following developments will focus exclusively on the particularities of the review by the *Cour de cassation,* which can be observed as to the application of the conflict of laws rule (A) and as to the application of foreign law (B). Some authors advocate for a stronger involvement of the *Cour de cassation* in the future (C).

A. *Conflict of Laws Rules*

If the conflict of laws rule has been applied erroneously by the court of appeal, the parties can appeal to the *Cour de cassation*. The situation is different, if the conflict of laws rule has not been applied at all by the court of appeal. The scope of the review by the *Cour de cassation* depends then on the nature of the rights involved. In case of unavailable rights, as far as the cross-border element is present in the case file, the conflict of laws rule can be pleaded by the parties for the first time before the *Cour de cassation*.[95] The applicability of foreign law is thus treated as a purely legal argument (*moyen de pur droit*), which is admissible before the *Cour de cassation*.[96] On the contrary, in case of available rights, when no party has pleaded foreign law in the first instance or in appeal, the conflict of laws rule cannot be pleaded for the first time before the *Cour de cassation*.[97] In case of silence of the parties, the application of the conflict of laws rule is not mandatory for the lower courts and the applicability of foreign law is treated as an argument combining factual and legal aspects (*moyen mélangé de fait et de droit*), which is not admissible before the *Cour de cassation*.

---

[94] The background idea is that the applicability of foreign law is not a new claim (*demande nouvelle*) but only a new argument (*moyen nouveau*): B. Audit, L. d'Avout, *op. cit.*, n° 326. In other words, the applicability of foreign law is not a claim, but only the legal basis of a claim: P. Mayer, V. Heuzé, *op. cit.*, n° 143.

[95] 1e Civ., 26.5. 1999, *Soc. Mutuelle du Mans*, *Rev. crit. DIP* 1999. 707, comm. H. Muir Watt. In this decision, the *Cour de cassation* required, as far as unavailable rights are involved, an *ex officio* application of the conflict of laws rule by the court of appeal, which means, logically, that the conflict of laws rule has not been pleaded before the lower courts. Hence, the argument is admissible for the first time before the *Cour de cassation*.

[96] H. Muir Watt, "Loi étrangère", Répertoire de droit international, Dalloz, 2010, n° 35.

[97] 1e Civ., 28. 11. 2006, n° 05–19838; 1e Civ., 20. 10. 2010, *Rev. crit. DIP* 2011. 53, comm. B. Ancel.

Despite these general principles identifying the situations where the appeal to the *Cour de cassation* is admissible, the *Cour de cassation* sometimes declares the appeal inadmissible. Indeed, one of the main concerns of the *Cour de cassation* is not to favour appeals whose sole objective is to delay the final outcome of the proceedings. Considerations of procedural economy require a more pragmatic approach. Thus, in order to discourage the parties from purely delaying appeals, the *Cour de cassation* developed an "exception of equivalence" which applies to available and unavailable rights. According to this exception, the appeal to the *Cour de cassation* is not admissible, if the applied law and the law which would have been applicable are equivalent as to the legal consequences of the dispute.[98] However, a specific condition must be fulfilled which limits considerably the usefulness of the exception of equivalence. The exception only applies if the court of appeal has ascertained the content of foreign law and duly explained its equivalence with French law.[99] In other words, the equivalence must be established by the court of appeal; it is not sufficient for the *Cour de cassation* to establish it *ex post*.[100] If the court of appeal has not applied the conflict of laws rule at all or has applied it erroneously, this specific condition is not fulfilled and the exception of equivalence cannot "save" the decision. Moreover, the concept of equivalence raises several questions which have not clearly been answered yet, especially as to the degree of similarity which is required.[101] Finally, it is not clear if the exception of equivalence is only deemed to be a remedy against the annulment – for merely formal reasons – of the decision of the court of appeal, or if the *Cour de cassation* uses it more generally as a new and less abstract approach to conflicts of laws.[102]

B. Foreign Law

In principle, lower courts are sovereign when applying and interpreting foreign law. In other words, the application and interpretation of foreign law are not subject to review by the *Cour de cassation*.[103] Only two exceptions are admitted. Firstly, the

---

[98] 1e Civ., 13. 4. 1999, *Rev. crit. DIP* 1999. 698, comm. B. Ancel and H. Muir Watt, *JDI* 2000. 315, comm. B. Fauvarque-Cosson; 1e Civ., 11. 1. 2005, *Rev. crit. DIP* 2006. 85, comm. M. Scherer; Com., 10. 7. 2012, n° 10–17325.

[99] 1e Civ., 23. 1. 2007, *Rev. crit. DIP* 2007. 760, comm. O. Boskovic.

[100] H. Muir Watt, op. cit., n° 72.

[101] H. Gaudemet-Tallon, "De nouvelles fonctions pour l'équivalence en droit international privé?", in *Le droit international privé: esprit et méthodes, Mélanges en l'honneur de Paul Lagarde*, 2005, Dalloz, p. 303.

[102] M.-L. Niboyet, G. de Geouffre de la Pradelle, *op. cit.*, n° 675.

[103] This has been a constant and general principle since Civ., 25. 9. 1829, *Sirey* 1830. 1. 151. For recent examples, see 1e Civ., 3. 6. 2003, *JDI* 2004. 520, comm. F. Mélin; 1e Civ., 3. 3. 2010, n° 09–13599; 2e Civ., 12. 7. 2012, n° 11–17487. O. Cachard, "Le contrôle de l'application du droit étranger par les juridictions suprêmes en droit français", in Cl. Witz (ed.), *Application du droit étranger par le juge national: Allemagne, France, Belgique, Suisse*, *op. cit.*, p. 107.

Cour de cassation controls if the court of appeal has distorted the foreign law. The control of distortion is limited to gross misinterpretations and the annulments of decisions on this ground are rare.[104] Historically, the control of distortion comes from the procedural regime of contractual matters in domestic law.[105] Lower courts are sovereign when interpreting a contract, unless clear and unequivocal contractual documents were distorted. This explains the current regime of review by the *Cour de cassation* regarding choice of law agreements. The interpretation of choice of law clauses and the characterization of implicit choices of law are left to the discretion of lower courts and are not subject to review by the *Cour de cassation*, except for distortion.[106] The second exception, which is becoming increasingly important in practice, is the review by the *Cour de cassation* of the grounds of the decision of the court of appeal. The *Cour de cassation* verifies the existence of a sufficient statement of reasons. Lower courts must sufficiently justify their decisions regarding the proof, the application, and the interpretation of the foreign law.[107] Indeed, since the recent case law requires the judge, when he has acknowledged that foreign law is applicable, to ascertain its content, a control is needed to make sure that the judge undertook sufficient steps to establish the content of the foreign law. The review of the grounds of the decision is the tool used by the *Cour de cassation* for that purpose.[108] As the obligation to state reasons is a formal requirement, the annulment of the decision that ensues is not grounded on an erroneous application of foreign law, but only on a lack of reasoning. Nevertheless, the control of the sufficient statement of reasons can also be a tool for the control of the decision as to its substance.[109] Indeed, either the court of appeal has not sufficiently justified its decision and the decision can be annulled on this ground, or the court of appeal has sufficiently provided reasons for it and the *Cour de cassation* can then annul the decision if the statement of reasons reveals a distortion of the foreign law.

---

[104] For example, 1e Civ., 1. 7. 1997, *Africatours, Rev. crit. DIP* 1998. 292, comm. H. Muir Watt, *D.* 1998. 104, comm. M. Menjucq; 1e Civ., 14. 2. 2006, *Rev. crit. DIP* 2006. 833, comm. S. Bollée; 1e Civ., 22. 10. 2008, *Rev. crit. DIP* 2009. 5., comm. H. Muir Watt.

[105] H. Muir Watt, *op. cit.*, n° 128.

[106] Regarding employment contracts, see F. Jault-Seseke, "L'office du juge dans l'application de la règle de conflit de lois en matière de contrat de travail", *Rev. crit. DIP* 2005. 253.

[107] For example, requiring the indication of the exact provision on which the decision is based: 1e Civ., 6. 3. 2001, *Rev. crit. DIP* 2001. 335, comm. H. Muir Watt, *JDI* 2002. 171, comm. M. Raimon; 1e Civ., 6. 2. 2007, n° 05–19333; 1e Civ., 20. 2. 2008, n° 06–19936; 1e Civ., 13. 2. 2013, n° 11–28259; requiring a comprehensive ascertainment of the foreign law: 2e Civ., 28. 2. 2013, n° 11–11170.

[108] H. Muir Watt, *op. cit.*, n° 127.

[109] H. Muir Watt, *op. cit.*, n° 136.

C. De Lege Ferenda

The limited review by the *Cour de cassation* regarding the application and interpretation of foreign law is traditionally justified by the specific role of the Supreme Court which is to ensure a uniform application of the law by French courts. This role relates only to the application of French law because the *Cour de cassation* is not the guardian of the unity of a foreign law.[110] Moreover, a passive attitude is considered to be more appropriate because it avoids an erroneous interpretation of foreign law by the *Cour de cassation* itself, which would necessarily damage the credibility of the court.[111] Finally, the limited review is also justified by pragmatic considerations i.e. avoid to overload the *Cour de cassation* with a mass of appeals. However, Horatia Muir Watt has shown that the recent strengthening of the role of the judge as to the ascertainment of foreign law is not consistent with the traditionally passive attitude of the *Cour de cassation* regarding the application and interpretation of foreign law.[112] The purpose is not to transform the *Cour de cassation* into a guardian of foreign law, but only to make sure that the lower courts apply the foreign law as it is applied in its country of origin. With regard to foreign laws which are regularly applied in France, for example the laws of the Maghreb countries in matters of personal status, divergent interpretations by the lower courts lead to unequal treatments, which are difficult to accept for the litigants. Their uniform application by French courts should be guaranteed by the *Cour de cassation.* Furthermore, as to the risk of overloading the *Cour de cassation*, it is difficult to understand why the *Cour de cassation* should not control the interpretation of foreign law, while some decisions omitting to apply the conflict of laws rule are subject to review even though no difference exists between the applied French law and the applicable foreign law. And one might add that the authority of the conflict of laws rule is similarly compromised by an omission to determine the applicable law as by an erroneous application of foreign law. Moreover, the distinction is too subtle to be feasible between, on the one hand, the requirement of a complete ascertainment of the foreign law by the lower courts – which leads to an annulment if the decision is not sufficiently justified – and, on the other hand, the absence of any control if the foreign law has been wrongfully applied because the court of appeal omitted some legal sources of the foreign law. All these arguments advocate for a stronger involvement of the C*our de cassation.* In recent years however, a slight shift in the attitude of the *Cour de cassation* has been perceivable regarding the review of the grounds of lower courts' decisions, which has become stricter and which is getting closer to a genuine review of the interpretation of foreign law.[113] If this evolution is to be confirmed and if the control really approaches a genuine review of interpretation, the regime would be satisfactory.

---

[110] See for example P. Mayer, V. Heuzé, *op. cit.*, n° 193.

[111] M.-L. Niboyet, G. de Geouffre de la Pradelle, *op. cit.*, n° 690.

[112] H. Muir Watt, "Loi étrangère", Répertoire de droit international, Dalloz, 2010, n° 118 f.

[113] H. Muir Watt, *op. cit.*, n° 136; M.-L. Niboyet, G. de Geouffre de la Pradelle, *op. cit.*, n° 692.

V. Foreign Law in Other Instances

The application of foreign law by non-judicial authorities has attracted less doctrinal attention than the application by judicial authorities and case law on this specific topic is rather limited.[114] However, this does not mean that proof and information about foreign law is not an issue for non-judicial authorities.

A. Civil Registrars

Civil registrars *(officiers de l'état civil)* are regularly confronted with the application of foreign law, especially when celebrating marriages. According to the conflict of laws rule, substantive conditions of marriage are governed by the law of the State of the nationality of each spouse. Hence, foreign law is to be applied every time at least one spouse is not French. The nationality is indicated in the documents required before the marriage, and the civil registrar is therefore always aware of the cross-border element. As marriage belongs to the category of unavailable rights, the application of the conflict of laws rule is mandatory. The recent law introducing same-sex marriage in France illustrates the somewhat demanding role of the civil registrar and that it is not always sufficient for him to apply simply the French conflict of laws rule codified in the *Code civil.* Indeed, civil registrars must also know all bilateral agreements, especially the older ones which conflict with the new French conflict of laws rule for same-sex marriage, whose aim is to favour same-sex marriages even though the law of the nationality prohibits this form of matrimonial union.[115] However, civil registrars are guided in their duties by administrative circulars explaining how to apply the conflict of laws rule and summarizing the current framework of French private international law.[116] The content of the foreign law must be proved by the spouses; it is not ascertained by civil registrars. They can produce a certificate of matrimonial capacity issued by the authorities of the State of nationality or a *certificat de coutume*.[117] If the content of the foreign law cannot be ascertained, the civil registrar must nevertheless celebrate the marriage as far as all conditions of French law are met and the spouses, informed of the risk that their marriage might not be recognized by their State of nationality, maintain their wish

[114] S. Fulli-Lemaire, D. Rojas-Tamayo, "France", in C. Esplugues, J. L. Iglesias, G. Palao (ed.), *Application of Foreign Law*, Sellier, 2011, p. 196.

[115] Art. 202–1 Code civil. See the administrative circular n° JUSC1312445C of 29. 5. 2013; P. Hammje, "'Mariage pour tous' et droit international privé. Dits et non-dits de la loi du 17 mai 2013 ouvrant le mariage aux couples de personnes de même sexe", *Rev. crit. DIP* 2013, p. 773.

[116] General Instruction on Civil Status (*Instruction générale relative à l'état civil*) of 11. 5. 1999, n° 527–556 and n° 567–567-6; administrative circular n° JUSC1312445C of 29. 5. 2013 presenting the law which introduces same-sex marriage into French law.

[117] General Instruction on Civil Status of 11. 5. 1999, n° 540.

to marry.[118] The same consequence also applies when the substantive conditions of marriage of the foreign law are not fulfilled, which is unanimously criticized because it contradicts the mandatory applicability of the conflict of laws rule in a matter involving unavailable rights, and should rather be addressed through recourse to the public policy exception if the conditions of the foreign law are too strict according to French standards.[119] The activities of civil registration, such as the drafting, modification or transcription of various civil-status records, are basically founded on the same principles. The conflict of laws rule is mandatory for civil registrars because unavailable rights are involved, but the content of foreign law is to be proved by the parties. The latter principle has been criticized because it introduces a difference between judges and civil registrars which is not really justified.[120] More particularly in matters of personal status, the laws of all Contracting States of the International Commission on Civil Status are summarized in an International Practical Guide to Civil Status, which is a useful tool for the ascertainment of foreign law.[121] If the parties fail to prove the content of foreign law, French law applies subsidiarily.[122]

B. Notaries (Notaires)

As a public official, the *notaire* is a forum and can be assimilated to a judge.[123] Thus, he must apply the conflict of laws rule of the forum when its application is mandatory, and has to ascertain the content of foreign law with the collaboration of the parties. In his advisory role, the *notaire* has the professional obligation to inform and advise his clients in order to draft valid legal deeds.[124] This implies the application of conflict of laws rules if necessary. However, just like judges, *notaires* are only subject to the *iura novit curia* principle, presuming that they know the law, as far as French law is concerned, which includes conflict of laws rules applicable in France, but not the foreign law designated by the conflict of laws rule. The *notaire* can require the parties to provide a *certificat de coutume* in order to establish the content of the foreign law. In practice, *notaires* often research the content of foreign law by themselves, because they are expected by their clients to provide

[118] General Instruction on Civil Status, n° 546.

[119] B. Bourdelois, "Mariage", Répertoire de droit international, Dalloz, 2011, n° 39.

[120] C. Bidaud-Garon, "Etat civil. – Autorités compétentes. – Loi applicable. – Réception des actes étrangers en France", *JurisClasseur Droit international*, fasc. n° 544, 2008, n° 187.

[121] http://www.ciec1.org/GuidePratique/index.htm

[122] General Instruction on Civil Status of 11. 5. 1999, n° 530.

[123] G. Droz, "L'activite notariale internationale", in *Collected Courses of The Hague Academy of International Law,* vol. 280, Martinus Nihjoff, 1999, p. 48.

[124] G. Droz, "L'activite notariale internationale", *op. cit.*, p. 49 f.; M. Revillard, *Droit international privé et communautaire: pratique notariale*, Defrénois, 2010; M. Revillard, "Notaire", Répertoire de droit international, Dalloz, 2012.

comprehensive legal advice. In their search, they can rely on the assistance of their local Center for notarial researches, information and documentation (*Centre de recherches, d'information et de documentation notariales, CRIDON)*, which provides legal consultancy services. These centres have, over the years, gathered together sources and documentation on numerous foreign laws and can generally provide *notaires* with sufficient information. Moreover, a Guide on comparative law, specifically intended for *notaires*, is available online.[125] If uncertainties remain as to the content of foreign law, the *notaire* has to inform the parties, and if these uncertainties cannot be clarified, the *notaire*, after explaining the difficulties he faces, applies French law. The regime of professional liability of *notaires* is very strict in French law.

The cooperation mechanism set up by the European Convention on Information on Foreign Law[126] is not available for non-judicial authorities.

[125] http://guidedroitcompare.com/. The guide has been elaborated and is regularly updated by an association of students of the master program in Notarial Law of the University of Paris Ouest Nanterre La Défense.

[126] Elaborated by the European Council and signed in London the 7. 6. 1968.

Germany: Proof of and Information About Foreign Law – Duty to Investigate, Expert Opinions and a Proposal for Europe

Oliver Remien

Abstract For some 140 years now foreign law is regarded not as a mere fact to be proven by the parties, but as law under s. 293 of the German Code of Civil Procedure. This implies specific duties for the German courts. The ways for ascertaining the foreign law are analyzed in detail in this report from Germany, especially the characteristic expert opinions on foreign law delivered by German academic institutes. Remarkably, the Federal Court of Justice has established a very strict case-law on the judges' duty to ascertain the content of the foreign law, although this Supreme Court does not rule on the content of the foreign law itself on appeal. De lege ferenda, this contribution argues for introducing – at least in the European Union – a reference procedure for preliminary rulings on the foreign law by a foreign court of the same level as the referring court hearing the case.

Proof of and information about foreign law is a topic often dealt with in German court practice and in German legal writing on conflict of laws and international civil procedure. And already in 1966 the Max-Planck-Institut für ausländisches und internationales Privatrecht in Hamburg has held an international symposium on just this topic in order to commemorate its foundation 40 years earlier as a Kaiser-Wilhelm-Institut in Berlin in 1926.[1] In fact, already in the second half of the nineteenth century, when in 1879 the German Civilprocessordnung of 1877, today Zivilprozessordnung or ZPO (Code of Civil Procedure), entered into force, it had a provision on this problem, today's § 293 ZPO. It then was § 265 CPO. This in some

[1] See *Müller* (ed.), Die Anwendung ausländischen Rechts im Internationalen Privatrecht, Festveranstaltung und Kolloquium anläßlich des 40jährigen Bestehens des Max-Planck-Instituts für ausländisches und internationales Privatrecht vom 6.-8. Juli 1966 in Hamburg, 1968.

O. Remien (✉)
Professor, Faculty of Law, Julius-Maximilians-University of Würzburg,
Domerschulstraße 16, 97070 Würzburg, Germany
e-mail: remien@jura.uni-wuerzburg.de

Y. Nishitani (ed.), *Treatment of Foreign Law - Dynamics towards Convergence?*,
Ius Comparatum – Global Studies in Comparative Law 26,
DOI 10.1007/978-3-319-56574-3_8

way innovative, though imperfect[2] provision still contains the core rule on this subject in Germany, though many other things in the meantime may have changed over time. This does not only apply for the general internationalization or globalization, but is especially true for the European integration which could or should have effects on this topic. This report from Germany follows the questionnaire provided by our General Reporter *Yuko Nishitani*. When appropriate it briefly addresses specific aspects of European legal integration.

I. Conflict of Laws Rules

1. Mandatory Application of Conflict of Laws Rules

The application of the conflict of laws rules in Germany is mandatory.[3] This also is the practice. In legal writing there is, however, since a long time a (small) current advocating a "facultative conflict of laws" (fakultatives Kollisionsrecht). It wants to apply the conflicts rules only if they are invoked by a party, but not *ex officio*. This opinion has most notably been advocated by *Axel Flessner*.[4] It particularly stresses the interests of the parties: they shall not be confronted with a foreign law (to the court) which they do not want. However, this endangers the applicability of mandatory rules[5] and clearly is a minority opinion which has found little support.[6]

---

[2] For some harsh, but partly unjust criticism see *Otto*, Der verunglückte § 293 ZPO und die Ermittlung ausländischen Rechts durch "Beweiserhebung", IPRax 1995, 299, 300 f. He entirely neglects the fact that the German provision is one hundred years older than comparable Swiss and Austrian provisions. Critical on § 293 ZPO also *Kindl*, Ausländisches Recht vor deutschen Gerichten, ZZP 111 (1998) 177.

[3] BGH 15.7.2008 – VI ZR 105/07, NJW 2009, 916, 917 at no. 8, with further references; *Kegel/Schurig*, Internationales Privatrecht, Ein Studienbuch, 9th ed. 2004, 497 f.; *Sonnenberger*, in: Münchener Kommentar zum Bürgerlichen Gesetzbuch, ed. by Säcker/Rixecker, Band 10: Internationales Privatrecht, 5th ed. 2010 (cited: MünchKomm-BGB/*Sonnenberger*) Einl. IPR nos. 220 ff., 619; *Leipold*, in: Stein/Jonas, Kommentar zur Zivilprozessordnung, 22nd edition 2008 (cited: Stein/Jonas(-*Leipold*), § 293 ZPO no. 30; *Geimer*, Internationales Zivilprozessrecht, 6th ed. 2009, nos. 2571 f., 2594; *Kropholler*, Internationales Privatrecht, 6th ed. 2006, 45 f.; *von Bar/Mankowski*, Internationales Privatrecht, Band I: Allgemeine Lehren, 2nd. ed. 2003, no. 5/64; *Schack*, Internationales Zivilverfahrensrecht, 5th ed. 2010, no. 699; *Müller,* in: Müller 66; *Mörsdorf-Schulte*, in: Prütting/Wegen/Weinreich (eds.), BGB, Kommentar, 8th edition 2013 (cited: Prütting/Wegen/Weinreich(-*Mörsdorf-Schulte*), Art. 3 EGBGB no. 28.

[4] Already in: *Flessner*, Fakultatives Kollisionsrecht, RabelsZ 34 (1970) 547–584; later in: *Flessner*, Interessenjurisprudenz im internationalen Privatrecht, 1990, 121–125; see also *Sturm*, Das Kollisionsrecht im Umbruch, StAZ 1977, 213, 215; on this concept see also *Wagner*, Fakultatives Kollisionsrecht und prozessuale Parteiautonomie, ZEuP 1999, 6, 7 ff.; *Trautmann*, Ausländisches Recht vor deutschen und englischen Gerichten, ZEuP 2006, 283, 287.

[5] See e.g. *Kreuzer*, Einheitsrecht als Ersatzrecht, Zur Frage der Nichtanwendbarkeit fremden Rechts, NJW 1983, 1943, 1946; in detail against „facultative conflict of laws"*Schurig*, Kollisionsnorm und Sachrecht, 1981, 49, 343 ff.; *von Bar/Mankowski* nos. 5/66 ff.

[6] In more detail see the doctoral dissertations by *Reichert-Facilides*, Fakultatives und zwingendes Kollisionsrecht, 1995; *Koerner*, Fakultatives Kollisionsrecht in Frankreich und Deutschland, 1995.

European integration could bring new aspects to our topic. In these last years, considerable though limited parts of conflicts laws in Germany and other EU Member States have been "europeanized" through enactment of EU-Regulations (Rome I, Rome II, Rome III, Succession etc.).[7] These regulations seem not to address expressly the question of mandatory or facultative application of their conflicts rules.[8] At least in Germany, this has not changed the mandatory application of conflict of laws rules in the areas concerned.

A preceding (or upstream) question to that of the mandatory or facultative character of the conflicts rule can be whether the Court is under a duty to ascertain whether the case presents facts constituting a foreign element giving rise to a conflicts question.[9] This depends on the procedural principles applying in a given procedure. In general civil procedure, according to the disposition maxim ("Dispositionsmaxime" or "Beibringungsgrundsatz"), pleading and proving the facts is the task of the parties alone and this would apply also here. Though, in some family matters the inquisitorial maxim ("Untersuchungsgrundsatz") reigns and also covers this question.[10]

2. *Frequency of Application of Foreign Law*

It is a common phenomenon that the German conflict of laws rules may lead to the application of foreign law. Of course this will depend on the individual conflicts rule, especially its connecting factor. A certain tendency to introduce habitual residence as a connecting factor is considered as reducing the frequency of referring to a foreign law. At any rate there are many court cases where foreign law has been ascertained and applied by German courts. The collection "IPRspr." is witness to it.[11] Especially notable are divorce and inheritance cases where foreign law has been applied. There even is a collection of legal opinions on foreign law which have been rendered by experts in order to help the court in ascertaining properly the content of the applicable foreign law and decide the case correctly ("IPG – Gutachten zum ausländischen und internationalen Privatrecht").[12]

---

[7] For a survey, see e.g. Prütting/Wegen/Weinreich(-*Mörsdorf-Schulte*) Art. 3 EGBGB no. 18.

[8] On the problem *Kieninger*, Ermittlung und Anwendung ausländischen Rechts, in: Leible/Unberath (eds.), Brauchen wir eine Rom 0-Verordnung?, 2013, 479 ff., 489 ff. with references, also 493 ff.; *Flessner*, Das Parteiinteresse an der lex fori nach europäischem Kollisionsrecht, in: Confronting the frotiers of family and succession law, Liber Amicorum Walter Pintens, 2012, 593 ff. holds all EU conflict of laws rules to be facultative.

[9] See *Schack* no. 701; MünchKomm-BGB/*Sonnenberger*, Einl. IPR no. 621; *Kieninger* 483 f.; *Trautmann*, Europäisches Kollisionsrecht und ausländisches Recht im nationalen Zivilverfahren, 2011, 44 ff.

[10] See e.g. *Schack* no. 701.

[11] IPRspr. – Die deutsche Rechtsprechung auf dem Gebiete des Internationalen Privatrechts, published annually at the Max-Planck-Institut.

[12] See infra 3 and II.3.b)ee) in more detail.

However, it may happen in practice that a court favours avoiding the complicated ascertainment and application of foreign law and shows a "homeward trend" ("Heimwärtsstreben").[13] This has often been criticized in legal writing.

3. The World's Laws Before German Courts

People and their laws may come from all corners of the World, also to German courts. The statistics on expert opinions on foreign law rendered by the Max-Planck-Institut in Hamburg[14] may give an impression of the relevant countries. The annual activity report of the institute[15] always contains some figures[16] on these expert opinions which indicate how many opinions on foreign law have been rendered in the different departments ("Referate") of the institute. Based on these figures here is a chart which may give some impression:

Short description of the department	Opinions rendered in the year									
	2004	2005	2006	2007	2008	2009	2010	2011	2012	Total
Scandinavia	1	1	4	2	–	–	4	2	2	16
Common Law-systems I (England I and II)	5	6	4	4	2	10	9	7	5	32
Common Law-systems II (Africa)	2	4	3	1	4	4	3	2	8	31
Common Law-systems III (India)	3	–	–	6	7	2	4	3	3	28
Netherlands	6	3	1	7	6	3	2	1	7	36
France (incl. francophone Africa)	3	6	3	10	1	4	1	2	1	31
Alpine countries (Switzerland/Austria/Liechtenstein)	3	2	–	2	2	–	1	3	1	14
Spain	1	1	–	1	1	–	8	10	8	30
Italy	1	1	–	1	–	3	5	3	6	20
South Eastern Europe	4	8	6	11	10	8	7	8	5	67
Greece	5	2	4	4	5	2	4	1	4	31
Eastern Europe (of that Poland)	–	4	2	2 (2)	4 (4)	–	1 (1)	–	–	13 (7)
Russia	3	–	–	2	1	2	1	2	1	12

[13] Cf. e.g. *Kropholler* 42 f., 113.

[14] On these expert opinions on foreign law in Germany see infra II.3.b)ee).

[15] Available at http://www.mpipriv.de/files/pdf4/taetigkeitsbericht_2012.pdf (mainly in German); for a list of the activity reports with links http://www.mpipriv.de/en/pub/about_us/informationsmaterial/institute_activity_rep.

[16] In this form since the year 2004.

Short description of the department	Opinions rendered in the year									
	2004	2005	2006	2007	2008	2009	2010	2011	2012	Total
Islamic legal systems (of those Turkey)	10	3	5	6	1	8	8 (2)	14 (7)	12 (8)	67 (17)
China/South East Asia	2	3	6	9	3	3	2	2	3	33
Japan	1	–	2	1	–	–	1	–	–	5
USA I and II	3	9	5	6	4	3	2	4	4	40
Latin America	–	2	10	4	3	3	4	7	4	37
Former GDR	–	–	–	–	–	–	–	1	–	1
Total	53	55	55	79	54	55	67	72	74	564

Thus, of these 564 or – deducting the single opinion on former GDR-law – rather 563 opinions on foreign law within nine years, 290, i.e. more than half of them, concerned the laws of other European countries (without Russia, but including francophone Africa). Russia only accounted for twelve expert opinions and the other continents show much lower figures than Europe, namely Asia (China and South East Asia 33, Japan 5, India 28:) 66, Anglophone Africa 31, the Americas (USA 40 and Latin America 37:) 77 and other common law jurisdictions – probably in different parts of the world, including Australia and Oceania – 32. This shows that especially the geographically close other European countries are involved, but that for the rest ascertaining the content of foreign law really is a global business. Of course, it cannot be taken for granted that these figures are representative for the entire sector of application of foreign laws in German courts, but they may give some insight.

Generally it is remarked that there are numerous cases which have applied Turkish or Iranian family law. There even is e.g. a series of articles on "Turkish divorce and effects of divorce law before German courts.[17] Islamic laws and especially talaq-divorces also play a role.[18] Notable are also cases applying English company law in cases where Limited companies registered in England and Wales have been active in Germany.[19] In case of traffic accidents in the EU, the injured person has the possibility to bring his claim against the foreign insurer in his home country; this often will lead to the application of the foreign traffic accident law of the place of accident, insurer and tortfeasor[20] within the EU and also to German courts.

[17] *Finger*, Türkisches Scheidungs- und Scheidungsfolgenrecht vor deutschen Gerichten, FuR 1997, 129–133, 1997, 195–199,1997, 236–238, 1997, 300–304, 1997, 340–347, 1998, 398, 2000, 193–198.

[18] *Jansen/Michaels*, Die Auslegung und Fortbildung ausländischen Rechts, ZZP 116 (2003) 3 ff., 42, 46 with references.

[19] Cf. *Mäsch*, Die Rolle des BGH im Wettbewerb der Rechtsordnungen oder: Neue Nahrung für den Ruf nach der Revisibilität ausländischen Rechts, EuZW 2004, 321, who even predicted that the application of foreign company law by German instance courts will become normal business („Normalität").

[20] *Tomson*, Der Verkehrsunfall im Ausland vor deutschen Gerichten, – Alle Wege führen nach Rom-, EuZW 2009, 204, 208.

4. *European Aspects*

Today, the European Union (EU) has inter alia the task to establish an area of Freedom, Security and Justice. In this framework and more specifically through the Judicial Cooperation in Civil Matters (JUSTCIV) it has to a considerable extent already unified the conflict of laws rules. But as already indicated, their practical impact may well be divergent in the Member States. This is a problem which will have to be addressed on the European level.

II. Foreign Law Before Judicial Authorities

1. *Nature of Foreign Law*

Foreign law in Germany is considered as "law" and not as a mere "fact".[21] This as such is well-settled and undisputed. It is even recognized in other areas than private law.[22] One can only ask the question whether due to practical problems this approach is – and can be – always observed 100%.[23] But it clearly is the applicable general rule. This is so since 1879 – before, in Prussia and other German states foreign law had been regarded as a fact.[24] The – as far as possible – equal treatment of foreign law calls for satisfactory means to acquire information about the applicable foreign law – insofar this issue has been considered as a kind of "secret king" of conflict of laws.[25]

[21] Stein/Jonas(-*Leipold*) § 293 ZPO nos. 2, 33; MünchKomm-BGB/*Sonnenberger*, Einl. IPR no. 624; MünchKomm-ZPO/*Prütting* § 293 ZPO nos. 1, 14; *Schack* no. 702; *Linke/Hau*, Internationales Zivilverfahrensrecht, Grundriss, 5th ed.2011, no. 321; *Geimer* no. 2577; *Kropholler* 212, 644; *von Bar/Mankowski* nos. 5/96 f.; *Rauscher*, Internationales Privatrecht, Mit internationalem Verfahrensrecht, 4th ed. 2012, no. 136; *Müller* in: Müller 68; *Kindl*, ZZP 111 (1998) 177, 179; *Otto*, IPRax 1995, 299, 301.

[22] Recently Bundesfinanzhof 13.6.2013 III R 63/11, BFHE 242, 34, no. 27, and III R 10/11, BFHE 241, 562 no. 29: public payments for children.

[23] See *Spickhoff*, Fremdes Recht vor inländischen Gerichten: Rechts- oder Tatfrage? ZZP 112 (1999) 265.

[24] See in more detail and also on innovative rules in Württemberg and Bavaria *Schellack*, Selbstermittlung oder ausländische Auskunft unter dem europäischen Rechtsauskunftsübereinkommen, 1998, 72 f.

[25] *Kegel*, Zur Organisation der Ermittlung ausländischen Privatrechts, FS Nipperdey, 1965, 453, 462: "eine Art 'heimlicher König'".

2. Application of Foreign Law

a) § 293 ZPO

The German Code of Civil Procedure – the Zivilprozessordnung, ZPO, of 1877 – contains a rule on application and ascertainment of foreign law in (today) its § 293 ZPO:

> "Das in einem anderen Staate geltende Recht, die Gewohnheitsrechte und Statuten bedürfen des Beweises nur insofern, als sie dem Gericht unbekannt sind. Bei Ermittlung dieser Rechtsnormen ist das Gericht auf die von den Parteien beigebrachten Nachweise nicht beschränkt; es ist befugt, auch andere Erkenntnisquellen zu benutzen und zum Zwecke einer solchen Benutzung das Erforderliche anzuordnen."

> "The laws applicable in another state, customary laws, and statutes must be proven only insofar as the court is not aware of them. In making inquiries as regards these rules of law, the court is not restricted to the proof produced by the parties in the form of supporting documents; it has the authority to use other sources of reference as well, and to issue the required orders for such use."[26]

According to § 293 sentence 2 ZPO (Code of Civil Procedure – Zivilprozessordnung) foreign law is to be ascertained and applied *ex officio*.[27] This has also been stressed in court practice.[28] But it is difficult to state in a general or abstract way[29] what the court has to do and how much effort it has to employ. The circumstances of the individual case can be considered.[30]

b) ... and the European Union

It may be noted that the Law of the European Union is not considered foreign law as Germany is one of the (founding) Member States of it. It is applied just in the same way as German law.[31] The law of other Member States of the European Union is, however, still considered foreign law. Thus, for other EU-Member State law, in

---

[26] Translation provided by Samson Übersetzungen GmbH, Dr. Carmen von Schöning, and published on the internet site of the Federal Ministry of Justice under http://www.gesetze-im-internet.de/Teilliste_translations.html, see infra V.

[27] *Schack* no. 703; *Linke/Hau* no. 321; Stein/Jonas(*-Leipold*) § 293 ZPO nos. 1 and 32; *Geimer* no. 2579; Bamberger/Roth BeckOK/*Lorenz*, BGB, Einl. IPR no. 79; Prütting/Wegen/Weinreich (*-Mörsdorf-Schulte*) Art. 3 EGBGB no. 52; *Kegel*, FS Nipperdey 453.

[28] BGH 23.6.2003 – II ZR 305/01, NJW 2003, 2685, 2686; already BGH 21.2.1962 – V ZR 144/60, NJW 1962, 961, 962; see also already *Müller* in: Müller 67, 69.

[29] See e.g. BGH 30.4.1992 – IX ZR 233/90, NJW 1992, 2026, 2029; *Otto*, IPRax 1995, 299, 303; Bamberger/Roth BeckOK/*Lorenz* Einl. IPR no. 81.

[30] OLG Hamm 5.6.2012 – I-19 U 20/11, juris: set-off in case of different currencies and provision of Polish law similar to German law.

[31] See e.g. Stein/Jonas(*-Leipold*) § 293 ZPO no. 8; MünchKomm-ZPO/*Prütting* § 293 ZPO no. 9.

principle the same rules as for third state law apply.[32] This means that the law of other Member States of the EU is treated differently from domestic – German and EU – law. One can ask whether this amounts to an unjustified discrimination,[33] but in an international perspective § 293 ZPO seems rather progressive because it treats foreign law as law; it also will not really result in an impediment to the internal market.[34]

However, where another EU-Member State has transposed a fully harmonizing EU-directive into its own legal order, this foreign transposing act has to be interpreted in conformity with the EU directive and this may be easy for the German court.[35]

3. Ascertainment of Foreign Law

a) Duty to Investigate Foreign Law

„*Da mihi facta, dabo tibi ius*" – "Give me the facts, so I will give you the law". "*Iura novit curia*" – "The Law is known to the Court" – Whereas according to these maxims[36] the German judge is under the unconditional obligation to know the German law,[37] this does not and cannot apply for foreign law.

Under § 293 ZPO, the Court has the duty to investigate the foreign law.[38] This is to be done *ex officio*.[39] Thus, the court has a duty to procure the information.[40] It

---

[32] See also *Schilken*, Zur Rechtsnatur der Ermittlung ausländischen Rechts nach § 293 ZPO, FS Schumann, 2001, 373, 374.

[33] *Schwartze*, Die Ermittlung und Anwendung des Vertragsrechts anderer EU-Staaten im deutschen Zivilprozeß nach § 293 ZPO – ein besonderer Fall, in: Recht in Europa, Festschrift für Fenge, 1996, 140 ff.

[34] Thus *Schilken*, FS Schumann 373, 374.

[35] See KG 26.9.2011, WRP 2012, 102 on the Danish transposition of the Unfair Trade Practices Directive.

[36] See e.g. MünchKomm-ZPO/*Prütting* § 293 ZPO no. 2.

[37] *Geimer*, in: Zöller, Zivilprozessordnung, Kommentar, 30th ed. 2014, (cited as:*Zöller/Geimer*), § 293 no. 1.

[38] *Schack* no. 702; Stein/Jonas(-*Leipold*) § 293 ZPO no. 9; MünchKomm-ZPO/*Prütting* § 293 ZPO no. 12; *Müller* in: Müller 67; *Huzel*, Zur Zulässigkeit eines „Auflagenbeschlusses"im Rahmen des § 293 ZPO, IPRax 1990, 77, 78; also BAG 10.4.1975, BAGE 27, 99, 109; *Ullrich*, in: Schwab/ Weth (eds.), Arbeitsgerichtsgesetz, Kommentar, 3rd ed. 2011, § 73 ArbGG no. 3.

[39] *Schack* no. 703; MünchKomm-ZPO/*Prütting* § 293 ZPO no. 12; Palandt(-*Thorn*), BGB, 73rd ed. 2014, Einl v EGBGB 3 (IPR) no. 34; *Lindacher*, FS Schumann 283; *Fastrich*, Revisibilität der Ermittlung ausländischen Rechts, ZZP 97 (1984) 423, 425; *Otto* IPRax 1995, 299, 302 with many references.

[40] Stein/Jonas(-*Leipold*) § 293 ZPO no. 33; *Remien*, Iura novit curia und die Ermittlung fremden Rechts im europäischen Rechtsraum der Artt. 61 ff. EGV – für ein neues Vorabentscheidungsverfahren bei mitgliedstaatlichen Gerichten, in: Aufbruch nach Europa, 75 Jahre Max-Planck-Institut für Privatrecht, 2001, 617, 618.

cannot in a general way just leave everything to the parties and proof provided by them.[41] But if in an individual procedure party argument about the foreign law becomes more detailed and controversial, then also the duties of the court increase more and more.[42] Ascertaining the foreign law by the court is, however, not a genuine proof-taking, because proof only concerns facts.[43] The court also has to mention in the reasons of its decision how it has proceeded in order to ascertain the foreign law.[44] The court enjoys discretion on how best to procure information on the foreign law,[45] but this is not an invitation to arbitrariness, but a duty and Supreme Court controlled discretion.[46]

Although the German court is not obliged to know the foreign law, it may in happy circumstances in fact happen to know it. It then can apply it on its own. This might happen when the judge has studied abroad, has had practical experience abroad or done academic research on the foreign law in Germany.[47] Especially, it can be the case if there are court divisions or chambers specialized in foreign law. In 1971 and 1982 German conflicts lawyers have recommended creating such specialized chambers.[48] At the regional court level at the Regional Court of Hamburg – Landgericht Hamburg – there exists the 5th,[49] now 27th,[50] Civil Chamber, specialized in foreign law. *Gerhard Luther* has reported that it only rarely has been in need of expert opinions.[51] In the 30s of the twentieth century, there has been such a senate at the Kammergericht, the Court of Appeals in Berlin.[52] Such specialized chambers or senates are frequently recommended today.[53] § 293 ZPO only applies where in

---

[41] *Müller* in: Müller 67.

[42] MünchKomm-ZPO/*Prütting* § 293 ZPO no. 16.

[43] MünchKomm-ZPO/*Prütting* § 293 ZPO no. 14.

[44] Cf. *Kindl*, ZZP 111 (1999) 177, 194 with references.

[45] *Schack* no. 706; Stein/Jonas(-*Leipold*) § 293 ZPO no. 36; *Lindacher*, Zur Mitwirkung der Parteien bei der Ermittlung ausländischen Rechts, FS Schumann 283; *Schilken* FS Schumann 373, 379; *Kindl*, ZZP 111 (1998) 177, 182; *Huzel*, IPRax 1990, 77, 78.

[46] See infra III.2.

[47] Stein/Jonas(-*Leipold*) § 293 ZPO no. 38; *Kronke*, Beweisrechtliche Havarie – Internationalsachenrechtliche gute Reise: Venezolanische Schiffspfandrechte vor deutschen Gerichten, IPRax 1992, 303; see also *Linke/Hau* no. 325.

[48] Zur Verbesserung der deutschen Zivilrechtsprechung in internationalen Sachen, Denkschrift vom 26.8.1970, RabelsZ 35 (1971) 323, and, after critique by public authorities and Bundesgerichtshof, shorter and more cautiously Deutscher Rat für Internationales Privatrecht, II. Denkschrift zur Verbesserung der deutschen Zivilrechtsprechung in internationalen Sachen /vom 27.4.1982/, RabelsZ 46 (1982) 743. See also *Luther*, Kollisions- und Fremdrechtsanwendung in der Gerichtspraxis, RabelsZ 35 (1973) 661, 668 ff.

[49] *Luther*, RabelsZ 35 (1973) 661, 671; see briefly *Kronke*, IPRax 1992, 303.

[50] See Geschäftsverteilungsplan des Landgerichts Hamburg für das Geschäftsjahr 2014.

[51] *Luther*, RabelsZ 35 (1973) 661, 672.

[52] See Denkschrift 1970, RabelsZ 35 (1971) 323, 328 with further references; also *Luther*, RabelsZ 35 (1973) 661, 669, also with some further examples.

[53] *Schack* no. 711; *Linke/Hau* no. 332. On an unfortunate and only temporary reformed rule for the appeal situation see *Schack* no. 712 and *Linke/Hau* op.cit.

the concrete case the court does not have knowledge about the content of the applicable law.[54]

The parties can have a duty to cooperate.[55]

b) Means Used to Ascertain Foreign Law

aa) Documents

The judge may study legal writings in the library in order to ascertain the foreign law.[56] It is reported that in easy structured and recurring family law cases this may already suffice.[57] Indeed, there is some remarkable legal literature on foreign laws in Germany. Especially in the area of family and succession law, there are two well-known big loose-leaf works of reference which will give access to the statute text and some further information, the *Bergmann/Ferid/Henrich* on International Marriage and Child Law[58] and the *Ferid/Firsching/Dörner/Hausmann* on International Succession Law.[59] They will be the first choice for getting some information.[60] To a certain extent, they may be considered part of the backbone of German foreign law information. And in these[61] and other fields such as company law[62] there are also further voluminous books on foreign laws. Also, there are many German introductions into the legal system or the business law of this or that country.[63] There even is a bibliography on foreign law in German language.[64] All this can be very useful, but will quite often not provide information which is sufficiently

[54] MünchKomm-ZPO/*Prütting* § 293 ZPO nos. 14, 16, also no. 24.

[55] See infra 2.b)cc).

[56] Stein/Jonas(-*Leipold*) § 293 ZPO no. 37; *Pfeiffer*, Methoden der Ermittlung ausländischen Rechts, FS Leipold, 2009, 285; *Müller* in: Müller 69; *Otto*, IPRax 1995, 299, 302.

[57] *Otto*, IPRax 1995, 299, 302.

[58] Internationales Ehe- und Kindschaftsrecht, mit Staatsangehörigkeitsrecht, loose-leaf.

[59] Internationales Erbrecht, Quellensammlung mit systematischen Darstellungen des materiellen Erbrechts sowie des Kollisionsrechts der wichtigsten Staaten, 88th ed. loose-leaf 2013.

[60] Expressly so also OLG Frankfurt am Main 2.3.1999–1 WF 36/99, NJWE-FER 1999, 194; further MünchKomm-ZPO/*Prütting* § 293 ZPO no. 24 with footnote 39; Prütting/Wegen/Weinreich(-*Mörsdorf-Schulte*), Art. 3 EGBGB no. 54; see also *Schack* no. 706; *Linke/Hau* no. 325.

[61] For succession law in Europe see *Süß*, Erbrecht in Europa, 2. edition, 2008.

[62] On English Limited companies see e.g. *Just*, Die englische Limited in der Praxis, 4th edition 2012.

[63] E.g. on Canada, Brazil, Turkey, Japan, India or Italy: *Handschug*, Einführung in das kanadische Recht, 2003; *Sester*, Brasilianisches Handels- und Wirtschaftsrecht, 2nd edition 2014; *Rumpf*, Einführung in das türkische Recht, 2004; *Baum/Bälz* (eds.), Handbuch Japanisches Handels- und Wirtschaftsrecht, 2nd edition 2011; *Podehl/Mathur/Agarwal*, Rechtsfragen des Indiengeschäfts, Praxishandbuch, 2nd edition 2012; *Kindler*, Italienisches Handels- und Wirtschaftsrecht, 2nd edition 2013.

[64] *Von Bar*, Ausländisches Privat- und Privatverfahrensrecht in deutscher Sprache, 9th edition 2013.

detailed to decide the case.[65] Often the court unsuccessfully tries this way and then has to take recourse to an expert.[66] Though, even then such a preliminary research may help the court in asking more precise questions to the expert.[67] Where, however, this autonomous research by the court is successful, it may be useful that the court by way of a kind of information decree ("Aufklärungsbeschluss") informs the parties about the content of the foreign law which it has ascertained so that they can take position on it and, in a proper case, may provide an opinion by a party appointed expert.[68] This apparently has been the practice at the 5th Civil Senate at the OLG (Higher Regional Court or Court of Appeals) Stuttgart under professor – and judge – *Stürner* and sometimes is labelled as "Stürner-System".[69]

bb) Internet Sources

The court may also take resort to internet resources. Some authors expressly point out that today the Internet offers many practical tools.[70] Others are more sceptic because much information is access restricted and in any event some familiarity with the foreign legal system might be required.[71] The EU has, in cooperation with notariat and academia, established a number of internet databases on specific areas of private law in the EU, "Couples in Europe" on marriage (and partnership) law[72] and "Successions in Europe" on Succession law.[73] But also beyond the EU internet sources may be helpful. Recently, in a procedure for legal aid concerning a divorce in Germany under the law of Kazachstan, an attorney successfully referred to the internet publication of the Kazakh Act and presented the applicable provisions in the original and his own German translation.[74]

---

[65] *Remien* 625.

[66] See also *Pfeiffer*, FS Leipold 286.

[67] *Pfeiffer*, FS Leipold 286 f.

[68] Thus *Schütze*, in: Gloy/Loschelder/Erdmann, Wettbewerbsrecht, 4th ed. 2010, § 11 Internationales Wettbewerbsverfahrensrecht no. 32.

[69] Ibid.

[70] E.g. Bamberger/Roth BeckOK/*Lorenz* Einl IPR no. 82 and also 81.

[71] See *Linke/Hau* no. 326.

[72] http://www.couplesineurope.eu.

[73] http://www.successions-europe.eu.

[74] OLG Nürnberg 31.1.2013–7 WF 1710/12, juris, see at no. 35.

cc) Assistance of the Parties

The parties of course have the right to procure information on the foreign law to the court.[75] But generally it is also held that the parties have a duty – or at least an incumbency[76] – to cooperate, see § 293 sentence 2 ZPO.[77] Legal basis and consequence of such a duty are, however, doubtful.[78] If one does not read it into § 293 ZPO, one could consider basing it on the general duty of the party to advance the procedure ("allgemeine Prozessförderungspflicht").[79] But only a minority opinion rejects such a duty.[80] Rather, it is even often held that the court may enjoin a party to bring the proof needed.[81] Sometimes, e.g. in commercial cases, access to information on the foreign law may be easier for the parties.[82] This duty may be even stronger where the parties have themselves chosen the foreign law.[83] But it is said that in practice party information on the foreign law is variable in form and quality.[84] Quite often parties provide statutory provisions and their translation into German.[85] More detailed party pleading on the content of foreign law can be of even more variable quality.[86] Courts are advised to be cautious.[87] At any rate, the duty of the parties only is to cooperate[88] – this can be a help to the court, but does not as such relieve it from its own duties.

[75] *Huzel*, IPRax 1990, 77, 79; *Lindacher* FS Schumann 283, 284.

[76] *Linke/Hau* no. 322; Bamberger/Roth BeckOK/*Lorenz* Einl. IPR no. 81; Prütting/Wegen/Weinreich(-*Mörsdorf-Schulte*) Art. 3 EGBGB no. 52; but no duty, *Kindl*, ZZP 111 (1998) 177, 192.

[77] *Leipold*, in: Stein/Jonas § 293 no. 47; *Pfeiffer*, FS Leipold 289; *Remien* 618; *Michael Becker*, Die Ermittlung und Anwendung ausländischen Rechts in der deutschen Rechtspraxis, FS Martiny, 2014, 631; contra: *Schilken*, FS Schumann 373, 379.

[78] Cf. *Huzel*, IPRax1990, 77, 80; *Kindl*, ZZP 11 (1998) 177, 192; *Rühl*, Die Kosten der Rechtswahlfreiheit: zur Anwendung ausländischen Rechts durch deutsche Gerichte, RabelsZ 71 (2007) 559, 571; on the legal consequences also *Michael Becker*, FS Martiny 632.

[79] In the latter sense *Huzel*, IPRax 1990, 77, 80; critical *Lindacher*, FS Schumann 283, 287.

[80] *Kindl*, ibid.; cf. also *Fastrich*, ZZP 97 (1984) 423, 426 f.; *Gruber*, Die Anwendung ausländischen Rechts durch deutsche Gerichte, ZRP 1992, 6, 7.

[81] See e.g. Stein/Jonas(-*Leipold*) § 293 ZPO no. 48; crit. *Huzel*, IPRax 1990, 77.

[82] Cf. *Schack* no. 707; see also the considerations by *Lindacher*, FS Schumann 283, 287. Cf. e.g. BGH 30.4.1992 – IX ZR 233/90, NJW 1992, 2026, 2029 (Liechtenstein).

[83] *Michael Becker*, FS Martiny 632.

[84] *Pfeiffer*, FS Leipold 289.

[85] Ibid.

[86] In more detail *Pfeiffer* ibid.

[87] *Schack* no. 707.

[88] *Huzel*, IPRax 1990, 77, 80; *Lindacher*, FS Schumann 283, 287.

dd) Expert Opinions Procured by a Party

Expert opinions procured by a party are treated as party argument on the foreign law.[89] In case of party expert opinions, the danger of one-sidedness of the opinion is considerable.[90] The court remains under its responsibility to evaluate this party opinion. When the party expert opinion is not challenged by the other party and it appears as convincing, the court may follow it.[91] Prominent as well as more ordinary court cases show that such private expert witness opinions are used in practice, e.g. on Venezuelan "prendas navales" (maritime charges)[92] or French rules on damages for loss of profits or compensation for deprivation of use of a semi-trailer.[93]

ee) Inquiry to an Expert or Expert Institute

Inquiry to an expert or expert institute probably is the most favoured way in German courts and may to some extent even be characteristic. It is an area where dogmatics and pragmatism meet. Some critics argue that sometimes a court may ask for an expert opinion too quickly although there are easier and more cost-efficient ways to obtain the information.[94] What is true is that this way is very convenient for the court.[95]

It may happen that a court requests an expert in an informal way to provide some information.[96] The court is considered to have much liberty ("Freibeweis", liberal proof-taking). However, the normal way will be that the court formally appoints an expert for a given case.[97] The court then issues an order for taking evidence ("Beweisbeschluss")[98] in the sense of § 358 ZPO naming the expert, see § 359 no. 2 ZPO. This is to say, it follows the rules of the ZPO – Code of Civil Procedure – on proof ("Strengbeweis", strict, i.e. rule-bound proof-taking).[99] Where a complete expert opinion is asked for, this probably is the only way.[100] As for the duties of the

---

[89] *Pfeiffer*, FS Leipold 291; *Samtleben*, NJW 1992, 3057, 3059; *Kronke*, IPRax 1992, 303, 304.

[90] See also *Pfeiffer*, FS Leipold 291 f.; *Schack* no. 707.

[91] *Huzel*, IPRax 1990, 77, 78.

[92] BGH 21.1.1991 - II ZR 49/90, NJW-RR 1991, 1211 and see *Samtleben*, NJW 1992, 3057, 3059.

[93] OLG Saarbrücken 16.1.2014 – 4 U 429/12, juris.

[94] *Otto*, IPRax 1995, 299, 303.

[95] Correctly *Otto*, IPRax 1995, 299, 303.

[96] Discussing this way *Pfeiffer*, FS Leipold 295; also *Leipold*, in: Stein/Jonas § 293 nos. 44, 45 and 46; MünchKomm-ZPO/*Prütting* § 293 ZPO no. 26, rightly mentioning "informal brief advice" ("formlose Kurzauskunft").

[97] See already *Müller* in: Müller 70 f.; MünchKomm-ZPO/*Prütting* § 293 ZPO nos. 26, 29.

[98] See e.g. MünchKomm-ZPO/*Prütting* § 293 ZPO no. 29; *Geimer* no. 2585.

[99] See e.g. MünchKomm-ZPO/*Prütting* § 293 ZPO nos. 29, 31.

[100] Stein/Jonas(-*Leipold*) § 293 ZPO no. 43 – but – no. 46 – not for (shorter) abstract legal information; *Otto*, IPRax 1995, 299, 303ff; *Schellack* 125 ff.; BGH 10.7.1975 – II ZR 174/74, NJW 1975, 2142.

expert, then the §§ 407, 407a ZPO apply.[101] Though, a minority opinion holds that under § 293 ZPO there exclusively is liberal, not rule-bound "Freibeweis" and the §§ 355 ff. ZPO on proof, especially §§ 402 ff. ZPO on experts, do not apply.[102] Generally, the court transmits the entire court file to the expert.[103]

An advantage of these court appointed experts is that, compared to party appointed experts, their neutrality will hardly be in doubt.[104] It regularly happens that institutes such as the Max-Planck-Institut für ausländisches und internationales Privatrecht in Hamburg or University institutes for comparative law or their individual professors are appointed as experts.[105] As far as the Max-Planck-Institute is concerned, this goes back to the aftermath of the First World War when with a view to the Mixed Arbitral Tribunals under the Versailles Treaty in 1926 the Kaiser-Wilhelm-Institut für ausländisches und internationals Privatrecht was founded in Berlin and due to the urgent needs of the time started a vast foreign law expert opinion practice under the directorship of *Ernst Rabel* which had a school-founding impact on comparative law in Germany.[106] Expert opinions by an institute are favoured to information provided by the services of a German Ministry of Justice.[107] In Bavaria, an announcement by the Bavarian Ministry of Justice even specifically names two institutes (in Munich and Regensburg) and gives some advice on how to proceed[108]: questions in writing, accompanied by the court file, by the court and not by individuals,[109] giving room for checking also the applicability of the foreign law and mentioning regional or personal factors in case of foreign laws not uniform in the entire state but having a regional or personal scission,[110] costs.[111]

Generally speaking, the expert may be an individual person,[112] but in practice very often – and not in Bavaria alone – an institute is appointed expert. There is some doubt about the admissibility of this,[113] but practice often procedes in this way.

---

[101] *Michael Becker*, FS Martiny 634.

[102] E.g. *Schilken*, FS Schumann 373 ff.; also *Linke/Hau* no. 329.

[103] Correctly *Müller* in: Müller 70.

[104] See also *Pfeiffer*, FS Leipold 294, 298.

[105] For a list of institutes see *Schütze*, Die Anwendung ausländischen Rechts durch deutsche Notare, BWNotZ 1992, 122, 124; somewhat outdated *Müller* in: Müller 70.

[106] Further see *Kegel*, FS Nipperdey 453, 461 with references; briefly also *Spickhoff*, ZZP 112 (1999) 265, 269 f.

[107] *Kegel*, FS Nipperdey 453, 468 f.

[108] Bekanntmachung des Bayerischen Staatsministeriums der Justiz vom 5.6.2008, Az.: 3134 – I -3701/2008 zum Sachverständigenwesen (Sachverständigenbekanntmachung), see there no. 2 with 2.1 to 2.5, available http://www.gesetze-bayern.de. On the older version see also Bamberger/Roth BeckOK/*Lorenz* Einl IPR no. 82.2.

[109] No. 2.3.

[110] No. 2.4.

[111] No. 2.5.

[112] *Pfeiffer*, FS Leipold 298 holds this to be the regular case.

[113] Ibid. 299.

A considerable number of individual experts on foreign and international private law are named in an unofficial list published by a judge since 1983, the so-called *Hetger*-list.[114] But this list has met with some criticism.[115] At the larger institutes, then a staff member of the institute will prepare the expert opinion of the institute which will be checked[116] by an experienced senior staff member in charge of coordinating the expert opinions delivered by the institute. The advantage of this way is not only that two persons – the drafting staff member and the coordinating senior staff member – check the case,[117] but also that the expert opinions are researched and drafted by a person with specific experience in the legal system concerned and not by a pretendedly globally all-competent lawyer or professor. The MPI has a number of staff members who each are in charge of the legal opinions relating to a number of foreign countries (so-called "Länderreferenten").

So, in either case, the experts are mostly German lawyers with international – and perhaps even country specific – experience.[118] Some say that a domestic expert on foreign law is better than a foreign expert, because thus the risk of misunderstanding between court and expert are reduced.[119] Of course the expert may inquire with foreign colleagues and cite the information obtained from them in his opinion.[120] This can happen in especially difficult cases. But it is also possible that foreign experts are appointed. But for them, it may be more difficult to handle the German court file.[121] However, in individual cases where a foreign colleague with very good knowledge of the German legal system was known to an institute, it has been possible to refer a German court to such foreign expert with very good results.[122] But this may be exceptional. That a court appoints a mixed German/foreign team of experts appears as, so far, exotic.[123] The court later may ask additional questions[124] and also hear the expert in court.[125] Many expert opinions delivered by the MPI and university institutes are annually published in the series "Gutachten zum internationalen und ausländischen Privatrecht" (IPG).[126]

---

[114] *Hetger*, Sachverständige für ausländisches und internationals Privatrecht, DNotZ 2003, 310, with references on earlier lists published by *Hetger* in footnote 3.

[115] *Otto*, IPRax 1995, 299, 303; *Schack* no. 710.

[116] Stressing this review by experienced colleagues *Samtleben*, NJW 1992, 3057, 3059.

[117] But thus *Pfeiffer*, FS Leipold 299.

[118] See also *Pfeiffer*, FS Leipold 284, 297.

[119] *Kegel*, FS Nipperdey 453, 467, 470; *Schack* no. 710; a bit more cautiously also MünchKomm-ZPO/*Prütting* § 293 ZPO no. 30; contra: *Linke/Hau* no. 327.

[120] Expressly so *Pfeiffer*, FS Leipold 299 f.

[121] See *Pfeiffer*, FS Leipold 297.

[122] Personal experience with a colleague from the Netherlands. In favour of foreign experts: *Linke/Hau* no. 327.

[123] *Pfeiffer*, FS Leipold 299 says it is not customary ("nicht üblich"), but points to party expert opinions in this format.

[124] *Pfeiffer*, FS Leipold 298.

[125] See infra 5.

[126] Ed. by *Basedow* et al.

The expert opinions very often provide carefully researched information on foreign law which is directly case-related. A drawback may be that the procedure is time consuming and expensive.[127] Further, the institutes, though praising this activity as "nobile officium", are primarily research institutes and therefore have other core tasks than delivering expert opinions.[128] These expert opinions bind considerable resources of the institutes.[129] To the reporter, it seems that the relative weight of expert opinions and free academic research in such institutes or at least some of them is changing over time. Probably, in the first decades after the Second World War (1945 ff.) with many refugees, expelled and displaced persons in a divided country and at the very heart of Europe, the expert opinions on foreign law were very important in matters of personal status, whereas later a shift towards a stronger focus on – not only, but often business related – research in an international competitive academic environment has taken place. Though, the system has also the merit of giving a number of young academics the chance to acquire really deep practical knowledge in conflict of laws and some foreign jurisdiction – in their capacity as "Länderreferenten". Work on the expert legal opinions can be difficult and strenuous. This may be illustrated by the half joking, half complaining use of the expression "Gutachtenknecht" – servant in charge of legal opinions – used for (former) staff members performing this function – not during practice at the institute, but when they look back to this activity in the earlier years of their academic career. But it can with very good reasons be argued that only a person having exercised this activity for a number of years does have a practice proven academic understanding of private international law. And that just this may shield such a person from falling into the traps of overly dogmatic, conceptualist or theory-centered conflicts thinking.

A further danger can be that the expert opinion in some way patronizes the court[130] or respectively that the court adopts it without much consideration or a sense for critique.[131] The court of course is not bound by it. Though, an instance court may feel comfortable in just relying on and following the expert legal opinion. Sometimes in extreme cases, this goes so far that the court does not really cite the foreign law, but just the expert opinion. In other cases, the court may be more critical and assertive, especially in case the expert tries to further develop the still unsettled foreign law.

[127] *Remien* 626; but contrast *Müller,* in: Müller 70.

[128] Denkschrift 1970, RabelsZ (35) 1971, 323; see also *Samtleben*, NJW 1992, 3057, 3059.

[129] See *Müller,* in: Müller 70.

[130] *Müller,* in: Müller 71.

[131] *Otto*, IPRax 1995, 299, 303.

ff) Inquiry to Domestic Judicial and/or Non-Judicial Authorities

The court can inquire with private or public bodies.[132] In some cases it may be possible to receive information from a public authority.[133] Inquiry with German embassies or consulates abroad is often seen quite critical.[134] It may be a matter of chance whether there an interested and qualified person is available.[135] However, there are also reports on cases where German embassies have been able to give very good information in status matters.[136] Much information about foreign commercial laws can also be obtained from a German institution active in promoting international trade – the "Germany Trade & Invest",[137] formerly Bundesagentur für Außenhandel or Bundesstelle für Außenhandelsinformation. It informs e.g. on "Egypt – Right to Adaptation of Contract in Case of Force Majeure"[138] or the "New Czech Civil Code".[139]

gg) Inquiry to Foreign Judicial and/or Non-Judicial Authorities

Germany takes part in the European Judicial Network – EJN.[140] In some family law matters such as child abduction this seems to be of practical importance.[141] Inquiry with diplomatic representations is said to produce limited success.[142]

hh) London Convention and Bilateral Treaties

Germany is a party to the London European Convention on Information on Foreign Law, CETS No. 062, and also its Strasbourg Additional Protocol, CETS No. 097, relating to criminal law.[143] In Germany there even is a specific Act on the Execution of the Convention, the AuRAG – Gesetz zur Ausführung des Europäischen Übereinkommens betreffend Auskünfte über ausländisches Recht und seines Zusatzprotokolls (Act on the Execution of the European Convention on Information

[132] MünchKomm-ZPO/*Prütting* § 293 ZPO no. 26.

[133] *Pfeiffer*, FS Leipold 286.

[134] E.g. Stein/Jonas(-*Leipold*) § 293 ZPO no. 40; *Schütze*, BWNotZ 1992, 122, 124.

[135] *Kegel*, FS Nipperdey 453, 465.

[136] *Otto*, IPRax 1995, 299, 302.

[137] http://www.gtai.de.

[138] See on the website under: 8.1.2014, Ägypten – Anspruch auf Vertragsanpassung bei "Höherer Gewalt".

[139] See ibid.: 5.2.2014, Neues Tschechisches Zivilgesetzbuch.

[140] Cf. also *Linke/Hau* no. 331.

[141] See *Carl/Menne*, Verbindungsrichter und direkte richterliche Kommunikation, NJW 2009, 3537.

[142] *Müller*, in: Müller 69.

[143] On the history and development of the Convention see *Schellack* 136 ff.

on Foreign Law). Outgoing (§§ 1–4 AuRAG) and incoming (§§ 5–8 AuRAG) requests are regulated therein. § 9 (1) AuRAG stipulates that the "receiving agency" is the Federal Ministry of Justice ((3) permits deviations by Regulation), whereas due to the fact that Germany is a Federal State, according to § 9 (2) and (4) AuRAG different bodies act as "transmitting agency". A German court "may" ("kann") use the London Convention, § 1 AuRAG. The OLG München (Higher Regional Court or Court of Appeals in Munich) has stated that a court in need of further information on the foreign law has to consider whether using the London Convention is a faster and more cost efficient way than an expert opinion of an institute for international and foreign private law.[144] The German court has to forward the request to the State Court Service Administration (Landesjustizverwaltung) as transmitting agency.[145] Where the German transmitting agency receives information on involved costs under art. 6 (3) London Convention, the transmitting agency according to § 2 AuRAG forwards this information to the requesting German court and the court then will inform the transmitting agency whether the request is upheld. Incoming requests related not to Federal law but to state (Land) law according to § 5 AuRAG are forwarded to the competent state authority. Generally, incoming requests can, in pursuance to art. 6 (2) London Convention, be forwarded to an attorney, a notary, a professor of law in public office or a judge if they consent, § 6 (1) 1 AuRAG. For a judge to be entrusted with answering the request, according to § 6 (1) 2 AuRAG the consent of his supreme service authority is required. On the relationship between the person appointed and the receiving agency certain provisions of the Code of Civil Procedure – ZPO – are applicable by analogy, states § 6 (2) AuRAG.

The London Convention is a most interesting instrument. However, it has not found much attention[146] and appears not to be used very much in practice.[147] Praise for the convention is scarce.[148] Each year there is a number of cases where the Convention is used,[149] in the 2 years 1999 and 2000 there were 32 outgoing requests,[150] and 25 incoming requests were received in 2001.[151] So Germany receives more requests than it itself transmits.[152]

---

[144] OLG München 18.1.2008, DAR 2008, 590 with comment *Riedmeyer* = IPRspr. 2008 Nr. 1, under no. 9: Austrian insurance or traffic accident law.

[145] See § 72 (1) of the Rechtshilfeordnung für Zivilsachen – ZRHO – (Ordinance on Judicial Assistance in Civil Matters) of 28.10.2011, available at https://bundesjustizamt.de/DE/SharedDocs/Publikationen/IRZH/ZRHO.pdf?__blob=publicationFile&v=5.

[146] *Tomson*, EuZW 2009, 204, 208.

[147] *Schack* no. 709; *Linke/Hau* no. 330; *Schellack* 156, 252.

[148] But see *Otto*, IPRax 1995, 299, 302; *Jastrow*, Zur Ermittlung ausländischen Rechts: Was leistet das Londoner Auskunftsübereinkommen in der Praxis? IPRax 2004, 402, 403, reporting regularly positive experience with the convention.

[149] *Otto*, IPRax 1995, 399, 302 with numbers for 1992 and 1993. For older numbers see *Schellack* 156, 269 ff.

[150] *Jastrow,* IPRax 2004, 402, 403.

[151] *Jastrow*, IPRax 2004, 402, 403.

[152] *Jastrow*, IPRax 2004, 402, 404. For earlier years *Schellack* 156 reports the opposite.

But the usefulness of the Convention is disputed. Some shortcomings prevent the Convention from being a real success. A main problem seems to be that only abstract questions are asked and the receiving authority does not have complete knowledge of the case.[153] But sometimes it would be necessary to know the entire content of the file or the argument.[154] There is a danger of misunderstandings.[155] So the information received may sometimes not suffice to decide the case.[156] In fact in some cases the Convention mechanism did not lead to the desired results so that finally an expert opinion has been asked for.[157] The London Convention probably is useful for simpler cases or simpler questions.[158] Perhaps this is the reason why in the framework of exequatur procedures the BGH has for technical questions of foreign law pointed to the Convention – in a case where it appeared as unclear whether some fee was an enforceable part of an Italian judgment[159] or where in a case French law might be decisive for the relevant point of time for converting a payment of French Francs in a French judgment and Deutsche Mark.[160] But in case of the question whether interest for default or only judgment interest had to be paid according to a Spanish judgment to be enforced in Germany, two requests under the convention did not suffice to ascertain the foreign law.[161]

Besides the multilateral London Convention, there is a similar bilateral treaty with Morocco of 29.10.1985, which has entered into force in 1994.[162] It provides for exchange of information on the law of the two states party between the two Ministries of Justice in Art. 18 and on exchange of information in the framework of judicial proceedings in its Art. 19 to 26. They have been developed on the basis of the London Convention and closely follow it.[163] Before World War II there had been

[153] Cf. *Hüßtege*, Zur Ermittlung ausländischen Rechts: Wie man in den Wald hineinruft, so hallt es auch zurück, IPRax 2002, 292, 293; *Spickhoff*, Die neue Sachverständigenhaftung und die Ermittlung ausländischen Rechts, FS Heldrich, 2005, 420.

[154] *Pfeiffer*, FS Leipold 289.

[155] *Luther*, RabelsZ 35 (1973), 660, 677.

[156] Cf. the interesting case BGH 29.6.1987 – II ZR 6/87, NJW 1988, 647, where in a claim against a casino in Belgium there had been an information request and answer under the Convention regarding art. 1965 Code civil on gaming, but where the OLG Düsseldorf with a view to the tolerated activitiy of casinos in Belgium had held the obligation to be enforceable due to a reliance principle on which it had not at all inquired into Belgian law. The BGH referred the case to the OLG.

[157] In this sense also *Pfeiffer* FS Leipold 288.

[158] *Leipold*, in: Stein/Jonas § 293 no. 91; *Pfeiffer*, FS Leipold 289; *Schellack* 157ff, especially 160; *Linke/Hau* no. 330.

[159] BGH 13.4.1983 – VIII ZB 38/82, IPRax 1985, 154, under no. 22.

[160] BGH 21.2.1985 – IX ZB 124/84, IPRspr. 1985 Nr. 173, juris.

[161] BGH 30.1.2001 – XI ZR 357/99, NJOZ 2001, 1 = IPRax 2002, 292 and article by *Hüßtege*, IPRax 2002, 292.

[162] See e.g. *Otto*, IPRax 1995, 299, 303; MünchKomm-ZPO/*Prütting* § 293 ZPO no. 27.

[163] Cf. Deutsche Denkschrift zum Vertrag – BT-Drucks. 11/20206, p. 9 f. and 10 (German memorandum on the Treaty), available at http://www.datenbanken.justiz.nrw.de/ir_htm/dt-marokk_rhv_denkschrift.html.

some bilateral treaties of Germany with other countries which provided for an obligation to give information on the laws of the states party, namely with Austria, Poland, Bulgaria.[164]

ii) Direct Communication of Judges

Direct communication of judges in Germany and abroad is not excluded, but probably difficult. In legal writing, some rules and practices for such a court-to-court communication are recommended.[165]

jj) Other Methods

As mentioned, under § 293 ZPO the courts are obliged to inquire into the foreign law, but free to choose the most appropriate ways. They are not limited to the formal proof-taking rules of the Code of Civil Procedure (ZPO).[166] So there is no exclusionary list of methods. Conversations with colleagues or other persons with expertise are, inter alia, mentioned.[167] Where it is impossible to obtain information on the foreign law in Germany or where diplomatic representations of Germany or the other country shall be requested, the court shall report to the State Court Services Administration.[168]

c) Specific Qualifications

There is not a specific definition of foreign law "expert" qualified for delivering expert opinions. However, the BGH sometimes – at least in the "prendas navales" case[169] – has applied a very strict standard for the qualification of the expert.[170] In some cases specific knowledge of the application in practice may be required, and then an expert having merely access to legal writing might not be considered appropriate.[171] Such standards can even become wholly unrealistic.[172] In Bavaria, an announcement of the Bavarian Ministry of Justice[173] specifically names two

---

[164] See ibid. p. 9 with references for the old treaties.

[165] *Carl/Menn*, NJW 2009, 3537, 3540 ff.

[166] Cf. Stein/Jonas(-*Leipold*) § 293 ZPO no. 39.

[167] See Stein/Jonas(-*Leipold*) § 293 ZPO no. 9.

[168] § 72 (2) 1 ZRHO, see above footnote 145.

[169] BGH 21.1.1991 – II ZR 49/90, NJW-RR 1991, 1211.

[170] Cf. Bamberger/Roth BeckOK/*Lorenz* Einl. IPR 82.2.

[171] MünchKomm-ZPO/*Prütting* § 293 ZPO no. 30, also on the prendas navales case.

[172] Cf. the critique of the decision by *Samtleben*, NJW 1992, 3057; *Kronke*, IPRax 1992, 303.

[173] See above II.3.b)ee).

institutes as expert for foreign law, the Private International Law Institute of the University of Munich and for Eastern European Law an institute in Regensburg.

d) No Binding Effect

The provided legal information never is binding on the court. Rather, the court retains its responsibility under § 293 ZPO and has to evaluate the information rendered.[174] But of course the court is bound by the applicable law, duly ascertained.[175] In case the court is not convinced by the information received, it will have to try further ways for ascertaining the content of the foreign law. For instance, a – further – expert opinion may be asked by the court from another legal expert. In fact there even can be – as e.g. in the prendas navales case –[176] a "battle of expert opinions" ("Gutachtenschlacht")[177] before the courts.

e) Examining the Reliability of the Provided Legal Information

When – as in case of a genuine expert legal opinion – the rules for formal proof-taking ("Strengbeweis") apply,[178] the parties under §§ 411 (2), 402, 397 (1) ZPO have a right to ask the court to call the expert into court[179]; however, this is disputed and denied by those who consider § 293 ZPO as always a form of not rule-bound "Freibeweis".[180] Generally, the expert may be called into court and questioned.[181] Sometimes but rarely this happens in practice. Often, it will not be worthwile,[182] because the expert will just repeat what is written in his legal opinion. In case additional research is necessary, the questions should be made known to the expert beforehand in writing.[183] In fact there are also cases where the court in the reasons of its judgment valuably refers to oral presentations made by the expert.[184] Further,

---

[174] Cf. Stein/Jonas(-*Leipold*) § 293 ZPO no. 59.

[175] This is emphasized by Stein/Jonas(-*Leipold*) § 293 ZPO no. 59.

[176] Above II.3.b)ee).

[177] Thus *Samtleben*, NJW 1992, 3057, 3058, heading of I 1.

[178] Cf. above II.3.b)ee).

[179] BGH 15.6.1994 – VIII ZR 237/93, NJW 1994, 2959; already BGH 10.7.1975 – II ZR 174/74, NJW 1975, 2142; Stein/Jonas(-*Leipold*) § 293 ZPO nos. 43 ff.; MünchKomm-ZPO/*Prütting* § 293 ZPO nos. 29, 31; Bamberger/Roth BeckOK/*Lorenz* Einl. IPR no. 82.2; *Michael Becker*, FS Martiny 626.

[180] Thus e.g. *Schilken*, FS Schumann 373, 383 ff., notably 387.

[181] Bamberger/Roth BeckOK/*Lorenz* Einl. IPR no. 82.2.

[182] Cf. *Schack* no. 714.

[183] See *Pfeiffer*, FS Leipold 298 FN 47; *Otto*, IPRax 1995, 299, 305; *Schack* no. 714.

[184] E.g. OLG Saarbrücken 16.1.2014 – 4 U 429/12, juris, at nos. 24 and 37.

other legal opinions may be provided e.g. by the parties in order to challenge the expert opinion.[185]

f) Bearing the Costs

Costs of ascertaining foreign law are part of the costs of the procedure and thus are governed by the general rules on costs. These are contained in the §§ 91 ff. ZPO. The losing party has to bear the costs and if the parties are partly winning, partly loosing costs are shared proportionally. This means that costs of ascertaining foreign law through expert opinions are added to the costs of the procedure so that the applicability of foreign law can make the procedure more expensive for the parties. Especially costs for expert opinions can be of importance.[186] The experts are paid according to fixed rates; the "Justizvergütungs- und Entschädigungsgesetz – JVEG", that is the Act on Remunerations and Compensations by the Court Services, today[187] regulates the details.[188] Whereas the rates allowed by the JVEG from the point of view of a legal professional are rather low – and do not correspond to market rates for legal advice –,[189] in smaller cases the expert's bill may be considerable or even out of proportion. Other additional costs arising because the case involving foreign law may be more complicated for the judges are not covered, but this has given rise to only one critical article favouring an increase of the court fees.[190] Cost recovery for private expert opinions is a question of its own.[191]

g) Interlocutory Relief? Liability?

Even in cases of interlocutory relief the applicable foreign law has, in principle, to be applied.[192] Though, this sometimes will not be possible. It therefore has been suggested to proceed in a more summarily manner on the basis of probability.[193]

---

[185] See e.g. BGH 13.5.1997 – IX ZR 292/96, NJW-RR 1997, 1154: first demand guarantee in Luxembourg; BGH 15.6.1994 – VIII ZR 237/93, NJW 1994, 2959: conclusion of contract under New York law.

[186] *Schwartze,* FS Fenge 136.

[187] Formerly the "Zeugen- und Sachverständigenentschädigungsgesetz – ZuSEG", i.e. Act on Compensation for Witnesses and Experts.

[188] The Bavarian announcement – above footnote 108 – expressly mentions this under no. 2.5.

[189] Correctly *Spickhoff,* FS Heldrich 420; cf. also already *Kegel*, FS Nipperdey 453, 465.

[190] *Rühl*, RabelsZ 71 (2007) 559, especially 572 f. and 584 ff.

[191] *Schwartze*, FS Fenge 136; *Mankowski*, Privatgutachten über ausländisches Recht – Erstattungsfähigkeit der Kosten, MDR 2001, 194.

[192] Stein/Jonas(-*Leipold*) § 293 ZPO no. 56; see also *Linke/Hau* no. 324.

[193] Stein/Jonas(-*Leipold*) § 293 ZPO no. 57, see also no. 58. See also *Schack* no. 704; *von Bar/Mankowski* nos. 5/102 ff.

In the overall area of ascertaining the content of foreign law, also the question of liability of experts can be raised. In Germany, it is now regulated in § 839a BGB.[194]

4. *Interpretation and Application of Foreign Law*

a) "As the Foreign Court Would Decide..."

According to standing case-law, German courts have to apply foreign law just in the same way as the judge of the country concerned would interpret and apply it.[195] *Gerhard Kegel* has succinctly stated that where according to conflict of laws rules foreign law is to be applied, we have to apply it correctly –[196] international harmony of decisions, interests of the parties, of commerce and public order, which may be at the origin of the conflicts rules, so demand.[197] The German court shall decide just in the same way as the foreign court would decide.[198] One may, however, ask the very good question which foreign judge is meant: first instance, appeal court, Supreme Court judge?[199] The relevant foreign sources of law have to be considered[200] – case law and/or legal writing.[201] The guiding principle is that the German court decision shall in the maximally possible way be approximated to a hypothetical decision in the foreign country – principle of the maximally possible approximation –[202] a demanding task![203] The mere textual interpretation of a statute text may not be sufficient,[204] foreign interpretation rules have to be followed.[205] Foreign law is to be applied as by the relevant foreign courts, even if other courts would interpret the same rule in a different way.[206] There is a famous saying by *Werner Goldschmidt*: whereas the jurist in applying his own law is an architect, in applying foreign law he

[194] Further see *Spickhoff*, FS Heldrich 419 ff.

[195] BGH 4.7.2013, NJW 2013, 3656, at no. 21 with further references; recently OLG Saarbrücken 16.1.2014 – 4 U 429/12, at no. 23, juris; *Schack* no. 705; *Linke/Hau* no. 323.

[196] *Kegel/Schurig* 504: "haben wir es *richtig* anzuwenden". See also Prütting/Wegen/Weinreich(-*Mörsdorf-Schulte*) Art. 3 EGBGB no. 57, who speaks of ‚authentic application' („authentische Anwendung").

[197] Ibid. 504.

[198] BGH 23.4.2002 – XI ZR 136/01, NJW-RR 2002, 1359, 1360 at II.2.b); already *Müller*, in: Müller 68. Also Stein/Jonas(-*Leipold*) § 293 ZPO no. 60.

[199] *Otto*, IPRax 1995, 299, 303.

[200] Kegel/Schurig 505.

[201] *Müller*, in: Müller 68 f.

[202] "Grundsatz größtmöglicher Annäherung", BVerwG 19.7.2012, BVerwGE 143, 369 at no. 14; *Michael Becker*, FS Martiny 625, also 629 and 633.

[203] *Becker*, ibid. 625.

[204] Kropholler 213.

[205] Kegel/Schurig 505 f.

[206] Cf. *Kegel/Schurig* 506 with some examples.

only is a photographer.[207] However, a certain liberty remains and this saying is commented upon a bit critically.[208] By some it is said that the German judge has the same liberty as the foreign judge.[209] Internationally, cases may arise which are not relevant in the court practice of the foreign jurisdiction and the German court then will have to try to decide the case in the same way as a foreign judge probably would do.[210] Certain critics object to the dominant approach that in case of application of foreign law it did not distinguish between describing the foreign law and deciding the case based on arguments and that a fiction of completeness of the foreign law ("Fiktion der Vollständigkeit des ausländischen Rechts") be inappropriately employed[211]; however, the limit between description and arguing decision for a court is blurred and could be ascertained only with complete knowledge of the foreign law, which the German court by definition will not have – the criticism therefore seems far too theoretic.

Questions of constitutional law can play a role. Although in international civil suits this will not happen very often, the situation shall be looked at here from a German perspective. When foreign law under German standards is contrary to the German constitution – the Fundamental Law ("Grundgesetz") of 1949 – the German ordre public may intervene.

When foreign law is contrary to the foreign constitution, the consequences before the German court should be the same as in the foreign country. The German rule which grants a monopoly to decide on the constitutionality of post-constitutional laws to the Bundesverfassungsgericht (Federal Constitutional Court) almost certainly does not apply in case of foreign law.[212] Thus, the constitutionality of the foreign rule may be scrutinized by the German Court and an interpretation in conformity with the (foreign) constitution may be applied.[213] Where foreign constitutional procedural law knows a reference procedure to a Constitutional Court in charge of scrutinizing the constitutionality of laws, it would be a tempting idea to have a reference of the German court to this foreign Constitutional Court.[214] However, this sometimes is not seen as desirable,[215] and at any rate probably is not really feasible.[216] It would also depend on the foreign Constitutional Court accepting such a German reference. In Germany, the reference procedure under art. 100 GG to the Bundesverfassungsgericht quite certainly is open only to German

---

[207] Cf. Kegel/Schurig 506.

[208] Kegel/Schurig 506; Kropholler 213.

[209] *Müller*, in: Müller 68.

[210] Kegel/Schurig 507; cf. also Kropholler 213.

[211] Jansen/Michaels, ZZP 116 (2003) 3.

[212] *Neumayer*, RabelsZ 23 (1958) 586 ff.

[213] MünchKomm-BGB/*Sonnenberger* Einl. IPR no. 337; *Schack* no. 705; *Neumayer*, RabelsZ 23 (1958) 590.

[214] See *Neumayer*, RabelsZ 23 (1958) 596 f., following *Niboyet*.

[215] MünchKomm-BGB/*Sonnenberger* Einl. IPR no. 337.

[216] Cf. *Michael Becker*, FS Martiny 630.

courts,[217] not to international[218] or foreign courts. Some think that in the absence of a foreign Constitutional Court decision the foreign substantive rule is to be applied,[219] whereas others let the German court scrutinize the foreign rule under the standards of the foreign Constitution.[220] Where a foreign Constitutional Court has declared the foreign rule as unconstitutional and not applicable, this is to be followed by the German court.[221] Where the foreign law unconditionally obliges the courts to follow the statute despite constitutional queries and only has some perhaps preemptive control, the constitutionality under the foreign Constitution is not to be checked by the German court.[222] However, the German ordre public might possibly intervene.

b) Gap-Filling and Development of the Law

As foreign law shall be applied just as in the foreign country, in principle also "gaps" have to be filled just as in the foreign country. However, this might prove particularly difficult.

An interesting question is whether the German court may in deciding the case further develop the foreign law and thus contribute to the development of this law ("Rechtsfortbildung"). It is sometimes said that the German judge should not shy away from it.[223] But there is also scepticism.[224] It seems realistic to expect a rather cautious attitude of the German courts in this respect. In legal writing a court case before the OLG Schleswig is mentioned where the buyer of a holiday chalet in Switzerland wished to oppose rights because of defects of the chalet to the financing bank which apparently had closely cooperated with the seller.[225] Swiss law permitted this in case of instalment sales of movables, but did not have a comparable general doctrine and in case of sale of real property. It seems that the German expert opinion on Swiss law favoured a tendency to further develop the Swiss law, but the court declined doing so.[226] Also in a complicated case on the insurance law of the Netherlands the court – LG Bonn – was cautious and did not follow the more pro-

---

[217] See *Menzel*, Internationales Öffentliches Recht, 2011, 608 FN 304; *Michael Becker*, FS Martiny 630 FN 44.

[218] Expressly in this sense *Maunz*, in: Maunz/Dürig, Grundgesetz, loose-leaf, Art. 100 no. 27.

[219] MünchKomm-BGB/*Sonnenberger* Einl. IPR no. 337.

[220] Jansen/*Michaels*, ZZP 116 (2003) 3, 31 ff., 54; see already the considerations by *Neumayer*, Fremdes Recht und Normenkontrolle, RabelsZ 23 (1958) 594 ff.

[221] *Michael Becker*, FS Martiny 630; *Neumayer*, RabelsZ 23 (1958) 591; implicitly MünchKomm-BGB/*Sonnenberger* no. 337.

[222] MünchKomm-BGB/*Sonnenberger* Einl. IPR no. 338; Prütting/Wegen/Weinreich(-*Mörsdorf-Schulte*) Art. 3 EGBGB no. 57; probably *Schack* no. 705.

[223] *Müller*, in: Müller 69; *Geimer* no. 2597; *Kropholler* 214; also *Schack* no. 705 in fine.

[224] Stein/Jonas(-*Leipold*) § 293 ZPO no. 61, but also with further affirmative references.

[225] *Michael Becker*, FS Martiny 627 ff.

[226] Ibid. 628.

gressive recommendations of the expert opinion.[227] Some foreign laws contain general rules advising their judges to further develop the law, e.g. art. 1 (2) Swiss CC. One could consider that such a rule may give more leeway also to the German judge applying such law,[228] but it is unclear under which circumstances and to which extent the German judge might really use it.

5. Failure to Establish Foreign Law

German law does not give a statutory solution for the problem of the applicable foreign law which cannot be ascertained.[229] A provision in a draft of the late nineteenth century stipulated that when the parties could not prove that the foreign law was different from German law it was presumed to be identical to German law.[230] This would lead to the lex fori.

Nowadays, the question in Germany is disputed: Whereas one opinion and notably case law[231] prefer application of the lex fori, other opinions intend to be more flexible and recommend application of general principles of law, the probable law, the most closely related law etc.[232] Even going back to the conflicts question and applying the law which subsidiarily would have to be applied ("kollisionsrechtliche Hilfsanknüpfung") is favoured by some.[233] A number of authors indicate a sequence of criteria and refer to the lex fori only as ultima ratio.[234] Some authors have noted that these more flexible standards can already be part of the interpretation of the foreign law[235] and *Sonnenberger* therefore considers the lex fori-solution as methodologically clearer.[236] However, in this solution there is, so it seems, the risk that the notion of interpretation of the foreign law is extended too far and beyond the standards of the applicable foreign law, or, on the other hand, that the lex fori is too

---

[227] LG Bonn 22.9.1987 – 7 O 210/85, which did not adopt the suggested "anticipatory interpretation" of art. 7.17.2.25 NBW.

[228] See *Becker*, FS Martiny 629 f.

[229] Cf. MünchKomm-BGB/*Sonnenberger* Einl. IPR no. 740; also *Kindl*, ZZP 111 (1998) 177, 196.

[230] See ibid. with references.

[231] See BGH 26.10.1977 – IV ZB 7/77, BGHZ 69, 387, 394 = NJW 1978, 496, 498, at least where there is a strong relation to Germany and with many references; *Kindl*, ZZP 111 (1998) 177, 197 with further references; *Lindacher*, FS Schumann 283, 284; *von Bar/Mankowski* nos. 5/104 ff.

[232] MünchKomm-BGB/*Sonnenberger* no. 741; *Schack* nos. 715 ff.

[233] E.g. *Kindl*, ZZP 111 (1998) 177, 200 f.; *Kreuzer*, NJW 1983, 1943, 1946 f.; *Schellack* 245; also Stein/Jonas(-*Leipold*) § 293 ZPO no. 67; contra e.g. *Schack* no. 721.

[234] MünchKomm-BGB/*Sonnenberger* Einl IPR no. 741; for the ultima ratio see *Schack* nos. 718, 722; *Michael Becker*, FS Martiny 633.

[235] MünchKomm-BGB/*Sonnenberger* Einl. IPR no. 742 with references.

[236] Ibid. no. 742 in fine.

easily taken resort to.[237] The flexible approach looking for the probable or most closely related rule therefore still seems preferable.

It also has been advocated to take resort to general principles[238] or to uniform law.[239] But also these solutions have shortcomings and may be not be any closer to the situation in the foreign country than the lex fori or other solutions.[240] Uniform law only exists on a limited scale.[241] For matters of contract law, it has been remarked that in the future restatements like the UNIDROIT Principles of International Commercial Contracts (UPICC) or the Principles of European Contract Law of the Lando-Commission might be useful.[242] Indeed the UPICC state in their preamble in the sixth paragraph: "They may be used to interpret or supplement domestic law." – and domestic here probably is better read as national, in contrast to international, not to foreign. Given many reforms and the international developments in the area of contract law much can be said in favour of such an approach. However, beyond contract law the situation hardly is the same.

Anyway, the court has got to decide and is not allowed to deny doing justice. Thus, it must find a solution even when the content of the applicable foreign law cannot really be ascertained.[243]

III. Judicial Review

1. Conflict of Laws Rules

The conflict of law rules are part of German or EU law and thus the general rules on appeals apply in case they have been misapplied. There is no restriction for appeals based on misapplication of conflict of laws rules.[244] And it may be borne in mind that conflict of laws rules are according to an opinion founded by *Gerhard Kegel*[245] often seen as an expression of "justice in conflicts matters" ("internationalprivatrechtliche Gerechtigkeit") and it seems this could additionally justify the possibility of appeal.

[237] Criticizing an homeward trend *Schack* no. 718; *Michael Becker,* FS Martiny 633. On the dangers of this approach also Stein/Jonas(-*Leipold*) § 293 ZPO no. 66.

[238] *Broggini*, Die Maxime "iura novit curia" und das ausländische Recht, Ein Beitrag zur Präzisierung des § 293 ZPO, AcP 155 (1956) 469, 483 f.

[239] *Kreuzer*, NJW 1983, 1943, 1947 f.

[240] Critically also *Schack* no. 720.

[241] Cf. the pertinent remark by *Kindl*, ZZP 111 (1998) 177, 198; also *Schack* no. 720. This is also admitted by *Kreuzer*, NJW 1983, 1943, 1947, who prefers the "kollisionsrechtliche Hilfsanknüpfung", but in lack of it wants to apply uniform law for which he gives a number of examples.

[242] *Schwartze,* FS Fenge 139 FN 74.

[243] Cf. Stein/Jonas(-*Leipold*) § 293 ZPO no. 64.

[244] Cf. e.g. *Schack* no. 725.

[245] *Kegel/Schurig* 55, 145 ff. et passim.

2. *Foreign Law*

In civil matters, there is an appeal against the decision of first instance by the Landgericht (Regional Court) to the Oberlandesgericht (Higher Regional Court or – roughly – Court of Appeals), respectively in small matters by the Amtsgericht (Local Court) to the Landgericht (Regional Court). On this appeal in principle there is the possibility of a review of the facts – in certain limits set by § 529 (1) Code of Civil Procedure (ZPO) – and of course also of the content of the foreign law applied.[246] On the next stage then an appeal on points of law called "Revision" may lie. It leads to the Bundesgerichtshof (Federal Court of Justice) or – in case of other jurisdictions than the ordinary one, e.g. labour matters – to one of the other four (altogether five) Federal Supreme Courts. Here on the level of "Revision", the question of foreign laws becomes complicated.

German law distinguishes between "Revision" based on erroneous application of foreign law (a) and "Revision" based on misapplication of German procedural rules on ascertaining the content of foreign law (b):

a) No "Revision" Based on Erroneous Application of Foreign Law

Whether in an appeal on points of law ("Revision") to the Bundesgerichtshof – the Federal Court of Justice as Supreme Court in Civil and Criminal cases – the application of foreign law may be reviewed, is disputed. The wording of the relevant provision of the ZPO – Code of Civil Procedure – used to be restrictive, but recently has been changed. In § 545 (1) ZPO it now runs: "Die Revision kann nur darauf gestützt werden, dass die Entscheidung auf einer Verletzung des Rechts beruht."/ "An appeal on points of law may only be based on the reason that the contested decision is based on a violation of the law."[247] Nevertheless, the BGH holds that here only domestic law is meant[248]: Otherwise, § 560 ZPO on laws which are not subject to "Revision" would be senseless because then there would be no laws at all which are not subject to "Revision".[249] Also the grounds for "Revision" would not fit in case of appeals concerning the content of foreign law.[250] The BGH could not really clarify the situation under foreign law, because the foreign practice would be decisive and even German instance courts could not rely on the BGH but would again and again have to check the latest state of the foreign practice.[251] In contrast to an opinion expressed

[246] Cf. Stein/Jonas(-*Leipold*) § 293 ZPO no. 70; see also e.g. OLG Saarbrücken 16.1.2014 – 4 U 429/12, juris, at no. 22; BGH 21.9.1995 – VII ZR 248/94, NJW 1996, 54, 55.

[247] Translation from the same source as mentioned supra in footnote 26.

[248] BGH 4.7.2013, NJW 2013, 3656 = JZ 2014, 102 with note by *Riehm*, Vom Gesetz, das klüger ist als seine Verfasser – Zur Revisibilität ausländischen Rechts, Zugleich Besprechung von BGH, Beschluss v. 4.7.2013 – V ZB 197/12, JZ 2014, 73 with many references.

[249] No. 20.

[250] No. 21.

[251] No. 21.

by some authors,[252] the BGH holds that this "Irrevisibilität" of foreign law is not discriminatory and thus also in intra-European cases does not violate the general prohibition of discriminations under art. 18 TFEU.[253] In legal writing, this "Irrevisibilität" has been criticized for a very long time[254] and the modification of the wording of § 545 ZPO for some authors gave rise to the hope for a procedural change –[255] but this has now been rejected by the BGH. Pragmatically and perhaps even wisely it sticks to its approach of firmly reviewing the application of § 293 ZPO but refrains from assuming the position of a foreign Supreme Court for foreign law. May be that in the European Union other specific arrangements could step in.[256]

However, there are some exceptions where foreign law can be reviewed on "Revision": This is particularly true for the question of *renvoi* by the foreign conflict of laws rules,[257] but can also be the case for some specific procedural questions.[258] And before the BGH in criminal cases, review of foreign law is said to be possible.[259]

Before the other Federal Supreme Courts, the situation is not uniform. It is all different in labour matters – the Bundesarbeitsgericht – Federal Labor Court – considers foreign law to be subject to "Revision".[260] However, there a special rule of the Act on the Labour Courts – Arbeitsgerichtsgesetz – applies, § 73 I 1 ArbGG. In administrative matters, however, the Bundesverwaltungsgericht shares the opinion of the BGH.[261] Also before fiscal courts, there is no appeal on a point of law to the Federal Fiscal Court (Bundesfinanzgericht)[262] and the situation is the same before the Federal Social Court (Bundessozialgericht) under § 162 SGG.[263]

---

[252] See Prütting/Wegen/Weinreich(-*Mörsdorf-Schulte*) Art. 3 EGBGB no. 58 with references.

[253] Ibid. no. 22; contra e.g. *Schack* no. 724; *Kieninger* 500 with references.

[254] E.g. *Spickhoff*, ZZP 112 (1999) 265, 276; *Kronke*, IPRax 1992, 303, 305; *von Bar/Mankowski* no. 5/109; and for further references see *Linke/Hau* no. 334 footnote 55. For a carefull comparative examination see *Kerameus*, Revisibilität ausländischen Rechts, Ein rechtsvergleichender Überblick, ZZP 99 (1986) 166.

[255] E.g. *Linke/Hau* no. 334; *Geimer* no. 2601; Palandt(-*Thorn*) Einl v EGBGB 3 (IPR) no. 37; critical to this hope already *Schack* no. 724 footnote 3 with references.

[256] See infra VI.3.

[257] *Schack* no. 725 with references; *Linke/Hau* no. 335; *Kerameus* ZZP 99 (1986) 166, 181 f.

[258] Further *Schack* no. 725; *Linke/Hau* no. 335; *Kerameus*, ZZP 99 (1986) 166, 180 f.

[259] *Graf*, in: Beck'scher Online-Kommentar StPO, 17th ed. 2013, § 337 StPO no. 8.

[260] BAG 10.4.1975, BAGE 27, 99, 109; also *Grunsky*, Arbeitsgerichtsgesetz, Kommentar, 7th ed., § 73 ArbGG no. 8; *Ullrich*, in: Schwab/Weth (eds.), Arbeitsgerichtsgesetz, Kommentar, 3rd ed. 2011, § 73 ArbGG no. 10; *Müller-Glöge*, in: Germelmann/Künzl et al. (eds.), Arbeitsgerichtsgesetz, Kommentar, 8th ed. 2013, § 73 ArbGG no. 6; very briefly *Friedrich*, in: Bader/Creutzfeld/Friedrich, ArbGG, Kommentar zum Arbeitsgerichtsgesetz, 5th ed. 2008, § 73 ArbGG no. 3; *Gross*, in: Natter/Gross (ed.), Arbeitsgerichtsgesetz, 2nd ed., § 73 ArbGG no. 4.

[261] BVerwG, BVerwGE 143, 369, at no. 16 with many references.

[262] *Hendricks*, Ausländisches Recht im Steuerprozess, IStR 2011, 711, 716 f.

[263] *Udsching*, in: Beck'scher Online-Kommentar Sozialrecht, 32nd ed. 2013, § 162 SGG no. 5; *Meyer-Ladewig*, in: Meyer-Ladewig/Keller/Leitherer, SGG, 10th ed. 2012, § 162 SGG no. 6c.

b) "Revision" Based on Misapplication of s. 293 on Duty to Investigate

As already pointed out, the court under § 293 ZPO has a duty to investigate the content of the foreign law. When this duty is not fully complied with, this procedural rule is infringed. This can be reviewed on appeal and even on appeal on points of law ("Revision").[264] The BGH is very strict, "remarkably strict"[265] and perhaps has become stricter and stricter.[266] It has even been said that the appeal as a rule is successful,[267] but this is an overstatement. *Thomas Pfeiffer* has shown that the BGH in some cases has reviewed himself the application of the foreign law and when he found it correct it dismissed the appeal although the inquiry into the foreign law by the instance court may not have been correct under the standards of § 293 ZPO.[268] Also the Federal Labour Court BAG seems, insofar, to go into the same direction.[269]

The strict standard of the BGH probably is best illustrated by the famous case of the "prendas navales", a kind of maritime charge, from Venezuela.[270] Before the OLG Bremen various expert opinions had been presented and the court had itself commissioned and received an expert opinion from the Max-Planck-Institut in Hamburg. Nevertheless, the BGH censored the OLG and the appeal on a point of law had success because under § 293 ZPO an expert opinion only based on "law in the books" was considered not sufficient and an inquiry into local practice was deemed necessary. "No mere treatise-opinion" ("Kein Lehrbuchgutachten") is held to be the message of this case –[271] the only problem is, that apparently Venezuelan practice was unclear and impossible to ascertain.[272] Some other cases are more convincing[273]: A girl had been killed in a jet-ski accident in Thailand and the court had applied a short Thai maritime law statute of limitations rule, although the German expert had indicated that he could not say whether this short maritime or the longer general tort statute of limitations rule would apply; the appeal on a point of law had

[264] E.g. Stein/Jonas(-*Leipold*) § 293 ZPO no. 71; *Schack* no. 727; *Linke/Hau* no. 335.

[265] Stein/Jonas(-*Leipold*) § 293 ZPO no. 72.

[266] *Kindl*, ZZP 111 (1998) 177, 195.

[267] *Kindl*, ZZP 111 (1998), 177, 178.

[268] *Thomas Pfeiffer*, NJW 2002, 3306, 3308.

[269] See BAG 10.4.1975, BAGE 27, 99, 111 on dismissal under US-American labour law.

[270] BGH 21.1.1991 – II ZR 49/90, NJW-RR 1991, 1211; further see *Samtleben*, NJW 1992, 3057; *Kronke*, IPRax 1992, 303.

[271] Cf. e.g. *Geimer* no. 2590; Zöller/*Geimer* § 293 ZPO no. 20; critical *Samtleben*, NJW 1992, 3057.

[272] According to the reports by *Samtleben*, NJW 1992, 3057 and *Kronke*, IPRax 1992, 303.

[273] Further interesting cases where the „Revision"was successful are e.g. BGH 26.6.2001 – XI ZR 241/00, NJOZ 2001, 1616 on liability of a Slowenian bank after the dismemberment of Yugoslavia, or BGH 25.9.1997 – II ZR 113/96, NJW 1998, 1321 on acquisition of property in a Spanish apartment; BGH 13.5.1997 – IX ZR 292/96, NJW-RR 1997, 1154 on first demand guarantee by a student and sole shareholder of a Panamanian corporation under the law of Luxembourg; BGH 19.9.1995 – VI ZR 226/94, NJWE-VHR 1996, 7 on interpretation of penalty clause under English law.

success because doctrine and case-law had not been inquired into by the court.[274] In a case where liability of a partner of a New York partnership was claimed, an academic expert opinion was held necessary, because the content of the provided party opinions was found insufficient on § 96 Partnership Law.[275] And in a recent case on Taiwanese transport law, an older and incomplete legal opinion by an institute had been presented by a party and the case was referred to the Court of Appeals because the Court should have procured a supplementary opinion.[276]

In addition to the arguments put forward by the BGH, some fear that the authority of German Supreme Federal Courts might be damaged in case of misinterpretations of foreign law.[277] Also, one may consider questionable that it is the task of the German Supreme Courts to judicially develop the foreign law more or less unfamiliar to them.[278]

IV. Foreign Law in Other Instances

1. Administrative Authorities

Administrative bodies can have to deal with foreign law, yet probably much less than civil courts. In the matter of driving licenses, foreign driving licenses may give the right to drive a motorcar also in Germany or may be recognized,[279] but this is more the recognition of a foreign administrative act and not the application of the foreign road traffic law by German authorities. Where public permissions for pharmaceuticals, insurance or banking activities are concerned, the situation appears to be similar. German public payments for children ("Kindergeld") may under § 65 (1) no. 2 Einkommensteuergesetz (Income Tax Act) not be due where comparable payments are granted abroad; the German administrative body then has to check whether there is a right to payment under foreign law.[280] In matters of immigration law, the existence of a family tie under foreign family law may be important where family reunion is sought for and then the applicable foreign family law has to be ascertained.[281] For matters of German taxes, it is reported that questions of foreign private or public law are of increasing importance, e.g. for the issues of deductability abroad, comparing the type of legal arrangement under foreign law to the German

[274] BGH 23.6.2003 – II ZR 305/01, NJW 2003, 2685.

[275] BGH 23.4.2002 – XI Z 136/01, NJW-RR 2002, 1359, 1360 at II.2. c) bb).

[276] BGH 21.12.2011 – I ZR 144/09, IPRspr. 2011 Nr. 3.

[277] *Schack* no. 724.

[278] *Remien* 630.

[279] For details see e.g. *Buschbell,* in: Beck'sches Rechtsanwalts-Handbuch, 10th ed. 2011, § 29 nos. 134 ff.

[280] Bundesfinanzhof 13.6.2013 – III R 63/11, BFHE 242, 34, and III R 10/11, BFHE 241, 562 with further references and also on the question of binding effect of foreign administrative decisions.

[281] See BVerwG 19.7.2012, BVerwGE 143, 369: Indian marriage law.

rule model, imputation of income to a certain legal person etc.[282] In case of an ensuing court procedure before the fiscal courts, § 293 ZPO applies via a reference in § 155 FGO – Finanzgerichtsordnung, Ordinance on the Fiscal Courts.[283]

2. Arbitration, Mediation or Other Alternative Dispute Resolution

The advantages of arbitration or other dispute resolution mechanisms are often praised and one of them is said to be the possibility for the parties to nominate specifically experienced persons as arbitrators. This can also include the arbitrators' knowledge of the applicable law – with the consequence that the issue of access to foreign law does not arise or is at least less problematic than in state courts. In fact, it is stated that in the area of arbitration the problems are substantially less important than before state courts.[284] Parties will, as a rule, nominate arbitrators which are at least supposed to know the applicable law –[285] one of the essential advantages of arbitration.[286] It is even said, that for the arbitrator there is no distinction between "domestic" and "foreign" law.[287] Nevertheless it is – perhaps not really coherently – found that it would be "utopic" to apply the principle of iura novit curia in a universalist manner.[288] Rather, it is said that where German arbitration procedure law applies, also § 293 ZPO applies,[289] at least by analogy.[290] The ways for ascertaining the content of the foreign law then are more or less the same as for a state court[291] and the same is true for the problems encountered.[292]

---

[282] *Hendricks*, Ausländisches Recht im Steuerprozess, IStR 2011, 711.

[283] For details see *Hendricks* ibid.

[284] *Schütze/Tscherning/Wais*, Handbuch des Schiedsverfahrens, Praxis der deutschen und internationalen Schiedsgerichtsbarkeit, 2nd ed.1990, no. 603.

[285] Ibid.

[286] Ibid.

[287] *Geimer*, Internationales Zivilprozessrecht, 6th ed. 2009, no. 3878; *Zöller*(-Geimer) § 1051 no. 13.

[288] Ibid.

[289] Ibid.; also MünchKomm-ZPO/*Prütting* § 293 ZPO no. 15.

[290] Schütze/Tscherning/Wais no. 604.

[291] Cf. the survey in *Schütze/Tscherning/Wais* no. 604.

[292] Cf. ibid. no. 605.

3. Attorneys, Notaries, etc.

Nowadays there are many international law firms active also in Germany and numbers of other law firms are part of international networks. This should substantially facilitate access to foreign law for such firms.

Especially interesting is the situation for the notariat.[293] In case foreign law has to be applied, German notaries have to inform parties about this fact and this has to be documented, § 17 (3) 1 BeurkG. But there is no duty to inform about the content of the foreign law.[294] It is recommended to resort to legal opinions.[295] Family and Inheritance, but also company law play a leading role.[296] Germany is a country of the Latin notariat and the notaries are organized in public bodies called chambers of notaries ("Notarkammern") on the State and united on the Federal level in the "Bundesnotarkammer". In 1993 some Notarkammern and the Bundesnotarkammer have founded the "Deutsche Notarinstitut" – DNotI – (German Notary Institute) in Würzburg.[297] Nowadays all the Notarkammern participate in the DNotI and the DNotI even is entrenched in the Statutes of the Bundesnotarkammer,[298] §§ 17–19. The DNotI through its "consulting service" gives legal advice to notaries – also on foreign law! Any German notary may inquire with the DNotI. Of the nearly 8000 inquiries each year some 24% concern foreign law or conflict of laws.[299] Not all of them will lead to foreign substantive law, because some are on German Conflict of Laws only – perhaps 10% –, and there will be a considerable number of cases of renvoi.[300] But be this as it may: This means that roughly there are some 1800, thus nearly 2000, inquiries about foreign law or conflict of laws which each year are answered by the DNotI – and at least many of them will also address foreign substantive law! There are no exact numbers about fields of law and countries, but it is said that approximately 40–50% concern succession law, 30% marriage law, 10–15% child law, while the importance of company law, after a flood of cases on English Limited companies, is varying.[301] Further fields are procedure, power of attorney, real property law, health care proxies, living wills (advance health care directives) etc.[302] The inquiries concern the whole world, but notably the laws of

---

[293] See in general *Schütze*, BWNotZ 1992, 122; Zimmermann, in: Beck'sches Notar-Handbuch, 5th ed. 2009, no. H 16.

[294] *Zimmermann*, in: Beck'sches Notar-Handbuch, 5th ed. 2009, no. H 15.

[295] Ibid.

[296] *Schütze*, BWNotZ 1992, 122.

[297] For details see http://www.dnoti.de – partly also in English, French, Italian or Spanish.

[298] Satzung der Bundesnotarkammer, available under http://www.bnotk.de/Bundesnotarkammer/Satzung/Satzung_BNotK.html

[299] 2012: 7700, see DNotI, Tätigkeitsbericht der Bundesnotarkammer im Jahre 2012 – VII Deutsches Notarinstitut, available on the homepage.

[300] Estimate by Dr. *Rembert Süß* of the DNotI, kindly communicated to the author.

[301] Communication by Dr. *Rembert Süß* of the DNotI. Partly similarly for the notaries already *Schütze*, BWNotZ 1992, 122.

[302] Id.

neighbouring countries, West and Eastern Europe, Northern America.[303] The service is financed by the notaries, but there is no fee for the individual opinions delivered to the notaries.[304] The DNotI cooperates with similar institutions in other countries, e.g. in France and Belgium. In Germany certificates of inheritance are issued by the courts and also the land register (Grundbuch) and the commercial register (Handelsregister) are kept by the courts, but requests for issuance respectively registration are commonly filed with a notary – the notary then can ask the DNotI for an opinion on foreign law and this may also be of use for the court which will have to decide on the request.[305]

V. Access to Foreign Law: Status Quo

Acts and regulations of the Federal Republic of Germany are published in the "Bundesgesetzblatt" (Federal Gazette) which is available online at http://www.bundesgesetzblatt.de. Decisions of the Bundesgerichtshof (Federal Court of Justice) are availbale at http://www.bundesgerichtshof.de, those of the Bundesverfassungsgericht (Federal Constitutional Court) under http://www.bundesverfassungsgericht.de. The Federal Ministry of Justice (Bundesministerium der Justiz) also offers a website with many translations of German Federal Acts into English under http://www.gesetze-im-internet.de/Teilliste-translations.html. Of course these are, however, "intended solely as a convenience to the non-German-reading public" and not binding.[306] These translations stem from different sources and may be of variable quality. Some translations of German statutes into English language are also provided on the private site http://www.iuscomp.org/gla/statutes/statutes.htm. The states ("Länder") also have their websites on state law and to a variable extent on the courts and their case law.

The European Judicial Network (EJN) (http://ec.europa.eu/civiljustice/index_en.htm) is available in Germany. Germany is party to the European Convention of 7 June 1968 on Information on Foreign Law ("London Convention").[307] In contrast, the Inter-American Convention of 8 May 1979 on Proof of and Information on Foreign Law ("Montevideo Convention") and Convention of 22 January 1993 on Legal Assistance and Legal Relations in Civil, Family and Criminal Matters ("Minsk Convention") stem from other parts of the World and Germany is not party to them. But Germany has a bilateral agreement similar to the London Convention with Morocco.[308]

[303] Id.

[304] Id.

[305] Id.

[306] See the note at the beginning of the internet page.

[307] For details see above II.3.b)hh).

[308] See already above II.3.b)hh).

In the European Union, there is the European Judicial Network (EJN) which to a certain extent might be helpful.[309]

VI. Access to Foreign Law: Further Developments

1. Practical Need

Foreign law being foreign, familiarity with it is often lacking. Access problems cannot be made disappear completely. For the different sectors one might be able to say:

(a) Improving access to foreign law for judicial authorities would be a good thing, although the German system seems to be functioning. A more internationally oriented training of the judges and more specialisation might bring improvements.
(b) As far as administrative and other non-judicial authorities are concerned, it is difficult to make a general statement, most probably the individual branches of administration would have to be considered. They cover a vast field which cannot be looked at in much detail here.
(c) For arbitrators, having knowledge and access to foreign law is part of their qualification. It is desirable that they, their associations and institutions take measures to maintain and increase this professional qualification.
(d) For attorneys, this to a certain extent may be similar. Their professional organizations should see to it that attorneys can, through suitable training, enhance their knowledge about foreign law and international cases.
(e) As far as notaries are concerned, with the German Notary Institute – DNotI -, there seems to be an attractive and well-functioning device for this sector. Having been founded in 1993 it recently has celebrated its twentieth year – with a symposium on European international succession law!
(f) For parties, especially those who cannot afford costly measures, one may also wish improvements, but most probably the problem has to be put in the broader perspective of access to law. This is a general problem and in an international perspective standards seem to be very divergent. Additional costs through involvement of foreign law perhaps cannot simply be put on the shoulders of the public in a general way, but partly will have to be borne by those exercising an international activity and partly should, where specific reasons exist, benefit from public help. Family matters may be a field to provide for. Also insurance for travel abroad and car driving abroad including legal costs seems especially important. Further, automobilists' associations such as in Germany most notably the Allgemeiner Deutscher Automobilclub – ADAC – offer legal advice to their members and partly to the public.[310]

---

[309] See already above II.3.b)hh) in fine.

[310] See http://www.adac.de with the possibility to ask for advice in case of an accident abroad for members and an important number of public information bulletins in case of damage abroad ("Schadenmerkblätter – Unfall im Ausland").

There are many different kinds of circumstances where access to foreign law is needed in Germany. Probably, divorce and inheritance cases count among the most important. But of course also businesses considering international activity or, possibly, private persons wishing to acquire real property abroad are in need of such information. Thus, divorce, succession and company law will be important areas of law – not to mention tax law. In contrast, in purely domestic cases, the problem nearly does not exist though Germany is a federal state: As far as civil law is concerned, this is nearly exclusively uniform federal law. Thus, the situation hardly arises in this sector. In other fields such as administrative law also there should be no too big difficulties: The judge or lawyer will have to research the law of the other state ("Land") in the library or databank and apply it. This may be some additional effort, but hopefully no unsurmountable difficulty at all.

2. Conflict of Laws Solutions

Savigny has shown that the law of the country where a legal relationship has its "Sitz", its seat or "Schwerpunkt", should govern the legal relationship. In the view of this author, this should not be changed.

In a comparative perspective, Germany appears to have a relatively open and equal treatment oriented approach to the application of foreign law. It is applied *ex officio*. Much effort is made to ascertain the content of foreign law. In the field of "Revisibilität", i.e. the possibility of an appeal on points of law, of foreign law, many authors wish a change, but it seems that case law, with its strict review of the obligations of the court under § 293 ZPO, more or less already has done what is realistically possible. In the framework of the European Union, a reference procedure on the lines of art. 267 TFEU would, as explained in the following paragraph, be most welcome. The unification of private international law in Europe also calls for a unification of the treatment of foreign law.

3. Methods of Facilitating Access to Foreign Law

As already outlined, a regional, i.e. European, initiative on access to foreign law would be useful. But a worldwide instrument would for the time being be very difficult to achieve and perhaps be of doubtful value. In an ideal world, an international convention could facilitate access to foreign law. But Switzerland and Somalia are (if – in the last case – at all), very different countries, also Canada, Cayman Islands, Czech Republic, Colombia, China, Cuba or the two Congos and many others. Not only the conditions of living, but also the development of a state of law are very different. Therefore, the idea of a global instrument on information on foreign law might promise more than it will be able to keep. Perhaps an intermediate approach might be to establish a network of information exchange between Supreme Courts willing and able to participate. This could be a step towards worldwide judicial cooperation and perhaps one day allow to forget about the question of "Failure to Establish Foreign Law" and a substitute law ("Ersatzrecht").[311]

For the sector of information on foreign law of another EU Member State, I champion the idea of a preliminary reference procedure similar to art. 267 of the Treaty on the Functioning of the European Union (TFEU). When in a court procedure the interpretation of the law of the EU is decisive, art. 267 TFEU permits and sometimes even requires references by national courts of EU Member States to the Court of Justice of the European Union in Luxembourg. Drawing a parallel to this, for cases where in a court procedure in an EU Member State the interpretation of the law of another EU Member State is decisive, a reference procedure to a court of this other (foreign) Member State could be established. This has been proposed by *Oliver Remien*[312] and also by *Andreas Schwartze*.[313] And further research even shows that decades ago in Italy *Edoardo Vitta* already had briefly mentioned, but then rejected, the similar idea of a reference procedure to the foreign Supreme Court.[314] In a contribution published in 2001 I have somewhat elaborated on this proposal[315]: any court should be allowed to make a reference,[316] the reference should go to a court of the same rank in the other EU Member State,[317] the Member States should be free to decide on concentration or decentralisation of the competence to decide on incoming references, e.g. courts of the capital or of courts close to this or that border of the country,[318] there should – in contrast to art. 267 TFEU – be no binding effect,[319] there should be no appeal against the decision of the foreign court answering the preliminary reference, but only against the final decision of the referring court,[320] costs and language could be regulated just as in the London

---

[311] See supra II.5.

[312] *Remien*, Illusion und Realität eines europäischen Privatrecht, JZ 1992, 277, 282; id., European Private International Law, the European Community and its Emergng Area of Freedom, Security and Justice, CMLRev. 38 (2001) 53, 78 f.; id, in: Aufbruch nach Europa 617, 627.

[313] *Schwartze*, FS Fenge 145. Somewhat vaguely also *Schellack* 251 considers information given by foreign courts and mentions preliminary references to the ECJ and abstract constitutional review of norms by the German Federal Constitutional Court under art. 100 GG ("Grundgesetz", i.e. Fundamental Law).

[314] See Per una convenzione europea sulla prova del diritto straniero, Diritto Internazionale 1963, 408 with a proposal („Proposta") and comments („Commento") for a Convention on a "Servizio giuridico europeo" by Edoardo Vitta; on this see also *Kegel,* FS Nipperdey 453, 466; *Schellack* 137. *Vitta* briefly mentions the forerunner provisions to today's art. 267 TFEU.

[315] *Remien*, in: Aufbruch nach Europa 617 ff.; welcomed by *Flessner*, Das ausländische Recht im Zivilprozess - die europäischen Anforderungen, in 30 Jahre österreichisches IPR-Gesetz, - Europäische Perspektiven -, 2009, 34, 41; critical *Jansen/Michaels*, ZZP 116 (2003) 3, 49 ff.; *Trautmann*, ZEuP 2006, 283, 306 f.; id., Europäisches Kollisionsrecht 429 – but ignoring the details of the proposal; neutral *Kieninger* 500; not yet realistic according to *Linke/Hau* no. 332.

[316] At 627.

[317] 627.

[318] 628.

[319] 629.

[320] 629.

Convention.[321] All this could apply also on the Supreme Court level –[322] and thus also the thorny question of review of foreign law by the Supreme Court – in Germany of the "Revisibilität" of foreign law before the BGH – could be solved.[323] This could contribute to the Judicial Cooperation in Civil Matters in the EU, but thus far it only is an academic proposal.

On the general global level, other less far-reaching measures might be interesting. Though, a global overall initiative appears to be difficult. But the Internet already now has remarkably improved the possibilities to get at least some information on many laws. Here, states could try to offer even more in order to get their law applied appropriately in other countries and judges and lawyers could for their part do more in order to have access to and properly understand this legal information.

[321] 629 f.

[322] 628 and 630.

[323] 630.

Greece: Foreign Law in the Greek Private International Law: Positive Solutions and Future Perspectives

Chryssapho Tsouca

Abstract In Greek Private International Law conflict of laws rules are of obligatory nature and foreign law is considered as jus to be applied ex officio, as provided for in Article 337 of the Code of Civil Procedure as well as in Article 144 (4) of the Code of Administrative Procedure. It is also admitted that the courts and other authorities, may use any means which is considered appropriate for acquiring knowledge of foreign law, usually a written information provided by the Hellenic Institute of International and Foreign Law. The application of both the conflict of laws rules and foreign law is subjected to the review of the higher courts. The solution prevailing regarding proceedings where the applicable foreign law could not be proved, is the application of the lex fori.

The improvement of the access to foreign law is of great importance for the international harmony pursued by conflict of laws system. The best way to make some progress in this direction is the use of new technologies and the international cooperation on the exchange of information about national laws. To the contrary modifying the status of foreign law in the sense that its applicability must depend exclusively on the parties' decision would be in principle a serious threat to the legal system's unity and the equality of parties. More useful is the unification of rules relative to the treatment of foreign law as a way to ensure the international harmony in the sphere of Private International Law.

C. Tsouca (✉)
Associate Professor, Law School, National and Kapodistrian University of Athens, Athens, Greece
e-mail: chtsouca@otenet.gr

Y. Nishitani (ed.), *Treatment of Foreign Law - Dynamics towards Convergence?*,
Ius Comparatum – Global Studies in Comparative Law 26,
DOI 10.1007/978-3-319-56574-3_9

I. Conflict of Laws Rules

As accepted in Greek Private International Law, conflict of laws rules are of obligatory nature[1] with the exception of cases where the interested parties have the right to choose the applicable law.[2] Another limit to the obligatory character of the conflict rules is the public policy, in the sense that, in case where the application of the *lex causae* is contrary to the forum's fundamental conceptions of justice, the private international law solution cannot fully apply.[3]

Even though there are no statistics available about the number of cases where the Greek courts have applied foreign law, the case law demonstrates that the application of private international rules leads quite often to the application of a foreign law. In that regard, it should be noted that the national origin of the foreign *lex causae* varies. Lately, however, there is an increasing number of cases, concerning family matters, where the applicable law is that of a Balkan country, due to the mobility of individuals originating from these countries.[4]

As put forward by several legal scholars, the frequency of the application of foreign law may also depend on the content of conflict of laws rule: as observed, regarding family law matters, the predominant connecting factor in Greek private international law is nationality. The rationale of this choice is to ensure the application of Greek law in relation to Greek citizens living abroad. Owning to the fact that Greece had been, for a long period of time, an emigration country, the application of the national law was obviously a political choice. Certainly, nowadays the situation has changed: Greece is now a host country for immigrants. Yet, it is insinuated that read in combination with the amendment of the Greek nationality code as regards the acquisition of the Greek nationality by second generation foreigners

---

[1] *N. Davrados*, The control by the Supreme Court of the application of the conflict of law rule, in Essays in honour of Spyridon Vl. Vrellis (2014) pp. 185–200 (in Greek), *D. Evrigenis*, Application of Foreign Law (1956) (in Greek), *A. Grammatikaiki-Alexiou*, Problems of Application of Foreign Law, especially in the Procedure of Issuing Certificates of Inheritance, Harmenopoulos 1976 pp. 527–540 (in Greek), *E. Michelakis*, Custom and Foreign Law as object of Proof, in Mélanges G. Streit vol. II (1963) pp. 253–268 (in Greek), *C. Pamboukis*, The Judicial Knowledge of Foreign Law, in Mélanges en l'honneur d'E. Krispis (1995) pp. 297–340 (in Greek), *K. Rokas*, in Institut Suisse de Droit Comparé The Application of Foreign Law in Civil Matters in the EU States and its Perspectives for the Future (2011) Part I Legal Analysis pp. 209–228 [http://ec.europa.eu/justice/civil/files/foreign_law_en.pdf] (in French), *E. Vassilakakis*, Judicial Review of Constitutionality of Foreign Law, in Charistiria Ioani Deliyani (1992) pp. 443–464 (in Greek), *E. Vassilakakis/V. Kourtis*, in C. Esplugues/J.L. Iglesias/G. Palao (eds.), Application of Foreign Law (2011) pp. 201–212, *Sp. Vrellis*, La preuve du droit applicable étranger, Koinodikion 1996 pp. 255–276.

[2] Technically speaking there is no exception regarding the obligatory nature of the conflict of laws rules in cases where a legal issue is subjected to another type Private International Law rules (such as *lois de police*) or to another method (such the method of recognition). In these cases it is not the nature of the conflict of laws rules which is affected but their applicability.

[3] See Article 33 of the Greek Civil Code ("The provisions of a foreign law shall not apply if the application thereof is contrary to morality or in general to public policy").

[4] *Sp. Vrellis*, The *ordre public* clause in the Greek case law on adoption, RHDI 64 (2011) pp. 157–182.

living in Greece in more favorable terms,[5] the aforementioned solution (*i.e.* application of the *lex patriae*) could still increase the number of cases governed by the *lex fori*.[6] An analogous reflection could also apply in respect of conflict of laws rules using the domicile or the habitual residence as connecting factors: having in mind that the number of foreigners living Greece has considerably increased, it is evident that such a private international law policy could equally increase the number of cases governed by Greek law.

Nonetheless, the thought that the use of the nationality or of the domicile/habitual residence as connecting factors could facilitate the application of the *lex fori* is not undeniable, not only because conflict of laws rules with the aforementioned content are principally based on the principle of proximity[7] but also because analogous private international law solutions are always of bilateral character, so that, in many instances, the judge (but not only) will apply a foreign law and not the *lex fori*. If sometimes the above solution permits the application of the *lex fori*, this is not the only effect of the rule in question. Regarding persons living abroad or having foreign nationality, the applicable law will be in principle a foreign law. In those cases the application of the *lex fori* will be exceptional: as always, when the *lex causae* is a foreign law, applying instead the *lex fori* is possible only when the application of the former is contrary to the public policy.

II. Foreign Law Before Judicial Authorities

A. *Nature of and Application of Foreign Law*

In principle, at the present stage, foreign law is considered in Greece as *jus* to be applied *ex officio* and not at party's request.[8] According to article 337 of the Civil Procedure Code (1967) entitled "*Proof of Foreign Law*", "*The court must take into account ex officio and without proof the law in force in a foreign country, the customary law and the business usages; if they are unknown to the court, the latter may order proof of the foreign law applicable or may use any other means judged appropriate without restricting to the evidence which the litigants have produced*".

---

[5] L. 4332/2015 Article 1a.

[6] *K. Rokas*, in Institut Suisse de Droit Comparé The Application of Foreign Law in Civil Matters in the EU States and its Perspectives for the Future (2011) Part I Legal Analysis pp. 210–211.

[7] *P. Lagarde*, Le principe de proximité dans le droit international privé contemporain. Cours général de droit international privé RCADI 196 (1986) pp. 9–238 (in French).

[8] This obligation is not without time limitation: according to case law, the parties have no right to propose the facts imposing the application of a foreign law and the subsequent court's obligation to proceed to the relevant research for the first time before the Supreme Court (Supreme Court 131/2012, NOMOS Legal Database, Court of Appeal of Piraeus 852/2013, NOMOS Legal Database).

The same solution is reproduced in the Code of Administrative Procedure. Article 144 (4) CAdmP provides that "*Foreign law, customary law and business usages shall be taken into account by the court ex officio, if they are known to it. If the court does not know them, it orders proof as described in article 152 [of the Code of Administrative Procedure]*".[9]

It must be observed that the term 'foreign law' encompasses not only legislative provisions but also customs and business usages. On the other hand, the Greek Supreme Court (Areios Pagos) has often indicated that the notion of 'foreign law' «*is not limited to foreign substantive provisions of private law*». Nonetheless, one must not overlook the court's tendency to avoid the application of a foreign *lex causae* by the misuse of different legal means, such as characterization or exception clauses.[10]

The aforementioned situation, *i.e.* the fact that foreign law is treated as *jus*, leads to the application of the principle *jura novit curia* not only as regards the *lex fori* but also concerning foreign law designated by a (Greek) conflict of law rule.[11] This principle applies as well regarding (ordinary and special) contentious proceedings as in the non-contentious proceedings.[12] On the contrary, the situation is somewhat blurred concerning the application of foreign law in proceedings for provisional protection and remedies. In those cases the courts have the tendency to deny the application of a foreign *lex causae* and to apply instead the *lex fori* because of the emergency which is typical of this kind of judicial protection: presumably, when the courts are asked to order provisional measures, they have no time to request and to await for the proof of a foreign law.[13] Nevertheless, this way of thinking is not shared by many legal scholars who, on the contrary, adopt 'a case by case' approach. Specifically, as argued, in case of provisional protection and remedies the courts should have recourse to the *lex fori* only when it is extremely difficult to ascertain the content of a foreign solution.[14]

---

[9] *P. Lazaratos*, Administrative Procedural Law (2013) p. 878–879 (in Greek), *Ch. Chryssanthakis* (ed.) Administrative Procedure – A Commentary on Greek Legislation of Administrative Procedure (2015) p. 450–451 (in Greek), *E. Vassilakakis/V. Kourtis*, in C. Esplugues/J.L. Iglesias/G. Palao (eds.), Application of Foreign Law p. 203. See in this sense Administrative Court of Appeal of Athens 1590/2014, Δ/νη (Justice) 2014 p. 1750].

[10] *T. Papadopoulou*, The role of the forum's judge in Private International Law (2000) p. 30 (in Greek).

[11] Multi-Member Court of First Instance of Syros 8/2013, NOMOS Legal Database [http://lawdb.intrasoftnet.com/nomos/nomos_frame.html].

[12] *E. Vassilakakis/V. Kourtis*, in C. Esplugues/J.L. Iglesias/G. Palao (eds.), Application of Foreign Law p. 205.

[13] One-Member Court of First Instance of Thebes 296/1990, Δ (Dike) 23 p. 258, One-Member Court of First Instance of Piraeus 788/1993, ΕΝΔ (Maritime Law Review) 1993 p. 332, One-Member Court of First Instance of Cephalonia, 468/2000, Δ (Dike) 2001 p. 759, One-Member Court of First Instance of Piraeus 56/2009 NOMOS legal data base, One-Member Court of First Instance of Thessaloniki 17765/2010, NOMOS Legal Database.

[14] *Sp. Vrellis*, Private International Law $(2008)^3$ pp. 118–119 (in Greek).

B. Ascertainment of Foreign Law

Irrespective of the above discussion, relative to the status of foreign law in cases of provisional protection and remedies, it is recognized that there are, in general, cases where the courts fail to ascertain the content of the applicable foreign law. This is the reason why it is admitted that, if the court has to apply *proprio motu* the foreign *lex causae*, it has also the possibility to "*use any means that it considers appropriate for acquiring knowledge of foreign law*" and not only "*the means of proof provided by the procedural law*".[15-16]

To that effect, the court may have recourse to the knowledge acquired in previous cases, where Greek courts had applied the same foreign law. In absence of such knowledge, courts usually request the litigants' assistance, consisting in a written opinion provided, in most cases, by the Hellenic Institute of International and Foreign Law[17] but also by legal experts or foreign judges. The cost of such assistance is financed by the parties. An analogous assistance can be provided both by foreign embassies in Greece or Greek embassies in foreign countries, even though such a solution is rarely used in practice.

In principle, there is no legislative specification of neither the qualifications possessed by the expert or institution which provides the legal information, asked by the court, nor of the legal value of this information. In fact, as to the latter question, only the court competent is to decide on the reliability and the applicability of the information regarding the foreign *lex causae*. On the other hand, given that in most cases the courts have recourse to the services of the Hellenic Institute of International and Foreign Law, one can presume that this solution is preferred because of the expertise of the aforementioned Institute in the field of comparative law; and that the same expertise must exist by other instances which could provide information on foreign law.[18] It must be also underlined that the Greek government has entrusted the Hellenic Institute of International and Foreign Law with the application of the European Convention of 1968 on Information on Foreign Law, as amended by the Additional Protocol of 1978. More precisely, the said Institute is appointed as receiving and transmitting authority in compliance with the article 2 of the Convention in question.

---

[15] *E. Vassilakakis/V. Kourtis*, in C. Esplugues/J.L. Iglesias/G. Palao (eds.), Application of Foreign Law p. 205.

[16] Court of Appeal of Thessaloniki 154/2010, ΕΠολΔ (Civil Procedure Review) 2011 p. 106, Administrative Court of Appeal of Athens 1590/2014, Court of Appeal of Athens 428/2009 (NOMOS Legal Database), Court of Appeal of Piraeus 852/2013, ΔΕΕ (Law of Business Establishments and Companies) 2013 p. 1192.

[17] *D. Evrigenis*, The problem of the knowledge of the applicable foreign law and the legal information given by the Hellenic Institute for International and Foreign Law, EEAN (Journal of Greek and Foreign Jurisprudence) 1957 pp. 224–236 (in Greek).

[18] Until the information is provided the court must suspend the procedure (Court of Appeal of Piraeus 428/2099, Court of First Instance of Athens 41/2010, Council of State 2866/2012, NOMOS Legal Database, Court of Appeal of Piraeus 852/2013, Administrative Court of Appeal of Athens1580/2014).

C. Interpretation and Application of Foreign Law

In respect of the interpretation of foreign law it must, first of all, be observed that the case law is not very "eloquent" on this matter. Nonetheless, in a recent decision of the Court of Appeal of Piraeus, where English law was applicable in respect to a maritime insurance contract, reference was made on the one hand to case law of the English courts and on the other hand to the relevant theoretical works.[19] On the contrary, Greek case law gives no answer to the question of the eventual gaps in the applicable foreign law. One can only presume that those cases must be treated in the same way as cases of failure to ascertain the content of the foreign *lex causae*. Certainly, the ideal solution would place oneself in the position of the foreign authorities when facing analogous cases. This approach is however unrealistic: the forum's judge is unable to imitate the way of thinking of foreign judges, placed in the framework of a different legal system, and often belonging to a different legal tradition. On the other hand, the court facing such a case could not remain silent, refusing, thus, to rule on the case submitted before it: a denial of justice is not permitted. This is the reason why the judge is obliged to find an alternative solution. Yet, it must be underlined that this solution must not differ from the one applied in cases in which the court fails to establish the content of the applicable foreign law.[20] The idea to dismiss the case because the foreign law does not regulate (either by legislative provisions or not) the legal issue concerned is not acceptable, in particular when the *lex fori*, on the contrary, provides for the necessary solution. Such an approach (i.e. the dismissal of the case) would not be in conformity neither with the local law nor with the foreign *lex causae*.

D. Failure to Establish Foreign Law

Although the legal theory has proposed other alternatives in respect of proceedings where the applicable foreign law could not be proved, such as the application of another law connected with the case, the solution prevailing in the Greek case law

[19] Piraeus Court of Appeal 480/2014, available in NOMOS Legal Database.

[20] See however a Supreme Court's decision (1577/2010, NOMOS legal database), in which the applicable Albanian law provided for no solution about the reparation of moral prejudice. The Court decided to proceed to the application by analogy of some other provision of the foreign *lex causae*. One could think that such an approach, if possible, is better, because in this way, i.e. by avoiding the application of the *lex fori*, we are able to ensure the international harmony. As fascinating as this thought may be, the question still remains whether the aforementioned solution "belongs" really to the foreign law or is it an *ad hoc* solution of the *lex fori*.

is the application of the *lex fori*.[21] In support of this practice legal scholarship underlines the practical advantages (more precisely, legal certainty) as well as the presumption that the unproved foreign provisions are similar to the legal solutions of the lex fori.[22] However, irrespective of the policy considerations of the prevailing practice, one must not oversee the fact that the application of the *lex fori* has been also highly criticized as not conforming to the essence of the conflict of laws system. According to those critiques, the main characteristic of private international law is the proximity principle and in that sense, instead of applying the local law, it would be better to identify subsidiary connecting factors which will ensure the application of the law of another country with which the legal relationship is also connected.[23]

III. Judicial Review

The application of both the conflict of laws rules and foreign *leges causae* is subjected to the review of higher courts, *i.e.* by courts of appeal and by the Greek Supreme Court, in order to ensure the binding force and the effective application of the *jura novit curia* principle in respect of the foreign law. The difference between the aforementioned twofold of judicial review (by courts of appeal and by the Supreme Court) is essential: it lies in the fact that the review operated by the courts of appeal concerns both the legal issues and the factual aspects of the case. On the contrary, the Supreme Court's control is restricted to points of law. More precisely, as regards the latter, article 559 (1) CCP provides that a judicial decision may be challenged for violation or incorrect interpretation of a substantive (not procedural) rule.[24] As expressly stated in the frame of the same provision, the term "substantive law" refers to statutory or customary law, irrespective of whether it is Greek, foreign or international law.[25]

---

[21] Court of Appeal of Piraeus 275/2012, One-Member Court of First Instance of Thebes 4/2014, NOMOS Legal Database.

[22] *E. Vassilakakis/V. Kourtis*, in C. Esplugues/J.L. Iglesias/G. Palao (eds.), Application of Foreign Law p. 208.

[23] *Sp. Vrellis*, Private International Law p. 119.

[24] Supreme Court 581/2010, ΕΕμπΔ (Review of Commercial Law) 2011 p. 142, Supreme Court 521/2010, ΕΕμπΔ (Review of Commercial Law) 2011 p. 146.

[25] No sanction is, on the contrary, imposed for court's errors as to the research of the content of the applicable foreign law (Supreme Court 581/2010). In theory this position is criticized on the ground that she is contrary to the letter and the spirit of Article 337 of the Code of Civil Procedure, especially in cases where the court has obviously made no effort to discover the foreign law's content [*A. Grammatikaki-Alexiou/Z. Papassiopi-Passia/E. Vassilakakis*, Private International Law (2013)^5 p. 83 (in Greek)].

IV. Foreign Law in Other Instances

Concerning the application of foreign law by non-judicial authorities, there is a debate between legal scholars in Greece as to the existence of an obligation to apply (conflict of laws rules and) foreign law. In accordance with one view, administrative authorities, just like courts, are equally obliged to apply and to ascertain foreign law by virtue of the article 144 (4) CAdmP. Nevertheless this view is not generally accepted. According to another opinion, non-judicial authorities are not empowered to request opinions in regard to the content of foreign law, as is the case with the judicial authorities. This limits the ability of non-judicial authorities to ascertain the content of foreign law".[26]

It is true that Article 337 CCP and Article 144 (4) CAdmP, both a legislative expression of the *jura novit curia* principle, concern cases brought before the courts. Nevertheless, one must not forget that there are cases where legal relationships with foreign elements have to be treated by non-judicial authorities, also bound by private international rules and, consequently, obliged to apply or at least to have recourse to foreign law. If we were to accept the contrary, *i.e.* that the Administration is exempted from the obligation to apply and to ascertain foreign law, it would undermine both the principle of legality which underlines the conduct of the Administration[27] and the goals of private international law, especially the international harmony aimed by the conflict of laws rules. Furthermore, such an approach would lead to a different treatment of one and the same relationship by judicial courts and administrative authorities and, in that sense, would threaten the unity of the forum's legal system.

The practice of non-judicial authorities demonstrates this school of thought: a significant part of the requests submitted to the Hellenic Institute of International and Foreign Law stem from other authorities rather than the judiciary, in particular form regional authorities asking questions on the nationality and the family status of foreigners.

At this point it is important to clarify that in many cases non-judicial authorities, having to treat an international legal relationship, do not apply, strictly speaking, foreign law – they must only take into account the foreign law, in the sense that they are not obliged (one must say, they are not authorized) to pronounce the legal consequences of a foreign provision.[28] This is the case of a land registrar who, having to register a sale contract of an immovable property concluded in another country, he must firstly ascertain its formal validity according to the relevant – foreign – law. In such a case, the land registrar is simply verifying that the foreign law has already been applied in the country where the contract has been concluded. A similar case, as to the treatment of foreign law, is the case of regional authorities verifying the

[26] *E. Vassilakakis/V. Kourtis*, in C. Esplugues/J.L. Iglesias/G. Palao (eds.), Application of Foreign Law p. 204.

[27] *E. Spiliotopoulos*, Treaty of Administrative Law (2011)[14] pp. 87–91 (in Greek).

[28] *P. Kinsch*, Le fait du prince étranger (1994) (in French).

alleged nationality of a foreigner: when asking information about a foreign nationality law, a regional (Greek) authority is not seeking to apply the foreign rules, but only to examine, if the person concerned can be considered as a national of that country, according to the latter's relevant legislation.

Furthermore, concerning, in particular, arbitration proceedings[29] and despite the lack of information on this matter, due to the confidentiality of the proceedings in those cases, the answer to the questions concerning the status and the ascertainment of foreign law must be viewed in the light of the particular nature of this dispute resolution mechanism.[30] More precisely, we must not forget that the arbitrators' power to decide about a case is not the result of a national law but of the parties' agreement to avoid the state courts. Because of this particularity, the arbitrators are bound only by the decisions of the persons concerned and not by the rules of any national law. As frequently said, regarding arbitration, there is no (national) *forum* which could designate the applicable law to the dispute. This element is also decisive for the status of conflict of laws rules and of foreign law: according to this logic, only the parties are competent to agree on the applicable law as to the substance of their relationship. If such agreement exists, the arbitrators are obliged to apply the law designated by the parties. On the contrary, if the parties have remained silent about the law applicable to their dispute, the arbitrator's' decision on this matter is almost unlimited.

As to the foreign law, firstly it should be stressed that, in the framework of the arbitration, because of the abovementioned non-existence of a *lex fori*, the applicable law, irrespective if designated by the parties or the arbitrators, will always be a 'foreign' law. Despite this legal technicality, in practice the only case in which there is no need to proceed to the ascertainment of the applicable law is when the latter is the national law of an arbitrator or if the arbitrator, irrespective of his nationality, is familiar with the law in question. Given that in the case of the arbitration, institutional or not, the arbitrators are chosen because of their authority, it is obvious why in such a case it will not be always necessary to proceed to the proof of the foreign *lex causae*.

On the other hand, we must not overlook the fact that the parties' autonomy concerns not only the substantive law applicable to the difference but also the procedural rules which must be respected.[31] Having that in mind, it is clear that the status of foreign law also depends on the parties' decision[32]: if the procedural law chosen

---

[29] *A. Mantakou*, The Misadventures of the Principle Jura Novit Curia in International Arbitration – A Practitioner's Approach, in Essays in honour of Spyridon Vl. Vrellis (2014) pp. 557–568 (where further bibliography).

[30] *Chr. Seraglini*, L'arbitrage commercial international, in *J. Béguin/M. Menjucq* (eds.), Droit du commerce international (2011) pp. 947 et seq.

[31] For the procedural aspects of arbitrations see *P. Mayer*, "L'autonomie de l'arbitre international dans l'appréciation de sa propre compétence," in Collected Courses of the Hague Academy of International Law, Vol. 217, Part V (1989).

[32] It is to be noted that according to A. Mantakou (Essays in honour of Spyridon Vl. Vrellis pp. 567–568) regarding the arbitration "the principle *Jura Novit Curia* seems to gradually take the shape of "*Jura non Novit Curia*". It follows that arbitrators depend on the parties' wishes as to the law applicable and its status.

by them provides for a particular way of ascertaining the content of foreign law, this must be respected. If not, or if the parties have not decided about the procedural aspects of their dispute, the arbitrators are free to ascertain the applicable law be any means they dispose. As important as those principles are, it is should not be forgotten that they apply only concerning non-institutional arbitration. In all the other cases, the regime of the dispute is governed by the specific rules of the institution concerned.

The above (the obligatory character of conflict of laws rules and the application of foreign solutions *proprio motu*) apply also in respect of other professionals taking part in the administration of justice in a wider sense, such as lawyers or notaries. Practitioners of this kind are equally bound by the conflict of laws rules and, hence, there are obliged to apply and to ascertain the applicable foreign law, using the same mechanisms as judges and other non-judicial authorities. Ignoring those aspects of the case would affect the quality of their work in a negative manner and occasionally adversely affecting the parties' interests. The parties will benefit from the knowledge of the legal personnel, in the sense that, if well advised, they will perhaps avoid an unnecessary litigation.

In practice, the 'use' of (conflict of laws rules and) foreign law in an advisory level is not rare, considering the growing number of foreigners living in Greece or of Greek citizens living abroad but still maintaining contacts with Greece, as well as the importance of Greece in the field of navigation. Because of these factors the number of cases with foreign elements has considerably increased, calling upon the application of private international law mechanisms irrespective if this happens before a court or in a prior stage, *i.e.* during the planning of the relationship or the preparation of the case.

V. Access to Foreign Law: *Status Quo*

The 'national' means of proof of foreign law, as important as they are, are not the only techniques available for the purpose of facilitating access to foreign law. Equally (if not more) important to this matter is international cooperation. Recognizing the particularity of the problems connected with the status of foreign law, Greece, as many other States, takes part in efforts of this nature. In particular, as a Member State of the European Union, Greece is member of the European Judicial Network on Civil and Commercial Matters.[33] Greece has also ratified the European Convention of 1968 on Information on Foreign Law[34] (and its additional

[33] Decision No 568/2009/EC of the European Parliament and the Council of the 18 June 2009 amending Council Decision 2001/470/EC establishing a European Judicial Network in civil and commercial matters.

[34] Ratified by the l. 593/1977.

Protocol of 1978).[35] In general, this Convention did not have the success expected: often unknown to potential beneficiaries, its application is not very often invoked.[36]

In addition, Greece has concluded a number of bilateral Conventions of judicial cooperation, which, among other issues, regulate the matter of the exchange of information on the legal system of the contracting States.[37]

The aforementioned cooperation would not be necessary, if every country possessed databases concerning its own legal system, translated in a foreign language (preferably in English). Apart from complicated cases (which in reality would not be so rare), such database will suffice for the regulation of cases connected with foreign countries. This is not the case of Greece. Indeed, Greece does not make information about the Greek legal system available in other languages than Greek: in official (but not only) websites one can find legislative texts as well as case law only in Greek language. It is obvious that such a situation has no or a little utility in cases in which a foreign authority has to apply the Greek law.

VI. Access to Foreign Law: Further Developments

A. Practical Needs

The improvement of the access to foreign law, if possible, is of great importance, in the sense that the application of the foreign *lex causae* is the ultimate condition of the conflict of laws system's efficacy. Failing to apply the foreign law designated by the national conflict of laws rules is a serious threat for the international harmony pursued by those rules. The best way to make some progress in this direction is to use new technologies, trying at the same time, not to increase the costs of legal information on this matter. The opposite would adversely affect the interests not only of the parties (occasionally unable to afford those costs) but also of States which, in times of economic crisis, must reduce their expenses.

If successful, such an effort will be to the benefit of everyone involved in an international relationship: the interested parties, the judges, the administration etc. If the courts are obviously the only ones which decide about a legal question in a binding manner, taking the right decision depends not only on the judge's knowledge and abilities. What is also decisive is the information furnished by other legal professionals who, if well informed, will help the courts (and the administration) to proceed to the regulation of each relationship according to the letter and the spirit of the law. In this way the parties' interests are equally well served: in this manner the

---

[35] Ratified by the l. 1709/1987.

[36] *C. Pamboukis*, The Judicial Knowledge of Foreign Law pp. 325–326.

[37] Greece has concluded analogous Conventions with Ukraine (l. 3281/2004, art. 15), Armenia (l. 3007/2002, art. 6), China (l. 2358/1995, art. 9), Albania (l. 2311/1995, art. 13), Tunisia (l. 2228/1994, art. 17), Syria (l. 1450/1984, art. 5), Czech Republic (l. 1323/1983, art. 13), Poland (l. 1184/1981, art. 4), Hungary (l. 1149/1981, art. 13) and Bulgaria (l. 841/1978, art. 13).

persons involved do not risk being exposed to judicial decisions (and acts) which may be challenged and possibly reversed. Legal certainty is, consequently, enhanced.

Of course, the frequency of the application or, more generally, the recourse to foreign law is not the same in every instance or regarding every kind of relationship with foreign elements: despite the lack of statistics, it is quite sure that courts and administrative authorities, because of the review to which their decisions are subjected, apply more frequently foreign law, concerning especially contracts and delicts/torts as well as family relations and successions, *i.e.* questions concerning the everyday life of persons.

B. Conflict of Laws Solutions

Regarding the techniques which could be used in order to resolve the problems raised by the application of a foreign law, it is important not to consider them as of procedural nature only. On the contrary, problems of this kind are rather accessory, depending, as to their solution, on the singularity of private international law and that the main concern of a specialist must be the quality of the solutions on this matter. This is the reason why the solution of technical problems (and the status of foreign law may be considered as one of them) must depend on how international relationships are regulated.

In the field of private international law, the method of conflict of laws rules and consequently the application of foreign law is the main way to respect the singularity of international relations. Systematically avoiding the application of foreign law designated by the conflict of laws rules would thus affect the quality of justice in this field and not in a positive way. More precisely, such an approach (systematically applying the *lex fori*) would render international harmony, necessary to international relationships, impossible to achieve.[38]

Of course, there are specific cases where such an attitude is not only permitted but also imposed. It is, however, important to be aware of the fact that in those cases an analogous solution is (occasionally) adopted not (or not only) for practical reasons and in particular in order to avoid the inconveniences related to the application of a foreign law; if regarding certain relations the application of the *lex fori* is preferred, this is a result of more substantial reasons. An illustrative example is found in the Hague Protocol of 2007 on the law applicable to maintenance obligations (and the EU Regulation 4/2009 on the same matter, imposing the application of this Protocol by the EU Member States) and specifically the Article 4 (2) and (3). According to these provisions, the application of the *lex fori* is, under certain conditions, a means to guarantee that the creditor of maintenance will be effectively protected. The legal basis of such a protection is the Protocol itself and there is no doubt

[38] About justice in the field of private international law see *Sp. Vrellis*, Conflit ou coordination de valeurs en droit international privé – À la recherché de la justice, RCADI T. 308 (2007) pp. 175–485 and *A. Bucher*, La dimension sociale du droit international privé (2010).

that in these cases the application of the *lex fori* is the result of substantive law considerations.[39]

One could argue that the *ex officio* application of the foreign law has negative consequences as to the financial cost of this procedure and the time required therefore and that, because of that, the Greek solutions on this matter, as illustrated before, must be modified in the sense that the status of foreign law must depend only on the parties' decision. Such a thought is logic but cannot be approved. Accepting that the treatment of foreign law will vary from case to case would be a serious threat to the legal system's unity and to the equality of the parties. In addition, such an approach would mean that in affairs with foreign elements the parties could dispose of their relationship and their rights irrespective of the interests involved, even if, in the field of the substantial law, the persons concerned do not have the same power. Is it possible to accept an analogous solution only for practical reasons (*i.e.* facilitate the life of the courts or of the parties) without considering the essence of the regulation obtained in this way? The answer must be negative.

As already said the status of the conflict of laws rules and of the foreign law, eventually designated by them, is not an autonomous problem which can be resolved regardless of its legal environment and especially without considering the purpose of private international law solutions. Of course, this is a general remark, which does not exclude certain exceptions. There are indeed areas of the substantial law where the parties' autonomy is nowadays recognized, even considering matters which in the past were not at the discretion of the parties. Family law is the most significant example one could mention in that regard. Nonetheless, we must not forget that if this really happens, the conflict of laws system is also affected: such a substantial law evolution entails in the field of private international law the recognition of the parties' right to choose the applicable law.[40] It is, thus, unnecessary to change the status of foreign law as regulated in the Greek law: if the parties want to

---

[39] About this legislative text see *A. Bonomi*, The Hague Protocol of 23 November 2007 on the Law Applicable to Maintenance Obligations, YPIL 2008 pp. 333–357. S. also *B. Ancel/H. Muir Watt*, Aliments sans frontières. Le Règlement CE 4/2009 du 18 décembre 2008 relatif à la compétence, la loi applicable, la reconnaissance et l'exécution des décisions et la coopération en matière d'obligations alimentaires, Rev. crit. DIP 2010 pp. 457–484, *A. Douga/V. Koumpli*, Cross-border maintenance obligations in Europe: The EU Maintenance Regulation, in Essays in Honour of Spyridon Vrellis (2014) pp. 239–250 (in Greek).

[40] See article 22 of the Council Regulation EU 2016/1103 implementing enhanced cooperation in the area of jurisdiction, applicable law and the recognition and enforcement of decisions in matters of matrimonial property regimes [regarding the initial Proposal for a Council Regulation on jurisdiction, applicable law and the recognition and enforcement of decisions in matters of matrimonial regimes see *M. Sotiropoulou*, The option given to spouses to choose the applicable law defined in the Proposal for a Council Regulation on jurisdiction, applicable law and the recognition and enforcement of decisions in matters of matrimonial property regimes: Progress or not?, RHDI 2013 pp. 21 et seq (where further bibliography)] and article 22 of the Council Regulation EU 2016/1104 implementing enhanced cooperation in the area of jurisdiction, applicable law and the recognition and enforcement of decisions in matters of the property consequences of registered partnerships.

avoid the difficulties connected with the application of foreign solutions, they can choose the *lex fori*.

Unification of rules relative to the treatment of foreign law at international or regional level would be most useful, not only *per se* but principally as a mechanism accessory to the unification to conflict of laws rules, i.e. in order to further promote the international harmony in the sphere of private international law.

The current discussion concerning the status of foreign law in the context of the EU private international law is a very significant indication of the practical importance of such an approach: as observed, the differences of the national laws of the EU Member States as to the question of foreign law can affect the efficacy of the EU Regulations on Private International Law.[41] Indubitably, there are many elements which must be taken into account when considering the problem of the most suitable way to treat foreign law in the European legal system, mainly the procedural autonomy of the Member States.[42] It is however clear that the *ex officio* application of a foreign *lex causae* designated by the European conflict of laws rules would increase the harmony of solutions in the European Union. Otherwise, some Member States, where there is no obligation to apply foreign law *proprio motu* but only on request of the parties, would be practically exempt from the obligation to apply the EU Regulations in question. In an analogous case, which in reality is the current situation in the European Union, the unification aimed by the latter, would be in danger: the law applicable in one and the same difference will differ according to the treatment reserved to foreign law by the national courts having competence on the matter. The forum shopping which the European legislator has vigorously tried to mitigate by adopting several Regulations on the applicable law, is now in the forefront.

C. Methods of Facilitating Access to Foreign Law

International cooperation on the exchange of information about the legal system of the concerned countries may be extremely advantageous, if well organized. In fact, the main problem to avoid in those cases is the bureaucracy which may considerably delay the cooperation as to this subject. Having in mind that such an information exchange aims to the regulation of a particular relation, it is important to remember

[41] For the relevant discussion see the site of the groupe européen de droit international privé http://www.gedip-egpil.eu/reunionstravail/gedip-reunions-23.htm#traitement. See also *St. Bariayti/E. Pattaut*, Codification et théorie générale du droit international privé, in: *M. Fallon/P. Lagarde/S. Poillot-Peruzzetto* (dir.), Quelle architecture pour un code européen de droit international privé? (2011) pp. 337–361 (342–347), *E.-M. Kieniger*, Ermittlung und Anwendung ausländischen Rechts, in: *St. Leible/H. Unberath* (Hrsg.), Brauchen wir eine Rom 0-Verordnung? (2013) pp. 479–501.

[42] See the CJEU' judgment in case C-93/12 ET Agrokonsulting-04-Velko Stoyanov v. Izpalnitelen direktor na Darzhaven fond «Zemedelie» – Razplashtatelna agentsia of 27 June 2013.

that the time spent to ascertain the applicable foreign law may have negative consequences for the persons involved.

This is why it is essential to establish a system of direct communication between the professionals concerned as well as to permit the use of such a system not only by the courts but also by other authorities or other legal personnel, occasionally called upon to deal with international relationships, such as lawyers or notaries.

Recourse to such a system of international cooperation regarding foreign law must be available only to legal professionals and not to individuals who don't usually possess sufficient knowledge to understand information concerning the law (foreign or not) and could be misguided as to the regulation of their legal affairs. In other words, a totally open system of exchange of information on foreign law could hinder the parties' interests.

However, as vital as it is an analogous system (of direct communication), it is not simple to be organized. Apart from the technical problems (if this direct communication is effected via internet), there are also more considerable questions, related to the information to be exchanged as to the persons engaged to this procedure. More precisely, such a concrete coordination system demands, first of all, the translation of the law of the collaborating countries, so that everyone understands the given information. And it is important to note that the translation would not be really useful if limited to the legislative texts. It should also concern the case law, as the latter reflects the real "image" of the applicable foreign law. If the purpose of private international law is to achieve that a legal relationship is treated in the same way in many countries, being informed on the real situation of the designated foreign *lex causae* is of great practical importance. Without such information, the law applied by the courts of the *forum* runs the risk of not being identical with the solutions applied by the foreign legal system and the international harmony will be a sole image without substance.

This is also the reason why the information given by the authorities of the foreign country (as defined by the international Convention, eventually establishing the international cooperation on this matter) must be binding. The contrary would endanger the effectiveness of the cooperation on this matter as well as the aim of the relevant law, *i.e.* the international harmony of solutions. If the judge, or any other competent authority or person, of the *forum* could proceed to further investigations as to the applicable law, then the whole system would be excessively time-and money-consuming. It is only exceptionally that deviation from this principle may be allowed to complete the information, given by the foreign authorities, as, for example, when the information is insufficient to answer the questions of the *forum*, the judge of the case has studied in the foreign State in question (and has, therefore, direct access to its law) and the parties can afford to pay for additional expertise on this matter.

If, in presence of a doubt, the court had, nevertheless, not proceeded to further investigations, the aforementioned position entails the risk for the court to rely on incorrect information. One could argue that in such a case the decision is subject to judicial review. An analogous conclusion is probably inaccurate: given the Greek

Supreme Court's position that there is no control of errors as to the research of the content of foreign law,[43] one can presume that in this case as well, the judgment could not be challenged. The best way to avoid this risk is to provide for judicial review in the framework of the Convention establishing the international cooperation itself, so that the procedural law of the contracting States could not hinder the judgment's control.

On the other hand, a direct exchange of information on foreign law, irrespective of her precise legal basis presupposes the training of the legal professionals (judges and others), occasionally involved to cases presenting foreign elements, concerning not only the use of new technologies but also how to trust the foreign authority about a case pending in the forum; more precisely how not to see such an exchange as an offence to the sovereignty of their own State and to their own authority to proceed to the regulation of the relation in question.

It follows from the foregoing that establishing a system ensuring an effective exchange of information on foreign law demands precise state actions that have a considerable cost, financial but not only. This situation could not be without effect on the services provided in relation to a specific difference: those services cannot be provided free of charge, especially not during periods of economic crisis and at least not before the system in question is well established.

Conclusions

In principle, is not easy to define the foreign law status in a manner that ensures certainty of law as well as respect of the international relations' particularities. Yet, Greek private international law manages to provide the courts (but not only) with sufficient legal tools to deal with problems arising out of the application of conflict of laws rules and of foreign law. This means not that there is no need for further improvement of the applicable solutions.

Indeed, as satisfactory as national solutions may be, they cannot resolve every problem of this kind without having recourse to the benefits of international cooperation in a larger scale as in the past with the support of new technologies. In a time period in which relations with foreign elements and the relevant provisions are more and more complicated, international cooperation is the only way to obtain accurate information about foreign law. It is, however, realistic to hope that such an ambitious project will be soon a reality? Considering the time required to that effect as well as the financial cost of operations of this kind, the answer to this question must be negative. For the time being, international cooperation exists only at regional level: the European Union is the most characteristic example of this kind.

At the same time and as important as the above remarks may be, we must realize that the treatment of foreign law is part of the conflict of laws system. Hence, any solution on this problem must be at the service of this system. It is also important

[43] See Supreme Court 581/2010.

not to forget that the policies of a national private international law system may differ from those of a system of unified provisions, such as the European private international law; and that a difference of this kind may affect the solutions relative to the status of foreign law.

Hungary: Inconsistencies Between Theory and Practice in the Treatment of Foreign Law in Hungary

László Burián and Sarolta Szabó

Abstract This article describes the present situation of the application and ascertainment of foreign law by analysing the Law Decree No. 13 of 1979 on Private International Law and its judicial practice in Hungary. In this Law Decree, which is the first legal instrument in the history of the Hungarian PIL, a more than hundred year old tradition was codified that foreign law should be treated as law, so according to the principle of "iura novit curia", the judge has to apply the foreign law ex officio. This approach is recognised by the Hungarian jurisprudence and the academic literature as well, but in most cases the problems stem from the fact that the tools and methods offered by the Hungarian PIL Code (e.g. experts), multilateral and bilateral treaties (e.g. London Convention) are not applied in all cases when they should and could be used. In addition, the article gives a short overview of interpretation of foreign law and failure to establish foreign law. Finally, based on a detailed analysis it concludes that there is a common need to improve the access of foreign law, and it is not just a technical issue, because the proper application of foreign law as a complex judicial task depends on the education and training of the judges and notaries as well.

I. Introduction

The Law Decree No 13 of 1979 on Private International Law (hereafter referred to as *Hungarian PIL Code*) is the first legal instrument in the history of the Hungarian private international law, which contains the domestic rules of jurisdiction, conflict of laws and recognition and enforcement of foreign judgements in their entirety in

L. Burián (✉) • S. Szabó
Professor, Faculty of Law and Political Sciences, Pázmány Péter Catholic University, Szentkirályi str. 28-30, H-1088 Budapest, Hungary
e-mail: burian.laszlo@jak.ppke.hu; szabo.sarolta@jak.ppke.hu

Y. Nishitani (ed.), *Treatment of Foreign Law - Dynamics towards Convergence?*,
Ius Comparatum – Global Studies in Comparative Law 26,
DOI 10.1007/978-3-319-56574-3_10

one statute. Despite the historical circumstances of the birth of the Hungarian PIL Code, it represented veritably modern approaches concerning PIL issues.[1]

However, the situation changed after the accession to the European Union (EU). It is a positive fact that the regulation of private international law (PIL) has profoundly changed in recent years, because – mainly during the last decade – the EU has undertaken an active role in the harmonisation of PIL rules. The growing series of EU PIL legislation – not unlike a "legal earthquake",[2] naturally – have a strong impact on the domestic legal system. Therefore, for example, after the adoption of the Rome I Regulation[3] the Hungarian PIL Code was modified significantly in the field of contract law in 2009,[4] and following the *Garcia Avello* decision[5] of the Court of Justice of the European Union (CJEU) a new provision was introduced regarding the bearing of names of natural persons.[6] In the last 2 years the amendments of the Hungarian PIL Code have only been technical or textual elaborations related to international marriages,[7] adoption[8] and succession.[9] Although PIL traditionally was and for a part still is an issue of national law, the priority of burgeoning union law may influence the divergent basic institutions (such as establishing the content of foreign law) of the national PIL rules also in the near future.

[1] For more details, see Burián, L. (2000). Hungarian Private International Law at the End of the 20th Century: Progress or Regress? In S. Symeonides (Ed.), *Private International Law at the End of the 20th Century: Progress or Regress?* (pp. 263–277.) Kluwer Law International.

[2] Esplugues, C., Iglesias, L., Palao, G., Espinosa, R., Azárraga, C. (2011). General Report on the Application of Foreign Law by Judicial and Non-Judicial Authorities in Europe. In C. Esplugues, J. L. Iglesias, G. Palao, (Eds.), *Application of Foreign Law.* (p. 4.). Sellier.

[3] Regulation (EC) No 593/2008 of the European Parliament and of the Council of 17 June 2008 on the law applicable to contractual obligations, OJ L 177, 4.7.2008, pp. 6–16.

[4] Act No IX of 2009. See more: Raffai, K., Szabó, S. (2010). Selected issues on recent Hungarian Private International Law Codification. *Acta Juridica Hungarica*, 51(2), 136–137.; Vékás, L. (2009). A nemzetközi magánjogi törvény módosításáról [On the Modification of the Act on Private International Law]. *Magyar Jog [Hungarian Law]*, 56(6), 321–326.

[5] C-148/02. Carlos Garcia Avello v. Belgian State [2003] ECR I-11613.

[6] According to the Act No IX of 2009, the new 10 (2) provision declares: "[h]aving regard to the right of any person to bear a name, the national law of the person shall apply. Upon request, the registration of a birth name shall be effected under the national law of the country of second citizenship [...]".

[7] Act No XCIII of 2012 and Act No. CCXXVIII of 2012 related to international marriage and registered partnership.

[8] Act No XXVII of 2013 related to international adoption.

[9] Act No LXXI of 2015 related to international succession.

II. The Application of the Hungarian Conflict of Laws Rules

A. The Application of the Hungarian Conflict of Laws Rules

Different approaches are employed by the countries when dealing with foreign law in the field of conflict of laws. The application of foreign law in civil proceedings depends on, *e.g.*, the status of the conflict of laws rules. As regards the binding force (or "the power"), the conflicts rules in Hungary have *mandatory character*. This character of the application of PIL rules is clearly stated in the Hungarian PIL Code which has been in force since 1 July 1979.[10] So the view that the conflict of laws rules are binding both on the judge and generally on the parties has never been questioned by Hungarian doctrine. This mandatory application of Hungarian conflict of laws rules is gleaned from Section 5 of the Hungarian PIL Code which stipulates that it is the judge's duty to ascertain the content and to apply the relevant foreign law.[11]

There is, however, another provision in the statute which expressly enables the parties to request jointly the non-application of the foreign law designated by the choice of laws rules. Section 9 of the Hungarian PIL Code states: "If the parties mutually request that the foreign law applicable in accordance with this Law-Decree be disregarded, the Hungarian law shall apply in place of that law [...]". So the parties have an opportunity to settle such "procedural agreements",[12] which means that they can always agree during proceedings to exclude the application of foreign law and subject their dispute to the Hungarian law.[13] But that provision is exceptional and it does not alter the basically mandatory character of Hungarian choice of law rules. There are unfortunately no statistics available, but it can be assumed that parties do not often make use of that possibility.[14]

---

[10] According to its Section 1 "The purpose of this Law-Decree is to determine the following in the interest of the development of peaceful international relations: – the law of which country is applicable if a foreign person, object of property or right (hereinafter: foreign element) is involved in a civil law, family or labour law relationship and the laws of several countries would be applicable [...]."

[11] For the establishment of the contents of a foreign law, Section 5 provides for as follows: "(1) A court or another authority shall, ex officio, enquire about a foreign law not known to it, shall, if necessary, obtain the opinion of an expert, and may also consider the evidence presented by the party."

[12] Swiss Institute of Comparative Law, The Application of Foreign Law in Civil Matters in the EU Member States and its Perspectives for the Future. 2011. http://ec.europa.eu/justice/civil/files/foreign_law_en.pdf. Accessed 12 September 2013. p. 20.

[13] It is necessary that the parties' request shall be mutually. As the Curia of Hungary pointed out, the plaintiff's unilateral declaration on the application of the Hungarian law *per se* could not enable the court to use the Section 9 of the Hungarian PIL Code and to apply Hungarian law instead of Austrian law (Gfv.IX.30.214/2006., EBH 2006.1520.). To contrast, in a former case the Curia stated that the parties' reference to the rules of the Hungarian Civil Code means that they wanted to disregard the foreign law by this implication. (Pfv. 23. 679/1997/5.).

[14] We found three cases in this respect. In one of them the parties mutually requested that the court of the second instance should disregard the law of Ecuador and apply the Hungarian substantive law to resolve their contractual dispute. (Curia of Hungary Pf.VI.21323/1996/4.).Two recent deci-

The mutual request to disregard the application of the foreign law designated by the choice of law rules might be typical in cases in which the parties are not interested in the application of the foreign law because in the end it does not make a significant difference whether foreign or Hungarian substantive law is applied (so-called false conflicts cases). This would of course presuppose that the parties have adequate information about the content of the applicable foreign law and can compare it with the relevant provisions of Hungarian substantive law.

It is, however, likely that in some cases the mutual request is made without detailed information about the applicable foreign law and the request is made "blindly", because, as a consequence of applying Hungarian substantive law, the case can be settled in a relatively short time.[15] The above solution is favourable for the parties because the ascertainment of the content of the foreign law and its application may be time-consuming, not to mention the cases when the content of the applicable foreign law cannot be ascertained at all. In the latter cases *lex fori* has to be applied. This is also favourable for the judge, since it does not have to ascertain the content of the foreign law. Among Hungarian authors, however, it is debated whether such a facultative application could be upheld under the EU PIL regime.[16]

B. The Scope and Frequency of the Application of Foreign Laws

Hungarian conflict of laws rules do often lead to the application of different foreign laws. According to the statistics of the Ministry of Justice of the last 3 years, Hungarian courts require information about the laws of various countries, but the overwhelming majority of the requests concern the laws of European countries. The most frequently invoked or applied laws are the laws of Austria,[17] Germany[18] and Romania.[19] Information is often required about the laws of Italy, Slovakia, Switzerland and the United Kingdom. In addition, according to the Ministry's statistics, some requests were submitted concerning the law of Croatia, Czech Republic, France, the Netherlands, Poland and Russia; and only one request occurred related

sions dealt with also contractual obligations, one of them was related to Spanish law (Pécs Regional Court of Appeal Gf. IV.30.010/2011/7.), and in the other case the parties avoided the application of Austrian law (Regional Court of Budapest-Capital 8.G. 40.635/2006/41.).

[15] As it happened in a case where the parties agreed on the application of Hungarian law instead of the designated law of Ecuador before the court of the second instance (Curia of Hungary Pf. VI.21323/1996/4.)

[16] Mádl, F., Vékás, L. (2012). Nemzetközi magánjog és nemzetközi gazdasági kapcsolatok joga [The Law of Conflicts and Foreign Trade]. Budapest: ELTE Eötvös Kiadó. 134.

[17] In the fields of traffic accidents, citizenship, contracts (agreements on loan, sale of goods, insurance) and guardianship.

[18] These cases concerned divorce, succession, maintenance of children and various contracts (e.g. carriage of goods, sale of goods, loan, insurance and maintenance agreement).

[19] These requests arrived mainly from the area of contract law and family law (e.g. placement of a child, presumption of fatherhood, name bearing and guardianship).

to the law of Angola, Canada, China, Cyprus, Egypt, Finland, Greece, Panama, Spain, Turkey and Vietnam. According to the Hungarian system of the proof of foreign laws (see 3.2), it is not necessary that the judge request the Ministry of Justice to ascertain the content of the applicable foreign law. Therefore, the few anonymous cases published on the website of the Curia of Hungary (formerly named: Supreme Court of Hungary) show that further foreign laws (e.g. the law of different US States) were applied in the last 5 years.[20] To sum up, it can be assumed that – at least – the laws of the EU Member States will be applied more frequently in the future because of the cornerstones of the single market, namely the 'four freedoms' (the free movement of persons, goods, services and capital).

III. Foreign Law Before Hungarian Judicial Authorities

A. *Nature and the Application of Foreign Law*

Considering the nature of the foreign law, Hungarian law has treated and still treats it as a *law*, a *legal matter* and not a fact. Thus, according to the principle of "*iura novit curia*", the judge has to apply (and know) *ex officio* the foreign law. This approach is recognised by the Hungarian jurisprudence and the academic literature as well.[21] Although there is no express legal provision which declares this legal character of the foreign law, it can be concluded from the relevant provisions (§ 5) of the Hungarian PIL Code on the ascertainment of the content of foreign law. Prior to the enactment of the 1979 Hungarian PIL Code,[22] the Code of Civil Procedure of 1952 also regulated the question in the same way. Its § 200 declared that "[t]he court shall inquire, ex officio, about the foreign law [...]". Thus, the legal character of foreign law – as it seemed to be a law – has never been questioned by Hungarian legal theory.[23] Although not mentioned by the relevant legal literature, this treatment of the foreign law follows from the equality of legal systems.

In relation to the application of foreign law, the above mentioned Section 5 Subsection (1) of the Hungarian PIL Code is clear on this subject. It declares that: "A court or other authority shall, ex officio, inquire about the foreign law not known to it [...]". This wording complies with the mandatory character of the Hungarian conflict of laws rules, that is the court has to apply foreign law whenever the conflict of law rules point to a certain foreign legal system. The same applies to the law

[20] For instance, the law of Delaware was applied in a case related to the preliminary question of the corporation's legal status before the Curia of Hungary (Pfv.IX.21.325/2007/4.).

[21] Burián, L., Czigler, T., Kecskés, L., Vörös, I. (2010). *Magyar nemzetközi kollíziós magánjog* [*Hungarian Private International Law*]. Budapest:KRIM Bt. 128.; Mádl and Vékás (2012) 133–134.; Harsági, V., Kengyel, M., Nemessányi, Z. (2011). Hungary. In C. Esplugues, J. L. Iglesias, G. Palao, (Eds.), *Application of Foreign Law*. (pp. 214–215). Sellier.

[22] The Hungarian PIL Code entered into force on 1 July 1979.

[23] Mádl and Vékás (2012) 134.; Harsági et al. (2011) 214.

chosen by the parties when validly chosen according to the relevant choice of law rules.

The application of foreign law can only be avoided in cases expressly regulated by the Hungarian PIL Code. These are the following:

- when the content of the foreign law cannot be ascertained [§ 5 subsection (3)]
- when there is a reference back to the Hungarian law by the choice of law rule of the applicable law (*renvoi*) [§ 4 last sentence]
- when the link to the foreign law was produced artificially or by simulation (fraudulent connection) [§ 8 subsection (1)]
- when to the application of foreign law reciprocity is required and the lack of reciprocity is proven (only in cases where one of the parties is a foreign state) [§ 17 subsection (2)][24]
- when the application of foreign law is contrary to the Hungarian public policy [§ 7 subsection (1)] and
- when the parties mutually request the non-application of the foreign law [§ 9]

B. Ascertainment of Foreign Law

Theoretically there is no difference between the application of the *lex fori* and foreign law. The maxim of "*iura novit curia*" applies for domestic law and there is no reason why it should be different when applying foreign law. The court is expected to have the necessary knowledge about foreign law and apply it without any reference made by the parties.

However, there is a certain difference in practice. The court is usually not familiar with the content of foreign law; therefore it has to be ascertained. Section 5 Subsection (1) of the Hungarian PIL Code does not only require the inquiry of the foreign law unknown to the court, it also indicates some of the means which can be used in order to establish its content. According to it a court shall, if necessary, obtain the opinion of an expert, and may also consider the evidence presented by the party.[25] Subsection (2) provides for a third way of establishing the content of foreign law. It refers to the possibility of seeking information from the Minister of Justice. Latter means is favoured and used most frequently in court practice.

---

[24] Section 17 states:

(1) The law of the Hungarian State shall apply to its legal relations falling under the scope of the Law-Decree, unless

a) the State expressly consented to the application of a foreign law, or

b) the legal relationship relates to a real property abroad owned by the State or intended to be acquired by the State, or

c) the legal relationship relates to participation in an economic organization with foreign interests.

(2) Subsection (1) may only apply to a foreign state in the case of reciprocity.

[25] Kecskés, L., The Application of Foreign Law and Private International Law. In L. Gáspárdy (Ed.), *Ünnepi tanulmányok dr. Novotni Zoltán 60. születésnapjára.* (p.169.). Miskolc.

Therefore, if we want to account what kinds of means are used to ascertain foreign law, the following methods can be mentioned. As indicated above, the judge is not bound by any means of ascertaining the content of foreign law. As far as documents are concerned, certificates of law are used. If they are not available, the inquiry to domestic authority, *i.e.,* the Ministry of Justice, is used most frequently. When the foreign law in question is the law of a Member State of the EU, the courts use the inquiry to foreign judicial and/or non-judicial authorities as well via the European Legal Network. Hungary is party to the European Convention of 7 June 1968 on Information on Foreign Law (known as the "London Convention"; see 6) and also contracting party of about thirty bilateral treaties (so called "agreements on mutual legal assistance"; see 6). Many of those contain a mutual obligation of the contracting parties to provide information about their legal regulations in force about their official interpretations and their court practice. So Hungarian courts can also obtain information related to contracting states to the London Convention and bilateral treaties.

However, even if it is not required, the court may use individual experts or institutions (universities or legal institutes) to know how the foreign statute (and of course the relating foreign legal practice and case-law) regulates the legal question to be granted.

It is worth mentioning that the rules of evidence embodied in Chapter X of the Hungarian Code of Civil Procedure are not applicable to the ascertainment of the content of foreign law according to the Hungarian academic literature, and in a decision of a Hungarian lower court it was confirmed stating that the ascertainment of the foreign law is not a question of evidence in a procedural sense.[26] Although, in the *dictum* of another case the Curia stated: "since the Ministry of Justice has not been able to inquire about the foreign law and the party has failed to prove it, its consequences shall be taken by the plaintiff".[27] This dictum shows that Hungarian court practice is not always consistent as far as the *ex officio* ascertainment of foreign law is concerned and tends to treat it as a matter of evidence in a procedural sense.

A further question is the costs concerning the application of foreign law. In principle these costs are usually borne by the court. Such expenses, therefore, are not classified as "litigation costs", since the judge has a duty to "know" the content of foreign law and to address an official request for information of the content of foreign law to the Hungarian Ministry of Justice (through the mechanism of the London Convention or via other diplomatic channels). So these expenses which rise from the use of these mechanisms should be covered by the Hungarian budget. In practice, this issue has divergent interpretations because of the lack of regulation.[28] Although the courts usually follow the view that the costs of the translation of the foreign legal regulation shall not be deemed to form part of the costs of the evidentiary procedure, they should be covered by the Hungarian budget.[29] When the ascertainment

[26] Regional Court of Baranya 8.G.40.036/2005/53. See: Harsági et al. (2011) 217.

[27] Curia of Hungary Gfv.IX.30.045/2010/3.

[28] See e. g. the No. 3/2006 and 1/2013 opinion of the Curia of Hungary

[29] See e. g. the No. 1/2013 opinion of the Curia of Hungary, point 1, last sentence.

of foreign law is requested by a party, the costs – such as experts' fees, honorariums for legal opinions, translation fees or public certification fees – are classified as litigation costs which must be assessed at the end of the procedure. The litigation costs under the Hungarian law are attributed to the losing party (i.e. Hungary follows the 'loser party pays all' principle), but the court has a discretional power to apportion the litigation costs between the parties according to the proportion of winning and losing the case.

It may be a drawback of the Hungarian system in relation to establishing the content of foreign law that there is no mechanism to examine the reliability of the provided legal information. It is solely for the court before which the dispute has been brought, and which must assume responsibility for the subsequent judicial decision, to establish the content of the foreign law in light of the circumstances of the case. Therefore, the only possibility to control the correct application of foreign law is the review performed by superior instances.

C. Interpretation and Application of Foreign Law and Gap Filling

Theoretically, foreign law shall be interpreted and applied in the same manner as in the country of origin. This requirement pertains primarily to the interpretation of foreign rules, but applies to other problems such as gap filling and analogy as well.[30] There is neither a universally accepted method of gap filling in the Hungarian legal literature, nor in the jurisprudence. Hungarian courts usually follow their own gap filling method when there is a legal gap in foreign law. The foreign law is applied according to its textual interpretation (that is governed by the relevant foreign statute provided by the authorities), or sometimes it is interpreted in the light of Hungarian law.[31]

Though the above mentioned method is characteristic in Hungarian court practice, there are a few cases when the Curia of Hungary applied foreign (Austrian and German) case law.[32] In the published judgements the main problem was not filling a gap in a foreign law, but rather the contradictory (or not precise) translation of the foreign rules, or the question of correct characterization of foreign legal institutions that are unknown or not recognised by Hungarian law.[33]

[30] Mádl and Vékás (2012) 137.

[31] Regional Court of Győr Gf.I.20072/2005/34. See: Harsági et al. (2011) 217. However, it is happen generally in proceedings of lower courts.

[32] Curia of Hungary Gfv. IX. 30.214/2006. (EBH 2006.1520.) and Pfv. II. 21.678/2012/7. In the latter decision the court compared the rules of the Danish, German and Hungarian law considering the validity of a matrimonial agreement concluded in Denmark between Hungarian and English citizens who lived in Germany.

[33] Both problem emerged e.g. before the Budapest-Capital Regional Court of Appeal where the court had to qualify such a marriage settlement which arranged the property relations not only in

D. Failure to Establish Foreign Law

If the foreign law cannot be ascertained by the court, Section 5 Subsection (3) of the Hungarian PIL Code declares: "If it is impossible to establish the contents of a foreign law, the Hungarian law shall apply". The application of the *lex fori* as a subsidiary law is a general method of the Hungarian PIL Code. *Lex fori* is used as a subsidiary law in all cases when the application of foreign law has to be avoided (see 3.1).

This solution has practical reasons. Applying the *lex fori* is not an invention of the Hungarian PIL Code. It had been practiced by Hungarian courts even long before the Code entered into force. Earlier legal theory severely criticised the automatic application of the *lex fori* as a subsidiary law. However, the alternative proposals made by legal scholars were too sophisticated and would have required judges to have such qualifications that could never have been fulfilled. The policy behind this solution adopted by the legislature is to simplify the judicial task and to avoid irrational continuance of litigation.

As a result, applying the law of the forum is possible as a last resort if the content of the foreign law cannot be established within a reasonable time. A good example in this respect is the judgment of the European Court of Human Rights (ECtHR) delivered in *Karalyos and Huber v Hungary and Greece* case.[34] It concerned a civil action in Hungary for recovery of damages incurred by two Hungarian citizens as a result of a fire on a vessel owned by a Greek company. Because the Greek authorities failed to provide the necessary information on the relevant Greek law, the Hungarian court has not rendered a decision yet. The ECtHR found Hungary to be in violation of Article 6 of the European Convention of Human Rights, since the length of proceedings was found to be excessive. The ECtHR declared that after a period of 9 years, the Hungarian court should have come to the conclusion that the content of the relevant Greek law could not be established through the Greek authorities, and the Hungarian court should have applied the *lex fori* (according to Section 5 Subsection 3 of the Hungarian PIL Code), and in this way it could have speeded up the proceedings.

---

respect during their life but in respect the death of one of the spouses. This French legal matter (regulated by Articles 1524 and 1525 of the French Civil Code) is subjected to matrimonial property, but it is unknown under the Hungarian law. (Budapest-Capital Regional Court of Appeal 1. Pf.20.214/2012/25.)

[34] ECtHR, 6 April 2004, Karalyos and Huber v Hungary and Greece, no 75116/01.

IV. Erroneous Application of Conflict of Laws Rules and Foreign Law

There is no difference between the preconditions of appeal based on the erroneous application of substantive law and conflict of laws rules.[35] Both are parts of Hungarian law and the second instance can overrule the decision of the first instance without any restrictions. When the case is decided on appeal by the second instance its decision cannot be appealed any more. However, if the final decision violates the law and this violation has an impact on the merit of the case, revision as an extraordinary legal remedy by the Curia of Hungary is possible. The rationale of this solution is that the improper application of Hungarian law at lower instances has to be corrected by higher courts. In this respect, there is no difference whether the improperly applied legal provisions are substantive or choice of law provisions.

The same principle applies to an erroneous application of foreign law. In Hungarian judicial practice, the Curia has a consistent attitude when dealing with incorrect application of conflicts or foreign law rules.[36] In such cases, the Curia sets aside the lower court decision and refers the case back for a new decision.[37] For instance, in a case of 2002 the lower court was obliged to request an inquiry from the Ministry of Justice related to the application of German rule on adoption.[38]

V. Foreign Law in Other Instances

When a question on foreign law in an administrative procedure occurs, then the domestic law determines what shall be done. For example, when it is about an entry in the register of births or in the marriage registry, according to the provisions on the registry procedure, the registration is done by the registrar upon the instruction of the superior authority. Prior to such an instruction, the Ministry of Justice examines the matter (e.g. examines the foreign documents, judgements) and delivers an official position on it. This opinion might be contested according to the rules of the Act CXL of 2004 on Administrative Procedure.

There are no official statistics as to the frequency of the application of foreign law before non-judicial authorities. However, the data bases given by the Ministry of Justice show that the public notaries, lawyers or other non-judicial authorities do not make use of the possibility of obtaining information on foreign law in their pro-

[35] For instance, related to an attorney agreement the first instance used the rule of the Hungarian PIL Code to determine the applicable law, but the appellate court declared that the correct PIL legal instrument to find the *lex contractus* is not the domestic PIL rule but the Rome I Regulation (Győr Regional Court of Appeal Pf.V.20.074/2011/5.). The same problem emerged before the Szeged Regional Court of Appeal (Gf.IV.30.147/2013/5.).

[36] Mádl and Vékás (2012) 134.

[37] See, e.g. the following cases of the Curia: Pf. III. 20,474/1992.; Pf. III. 20,998/1995.

[38] Curia of Hungary Pfv. II. 20.996/2000., BH2002.492.

ceedings (*inter alia*, probate proceedings, drafting of wills) from the responsible department of the Ministry.[39]

In domestic arbitration – in cases decided almost exclusively before the Permanent Court of Arbitration attached to the Hungarian Chamber of Commerce and Industry –, Hungarian law applies in 99 per cent of the cases. In international arbitration before these arbitral tribunals, there is usually one arbitrator for whom the applicable law is his own domestic law. In such cases, she/he informs the other members of the tribunal about the content of the applicable law. In cases when the applicable law is not known to any member of the tribunal, an expert opinion can be obtained in order to ascertain the content of the foreign law. The same applies for mediation and other alternative dispute resolution.

As regards ascertaining foreign law in the advisory work of attorneys, notaries, etc., we can say that there are no universal methods in this respect. Large law firms have an easier access to foreign law than smaller ones or individual attorneys. They can contact their partner law firms in the respective countries whose laws are in question. There is a general possibility to consult university lecturers who are specialised in the field of law in question, doing comparative research. Another method can be to do research in law-libraries of legal faculties of universities or other specialised public libraries. And finally, legal literature and legal sources are also, to some extent, available on the Internet. For example, the European Judicial Network,[40] the European e-Justice Portal[41] or the European Notarial Network[42] and the website of Notaries of Europe[43] can provide useful information as well.

VI. Access to Foreign Law: Status Quo

Hungary provides legal information through its official (government) website in Hungarian.[44] The European Judicial Network[45] is also available in Hungary for the judge to communicate directly with a foreign judge to obtain legal information. Besides, an international instrument also can provide the forum information on foreign law, because Hungary is a party to the London Convention. This Convention provides a system to assist national courts in determining the application of foreign law in fields of civil and commercial law.[46] Hungary is not party to other multilateral

[39] In the Ministry's data bases only four cases were found.

[40] http://www.ejn-crimjust.europa.eu/ejn/

[41] https://e-justice.europa.eu/home.do?action=home&plang=en

[42] http://www.enn-rne.eu/reseau-notarial-europeen-en/001/index.html

[43] http://www.cnue.eu/

[44] www.magyarorszag.hu; https://kereses.magyarorszag.hu/jogszabalykereso

[45] http://www.ejn-crimjust.europa.eu/ejn/. Established by 2001/470EC Council Decision (OJ L 174.).

[46] The London Convention was transposed into Hungarian law by the Government Decree No 140 of 1992, and entered into force in relation to Hungary on 16 February 1990. More about the mecha-

conventions, but it has concluded twenty-seven bilateral agreements on mutual legal assistance on civil and commercial matters.[47] A considerable number of those States are now Member States of the EU. The latter agreements were signed with China (in 1997), Egypt (in 1999) and Ukraine (in 2002). Most of the bilateral agreements contain the mutual obligation to provide information about the content of foreign law.[48] In agreements on mutual legal assistance on civil, family (and sometimes criminal) matters contracting Parties committed themselves that their Ministries of Justice – in case of a request – jointly inform each other about their own statutes and case-laws. It is worth emphasizing that a special (separate) agreement was signed with Belgium on the exchange of legal information.[49]

As far as the effectiveness of these above mentioned instruments is concerned, their actual functioning depends on the complexity of the case. In simple cases, the requests are mostly answered in due time. In more complex cases, however, there might be undue delays and, in a small number of cases, foreign authorities do not give the information required even if there is no legal ground for denying it. The system is time-consuming, but this is a natural consequence of the complexity of the subject matter and the rather complicated method of its functioning. One of the reasons for the shortcomings might be that the questions asked by the referring court are not always detailed or precise enough to be answered adequately or the translation does not completely match the original question. Therefore, the court gets only some general or partial information and based on that information the specific case cannot be decided and further information is needed.

---

nism and practice see: Rodger, B. J. and Van Doorn, J. (1997). Proof of Foreign Law: The Impact of the London Convention. *International and Comparative Law Quarterly*, 46(1), 151–173.

[47] Ukraine: Act XVI of 2002; Egypt: Act CII of 1999; China: Act LXII of 1997; Turkey: Act LVII of 1992; Czech and Slovakia: Act LXI of 1991; Syria: Law-Decree No 9 of 1988; Vietnam: Law-Decree No 8 of 1986; Alger: Law-Decree No 15 of 1985; Tunisia: Law-Decree No 2 of 1985; Belgium: Law-Decree No 64 of 1984; Cuba: Law-Decree No 4 of 1984; Cyprus: Law-Decree No 19 of 1983; Finland: Law-Decree No 25 of 1982; France: Law-Decree No 3 of 1982; Greek: Law-Decree No 21 of 1981; Italy: Law-Decree No 11 of 1981; Iraq: Law-Decree No 11 of 1978; former Soviet Union (current successor States): Law-Decree No 18 of 1972 on the modification and supplement of Law-Decree No 38 of 1958; North Korea: Law-Decree No 12 of 1971; Mongolia: Law-Decree No 11 of 1969; former Yugoslavia (current successor States): Law-Decree No 1 of 1969; Austria: Law-Decree No 24 of 1967; Bulgaria: Law-Decree No 6 of 1967; Albania: Law-Decree No 25 of 1960; Poland: Law-Decree No 5 of 1960; Romania: Law-Decree No 19 of 1959.; Britain: Act XIII of 1936.

[48] Except ones, which were concluded with Britain and with Iraq.

[49] Law-Decree No 28 of 1983.

VII. Access to Foreign Law: Further Developments

A. Practical Need

In most cases the problems stem from the fact that the infrastructure offered by multilateral and bilateral treaties – though known – is not used in all cases when it should and could be used. Courts and other judicial authorities almost automatically try to obtain information through the Ministry of Justice. In the majority of cases those questions are either based on the London Convention or on a bilateral agreement. In those cases the Ministry tries to obtain information based on those agreements. In a relatively small part of those cases the Ministry cannot give the information required, because in spite of the international agreement it does not receive the required information from the respective authority of the state whose law is concerned.

The other type of request concerning the ascertainment of foreign law stems almost exclusively from notaries who need information on foreign succession law in probate proceedings. Those requests are often not based on any international agreement. In those cases, the Ministry tries to obtain the information needed by consulting experts and studying foreign statutes, their legal practice and respective legal literature. Obtaining information in such a way may be time-consuming and may lead to an undue delay in solving the case. When the required information arrives, it is sometimes already too late. On the other hand, the information obtained is often only an extract from the text of the relevant foreign act without reference to court practice. In such cases the application of foreign law might be only formal and does not meet the high standards and requirements set forth by the theory of Hungarian PIL.

With respect to the areas of law, access to foreign law is mostly needed in civil and commercial matters. Nowadays there is a growing need for access to foreign law in matters of family law and succession because of the tendency of internalisation of personal relationships and the growing number of mixed marriages, foreign citizens and foreign couples etc. living in Hungary.

B. Conflict of Laws Possibilities and Solutions to Reduce the Application of Foreign Law

Hungarian PIL rules regarding the application of foreign law are adequate but should be refined in the near future (considering the ongoing codification of the Hungarian PIL Code). The number of cases in which foreign law applies cannot and should not be reduced by administrative means. Even if – but this is absolutely unlikely – the Hungarian legislation had the intention of modifying the Hungarian PIL Code in order to reduce the number of cases in which foreign law applies, such a modification would have no effect because of the growing importance of the EU conflicts-legislation. It should be noted that, as the EU PIL legislation is broadening, Hungarian judges have to apply foreign law more and more frequently pursuant to conflict of laws rules unified by EU regulations. According to the unanimous view held by scholarship, there is no place in those cases for the parties to jointly request the non-application of the governing foreign law according to Section 9 of the Hungarian PIL Code. Therefore, the trend is that the number of cases when application of foreign law is needed will be growing.

Another factor pointing towards this trend is the exclusion of *renvoi* – except in succession matters – by the EU PIL rules. Hungarian judges could often apply the *lex fori* by accepting the reference-back by the choice of laws rules of the *lex causae* based on Section 4 of the Hungarian PIL Code. This is not possible when the application of foreign law is based on the choice of law rules of EU regulations which exclude *renvoi*. On the other hand, the growing importance of party autonomy in the EU PIL rules and the possibility of choosing the *lex fori* may lead to a certain reduction of the number of applicable foreign laws in those areas.

To answer the question on the necessity to change the treatment of foreign law, we can say that it is a more than hundred year old tradition codified in the Hungarian PIL Code that foreign law should be treated as law. There is no reason why this attitude should be changed. Even if it would seem reasonable to give the judge a possibility to put the burden of proof of the foreign law on the party who relies on it in a limited area – for example, following the example of the Swiss PIL Code – the clear tendency in the EU law is exactly the opposite. The Madrid Principles clearly opt for the application of foreign law *ex officio* and so will the planned regulation on the application of foreign law.[50] So the Madrid principles and the possible EU regulation would be of great importance because it would unify the treatment of foreign law in EU Member States and ensure the proper operation of the existing and future EU regulation on PIL. Similar international instruments might have less effect, because the countries with different traditions are unlikely to ratify such an instrument.[51]

[50] Esplugues Mota, C. (2011). Harmonization of Private International Law in Europe and Application of Foreign Law: the "Madrid Principles" of 2010. *Yearbook of Private International Law* (pp. 273–298.) Sellier.; Lalani, S. (2011). A Proposed Model to Facilitate Access to Foreign Law. *Yearbook of Private International Law* (pp. 299–313.) Sellier.

[51] For instance, at the international level the Hague Conference on Private International Law has been working on a similar project for ages. And the difficulties of this sophisticated and complex project are evident if the conclusions of the joint conference with the EU in 2012 are read. As it stated in point 5: "Any future instrument in this field should not be exclusive in nature, but rather should be complementary to existing and future mechanisms that also facilitate access to and the treatment and application of foreign law." See: Access to Foreign Law in Civil and Commercial Matters, Conclusions and Recommendations (2012). http://www.hcch.net/upload/foreignlaw_concl_e.pdf. Accessed 12 September 2013.

C. Methods for Facilitating Access to Foreign Law

In our opinion, the existing international and regional legal instruments – when properly used – can serve as a good basis for facilitating the access to foreign law. Opening these instruments also for non-judicial authorities might be useful but opening it to individuals seems to be going too far. It would overburden the infrastructure and would lead to malfunctioning of the system. If a request should be directly sent to the competent authority or designated expert body of the foreign state, instead of being transmitted by the competent authority of the requesting state, this solution might speed up the access to information, as it has already happened in the EU countries via the European Judicial Network. In our view, the answer provided by the requested state should not be binding.

As far as costs of services on legal information are concerned, in our opinion the reasonable costs should be reimbursed by the requesting party. The other solution would result in serious financial problems and would frustrate the functioning of the whole system.

To conclude, it is no doubt that there is a need to improve the access to foreign law. Considering other feasible methods of facilitating access to foreign law, the direct communication of judges might not work smoothly between judges who do not share a common language. Those methods which improve and strengthen the existing networks for other legal professionals (*e.g.*, law firms) or qualified experts or expert institutes (*e.g.*, creating a list of experts) may prove useful. The method which provides widespread information on national laws on the Internet would be necessary. An electronic access to foreign law through a database in English or translated into other languages, which also contains case law, academic literature and incidentally, former anonymous expert opinions or information provided by the foreign authorities may serve as a first step to know much more about each other's legal systems, providing effective, cost-efficient and prompt access to foreign law.

Undisputedly, all these methods are likely to facilitate the access to foreign law but will not be able to solve the other main problem which is not a technical one: the proper application of foreign law which remains a complex judicial task. That is why we think that the education and training of judges and notaries both on PIL rules (on EU and domestic level) and on frequently applied foreign law should have priority in this question.

Italy: Proof and Information about Foreign Law in Italy

Nerina Boschiero and Benedetta Ubertazzi

Abstract This Report was prepared with regard to cross-border cases where foreign law is determined as the applicable law by the Italian PIL statute. Attention is given not only to the Italian PIL Statute of 1995, but also to the former Italian PIL system, with a focus on its Italian literature and application in case law. In particular, the Report analyses a landmark judgment of the Supreme Court, of May 26, 2014, which highlights the binding force of the Italian PIL rules and which has wide implications on the state of art of pleading and proofing of foreign laws in Italy.

1. Methodological Premise

1.1. International and EU Conflict of Law Rules

This Report was prepared according to the domestic private international law (hereinafter: PIL) system, with a focus on its Italian literature and application in case law. Attention was given not only to the Italian PIL Statute of 1995 (hereinafter: Italian PIL statute),[1] but also to the former Italian PIL system (hereinafter: previous Italian PIL system).[2] PIL rules deriving from international treaties or the EU regulations are only considered within this framework.

The methodological premise and paragraphs 1.1, 1.2 and 2.1 were written by Nerina Boschiero. The remainder of the paper was written by Benedetta Ubertazzi.

[1] See Legge 31 maggio 1995 n. 218. Riforma del sistema italiano di diritto internazionale privato, in *Gazzetta Ufficiale* n. 128 of 3 June 1995.

[2] See Sections 16 to 31 of the general legal provisions of the Civil Code, which were abrogated by the Italian PIL Statute, except for Art. 16 on which see para 1.3.

N. Boschiero (✉)
Professor, School of Law, University of Milan, Via Festa del Perdono, 7, 20122 Milan, Italy
e-mail: nerina.boschiero@unimi.it

B. Ubertazzi
Full Tenured Aggregate Professor, University of Milan-Bicocca, Milan, Italy
e-mail: benedetta.ubertazzi@unimib.it

Y. Nishitani (ed.), *Treatment of Foreign Law - Dynamics towards Convergence?*,
Ius Comparatum – Global Studies in Comparative Law 26,
DOI 10.1007/978-3-319-56574-3_11

Regarding PIL rules, their binding nature was already recognized under the previous PIL system. Leaving their application to judicial authorities' and parties' discretion could in fact expose Italy to liability for breaching international obligations.[3] Due to the 2003 Constitutional amendment (Art. 117.1 of the Italian Constitution), a treaty duly incorporated into national law acquires a status which is not higher than the Italian Constitution, but definitively higher than "ordinary" national legislation. Thus, in case of conflict, the former will prevail and override national legislation (including domestic PIL rules). Consequently, failing a "manifest" intention by the Italian lawmakers to repeal the law implementing a treaty, thereby casting off the international undertakings, "one ought to think that the legislature intended to abide by the general and fundamental rule of international law commending respect for the treaties".[4] Art. 2 of Italian PIL Statute reminds that the national conflict of law rules "do not prejudice" the application of international rules in force within the Italian legal system.

Regarding PIL rules of the EU, particular attention is given to the Rome I Regulation,[5] the Rome II Regulation,[6] and the Rome III Regulation.[7] These Regulations do not state explicitly whether their PIL rules are of mandatory or facultative nature. Yet, Italian literature unanimously agrees on their mandatory nature.[8]

---

[3] F. Pocar, L'assistenza giudiziaria internazionale in materia civile, Padova, 1967, p. 209; N. Boschiero, *Norme di diritto internazionale privato "facoltative"?*, in *Riv. dir. int. priv. e proc.* (hereinafter: *RDIPP)* 1993, p. 573.

[4] See Corte Cass., 16.71954 n. 2539, in *Foro Italiano* 1955, I, p. 33 ff.

[5] Regulation (EC) No 593/2008 of the European Parliament and of the Council of 17 June 2008 on the law applicable to contractual obligations. In *OJ* L 177, 4.7.2008, pp. 6 ff. For Italian literature on this Regulation see P. Franzina (Ed.), *La legge applicabile ai contratti nella proposta di regolamento "Roma I", Atti della giornata di studi – Rovigo, 31 marzo 2006,* Cedam, Padova, 2006, pp. 180; B. Ubertazzi, *Il regolamento Roma I sulla legge applicabile alle obbligazioni contrattuali*, Giuffré, Milano, 2008, pp. 207; F. Salerno and P. Franzina (eds.), *Regolamento (CE) n. 593/2008 del Parlamento europeo e del Consiglio del 17 giugno 2008 sulla legge applicabile alle obbligazioni contrattuali ("Roma I") – Commentario*, in *Le nuove leggi civili commentate*, 2009, pp. 521–954; N. Boschiero (Ed.), *La nuova disciplina comunitaria della legge applicabile ai contratti (Roma I),* Giappichelli, Torino, 2009, pp. XVI–548.

[6] Regulation (EC) No 864/2007 of the European Parliament and of the Council of 11 July 2007 on the law applicable to non-contractual obligations. In *OJ* L 199, 31.7.2007, pp. 40 ff. For Italian literature on this Regulation see P. Franzina, *Il regolamento n. 864/2007/CE sulla legge applicabile alle obbligazioni extracontrattuali ("Roma II"),* in *Le nuove leggi civili commentate* 2008, pp. 971–1044; C. Honorati, *Regolamento n. 864/2007 sulla legge applicabile alle obbligazioni non contrattuali*, in F. Preite and A. Gazzanti Pugliese (Eds.), *Atti notarili. Diritto comunitario e internazionale,* Utet, Torino, 2011, pp. 483–558.

[7] Council Regulation (EU) No 1259/2010 of 20 December 2010 implementing enhanced cooperation in the area of the law applicable to divorce and legal separation. In *OJ* L 343, 29.12.2010, pp. 10 ff. For Italian literature on this Regulation see P. Franzina, *The Law Applicable to Divorce and Legal Separation under Regulation (EU) No. 1259/2010 of 20 December 2010*, in *Cuadernos de derecho transnacional* 2011, 2, pp. 85–129; Id. (ed.), *Regolamento (UE) n. 1259/2010 del Consiglio del 20 dicembre 2010 relativo all'attuazione di una cooperazione rafforzata nel settore della legge applicabile al divorzio e alla separazione personale – Commentario*, in *Le nuove leggi civili commentate* 2011, pp. 1435–1543.

[8] L. Fumagalli, Diritto straniero (applicazione e limiti), in Enciclopedia del diritto, Giuffrè, Milano, 2011, p. 471 ff.

In fact, EU PIL benefits from the same "supremacy" over domestic legislation that is recognized in all self-executing provisions of EU Regulations.[9]

Furthermore, the mandatory nature of EU PIL rules and their supremacy over ordinary domestic choice of law norms has been further motivated by their rationale. These rules are enacted to advance fundamental EU principles and objectives, such as "effet utile", effectiveness and equivalence between situations covered by domestic laws and cases regulated by EU norms, foreseeability and legal certainty, and uniform application of EU Regulatory norms.[10] To allow EU PIL rules to achieve these objectives, they must be concretely applied in each Member State, rather than subject to parties' willingness with the consequent risk of remaining unapplied.[11]

1.2. Foreign Law in Proceedings on Recognition and Enforcement of Foreign Judgments

This Report was prepared with regard to cross-border cases where foreign law is determined as the applicable law by the Italian PIL statute.

Consideration was not given to cases where information on foreign law is gathered to decide issues of recognition and enforcement of foreign judgments in Italy,[12]

---

[9] N. Boschiero, *Norme* cit., p. 573.

[10] G.P. Romano, *Italy*, in Swiss Institute of Comparative Law, *The Application of Foreign Law in Civil Matters in the EU Member States and its Perspectives for the Future,* JLS/2009/JCIV/PR/0005/E4, Part I, Legal Anlysis, Avis 09-184, Lausanne, 11 July, 2011, p. 273, available at http://ec.europa.eu/justice/civil/files/foreign_law_en.pdf (hereinafter G.P. Romano, *Italy*); L. Fumagalli, cit., p. 471; Tuo C., *Obbligazioni contrattuali ed applicazione della legge straniera: un preoccupante segnale di regresso da parte della Corte di Cassazione*, in *RDIPP* 2010, p. 74 ff.

[11] G.P. Romano, *Italy*, cit., p. 273; Fumagalli L., cit., 471; C. Tuo, cit., 74. In this line, an EU position favorable to the mandatory nature of EU conflict of laws rules is taken by the EU Commission, and by the Rome III Regulation, according to which the European Judicial Network "could assist the courts with regard to the content of foreign law". According to the Commission "different practices [are] followed in the Member States regarding the treatment of foreign law". Therefore, the Commission is prepared to take appropriate measures if necessary. In *OJ* L 199, 31.7.2007, pp. 40 ff. See L. Fumagalli, cit., p. 470–471. See also 2001/470/EC: Council Decision of 28 May 2001 establishing a European Judicial Network in civil and commercial matters, in *OJ* L 174, 27.6.2001, pp. 25 ff., Recital 14. See P. Franzina, *Il ruolo della rete giudiziaria europea nell'applicazione e nello sviluppo degli strumenti della cooperazione giudiziaria in materia civile,* in N. Boschiero and P. Bertoli (Eds.), *Verso un "ordine comunitario" del processo civile – Atti del Convegno interinale della Società italiana di Diritto internazionale (Como, 23 novembre 2007),* Editoriale Scientifica, Napoli, 2008, pp. 185–199.

[12] According to Arts. 64, 65 and 66 of the Italian PIL Statute. Regarding these rules, see A. D'Alessandro, *Il riconoscimento delle sentenze straniere,* Giappichelli, Torino, 2007, pp. XIX-400; O. Lopes Pegna, *I procedimenti relativi all'efficacia delle decisioni straniere in materia civile*, CEDAM, Padova, 2009, pp. XIII–313.

or on the validity of clauses vesting or denying jurisdiction in cross-border situations,[13] even though foreign law plays a crucial role in these matters too.[14]

1.3. Foreign Law Applied to Establish Reciprocity

This Report was prepared with regard to cross-border cases where foreign law is determined as the applicable law by the Italian PIL statute. In contrast, relevance was not given to cases where information on foreign law is gathered to decide on reciprocity. According to the principle of reciprocity, before Italian judicial authorities foreigners may claim civil rights only if in their countries of origin Italians may claim rights similar or corresponding to the ones claimed by the foreigners in Italy.[15]

One approach requires foreigners to prove that the law of his or her country of origin grants Italians rights analogous to those at issue in Italy as a question of

[13] For instance, recently the issue arose of whether Italian courts had jurisdiction to hear a case related to an alleged breach of contracts, raised by an Italian company against the US governmental agency Navy Engineering Field Activity Mediterranean. Ultimately, Italian jurisdiction was declined by the Supreme Court in 2012, since parties agreed "to renounce acting against the Government of the United States, save where so allowed by the clauses concerning the termination of the present agreements and the relevant US federal legislation". According to the Supreme Court, the relevant US federal legislation was to be ascertained by the Court of first and second instance ex officio and according to the principle of *iura novit curia*. The legislation in question ascertained no contractual action against US governmental agencies before Italian courts. See Corte Cass. 7.6.2012 n. 9189, in *RDIPP* 2013, pp. 433 ff.

[14] See the survey conducted by the Swiss Institute of Comparative Law within the study previously mentioned on "the application of foreign law in civil matters in the EU Member States and its perspective for the future". This survey consisted of sending fifty-two questionnaires concerning the application of foreign law to a number of Italian legal professionals, namely judicial authorities, both Courts of Appeal and Tribunals of first instance, public registrars, lawyers and notaries, and then by analysing their respective replies. Particularly, two out of eight judicial authorities surveyed emphasized that foreign law also plays a crucial role in Italy when deciding upon the recognition and enforcement of foreign judgments and when implementing letters of rogation. See Swiss Institute of Comparative Law, *The Application of Foreign Law in Civil Matters in the EU Member States and its Perspectives for the Future,* JLS/2009/JCIV/PR/0005/E4, Part I, Legal Analysis, Part II, Empirical Analysis, Part III Synthesis Report with Recommendations, Avis 09–184, Lausanne, 11 July, 2011, pp. 224–238, available at http://ec.europa.eu/justice/civil/files/foreign_law_en.pdf, http://ec.europa.eu/justice/civil/files/foreign_law_ii_en.pdf, http://ec.europa.eu/justice/civil/files/foreign_law_iii_en.pdf (hereinafter Swiss Institute Study). See C. Leuzzi and G.P. Romano, *Italy*, in Swiss Institute of Comparative Law, *The Application of Foreign Law in Civil Matters in the EU Member States and its Perspectives for the Future,* JLS/2009/JCIV/PR/0005/E4, Part II, Empirical Analysis, cit., pp. 226 ff.

[15] See Art. 16 of the Preliminary Dispositions of the Italian Civil Code (hereinafter: disp. prel. c. c.). Reciprocity does not concern either foreigners regularly resident in Italy and benefitting from non-discrimination treatments, or fundamental human rights, which can be claimed by any foreigner in Italy. B. Nascimbene, *La capacità dello straniero: diritti fondamentali e condizione di reciprocità*, in *RDIPP* 2011, pp. 307 ff.

fact.[16] To successfully prove reciprocity the interested foreigners must produce official translations of relevant parts of the foreign law at stake.[17] If the foreigner fails to prove the content of the foreign law or its reciprocal application, then Italian authorities shall refuse to grant the right in Italy.

This first approach was recently overturned by the Italian Supreme Court in 2009.[18] This judgment applied Art. 14 of the Italian PIL statute, which will be analysed in the following sections. Although Art. 14 concerns the ascertainment of foreign law invoked as the applicable law by Italian PIL norms, the Supreme Court in 2009 maintained that Italian judicial authorities shall apply it even to foreign law that is invoked to prove reciprocity. Thus, considering this foreign law as a "law", rather than a fact, whose content must be ascertained *ex officio*.[19]

1.4. Sources of Information

To prepare this Report, Italian legislation, literature and case-law published with commentaries in various legal journals of a general nature or of a specialized character were consulted.[20] Useful data were drawn from the Italian Reports on the topic of foreign law before national courts: (1) the survey of the Swiss Institute of

[16] See Trib. Vicenza 27.4.2000, in *RDIPP* 2001, p. 130 ff.; Corte Cass. 7.5.2009 n. 10504, *Ibidem* 2010, p. 776 ff.; Corte Cass. 11.2. 2010 n. 3098, *Ibidem*, p. 748 ff.; Corte Cass. 30.10. 2008 n. 26063, *Ibidem* 2009, pp. 661.

[17] Court of Appeal of Torino 10.12.2004, *Ibidem* 2005, p. 777.

[18] See Corte Cass. 24.6.2009 n. 14777, in Diritto commercio internazionale 2010, p. 217 ff. See the comment to this judgment of M.E. De Maestri and F. Pesce, La possibile estensione applicativa dell'art. 14 della legge 218 del 1995 alla luce di una recente sentenza della Corte di Cassazione, ibidem, p. 223 ff.

[19] See I. Queirolo, *Conoscenza del diritto straniero e contraddizioni della giurisprudenza italiana,* in *RDIPP* 2010, p. 603 ff. This judgment is interpreted by part of the Italian literature as transforming Art.14 into a rule posing a general principle of procedural law, applicable as such not only to PIL cases but also to other situations where foreign law is invoked to demonstrate reciprocity. See B. Nascimbene, *La capacità* cit., p. 307 ff. Another approach could consider Art.16 disp. prel. c. c. as posing a PIL rule itself, namely a rule on the capacity of physical persons, and therefore as a norm included in the PIL system. B. Ubertazzi, *La capacità delle persone fisiche nel diritto internazionale privato,* Cedam, Padova, 2006, *passim*. According to this approach, then, Art.14 PIL also applies to (PIL) cases falling under Art.16 disp. prel. c.c., with the positive result of avoiding discriminations between the parties obliged to prove the content of foreign laws and the parties not obliged to do so. This approach seems to have been confirmed by the Supreme Court judgment of 2009.

[20] As published with commentaries in various legal journals of a general nature or of a specialized character. Namely Rivista di diritto internazionale privato e processuale, Rivista di diritto internazionale, Diritto del commercio internazionale, Le Nuove Leggi Civili e Commentate, Giurisprudenza italiana, Giustizia Civile, Enciclopedia del diritto, Enciclopedia giuridica Treccani, il Foro Italiano. Also, on-line data bases were accessed, namely Juris data, DeJure, il Foro italiano, and the data bases available at the web-sites of the Italian Supreme Court, of the Constitutional Court and of the Italian Official Journal (Gazzetta Ufficiale).

Comparative Law[21]; (2) the Madrid Principles for a future EU Regulation on the application of foreign law[22]; and (3) the Hague Conference of Private International Law's "Feasibility study on the treatment of foreign law".[23]

2. Conflict of Laws Rules

2.1. National Conflict of Laws Rules. In Particular, Art. 14 of the PIL Statute and the Supreme Court Judgment of 2014

The matter of proof and information of foreign law is governed by recently adopted PIL provisions of both normative nature and of case-law character.

Regarding the PIL provision of a normative nature, Art. 14 of the Italian PIL Statute on "ascertainment of foreign law" reads as follows:

> 1. The content of foreign law is to be ascertained ex officio by the competent authority. To ascertain foreign laws the competent authority may use the means provided by the International conventions or the information provided by the Italian Ministry of Justice. Also, the competent authority may seek the assistance of experts or specialized institutions.
> 2. Should the judicial authority fail to ascertain the content of the applicable foreign law notwithstanding the parties' assistance, this authority shall apply the law determined by other relevant and existing choice of law rules. Otherwise, Italian law shall be applied.

Art. 14 poses on competent authorities a clear obligation to ascertain *ex officio* foreign laws. This is contrary to the previous PIL system that lacked an express rule on the mandatory application and ascertainment of the foreign law.

Regarding the PIL provision of a case-law nature, with a landmark judgment of May 26, 2014 (hereinafter the "2014 Supreme Court Judgment"), the Supreme Court of Cassation expressed the binding force of the Italian PIL rules.[24]

---

[21] See G.P. Romano, *Italy*, cit., pp. 266–287 and C. Leuzzi and G.P. Romano, *Italy*, cit., p. 226 ff.

[22] These Madrid Principles were devised as part of the EU project on "the Application of Foreign Law by Judicial and Non-Judicial Authorities in Europe": "Team European Union Action Grant Project-Civil Justice JLS/CJ/2007-1/03". See I. Queirolo (coordinator) and S.M. Carbone, P. Ivaldi, L. Carpaneto, C. Tuo, M.E. De Maestri, F. Pesce, *Italy*, in C. Esplugues, J.L. Iglesias and G. Palao (Eds.), *Application of Foreign Law*, Sellier, Munich, 2011, pp. 237–253. The Madrid Principles for a future EU Regulation on the application of foreign law are available at www.elra.eu/wp-content/uploads/file/Valencia.doc

[23] Available at the Hague Conference website: http://www.hcch.net/upload/hidden/2012/xs2foreignlaw.html; and http://www.hcch.net/upload/wop/gap2013concl_e.pdf. Particularly from the "verbal notes" of February 5, 2008, with which the Embassy of Italy in The Hague forwarded to the Permanent Bureau of the Hague Conference of Private International Law the responses to the questionnaire related to this study. Available at the Hague Conference website: http://www.hcch.net/upload/wop/genaff_pd09it.pdf

[24] See Corte Cass. 26.5.2014 n. 11751, in *Foro it.* 2014, 6, I, 1738 commented by G. Casaburi, *ibidem.*

In its task of judicial control of the decisions of the lower courts as far questions of law are concerned, the Supreme Court overruled a judgment of the Court of Appeal of Milan on the ground that the judges had failed to apply the applicable foreign law as required by the relevant conflict of law rules of the forum.

The lawsuit had been brought in front of an Italian trial court by a foreign national person (born out of wedlock, with only her mother being named in the birth record) seeking to establish her legal parentage with an Italian famous fashion designer, after the her mother claimed the designer was her putative natural/genetic father. The applicant claimed a judgment of paternity along with the right to add his surname and the damages suffered by the putative father's refusal to voluntary acknowledge the legal parentage during the years of her childhood.

Like many other States' private international law rules concerning the question of a child's legal parentage, in cases with foreign elements, the Italian PIL Statute also refers to the national law of the child at the moment of birth as the main connecting factor on the basis in which to determine the applicable law. According the new Italian choice-of-law rules, the child's status is determined by the national law under the jurisdiction of which it was born. A child is considered legitimate if considered such under the law of the State of which one of the parents is a citizen at the moment of the child's birth. The means for investigating or disputing the status of a child are equally governed by the national law applicable to the child at the moment of its birth. The status of legitimate child, obtained on the basis of the nationality of one of its parents, may be disputed only on the basis of this law. The condition for recognition of a natural child are again governed by the national law applicable to the child at the moment of its birth or, if more favourable, by the national law of the parent who recognizes the child (Articles 33–35).

After having ascertained their (international) jurisdiction to hear the case against a defendant domiciled and having his habitual residence in the forum, the judges of the trial court tackled the question of the applicable law coming to the right conclusion that the disputed status of the applicant should have been ascertained on the basis of the Canadian law. Since the child, born in France from a Canadian mother, had acquired the nationality of her mother at the time of her birth by right of blood. Nevertheless, confronted with the evidence that the Canadian legal system is a foreign plural-legal system with a multiplicity of applicable legal systems, the trial court rejected the claimant's applications on the ground that she did not disclose to the court any legal criteria to identify the applicable sub-legal system, with the consequence that it was allowed to resort to the *lex fori*. In particular, in order to justify the violation of the duty to determine ex officio the applicable foreign *lex causae*, the trial court invoked the operation of an Italian provision (article 253 of the Italian civil code) that it characterized as a *lex fori* rule of public policy with an overriding effect over the general rules of conflict of laws in so far it prohibits the declaration of the status of recognized child in contrast with a status of "legitimate child" otherwise established. The trial court argued that the status of legitimate child of the claimant was already proven by a foreign public document (a Californian certificate of registry of marriage) in which the bride/applicant had declared at the time of her marriage to be the daughter of the husband of the mother, married 4 years after the birth of the child in 1968.

The Court of Appeal of Milan, where judgment had been sought on the ground that the foreign law had not been searched and therefore not applied, partially revised the lower court's judgment on the basis of an "innovative" distinction among the Italian private international law rules on filiation. It stated that the trial court was right in applying the *lex fori* in absence of proof by the party of the content of the foreign law in cross-border cases only when the issue at stake was a petition for a sentence establishing natural paternity. On the contrary, in matters relating to a disputed status of a legitimate child, the "status" should have been characterized as a "question of fact" that might have been proven by a foreign public document. According to the Court of Appeal, in matter of establishment and contestation of legal parentage, both the Italian conflict of law rules and the courts practice require to rely upon the principle of "full recognition" of foreign certificates *i.e.*, recognition of the legal relationship established or evidenced therein. In this respect, the Court of Appeal dismissed a medical document attesting the non-genetic paternity of the husband of the mother produced by the claimant, in so far as ex parte, as well as the refusal of the putative father to submit himself to a DNA evidence, and simply concluded that the refusal of the lower court to ascertain the status of the child could not be censored as an error in law, being the simple consequence of a "fact"; precisely, according to the Court of Appeal, the possession of a status of legitimate child by the claimant was already fully attested "beyond any reasonable doubt" by the foreign certificate of marriage. Therefore, it declared inadmissible the judicial petition for a recognition of natural child by resorting to the same Italian civil law provision relied upon by the lower court.

The Claimant attacked the appeal judgment in front of the Supreme Court on the ground that again the foreign law applicable to the substance of the case in order to determine the *status filiae* of the claimant has not been applied by the Court.

According to the Supreme Court of Cassation, in the case at hands, the status of the child should have been investigated and established by the lower Courts only on the basis of the foreign applicable law designated by the Italian conflict of law rules (Article 33 and 18 of the Italian PIL Statute): precisely according to the Canadian Law, the undisputed national law at the time of the birth of the child that corresponds to the foreign element of the dispute and also to the connecting factor of the relevant conflict of law rule. By considering that the entire conflict of law process was impeded by the failure of the claimant to reveal to the Courts the applicable legal criterion to identify the sub-legal system, the lower Courts seriously erred in law by consistently ignoring the express provision in the new Italian Statute (Article 14) on the mandatory (*ex officio*) application of the designated foreign law.

The Supreme Court recalled to the judges that the first section of this article codified the generally accepted principle that when a trial judge has to apply a foreign law, he is under an obligation to investigate, interpret and apply such law on his own motion; they have voluntary ignored to resort to the various methods of ascertaining foreign law enumerated in the rule in order to implement the principle *jura aliena novit curia*. In addition to the instruments referred to in international conventions and information obtained through the Ministry of Justice, the PIL Statute provides that the trial judges may hear experts or specialized institutions. The second indent of the PIL provision states that in case of failure to determine foreign law, "also even with the aid of the parties", the judge has the duty to search for alternative laws designated by other connecting factors, contained in the relevant PIL norms. This is precisely the case of the Italian PIL rules on filiation that use multiple connecting factors applying either in the alternative or in a "cascade", according to the principle "*favour recognitionis*". Therefore, the application of the *lex fori* by Italian Courts is only possible as a *last resort* when there is a failure to determine any alternative foreign law.

The Supreme Court of Cassation, therefore, rightly reproached the lower Italian courts for (1) incorrectly appling both of the relevant conflict of law rules under the Italian legal system and (2) ignoring their duty to search, investigate and apply *ex officio* the applicable foreign law.

The most important part of the Supreme Court's Cassation judgment is the part in which it censored the lower Courts for having treated not only the foreign law, but also the connecting factor leading to the reference to foreign law, as simple questions of fact to be proven by the claimant and not as questions of law, governed by the principle "iura novit curia".

To summarize, the latest judgment of the Italian Supreme Court of Cassation has wide implications on the state of art of pleading and proof of foreign law in Italy. The status of foreign law in domestic proceedings is undoubtedly a question of law. Thus the Italian courts have an explicit statutory duty to discover ex officio the foreign applicable law (as a logic and inherent consequence of the mandatory nature of conflict of law provisions), even if the parties are unwilling to submit their case to the foreign law application or are unaware of its applicability.

2.1.1. The Binding Force of Conflict of Law Rules

The Italian literature unanimously interprets Art. 14 as implying a series of obligations: namely, to qualify Italian PIL norms as mandatory in nature; to ascertain *ex officio* not only the content of applicable foreign laws but the presence of elements connecting the case to a foreign legal system, to consider the applicable foreign laws as "foreign laws" and not "facts", and to subject to judicial review by superior instances the incorrect application of the relevant PIL rule and foreign law.[25]

These are the same conclusions reached by the Italian scholars in respect to the previous PIL system. PIL rules had a mandatory nature because of the general principle that all domestic provisions are binding on judges and subject to the *iura novit curia* principle. This approach is followed even today. Thus the judges have to apply PIL rules *ex officio* even when the relevant PIL rules allow for party autonomy or for free disposition (principle dispositive) relating to the *dispositive* or *non-dispositive* nature of the disputed rights. In fact, judges are obliged to raise the applicable law

[25] G.P. Romano, Italy, cit., p. 268; N. Boschiero, *Norme* cit., p. 541 ff.; I. Queirolo (coordinator) and S.M. Carbone, P. Ivaldi, L. Carpaneto, C. Tuo, M.E. De Maestri, F. Pesce, cit., p. 241; I. Queirolo, *Conoscenza* cit., p. 622; S.M. Carbone, *La conoscenza* cit., p. 195.

issue on their own motion, even if it has not been invoked by either party; they cannot simply deduce "tacit agreements" from the procedural passivity of the parties with regard to the issue of foreign law.[26]

2.1.2. The Procedural Status of Foreign Elements

These conclusions are not completely shared by the Italian jurisprudence. It is true that even under the previous PIL system the Supreme Court had already authoritatively ruled on the duty of the judges to establish *ex officio* the content of foreign law to be considered as "law"[27] and to ascertain its contents *suo moto*.[28] It is also true that, in interpreting the new Art. 14 of the Italian PIL statute, the case-law has tackled the mandatory nature of Italian conflict of laws rules in *obiter dicta* but never in the *ratio decidendi* of the judgments.[29]

Nevertheless, the Italian jurisprudence has always been "ambiguous" and "hesitant"[30] on the procedural treatment of the "foreign elements" of a case. These elements form an integral part of the PIL rules as connecting factors.[31] In contrast with the unanimous opinion of Italian literature (both under the previous PIL system and the current PIL Statute), according to which the mandatory nature of conflict of law rules implies also the obligation for judges to raise *ex officio* the question of the existence of foreign elements,[32] the Italian jurisprudence has shown a swinging tendency. In fact, this case law treated any foreign element as a "simple matter of fact" subject to the "dispositive principle" ex Art. 115 of the Italian Code of Civil Procedure (hereinafter: CCP). Under this principle, judicial authorities shall only give relevance to evidence related to the elements that have been routinely acquired during the proceedings, so that foreign elements shall be discovered as any other fact of the case.

The Italian Supreme Court maintained in 1982[33] that the existence of foreign elements had to be raised and proved by parties. The Italian Supreme Court stated

[26] See N. Boschiero, *Norme* cit., pp. 571–574. See also the references provided for by G.P. Romano, *Italy,* cit., p. 266, fnt. 1.

[27] See Corte Cass. 26.5.1980 n. 3445, in *RDIPP* 1981, p. 79 ff.

[28] See Corte Cass. 23.2.1978 n. 903, in *RDIPP* 1979, p. 814 ff. Even before the previous PIL system see Cassazione del Regno 28.6.1940, in *Riv. diritto internazionale* 1942, p. 212 ff. See N. Boschiero, *Norme* cit., 545.

[29] See I. Queirolo, *Conoscenza* cit., p. 622; G.P. Romano, cit., p. 269.

[30] See G.P. Romano, cit., p. 269.

[31] See N. Boschiero, *Norme* cit., p. 571.

[32] N. Boschiero, *Norme* cit., 541 ss.; G.P. Romano, *Italy* cit., p. 268; I. Queirolo (coordinator) and S.M. Carbone, P. Ivaldi, L. Carpaneto, C. Tuo, M.E. De Maestri, F. Pesce, cit., p. 241; I. Queirolo, *Conoscenza* cit., p. 622; S.M. Carbone, *La conoscenza* cit., 195; L. Fumagalli, cit., p. 471.

[33] See Corte Cass 29 marzo 1982, n.1936, in *RDIPP* 1983, 625. See Corte Cass. (s.u.) 13.1.1990 n. 362, in *Giur it.* 1990, I, p. 1260 ff.; Corte Cass. 19.2.1986 n. 995, in *RDIPP* 1987, p. 823 ff.; Corte Cass. 19.1.1985 n. 149, in *RDIPP* 1986, p. 344 ff.; Corte Cass. 21.3.1980 n. 1906, in *RDIPP* 1981, p. 498 ff. See N. Boschiero, *Norme* cit., 545; I. Queirolo, *Conoscenza* cit., p. 611; M. Rubino-Sammartano, *Il giudice nazionale di fronte alla legge straniera,* in *RDIPP* 1991, p. 317.

again in 2009 that the foreign elements of a case have a *factual nature* and therefore shall be acquired procedurally though the burden of proof rests on the interested parties.[34]

However, the Supreme Court implicitly established in 2011 that the existence of foreign elements in a case have to be proven by judicial authorities, rather than by the parties.[35] Therefore, in order to maintain the binding force of PIL rules, foreign elements shall be treated in a procedural way different than all other facts of a case.[36] In fact, according to one opinion, the *dispositive principle* shall be complemented by the one of "acquisition", ex Art. 245 Italian CCP, under which the factual elements of a case are formally integrated in the proceedings when produced by any party, rather than just by the one invoking them.[37] Thus, in ascertaining the transnational nature of a case, relevance shall be given to the elements that must be proven by any party, rather than just by the party who invokes the application of choice of law rules.[38] According to a second more "rigorous" opinion, foreign elements are part of PIL rules that can be either indicated explicitly by the rules themselves or that can indirectly result from the connecting factors through which PIL norms determine the applicable laws. Therefore, as an integral part of the forum legal norm, they must be assessed by judges ex officio.[39]

Ultimately, the Supreme Court Judgment confirmed in 2014 this 2011 Supreme Court approach, as mentioned in paragraph 2.1.

---

[34] Corte Cass. 5.6.2009, in *RDIPP* 2010, 140.

[35] See Corte Cass. 4.4.11 n. 7599, in *Giust. Civ. Massimario* 2011, 4, 536. In this divorce case involving spouses of different nationalities, the Court required the parties to prove where their matrimonial life was predominantly located in order to determine the applicable law. The Supreme Court, however, found that the court of first instance erred in its assessment of this issue and overturned its ruling. This judgment was welcomed by the Italian literature according to which conflict of law rules can only be applied if the factual pattern of the case calls for such application; whereas leaving this issue to the parties' initiative would render the Italian choice of laws rules *in concreto* "facultative", contrary to Art. 14 Italian PIL statute. See the comment of C. Tuo, *Obbligazioni contrattuali e applicazione della legge straniera:: un preoccupante segnale di regresso da parte della Corte di Cassazione,* in *RDIPP* 2010, p. 55 ss. See also the partial critics and the references to case-law in I. Queirolo, *Conoscenza* cit., p. 633 fnt. 82.

[36] S.M. Carbone, *La conoscenza* cit., p. 198.

[37] I. Queirolo, *Conoscenza* cit., 633 and footnote 82 for references.

[38] Ibidem.

[39] N. Boschiero, Norme cit., p. 578; N. Boschiero, sub Art. 14, in S. Bariatti (Ed.), Legge 31 maggio 1995 n. 218, Riforma del sistema italiano di diritto internazionale privato, Commentario, in Le Nuove Leggi Civili e Commentate 1996, p. 1038 ff.

2.2. *Designation of Foreign Laws by Conflict of Laws Rules*

Italian PIL rules are mainly bilateral, and therefore capable of designating either foreign law or the law of the forum as the applicable law. Thus, Italian PIL norms frequently determine foreign laws as the applicable law. However, in only a few cases Italian judges choose to apply foreign laws.[40]

In this context, attention will be given to the aforementioned survey of the Swiss Institute of Comparative Law (hereinafter: the survey). In fact, this Institute sent fifty-two questionnaires (hereinafter: the questionnaire) concerning the application of foreign law to a number of Italian legal professionals. There was a total of nineteen responses. In Italy the areas of litigation most commonly subject to foreign law are contract, inheritance and tort law; however, family, competition and maritime law also play an important role. With the exception of judges, all categories involved highlighted that their resort to foreign law was increased frequently for a number of reasons including rising immigration trends, the increased migration of individuals and workers into Italy from other EU member States and the growth in the number of foreign companies operating in Italy.[41]

In contrast, Italian judicial authorities responding to the questionnaire declared that the frequency of their application of foreign law is extremely low, less than 25%, and has not increased. In fact, information on foreign law is not easily available, which causes procedural delays. Also, judges are not well trained in the application of foreign law, which creates a risk of committing errors. Thus, judicial authorities avoid applying foreign law as much as possible, discouraging parties from requesting its application. However, in the case of a foreign law that is that of a EU member State, the European Judicial Network facilitates the ascertainment of the foreign law of an EU member State, and EU laws are highly harmonized.[42]

---

[40] See Swiss Institute Study, Part III, Synthesis Report with Recommendations, cit., p. 6. The exact number of these cases is unknown due to the fact that Italy does not collect statistical data on this issue (See *supra*, para 1.1.).

[41] Ibidem, pp. 224–226 ff.

[42] Ibidem, pp. 226–230. These results are confirmed by an analysis of the judgments that apply foreign laws and that are published in the 2005–2013(1–2) issues of the main Italian law legal journal reporting on judgments on conflict of laws issues, namely the aforementioned "Rivista di diritto internazionale privato e processuale". Just thirty-four judgments applied foreign laws as designated by conflict of laws rules of the Italian PIL statute. Foreign laws are most typically applied in family law, contract law and in the context of employment relationships. The States whose laws are most frequently applied are Morocco and the US, while German, Egyptian, Canadian, Tunisian, Spanish and Brazilian laws also play relevant roles. The judgments at stake are hereinafter listed in chronological order: Corte Cass. 21.1.2013 n.1302, in *RDIPP* 2013, p. 472 (US law); Corte Cass. 7.6.2012 n. 9189, *Ibidem*, p. 433 ff. (US law); Corte Cass. 30.4.2012 n. 6622, *Ibidem*, p. 165 (Swiss law); Trib. Belluno 30.12.2011, *Ibidem* 2012, p. 452 (Moroccan law, Moudawana); Trib. Chiavari 12.12.2011, *Ibidem*, p. 937 (Australian law, South Australia State law); Trib. Novara 14.7.2011, *Ibidem*, p. 958 (Rumanian law); Trib. Treviso 9.5.2011, *Ibidem*, p. 383 (Moroccan law, Moudawana); Corte Cass. 4.4.2011 n. 7599, *Ibidem* 2011, p. 1092 (Canadian law); Corte Cass. 25.11.2010 n. 23933, *Ibidem*, p. 474 (German law); Trib. Torino 20.7.2010, *Ibidem* 2012, p. 227 (Spanish law); Trib. Prato 16.7.2010, *Ibidem*, p. 145 (Brazilian law); Trib.

3. Foreign Law Before Judicial Authorities

3.1. Nature of Foreign Law

The nature of foreign law before Italian judicial authorities was already stated in paragraphs 1 and 2.

3.1.1. Foreign Law Recalled by Conflict of Laws Rules

Art.14 of the Italian PIL Statute does not explicitly clarify if foreign law shall be considered as "law" or rather as "fact". Italian literature, however, unanimously maintains that Art. 14 poses on the competent adjudicating authorities the obligation to ascertain foreign laws *ex officio*, which implies the "law" nature of foreign law.[43] Art. 14 thus implicitly adopts the approach followed by the prevailing Italian literature in the framework of the previous PIL system.[44]

However, the previous PIL system Italian case-law considered foreign laws as a fact.[45] The Supreme Court started following a new approach. According to this new approach, foreign laws were considered as "laws", and therefore their erroneous application could be reviewed by the same Supreme Court. According to the same approach, adjudicating authorities had to raise *ex officio* the question of the application of PIL rules and had to apply *ex officio* foreign laws, in line with the principle

---

Aosta 25.6.2010, *Ibidem* 2011, p. 437 (Moroccan law, Moudawana); Trib. Tivoli 4.8.2009, *Ibidem*, p. 160 (US law, State of Virginia); Trib. Firenze 18.5.2009, *Ibidem*, p. 145 (Spanish law); Corte Cass. 19.4.2010 n. 9276, *Ibidem*, p. 195 (Tunisian law); Trib. Firenze 15.4.2009, *Ibidem* 2010, p. 769 (US law, State of Georgia); Trib. Belluno 6.3.2009, in *Ibidem* 2011, p. 140 (Indian law, Hindu Marriage Act); Trib. Reggio Emilia 31.7.2008, *Ibidem* 2009, p. 737 (Tunisian law); Corte Cass. 26.5.2008 n. 13547, *Ibidem*, p. 409, (US law, State of New York); Trib. Reggio Emilia 3.9.07, in *Ibidem*, p. 638 (Vietnamese law); Corte Cass. 19.7.07 n. 16017, *Ibidem* 2008, p. 533 (US law, State of New York); Trib. Reggio Emilia 14.5.2007, *Ibidem* 2009, p. 729 (Jersey law); Trib. Rovereto 15.3.07, *Ibidem* 2008, p. 179 (UK law); Trib. Milano 2.2.2007, *Ibidem*, p. 137 (Pachistani law); Corte Cass. 28.12.06 n. 27592, *Ibidem* 2007, p. 443 (Egyptian law); Corte Cass. 23.2.2006 n. 4040, *Ibidem*, p. 157 (US law, State of New York); Corte Cass. 7.12.2005 n. 26976, *Ibidem* 2006, p. 1053 (US law); Corte Cass. 4.11.2005 n. 21395, *Ibidem*, p. 791 (Moroccan law); Corte Cass. 28.9.2005 n. 18944, *Ibidem*, p. 774 (British Virgin Islands); Trib. Pordenone 14.9.2005, *Ibidem*, p. 181 (Moroccan law, Moudawana); Corte Cass 29.7.2005 n. 15956, *Ibidem*, p. 1097 (German law); Corte Cass. 9.6.2005 n. 12169, *Ibidem*, p. 438 (Moroccan law); Corte Cass. 21.4.2005 n. 8296, *Ibidem* 2005, p. 1088 (Brazilian law); Corte Cass 26.11.2004 n. 22332, *Ibidem*, p. 771 (Canadian law).

[43] See F. Pocar, cit., p. 35; N. Boschiero, *Norme* cit., 541 ff; I. Queirolo (coordinator) and S.M. Carbone, P. Ivaldi, L. Carpaneto, C. Tuo, M.E. De Maestri, F. Pesce, cit., 241; I. Queirolo, *Conoscenza* cit., p. 622; S.M. Carbone, *La conoscenza* cit., 195; L. Fumagalli, cit., p. 470; G.P. Romano, *Italy*, cit., p. 268.

[44] See I. Pittaluga, La prova del diritto straniero: evoluzioni giurisprudenziali in Francia e in Italia, in RDIPP 2002, p. 688 ff.; G.P. Romano, Italy, cit., p. 266.

[45] See the references in N. Boschiero, *Norme* cit., p. 545.

of *iura novit curia*.[46] However, other judgments continued to maintain the factual nature of foreign law.[47]

After the entry into force of Art. 14 of the Italian PIL statute, Italian case-law has unanimously affirmed that Art. 14 implies that foreign law is inserted as "law" in the Italian legal order and therefore is subject to the same procedural treatment as Italian norms.[48] This approach was recently confirmed by the 2014 Supreme Court Judgment, as mentioned in paragraph 2.1.

3.2. Application of Foreign Law

Art. 14 of the Italian PIL Statute does not explicitly say if foreign law shall be applied *ex officio* or rather at a party's request. Italian literature, however, unanimously maintains that Art. 14 obliges the adjudicating authorities to ascertain foreign laws *ex officio*, and therefore to apply *ex officio* foreign laws.[49] This unanimous approach of Italian literature corresponds to the one adopted in the frame of the previous PIL system by the majority of scholars.[50]

However, during the previous PIL system Italian case-law considered foreign law as a fact, to be applied at a party's request.[51] After the entry into force of Art. 14 of the Italian PIL statute, Italian case-law unanimously affirms that foreign laws are to be applied *ex officio* by judicial authorities.[52] This approach was recently confirmed by the 2014 Supreme Court Judgment, as mentioned in paragraph 2.1. This Judgment overcame past case-law hesitations[53] stating that foreign elements and connecting factors cannot be treated procedurally as a question of fact, since judges are obliged to search them ex officio.

---

[46] See Corte Cass. 16.2.1966 n. 486, in *RDIPP* 1966, p. 571 ff.; Corte Cass. 13.4.1959 n. 1089, in *Giur. it.* 1960, I, 1, p. 583 ff. See N. Boschiero, *Norme* cit., p. 543; G.P. Romano, *Italy*, cit., p. 269.

[47] See *supra*, fnt. 33.

[48] See Corte Cass. 9.5.2007 n. 10549, in *RDIPP* 2008, p. 216 ff.; Corte Cass. 29.3.2006 n. 7250, *ibidem* 2007, p. 787 ff.; Corte Cass. 9.1.2004 n. 111, *ibidem* 2005, p. 172 ff.; Corte Cass. 12.11.1999 n. 12538, *ibidem* 2001, p. 651 ff. See G.P. Romano, Italy, cit., p. 276.

[49] See I. Pittaluga, cit., p. 688; G.P. Romano, *Italy*, cit., p. 270; S.M. Carbone, *La conoscenza* cit., p. 198. This obligation arises from the general rule codified by Art. 113 of the CCP, according to which Italian judicial authorities must determine *ex officio* the applicable norms in a case. Yet, judicial authorities shall inform parties on the decision to apply one or the other foreign laws, granting them the right to be heard on the point ex Art. 101 CCP. L. Fumagalli, cit., p. 473; G.P. Romano, *Italy*, cit., p. 272.

[50] As opposed to the 1960s, when some authors claimed that judicial authorities had to apply foreign law solely at a party's request. See G.P. Romano, *Italy*, cit., p. 266 fnt 1 for references.

[51] See the references in N. Boschiero, *Norme* cit., p. 545.

[52] Corte Cass. 5.6.2009 n. 13087, in *RDIPP* 2010, p. 140 ff. See the comment of Tuo C., cit., p. 74 ff. See also the case-law referred to by G.P. Romano, *Italy,* cit., p. 269.

[53] See *supra*, para 2.1.

3.3. Ascertainment of Foreign Law

Art. 14 of the Italian PIL Statute explicitly states that judicial authorities shall ascertain foreign laws according to the principle *iura novit curia*. This Article codifies the unanimous approach of the Italian literature in the frame of the previous PIL system.

However, during the previous PIL system, Italian case-law considered foreign law as a fact to be proven by parties, who had to demonstrate that the content of foreign law differed from Italian law.[54] In cases where parties failed to prove this, judicial authorities applied Italian law under the assumption that it was identical to foreign law.[55] When the Supreme Court took the new approach that foreign laws were to be considered as "laws" rather than as facts, adjudicating authorities had to ascertain foreign law according to the principle *iura novit curia*. Parties had to assist judicial authorities in ascertaining foreign laws, without having any burden of proof in this respect.[56] Other Supreme Court judgments, however, maintained that foreign law had to be ascertained at a party's request or through cooperation between the courts and parties.[57]

Despite the entry into force of Art. 14 of the Italian PIL Statute, Italian case-law is divided on the ascertainment of foreign law. The reason is that the "Sezioni Unite", namely the entire Supreme Court Body competent to solve jurisprudential discrepancies, has yet to decide on this issue, whereas the previous decisions, including that of 2014 just examined, have not been adopted by this Body.

One approach of the Supreme Court recognizes that foreign law is a "law" rather than a fact, which is inserted into the Italian legal system and therefore subject to the same procedural treatment as Italian law. Thus, foreign law shall be ascertained by judicial authorities according to the principle *iura novit curia*, and irrespective of any cooperation of the parties.[58] A second approach followed by the Supreme Court still considers foreign law as a matter falling outside the scope of the *iura novit curia* principle and one to be proven by parties.[59] Recently, the first approach was confirmed by the 2014 Supreme Court Judgment, as mentioned in paragraph 2.1.

---

[54] See the case-law abovementioned, *supra*, fnt. 33. See G.P. Romano, *Italy*, cit., p. 275.

[55] See Corte Cass. 1312.1.1978 n. 135, in *RDIPP* 1979, p. 677 ff. See G.P. Romano, *Italy*, cit., p. 275.

[56] See Corte Cass. 16.2.1966 n. 486, cit., p. 571 ff.; Corte Cass. 13.4.1959 n. 1089, cit., p. 583 ff. See N. Boschiero, *Norme* cit., p. 543; G.P. Romano, *Italy*, cit., p. 275.

[57] Corte Cass. 23.2.1978 n. 903, cit., p. 814 ff.

[58] This approach is adopted for proceedings commenced prior to the entry into force of the Italian PIL Statute too, provided that the judgments related to these proceedings have not become final. See Corte Cass. 17.11.2003 n. 17388, in *RDIPP* 2004, p. 1042 ff.; Corte Cass. 12.111.1999 n. 12538, cit., p. 651 ff. See I. Queirolo (coordinator) and S.M. Carbone, P. Ivaldi, L. Carpaneto, C. Tuo, M.E. De Maestri, F. Pesce, cit., p. 241; G.P. Romano, *Italy*, cit., p. 276.

[59] This approach has been adopted by lower level courts, with regard to proceedings instituted not only before, but also after the entry into force of the Italian PIL Statute. See Corte Cass. 19.4.2010 n. 9276, *Ibidem*, p. 195; Corte Cass. 20.7.2007 n. 16089, in *RDIPP* 2008, p. 1121 ff.; Corte Cass. 15.6.2007 n. 14031, in *RDIPP* 2007, p. 1116; Corte Cass. 29.3.2006 n. 7250, cit., p. 787 ff.; Corte

In ascertaining foreign laws, judicial authorities may avail of the means referred to in Art. 14, namely the information provided for by International conventions and by the Italian Ministry of Justice, and the assistance of experts, specialized institutions and the same parties. Yet, judicial authorities may also adopt means other than the ones listed in Art. 14. This list is non-exhaustive and its aim is to allow Italian judicial authorities to benefit from any means and sources of information, even of an informal nature, to reach an effective application of foreign laws.[60]

In particular, judicial authorities may acquire information on the applicable foreign law through the assistance of:

(i) mechanisms established by international conventions. Italy is party to the London Convention,[61] to several multilateral treaties that are relevant to the matter of proof of and information on foreign law,[62] and to a number of bilat-

---

Cass. 19.1.2006 n. 22406, in *RDIPP* 2007, p. 769 ff.; Corte Cass. 9.1.2004 n. 111, in *RDIPP* 2005, p. 172 ff.; Corte Cass. 11.11.2002 n. 15822, in *RDIPP* 2003, p. 978 ff.; Corte Cass. 10.8.2002 n. 11434, *Ibidem* 2003, pp. 505; Corte Cass. 30.5.2001 n. 7365, *Ibidem* 2002, p. 745 ff.; Corte Cass. 20.5.2001 n. 7365, in *Repertorio: 2001, Diritto internazionale privato [2290]*, n. 39; Corte Cass. 29.3.2001 n. 6757, in *RDIPP* 2002, pp. 450 ff. See I. Queirolo (coordinator) and S.M. Carbone, P. Ivaldi, L. Carpaneto, C. Tuo, M.E. De Maestri, F. Pesce, cit., p. 241. See also Milan Court of Appeal, specialized section in intellectual property 4.5.2012, registrar number 2935/2009, not yet published, p. 14 according to which the principle *iura novit curia* concerns exclusively the *lex fori* and does not extend to foreign laws.

[60] See L. Fumagalli, cit., p. 473; G.P. Romano, *Italy,* cit., p. 275. See Corte Cass. 26.2.2002 n. 2791, in *RDIPP* 2002, p. 463 ff.

[61] See the multinational European Convention on Information on Foreign Law, adopted in London, on June the 7th 1968 and its Additional Protocol and designated the Ministry of Justice (Ministero di Grazia e Giustizia) as the receiving and transmitting agency in pursuance of Art. 2, paragraph 3, and of Art. 4 of this Convention and its Additional Protocol. Particularly, see the Italian declaration contained in a letter from the Permanent Representative of Italy dated 10 April 1972 handed to the Secretary General of the London Convention at the time of deposit of the instrument of ratification on 10 April 1972, and respectively the Italian declaration contained in a letter from the Permanent Representative of Italy dated 5 February 1982, handed to the Secretary General of the Addition Protocol to the Convention at the time of deposit of the instrument of ratification on 11 February 1982. This Convention and its related Protocol were adopted under the framework of the Council of Europe. The texts of the Convention and the Protocol together with the list of declarations, reservations and other communications by States parties is available on the official website of the Council of Europe at http://conventions.coe.int/Treaty/Commun/QueVoulezVous.asp?NT=062&CM=1&CL=ENG. The London Convention was welcomed by Italian literature as being particularly innovative, in that it obliges the receiving agency of the State party to reply on the content of its legal system in a detailed way upon request. Yet this Convention was very rarely applied in Italy due to the difficulties to activate its complex operational mechanisms. See S.M. Carbone, *La conoscenza* cit., p. 199; G.P. Romano, *Italy*, cit., p. 277; I. Queirolo (coordinator) and S.M. Carbone, P. Ivaldi, L. Carpaneto, C. Tuo, M.E. De Maestri, F. Pesce, cit., p. 249.

[62] Such as: (a) the Hague Convention of 18 March 1970 on the Taking of Evidence Abroad in Civil or Commercial Matters (this Convention was adopted in the framework of the Hague Conference of Private International Law. Italy ratified the Convention on 22.6.1982. See the status table on the official website at http://www.hcch.net/index_en.php?act=conventions.status&cid=82. Particularly, see Art. 1.); (b) the Hague Convention of 25 October 1980 on the Civil Aspects of International Child Abduction (this Convention was adopted in the framework of the Hague

eral treaties that relate to cooperation in civil matters and include provisions regarding the exchange of information on the State parties' respective legal systems.[63]

(ii) the Italian Ministry of Justice, which has a corresponding duty to provide the interested judicial authority with the required information.[64]

(iii) experts and specialized institutions, which are named typically consultants of "consulenti tecnici d'ufficio" (hereinafter: "CTU"). This means is the most frequently used and the most efficient in ascertaining foreign laws in Italy. CTUs are selected by judicial authorities in line with Arts 191–202 CCP.[65]

Conference of Private International Law. Italy ratified the Convention on 22.3.1985. See the status table on the official website at http://www.hcch.net/index_en.php?act=conventions.status&cid=24. Particularly, see Art. 14.). In contrast, Italy is not part of (a) the Hague Convention on 19 October 1996 on Jurisdiction, Applicable Law, Recognition, Enforcement and Co-Operation in Respect of Parental Responsibility and Measures for the Protection of Children (this Convention was adopted in the framework of the Hague Conference of Private International Law. Italy did not ratify this Convention. See the status table on the official website at http://www.hcch.net/index_en.php?act=conventions.status&cid=70. Particularly, see Art. 35.); (b) of the Hague Convention of 13 January 2000 on the International Protection of Adults (this Convention was adopted in the framework of the Hague Conference of Private International Law. Italy did not ratify this Convention. See the status table on the official website at http://www.hcch.net/index_en.php?act=conventions.status&cid=71. Particularly, see Art. 29.); and of the Minsk Convention of 22 January 1993 on Legal Assistance and Legal Relations in Civil, Family and Criminal Matters (this Convention was adopted in the framework of the Commonwealth of Independent States. Italy did not ratify this Convention. See the Convention at http://www.unhcr.org/4de4edc69.html).

[63] These bilateral Conventions are published, together with all multilateral Conventions ratified by Italy, in the Italian Ministry of Foreign Affairs data base. See "ITRA – Banca dati dei Trattati Internazionali, Data base of the International Treaty", accessible on the official website at http://itra.esteri.it/Ricerca_Documenti/Ricerca_Documenti2.aspx. Multilateral and bilateral treaties to which Italy is a party are published also in M. Giuliano, F. Pocar and T. Treves (Eds.), *Codice delle convenzioni di diritto interanzionale privato e processuale,* 2 ed., Giuffrè, Milano, 1981. See also G.P. Romano, *Italy,* cit., p. 278.

[64] If the Italian Ministry does not possess this information, it shall use any instruments of international conventions or diplomatic channels to acquire it, and may also request it from the Ministry of Justice of the foreign State in question. Once acquired, the information shall be transferred by the Ministry to the interested judicial authorities. G.P. Romano, *Italy*, cit., p. 278; L. Funagalli, cit., p. 474 fnt 30.

[65] Firstly, judicial authorities may select CTUs that are inscribed in apposite registers, which are kept by the chancellery of every court and are divided into various categories (Art. 13 of the norms executing Italian CCP, so called "disposizioni di attuazione del codice di procedura civile", hereinafter "disp. att. CCP."). To be included in the registers candidates must possess specific technical competences, must be "morally impeccable", must be members of their respective professional associations (Art. 14 disp. att. CCP), and have to be selected by a Committee formed by the Public Prosecutor and by a professional of these associations (Art. 15 disp. att. CCP). Secondly, judicial authorities may select CTUs that are not inscribed in apposite registers. However, in this case the President of the judicial authority in question shall approve the appointment, and may require an explanation for why it was necessary to appoint a CTU inscribed in no registers. This second procedure is usually adopted with regard to CTU experts in foreign laws, since few of them are inscribed in registers. For instance the section on expert in foreign laws of the CTU register at the disposal of the Court of Verona indicates just one expert in German law and one expert in the law of Islamic countries: http://www.tribunale.verona.giustizia.it/it/Content/Ctu/13335?nominativo=&professione=103953&lemma=&Idlink=13335. See also L. Fumagalli, cit., p. 474 fnt. 28.

CTUs shall provide information not only on the norms of the foreign law at stake, but also on their literature and case-law interpretation and on any other relevant material. The information provided by CTUs is not binding upon the judicial authorities, and shall be questioned also by the experts that are appointed by parties as "consulenti tecnici di parte" ("CTP").[66]

(iv) litigating parties. Parties do not carry any burden of proof in this respect. However, if they unjustifiably refuse to provide assistance to judicial authority, their procedural behaviour could be negatively evaluated by this same authority.[67]

(v) means that are not listed by Art. 14: a) Consular documentation, since Art. 49 of the Italian Statute on Consular functions and competences establishes that Consuls may release attestations on laws and customs existing in their State of residence,[68] b) assistance from foreign Consuls that are resident in Italy and that may grant this assistance on the basis of a discretionary power,[69] c) the European Judicial Network in Civil and Commercial Matters,[70] d) direct communication with foreign judicial authorities, that may answer an Italian request of information for reasons of courtesy,[71] e) official sources of foreign law available on the internet,[72] f) their own knowledge and personal research.

All these conclusions are confirmed by the 2014 Supreme Court Judgment, as mentioned in paragraph 2.1. Also, the same conclusions are supported by the recent analysis of the questionnaire on the application of foreign law that was sent by the Swiss Institute of Comparative Law to a number of Italian judicial authorities.[73]

---

[66] In including experts/consultants and specialized institutions in the list of means of ascertaining foreign laws, Art. 14 reaffirms what had previously been established by Arts. 61–64 and 68 of the Italian CCP, according to which judicial authorities may avail themselves of the assistance of qualified experts or consultants. See I. Queirolo (coordinator) and S.M. Carbone, P. Ivaldi, L. Carpaneto, C. Tuo, M.E. De Maestri, F. Pesce, cit., p. 244; G.P. Romano, *Italy*, cit., p. 279; S.M. Carbone, *La Conoscenza* cit., p. 199.

[67] In assisting judicial authorities parties typically produce opinions *pro veritate* that are rendered by experts (appointed by the parties) in the applicable foreign law. Parties also avail themselves of expert witnesses and CTPs who are selected on the basis of their professional reputation. See I. Queirolo (coordinator) and S.M. Carbone, P. Ivaldi, L. Carpaneto, C. Tuo, M.E. De Maestri, F. Pesce, cit., p. 245; S.M. Carbone, *La conoscenza* cit., p. 200; G.P. Romano, *Italy*, cit., p. 276.

[68] This method has limits since Consuls are not obliged to assist judicial authorities and their assistance is limited to providing texts of existing laws and customs, rather than their literal or case-law interpretations. See G.P. Romano, *Italy*, cit., p. 279; L. Fumagalli, cit., p. 475.

[69] See F. Pocar, cit., p. 41; G.P. Romano, *Italy*, cit., p. 279.

[70] In fact, Recital 10 of the Decision establishing this network states that it seeks to facilitate judicial cooperation between the Member States in civil and commercial matters, both in sectors to which existing international instruments apply and in areas where no instrument is currently available. See L. Fumagalli, cit., p. 475 fnt. 32.

[71] See G.P. Romano, *Italy*, cit., p. 279.

[72] See C. Leuzzi and G.P. Romano, *Italy*, p. 224.

[73] Ibidem. Finally, in cases where the London Convention is applied in Italy, judicial authorities rely on its specific rules on the bearing of costs of ascertaining foreign law. In contrast, Italian law

3.4. Interpretation and Application of Foreign Law

Art. 15 of the Italian PIL Statute on "interpretation and application of foreign law" states that "foreign law is applied according to the criteria posed by its country of origin in relation to its interpretation and temporary application". The solution codifies the approach followed by Italian literature in the frame of the previous PIL system, according to which in cases where foreign law is applied in Italy, it should not be considered as "transformed", "nationalized" or assimilated to domestic rules by judicial authorities. Rather foreign law is considered as an autonomous legal system, which shall be interpreted and applied by judicial authorities as if they were sitting in the country of origin of the foreign law in question.[74] As a consequence, according to Italian literature the foreign legal system has to be interpreted and applied in its entirety, including then not only the statutes, but also their case law and doctrinal interpretation, even when this interpretation seems manifestly incorrect to said authorities.[75] In cases where the applicable foreign laws establish norms on the relevant matter that have not yet been interpreted by the domestic literature or case law, Italian judicial authorities shall interpret these norms themselves by considering also parties' agreements on the interpretation and application of the relevant foreign law related to disposable rights.[76]

Moreover, since the Italian PIL Statute partially accepts "renvoi", the principles derived from Arts. 14 and 15 of this Statute apply not only with regard to substantive foreign law applicable, but also in relation to the conflict of laws rules belonging to the foreign law that is determined as applicable by the Italian PIL Statute or by the foreign conflict of law rules in cases of second accepted renvoi.[77] Consequently, the foreign relevant PIL rules shall be interpreted and applied by Italian judicial authorities as if these authorities were sitting in the country of origin of the rules at stake. Therefore, Italian judicial authorities shall apply PIL rules included in the legal system of the foreign law determined as applicable by the Italian PIL Statute according to the characterization followed in this foreign legal system, rather than in Italy, and thus even in cases of conflict of characterizations.[78]

---

does not rule on the costs of ascertaining foreign laws. However, in practice the costs of CTUs are typically not borne solely by the party who invokes this method of ascertainment of foreign law but rather are equally distributed between the parties. Judicial authorities are fee to distribute CTUs' costs on a different basis. Furthermore, each party bears the costs related to the means adopted to assist judicial authorities in ascertaining foreign law. See G.P. Romano, *Italy*, cit., p. 280.

[74] N. Boschiero, sub art. 15, in S. Bariatti (Ed.), cit., p. 1043; L. Fumagalli, cit., p. 476; I. Queirolo (coordinator) and S.M. Carbone, P. Ivaldi, L. Carpaneto, C. Tuo, M.E. De Maestri, F. Pesce, cit., p. 246.

[75] N. Boschiero, sub art. 15, cit., p. 1045.

[76] Ibidem, p. 1043.

[77] Ibidem, p. 1044.

[78] In situations where the second accepted renvoi applies, Italian judicial authorities shall characterize the case before them a third time according to the PIL system of the legal system applicable by the conflict of laws rules included in the legal order of the foreign law that was initially found applicable by the Italian PIL Statute, and so on and so forth in cases of further grades of renvoi. Ibidem, p. 1044–1045.

Furthermore, even when foreign law seems incompatible with the Constitution of the country of origin, Italian judicial authorities shall still apply it if its control of constitutionality is entrusted by the country of origin to a single judicial body, like a Constitutional Court.[79] In contrast, Italian judicial authorities can determine this compatibility only in cases where the legal system of the country of origin entrusts the question of national law's constitutionality to any domestic judicial authorities.[80]

In addition, when foreign law is recalled by conflict of laws rules aimed at favoring substantive results, like the *favor filiationis*, then this law shall be interpreted and applied according to the criteria of its country of origin that better allow it to satisfy the *favor* at stake.[81]

The consequence of the literature's approach is that eventually existing gaps in the relevant foreign law shall be filled out by Italian judicial authorities through the ascertainment of the entire foreign legal system. Thus a failure to establish foreign law never occurs. Then, judicial authorities can avoid the application of foreign law only if this law is interpreted and applied by the relevant authorities of its countries of origin in a way incompatible with international public policy ex Art. 16 of the Italian PIL Statute.

Italian case law follows, however, a different approach than Italian literature. In fact, during the previous PIL system Italian jurisprudence either pronounced itself on the interpretation and application of foreign law with manifest substantive ambiguity,[82] or even maintained that when applied in Italy foreign law shall be interpreted and applied according to the rules of the Italian legal system.[83] After the entry into force of the Italian PIL statute, with the Regoli judgment of 2002 the Italian Supreme Court correctly stated that Article 15 implies that foreign law shall be interpreted and applied by Italian judicial authorities as if they were judges of its country of origin and as if the foreign law at stake was a "living legal system".[84] Yet the same Regoli judgment maintained that in interpreting and applying foreign law

---

[79] Ibidem, p. 1045.

[80] See P. Ivaldi, *In tema di applicazione giudiziale del diritto straniero*, in *RDIPP* 2010, 594; I. Queirolo (coordinator) and S.M. Carbone, P. Ivaldi, L. Carpaneto, C. Tuo, M.E. De Maestri, F. Pesce, cit., 247. See also the Report on Art. 15 of the Italian PIL statute, recalled by P. Ivaldi at p. 594, fnt. 42. Finally, see G. Morelli, *Controllo di costituzionalità di norme straniere*, in *Riv. it. scienze giuridiche* 1954, p. 27; G. De Nova, *Legge straniera e controllo di costituzionalità*, in *Il foro pad.* 1955, IV, c 1; R. Quadri, *Controllo sulla legittimità costituzionale delle norme straniere*, in *Diritto internazionale* 1959, p. 31; F. Mosconi, *Norme straniere e controllo di costituzionalità e legittimità internazionale*, in *Diritto internazionale* 1960, p. 426; S.M. Carbone, *Sul controllo di costituzionalità della norma straniera richiamata*, in *RDIPP* 1965, p. 689; G. Badiali, *Il ruolo del giudice nel controllo della costituzionalità delle norme straniere richiamate*, in *Riv. dir. int.* 2006, p. 611.

[81] See P. Ivaldi, *In tema* cit., 593; I. Pittaluga, cit., p. 693.

[82] See Corte Cass. 16.2.1966 n. 486, cit., p. 571 ff. See P. Ivaldi, *In tema* cit., p. 587.

[83] See the references in P. Ivaldi, *In tema* cit., p. 587, fnt. 12.

[84] See Corte Cass. 26.2.2002 n. 2791, cit., 464. See P. Ivaldi, *In tema* cit., p. 585 ss.; L. Fumagalli, cit., p. 476; I. Queirolo (coordinator) and S.M. Carbone, P. Ivaldi, L. Carpaneto, C. Tuo, M.E. De Maestri, F. Pesce, cit., p. 246; G.P. Romano, *Italy*, cit., p. 276. See also Corte Cass. 4.11.2005 n. 21395, *Ibidem*, p. 791.

ex Art. 15 of the Italian PIL statute, judicial authorities shall limit themselves to interpret and apply foreign law as translated by a competent translator, provided that their interpretation and application is not arbitrary or inconsistent.[85] According to the Regoli judgment, in cases of manifest practical difficulties, Italian judicial authorities shall not examine further how foreign law is concretely interpreted and applied by the literature and case-law of its country of origin.[86] Another judgment of the Supreme Court, this one in 2009, went even further in maintaining that judicial authorities shall interpret and apply foreign law on the basis of their mere acquisition of a non-officially translated partial text of the relevant norms or extracts of the Constitution of its country of origin.[87] Furthermore, according to a case-law minority opinion, in proceedings related to provisional measures, establishing foreign law judicial authorities shall not avail themselves of the means of assistance provided for by Art. 14 of the PIL Statute.[88]

This approach of Italian case-law leads to the consequence that, since foreign laws are only partially ascertained by judicial authorities, several gaps arise.[89] Yet, when gaps exist in the ascertainment of foreign law, Italian judicial authorities maintain that a failure to establish foreign law occurs, with the consequences highlighted in the following paragraph.

3.5. Failure to Establish Foreign Law

When judicial authorities fail to establish the applicable foreign law, Art. 14.2 of the Italian PIL Statute maintains that where the relevant PIL norms adopt more than one (subsidiary or alternative) connecting factors for the same factual relationship, designating more than one applicable law, Italian law shall not be applied automatically, but rather other foreign laws shall be applied as determined applicable by the connecting factors of the PIL norms in question.[90] Thus, Italian law can be applied

---

[85] Corte Cass. 26.2.2002 n. 2791, cit., p. 470. See P. Ivaldi, *In tema* cit., 589 ss.; I. Queirolo (coordinator) and S.M. Carbone, P. Ivaldi, L. Carpaneto, C. Tuo, M.E. De Maestri, F. Pesce, cit., p. 247; F. Marongiu Buonaiuti, *Un ritorno al "diritto internazionale privato facoltativo" in una recente sentenza della Corte di Cassazione,* in *Riv. dir. int.* 2002, p. 962 ff.

[86] Corte Cass. 26.2.2002 n. 2791, cit., p. 731. See also Corte Cass. 9.1.2004 n. 115, in *RDIPP* 2004, p. 1379. See P. Ivaldi, *In tema* cit., p. 589 ss.; I. Queirolo (coordinator) and S.M. Carbone, P. Ivaldi, L. Carpaneto, C. Tuo, M.E. De Maestri, F. Pesce, cit., p. 247.

[87] See Corte Cass. 24.6.2009 n. 14777, cit., p. 217 ff. See the comment to this judgment of M.E. De Maestri and F. Pesce, cit., p. 223 ff. See also G.P. Romano, *Italy,* cit., p. 281.

[88] Trib. Modena 12.8.1996, in *Giur.it* 1997, I, 2, 368; Trib. Modena 11.7.1998, in *Giur. it.* 1999, p. 50. See G.P. Romano, *Italy,* cit., p. 281.

[89] G.P. Romano, *Italy,* cit., p. 281.

[90] See P. Picone, *La teoria* cit., 344. See also G.P. Romano, *Italy,* cit., pp. 282–283; S.M. Carbone, *La conoscenza* cit., p. 204; I. Queirolo (coordinator) and S.M. Carbone, P. Ivaldi, L. Carpaneto, C. Tuo, M.E. De Maestri, F. Pesce, cit., p. 246; L. Fumagalli, cit., p. 475. See, however, P. Picone, *La teoria generale del diritto internazionale privato nella legge italiana di riforma*

only when the relevant conflict of laws rule does not establish any connecting factor different than the one adopted to invoke the foreign law which remained unascertained. Also, Italian law shall be applied when judicial authorities fail to establish all other foreign laws implicated by the connecting factors adopted by the conflict of laws norm for the case in question.[91]

Recourse to Italian law is then a subsidiary and residual option, aimed at ensuring the administration of justice in the concrete case at stake. These conclusions are confirmed by the 2014 Supreme Court Judgment, as mentioned in paragraph 2.1.[92]

4. Judicial Review

4.1. Conflict of Laws Rules

Under the Italian PIL Statute, Italian literature and case law unanimously maintain that when conflict of laws rules have erroneously been applied and Italian law has been applied instead of foreign law, parties can appeal to the Italian Supreme Court according to Art. 360 Section 1 n. 3 of the Italian CCP.[93] Some of the Italian literature also emphasizes that this judicial review includes cases where judicial authorities apply Italian law rather than foreign law as a result of a failure to ascertain its content.[94]

---

della materia, in *Riv. dir. int.* 1996, p. 344, according to whom Art.14 Section 2 should apply only to subsidiary connecting factors, since the rationale behind alternative connecting factors is to determine different applicable laws for different cases, not multiple laws in the same case.

[91] G.P. Romano, *Italy,* cit., pp. 282–283; S.M. Carbone, *La conoscenza* cit., p. 204; I. Queirolo (coordinator) and S.M. Carbone, P. Ivaldi, L. Carpaneto, C. Tuo, M.E. De Maestri, F. Pesce, cit., p. 246; L. Fumagalli, cit., p. 475.

[92] N. Boschiero, sub art. 14, cit., p. 1042; G.P. Romano, *Italy,* cit., p. 282; I. Queirolo (coordinator) and S.M. Carbone, P. Ivaldi, L. Carpaneto, C. Tuo, M.E. De Maestri, F. Pesce, cit., p. 246; L. Fumagalli, cit., p. 476. During the previous PIL system, in fact, in the absence of any explicit rules on the issue of the failure to establish foreign law, Italian case law typically adopted two different approaches. The first more rigorous approach consisted of entirely rejecting the claims of the party invoking the application of a foreign law in cases where this party failed to establish its content (Corte Cass. 4.5.1985 n. 2805, in *RDIPP* 1986, p. 648; G.P. Romano, *Italy,* cit., p. 282; I. Queirolo (coordinator) and S.M. Carbone, P. Ivaldi, L. Carpaneto, C. Tuo, M.E. De Maestri, F. Pesce, cit., p. 246 fnt. 25). The second approach, followed by the majority of Italian jurisprudence, consisted of imposing the application of Italian law in cases where the interested party failed to establish foreign law (Corte Cass. 1.4.1980 n. 2094, in *RDIPP* 1981, p. 500; Corte Cass. 21.3.1980 n. 1906, cit., p. 499. See G.P. Romano, *Italy,* cit., p. 282; I. Queirolo (coordinator) and S.M. Carbone, P. Ivaldi, L. Carpaneto, C. Tuo, M.E. De Maestri, F. Pesce, cit., p. 246 fnt. 25), assuming that Italian law had a primacy nature over any foreign laws and was either identical to the foreign law invoked or inspired by general principles analogous to those of the appropriate law (G.P. Romano, *Italy,* cit., p. 282; N. Boschiero, sub art. 14, cit., p. 1042).

[93] P. Ivaldi, *In tema* cit., p. 600; G.P. Romano, *Italy,* cit., p. 283. See Corte Cass. 21.4.2005 n. 8360, in *RDIPP* 2006, p. 739.

[94] P. Ivaldi, *In tema* cit., p. 600; G.P. Romano, *Italy,* cit., p. 283. See the opposite view as referred to by P. Ivaldi, *In tema* cit., p. 600 fnt. 63.

Recourse for erroneous application of conflict of law rules is available even when the plaintiff does not enumerate the rules of the foreign law that were not applied or their specific content. However, the plaintiff shall invoke before the Supreme Court the relevant "principle of law" which derives from the (foreign) law that was not applied and which would have been capable of supporting a different judgment than the one rendered.[95] Recourse for erroneous application of conflict of law rules is possible even in the absence of this invocation. In cases where foreign law was not applied because of a failure to follow the principle of *iura novit curia*, the Supreme Court typically refers the case to lower instance courts, mandating application of foreign law in accordance with this principle.[96]

Furthermore, since *renvoi* is partially admitted by the Italian PIL Statute, the judicial review at stake shall concern the application by lower instance courts of the entire foreign legal system, including its PIL norms and those of a different legal order that might be determined as applicable in cases of second accepted *renvoi*.[97] Thus, this review shall apply for instance to cases where the characterisation of the relevant foreign conflict of laws rules have been erroneously rendered in order to apply Italian law rather than the appropriate foreign law.[98]

Finally, Italian literature and case-law do not address cases where, due to an erroneous application of PIL norms, foreign law has been applied instead of Italian law. One opinion invokes the same reasons allowing judicial review in cases of application of foreign law rather than Italian law and recalls the need to avoid discriminating against Italian law in favor of foreign law.[99] This opinion thus maintains that even in cases where foreign law was applied in place of Italian law, parties can appeal to the Italian Supreme Court according to Art. 360 Section 1 n. 3 of the Italian CCP.[100]

4.2. Foreign Law

Judicial authorities may correctly apply conflict of laws rules and correctly identify the applicable foreign law recalled by these rules, but then erroneously ascertain the content of this law and consequently render an erroneous judgment. In such cases, the case-law under the previous PIL system excluded the parties from appealing to the Supreme Court.[101]

---

[95] Corte Cass. 25.3.02 n. 4203, in *Giur. it.* 2002, p. 1649; Corte Cass 11.11.2002 n. 15822, in *RDIPP* 2003, p. 978; Cass. 29.3.2006 n. 7250, cit., p. 787; Cass. 5.6.2007 n. 13184, in *RDIPP* 2008, p. 836; Corte Cass. 15.6.2007 n. 14031, cit., p. 1116; Cass. 21.1.2004 n. 886 in *RDIPP* 2005, p. 173. See P. Ivaldi, *In tema* cit., pp. 600–601; G.P. Romano, *Italy,* cit., pp. 283–284.

[96] Cass. 17.11.03 17388 in *RDIPP* 2004, p. 1042. See P. Ivaldi, *In tema* cit., pp. 601–602; G.P. Romano, *Italy,* cit., pp. 283–284.

[97] See *supra*, para 3.4. See N. Boschiero, sub art. 14, cit., p. 1044.

[98] Ibidem.

[99] G.P. Romano, *Italy,* cit., p. 283.

[100] Ibidem.

[101] This case-law, in fact, emphasized that judicial review concerned only erroneous application of laws, whereas foreign law had to be considered as a fact, rather than as a law. This approach was

After the adoption of the Italian PIL Statute, since foreign law rules are considered as laws rather than as facts, Italian literature and case law unanimously maintain that when these laws have erroneously been applied, parties can appeal to the Italian Supreme Court according to Art. 360 Section 1 n. 3 of the Italian CCP.[102] The "nomophylactic function" of the Supreme Court, by which it acts as a guardian of the correct application of laws, extends to foreign laws as well.[103] The judicial review at stake therefore concerns the choices and methods adopted in interpreting foreign law by the judges.[104] During this review, consideration should be given also to an analysis of the costs and benefits, so that the nature of the dispute and the advantages that parties might derive on the one side and the costs and lengthiness of a thorough examination in this respect on the other are taken into account.[105] In cases where the rationale behind the choice related to the application of foreign law and the criteria adopted to ascertain such law are not apparent, a lack of reasonableness can be claimed. Consequently, the judgment can be overturned.[106]

Finally, the requirements for appealing to the Supreme Court in cases where foreign law was erroneously ascertained and applied are analogous to the ones mentioned above in relation to the erroneous application of the conflict of laws rules.[107]

5. Foreign Law in Other Instances

5.1. Foreign Law Before Administrative and Other Non-judicial Authorities

The Italian PIL Statute does not establish any rule on the application and ascertainment of foreign law before administrative and other non-judicial authorities, such as civil registry officers. In fact, Arts. 14 and 15 insist on limiting their scope to the application and ascertainment of foreign law by "judicial authorities". Italian literature, however, recalls that the Italian PIL Statute addresses a certain number of cases

---

partially overruled by a 1959 Supreme that overturned the Court of Appeal's judgment because of an erroneous application of the relevant Pennsylvanian law. Moreover, the Supreme Court ascertained this same applicable law itself, by recalling doctrinal and jurisprudential case-law. Yet after this judgment, other case law still denied judicial review to judgments based on erroneous application of foreign laws. Corte Cass. 13.4.1959 n. 1089, in *Giur. it.* 1960, I, 1, p. 583 ff. See N. Boschiero, *Norme* cit., p. 543; G.P. Romano, *Italy*, cit., p. 269.

[102] See P. Ivaldi, *In tema* cit., p. 600; G.P. Romano, *Italy,* cit., p. 284.

[103] Corte Cass. 21.4.2005 n. 8360, cit., p. 742. See P. Ivaldi, *In tema* cit., p. 600; G.P. Romano, *Italy,* cit., p. 284.

[104] S.M. Carbone, *La conoscenza* cit., p. 200; G.P. Romano, *Italy,* cit., p. 285.

[105] Ibidem.

[106] Ibidem.

[107] G.P. Romano, *Italy,* cit., p. 285.

where conflict of laws rules are applied by administrative and other non-judicial authorities, namely civil registry officers.[108]

These conclusions are confirmed by the survey of the Swiss Institute of Comparative Law, which sent the aforementioned questionnaire concerning the application of foreign law to a number of civil registry officers and to the National Association of Civil Registry Officers. Just one registrar responded. The registrar highlighted that she frequently applies foreign law since Italian PIL norms refer to foreign law in most of the transnational cases concerning family matters.[109] Also, the public registrar in question maintained her obligation to apply foreign law since the Italian PIL Statute mandates such application.[110] Moreover, to ascertain foreign law, the interested registrar from time to time utilizes just the opinions of legal experts or diplomatic channels.[111]

5.2. Foreign Law in Arbitration

The Italian PIL Statute does not establish any rule on the application and ascertainment of foreign law in arbitration, mediation and other alternative dispute resolution mechanisms, and little case law exists on the point.[112] The regulation of the Arbitral Chamber of Milan, however, states that the Arbitral Tribunal shall make decisions according to the rule of law and the uses of international trade, even in the absence of any express agreement by the parties in this respect, unless they have agreed that the case shall be decided *ex aequo et bono* (art. 3 para 4).[113]

---

[108] For instance, according to Italian civil code, in order to recognise a marriage between spouses one or both of which possess foreign nationalities, civil registry officers must ascertain the fulfilment of all matrimonial conditions that are required by the same code. See I. Queirolo (coordinator) and S.M. Carbone, P. Ivaldi, L. Carpaneto, C. Tuo, M.E. De Maestri, F. Pesce, cit., p. 250; G.P. Romano, *Italy,* cit., p. 285.

[109] See C. Leuzzi and G.P. Romano, *Italy,* cit., p. 228.

[110] Ibidem, p. 229.

[111] Ibidem, p. 232.

[112] See R. Luzzatto, International Commercial Arbitration and Municipal Law of States, in 157 RC 1977-IV, pp. 83 ff.; L. Radicati di Brozolo, Arbitrage commercial international et lois de police: considérations sur les conflits de juridictions dans le commerce international, in 315 RC 2005, p. 463 ff.; A. Carlevaris, L'accertamento del diritto nell'arbitrato internazionale tra principio iura novit curia e onere della prova, in Riv. Arb. 2007, p. 525 ff.; S.M. Carbone, L'autonomia privata nei rapporti economici internazionali ed i suoi limiti, in RDIPP 2007, p. 891 ff.; P. Bernardini, L'arbitrato nel commercio e negli investimenti internazionali, 2ed., Giuffrè, Milano, 2008; A. Atteritano, L'enforcement delle sentenze arbitrali del commercio internazionale, Giuffrè, Milano, 2009, pp. 266 ff.; S.M. Carbone, Iura novit curia e arbitrato commerciale internazionale, in RDIPP 2010, p. 355 ff.

[113] This norm is consistent with Recommendation 1 of the International Law Association Resolution on "Ascertaining the content of the applicable law in international commercial arbitration", adopted in Rio de Janeiro on 2008. See P. Bernardini, cit., pp. 203–204; S.M. Carbone, Iura novit curia cit., p. 355.

In applying the rule of law to establish which legal discipline shall regulate their case, arbitrators shall also refer to the conflict of laws norms of the State of their seat, which are considered mandatory, rather than facultative, even in arbitrations.[114] The law determined as applicable by these conflict of law norms will be recalled here as "foreign law" just for simplicity reasons, since it is well known that in international commercial arbitration no *lex fori* and consequently no foreign laws exist. The foreign law applicable in arbitration shall be considered as a law rather than as a fact. Arbitral Tribunals shall then ascertain foreign laws according to the principle *iura novit curia*.[115]

Also, according to Italian literature, in international commercial arbitration mandatory norms (*lois de police*) of both the legal system of the State of the seat (for simplicity reasons here improperly renamed State of the forum) and those of other States (for simplicity reasons here improperly renamed third States) shall be applied by arbitrators ex officio and according to the principle *iura novit curia*, to protect against challenges to the award.[116]

In ascertaining foreign law and mandatory foreign norms (hereinafter for simplicity reasons "foreign law and mandatory foreign norms" will be altogether referred to as "foreign law"), arbitrators shall utilize information provided by the parties and shall also use experts appointed by the same arbitrators or expert witnesses chosen by the parties. Foreign law shall be interpreted and applied encompassing the entire legal system of its country of origin. Also, arbitrators shall always respect the principle of "dispositivo" by keeping the parties informed of their ascertainment of foreign law and by granting them the right to be heard on the relevant points.[117] This is especially true since arbitrators shall never exceed the parties' *petita*, which might occur in cases where they apply a law whose content is not anticipated by the parties.[118]

In cases of failure to ascertain foreign law, arbitrators shall apply *ex officio* rules and principles founded at the international level, by benefitting from the experience acquired in the arbitral practice, as codified by the International Bar Association and Unidroit.[119]

Finally, Italian literature excludes that judicial review of arbitral awards may be based on an erroneous application of conflict of law rules or of foreign laws. This

---

[114] The Resolution is available on the official website at http://www.ila-hq.org/en/committees/index.cfm/cid/19. See the report to this Resolution on "Ascertaining the Contents of the Applicable Law in International Commercial Arbitration" written by "Professor Filip De Ly (Netherlands): *Chair*, Professor Luca G Radicati di Brozolo (Italy): *Co-Rapporteur*, Mr. Mark Friedman (UK): *Co-Rapporteur*". See generally S.M. Carbone, Iura novit curia cit., p. 355 ff.

[115] Yet this principle applies with peculiarities in arbitration as articulated in Recommendation 4 of the ILA Resolution of 2008 mentioned above. See S.M. Carbone, Iura novit curia cit., p. 355.

[116] This follows from the deontological duty of arbitrators to render an effective and enforceable award, as stated in Recommendation 13 of the ILA Resolution of 2008. See S.M. Carbone, Iura novit curia cit., p. 363; S.M. Carbone, *L'autonomia* cit, 904–906; L. Radicati di Brozolo, *Arbitrage* cit., p. 463.

[117] S.M. Carbone, Iura novit curia cit., pp. 356 and 366.

[118] This is consistent with Recommendation 8 of the ILA Resolution of 2008. S.M. Carbone, Iura novit curia cit., pp. 361 and 366; A. Carlevaris, *L'accertamento* cit., pp. 525–527.

[119] S.M. Carbone, Iura novit curia cit., p. 358.

interpretation is in line with the understanding of Art. V of the New York Convention of 1958 on the Recognition and Enforcement of Foreign Arbitral Awards.[120]

5.3. Foreign Law in Advisory Work by Notaries and Lawyers

The Italian PIL Statute does not establish any rule on the application and ascertainment of foreign law in advisory works and no case law exists on this point. Italian notaries are confronted with the need to apply and obtain information on foreign law when drafting legal documents (such as wills, contracts, minutes of shareholders meetings, spouses' agreements etc.), in verifying the legal status of an applicant's person or assets abroad, and in the context of legal counselling. In these cases notaries shall exercise their authority by applying relevant rules of the Italian legal system, including the PIL statute and therefore the conflict of laws rules which might invoke a foreign law also in transnational cases, for instance when spouses possess different nationalities. Thus, in these cases notaries shall apply foreign law.[121]

These conclusions are confirmed by the survey of the Swiss Institute of Comparative Law, which sent the abovementioned questionnaire concerning the application of foreign law to a number of Italian notaries. Four notaries responded. According to their responses foreign law plays an important role before them in matters related to corporate, matrimonial property and international inheritance law.[122] Italian notaries highlighted that they are obliged to apply foreign law by virtue of their status as public officials and by their consequently being subject to the entire Italian legal system, which includes the current Italian PIL statute, which considers choice of law rules mandatory.

To ascertain foreign law notaries mainly use the official sources of foreign laws available on the internet, in national libraries or from cooperation of foreign colleagues, and from time to time notaries use the European Judicial Network or the network among National Confederations of notaries.[123] Yet the notaries denounced an insufficient level of information about the content of foreign laws in Italy that

---

[120] Ibidem, p. 358; R. Luzzatto, *International* cit., pp. 83 ff.; A. Atteritano, cit., pp. 266 ff.

[121] I. Queirolo (coordinator) and S.M. Carbone, P. Ivaldi, L. Carpaneto, C. Tuo, M.E. De Maestri, F. Pesce, cit., p. 250; G.P. Romano, *Italy*, cit., p. 285.

[122] in corporate matters, foreign law plays an important role before Italian notaries when companies move abroad or in mergers when at least one of the corporations involved is not Italian. In matrimonial property and international inheritance law, in order to draft real estate contracts when at least one of the parties is a foreigner, notaries are required by law to verify both the contractual capacity of parties and the seller's and purchaser's marital status and matrimonial property regime. C. Leuzzi and G.P. Romano, *Italy*, cit., p. 227.

[123] In contrast, notaries rarely refer to paid foreign legal databases or opinions of legal experts because of their extremely high costs nor do they use diplomatic channels because of their lengthiness. Ibidem, p. 237. See also E. Calò, *Le Nouveau Réseau Mondial du Notariat institué au sein de l'Union international du Notariat*, 15–17 février 2012, 2, available on the official website of the Hague Conference of Private International Law at www.hcch.net

puts them at risk of erroneously applying these laws. The issue of the notaries' responsibility in cases of erroneous application of foreign law, however, still remains unclear and should be further examined by Italian literature.[124]

In addition, the Swiss Institute of Comparative Law sent the aforementioned questionnaire concerning the application of foreign law to a number of Italian lawyers, academics amongst them. Six lawyers responded. According to their responses, the application of foreign law is frequent and is considerably increasing in both contentious and non-contentious cases. Italian lawyers highlighted that they are not obliged to apply foreign law in Italy in their advisory functions. Therefore, these lawyers admitted avoiding applying foreign law as much as possible, particularly because they are not familiar with foreign systems, especially of a non EU nature, and therefore they risk incurring professional liability.[125]

To ascertain foreign law lawyers mostly use the official sources of foreign laws available on the internet or in national libraries and the cooperation of foreign colleagues[126] and from time to time lawyers use the European Judicial Network in Civil and Commercial Matters. Yet, the lawyers emphasized the prohibitively high cost of access to foreign law and highlighted the difficulty in accessing information on foreign laws in Italy, which carries the risk of their erroneous application of these laws.[127]

6. Access to Foreign Law: Status Quo

Italy offers free access websites containing legislative and jurisprudential information of the Italian Constitutional Court and the European Union legal system.[128] Other Italian websites offering doctrinal and jurisprudential (Supreme Court, Court of Appeal, first instance courts) information are not freely accessible and require registration fees.[129] Some are even limited to practitioners, namely lawyers, notaries etc.[130] Moreover, Italian legislation and case-law (Italian Constitutional Court,

---

[124] G.P. Romano, *Italy,* cit., p. 286 ff.; E. Calò, cit., p. 2.

[125] Particularly, in litigation and in drafting legal documents related to inheritance law, family law, bankruptcy law, international and cross-border taxation, tort and contractual law. C. Leuzzi and G.P. Romano, *Italy,* cit., p. 225.

[126] In contrast, lawyers rarely refer to diplomatic channels, paid foreign legal databases, or opinions of legal experts because of their extremely high costs and they never use the mechanisms of the London Convention or bilateral mechanisms of judicial cooperation. Ibidem, p. 232.

[127] Ibidem, pp. 230–236.

[128] See the site for the official gazette (Gazzetta Ufficiale) See *supra*, para 1.4. See also See http://www.gazzettaufficiale.it/homePostLogin;jsessionid = 04Inf66nVoY88 + XXQ7RIvw__.ntc-as2-guri2a. See http://www.giurcost.org/. See *supra*, para 1.4.

[129] See the data bases mentioned by the Central Library of the Ministry of Justice: http://www.giustizia.it/giustizia/it/mg_7_4_3.wp. See *supra*, para 1.4.

[130] See the databases established by the competent services of the Supreme Court: http://www.cortedicassazione.it/AreaRiservata/AreaRiservata.asp. See *supra*, para 1.4.

Supreme Court, Court of Appeal, first instance courts) are published with commentaries in various legal journals.[131] Italy is included in the European Union's N-Lex website named "a common gateway to National law", which was launched in 2006 and provides a single access point with a common search interface for national legislation.[132]

Italy is not included in the meta-search engine of National Case Law that was created by the Network of the Presidents of the European Supreme Courts and released in April 2007. This meta-search engine allows one to simultaneously query several search engines of 20 EU Member States, and provides information on supreme court justices and legislation, including automatic translation facilities.[133]

The abovementioned European Judicial Network is available in Italy for judges to directly communicate with foreign judges in order to obtain legal information on foreign laws.[134] Yet, Italian judges and specialists are often unaware of this system's capacity in relation to the sharing of information on foreign laws.[135] The Hague Judicial Network is not available in Italy for judicial authorities to directly communicate with a foreign colleague to obtain legal information.[136]

As abovementioned, Italy is part of several multilateral and bilateral treaties concerning proof of and information on foreign law. With particular regard to the London Convention and the aforementioned "verbal notes" of the Embassy of Italy in The Hague, in 2006 Italy received 25 requests for assistance in ascertaining for-

[131] See the journals mentioned in the catalogue of the central library of the Ministry of Justice: http://opac.giustizia.it/SebinaOpac/Opac. See *supra*, para 1.4.

[132] This website is operated by the EU and allows access to each official database of national law of the 28 EU countries via a standard search screen, in all official languages. See the database at http://eur-lex.europa.eu/n-lex-s/index_en.htm. See the Italian database at http://eur-lex.europa.eu/n-lex-s/info/info_it/index_en.htm. See C.M. Germain, *Digitizing the World's Laws. Woking Paper*, in R.A. **Danner and J. Winterton,** *International Legal Information Management Handbook*, London, Ashgate, 2010, p. 181 ff.

[133] See the meta-search engine here: http://network-presidents.eu/rpcsjue/?lang=it. See C.M. Germain, *Digitizing* cit., p. 181 ff. The list of participating countries is available at http://network-presidents.eu/rpcsjue/status.php

[134] See the official website of the Italian Ministry of Justice http://www.giustizia.it/giustizia/it/mg_2_1_2_4.wp. Official statistical data on how frequently this system is used in Italy does not exist. According to the Swiss Institute Study, there is a general consensus among practitioners (judges, notaries, lawyers, public official registrars) that the European Judicial Network has enormous potential that has yet to be fulfilled.

[135] The sharing of information on foreign laws through the Network only appears in the aforementioned Recital 14 of the Rome III Regulation, according to which the European Judicial Network, "could play a part in assisting the courts with regard to the content of foreign law" (see *supra*, para 1.1.). Yet the sharing of information on foreign laws does not appear in the list of "recitals" of the Decision instituting the European Judicial Network or on any part of the Commission's website on the "Synthesis" of this Network. See Swiss Institute Study, Part III Synthesis Report with Recommendations, cit., p. 87.

[136] In fact, Italy has not yet fulfilled the requirement posed by Art. 2 of this resolution, according to which "States that have not designated Network judges are strongly encouraged to do so". See the official website at http://www.hcch.net/upload/haguenetwork.pdf

eign law, and directed 38 requests to foreign States.[137] This Convention establishes then a promising mechanism of cooperation. Yet, the potential of this mechanism remains unknown and unused in the European Judicial Area due to the complexities of this mechanism as a flaw of the Convention.[138]

7. Access to Foreign Law: Further Developments

7.1. *Practical Needs*

Given the reality of globalization and the cross-border movement and activity of persons and companies, the laws of foreign States inevitably affect more and more frequently those implicated in transnational circumstances. Thus, there is an increased need to improve access to foreign law. According to the survey of the Swiss Institute of Comparative Law, access to foreign law is needed by Italian practitioners most in the following areas: (i) Regarding lawyers, in the field of contracts, particularly when there is need to choose a foreign law to govern contractual obligations, or when one of the parties at least is a foreigner or when foreign law might be applicable due to PIL norms related to contracts. Also, commercial operations connected to more than one jurisdiction imply the issue of the application of foreign law by lawyers. Finally, Italian lawyers deal with foreign laws in inheritance law, bankruptcy law, international and cross-border taxation, and tort law.[139] (ii) Italian judges are faced with the issue of the application of foreign law in international cases related to contract law, inheritance law, tort law, competition law and maritime law. Also, Italian judges deal with the application of foreign law in proceedings related to the recognition and enforcement of foreign judgments and when implementing letters of rogation.[140] (iii) Italian notaries highlight being involved in the application of foreign law when drafting legal documents such as wills, contracts, minutes of shareholder meetings and matrimonial agreements·. Also, public notaries have a need to obtain information on foreign law when verifying the legal status of an applicant's person, namely for legal persons or assets abroad and in the context of legal counselling. In addition, reference to foreign law is implied in cases before

---

[137] Available at the Hague Conference website: http://www.hcch.net/upload/wop/genaff_pd09it.pdf. See *supra*, para 1.4.

[138] See *supra*, para 3.3. Furthermore, according to the survey of the Swiss Institute of Comparative Law, the reasons for not using the London Convention are threefold: a lack of awareness of the mechanism, the length of this mechanism, and the unavailability of the Convention to practitioners other than judges, namely notaries, lawyers and public official registrars. In addition, this Convention requests complex translations, increases the costs of the proceedings and allows information on the relevant foreign law to be given without knowledge of the factual elements of the specific case. See Swiss Institute Study, Part III Synthesis Report with Recommendations, cit., p. 59.

[139] See C. Leuzzi and G.P. Romano, *Italy*, cit., p. 224.

[140] Ibidem, pp. 225–226. See also above, para 2.2.

notaries related to corporation matters (for instance when a company relocates in Italy or abroad, or when a foreign company merges with an Italian one, or concludes agreements in Italy, which imply that the notary verifies the legal person's right to sign according to the applicable law), matrimonial property (for instance, when a notary drafts a real estate contract when a party is a foreigner, shall verify the contractual capacity of this foreign party and the sellers' and purchaser's marital status and matrimonial property regime), and inheritance issues (for instance when a notary drafts a will related to properties located abroad).[141] (iv) In Italy the single public registrar officer that replied to the questionnaire of the Swiss Institute of Comparative Law highlighted that she is faced with the issue of application of foreign law mainly in family law and personal rights cases.[142]

7.2. Conflict of Laws Solutions

Italian PIL norms are mainly bilateral in nature, and are therefore equally capable of determining whether Italian law or foreign law is applicable as the proper law in a transnational case. To fulfil this equality principle, the Italian PIL Statute purports to ascertain and apply the relevant foreign law ex officio and in line with the principle of *iura novit curia*. Also, in cases of failure to ascertain the applicable foreign law, Italian law can be applied only when the relevant conflict of laws rule does not establish any connecting factor other than the one adopted to invoke the foreign law which remained unascertained or when judicial authorities fail to establish even the other foreign laws recalled by other connecting factors adopted by the conflict of laws norm for the case in question.[143] Recourse to Italian law is then a subsidiary and residual option[144] and the Italian PIL system is in line with and goes even further than the resolution of the Institute of International Law on Equality of Treatment of the Law of the Forum and of Foreign Law,[145] the already mentioned Madrid Principles for a future EU Regulation on the application of foreign law; and the Principles of Transnational Civil Procedure of the American Law Institute.[146]

---

[141] C. Leuzzi and G.P. Romano, *Italy*, cit., pp. 226–227.

[142] In fact, Italian PIL rules in these matters typically adopt nationality as the prevalent connecting factor and the relevant parties are usually foreigners. Ibidem.

[143] See G.P. Romano, *Italy*, cit., pp. 282–283; S.M. Carbone, *La conoscenza* cit., p. 204; I. Queirolo (coordinator) and S.M. Carbone, P. Ivaldi, L. Carpaneto, C. Tuo, M.E. De Maestri, F. Pesce, cit., p. 246; L. Fumagalli, cit., p. 475.

[144] N. Boschiero, sub. Art. 14 cit., p. 1042; G.P. Romano, *Italy*, cit., p. 282; I. Queirolo (coordinator) and S.M. Carbone, P. Ivaldi, L. Carpaneto, C. Tuo, M.E. De Maestri, F. Pesce, cit., p. 246. S.M. Carbone, *La conoscenza* cit., p. 204.

[145] The Resolution was adopted in Saint-Jacques-de-Compostelle on September the 12th, 1989, under the Rapporteur *Mr. Pierre Gannagé*, and is available on the official website at http://www.idi-iil.org/idiE/resolutionsE/1989_comp_02_en.PDF

[146] See Principle 2, available on the official website at http://www.unidroit.org/english%20/principles/civilprocedure/main.htm

However, reliable and accessible global mechanisms with regard to the application of foreign law are not in force in Italy. Therefore, an increased burden on those affected by cross-border situations exists. Thus, when allowed by the Italian legal order according to the parties' wishes and their lawyers' advice,[147] Italian practitioners should avoid the application of foreign law, fearing irregular access to this law and delays in proceedings.[148] Yet, as highlighted by the European Commission and the Hague Conference on Private International Law in 2012, "access to foreign law is an important component of access to justice" (and therefore also of the human right to a fair trial), which "strengthens the rule of law and is fundamental to the proper administration of justice".[149] Thus, rather than reducing the application of foreign law and therefore the access to foreign law in Italy, more systemic measures on access to foreign law should be adopted at the global level through international treaties. It seems then feasible and desirable to harmonize through international multilateral or regional (i.e. EU) instruments the mechanisms to access foreign law.[150] However, since domestic rules concerning the status of foreign law in national proceedings, namely its being considered as a law or as a fact, that are in force in the various jurisdictions of the world are extremely heterogeneous, there is little likelihood of success for any attempt to harmonize through international multilateral or regional instruments this status.[151]

7.3. Methods of Facilitating Access to Foreign Law

The international instruments harmonising the mechanisms to access foreign law should focus on cross-border administrative and legal cooperation under the auspices of the Hague Conference of Private International Law. This instrument should not be exclusive in nature, but rather should be complementary to existing and future mechanisms that also facilitate access to the text and treatment foreign law. The instrument should facilitate:

---

[147] See C. Leuzzi and G.P. Romano, *Italy,* cit., p. 224.

[148] Ibidem.

[149] See Access to Foreign Law in Civil and Commercial Matters, Conclusions and Recommendations, number 3, available on the official website at http://www.hcch.net/upload/foreignlaw_concl_e.pdf (hereinafter: Access to Foreign Law).

[150] Swiss Institute Study, Part III Synthesis Report with Recommendations, cit., p. 7.

[151] See Access to Foreign Law number 4. See also the conclusion of the Hague Conference Works on Foreign Law, as recalled by its First Secretary, Lortie Philippe in *The Evolution of Work on Foreign Law at the Hague Conference on Private International Law,* pages unnumbered, available at http://www.legalaccess.eu/IMG/pdf/lortie-hcch-acces-droit-etranger.pdf (hereinafter: the Hague Works on Foreign Law). See also Swiss Institute Study, Part III Synthesis Report with Recommendations, cit., p. 8. Yet, according to the already recalled Madrid Principles an EU Regulation should be adopted to achieve uniformity in the various Member States on the topic of the status of foreign law also. See Madrid Principles I–XI. See C. Esplugues, J.L. Iglesias, G. Palao, cit., *passim.*

(i) improved online access to legal information on foreign law, namely by providing "free access", "reproducing and re-use", "integrity and authoritativeness", "preservation", "open formats, metadata and knowledge-based systems", "protection of personal data", "citations", "translations", "support and co-operation"[152];
(ii) additional access to foreign law via cross-border cooperation, not only for judicial authorities but also for practitioners, administrative bodies and other government officials, thus enhancing direct communication between judicial and non-judicial authorities[153];
(iii) access to foreign law via a global network of institutions and experts for more complex questions.[154]

---

[152] See the recommendations of the experts' works carried out between 2006 and 2009 in the frame of the Hague Conference of Private International Law, of the conference organised jointly by the European Commission and the Hague Conference on Private International Law from 15 to 17 February 2012, and of the Swiss Institute of Comparative Law. Swiss Institute Study, Part III Synthesis Report with Recommendations, cit., p. 8. See Access to Foreign Law, number 4. See also the Hague Works on Foreign Law.

[153] See Access to Foreign Law, number 4. See also the Hague Works on Foreign Law.

This part of the system on references of questions of foreign law should develop based on the model provided for by the court to court Memorandum of Understanding signed in 2010 between the Supreme Courts of New South Wales (Australia) and Singapore, and between the Chief Justices of the Supreme Court of New South Wales and of New York State (). This mechanism allows a court to request foreign courts to determine questions related to the applicable foreign law that are in issue in the proceedings before the requesting court, provided the parties consent. See Hon Justice P.L.G. BRERETON, *Proof of Foreign Law: Problems and Initiatives*, in 85 *American Law Journal* 2011, p. 1 ff.; J. SPIGELMAN, *Proof of Foreign Law by Reference to the Foreign Court*, in 127 *Law Quarterly Review* 2011, 208 ff.

[154] The Permanent Bureau, then, might facilitate a series of networks of qualified organisations (bar associations, comparative law institutes, organisations of notaries and other specialists), but the services of these organisations would not be provided on a free basis. See Access to Foreign Law, number 4. See also the Hague Works on Foreign Law.

Poland: Proof and Information About Foreign Law – Theory and Reality

Michal Wojewoda

Abstract Polish law is based on the assumption of equality of legal systems. All transborder cases are to be decided according to the law – be it Polish or foreign – which is indicated by a relevant conflict rule (applied *ex officio*). Whenever foreign law turns out to be applicable, the task of ascertaining its contents and applying it encumbers the judge who should use one of many methods available in this respect (including some international measures concerning the exchange of information on foreign law). In practical terms, though, courts usually involve the Ministry of Justice requesting texts of foreign regulations and information on foreign judicial practice.

On the other hand, outside judicial proceedings (e.g. in arbitration cases or when transborder issues are dealt with by Civil Registry Officers), the burden of applying foreign law appears to be even more cumbersome since no assistance of the Ministry of Justice is offered here.

Looking from a more general perspective, however, the real problem in cases with a foreign element seems to be more practical than legal. The truth is that lawyers in Poland are, by and large, very skeptical about applying foreign law and they tend to strongly support the *lex fori* approach.

Introduction

Polish law – as it stands on the books – does not devote too much attention to the problems of ascertainment, proof and application of foreign law. There are few statutory rules and they touch upon very basic issues only. Still, the problem is covered by abundant literature with most commentators (including judges of the Polish Supreme Court) taking similar views. These views will create the main point of reference for the current publication.

M. Wojewoda (✉)
Associate Professor, Faculty of Law and Administration, University of Lodz, Lodz, Poland
e-mail: michalw@uni.lodz.pl

Y. Nishitani (ed.), *Treatment of Foreign Law - Dynamics towards Convergence?*,
Ius Comparatum – Global Studies in Comparative Law 26,
DOI 10.1007/978-3-319-56574-3_12

There exists, however, a darker side of the problem. Not infrequently 'the law in action' does not follow theoretical guidelines. Lack of sufficient training in private international law, unwillingness to make efforts to ascertain the content of foreign regulations and reluctance to embark on the task of understanding and applying the rules of an 'alien' legal system ('fear of the unknown' syndrome) – such considerations are often present in a day-to-day courts' practice in Poland. They lead to situations when a civil case with a clearly visible international element is solved according to the *lex fori* with no reference to conflict of laws issues. What is more, the above attitude seems to be present not only in courts, where it meets with tacit endorsement of professional counsels representing the parties, but also in non-judicial practice.

I. Conflict of Laws Rules

Conflict of laws rules in Poland are to be found both in domestic and international sources. The most important piece of national legislation is the statute of 4th February 2011 on Private International Law (hereinafter 'the PIL Statute'),[1] which replaced the former statute of 12th November 1965. The non-domestic sources, which in fact enjoy precedence over national law in their respective spheres of application, are various international conventions (bilateral and multilateral) as well as the conflict-of-laws regulations of the European Union.

Despite the lack of a clear provision in this respect, it is universally agreed and have never been disputed by the Polish doctrine, that conflict of law rules – whatever their origin – should be mandatorily applied if a given situation has links with more than one legal system. From the constitutional point of view, all rules of private international law (both domestic and international) are a part of Polish law which ought to be observed and applied *ex officio* in any judicial or extrajudicial proceedings.[2]

Polish private international law consists predominantly of bilateral conflict rules which – employing various connecting factors – indicate the law applicable to particular types of issues. Depending on the factual situation, the governing legal system may be either Polish or foreign law. Similarly, in those cases when parties are free to choose applicable law, their choice may result in the application of either local or foreign provisions. One can make here some general remarks with regard to various types of civil cases:

---

[1] Dz.U. 2011, no. 80, item 432.

[2] See P. Rylski, Stwierdzenie treści prawa obcego i obcej praktyki sądowej w polskim postępowaniu cywilnym [Ascertaining the contents of foreign law and foreign court practice in the Polish civil procedure], in: *Aurea praxis aurea theoria. Księga pamiątkowa ku czci Profesora Tadeusza Ereciński ego* [*Aurea praxis aurea theoria. Book in honour of Professor Tadeusz Ereciński*], ed. J. Gudowski, K. Weitz, vol. I, Warszawa 2011, p. 1307; cf. W. Popiołek, M. Zachariasiewicz, Poland, in: *Application of Foreign Law*, ed. C. Esplugues, J.L. Iglesias, and G. Palao, Munich 2011, p. 280.

Taking into account that the most popular connecting factors in *personal matters* (incl. problems of capacity and issues of family or succession law) are nationality, domicile or habitual residence, it must be observed that cases concerning foreign nationals and/or persons living outside the territory of Poland are often decided according to foreign law. Moreover, it is not surprising that the applicable law will often be the law of one of the neighbouring states.

In *commercial cases*, on the other hand, it is the law of countries with which Poland maintains strong business links that is frequently applied. One has to remember that in such cases, in the absence of parties' choice, personal law of one of the contractors is usually applicable.[3] Thus, it may well be the law of a foreign business partner.

There is also a growing number of *cases concerning traffic accidents* that took place abroad. In these cases foreign law applies (*lex loci delicti*) pursuant to Art. 3 of the Hague Convention of 1971 on the Law Applicable to Traffic Accidents.

According to the data provided by the Polish Ministry of Justice for the purposes of this article, the greatest number of requests for information on foreign law were made in recent years with regard to:

- in succession matters: the law of Germany or of the United States;
- in family (matrimonial) matters: the Ukrainian law;
- in commercial matters: German, Italian or Spanish law.

Although the courts' inquiries with the Ministry of Justice (which constituted the basis for the above generalization) are not obligatory, they are definitely the most popular tool used to ascertain foreign law in courts' practice (see *infra* II.C.1) and therefore the statistics presented here seem quite representative.

II. Foreign Law Before Judicial Authorities

A. Nature of Foreign Law

The Polish legal system operates upon a basic assumption of the equality of laws of all countries.[4] There is no general rule which would give any precedence to the local (Polish) system and thus the application of foreign law should not be treated as an exception.[5] The decision as to which law is applicable should be taken impartially in each and every case on the basis of relevant conflict rules.

---

[3] See Art. 4–8 of the Regulation (EC) No 593/2008 of the European Parliament and of the Council of 17 June 2008 on the law applicable to contractual obligations (Rome I), O.J. UE 2008, L 177/6.

[4] T. Ereciński, J. Ciszewski, Międzynarodowe postępowanie cywilne [International civil procedure], Warszawa 2000, p. 266.

[5] M. Pazdan, Prawo prywatne międzynarodowe [Private international law], 15 ed., Warszawa 2012, p. 82.

Foreign law is treated on equal footing as Polish law. It is considered as 'law' and not merely as a problem of facts. At the same time, the external character of foreign rules is specifically acknowledged. It is well accepted that Polish courts will sometimes decide the case according to substantive rules enacted by a foreign legislator. Still, the sovereignty of the Polish judge is not affected since the application of foreign law is based on the imperative command of a conflict rule, which – whether found in the PIL Statute, some international treaty or in one of the European Union regulation – will always possess the authority of a constitutional source of Polish law. Thus, one must come to a conclusion that it is the will of the Polish lawmaker that constitutes formal grounds for applying in Poland legal provisions enacted in another country.

Notwithstanding the points mentioned above, it has to be remembered that there are certain restrictions concerning the application of foreign rules before Polish courts.[6] The most important role in this respect is played by the *ordre public* exception (Art. 7 of the PIL Statute). According to this provision, foreign law shall not be applied if its application would lead to a result that is contrary to the fundamental principles of the Polish legal order.

B. Application of Foreign Law

Art. 1143 §1 of the Polish Code of Civil Procedure (hereinafter 'PCCP') makes it clear in its first sentence that foreign law in Poland is always applied by the court *ex officio*. If relevant conflict rules point towards a foreign legal system making it applicable in a given case, the court is obliged to apply that law on its own motion. This statutory obligation is not circumscribed by any additional condition. In particular, the application of foreign rules is not subject to reciprocity in relations with states whose law is to be applied, nor does it depend on any formal request by the parties. Naturally, it is quite common that the parties would express their views as to which law is applicable (especially if there are doubts concerning the final outcome of the choice-of-law reasoning), but parties' opinions are not binding upon the court.

The judge must always take an independent decision based on the content of relevant choice-of-law provisions. Also in cases where the parties are free to choose the applicable law, the court should *ex officio* verify the effectiveness and validity of such choice in the light of the underlying conflict rule. It may also happen that the parties would change or revoke their original choice (even during court proceedings). Still, it must be kept in mind that the will of the parties may play some role only at the stage of ascertaining which law is applicable. Once it is established that the case is governed by a particular (foreign) legal system, the judge must proceed to apply the provisions of that system *ex officio*. Sometimes – when *renvoi* comes into play – the court will first check the conflict rules of foreign law, otherwise it will proceed to the merits of the case applying relevant substantive provisions.

[6] See T. Ereciński, J. Ciszewski, *op.cit.*, p. 290 ff.

C. Ascertainment of Foreign Law

The same provision of the PCCP (Art. 1143 §1 first sentence), which makes it obligatory to apply foreign law whenever conflict rules so require, determines also the question of ascertaining the content of foreign law. It is again the court that is encumbered with the task of getting to know what the position of foreign applicable law is with regard to the dispute at hand. The court, on its own motion, must take all possible steps to ascertain the applicable rules of the foreign system.

This does not mean, however, that the '*iura novit curia*' principle is accepted in Poland with regard to foreign law. The prevailing doctrinal view holds that the obligation to act *ex officio* does not amount to a (fictitious) presumption that the court actually knows foreign rules and regulations.[7] On the contrary, in practical terms it may be taken for granted that a Polish judge shall not be familiar with foreign law and therefore its contents must be proved by appropriate means. This marks an important difference with the situation when domestic law is applicable. Here the '*iura novit curia*' principle is fully operative and it leads to a conclusion that Polish law must never be subject to proof (thus, even expert legal opinions that are sometimes submitted in course of disputes based on Polish law are treated exclusively as private views of the plaintiff or the defendant).

Unlike the internal law, foreign rules will have to be identified and ascertained in a special process that will be inspired, or at least closely monitored, by the judge. This process shows close resemblance to regular evidentiary proceedings undertaken to establish facts relevant for a given case. Still, it is argued that proof of foreign law will have a distinct nature. Three main differences are usually mentioned here.[8] Firstly, the methods of ascertaining foreign law are not limited to means of proof envisaged by procedural law for proving facts. Secondly, the roles of the court and the parties are totally different. And, last but not least, the consequences of wrong ascertainment of foreign law will differ in comparison to errors made in taking factual evidence.

All the above points deserve additional commentary – the first two are dealt with immediately below while the problem of potential faults while proving foreign law will be presented in part III, infra, in the context of judicial review.

1. As far as means of proof of foreign law are concerned, the PCCP expressly mentions only two possibilities. These are:
    (i) the request to the Ministry of Justice concerning the text of foreign law and information on foreign judicial practice (Art. 1143 §1 PCCP second sentence), and
    (ii) the expert opinion (Art. 1143 §3 *in fine* PCCP).

At the same time, Art. 1143 §3 PCCP makes it clear that the court may also avail itself of 'other means' of ascertainment. There are, for instance, special methods

[7] See W. Popiołek, M. Zachariasiewicz, *op.cit.*, p. 279.

[8] See P. Rylski, *op.cit.*, p. 1319.

envisaged in various international instruments such as bilateral and multilateral conventions as well as the European Union law.[9] The *communis opinio* holds that in fact any possible source of information on foreign law may be utilized.[10] Consequently, a non exhaustive list of informal possibilities which are open to the judge includes:

- consulting foreign official journals, case law publications, various commentaries, academic textbooks, monographs and other legal literature;
- exploring Internet sources, especially official databases containing legal texts and/or relevant judgments of foreign courts.

It is also conceivable that the court will use its private knowledge acquired in former cases, during professional training, through personal contacts with foreign lawyers or otherwise. It is advised, though, that the court always inform the parties of the source of its knowledge and whenever possible it should attach a copy of relevant documents to the case dossier so that the parties could comment and present their views. It is also recommended that when looking for the best way of finding the contents of foreign law in a given case, the court should consider more than one method. The final choice ought to be based on such considerations as reliability, efficiency and cost.[11] The value and the subject matter of the case should also be taken into account.[12] On the other hand, it is admitted that speed and immediacy plays a relatively smaller role in cases with an international element than in purely domestic disputes. One has to accept that arriving at the right decision will normally take more time when foreign law applies.[13] Regrettably, not always are the above considerations strictly followed in practice.

The only means of ascertainment that should not be utilized, as wholly inappropriate, is the questioning of witnesses or of the parties themselves. These methods are used only when establishing the facts of the case. At the same time, it is clear that no formal testimonies will be accepted in the process of ascertaining the content and meaning of foreign rules.[14] Persons having specialized legal knowledge in a given field may be summoned as experts but not as witnesses. And the parties are naturally welcome to help the judge with proof of foreign law, just as they are free to comment upon all court's findings in this respect, but they should never be called to formally testify to that.

The expert opinion on foreign law is rarely used in civil proceedings in Poland despite its clear advantages. It may help the court not only with finding all the applicable

---

[9] These methods are presented in more detail in part V below.

[10] K. Sznajder-Peroń, in: System Prawa Prywatnego [System of Private Law], vol. 20A - Prawo prywatne międzynarodowe [Private International Law], ed. M. Pazdan, Warsaw 2014, ch. III, §17, p. 523.

[11] P. Rylski, *op.cit.*, p. 1320–1321.

[12] M. Margoński, Ustalanie treści obcego (czeskiego) prawa w sprawie o wyrównanie szkody doznanej w wypadku komunikacyjnym [Ascertaining the contents of foreign (Czech) law in a case for damages concerning a traffic accident], *Glosa* 3/2013, p. 86.

[13] Cf. T. Ereciński, J. Ciszewski, *op.cit.*, p. 281.

[14] See K. Sznajder-Peroń, *op.cit.*, p. 524.

rules but also with understanding and interpreting them in the actual circumstances of the case (the expert will have access to the whole case dossier). There are no special requirements with regard to persons acting as potential experts, except that they should possess sufficient expertise on the subject. Experts may be individual persons – either Polish nationals or foreigners – such as academics knowledgeable in foreign law or private lawyers with practical experience. It is equally possible to make inquiries to a scientific institute (domestic or international) with a view to acquiring their opinion.

The rules on civil procedure require that experts be impartial. They should be released from their duty (also upon party's request) if there are reasons to believe that their opinion may not be fully objective e.g. when there are family or business links or other close liaisons with either party.

The main reason why expert opinions are not very often used in practice seems to be practical difficulties in finding a good expert and potentially high costs, especially when an international institute is asked for assistance.

Despite the prevailing view, which finds support in the Supreme Court case law,[15] that the request to the Ministry of Justice should be used after the court has explored other possible means of ascertaining foreign law, this particular method appears to be a default choice in a majority of cases. There is a special department in the Ministry of Justice which gathers information on foreign law through various channels (see *infra* V.E). Depending on availability, the Ministry shall provide legal texts as well as other materials which might help to solve the relevant legal issues. The formal procedure requires that the inquiry to the Ministry of Justice be accompanied by the case dossier. This allows for additional commentaries or (informal) hints by the Ministry to be given to the court in order to avoid serious mistakes in the choice-of-law reasoning, such as forgetting about the *renvoi* mechanism or applying the PIL Statute when international conflict rules are applicable. Still, the legal texts or recommendations provided by the Ministry are not binding upon the court when deciding the case. All gathered materials as well as possible comments from the parties must be independently assessed by the judge so that a substantive judgment is handed down. This judgment, based on foreign law, may still be subject to control if an appeal is lodged by either party. Such appeal could concern any mistakes that influenced the final decision of the court including potential faults in ascertaining, interpreting and applying foreign law (for judicial review, see *infra* III).

It is admitted that one of the vital problems (difficult to resolve in practice) is the reliability of information on foreign law. There are no institutional methods of checking whether texts provided by the parties, found on the Internet or even sent by the Ministry of Justice are accurate and up to date. Similarly, it is hard to establish whether a decision of a foreign court cited as a point of reference is really a leading case or, possibly, an aberration from a long established line of judgments. Some of these problems may be avoided when special tools are employed with regard to proof of foreign law, such as the London Convention or the European Judicial Network, as they involve communication with competent institutions of the state whose law is applicable. These methods, which are definitely more reliable, are commented upon in more detail in part V below.

[15] See e.g. the Supreme Court judgment of 5 October 2012, IV CSK 68/12.

2. The second peculiarity of ascertaining the content of foreign law in judicial proceedings in Poland is the distribution of tasks between the court and the parties. It is well established that the main responsibility in this respect lies with the court and there is no obligation of the parties whatsoever to participate in the process of proving foreign law. Case law of the Polish Supreme Court is very consistent on this issue.[16] The parties are not obliged to provide information on foreign law and they must not be sanctioned in any way for not helping the court. On the other hand, the parties are always welcome to assist the judge by providing relevant information or by verifying the reliability of materials already gathered. They may also present – throughout the proceedings – their views on how foreign law should be applied in a given case. Parties' rights in this respect are not always exercised in practise. Sometimes it is a result of the adopted tactics. A party to civil proceedings (especially the defendant) is not always interested in a prompt judgment. Similarly, any mention of foreign law can be intentionally avoided for fear of an unfavourable solution offered by an 'alien' legal system. However, if a party decides to be active, appropriate steps can be taken at any stage of the proceedings. Assuming that parties' arguments concerning foreign law (its applicability or its contents) are accurate, the court should not dismiss them on the grounds of late submission. It does not matter, either, that the initial position of the party in question was completely different. The problem of applicability of foreign law, its contents or its interpretation can be raised as late as in the party's final speech before the court of first instance or even in the course of appellate proceedings.[17]

Ascertaining foreign law by the court may entail certain costs. The most obvious ones are the costs of translations (even texts provided by the Ministry of Justice are often in original language). Expert opinions may prove quite expensive, too, especially when a foreign institute is asked for assistance. All expenditure provisionally covered by the court will ultimately be treated as a part of the costs to be apportioned between the parties according to the final outcome of the case. Normally, these costs will be paid by the losing party and if there is no clear winner, they will be divided proportionally.

D. Interpretation and Application of Foreign Law

If a Polish court comes to a conclusion that foreign law is applicable in the case at hand, efforts should be made to solve the case exactly in the same way as it would be done in the country of origin. With regard to all substantive issues that await resolution, the Polish judge should follow, as far as possible, the approach normally

[16] See e.g. judgments of the Supreme Court of 3rd March 2011, II PK 208/10 and of 14th July 2010, V CSK 7/10.

[17] See the Supreme Court judgment of 9th May 2007, II CSK 60/07.

adopted in the applicable legal system. This presupposes that when familiarizing themselves with texts of foreign regulations the judges should apply methods of interpretation typical of the system in question. If necessary, recourse should be made to legal commentaries and/or to relevant case law of foreign courts. It would be a clear mistake to use interpretation methods based on Polish law or to apply analogies to solutions adopted in similar cases with no international element. It has to be kept in mind that even if the wording of applicable foreign regulations is identical with Polish law, there might still be differences concerning the interpretation and application of a given rule.

One of important implications that follow from the above remarks is the conclusion that also in cases when a gap in foreign law is encountered, the judge should embark upon the task of filling such gap in exactly the same way as it would be done in the country of origin. Local methods – which are normally employed by the Polish court in other cases – are prohibited.

This way of reasoning is rather unanimously accepted in legal writings.[18] It also finds support of the Supreme Court whenever problems of interpretation and application of foreign law appear before that court.[19] However, the day-to-day reality is less encouraging. The access to foreign materials is often limited. Not infrequently must the court solve the case relying only on a bear text of a foreign statute with no supplementary materials. What is more, the judge will normally not be able to read and understand the text in its original version. Translations into Polish language, which are used, are not always accurate. Since there are no dedicated court interpreters who would specialize in translating legal texts, a risk that a gist of legal controversy may simply be lost in translation is relatively high.[20]

E. Failure to Establish Foreign Law

If the application of conflict rules results in a conclusion that foreign law is applicable but – despite court's efforts – the contents of foreign law is not established in reasonable time, then Polish law becomes applicable as a substitute legal system pursuant to Art. 10 section 2 of the PIL Statute.

It is universally acknowledged that the above provision must not be an excuse to avoid the application of foreign law. The recourse to the *lex fori* is the *ultimum refugium* to be used when all efforts made by the court with regard to proof of foreign law have failed.[21] One has to remember that this possibility was introduced in order to avoid the denial of justice. The solution is based on the assumption that if the

---

[18] See T. Ereciński, J. Ciszewski, *op.cit.*, p. 283 ff.

[19] Cf. the Supreme Court judgment of 5 October 2012, IV CSK 68/12.

[20] All texts in foreign languages, which serve as 'evidence' in civil proceedings must be 'processed' by certified sworn translators - they are not legal specialists, though, but people with general linguistic competence.

[21] Cf. P. Rylski, *op.cit.*, p. 1334.

court has jurisdiction and there are no formal obstacles which would thwart the proceedings, the case should end with a substantive judgment. This judgment must always be based on some legal system and the use of local law is a natural choice when rules of a generally applicable foreign system cannot be accessed.

It should be pointed out that art. 10 section 2 of the PIL Statute is a general clause whose sphere of application was intentionally left unclear.[22] The open ended character of the provision in question results from the referral to 'reasonable time' during which foreign law should be ascertained. In an attempt to make the use of the above rule more predictable following remarks can be made:

- Art. 10 section 2 must not be relied upon unless the court has undertaken serious efforts with regard to finding the content of foreign law; the absolute minimum seems to be the inquiry with the Ministry of Justice resulting in a negative response;
- the 'reasonable time' criterion should be seen in the special context of proceedings involving international elements where foreign law turns out to be applicable; it is submitted that in such proceedings the necessity to thoroughly assess all circumstances of the case and to apply foreign rules in a proper manner should be given precedence over the need for a prompt solution (in urgent situations temporary measures may be taken based on domestic law).[23] By and large, such cases may be expected to last longer than disputes of purely internal character where Polish law applies;
- in assessing how much time should be devoted to establishing the contents of foreign law, the subject matter of the proceedings and its value should be taken into account;
- the court shall not be excused from its obligation to ascertain foreign law even if the parties express their readiness to revert to the Polish system as a substitute option (the situation is naturally different if – further to relevant conflict rules – the parties are free to choose local law as applicable also during court proceedings).

Some authors observe[24] that difficulties with ascertaining foreign law should not be validly raised with regard to legal systems of the Member States of the European Union, especially now when the European Judicial Network has become operational (see *infra* V.B). One can also find a more radical view that in all situations when a legal system of a country with which Poland has diplomatic relations applies, art. 10 section 2 of the PIL Statute should never come into play.[25]

---

[22] Cf. P. Czubik, Klauzula generalna przewidująca "rozsądny termin" dla ustalenia treści prawa obcego – rzekome czy rzeczywiste niebezpieczeństwo dla praktyki notarialnej [The 'reasonable time' clause for ascertaining the contents of foreign law – an imaginary or real threat to the notarial practice], *Nowy Przegląd Notarialny* 3(53)/2012, p. 11.

[23] See T. Ereciński, J. Ciszewski, *op.cit.*, p. 281.

[24] M. Cichomska, Metody ustalania treści prawa obcego a Europejska Sieć Sądownicza [Methods of ascertaining the contents of foreign law and the European Judicial Network], *Polski Proces Cywilny* 2(7)/2012, p. 307.

[25] See P. Czubik, *op.cit.*, p. 8 and p. 10.

In any event, it is clear that courts must not give up their efforts to ascertain the contents of applicable law too easily. Art. 10 section 2 of the PIL Statute does not provide a legitimate way to circumvent the conflict of laws mechanism making it possible to try an international case according to the *lex fori*.

Notwithstanding the above, one has to remember, too, about a special provision present in the PIL Statute (*lex specialis*), which takes precedence over art. 10 section 2. It is art. 3 section 1 of the PIL Statute, which comes into play when there are problems with ascertaining the national law (*lex patriae*) of a given person. In such a case, first of all an attempt should be made to get access to the relevant provisions of the law of domicile or habitual residence. Only if this special rule does not help and the applicable law is still not ascertained, as an *ultima ratio* recourse can be made to Polish law further to art. 10 section 2 of the PIL Statute.

III. Judicial Review

A. Conflict of Law Rules

Any defects in the interpretation or application of conflict of law rules may constitute the basis for an appeal to the court of second instance. As it was already mentioned, private international law regulations are a part of Polish law and thus all errors relating to their use by the court are treated exactly in the same way as other errors in law.

In practice several different types of mistakes may appear. The most evident ones will include:

- applying conflict rules of the domestic PIL Statute when an international convention or an EU regulation should be used;
- wrong characterization of the claim resulting in identifying the applicable law on the basis of conflict rules devoted for a different sort of problems (e.g. treating the case as contractual when conflict rules for delicts should rather be used);
- faulty interpretation of a conflict rule leading to the application of an inappropriate legal system;
- an error concerning one of general mechanisms of private international law such as *renvoi* or the *ordre public* clause.

B. Foreign Law

By way of introduction, it should be pointed out that all potential mistakes with regard to applicable foreign law would also constitute – by itself – an offence of Polish law. That is because all such mistakes can be treated as a breach of private international law of the forum whose rules require that foreign law ought to be applied correctly.[26] However, it is universally accepted in Poland that errors in applying or interpreting foreign law may, and in fact should, be invoked directly. They are all errors in law and as such they are subject to revision in appellate proceedings.

Moreover, since the appeal model adopted in Poland requires total reappraisal of the case merits, the court of second instance should take into account, *ex officio*, also those substantive errors that are not indicated by the appellant.[27]

It can be added that mistakes concerning foreign law will not be different from those which appear in domestic cases with regard to Polish substantive provisions. One could mention here, for example, choosing a wrong set of applicable rules, applying provisions which are no longer in force, wrong interpretation of foreign law or an incorrect filling up of a legal gap in the applicable legal system.[28]

C. The Supreme Court Appeal

In both types of cases – including breaches of Polish conflict rules and breaches of foreign law – there might be a possibility to lodge an appeal to the Supreme Court for the cassation of the decision of the court of second instance. This is an extraordinary type of appeal under Polish law. Generally, there must be a good reason for the case to be heard by the Supreme Court (these reasons are listed in the PCCP). There are also certain negative conditions barring cassation in some types of cases. Consequently, the first stage of review proceedings in the Supreme Court involves a general (formal) appraisal of the case in order to grant or deny leave to appeal.

The material grounds to lodge a cassation – to be assessed at the second stage of review – are also rather limited. In cases with an international element, the cassation may be successful if a fault in applying or interpreting the law is alleged and proved by the appellant. Such fault may concern either rules of private international law or the substantive provisions of foreign law. In the latter case, it will normally be the task of the appellant to present necessary justification and to prove the alleged fault in the application of foreign law (otherwise no leave to appeal will probably be granted).[29] This may involve a private expert's opinion that would authoritatively explain the way in which foreign law should be applied. If necessary, the Supreme Court may, by itself, take required steps to ascertain foreign law in order to review the case on its merits and to rectify faulty judgments of lower courts. In practice, however, if the arguments of the appellant are persuasive, the case will be sent back for reappraisal to the court of second instance with some binding guidelines. These guidelines will normally highlight the most important legal points to be reconsidered, including problems of foreign law.

[26] T. Ereciński, J. Ciszewski, *op.cit.*, p. 294–295.

[27] P. Rylski, *op.cit.*, p. 1339.

[28] Cf. T. Ereciński, J. Ciszewski, *op.cit.*, p. 298.

[29] Cf. W. Popiołek, M. Zachariasiewicz, *op.cit.*, p. 283.

Summing up, it has to be stressed that the sheer fact that private international law issues are at the bottom of an appeal (to the court of second instance or to the Supreme Court) will mark no practical difference during appellate (cassation) proceedings.

IV. Foreign Law in Other Instances

Due to a constant increase of the cross-border relations in civil matters, which is observed in Poland, problems of ascertainment, interpretation and application of foreign law become more and more popular also in non-judicial proceedings. Conflict rules are addressed to all persons and thus they should be observed not only by courts. In fact, there is a number of institutions that become involved – in their various capacities – in private law cases with foreign element.

Regrettably, no special rules have been put in place to facilitate access to foreign law in such instances. The Code of Civil Procedure as well as relevant international instruments apply only in judicial proceedings. No other bodies may avail themselves of special procedures which are designed to help ascertain the contents of foreign law (see II.C and V).

The most important instances when foreign law may prove applicable outside the courtroom settings are briefly presented below.

A. Civil Registry

As far as public bodies are concerned, private international law issues are most commonly present in the activities of the Civil Registry. It is an administrative authority entrusted with various tasks with regard to civil status of natural persons. To take some examples, Civil Registry Officers shall evaluate the capacity of spouses to enter into marriage, are competent to receive declarations of paternity with regard to illegitimate children or may assist in the process of making a will (testament).

It is not unusual anymore that foreign elements would appear in the course of such activities. Typically, it will be a non-Polish nationality of the interested person that causes private international law questions. Since nationality is a popular connecting factor in family matters, foreign law can prove applicable. Surprisingly, though, there are no special procedures nor any officially authorized methods available to Civil Registry Officers that would help to find the applicable foreign rules.[30] The Ministry of Justice turns down potential requests to provide the text of foreign law since Art. 1143 PCCP does not apply in non judicial proceedings. That is why

[30] The difficult situation of the Civil Registry Officers is analyzed by M. Wojewoda, Prawo obce w praktyce polskich urzędów stanu cywilnego [Foreign law in Polish Civil Registry practice], *Metryka* 1/2014, p. 33 ff.

an unofficial tool is often employed in practice whereby inquiries are made with local diplomatic posts of the countries whose law is applicable. It is to be remembered, though, that such addressees are under no obligation to provide legal information and when they do, it is only out of international courtesy.[31]

B. Notaries

Another typical group of situations where problems of foreign law may turn up is the daily practice of notaries. Notaries in Poland are qualified private lawyers performing certain public functions (Latin notaries). In particular, some legal acts, transactions or declarations must be made before or at least be authorised by a notary. Sometimes a special form of a notarial deed is necessary.

In all such situations notaries are obliged to make sure that acts performed before them are not illegal and are not effected *in fraudem legis*. This principle applies with regard to all activities undertaken under Polish law, but it is not clear to what extent it should be used in cases with an international element.[32] It is submitted that notaries should know and apply conflict rules which are in force in Poland. They ought to be prepared to advise their clients whether the Polish or foreign law applies in the situation in question. However, the notary is not expected to know foreign law. Thus, they may refuse to assist in a legal transaction if they cannot secure its legality and correctness.[33] It is possible, though, that a notary will be ready to make a (private) effort to ascertain the contents of the relevant legal system (in order not to lose clients).[34] Sufficient knowledge of foreign law will make it possible that a legal act in question is performed in a respective notarial form.

Although no formal help in this respect has been offered so far to notaries by the Polish legislator,[35] projects are made to open the possibility to make inquiries with the Ministry of Justice also for the purposes of the notarial practice.[36]

[31] Cf. M. Margonski, Metodyka ustalania treści obcego prawa spadkowego [The methodology of ascertaining the contents of foreign succession law], *Przegląd Sądowy* 6/2009, p. 76.

[32] M. Pazdan, Czynności notarialne w międzynarodowym prawie spadkowym [Notarial activities in the international law of succession], *Rejent* 4(84)/1998, p. 100.

[33] A. Oleszko, Stosowanie prawa obcego przez polskiego notariusza [The application of foreign law by a Polish notary], in: II Kongres Notariuszy Rzeczypospolitej Polskiej. Referaty i opracowania [2nd Congress of Notaries of the Republic of Poland. Papers and Essays], Poznań/Kluczbork 1999, p. 212.

[34] See M. Pazdan, *op.cit.* 1998, p. 100–101.

[35] A. Oleszko, *op.cit.*, p. 210–212.

[36] At the time when this publication went to print (Autumn 2016) Polish notaries already enjoyed limited possibility of requesting the assistance of the Ministry of Justice with regard to ascertaining the text of foreign law. According to Art. 95da §2 of the Notarial Law of 1991 (as amended in 2015) such possibility opens in a transborder case when a certificate of succession is to be issued by a notary.

C. Arbitration

Currently, there exist no special regulations concerning proof of foreign law in arbitration proceedings. If a given case is to be decided according to foreign rules, the arbitrators will not enjoy any of the official possibilities which are open to the state judge. In particular, no assistance from the Ministry of Justice will be available or the possibility to use the London Convention and the European Judicial Network (see *infra* V). Nevertheless, as it becomes clear from the experience of one of the permanent courts of arbitration in Poland (the court attached to the Polish Confederation Lewiatan), foreign law is hardly ever invoked in arbitration proceedings.

D. Counsels

Finally, a couple of words should be said with regards to advocates, legal counsels and other private lawyers, whose role consists in advising or representing their clients. Whenever they come across private international issues in their professional practice, e.g. when preparing a contract or drafting a will in a case where foreign law applies, they will normally take recourse either to Internet sources, various databases and library materials or they will try to use unofficial contacts with their counterparts in other countries to obtain sufficient legal feedback. Again, it has to be repeated that there are no institutionalized methods whatsoever that could be utilized in this respect.

V. Access to Foreign Law

A. General Remarks

The Republic of Poland participates in various international schemes concerning the information on foreign law. Generally they are based on multilateral or bilateral conventions but there is also a relatively new mechanism – the European Judicial Network – that was introduced by the European Union in recent years. All these schemes are used as means of acquiring knowledge about foreign law in cases with an international element but they are designed to help the state courts only. As it will be explained below, the central role in the whole process is always played in Poland by the Ministry of Justice.

It should be remembered that the same channels of communication are utilized when information on Polish law is needed in other countries. Still, it is worth adding that the Polish Sejm (the lower chamber of Parliament) runs also a special on-line database[37] where all legal acts enacted in Poland from the year 1918 until today (both binding and obsolete) can be accessed free of charge. Those who visit the website can use an automated search engine to find the particular texts, but no acts are delivered on individual demand and no hints concerning interpretation of Polish law are given. All texts are available exclusively in Polish language. The particular texts are accompanied by a bibliographic note explaining, among other things, when a given act entered into force and if it is still binding. Consolidated versions are also available with regard to those acts that underwent revision.

Another important internet site that should be mentioned here is the official database with decisions (judgments) of selected state courts of all levels (with the exclusion of the Supreme Court).[38] The search engine makes it possible to look for decisions of a particular court, to track down decisions concerning a given legal problem or to find an individual case identified by its official index. The number of judgments available to the public (in both civil and criminal cases) is still growing and currently exceeds 33,000.[39] Still, only the original Polish version of the decisions and their motives is published. A similar service concerning case law of the Supreme Court is available.[40] There is also a separate database with judgments of administrative courts.[41]

Alongside public databases, there are many commercial ones (run on-line or available on CDs) which provide information on Polish law. These databases would normally contain both legal texts, court decisions, commentaries, articles as well as templates of typical contracts, court petitions and other legal motions. At least some portion of the materials will normally be accessible in selected foreign languages such as English or German. The translations are not officially authorized but they are quite reliable. The fees for using such databases depend on the type and scope of required access.

B. European Judicial Network

Being a member of the European Union, Poland participates in a project called the European Judicial Network. It is based on the Council Decision of 28 May 2001[42] but the initiative got a new impetus following the amendments introduced by the Decision of the European Parliament and of the Council of 18 June 2009 (effective as from 1 January 2011).[43]

37 http://isip.sejm.gov.pl

38 http://orzeczenia.ms.gov.pl

39 The database last accessed on November 1, 2014.

40 http://www.sn.pl/orzecznictwo

41 http://orzeczenia.nsa.gov.pl

42 Council Decision 2001/470/EC.

43 Decision 568/2009/EC of the European Parliament and of the Council.

The objectives of the network are twofold. On the one hand, basic information on national laws of particular Member States is made available to the general public through a special internet site[44] where relevant data is available in 22 languages of the European Union. On the other hand, judicial cooperation in civil and commercial matters is facilitated, as between the Member States, by establishing a special system of exchange of legal information. The network consists of many contact points which are established internally in all Member States. In Poland, the responsibilities of a contact point have been assigned first of all to the Ministry of Justice. Acting in this capacity, the Ministry provides information on Polish law on request from other contact points, but at the same time it gathers information on foreign law when it is needed in Polish courts. The network was meant to be flexible as well as reliable. Accordingly, there are no formal requirements concerning languages or methods of communication between contact points and the reliability of the system is guaranteed by designated (experienced) judges who are involved in the activities of contact points. Interestingly, the participation of associations of other legal professions has been also envisaged in the network.

It still remains to be seen how the new possibilities will be explored in practice. For the time being, it seems that local judges in Poland are not sufficiently acquainted with the functioning of the network (see *infra* E).

C. London Convention

Another important international instrument that has been applicable in Poland for more than 20 years now is the 1968 London Convention on Information on Foreign Law.[45] It allows Polish courts to request legal information from abroad whenever law of another participating country proves applicable in a case at hand. Here again, it is the Ministry of Justice that acts as an intermediary who will pass the local court's request to the competent institution of another state. Taking into account that the number of signatories applying this international act counts 45, the London Convention seems to be a mighty instrument.

But the reality is not so encouraging. There are certain drawbacks that make the whole system rather unpopular. The request must be prepared in the official language of the addressee, which involves translations. Only the traditional methods of communication are used, which makes the process slow, especially that not all countries react with desired urgency. Finally, it has to be remembered that the request is not accompanied by the dossier of the case so replies are often very general and not really tailored to the facts of the dispute. It is observed that in some instances the internet search for a text of applicable law may bring similar results as a lengthy procedure of the formal request under the Convention.[46]

---

[44] Originally http://ec.europa.eu/civiljustice, now https://e-justice.europa.eu.

[45] Poland ratified the London Convention in 1992.

[46] Cf. M. Cichomska, *op.cit.*, p. 302.

D. Bilateral Treaties

When presenting, from the Polish perspectives, the instruments allowing for the exchange of information concerning various legal systems, one should also mention bilateral acts i.e. the consular conventions as well as numerous agreements on judicial cooperation in civil (and criminal) matters. Over the past years Poland has signed such conventions with some 30 countries. There is also one special instrument devoted exclusively to proof of foreign law, which is the treaty of 1986 between Poland and Belgium on the exchange of legal information. All the above international agreements provide for the possibility of requesting information concerning the legal system of the other contracting state. This will ensure access to legal texts and – in some cases – also to case law or other materials that can help with the interpretation of foreign rules.

E. The Role of the Ministry of Justice

An important factor in all cases when information on foreign law is officially gathered in Poland is the involvement of the Ministry of Justice. To be more precise, it is the Department of International Cooperation and Human Rights that will process all inquiries concerning foreign legal systems. It is a regular practice that the Polish court seized of the case where foreign law applies would address the Ministry of Justice on a general procedural basis of Art. 1143 §1 PCCP and the Ministry would then be free to choose the best way of gathering requested information. Sometimes bilateral treaties are put into operation and in other cases the European Judicial Network is utilised. Some authors assert, though, that the Ministry must not decide for itself and it should always turn back to the court for clarifications if an international instrument is to be used.[47] This definitely holds true with regard to the London Convention which must be always expressly invoked by the very court that makes an inquiry and where some additional conditions specified by the Convention (e.g. translations) must be met at the time of preparing the original request.

As far as statistical data is concerned, in the year 2012 the Ministry of Justice received 988 court inquiries regarding foreign law. The majority of cases concerned European legal systems (659), then the laws of various North American (138) and Asian (108) countries, with the rest distributed between the states of Africa (37), South America (32) and Australia (14). In 2013 (until October), the number of requests reached 1171 (which reflects the ongoing intensification of international relations in civil matters). The regional distribution of cases follows roughly the same pattern as in the preceding year – Europe (791), North America (157), Asia (134), Africa (41), South America (34) and Australia (14).[48]

---

[47] M. Cichomska, *op.cit.*, p. 308–309.

[48] All data based on information received from the Ministry of Justice for the purposes of this publication.

It has to be added that sometimes, in more standard cases (e.g. when the capacity of a foreigner to marry is at stake), the Ministry of Justice will be able to provide requested information from its own archives without launching any extended search.

As a final remark it must be reiterated, that whatever materials are received by the court from whatever source, they must be always critically analysed as to their suitability in the dispute at hand. What is more, as far as the substantive solution is concerned, the court should take the approach that would conform, as far as possible, to the attitude adopted in the country of origin. One has to remember that every case where foreign law applies should ultimately be solved *aliena lege artis*.

VI. Access to Foreign Law: Further Developments

The remarks in this final part of the article will be rather subjective as they reflect personal beliefs of the author. These beliefs are based on the author's professional experience as a legal counsel and on his academic involvement as a university teacher. The conclusions can be made in several points:

In relation to the present situation concerning access to foreign law in Poland, no serious reform seems necessary. As far as judicial authorities are concerned, a few methods of ascertaining foreign law are expressly envisaged and regulated by the law but at the same time the judge is invited to use any other means in order to acquire sufficient knowledge of the applicable legal system. This solution is satisfactory. As it is argued below, it is not the law but the awareness and attitude of judges that should be changed so that the challenge of applying foreign law is properly tackled.

Admittedly, the use of expert's opinions could be more popularised. It has to be realised that especially in complex cases when foreign law applies, the court will hardly be able to hand down a correct judgment if no assistance is provided from an impartial expert, with an inside view of the applicable legal system, who is given full access to the facts of the case. To this end experience of other European countries (e.g. Germany) could be used where experts on foreign law are often invited to assist in the proceedings. Possibly, some international courses could be organised – under the aegis of the European Union or otherwise – to train potential experts, to make them understand their role in international cases and to teach them proper methodology of writing opinions on foreign law.

In case of non-judicial bodies – such as Civil Registry – some reform of the law could probably be undertaken. Still, it appears that what would do here is the extension of the sphere of operation of Art. 1143 PCCP whereby all public institutions, competent in cases where international elements may turn up and where foreign law might apply, are allowed to make inquiries to the Ministry of Justice.

As far as private lawyers (including notaries) are concerned, it seems that they should develop their own ways of getting information on foreign law – either obtaining it from the Internet, the official or commercial databases, or acquiring it through a network of professional connections with lawyers from other countries. However, it should be noted here that in 2014 a revision of the law concerning notaries has been proposed with a view to giving notaries the possibility to apply to the Ministry of Justice for information on foreign law (cf. footnote 36).

Also in the course of proceedings before arbitral tribunals, there appears to be no compelling reasons to introduce major changes. Parties that decide for arbitration ought to be aware that institutionalised methods of proof of foreign law are not available here. At the same time they should know that other ways are still open. And although the task of ascertaining foreign law would normally lie with the parties and not with the arbitral tribunal, this outcome is not surprising. Arbitration proceedings are generally less restrictive. It is to be remembered that powers of the arbitral tribunal are limited both in relation to proving facts as well as ascertaining applicable law. Still, it is quite possible that the arbitrators themselves will possess sufficient knowledge of foreign law. Such knowledge will often be a good reason for appointing a particular arbitrator (arbitrators attached to permanent courts of arbitration in Poland are often people with good command of foreign languages and with considerable experience acquired under foreign legal systems).

It should not be overlooked, either, that the parties to arbitration proceedings may decide to have their case decided not according to some national law of a given country but rather *ex equo et bono* pursuant to Art. 1194 §1 PCCP.

As far as conflict rules in Poland are concerned it does not seem proper to change them in a way which would reduce the number of cases where foreign law applies. The *lex fori* approach is not the right answer for the challenges of present times. Indeed, private international law could be simplified in many respects but this does not mean that there should be extra privileges for the law of the forum.

What is really necessary, in the opinion of this author, are serious changes concerning the formation and training of professional lawyers. They should be taught to accept the simple truth that various national laws are equal and that the local system does not enjoy any precedence over foreign law. They should be well trained in private international law and be able to identify the applicable legal system whenever an international element appears. In the ideal world, they should be accustomed to actively looking for information on foreign law by utilising modern techniques, especially by exploring available internet sources. They should also be proficient in using electronic databases and various search engines.

It is clear that all such skills take time and effort to develop. Thus, it seems necessary to adapt, accordingly, the university curricula and internship programmes as well as various schemes of on-going training addressed to fully fledged professionals. Lawyers should be aware how important the command of foreign languages is and what benefits may be taken from learning comparative law. The current situation in Poland is not satisfactory in this respect. Suffice it to say that in most law schools private international law is not a compulsory subject. Also special training programmes for future advocates and legal counsels do not cover conflict of laws issues. As a result, it is quite possible that a legal professional admitted to the bar in Poland will not be aware that sometimes the Polish court is obliged to solve the case according to foreign law, let alone helping the judge with finding what that law is.

Portugal: Proof of and Information About Foreign Law in Portugal

Rui Manuel Moura Ramos

Abstract The subject of this contribution is to assess Portuguese legal order position concerning application of foreign law. It encompass the procedural status of conflict rules, the status of foreign law in courts (nature, application, knowledge and interpretation), existence of judicial review of application of foreign law, status of foreign law before other entities (arbitral tribunals, notaries and administrative authorities), and access to foreign law (either in the present situation or in the light of the foreseeable evolution, here with regard to practical needs, retained conflict of laws solutions and methods of facilitating access to foreign law).

I. Conflict of Laws Rules

In Portuguese legal order, application of conflict of laws provisions has a mandatory nature,[1] their binding character beeing recognised by jurisprudence and legal thinking,[2] in the absence of an express rule of law with that content. Such a silence,

[1] In Portugueese legal doctrine, the binding force of conflict of laws rules is not directly discussed, these rules beeing subject to a codification that is included [Chapter III – "Law of Aliens and Conflict of Laws" (Articles 14 to 65)], in the introductory part [Title I – "On Laws, its interpretation and application" of the General Part (Book I) of the Civil Code (1966, amended in 1977)].

[2] The doctrine supporting the facultative character of conflict rules (professed in Germany, among others, by Axel Flessner) has no supporters in Portuguese legal thinking. On this point see Moura Ramos, *Da Lei Aplicável ao Contrato de Trabalho Internacional*, Coimbra, 1990, Almedina, p. 131–154, and, for a broader analysis, T. De Boer, "Facultative choice of law: the procedural status of choice of law and foreign law", *Recueil des Cours*, 257 (1996-I), p. 223–428.

A restriction to the binding nature of the conflicts rule appears also, in french jurisprudence, with the construction of "accord procédural". On this notion, see Manuel Jorge, "La loi étrangère devant le juge du fond. Accord procédural et equivalence des lois", *in Estudos em Homenagem à Professora Doutora Isabel de Magalhães Collaço*, v. I, Coimbra, 2002, Almedina, p. 217–229, and Bénédicite Fauvarque-Cosson, "L'accord procédural à l'épreuve du temps. Retour sur une notion française controversée", *in Le droit international privé: esprit et méthodes. Mélanges en l'honneur de Paul Lagarde*, Paris, 2005, Dalloz, p. 263–284.

R.M. Moura Ramos (✉)
Professor, Faculty of Law, University of Coimbra, Coimbra, Portugal
e-mail: rmmramos@fd.uc.pt

Y. Nishitani (ed.), *Treatment of Foreign Law - Dynamics towards Convergence?*,
Ius Comparatum – Global Studies in Comparative Law 26,
DOI 10.1007/978-3-319-56574-3_13

in the light of the presence of legal rules concerning the operation of conflict rules [characterization (article 15 of Civil Code) and reference to a complex legal order (article 20 of the same code)], the limits on its special application [*renvoi* (articles 16 to 19) and recognition of vested rights under a law whose competence is not determined by *forum* conflicts rules (article 31, number 2)] should notwithstanding be construed as implying recognition of the mentioned binding force of conflict rules.

These provisions, that besides the Civil Code[3] are also inserted in several other domestic substantive law codifications[4] and nowadays include a large number of rules coming from international treaties[5] and European Union acts[6] applied in Portuguese legal order,[7] are mainly of a multilateral character, pointing in the same conditions either to the application of *forum* law (portuguese law) or to foreign law.[8] In such circumstances, these rules lead frequently to the application of foreign law, that is to say, in all the cases when the connecting factor of those rules points to a foreign legal order.

---

[3] See *supra*, note 1.

[4] For example, Commercial Code of 1888 (article 4), Commercial Societies Code of 1986 (article 3), Securities Market Code of 1999 (articles 3, 39 to 42 and 108), Labour Code of 2009 (articles 5 to 8), Industrial Property Code of 2003 (articles 3 and 4) and Copyright Code of 1985 (articles 37, 63 to 66 and 108). For some other domestic legal acts containing conflict of laws provisions, see the collections of Dário Moura Vicente (*Direito Internacional Privado. Textos Normativos Fundamentais*, Coimbra, 2012, Coimbra Editora, p. 81–150) and António Marques dos Santos (*Direito Internacional Privado. Colectânea de Textos Legislativos de Fonte Interna e Internacional*, 2nd edition, Coimbra, 2002, Almedina, p. 26–474).

[5] Some of them (but not all of them) coming from Hague Conference of Private International Law. For an enumeration, see the collections quoted in the previous note, respectively p. 569–608 and 849–1147.

[6] See mainly Regulations 1346/2000 of 29 may 2000 on Insolvency Proceedings, 864/2007 of 11 July 2007 on the Law Applicable to Non-Contractual Obligations (Rome II), 593/2008 of 17 June 2008 on the Law Applicable to Contractual Obligations (Rome I), 4/2009 of 18 December 2008 on Jurisdiction, Applicable Law, Recognition and Enforcement of Decisions and Cooperation in Matters Relating to Maintenance Obligations, 1259/2010 of 20 December 2010 Implementing Enhanced Cooperation in the Area of the Law Applicable to Divorce and Legal Separation (Rome III), 650/2012 of 4 July 2012 on Jurisdiction, Applicable Law, Recognition and Enforcement of Decisions and Authentic Instruments in Matters of Successsion and the Creation of an European Certificate of Succession, and 606/2013 of 12 June 2013 on Mutual Recognition of Protection Measures in Civil Matters. For an indication of some more regulations and directives containing provisions on conflict of laws matters, see Michael Bogdan, *Concise Introduction to EU Private International Law*, 2nd edition, Groningen, 2012, European Law Publishing, p. 155–161 and 165–168, and Moura Ramos, "Direito Internacional Privado e Direito Comunitário. Termos de uma interacção", *in Nos 20 Anos do Código das Sociedades Comerciais. Homenagem aos Profs. Doutores A. Ferrer Correia, Orlando de Carvalho e Vasco Lobo Xavier*, v. III – Vária, Coimbra, 2007, Coimbra Editora, p. 1045–1098 (1058–1065).

[7] On this question, see article 8, numbers 2 to 4, of the Portuguese Constitution (1976).

[8] On this equality principle and the consequences derived from it on conflicts law system, see mainly Ferrer Correia, "O direito internacional privado português e o princípio da igualdade", *in Temas de Direito Comercial e Direito Internacional Privado*, Coimbra, 1989, Almedina, p. 413–450.

Even if it is difficult to advance statistical data on this matter, one may assume that brazilian, venezuelan, capverdian, french, swiss, spanish, german and belgian law are the most frequently invoked. The reason lies on the movement of persons between Portugal and those countries.

II. Foreign Law Before Judicial Authorities

A. *Nature of Foreign Law*

It is stated in portuguese legal order that foreign law is applied as law.[9] Under article 348, 1 and 2 of Civil Code, courts must obtain *ex officio* knowledge on the contents on foreign law, even when it has not been invoked by the parties in the procedure and it is considered applicable by the system of conflict rules, the contested party had recognized its existence and contents or has not opposed to it.[10]

---

[9] For the presentation of different views on this matter, see Cyrille David, *La loi étrangère devant le juge du fond*, Paris, 1965, Dalloz, AAVV, *Les Problèmes Actuels posés par l'application des lois étrangères*, Paris, 1988, L.G.D.J., Trevor Hartley, "Pleading and proof of foreign law: The major european systems compared", 45 *The International and Comparative Law Quarterly* (1996), p. 271–292, François Mélin, *La Connaissance de la Loi Étrangère par les Juges du Fond (Recherches sur l'infériorité procédurale de la loi étrangère dans le procès civil)*, Aix-en Provence, 2002, Presses Universitaires d'Aix-Marseille, Maarit Jantera Jareborg, «Foreign Law in National Courts: A Comparative perspective», *Recueil des Cours* 304 (2003-IV), p. 181–386, and Sofie Geeroms, *Foreign Law in Civil Litigation. A Comparative and Functional Analysis*, Oxford, 2004, Oxford University Press. For a more theoretical approach on this subject, see Paolo Picone, "Die "Anwendung" einer auslandischen "Rechtsordnung" im Forumstaat: ...perseverare est. diabolicum!", *in Private Law in the International Arena. From National Conflict Rules towards Harmonisation and Unification. Liber Amicorum Kurt Siehr*, The Hague, 2000, T.M.C. Asser Press, p. 567–589.

[10] The point is established in portuguese legal doctrine. See Ferrer Correia, *Lições de Direito Internacional Privado*, I Coimbra, 2000, Almedina, p. 427, Baptista Machado, *Lições de Direito Internacional Privado*, 2nd edition, Coimbra, 1982, Almedina, p. 247–248, Marques dos Santos, "Aplicação do Direito Estrangeiro", 60 *Revista da Ordem dos Advogados* (2000), II, p. 647–668 (660–664), Lima Pinheiro, *Direito Internacional Privado, v. I – Introdução e Direito de Conflitos. Parte Geral*, 2nd édition, Coimbra, 2008, Almedina, p. 576–578, and Dário Moura Vicente/Maria Helena Brito, "Portugal", *in Application of Foreign Law* [Carlos Esplugues/José Luís Iglesias/ Guillermo Palao (eds)], Munich, 2011, Sellier. European law publishers, p. 301–315 (301). For a comparison with the situation under spanish law, see Mercedes Sabido Rodriguez, "El Derecho extranjero designado aplicable por la norma de conflicto del foro. Soluciones adoptadas en los sistemas de derecho internacional privado português y español", *in Estudos em Memória do Professor Doutor António Marques dos Santos*, v. I, Coimbra, 2005, Almedina, p. 356–379. In french law, see Cyrille David, *La loi étrangère devant le juge du fond* (*cit. supra*, note 9), p. 21–93, François Mélin, *La Connaissance de la Loi Étrangère par les Juges du Fond (Recherches sur l'infériorité procédurale de la loi étrangère dans le procès civil)* (*cit. supra*, note 9),and, recently, Hélène Gaudemet-Tallon, "Le point sur l'évolution de la condition du droit étranger en droit international privé français", *in Essays in honour of Konstantinos D. Kerameus*, I, Athens, 2009, Ant. N. Sakkoulas, p. 359–378.

B. Application of Foreign Law

As pointed out in the previous answer, foreign law is applied before judicial authorities *ex officio*, these ones having the duty to know foreign law *ex officio*, even if it has not been invoked or alleged by the parties. Article 348, 1 of Civil Code imposes also to the parties, in the light of the difficulties that possibly can arise, a duty of collaboration with the judge[11] in ascertaining the existence and contents of foreign law.

C. Ascertainment of Foreign Law

In Portuguese legal system,[12] when ascertaining foreign law, "*iura novit curia*"principle applies, as it derives from the provisions quoted in the two precedent answers, the parties beeing bound by the duty of collaboration with the judiciary that has also been mentioned.

---

[11] This duty is expressed referred in article 348, number 1, of Civil Code, that states that one that invokes foreign law must prove its existence and content, even if it is up to the courts to obtain *ex officio* its knowledge; see also Dário Moura Vicente/Maria Helena Brito, "Portugal", *in Application of Foreign Law* [Carlos Esplugues/José Luís Iglesias/Guillermo Palao (eds)] (*cit. supra*, note 10), p. 303. On the same duty see also, expressly, Article 14, 2, first part, of 1995 Italian Statute of Private International Law (on the solutions embodied in this article 14 and on the problems that arise in their application to different kinds of conflicts rules, see Paolo Picone, "La prova del diritto straniero nella legge italiana di riforma del diritto internazionale privato", *in Festschrift fur Erik Jayme* (hrsg. von Heinz-Peter Mansel / Thomas Pfeiffer / Herbert Kronke / Christian Kohler / Rainer Hausmann), Band I, Munchen, 2004, Sellier. European Law Publishers, p. 691–700), and, even if in less binding terms, Article 15, 2, first sentence, of Belgian Code of Private International law of 16th July 2004 (see in this respect Marta Pertegás, "Artikel 15", in *Le Code de Droit International Privé Commenté* [J. Erauw/M. Falon/E. Guldix/J. Meeusen/M. Pertegás Sender/H. van Houtte/N. Watté/P.Wautelet (eds.)], Bruxelles, 2006, Intersentia, p. 84–88. On the recent evolution in spanish law on this topic, see Alfonso Luis Calvo Caravaca/Javier Carrascosa Gonzalez, "Aplicación del Derecho extranjero en España y la nueva Ley de Enjuiciamiento Civil", *Tribunales de Justicia*, N.° 11 (Noviembre 2000), p. 1155–1169, and Federico F. Garau Sobrino, "La nodoctrina constitucional sobre la alegación y prueba del derecho extranjero", *in Entre Bruselas y La Haya. Estudios sobre la unificación internacional y regional del Derecho internacional privado. Liber Amicorum Alegria Borràs*, Madrid, 2013, Marcial Pons, p. 431–443, and, in french jurisprudence, *Cour de Cassation (1st Civ. Ch.)*, 17 may 1989, 77 *Rev. crit. dr. internat. privé* (1988), p. 329–336, note Bertrand Ancel.

[12] For a comparative picture on the different methods used to ascertain foreign law, see Shaheeza Lalani, "Establishing the content of foreign law: a comparative study", 20 *Maastricht Journal of European and Comparative Law* (2013), p. 75–112, and, for a more specific perspective, Tiong Min Yeo, "Common law innovations in proving foreign law", 12 *Yearbook of Private International Law* (2010), p. 493–502.Some legal systems foresee a non unitarian approach, providing for a distinct solution concerning certain (for example, patrimonial) matters. On this respect, see article 16 of 1987 swiss federal private international law act, and Fritz Sturm/Gudrun Sturm, «Art. 16 Abs 1 Satz 3 schweizerisches IPRG – Patrone ohne Pulver?», *inMélanges en l'honneur de Spyridon Vl. Vrellis*, Athens, 2014, Nomiki Bibliothiki, p. 899–908.

Besides the assistance of the parties implied by this duty of collaboration, the judge may use all other means useful to ascertain the content of foreign law, such as documents and internet sources, expert witness, inquiry to domestic non-judicial authorities,[13] inquiry via multilateral treaties for access to legal information[14] and direct communication of judges.

Individuals and institutions providing legal information must be qualified, these qualifications beeing freely appreciated by the courts. The provided legal information is not binding upon judicial authorities, these one having the possibility to check its accuracy and to complete it by all other means at their disposal. So far, there is not a specific established mechanism to examine the reliability of the provided legal information, the judiciary having the possibility to use all the means at its disposal to such a goal. The costs of ascertaining foreign law are supported by the judiciary system as a whole, and, in the case of the mentioned collaboration of the parties, by the party involved.

D. Interpretation and Application of Foreign Law

According to law (article 23, n.° 1, of Civil Code), "foreign law must be interpreted inside the system where it belongs and according with the rules of interpretation fixed thereof". The legislator took a clear position on this problem,[15] along the lines

[13] Mainly the Documentation and Comparative Law Office (*Gabinete de Documentação e de Direito Comparado* – GDDC), established within the Attorney General's Office (*Procuradoria-Geral da República*). This Office provides assistance to the judiciary in matters relating to international cooperation, legal information, publishing of law journals and the use of the new technologies of information. According to the law [article 161 of Framework Law on International Judicial Cooperation (Act n.° 144/99, of 31 August)], the GDDC will furnish information on foreign law upon request from a Portuguese judicial authority (and provides also information at the request of a foreign judicial authority on relevant Portuguese law to be used in criminal proceedings). The GDDC is also the national body appointed under the European Convention on Information on Foreign Law to receive and transmit information on foreign and domestic law.

[14] See *infra*, V.

[15] For a detailed consideration of this question, see Cyrille David, *La loi étrangère devant le juge du fond* (*cit. supra,* note 9), p. 241–290, Javier Maseda Rodriguez, "La Interpretación judicial del Derecho Extranjero", *Revista de Derecho Privado*, Noviembre 1997, p. 793–822, Spyridon Vrellis, "Uberlegungen bettreffend die Auslegung fremder Rechtsnormen", *in Private Law in the International Arena. From National Conflict Rules towards Harmonisation and Unification. Liber Amicorum Kurt Siehr* (*cit. supra*, note 9), p. 829–841, and specially on the question of taking in consideration a different legal order than the *lex causae*, see Laura Garcia Gutierrez, "El "doble escalón" del derecho internacional privado: sobre la toma en consideración de outro ordenamiento jurídico en la interpretación del derecho material aplicable", *in Pacis Artis. Obra Homenaje al Professor Júlio D. Gonzalez Campos*, t. II – Derecho Internacional Privado, Derecho Constitucional y Varia, Madrid, 2005, Eurolex, p. 1547–1561.

that are shared by portuguese legal doctrine[16] and that emphasize the completeness of the foreign system as a whole, recognizing the importance of interpretative criteria and pursuing the goal of harmony of results.[17]

Concerning filling of possible gaps in foreign law, the same position (application of criteria put forward in foreign law) should be taken, as it is advanced in portuguese legal thinking,[18] notwithstanding the silent of the law in this respect.

E. Failure to Establish Foreign Law

When after the utilisation of all the relevant means mentioned *supra*, in (C), foreign law cannot be ascertained (either because it is not possible to identify it[19] or because its content cannot be established), the law that would be subsidiarily applicable[20] shall be the law applied by the courts, under Article 23, number 2, of the Civil Code. If it is also not possible to establish the content of such a law, then under article 348, number 3, of Civil Code common portuguese law (*lex fori*) will be applied.[21] In portuguese doctrine it is disputed if it is possible, in a situation where difficulties arise in the process of establishing foreign law, to use a principle of greater

[16] See Ferrer Correia, *Lições de Direito Internacional Privado* (*cit. supra*, note 10), p. 434–435, Baptista Machado, *Lições de Direito Internacional Privado* (*cit. supra*, note 10), p. 244–246, Marques dos Santos, «Aplicação do Direito Estrangeiro» (*cit. supra*, note 10), p. 656–658, Lima Pinheiro, *Direito Internacional Privado, v. I – Introdução e Direito de Conflitos. Parte Geral* (*cit. supra*, note 10), p. 575–576, and Dário Moura Vicente/Maria Helena Brito, "Portugal", *in Application of Foreign Law* [Carlos Esplugues/José Luís Iglesias/Guillermo Palao (eds)] (*cit. supra*, note 10), p. 306.

[17] Such a position may lead to the defense of a restritive position on control of interpretation of foreign law. See, in this respect, Bertrand Ancel, note on *Cour de Cassation (Ch. Crim)*, 17 may 1989, 78 *Rev. crit. dr. internat. privé* (1989), p. 511–519.

[18] See Marques dos Santos, "Aplicação do Direito Estrangeiro" (*loc.cit. supra*, note 16).

[19] The law refers explicitly to the situation where it is not possible to determine the factual or juridical elements that comand the determination of the applicable law (the connection).

[20] Under portuguese law (article 32, number 1, concerning stateless) law of habitual residence appears as the law subsidiarily applicable in matters of personal status (status, legal capacity, family law and successions – article 25 of Civil Code). See also Marques dos Santos, "Aplicação do Direito Estrangeiro" (cit. supra, note 10), p. 665–666.

[21] On the same subsidiary competence of forum law, see, in french jurisprudence (Cour de Cassation (1st Civ. Ch.), 2 february 1988, 78 Rev. crit. dr. internat. privé (1989), p. 55–63, note Bertrand Ancel.

Concerning such approach, see, recently, in a specific context, Aurelio López Tarruella, "Constitue la aplicación de la lex fori en defecto de prueba del Derecho extranjero designado por una norma de conflicto unionista un incumplimiento delDerecho de la Unión Europea?", in Nuevas Fronteras del Derecho de la Unión Europea. Liber amicorum José Luis Iglesias Buhigues [Carlos Esplugues Mota/Guillermo Palao Moreno (eds.)], Valencia, 2012, tirant lo blanch, p. 537–554.

similarity and even to make recourse to presumptions,[22] even if this last possibility is contested.[23] We understand that absolute certainty is in some cases difficult, when applying foreign law, and that it should be enough a proof that could form the conviction of the judge on this point.[24] But nowadays there are plenty more means to establish foreign law, and one must put aside any possibility that should construe, eventually by means of presumptions, the content of the applicable law in a way different from the one that is in force in the legal system considered.

The main policy consideration under this solution is the assumption that application of foreign law, in a system of bilateral conflict rules, must correspond to the living law in force (the *law in action*, one could say),wherever it comes from, in the considered system. If the goal of the legislator is the one of protect the expectations that have grown up on the application of foreign law, then one shall apply this law as it is in force and is really applied in the considered legal system. In this context, there is no more room to the application of a foreign law if one cannot establish its content, and one may then rely on the applicability of the law subsidiarily applicable (in the sense it could also have led to the creation of parties'expectations), or, as a last resort solution (and just in the measure required to escape a *déni de justice*), to *forum law*. The most important goal is the one of reducing the application of *forum law*, in non domestic situations, to this last resort solution. Under the background ideas of portuguese conflict-of-laws system, where equality principle in the application of *forum law* and foreign law plays a very important function,[25] the application of that law, when not required by the connecting factor present in a conflicts rule, should in reality not take place, because it does not rely on the policy considerations just mentioned.

---

[22] In this sense, see Ferrer Correia, Lições de Direito Internacional Privado (cit. supra, note 10), p. 431–432, Baptista Machado, Lições de Direito Internacional Privado (cit. supra, note 10), p. 248–249, and Marques dos Santos, «Aplicação do Direito Estrangeiro» (cit. supra, note 10), p. 665.

[23] See Lima Pinheiro, Direito Internacional Privado, v. I – Introdução e Direito de Conflitos. Parte Geral (cit. supra, note 10), p. 579.

[24] On this sense Baptista Machado, Lições de Direito Internacional Privado (cit. supra, note 10), p. 248.

It is also true, in this matter, that "the judge may and must always content himself with a degree of certainty that is appropriate for practical life, one which silences doubts without entirely excluding them". See, in this respect, Kevin M. Clermont/Emily Sherwin, "A Comparative Puzzle: Standards of Proof", in Law and Justice in a Multistate World. Essays in Honor of Arthur T. von Mehren (edited by James A.R. Nafziger/Symeon C. Symeonides), Ardsley, 2002, Transnational Publishers, p. 629–644, p. 629.

[25] See Ferrer Correia, "O direito internacional privado português e o princípio da igualdade" (cit. supra, note 8) and Moura Ramos, Da Lei Aplicável ao Contrato de Trabalho Internacional (cit. supra, note 2), p. 224–263, in the sense that equality principle between forum law and foreign law is the basic structure of contemporary private international law (p. 256).

III. Judicial Review

A. Conflict of Laws Rules

In case of erroneous application of a conflicts rule, the parties can appeal to higher courts (including the *Supreme Court*) in the same conditions such an appeal is possible, on domestic situations, on the erroneous application of a substantive law provision. Even if there is no provision with such a content, the point comes as a direct consequence of the legal and binding character of the conflict of laws rules.[26]

The background ideas of such a solution are, as mentioned, the prevailing consideration of the legal character of the conflict rules and the policy considerations[27] that justify the application of foreign law in portuguese legal order.

B. Foreign Law

In case of erroneous application of foreign law, the parties can appeal to higher courts, including the Supreme Court. The point is expressly mentioned in Article 674, number 1, alínea a) and number 2, of Civil Procedure Code.[28] According to these provisions, appeal to the Supreme Court is possible if based on violation of "substantive law", the meaning of this expression including norms and principles of general or common international law and the general dispositions, of a substantive character, coming from domestic or foreign sovereignty organs,[29] or placed in international conventions or treaties.

This solution comes as a recognition of the legal character of foreign law, that is applied as *law* and not as *fact*.[30] Such a position is also in line with the main goal of

---

[26] See supra, point I.

[27] Refered also supra, point II, E.

[28] The Code has been approved by Law n.° 41/2013, of 26 June, but the solution is traditional in portuguese law. See on this respect Ferrer Correia, Lições de Direito Internacional Privado (cit. supra, note 10), p. 427, Baptista Machado, Lições de Direito Internacional Privado (cit. supra, note 10), p. 248, Marques dos Santos, "Aplicação do Direito Estrangeiro" (cit. supra, note 10), p. 662–663, Lima Pinheiro, Direito Internacional Privado, v. I – Introdução e Direito de Conflitos. Parte Geral (cit. supra, note 10), p. 578, and Dário Moura Vicente/Maria Helena Brito, "Portugal", in Application of Foreign Law [Carlos Esplugues/José Luís Iglesias/Guillermo Palao (eds)] (cit. supra, note 10), p. 311.

[29] This formulation excludes violation of foreign customary law as a basis for appeal to the Supreme Court; on this point, Lima Pinheiro, Direito Internacional Privado, v. I – Introdução e Direito de Conflitos. Parte Geral (cit. supra, note 10), p. 578. Pretending that such an exclusion is based on practical reasons (the serious difficulty of proof of foreign customary law), see Marques dos Santos, "Aplicação do Direito Estrangeiro" (cit. supra, note 10), p. 663.

[30] In this sense Ferrer Correia, *Lições de Direito Internacional Privado* (*cit. supra*, note 10), p. 427, Baptista Machado, *Lições de Direito Internacional Privado* (*cit. supra*, note 10), p. 248, Marques dos Santos, "Aplicação do Direito Estrangeiro" (*cit. supra*, note 10), p. 660–663, and Lima

application of foreign law under a system of multilateral conflict of law rules: to enable protection of juridical expectations based on application of foreign law and, therefore, the continuity of juridical life of persons in relationships connected with more than one legal system.

IV. Foreign Law in Other Instances

Foreign law is also applied before non judicial (mainly administrative) authorities, since these authorities exercise some competences (in family matters, for example) that require such application. This is more and more frequent in view of the progressive "dejudicialization" of some state competences, as is the case in marriage and divorce matters. When applying foreign law these administrative authorities are in principle bound by the same legal rules that govern such application by judicial authorities,[31] even if in some cases[32] special rules must be taken in account.

In case of arbitration, and in view of the fact this activity is placed by portuguese law on the same foot of the judicial one,[33] and since that in arbitration procedures that take place in Portugal the parties may freely choose, in international arbitrations, the rules of law to be applied by arbitrators,[34] application of foreign law is equally frequent, and the same principles that we have considered concerning judicial authorities are also applied.[35]

Pinheiro, *Direito Internacional Privado, v. I – Introdução e Direito de Conflitos. Parte Geral* (*cit. supra*, note 10), p. 577. On the situation in french law, see Jean-Pierre Ancel, "L'invocation d'un droit étranger et le contrôle de la Cour de cassation", *in Vers de nouveaux équilibres entre ordres juridiques. Mélanges en l'honneur d'Hélène Gaudemet-Tallon*, Paris, 2008, Dalloz, p. 3–10.

[31] In this sense Lima Pinheiro, *Direito Internacional Privado, v. I – Introdução e Direito de Conflitos. Parte Geral* (*cit. supra*, note 10), p. 581, and Dário Moura Vicente/Maria Helena Brito, "Portugal", *in Application of Foreign Law* [Carlos Esplugues/José Luís Iglesias/Guillermo Palao (eds)] (*cit. supra*, note 10), p. 312 and 313.

[32] Concerning marriage by foreigners, and proof of capacity to marry, when there are difficulties to present a certificate to marry based on the personal law (nationality law) of the future spouse, Article 166, number 2, of Civil Registration Code establishes a special procedure where decision powers are granted to the civil state officer.

[33] According to Article 42nd, number 7 of Portuguese Arbitration Act (Law n.° 63/2011, of December 14th), a final arbitral award has the same binding character between the parties and the same executory character that a sentence from a judicial court.

[34] See articles 61, 49, number 1, and 52, number 1, of Portuguese Arbitration Act, and, on this subject, Moura Ramos, "L'arbitrage international dans le nouveau droit portugais de l'arbitrage", *in Entre Bruselas y La Haya. Estudios sobre la unificación internacional y regional del Derecho Internacional Privado. Liber amicorum Alegria Borràs* (*cit. supra*, note 11), p. 611–624.

[35] In this sense, in Portuguese legal thinking, António Pinto Leite, "*Jura novit curia* e a arbitragem internacional", *in VI Congresso do Centro de Arbitragem Comercial*, Coimbra, 2013, Almedina, p. 151–168.

In other situations, the question presents itself in a different way.[36] So, in the case of notaries,[37] they must apply foreign law when this is the applicable law, but they are not obliged to know it *ex officio*; in these circumstances, if applicable law is a foreign one, they will perform the act if they know the content of the foreign applicable law or if it would be established by the parties.[38] And, recently (Decree Law n.° 125/2013, of August 30th), the new article 43.°-A of Immovables Registration Code stated that when the viability of the registration demand must be considered on basis of a foreign law, the person concerned must, by an idoneus document, provide the proof of its respective contents.

V. Access to Foreign Law: Status Quo

In Portugal, legal information is provided through official websites, either governmental ones (for example, those ones from Ministry of Justice (www.publicações.mj.pt) or from the *Procuradoria-Geral da República*(Attorney-General) (www.pgr.pt) or some of their departments (www.pgdlisboa.pt and www.gddc.pt), or those from some courts, like the Constitutional Court (www.tribunalconstitucional.pt). The website from the government (www.portugal.gov.pt) also publishes daily legislation and the Portuguese official journal is eletronicly published (dre.pt).

As to the possibility for the judge to directly communicate with a foreign judge to obtain legal information, Portugal has not integrated until now the Hague Judicial Network,[39] but the European Judicial Network (EJN), is available. On the website of this last network it is possible to have access to fact sheets containing information on the legal situation in the countries concerned.

---

[36] A recent survey on this question is provided by the essay of Afonso Patrão, "Poderes e Deveres do Notário e Conservador na Cognição de Direito Estrangeiro", *inCadernos do C.E.No.R. Cadernos de Estudos Notariais e Registais*, n.° 2, p. 9–38.

[37] See also Dário Moura Vicente/Maria Helena Brito, "Portugal", *in Application of Foreign Law* [Carlos Esplugues/José Luís Iglesias/Guillermo Palao (eds)] (*cit. supra*, note 10), p. 312 and 313. For some notes on the characterization of the role played by these professionals, see at last A. (Teun) V.M. Struycken, "Notaires. Piliers de l'Ordre Juridique", *in De Rome à Lisbonne: Les Juridictions de l'Union européenne à la croisée des chemins. Mélanges en l'honneur de Paolo Mengozzi*, Bruxelles, 2013, Bruylant, p. 475–488, mainly p. 477–487.

[38] Article 85, number 2, of Civil Law Notary Code disposes that when applicable law on succession is not portuguese law, and it is not known by the judge, the act must be instrued with a idoneous document assessing the proof of foreign law. See on this respect Lima Pinheiro, *Direito Internacional Privado, v. I – Introdução e Direito de Conflitos. Parte Geral* (*cit. supra*, note 10), p. 580–581, and, on the situation under spanish law, José Carlos Fernandez Rozas, "La aplicación del derecho extranjero por los notários", 35 *Anales de la Academia Matritense del Notariado* (1996), p. 171–209.

[39] On the development of this network and on general principles guiding these communications, see recently *Communications Judiciaires Directes*, 2013, Conférence de La Haye de Droit International Privé.

Portugal is also part to several international and regional instruments on proof and/or information on foreign law, such as the European Convention of 7 June 1968 on Information on Foreign Law (London Convention), Additional Protocol to this Convention of 15 March 1978 and Convention on Information in Juridical Matters Related to Law in Force and its Application[40] (Brazilian Convention) of 22 September 1972.[41]

Besides, in Portugal it is also possible for the judge,[42] in order to facilitate access to foreign law, to have recourse to other regional settings, like the *IberRede* (*Rede Iberoamericana de cooperação jurídica internacional*) (www.iberred.org), established in 2004 by the *Conferência de Ministros da Justiça dos Países Iberoamericanos*, and the *Rede de cooperação jurídica e judiciária internacional dos países de língua portuguesa* (*RJCPLP*) (www.rjcplp.org), established in 2005 by the *Conferência de Ministros dos Países de Língua Portuguesa*. In criminal matters, the European Judicial Network for criminal matters is also available, and, as for the notaries, they may also use the European Notarial Network.

One can say that the European Judicial Network is frequently used (247 requests of cooperation in 2012, an increase of 71.25% concerning the precedent year).[43] This number refers to requests of cooperation by judges. Furthermore, it must be said that the entities that may not use directly this network (lawyers, citizens, solicitors and notaries) can visit the website of the network (235.820 visitors in 2012 and 1.784.649 appearances of the page in 120 countries).[44] The other settings, meanwhile, are not so frequently used (4 requests for the *Iberrede*, and 7 for the *RJCPLP* in the same period).[45]

The settings are very useful concerning the generic information that they provide, in the matters to whom the fact sheets are available. Specific information is also avail-

---

[40] This instrument, established by the Conference of Ministers of Justice of Spanish-Luso-American Countries and Phillipines, is only in force between Portugal and Argentina. The contracting parties engage themselves to mutually render information on juridical matters (article 1), by means of the establishment of a system of central authorities (article 2). It enables judicial authorities and organs having functions of jurisdictional nature to procure information (article 3), indicates the required content of the information demand (article 4), the competent authorities to provide an answer, its content and effects (article 5), disposes on the mandatory character of the answer and on the delay imposed to it (article 6), foresees the possibility of complementary information and imposes the gratuity of the answers (article 7).

[41] Portugal is not part either to Inter-American Convention of 8 May 1979 on Proof of and Information on Foreign Law ("Montevideo Convention") or to Convention of 22 January 1993 on Legal Assistance and Legal Relations in Civil, Family and Criminal Matters ("Minsk Convention").

Emphasizing the need of further codification instruments, see Philippe Lortie/Maja Groff, "The missing link between determining the law applicable and the application of foreign law. Building on the results of the joint conference on Access to foreign law in civil and commercial matters (Brussels, 15–17 February 2012)", *in A Commitment to Private International Law. Essays in honour of Hans van Loon*, Cambridge, 2013, Intersentia, p. 325–341.

[42] The same information is also available for public prosecutors and bailiffs (judicial officers).

[43] See 2012 Annual Report, Judiciary Superior Council (Conselho Superior da Magistratura), p. 92.

[44] *Idem, ibidem*, p. 88.

[45] *Idem, ibidem*, respectively, p. 93 and 94.

able to judges, public prosecutors, bailiffs and central authorities, that can get an answer on concrete questions by having recourse to the national contact points of the network. In some cases, the Portuguese contact point had also assisted directly the citizens (for example, on the question of the definitive character of a foreign decision).

The more problems of these networks are the lack of knowledge of their virtualities and of the legal instruments (conventions and EU regulations) that refer to international relations and the lack of training of the legal professions in these matters.

VI. Access to Foreign Law: Further Developments

A. Practical Need

In my opinion, there is need to improve access to foreign law,[46] particularly for non-judicial authorities, lawyers, notaries and the parties, especially those who cannot afford costly measures. The situation on this topic is better concerning judicial authorities, that have at their disposal some means[47] that are not, at the least in the same way, available to other concerned persons and entities. It would be useful to answer the needs of these entities, mainly taking in account the growing presence of non-judicial entities (in such different areas such as family law, successions, and commercial law) having jurisdiction in the international arena. Concerning judicial authorities, the effort should be put on training the operators and on assuring a larger knowledge of the instruments that must be used in international relations.

It is very difficult to say in which circumstances access to foreign law is most needed in Portugal. One can certainly think that this quest appears either before doing business or in the course of litigation or in the context of international relocation.

If we think which areas of law are the most needed, it is sure that family matters (mainly divorce, parental responsibility and legal Kidnapping) and legal obligations are certainly the matters where people look more for legal information.

B. Conflict of Laws Solutions

I don't think portuguese conflict of laws rules should be modified *de lege ferenda* to reduce the number of cases in which foreign law is applied (and I rather would think in a similar way concerning other conflict-of-law systems). In fact, in general,

[46] Also stressing this need, and favouring the adoption of a new EU instrument aimed at harmonising the treatment of foreign law in EU Member States, and considering that the current state of affairs is against predicability and harmony of results, impairing the achievement of a real space of civil justice, see Carmen Azcárraga Monzonís, "The urgent need for the harmonisation of the application of foreign laws by national authorities in Europe", 3 *International Journal of Civil Procedure* (2013), 1, p. 104–125.

[47] Mainly those refered *supra*, in point V.

private international law expresses one particular idea of justice[48] and this idea should not be sacrified because the difficulties that may appear in its concretisation. Concerning in particular the portuguese conflicts system, it is mainly based, as we have said,[49] in multilateral conflict rules, where foreign law comes on the same foot as *forum* law, the application of one or of the other depending just on the concretisation of the connecting factor. I think this is the best system to poursue justice and international harmony in private international law cases, and therefore I will not support the change of the basic pattern of this construction.

I also do not think that the treatment of foreign law in Portugal (its application *ex officio*, as law and not as fact)[50] should be changed *de lege ferenda*. Application *ex officio* comes as a natural consequence of the recognition that private international law justice commands application of foreign law; in these circumstances, its status in *forum* must not depend on its allegation by the parties. This is also a consequence of equality principle between *lex fori* and foreign law that is embodied in portuguese system.[51]

International or regional instruments unifying the treatment of foreign law would certainly be useful. Even those that do not completely share the analysis of what is referred as the "devastating effects of the absence of a common set of rules governing the application of foreign law" in european private international law[52] must recognize that, mainly in unified spaces, such a unification should be welcomed.[53]

C. Methods of Facilitating Access to Foreign Law

Establishment of administrative and/or judicial cooperation to exchange information on Member States'law have been until now a useful tool to facilitate access to foreign law.[54] So far, it is possible to think that international or regional

[48] For the characterization of this idea in more developped terms, see Moura Ramos, *Da Lei Aplicável ao Contrato de Trabalho Internacional* (*cit. supra*, note 2), p. 224–263.

[49] Cfr. *supra*, I.

[50] Cfr. *supra*, II, A.

[51] Cfr. *supra*, I, and *op. cit. supra*, note 8.

[52] See Carlos Esplugues Mota, "Harmonization of private international law in Europe and application of foreign law: The "Madrid Principles" of 2010", 13 *Yearbook of Private International Law* (2011), p. 273–297, p. 275. For a prior stage of this last initiative, see Urs Peter Gruber/Ivo Bach, "The Application of Foreign Law. A progress report on a new european project", 11 *Yearbook of Private International Law* (2009), p. 157–169.

[53] For a presentation of the difficulties on this topic and some proposals of solutions, see Carlos Esplugues Mota (*op. cit. supra*, note 52).

[54] On the role played, in particular, by the European Judicial Network, see Georgina Garriga Suau, «La creciente potencialidad de la Red Judicial Europea en matéria civil y mercantil en la construcción del espacio judicial europeo», 8 *AEDIPr* (2008), p. 237–255.

instruments on this matter could improve access and facilitate correct application of foreign law.[55]

In face of the growing presence of exercise of jurisdiction by non-judicial authorities in the international arena, such international instruments should be open to these authorities, and, hopefully, to individuals (even if one could think that the status of judicial authorities inside these mechanisms should be a distinct one).

Should the competent authorities or designated expert bodys of foreign state be known by advance and indicated in the instrument, I see no reason to exclude direct communication of the request between them and the interested judge, without the necessary intervention of central authority of requesting state.

In any case, meanwhile, I think the answer provided by the requested state should not be binding. There is no possibility to give an "authentique" picture of state of art in the requested state, as application of law is concerned, and the responsibility of ascertaining the contents of foreign law must stay with the judge that bears the responsibility of applying it, also taking in account that he may also use all other different means to establish its contents.

As to costs of services on legal information, they should in no circumstance be beard by the requesting entities. In the framework of a system where cooperation between authorities is organized, the correct application of foreign law in each case is not only in the interest of the requesting entity itself but of the legal community as a whole. In these case, costs implied by this correct application should in principle lie with the system itself and not be transferred to those that use it. The opposite solution would improve the difficulties and cause inequalities in recourse to mechanisms of facilitation of access to foreign law.

Besides this possibility, one should not forget to act in all other useful ways to facilitate access to foreign law. In this context, promotion of information on national law on the Internet is certainly a first step that can be made. The identification of qualified experts or expert institutes (like Swiss Institute of Comparative Law and Max-Planck Institute for Comparative and International Private Law) is also useful, provided that the judicial and non-judicial authorities should have the possibility to have recourse to them. And the establishment of networks for other legal professionals, like the reinforcement of direct communication between judges[56] and the connections between lawyers offices can surely be important means in achieving the some goal of permitting better and more accurate knowledge of the contents of foreign law.

[55] For a suggestion on facilitation of access to information on foreign law, see Shaheeza Lalani, "A proposed model to facilitate access to foreign law", 13 *Yearbook of Private International Law* (2011), p. 299–313.

[56] As the Hague Judicial Network; see *supra*, note 39.

Romania: Proof of and Information About Foreign Law in Romania

Flavius George Păncescu

Abstract The legal regime of foreign law in Romania has received relatively recently a new expression in the New Civil Code. The relevant provisions are presented, accompanied by comments, practical information and statistical data.

The procedure of obtaining information on Foreign or Romanian law is also presented from a practical point of view, with regard to the latest legislative modifications.

I. Conflict of Law Rules

The conflict of law rules are included in the Seventh Book of the Romanian Civil Code from 2009 (Articles 2557–2663), which has entered into force in 2011. Previously these rules were part of Law No. 105/1992 on the private international law relations. Further, this book is divided in nine titles, as follows: General Provisions; Persons; Family; Goods; Successions; Legal Act; Obligations; Bill of exchange, promissory note and cheque; Trusts; Limitation. The most important novelties are: 1. the alignment of the majority of the conflict of law rules with those from the most European Regulations and International Conventions[1]; 2. the introduction and definition of new concepts such as habitual residence, torts etc.

As a rule, the application of the Romanian conflict of law rules is mandatory. This rule has no legislative expression, but it was constantly retained by the doctrine and jurisprudence.

On the proportion of the application of foreign law, when the conflict of law rules to them cannot be assessed in numbers, but certainly there are many situations in which such occasions occur. The states whose laws are most frequently applied or invoked before judicial authorities in Romania are Germany, Italy, France and the United States of America.

[1] Such as Rome I and II Conventions on Contractual and Non-Contractual Obligations; Maintenance Regulation No. 4/2009, 1996 Hague Convention on Applicable Law in Respect of Parental Responsibility and Measures for the Protection of Children.

F.G. Păncescu (✉)
Dr. Romanian Ministry of Justice, Str. Apolodor, nr. 17 sector 5, Bucureşti 050741, Romania

Romanian Academy, Bucureşti, Romania
e-mail: fgpancescu@gmail.com

Y. Nishitani (ed.), *Treatment of Foreign Law - Dynamics towards Convergence?*,
Ius Comparatum – Global Studies in Comparative Law 26,
DOI 10.1007/978-3-319-56574-3_14

II. Foreign Law Before Judicial Authorities

The foreign law is considered in Romania as element of law, not of fact.[2] This rule derives in present from Article 2559 (1) of the Civil Code, accordingly to which foreign law includes substantive law as well as conflict of law rules, when not otherwise provided. But it retains its foreign character and does not become national.[3]

According to Article 2562 (1), (2) of the Civil Code and Article 22 of the Code of Civil Procedure, the foreign law is applied *ex officio*. If the conflict rule is not mandatory, the application of foreign law is leaved at the parties' agreement. The application of foreign law is, in principle, independent from the condition of reciprocity. However, if in certain matters the condition of reciprocity is requested, the fulfillment of it is presumed. Otherwise, the existence of the reciprocity is established by the Ministry of Justice, after consulting the Ministry of Foreign Affairs[4] (Article 2561 of the Civil Code).

The principle "*iura novit curia*" does not apply to foreign law. Therefore, the content of foreign law is established by the Romanian court together with the parties. The party who invokes foreign law has to prove its content (Article 2562 (2) of the Civil Code).

As a rule, foreign law has been ascertained in practice based on inquiries via bilateral or multilateral treaties for access to legal information.[5] On some occasions, in the absence of any treaties supporting exchange of legal information, foreign law has been obtained upon Internet sources, provided by the Romanian or foreign consular or diplomatic offices. Direct communication of judges is mostly used in the frame of judicial networks, as it will be described further below. The provided legal information is binding upon judicial authorities if it has an official character. On the costs of ascertaining foreign law, these are beard by one or both of the parties, even if it was ordered *ex officio* (Article 262 of the Code of Civil Procedure). The interpretation and application of the foreign law follow the rules of the country of origin (Article 2563 of the Civil Code).

According to Article 2562 (3) of the Civil Code, if the content of foreign law cannot be established within a reasonable time, the Romanian law will be applied in subsidiary. The background idea is that, since the Romanian court has jurisdiction over the case, the Romanian law has the most connections to the circumstances of the case. In respect to the stateless persons, respectively the determination of the applicable law what concerns their personal status, there is a special provision (Article 2568 (3) of the Civil Code).

---

[2] *I. Nestor*, Principiul jura novit curia în cazul aplicării legii străine de către instanţele române, Studii şi Cercetări Juridice nr. 2/1965, pp. 245–246.

[3] *I.P. Filipescu, A.I. Filipescu*, Tratat de drept internaţional privat, Editura Univers Juridic, Bucureşti, 2007, p. 151.

[4] Such situations occur relatively rare in practice, most cases being with the different states of the United States of America, in matrimonial matters.

[5] More details *infra*, point V.

III. Judicial Review

When conflict of law rules have erroneously been applied, the interested party can use ordinary (appeal) and extraordinary (appeal in cassation, contestation for the annulment and the motion of revision) means of review. According to Article 479 of the Code of Civil Procedure, the judge of appeal is verifying, in the limits of the request for appeal, the factual and legal aspects retained by the first instance judge. What concerns the appeal in cassation, a ground for this mean of review is the erroneously application or breach of the material law provisions (Article 488 (1) point 8 of the Code of Civil Procedure), including conflict of law rules.

If the legal issues which have formed the object of the trial have been differently solved by different final judicial decisions the General Prosecutor, the College of the courts of appeal or the Ombudsman can file for an appeal in the interest of law, at the High Court of Cassation and Justice. According to Articles 514 of the Code of Civil Procedure, the appeal in the interest of law is used to ensure the unitary interpretation and application of the law by all the courts.

If the foreign law has erroneously been applied, the interested party can use all the above-mentioned means of review. However, the appeal in the interest of law cannot be used, since its object is the unitary interpretation and application of the national law.[6]

IV. Foreign Law in Other Instances

Foreign law can be frequently occurring before notaries (wills and successions matters) as well as administrative authorities (public registry offices).

In international arbitration foreign law has a large incidence. According to Article 1120 of the Code of Civil Procedure, the arbitral tribunal shall apply the rules of law to be applied to the merits of the dispute agreed by the parties. In the absence of any such agreement, the arbitral tribunal shall apply the rules of law which it determines to be adequate. The arbitral tribunal shall always take account of any relevant trade and professional usages. The arbitral tribunal shall decide *ex aequo et bono* only if the parties have agreed to give it such powers.

V. Access to Foreign Law: Status Quo

The Ministry of Justice of Romania acts as Central Authority for incoming and outgoing requests in this matter, according to Article 29 of Law No. 189/2003 on the international judicial assistance in civil and commercial matters, republished.

---

[6] *D.A. Sitaru*, Drept internaţional privat, Editura Lumina Lex, Bucureşti, 2001, pp. 105–106.

What concerns incoming requests, the Ministry of Justice of Romania does not provide legal information on its website for official use. However, some important legislative acts are present here, such as the Civil Code, Code of Civil Procedure, Legal Aid Act etc. In such cases, the Ministry of Justice provides a reply or forwards the request to another authority, being competent in that matter, but not to a private body or to a qualified lawyer. This reply, drafted in an objective and impartial manner, might be accompanied by complementary documents (Article 31 (1), (2) of Law No. 189/2003). It must be also underlined that the reply has no special form, as a certification of the content of the legal provision.

The Hague Judicial Network is used by Romanian judges, mostly in child abduction cases. The European Judicial Network is used as well by the judges in order to obtain legal information, but through the intermediary of the Contact Points from the Ministry of Justice of Romania.

Romania is party at the European Convention of 7 June 1968 on Information on Foreign Law ("London Convention"). Almost all the bilateral conventions in international judicial assistance concluded by Romania with other states contain provisions facilitating the exchange on information of national law.

In practice these conventions are rarely used (20 requests in average per year). The London Convention is the most commonly used instrument, even with Member States of the European Union.

As a rule, these instruments work well. However, sometimes they are time-consuming (6 months), due to the slow reaction of some of the requested authorities. For incoming requests, the Ministry of Justice furnishes a reply as rapidly as possible. However, if the preparation of the reply requires a longer time – a situation which appears rarely in practice, the Ministry of Justice informs the requesting foreign authority (Article 31 (4), (5) of Law No. 189/2003).

VI. Access to Foreign Law: Further Developments

A. *Practical Need*

For some categories of persons, an improvement of access to foreign law is welcomed, especially to attorneys and parties. In this sense, the practice of providing legal information on official websites would be useful. However, an extension of the above-mentioned instruments to these persons is not practical.

Access to foreign law is mostly needed in the course of arbitration and litigation. Sometimes they are needed even to prepare such procedures.

What concerns the areas of law in which access to foreign law are frequent are contract law (civil and commercial), law of traffic accidents, family law, law of successions and tax law. The reason is the increased freedom of movement of persons and circulation of capital between Romania and other countries, which lead even to disputes who arise from the legal relations derived from this mobility.

B. Conflict of Law Solutions

As mentioned at the beginning of the report, the conflict of law rules in Romania were recently revised. The majority of them is in accordance with the European Law on the conflict of laws in different matters, or even redirects to this which leads to the conclusion that a revisal of these provisions is not necessary.

Furthermore on this aspect, the duty of the judge to have an active role in the course of the trial is one of the principles of the Romanian civil procedure, which leads us to the conclusion that the treatment of foreign law in Romania before the judiciary should remain unchanged.

Finally, having in regard the variety of concepts towards the treatment of foreign law and the tradition on this aspect, a unification by way of international or regional instruments of them seems unfeasible and perhaps, undesired.

C. Methods of Facilitating Access to Foreign Law

In our opinion, these instruments facilitating exchange of information on foreign law are useful tools. However, a more direct communication between requesting and requested authorities would be more effective. Having this in regard, an opening to other authorities and individuals would be an option, but not without costs, which could be beard by the legal aid system.

On the binding character of the reply to requests on foreign law is complex and depends amongst other things on the authority from which it emanates, which stay for a negative approach.

Nevertheless, the use of qualified experts or expert institutions[7] is in our opinion delicate and raises difficulties in practice, since it regards more the procedure of obtaining evidence abroad.

---

[7] For examples of such cases, *I.P. Filipescu, A.I. Filipescu*, op. cit., p. 155.

Spain: The Application of Foreign Laws in Spain – Critical Analysis of the Legal Novelties of 2015

Carmen Azcárraga Monzonís

Abstract The Spanish system about treatment of foreign laws is regulated in different legal sources including the recent Act 29/2015 on International Legal Cooperation. The inconsistency between the mandatory nature of conflict of laws rules and the burden of parties of proving the foreign law makes the system unsatisfactory in the judicial scope whereas more flexible solutions -and consequently more satisfactory outcomes- can be evidenced in the non-judicial scope. This research approaches both scenarios from a legal and practical perspective and analyses the current solutions and some proposals of improvement.

I. Introduction

In Spain there is no a single Act or Code of Private International Law unlike in other countries. The Spanish system of Private International Law is scattered throughout a set of rules of different origin, nature and purpose and this feature also affects the legal regime of the application of foreign laws, a field which has been recently amended as a consequence of the entry into force of the new Act 29/2015, of 30 July, on International Legal Cooperation.[1]

The whole system of application of foreign laws in Spain derives from the rule contained in Article 12(6) of the Spanish Civil Code (CC hereinafter) under which "Spanish authorities and courts must apply *ex officio* the conflict of laws rules of Spanish law". In accordance with this provision and following the interpretation of the Spanish Supreme Court,[2] parties do not need to invoke the applicability of a specific conflict of laws rule when a foreign element is involved in the private international situation, and they cannot agree to avoid its application either.

[1] BOE (Spanish Official Journal) n. 182 of 31.7.2015.

[2] Judgments 436/2005 of 10.6.2005 (RJ \2005\6491).

C. Azcárraga Monzonís (✉)
Assistant Professor, Faculty of Law, University of Valencia, Avda/Los Naranjos, s/n, Valencia 46022, Spain
e-mail: carmen.azcarraga@uv.es

Y. Nishitani (ed.), *Treatment of Foreign Law - Dynamics towards Convergence?*,
Ius Comparatum – Global Studies in Comparative Law 26,
DOI 10.1007/978-3-319-56574-3_15

Spanish authorities shall verify the presence of a foreign element in the case at hand –although first notice is usually provided by parties in their respective allegations- and then proceed to implement of their own motion the relevant conflict of laws rule which may lead to the application of a foreign law. Hence, the application of foreign laws following the application of mandatory conflict of laws rules does not depend on the will of either the parties or the competent authority. It is a direct consequence of the mandatory nature of conflict of laws rules.

Nevertheless, once the above has been clarified, a significant distinction must be made between the absence of the need to plead the applicable foreign law as a consequence of the mandatory nature of conflict of laws rules and its final and proper application in practice by Spanish authorities once its content has been proved. In this regard judicial and non-judicial scopes should be differentiated when approaching the proof of foreign laws as a previous step to their application by Spanish authorities.

While in the judicial scope the Spanish system makes the ultimate application of foreign laws depend on the proactive will of the parties given that the burden proof of the relevant applicable law rests with them, this rule is more flexible in the non-judicial scope. As previously explained, Article 12(6) CC is applicable to the activity of every authority acting in Spain – they are all bound by the mandatory nature of conflict of laws rules – but this rule must be interpreted together with other provisions specifically focused on the application of foreign laws by judicial and non-judicial authorities, as will be explained for each of these scopes at the relevant section.

Historically most Spanish conflict of laws rules have potentially led to the application of foreign laws particularly on the basis of two factors: first, international migrations where Spain is a destination country; second, the fact that "nationality" as connecting factor has traditionally had a prominent role namely in fields like personal status, family and succession matters. Even though in the recent years (above all since the European Union acquired legislative competence to deal with these issues), Spanish Private International Law has gradually welcomed in many fields other connecting factors such as "residence" (which leads to reduce the application of foreign laws) and "party autonomy" (which may also favour the coincidence *forum-ius*), the application of foreign laws in Spain is still possible due to the participation of our country in international migrations.[3]

[3]According to the information provided by the Spanish Ministry of Employment and Social Security on 30 June 2016 more than 5 million foreigners were (legally) residing in Spain, most of them from Romania and Morocco. Information available at (accessed 26.10.2016): http://extranjeros.empleo.gob.es/es/estadisticas/operaciones/con-certificado/201606/Residentes_Principales_Resultados_30062016.pdf

II. Foreign Law Before Judicial Authorities

II.1. Nature of Foreign Law

Foreign law has been granted a hybrid nature in Spanish Private International Law. The procedural treatment of foreign law leads to consider it as a *tertium genus*[4] between "fact" and "law". It is a matter of fact since it must be proven by parties (who must also cover the costs of proving it) but it is accepted to be more than a pure fact given that it is granted a different regime of evidence. At the same time it is considered law because once proved authorities will apply foreign law as authentic law but they do not apply it *ex officio* so it cannot be deemed law strictly speaking, at least not like Spanish substantive law.

As a starting point it is unanimously understood that Spanish judges do not have the duty to know the content of foreign laws.[5] The principle *iura novit curiae* is then exclusively confined to the knowledge of Spanish law and furthermore this rule is applied in a very rigid manner till the point that even when the judge knows the content of a foreign law, he shall not apply it if it has not been properly proved by the parties.

The hybrid nature of foreign law in the judicial scope derives from the joint interpretation of Article 12(6) CC and Article 281 of *Ley de Enjuiciamiento Civil* of 2000 (Civil Procedure Act of 2000 (CPA hereinafter).[6] As pointed out above, the first provision states the mandatory nature of conflict of laws rules such that parties would not have to plead the foreign law if it were not because they have to base their respective arguments on the relevant applicable law. However, at the same time, this rule collides with the procedural treatment of foreign laws provided by the CPA of 2000.[7]

The main inconsistency would lie on the fact that the mandatory character awarded to conflict of laws rules does not entail the correlative burden for authorities to ascertain the content of the foreign law to be applied.[8] Article 282 CPA states that "Evidence shall be taken at the request of the parties. (…)" and Article 281 CPA clarifies explicitly the evidence regime of foreign laws and distinguishes it from the one governing the proof of "facts", in the following terms:

Article 281 CPA: Object and need of proof.

---

[4] VALLESPÍN PÉREZ, D.: "La prueba del Derecho extranjero en la Ley 1/2000, de Enjuiciamiento Civil", *Justicia: Revista de Derecho procesal,* No 1, 2000, p. 36.

[5] Judgment of Spanish Supreme Court 797/2007 of 4.7.2007 (RJ\2007\4937) and others listed in it. Some authors believe that the *ex officio* application of foreign laws is unreasonable. FORNER DELAYGUA, J.: *La prueba de los hechos en el proceso: aspectos de ley aplicable*, Bosch, Barcelona, 2006, p. 95.

[6] BOE n. 7 of 8.1.2000.

[7] Article 33.1 Act 29/2015: "The proof of the content and validity of foreign laws shall be governed by the Civil Procedure Act and other provisions applicable to this matter".

[8] IGLESIAS, J.L., ESPLUGUES, C., PALAO, G., ESPINOSA, R., AZCÁRRAGA, C.: "Spain" in IGLESIAS, J.L., ESPLUGUES, C. and PALAO, G.: *The Application of Foreign Laws by Judicial and Non-Judicial Authorities in Europe*, Sellier, Munich, 2011, p. 356.

1. Facts related with the access to justice sought in the procedure at hand shall be object of proof.
2. Custom and foreign law shall also be object of proof. The evidence of custom shall not be needed when the parties agree on its existence and content and its rules do not violate public policy. Foreign law shall be proved as regards its content and validity; the court may make use of all means of ascertainment deemed necessary for its implementation.
3. Facts on which there is full agreement of the parties are exempted from evidence, except in cases where the subject matter is not available for litigants.
4. Evidence of facts that are absolutely and generally known shall not be necessary.

Therefore facts must be proven by parties as a general rule and even though the Civil Procedure Act provides for some exceptions (evidence of facts is not required if parties are in full agreement on them and in case of facts that are absolutely and generally known), these rules are not applicable to foreign laws.

Article 281(2) CPA states that "Custom and foreign law shall also be object of proof" and they are provided for a different regime than the one established for "mere facts". Furthermore the treatment of foreign law does not include the possibility to skip evidence "when the parties agree on its existence and its rules do not violate public policy". This is only provided for custom. Foreign law shall be proved by parties in every case and this includes proving not only its content and validity, but also, as case law has traditionally supported,[9] the way it is interpreted or implemented by the authorities of the country of origin in such manner that Spanish judges will obtain certainty about the proper application of the relevant law.

If foreign laws are not proved or judges believe that they have not been evidenced sufficiently, they cannot be applied by courts and consequently the active or passive attitude of parties as regards the fulfilment of this procedural duty directly impacts on the mandatory nature of conflict of laws rules till the point that the current system is providing them *de facto* with a purely optional nature –thus contrary to the mandatory nature of Article 12(6) CC-.

We will explain in this Chapter the role of the authorities in this context and the accurate application of the rule contained in Article 281(2) CPA under which "the court may make use of all means of ascertainment deemed necessary for its implementation". But apart from some particular situations where court activity will be possible, the fact that the burden of proof rests with the parties makes the whole system unsatisfactory because it directly affects the final outcome of controversies governed by foreign laws.

II.2. Ascertainment of Foreign Law

As previously stated, the burden of proving foreign laws before judicial authorities rests with the parties. However, support activity of courts to this end has been accepted in particular situations by the Spanish Constitutional Court.[10] As a result, ascertainment of foreign law should be approached differently depending on the

[9] See in this regard, *ad ex,* judgment of the *Audiencia Provincial* of Valencia of 15.11.1993 (AC 1993\2234) or judgment of the *Audiencia Provincial* of Santa Cruz de Tenerife of 13.6.1994 (AC 1994\1003). "*Audiencias Provinciales*" are Appeal Courts of regional scope.

[10] Judgment 10/2000 of 17.1.2000 (RTC 2000\10). BOE n. 42 of 18.2.2000.

person performing this task, either parties or judicial authorities. Therefore, the different means that can be used to ascertain foreign laws will also differ depending on that same aspect.

II.2.1. Ascertainment of Foreign Law by Parties

Since the Spanish Civil Procedure Act of 2000 does not contain any specific provision on this issue, the general rules on evidence in Article 299 CPA shall apply as regards the means of proof of foreign laws available for parties. Among the limited means established (the list provided in Article 299(1) CPA is conceived as a *numerus clausus),* documentary evidence stands out from the rest (Article 299(2) and (3) CPA and 317 ff CPA), as well as the use of experts' opinions (Article 299(4) CPA and 335 ff CPA).[11]

Regarding documentary evidence, documents of public nature (issued by public authorities, such as certificates issued by Consulates) bear more relevance than private documents. Although the latter (doctrinal works, copies of legal instruments or case law) can also be presented as evidence of a foreign law, the court may consider that they are not sufficient to this end. When it comes to evidence based on experts' opinions, legal opinions of at least two prestigious jurists of the foreign country are traditionally admitted.[12] However, it must be noted that Article 33.4 Act 29/2015 states that "No report or opinion, national or international, on foreign law, shall be binding for Spanish courts".

II.2.2. Ascertainment of Foreign Law by Courts

As regards the possibility of courts to ascertain the content of the foreign law it is important to remember that Article 281(2) CPA states that "the court may make use of all means of ascertainment deemed necessary for its implementation". The interpretation of this provision requires clarifying two different issues. In first place, the particular situations where this rule can be applied; in second place, the accurate meaning of the terms "means of ascertainment".

The enactment of the Civil Procedure Act of 2000 was conceived at that moment as increasing the power of judges to this respect comparing with the former regulation but a remarkable continuity of the former situation has been evidenced in practice[13] as a consequence of the Constitutional Case Law mentioned above. Such doctrine does not accept the existence of a generic duty of collaboration of judges

[11] IGLESIAS, J.L. and ESPLUGUES, C.: *Derecho internacional privado*, Tirant Lo Blanch, Valencia, 2016, pp. 306–307.

[12] Judgments of Spanish Supreme Court of 22.5.2001 (RJ 2001\6477) and of 15.3.1984 (RJ 1984\1574).

[13] For instance, Judgment *Audiencia Provincial* of Málaga 120/2005 of 10.2.2005 (JUR\2005\139773) about separation of Moroccan spouses governed by Moroccan Law. The court holds that despite the resources available for judges, the burden of proving the content of the foreign law rests with the parties.

so that judicial collaboration is actually limited to those cases in which the parties have shown a minimum level of diligence in proving the foreign law.

If parties have tried to prove the foreign law with no success or in case the fulfilment of this obligation becomes really impossible (for instance, regions involved in armed conflicts or having acquired independence recently), the judge should cooperate with parties in this task following Article 281(2) CPA in order to avoid a possible violation of the right of access to justice.[14] On the contrary, in case this diligence of parties is not established, judges are not compelled to provide them with assistance[15] and of course they are not in any case forced to apply the foreign law *ex officio*. Judges cannot replace the parties in the search of the content and validity of foreign laws irrespective of their activity. They may cooperate with the parties but cannot substitute them in this task.

On the other hand, the use of the wording "means of ascertainment" instead of "means of proof" has been granted a broad interpretation in the sense of providing judges with more possibilities than parties to undertake this task, since they can make use of all means of evidence listed in the procedural legislation (like parties) as well as other channels such as[16] their own knowledge in certain cases (for instance, because the court has applied the same foreign law several times); the mechanisms provided by some international conventions, both bilateral or multilateral; or the access to the European Judicial Network in Civil and Commercial Matters[17] or the new European e-Justice Portal.[18]

Whether the foreign law is considered sufficiently proved or not depends on the personal assessment made by the authority hearing the case, this said for both scopes covered by this Chapter, judicial and non-judicial authorities. In case it is deemed to be sufficiently proved, it will be treated as authentic law and will be applied by Spanish authorities the same way it would be applied in the country of origin.

II.3. Failure to Establish Foreign Law

Before the adoption of Act 29/2015 there was no explicit solution in case of failure to establish the foreign law and this situation generated different outcomes and legal uncertainty[19] depending on the court dealing with the particular case. The introduction of an explicit solution appears consequently as one of the main novelties of Act 29/2015.

---

[14] This is clearly reflected in the above mentioned Judgment of the Constitutional Court 10/2000 of 17.1.2000. The Court held that the claimant's right of access to justice had been violated by the *Audiencia Provincial* of Vizcaya because it had frustrated the possibility of ascertaining Armenian law to her divorce after having sufficiently proved that she was diligent in trying to prove it.

[15] See, for instance, Judgment of *Audiencia Provincial* of Guadalajara 12/2004 of 14.1.2004 (AC\2004\371). ESPINOSA CALABUIG, R.: "Nota a la SAP de Guadalajara de 14 de enero de 2004", *Revista Española de Derecho Internacional,* n. 57, 2005, pp. 350 ff.; or Judgment of *Audiencia Provincial* of Castellón 64/2009 of 15.7. 2009 (AC\2009\1876).

[16] CALVO, A.L. and CARRASCOSA, J.: "La prueba del Derecho extranjero ante los tribunales", *Estudios de Deusto*, vol. 54-2, 2006, p. 80.

[17] http://ec.europa.eu/civiljustice/index_en.htm (accessed 26.10.2016).

[18] https://e-justice.europa.eu/home.do?action=home&plang=en (accessed 26.10.2016).

[19] ÁLVAREZ GONZÁLEZ, S.: "Aplicación judicial del Derecho extranjero: la desconcertante

Before the new regime, the absence of a rule had led to two different possibilities in the Spanish *praxis*[20]: the traditional choice of applying Spanish law instead of the foreign law pointed by the conflict of laws rule; or the dismissal of the cause of action brought before the courts according to Article 217 CPA.

Among these options, the subsidiary application of Spanish law in case of lack of proof of foreign law appeared to be the most followed solution in lower courts and was supported by the Supreme Court[21] despite admitting criticism as well because it rewards the negligence of the parties when undertaking this task and favours the resort to strategies when they prefer Spanish law to be applied instead of the applicable foreign law.[22] However, we agree upon the inconvenience of the solution supporting the dismissal of the claim because, as the Constitutional Court has also said, the subsidiary application of Spanish law is more respectful with the citizens' right of access to justice than rejecting the claim.[23] And this is actually the explicit solution currently stated in Article 33.3 Act 29/2015: "Exceptionally, in cases where the content and validity of foreign law cannot be evidenced by the parties, Spanish law may[24] be applied".

II.4. Judicial Review

In case of judicial decisions, the system of challenges provided for in the procedural legislation shall be applied. In case of extrajudicial decisions, an administrative challenge before a public body within the Ministry of Justice, i.e. General Directorate of Registries and Notaries (*Dirección General de los Registros y del Notariado*) is established.

Focusing on judicial decisions, four different situations may be distinguished[25]: Firstly, the court has not applied the conflict of laws rule or it has applied it wrongly. Secondly, the court has correctly applied the conflict of laws rule but the foreign law has not been validly proved by the parties and Spanish law has been finally applied. Thirdly, the court has correctly applied the conflict of laws rule, the parties have proved the content and validity of the foreign law but Spanish law has been finally

---

práctica judicial, los estériles esfuerzos doctrinales y la necesaria reforma legislativa", *La Ley. Revista jurídica española de doctrina, jurisprudencia y bibliografía,* n. 6287, 2005, p. 2004.

[20] PALAO MORENO, G.: "Das Fehlen von Vorbringen, Darlegung und Beweis auslandischen Rechts im spanischen Zivilprozess", *ZZPInt*, n. 13, 2008, pp. 39–45.

[21] Judgment 436/2005 of 10.6.2005 and related decisions listed in it.

[22] DESDENTADO BONETE, A.: "Otro cierre en falso? La prueba del Derecho extranjero", *Diario La Ley*, n. 1, 2005, p. 1789.

[23] Judgments of Constitutional Court 10/2000 of 17.1.2000 (RTC\2000\10), 155/2001 of 2.7.2001 (RTC\2001\155) and 33/2002 of 11.2.2002 (RTC\2002\33). A summary of these three Constitutional decisions is provided in Judgment of the Supreme Court 2652/2003 of 4.11.2004 (RJ 2005\1056).

[24] Please note that the facultative drafting of the rule still permits the adoption of other measures. It would have been advisable to include a mandatory rule.

[25] IGLESIAS, J.L., ESPLUGUES, C., PALAO, G., ESPINOSA, R., AZCÁRRAGA, C.: "Spain", *cit.*, p. 364.

applied to the merits. Lastly, a fourth possibility exists where the judge has properly applied the Spanish conflict of laws rule, the foreign law has been validly proved by the parties and the court has applied the foreign law, but the parties consider that it has been wrongly applied.

Starting from these four situations, the CPA of 2000 provides for several appeals before different judicial instances. On the one hand, Articles 207(1) and 455 CPA admit the possibility of a general appeal *("recurso de apelación")* of first instance decisions before *Audiencias Provinciales* (Provincial Courts). This possibility is said to be applicable to every situation previously stated. On the other hand, Article 477(1) CPA also states the possibility to challenge a previous decision rendered by a Provincial Court (if some conditions are met) through cassation before the Supreme Court *("recurso de casación")*. This is deemed to be applicable with no doubt to the three first situations but the fourth one is more controversial since the Spanish legislator says nothing to this respect and scholars and case law do not follow a sole interpretation.

While some believe that this challenge should also be granted in cases where the foreign law has not been properly applied, others do not think the violation of a foreign law can be object of cassation. Starting with the positive position, some Spanish authors argue the possibility of challenging a judgment before the Supreme Court in these cases on the grounds that the wrong application of a foreign law is a consequence of the mandate of conflict of laws rules under Article 12(6) CC.[26]

By contrast, the negative view, which has also been supported by the Spanish Supreme Court in Judgment of 15.7.1983,[27] has been grounded on several reasons.[28] In first place, foreign law is conceived as a fact; hence cassation is not available in this case because this challenge is solely envisaged *"as a unique ground"* for violations of legal rules under Article 477(1) CPA. Secondly, one of the aims of this cassation challenge is to maintain the uniformity of case law of the Supreme Court in its task of interpretation of the Spanish legal system. And thirdly, to admit this possibility could lead to contradictory interpretations of the foreign law between the one held by national authorities of such country and Spanish case law.

Finally, a third path supports the possibility of reviewing in cassation the application of foreign law by the Supreme Court without considering the judgment as being part of the Spanish case law (as an exception of what it is stated in Article 1(6) CC, which deals with the sources of our legal system). This has actually been the position of the Supreme Court in Judgment of 4.7.2006[29] where it held the possibility of challenging in cassation before the highest Court but not the obligation of including the relevant judgment in the Spanish jurisprudence. Otherwise it might imply a denial of justice and would also lead to violate the mandatory nature of conflict of laws rules.

---

[26] CALVO CARAVACA, A.L. and CARRASCOSA GONZÁLEZ, J.: "Aplicación del Derecho extranjero en España y la nueva Ley de Enjuiciamiento Civil", *Anales de Derecho. Universidad de Murcia*, n. 17, 1999, pp. 302–303.

[27] RJ 1983\4228.

[28] MIRALLES SANGRO, P.P.: Aplicación del Derecho extranjero en el proceso y tutela judicial, Dykinson, Madrid, 2007, p. 213.

[29] RJ 2006\6080.

III. Foreign Law in Other Instances

As previously said, in accordance with Article 12(6) CC "Spanish authorities and courts must apply *ex officio* the conflict of laws rules of Spanish law". Therefore all Spanish authorities are obliged to apply conflict of laws rules to private international relationships and this entails potentially that all authorities dealing with these situations –non-judicial authorities as well- may be involved in the task of applying foreign laws.

For instance, authorities in charge of Civil Registries may apply foreign laws when determining the capacity of foreigners to get married in Spain. Notaries may also need to apply the law of another country when establishing the capacity of a foreigner to enter into a contract or to establish a last will. International successions governed by foreign laws may also have consequences in the registration of immovable properties in Land Registries. And the same can be said as regards Commercial Registrars who deal with transactions with foreign elements.

III.1. Non-judicial Authorities

The legal regime governing the application of foreign laws outside courts is not the same as in the judicial scope. As will be explained in this section, more flexible solutions are provided for and this usually leads to more satisfactory outcomes. We will approach the legal regime applicable to public registries and notarial activity.

III.1.1. Application of Foreign Laws by Authorities in Charge of the Civil Registry

Legal sources in this scope are contained in Article 15 of Civil Registry Act (*Ley del Registro Civil*) of 1957 (CRA hereinafter)[30] and Article 91 and 152 of Civil Registry Regulation (*Reglamento del Registro Civil*) of 1958 (CRR hereinafter).[31] In accordance with Article 15 CRA registrable facts shall include those affecting Spaniards and the events occurred in Spanish territory affecting foreigners. In any case events occurred abroad shall also be registered when the corresponding entries constitute the basis for registration required by Spanish law.

Article 91 CRR states that the adequacy of a fact or a document to the relevant foreign law can be established by the authority *ex officio* and in case he does not know the relevant foreign law its content can be ascertained by different means: either by a testimony of the Consul of the country of origin in Spain, or by a testimony of the Consul of Spain in the country of origin, or by a testimony of a Spanish Public Notary who knows such foreign law.

---

[30] BOE n. 151 of 10.6.1957. A new Civil Registry Act will enter into force in July 2017.

[31] BOE n. 296 of 11.12.1958.

Article 152 CRR states that registration of civil status under a foreign law or the existence or inexistence of a fact or resolution affecting the civil status requires presenting the corresponding public title, the authentic certificate of the foreign Registry or the official declaration issued abroad.

III.1.2. Application of Foreign Laws by Land Registrars

Legal sources in this scope are contained in Article 36 and Article 37 of Land Registry Regulation (*Reglamento Hipotecario*) of 1947 (LRR hereinafter).[32] Article 36(I) LRR admits as a general rule the possibility of registering in the Land Registry any document issued abroad insofar it complies with the requirements set out by Spanish Private International Law rules, i.e. legalization and any other formal conditions deemed necessary for the document to be formally valid in Spain. Furthermore the fulfilment of foreign forms and solemnities, as well as the legal aptitude and legal capacity to perform acts and render documents must be proved. This can be done, *inter alia*, by way of a report or asseveration issued by different authorities mentioned in this provision: a Spanish Public Notary, a Spanish Consul or a competent Diplomat, Consul or Civil Servant of the country whose legislation must be applied. However, Article 36(III) LRR states that the Land Registrar is allowed not to use those three methods under his own responsibility in case he knows sufficiently the foreign law. In doing so he must state it in the relevant entry.

On the other hand, under Article 37 LRR these documents must be translated into Spanish or any other language granted official character in Spain.[33] However, again and in similar terms as above, the Land Registrar may leave aside the translation if he knows the foreign language in which the document is drafted.

III.1.3. Application of Foreign Laws by Commercial Registrars

Legal sources in this scope are contained in Article 5(3) of Commercial Registry Regulation (*Reglamento del Registro Mercantil*) of 1996 (CRR hereinafter).[34] Article 5(3) CRR states in particular that registration in Commercial Registries of foreign documents shall be governed by the regulation governing Land Registries (LRR *supra*). Existence and valid constitution of registered corporations and the continuity of the position and the powers of the persons who represent them may also be accredited by means of a certification duly legalized or "apostilled", issued either by the competent Civil Servant of the public Registry referred to by the European Directive 68/151/EEC of 9.3.1968[35] or of a similar office in those countries not having an institutional equivalence.

[32] BOE n. 106 of 16.4.1947.

[33] Other languages coexist with Castilian in some Spanish regions (Catalonia, Valencia, Galicia, Basque Country, Balearic Islands and Navarra).

[34] BOE n. 184 of 31.7.1996.

[35] OJ L 65 of 14.3.1968.

III.1.4. Application of Foreign Laws by Notaries

The source in this field is Article 168 of Notarial Regulation (*Reglamento de Organización y Régimen del Notariado*) of 1944 (NR hereinafter).[36] If Notaries render documents affecting foreigners, Article 168(I)(4) NR provides for two different rules which show once again that the legal regime of the application of foreign laws is more flexible outside courts than in the judicial system. In the notarial scope the capacity of foreigners will be ascertained by the Notary himself if he knows the relevant foreign law. And in case he does not know whether the foreigner is capable or not in accordance with the law governing his or her capacity, this matter will be accredited by means of a certification of the Consul. If this is not possible, accreditation will be performed by the diplomatic representative of such country in Spain.

Together with the above, Article 168(II) NR states that in case the country of origin of the foreigner only uses the first name and one family name, the Spanish Notary is prevented from asking him the second family name, even if the name is to be included in a document which will be registered in the Land Registry.

III.2. Failure to Establish Foreign Law

The nature and purpose of the activity of non-judicial authorities leads to a different treatment of the failure to establish foreign laws comparing with the judicial scope. As explained above, the application of foreign laws is not directly linked to the proof of its content by the parties. Outside courts several means are available for authorities and this flexibility should benefit the accomplishment of better results. However, even in this framework foreign laws may not always be ascertained.

If the latter happens none of the regulations mentioned above provide for explicit solutions. Concerning the notarial scope, the failure to establish the foreign law will affect the substantial performance of the requested legal act. As regards the above mentioned Registries (Civil Registry, as well as Land or Commercial Registries) it has been suggested that the requested registration should be refused unless an international agreement providing otherwise could be applied. For instance, concerning Civil Registries Article 5(1) of the Munich Convention on the Law Applicable to Surnames and Forenames of 5.9.1980[37] compels to apply domestic law in such cases.

III.3. Foreign Law in Arbitration and Mediation

Arbitration is regulated in the Spanish Arbitration Act 60/2003 of 23 July (AA hereinafter).[38] The Spanish Constitutional Court has considered arbitration as a "jurisdictional equivalent" since long ago. Constitutional case law has confirmed

[36] BOE n. 189 of 7.7.1944.

[37] BOE n. 303 of 19.12.1989.

[38] BOE n. 309 of 26.12.2003.

this view (Judgment 62/1991) while ascertaining that the right of access to justice (stated in Article 24 of the Spanish Constitution) is not violated by the decision of submitting a controversy to arbitration.

Foreign laws are also applied by arbitrators in Spain although this particular issue is not clarified in the Spanish legislation.[39] Article 34 AA regulates the rules governing the merits of the controversy in the following terms:

Article 34 AA: Rules applicable to the merits of the controversy.

1. Arbitrators will only resolve in equity if the parties have authorised them explicitly to do so.
2. Without prejudice of the previous paragraph, in international arbitrations arbitrators will resolve the controversy under the legal rules chosen by the parties. Unless provided otherwise every reference made to a national legal system will refer to the substantive rules of such country and not to its conflict of laws rules.

   If parties do not establish the applicable legal rules arbitrators will apply the rules they will consider more appropriate.
3. In any case, arbitrators will resolve the controversy under the terms of the contract and will consider the applicable uses".

Paragraph 2 states that "in international arbitrations arbitrators will resolve the controversy under the legal rules chosen by the parties". It should then been understood that the parties should bring evidence of those "chosen rules" for them to be applied by arbitrators (by means of experts' opinions, for instance). The situation changes if the parties do not provide the arbitrator with the applicable legal rules. In such a case "arbitrators will apply the rules they will consider more appropriate" and therefore they will be forced to establish their content on their own.

As regards mediation, a new Act of national scope was adopted in 2012 as a consequence of the transposition of Directive 2008/52/CE of 21 May 2008 on certain aspects of mediation in civil and commercial matters[40]: the Spanish Act 5/2012, of 6 July 2012, on Mediation in Civil and Commercial Matters (MA hereinafter).[41] Under Article 2 MA this new regulation shall be applied if it is explicitly or implicitly chosen by the parties or, in the case of lack of choice, when one party at least is domiciled in Spain and the mediation takes place in Spain. Furthermore such legal regime shall be applied to "mediation in civil and commercial matters, including cross-border disputes, provided that they do not affect rights and duties which are not available for the parties under the relevant applicable law".

The consequent problem would be to fix such "relevant applicable law". The new Act does not clarify this matter but in cross-border cases it shall be understood that the relevant conflict of laws rule in the particular matter will point the applicable law and if it turns to be a foreign law, its ascertainment and subsequent application is affected by the very nature of mediation, a system where the mediator does not resolve the controversy like in arbitration but the parties themselves. In this sense,

---

[39] Arbitration procedures developed within arbitration entities are also governed by the Arbitration Rules of those entities but none of the Regulations which have been consulted for this contribution deal with the application of foreign laws.

[40] OJ L 136 of 24.5.2008.

[41] BOE n. 162 of 7.7.2012.

legal advice is especially significant in international controversies because settlements are usually expected to be granted efficacy in more than one country.

Moreover, the final settlement reached by the parties as the culmination of the mediation procedure may be notarised in order to be converted into an enforceable title (Article 23(3)(II) MA) and the Notary will have to verify the fulfilment of all the requirements established by the MA as well as that the mediation settlement is not contrary to the law (Article 25 MA). At this moment the Notary would have to ascertain the content of such law and the rules on the application of foreign laws in the notarial activity explained above should be applied in case it would be the law of another country.

IV. Access to Foreign Law: Status Quo

The issue concerning the information about foreign laws has been object of regulation in the recent Act 29/2015 on International Judicial Cooperation. Article 34 states that such "information" may include aspects like the legal provisions themselves, their validity, content, sense and scope, the case law, the procedural framework, the judicial organization and any other relevant legal information.

On the other hand, Articles 35 and 36 regulate the procedural treatment of information requests in two different situations: in case Spanish authorities ask for assistance abroad, and conversely, in case foreign authorities request such assistance to our authorities. Without prejudice of the possibility of direct contact between authorities, these two provisions refer to the possible intermediation of the Spanish Central Authority, i.e. the Ministry of Justice in accordance with Article 7 Act 29/2015.

Besides this new regime, it should be noted that information about Spanish law is also available on the Internet in a number of official Websites (although it is not always updated). For instance, the Official Journal (*Boletín Oficial del Estado*),[42] Labour legislation provided by the Ministry of Employment and Social Security,[43] Electronic Codes on different fields of law[44] or even legislation translated into French or English provided by the Ministry of Justice.[45]

On the other hand, Spain is a member of several networks of international cooperation such as The Hague Judicial Network of The Hague Conference on Private International Law,[46] the European Judicial Network in civil and commercial

[42] Available at (accessed 26.10.2016): https://www.boe.es/legislacion/legislacion.php

[43] Available at (accessed 26.10.2016): http://www.empleo.gob.es/es/sec_leyes/

[44] Available at (accessed 26.10.2016): https://www.boe.es/legislacion/codigos/codigo.php?id=034_Codigo_Civil_y_legislacion_complementaria&modo=1

[45] Available at (accessed 26.10.2016): http://www.mjusticia.gob.es/cs/Satellite/es/1288774502225/ListaPublicaciones.html

[46] The Spanish representative of this network is The Honourable Judge Francisco Javier Forcada Miranda, Court of Appeal, Madrid. Information available at (accessed 26.10.2016): http://www.hcch.net/upload/haguenetwork.pdf

matters,[47] the Ibero-American Network of Judicial Assistance (IberRed)[48] or the Network for legislative cooperation between the Ministries of Justice of the European Union.[49]

Furthermore, Spain has ratified a set of international conventions on information of foreign law, both multilateral and bilateral. While multilateral conventions are more used in practice, bilateral agreements are rarely used by Spanish judges.[50] Moreover more requests are received than emanated from Spanish authorities.[51] Regarding multilateral conventions, we refer to the European Convention of 7 June 1968 on Information on Foreign Law ("London Convention") and the Inter-American Convention of 8 May 1979 on Proof of and Information on Foreign Law ("Montevideo Convention"). And bilateral agreements on legal cooperation regulating the commitment to provide information on the content of the respective legal systems include[52]:

(a) Convention of 23 May 1993 on Mutual Assistance in Civil Matters between the Kingdom of Spain and the Republic of Bulgaria.
(b) Convention of 4 May 1987 on Legal Assistance Recognition and Enforcement of Judgments in Civil Matters between the Kingdom of Spain and the Czechoslovak Socialist Republic.
(c) Convention of 26 October 1990 on Judicial Assistance in Civil Matters between the Kingdom of Spain and Union of Soviet Socialist Republics (USSR).
(d) Cooperation Agreement of 1 December 1984 on Legal Information Exchange in Civil and Commercial Matters between the Kingdom of Spain and the Mexican United States.
(e) Convention of 24 February 2005 on Judicial Assistance in Civil and Commercial Matters between the Kingdom of Spain and the People's Democratic Republic of Algeria.
(f) Convention of 13 April 1989 on Legal Cooperation in Civil Matters between the Kingdom of Spain and the Federal Republic of Brazil.
(g) Convention of 2 May 1992 on Mutual Assistance in Civil and Commercial Matters between the Kingdom of Spain and the People's Republic of China.

[47] Available at (accessed 26.10.2016): http://ec.europa.eu/civiljustice/index_en.htm

[48] Available at (accessed 26.10.2016): https://www.iberred.org/

[49] Available at (accessed 26.10.2016): http://legicoop.eu/

[50] IGLESIAS, J.L., ESPLUGUES, C., PALAO, G., ESPINOSA, R., AZCÁRRAGA, C.: "Spain", *cit.*, p. 368.

[51] See Spanish answer to the questionnaire of 2007 of The Hague Conference on Private International Law concerning the treatment of foreign law. Available at (accessed 26.10.2016): http://www.hcch.net/upload/wop/genaff_pd09es.pdf

[52] Please note that the implementation of bilateral agreements may be affected by the fact that some of the countries with which those agreements have been negotiated are also parties to the London or Montevideo Conventions. For instance, Bulgaria, Slovakia and Czech Republic are also parties to the London Convention. Mexico is a party to the London and Montevideo Conventions. Russia is also a party to the London Convention.

(h) Convention of 15 September 2003 on Mutual Assistance in Civil and Commercial Matters between the Kingdom of Spain and the Dominican Republic.
(i) Convention of 30 May 1997 on Judicial Cooperation in Civil, Commercial and Administrative Matters between the Kingdom of Spain and the Kingdom of Morocco.
(j) Convention of 15 June 1998 on Mutual Assistance in Civil and Commercial Matters between the Kingdom of Spain and the Kingdom of Thailand.
(k) Convention of 4 November 1987 on Legal Cooperation between the Kingdom of Spain and the Oriental Republic of Uruguay.

V. Access to Foreign Law: Further Developments

V.1. Practical Need

The Spanish system governing the application of foreign laws was amended in 2015 including some improvements such as the explicit reference to the solution to be adopted in case of failure proving the applicable law or the procedural treatment of requests about information, but the main solutions have been preserved and no substantial changes have been adopted.[53] Hereinafter, any attempt of further developing the system will be fostered by international organisations like the European Union or The Hague Conference on Private International Law.

Despite the entry into force of very recent rules in this field, we support the urgent need of adopting international initiatives in order to resolve the practical problems still existing in this field, above all in the judicial scope. Other fields like arbitration or the activity developed in public registries are more flexible in the search of solutions, but access to foreign law in the judicial scope needs urgently to be improved because the final success of the whole system is today made dependant on the will of the parties and their available means.

The problems existing in the treatment of foreign laws are particularly worrying for those matters in which conflict of laws rules have already been harmonised in the EU. The most common areas of foreign law applied by or invoked before Spanish judicial authorities include marriage and nullity of marriage, divorce and legal separations, parental responsibility, parent-child relationship, international child protection including child abduction and child adoption, maintenance, commercial contracts, sale of goods, securities transactions, property and inheritance.[54] Within this list harmonisation of conflict of laws rules has already been accom-

[53] We share the disappointed view of the Spanish doctrine: CALVO CARAVACA, A.L.: "Aplicación judicial Derecho extranjero en España. Consideraciones críticas", *Revista Española de Derecho Internacional*, n. 68, 2016, p. 155.

[54] See the Spanish answer to the questionnaire of 2007 of The Hague Conference on Private International Law concerning the treatment of foreign law. Available at (accessed 26.10.2016): http://www.hcch.net/upload/wop/genaff_pd09es.pdf

plished in matters like contractual and non-contractual obligations, divorce and separation, maintenance or successions.

The main objective of applicable law instruments is the application of the same law to the same controversy regardless of the European court seized by the parties. But the still existing divergences between EU Member States as regards the application of foreign laws[55] frustrates this objective because the effective –and correct- application of the relevant foreign law still depends on the domestic system of the Member State where the case is heard.

This reality hinders the creation of a real space of civil justice throughout the EU because the same case may be resolved differently depending on the Member State where the litigation is taking place. This generates an undesirable state of legal uncertainty affecting citizens' expectations and favours *forum shopping* and "races to court" because despite the harmonisation of conflict of laws rules parties can still select the more convenient court for their interests taking advantage of this heterogeneity.[56]

The European legislator has started to show a first interest in dealing with the treatment of foreign laws at a supranational level but there is still much to do.[57] The same can be said in the scope of the works developed by The Hague Conference on Private International Law.[58] Both organisations have even organised a joint EC-HCCH Conference on access to foreign law held in Brussels on 15-17 February 2012.[59] If any of these initiatives is finally culminated the impact for the Spanish regime will probably be positive, above all if they support the establishment of an *ex officio* system of application of foreign laws.

[55] See IGLESIAS, J.L., ESPLUGUES, C. and PALAO, G.: The Application of Foreign Laws by Judicial and Non-Judicial Authorities in Europe, Sellier, Munich, 2011.

[56] AZCÁRRAGA MONZONÍS, C.: "The Urgent Need for Harmonisation of the Application of Foreign Laws by National Authorities in Europe", *International Journal of Procedural Law*, 2013-3, pp. 107–109.

[57] See in this regard AZCÁRRAGA MONZONÍS, C.: "The Urgent Need for …", *cit.*, pp. 105–126. We have supported in the past that the adoption of an initiative about this issue at EU level is not only convenient but even necessary to overcome the current unsatisfactory scenario. Such proposal supports the adoption of a new EU Regulation on the treatment of foreign laws covering every situation where judicial and non-judicial authorities have to face this task no matter the source -international or domestic- of the relevant conflict of laws rule pointing the applicable law.

[58] See LORTIE, P.: "The Evolution of Work on Foreign Law at the Hague Conference on Private International Law", 2012, available at (accessed 26.10.2016): http://www.hcch.net/upload/hidden/2012/lortie.pdf

[59] All information available at (accessed 26.10.2016): http://www.hcch.net/upload/hidden/2012/xs2foreignlaw.html

V.2. *Conflict of Laws Solutions*

While waiting for the development of the above mentioned initiatives at international level, other conflict of laws solutions -mostly incorporated by EU law- have also helped to reduce the number of cases in which foreign law is applied through favouring the coincidence *forum-ius*. The application of the substantive law of the authority hearing the case (*lex fori*) can be achieved either by choice of law made by the parties or by means of the application of objective criteria.

"Party autonomy" as connecting factor has been introduced in every matter regulated so far in European Private International Law. Parties have broader or narrower possibilities to choose the law governing the relationship under a number of EU Regulations and they usually have the possibility to select as applicable law the legal system of the competent authority hearing the case thus favouring the coincidence *forum-ius*. The same can be ascertained following the application of objective criteria since "habitual residence" is displacing "nationality" as the main connection in many fields.

V.3. *Methods of Facilitating Access to Foreign Law*

Several methods of access to foreign law have already been implemented in Spain; for instance, the use of Information Communication Technologies (ICT) and international judicial and administrative cooperation, but the main problem still rests with the premise from which the whole system derives. The fact that in the judicial scope it all depends on the activity of the parties frustrates a successful outcome. Therefore, the author of this Chapter supports changing the existing system and implementing an *ex officio* model as already exists in other European countries.[60]

The implementation of a system based on a more active role of authorities may even entail the creation of new jobs, entities and networks of professionals specialized in proof of national legal systems. These may include lawyers and other jurists as legal experts, public or private research entities and translators. The creation of networks of entities and professionals working in all those fields which may be contacted by authorities for support –which would consist of drafting non-binding reports and providing legal translations- could be certainly useful. Obviously, this proposal would need to be accompanied by financial support. If ascertainment of foreign laws is going to be converted into a public issue, the provision of research and translation services must be covered by public means and this would probably be a controversial issue at the present moment taking into account the situation of crisis Spain is experiencing today.

[60] ESPLUGUES, C. (Rapporteur), IGLESIAS, J.L., PALAO, G., ESPINOSA, R. and AZCÁRRAGA, C.: "General Report on the Application of Foreign Law by Judicial and Non-Judicial Authorities in Europe", in IGLESIAS, J.L., ESPLUGUES, C. and PALAO, G.: *The Application of Foreign Laws by Judicial and Non-Judicial Authorities in Europe*, Sellier, Munich, 2011, pp. 38 ff.

But while we wait for that change to happen (maybe someday through the intervention of the European legislator), it may be useful to remind that international or regional instruments on information of foreign law in force in Spain already provide for useful channels of cooperation but these are not always applied in practice or are even unknown. Training about this issue should also be fostered in order to inform authorities about existing methods and promote their use consequently. The role of the Spanish General Council of the Judiciary (*Consejo General del Poder Judicial*) is significant to this end.[61]

VI. Conclusion

Despite the adoption in 2015 of new rules in this field, the current Spanish system provided for in the judicial scope still raises serious concerns and should be improved. Making the application of foreign laws dependant on the activity of the parties is disproportionate, taking into account their means and the costs this process may entail,[62] not to mention those situations where the parties are not even interested in proving. Furthermore, the system is inconsistent insofar it provides for mandatory conflict of laws rules while courts shall wait for the parties to prove the relevant applicable law. This solution undermines the very nature of conflict of laws rules, as well as the policies underlying the choices of the legislator.

The situation appears to be more coherent in the non-judicial arena, where ascertainment of foreign law is performed by Registrars and Notaries in a more flexible manner. This possibility is not only evidenced in law –as explained above- but also in practice.[63] Extrajudicial authorities are empowered to apply foreign law despite the lack of proof by the parties and this rule should be extended to the judicial scope. This proposal is not going to be implemented at a national level but it may derive in the future from the boost of the European legislator.

---

[61] Two more networks which have been created within this public body are also worth mentioning in the scope of international cooperation: REJUE (*Red Judicial Española*, Spanish Judicial Network) and REDUE (*Red de Expertos en Derecho de la Unión Europea*, Network of Experts in European Law). Further information at (accessed 26.10.2016): http://www.poderjudicial.es/cgpj/es/Temas/Redes-Judiciales

[62] CARBALLO PIÑEIRO, L.: "El carácter imperativo de la norma de conflicto y la prueba del Derecho extranjero. Una relectura en clave procesal y constitucional", *Anuario Español de Derecho Internacional Privado,* 2001, p. 493.

[63] RODRÍGUEZ SÁNCHEZ, J.S.: Una introducción al Reglamento de Sucesiones de la UE –desde la perspectica de los derechos reales sobre bienes inmuebles y el Registro de la Propiedad de España-, Cuadernos de Derecho Registral, Fundación Registral, Madrid, 2013, p. 41. The author explains how Registrars have traditionally make efforts to find out the content of foreign succession laws. At least the most commonly applied in Spain such as French or German laws.

Sweden: Proof of and Information About Foreign Law in Civil and Commercial Matters – Swedish Perspectives

Ulf Maunsbach

Abstract The treatment of private international law in Sweden, including proof and information about foreign law, is influenced both by Sweden's membership in the European Union and by Sweden's close relationship with its neighboring Nordic countries (e.g. Denmark, Finland, Iceland and Norway). Another feature of relevance that impacts the possibility to draw firm conclusions regarding the treatment of foreign law in Sweden is the fact that there are few cases to draw conclusions from. However, some distinctive features regarding the treatment of foreign law in Sweden will be presented. It will be discussed to what extent Swedish courts are to apply foreign law *ex officio* and a distinction between mandatory and non-mandatory issues are made. It is highlighted that foreign law is treated as law (and not fact) in Sweden and that it is to be applied loyally, in conformity with how the law is applied in the country of origin. It is presented that a failure to determine the content of foreign law may be cured in different ways and it is concluded that a wrongful application of foreign law may be appealed in accordance with a normal appeal. It is further concluded that Swedish courts (and other instances that apply foreign law) rather use informal network in order to ascertain the content of foreign law than official networks (like the London rules). A concluding comment is that the treatment of foreign law in Sweden would benefit from a more developed system through which judges will be able to contact colleagues in other countries.

I. Introduction

Sweden is a Member State of the European Union and as such all binding EU legal acts are applicable in Sweden. Due to the development towards a full scale harmonisation in the field of private international law it can, on a general note, be stated that Sweden's legislation in this field is increasingly a result of the membership in EU.

U. Maunsbach (✉)
Associate Professor, Faculty of Law, University of Lund, P.O. Box 207, Lund 221 00, Sweden
e-mail: Ulf.Maunsbach@jur.lu.se

Y. Nishitani (ed.), *Treatment of Foreign Law - Dynamics towards Convergence?*,
Ius Comparatum – Global Studies in Comparative Law 26,
DOI 10.1007/978-3-319-56574-3_16

Another feature that affects the Swedish legal system is Sweden's close relation to the other Nordic countries and the developed co-operation that exists in this region.[1] One area that has been important is co-operation in the field of private international law, not the least within the area of family law. Although much of the development is now due to initiatives from EU, there still exist a tradition of specific Nordic regulatory co-operation.[2] So far none of the inter-Nordic regulations in the field of private international law has been revoked due to the increased influence of EU-law, but many of the Nordic regulations has been amended to better adopt to the European framework. It may also be stated that the importance of the inter-Nordic regulations is affected by the fact that an increasing number of areas are governed by directly applicable EU-law.[3]

Irrespective of the fact that private international law is harmonised, the judicial system is still, to a large extent, a national concern. Consequently issues as to proof and information about foreign law may be dealt with differently by courts in different EU states (and/or Nordic states).

I will henceforth focus on the Swedish judiciary system and I will primarily deal with application of foreign law within a private-law context. Consequently criminal proceedings and the application of foreign criminal law will not be covered. In Sweden there are three kinds of courts, all of which may encounter situations where foreign private law is to be applied. The first group is the general courts, which comprise 48 district courts, 6 courts of appeal and the Supreme Court. A second group is the general administrative courts, which comprise 12 administrative courts, 4 administrative courts of appeal and the Supreme Administrative Court. Finally there are also special courts, which determine disputes within special areas, for example, the Labour Court, Land and Environmental Courts, the Migration Court and the Patent and Market Courts.[4]

In the following I shall focus on the general court system that is governed by the Swedish Code of Judicial Procedure,[5] but most of the analysis as to proof of and

---

[1] The Nordic region is the name for the north European region consisting of Denmark, Finland, Iceland, Norway and Sweden, and the three autonomous regions of Faroe Islands, Greenland and Åland. The Nordic Council and The Nordic Council of Ministers represent the official Nordic co-operation. The Nordic Council was formed in 1952 and is the forum for inter-parliamentary co-operation. The Nordic Council of Ministers was formed in 1971 and is the forum for inter-governmental co-operation. Since early 1930s, a series of private international law conventions have been adopted to govern inter-Nordic relations, primarily within family and succession law. See further: http://www.norden.org/en

[2] One such example would be Förordning (1931: 429) om vissa rättsförhållanden rörande äktenskap, adoption och förmyndarskap. [Ordinance (1931: 429) on Certain Aspects Regarding Marriage, Adoption and Guardianship].

[3] For a more thorough analysis as to inter-Nordic regulation and Nordic co-operation see: Jänterä-Jareborg, M. "The Nordic Input on the EU's Cooperation in Family and Succession Law – Exporting Union Law Through "Nordic Exceptions"", in EU Civil Justice: Current Issues and Future Outlook, Hart 2016.and Jänterä-Jareborg, M. "Den internationella familjerätten i Europa", SvJT 2014 s. 226–243.

[4] See further http://www.domstol.se/Funktioner/English/The-Swedish-courts/

[5] Rättegångsbalk (1942: 740) [The Swedish Code of Judicial Procedure].

information about foreign law is applicable also in situation where those questions arises before the administrative and specialised courts, although those courts are governed by specific rules of procedure.[6]

Questions as to proof of and information about foreign (private) law may also appear before other instances than judicial authorities. I will briefly cover this aspect with a certain focus on family law issues. In relation to administrative authorities a separate judicial structure is applicable, and decisions are appealed to the administrative courts, with its specific procedural legislation.[7] However, general issues as to foreign law are, irrespective of the different context, treated in a similar way as in the general courts, and much of the findings in this report is therefore of general relevance.

While preparing this national report I have, as a starting point, been using the national report that I wrote within the frames of the study "The Application of Foreign Law in Civil Matters in the EU Member States and Its Perspectives for the Future" performed by the Swiss Institute of Comparative Law on behalf of the European Commission.[8] From that starting point this report may been seen as a developed and up-dated presentation as to Swedish perspectives on questions regarding proof of and information about foreign law in civil and commercial matters. However, it is to be stressed that a brief report like the one at hand hardly manages to present a comprehensive analysis as to all relevant aspects regarding the application of foreign law. This report is rather to be seen as an overview of issues and a brief analysis regarding potential problems and solutions.[9]

II. Identifying a Foreign Dispute in the Realm of Private Law

In Sweden there are no explicit formal provisions with regard to discovery of foreign elements in a dispute. Private law disputes are to be regarded as covered by the general regulation in the Code of Judicial Procedure, irrespective of potential foreign elements. As to the question to what extent Swedish judges have a duty to discover on their own initiative (*ex officio*) the foreign elements that require application of foreign law in a given case, it is appropriate to differentiate between mandatory and non-mandatory issues.

It may be regarded as a problem on its own to develop a proper terminology as to the closer delimitation between mandatory and non-mandatory issues and how such

[6] See e.g. Förvaltningsprocesslag (1971: 291) [The Administrative Court Procedure Act] and Lag (1971: 289) om allmänna förvaltningsdomstolar [The Administrative Court Act].

[7] See supra footnote 6.

[8] See further http://ec.europa.eu/justice/civil/files/foreign_law_en.pdf

[9] See further: Bogdan, M. "Svensk internationell privat- och processrätt" [Swedish Private International Law], 8th Ed. Norstedts Juridik 2014 (cit. Bogdan 2014), Jänterä-Jareborg, M., "Svensk domstol och utländsk rätt" [Swedish Courts and Foreign Law], Iustus förlag 1997 (cit. Jänterä-Jareborg 1997) and Jänterä-Jareborg, M., "Foreign Law in National Courts – a Comparative Perspective", Recueil des course, Volume 304, 2003 (cit. Jänterä-Jareborg 2003).

issues affect cases in the realm of civil procedure. In this report I choose to address the problem by separating non-mandatory issues from mandatory issues and I choose to relate this to whether or not a case is amenable for out-of court settlement, which is the situation if the case regards a non-mandatory issue. A more developed explanation would be to separate between permissively regulated issues, falling within the parties' free disposition and mandatorily regulated issues falling outside the parties' rights of disposition.[10] Irrespective of which terminology that is used it is clear that the nature of the case is directly affected by the nature of the issues that is to be adjudicated and it is, consequently, important to be attentive to the importance of a correct classification of the issues involved.

Usually it appears directly from the facts in the case whether or not they are to be regarded as mandatory or non-mandatory. However, the demarcation is not always distinct and it is quite common that both mandatory and non-mandatory elements appear in the same proceeding (i.e. a "mixed-case").[11] A simple rule of thumb would be that issues regarding status (e.g. divorce, marriage, declaration of fatherhood) are usually regarded as mandatory.[12]

A general rule in Swedish private international law is that foreign elements are to be discovered *ex officio* if the proceeding deals with mandatory issues, whereas that is not the case in relation to non-mandatory issues.[13]

Specifically regarding cases dealing with mandatory issues it may be questioned to what extent the parties may, with binding effect, enter into agreements as to applicable law. However there are elective choice-of-law rules that provide the parties with choices, also in relation to mandatory issues.[14]

As to cases dealing with non-mandatory issues, the judgment may not be based on circumstances other than those pleaded by a party as the foundation for his or hers action.[15] Regarding such cases, it may be concluded that the foreign element is

[10] As to the use of the term "permissively regulated issues" see further Jänterä-Jareborg, M., "The Foreign Law Problem" In Essays on Tort, Insurance, Law and Society in Hounour of Bill W. Dufwa, Jure, Stockholm 2006.

[11] One example from Swedish case-law is NJA 1985 p. 338 in which divorce, guardianship and maintenance was adjudicated. In the case the Supreme Court decided to treat all issues involved as mandatory as regards the procedure, but as to the adjudication of the different substantive issues involved it is stated that it is to be possible to separate mandatory (e.g. the divorce) and non-mandatory (e.g. the question regarding maintenance) elements.

[12] For a more comprehensive discussions as to proceedings regarding mandatory and non-mandatory issues see Ekelöf, P.O. and Edelstam, H. "Rättegång I [Procedural Law I]", Norstedts Juridik 2002 (cit. Rättegång I), pp 59–65 and Jänterä-Jareborg 1997.

[13] Bogdan 2014, pp 37–42 and Jänterä-Jareborg 1997, pp 119–234.

[14] Examples of elective choice-of-law rules are to be found in Förordning (1931:429) om vissa internationella rättsförhållanden rörande äktenskap, adoption och förmyndarskap [Ordinance (1931:429) on Some International Marriage, Adoption and Guardianship Relationships]. There are also examples in this field where the applicability of foreign law is made dependent on the parties choice, e.g. chapter 3 paragraph 4 section 3 in Lag (1904:26) om vissa internationella rättsförhållanden rörande äktenskap och förmynderskap [Act (1904:26) on Some International Marriage and Guardianship Relationships].

[15] The Swedish Code of Judicial Procedure, Chapter 17, Section 3.

to be referred to by the parties if it is to be possible for the judges to consider it. However, it lies (at least partly) within the frames of the court's discretionary power to inform parties of circumstances that may affect the out-come of the dispute, e.g. facts that may lead to the application of foreign law. During the preparations it is, according to Swedish law, possible for the court to clarify the nature of the case by encouraging the parties to state everything that they wish to invoke in the case. By questions and observations the court shall attempt to remedy unclear and incomplete statements made by the parties.[16]

The magnitude of the courts discretionary power is one of the most debated questions in Swedish procedural law.[17] However, as to the question regarding foreign elements it seems to be quite clear that Swedish courts within the frames of its discretionary power, ought to inform the parties of potential consequences that referred facts may have in relation to the applicability of foreign law, thus giving them the opportunity to retract the reference if they prefer Swedish law to be applied. In this respect one can state that Sweden applies a "soft" ex-officio principle in relation to disputes of a non-mandatory nature. In practice this creates a situation very similar to a situation in which foreign elements are to be considered only when actually invoked by the parties, due to the fact that courts in those situations usually are presupposed to use their discretionary power to inform the parties that there may be foreign element that they might invoke.[18]

In relation to cases dealing with mandatory issues the duty to discover foreign elements comprises a possibility for the court to require the parties to provide information regarding the international character of the dispute e.g. the location of certain elements of the case. However, in practice, it is highly unlikely that courts will use the discretionary power to discover elements (foreign or non-foreign) that are not clearly manifest in the case.

As to cases dealing with non-mandatory issues it is possible for the parties to avoid the application of foreign law, by refraining from revealing to the judge the foreign elements in their case. This may even be a possibility in certain cases dealing with mandatory issues, in which (as stated above) there are elective choice-of-law rules that may be applicable. One example is the above mentioned rule in Ch. 3, article 4, subsection 3, of Act (1904:26)[19] in which application of foreign law in matters regarding divorce in relation to foreign citizens (which is to be regarded as a mandatory issue) are dependent of whether or not one of the spouses invokes that the divorce would be contrary to the applicable law in his/hers country of nationality (*lex patriae*).[20]

Statistic data as to court decisions is not readily available in Sweden. Consequently it is not possible to indicate, in real numbers, how often foreign law is applied. A gen-

---

[16] The Swedish Code of Judicial Procedure, Chapter 42, Section 8.

[17] See e.g. Rättegång V [Judicial Procedure V], Norstedts Juridik 2010, p. 44 (with further references).

[18] See further Bogdan 2014 and Jänterä-Jareborg 1997.

[19] Lag (1904:26) om vissa internationella rättsförhållanden rörande äktenskap och förmynderskap [Act (1904:26) on Some International Marriage and Guardianship Relationships].

[20] For further discussions see Bogdan 2014, pp 171–172.

eral observation is that it is not particularly frequent in courts, even though it occurs more frequently in certain areas (often within the realm of family law).

As to the geographic origin of the applicable foreign legal system, it is, for obvious reasons, the laws of the different neighboring Nordic countries that are most common, followed by the laws of the different EU Member States.

III. Foreign Law Before Judicial Authorities

A. Nature of Foreign Law

Foreign law is regarded as law and not fact in Sweden, but the special foreign nature of the law applied may be taken into account in the application (as will be shown below). Thus there is a difference between application of national (Swedish) law and foreign law, although both are regarded as law.

B. Application of Foreign Law

Courts in Sweden are governed by the principle of *iura novit curia* which implies that there is no need to prove the content of legal rules. The Court is to be able to assess which rules to apply when examining the facts invoked. This principle is generally accepted and partly formalised in the Code of Judicial Procedure, in which it is stated that no proof is required as to legal rules.[21] The principal rule therefore is that choice-of-law rules are to be applied *ex-officio*, if the factual circumstance in the case is making them applicable.

However, in non-mandatory proceedings, the parties may choose not to invoke the foreign elements that activate a certain choice-of-law rule and there is a wide range of possibilities for the parties to enter into agreements as to applicable law.

Furthermore, there are conflict-of-law rules that by themselves require the parties to invoke the application of foreign law. One example is the rule in article 1, subsection 1 in Act (1931: 429)[22] in which application of *lex patriae* in relation to matters regarding impediment to marriage is (in certain situations) made dependent on whether or not application of *lex patriae* is requested by the parties.[23] The fact that the parties may refrain from the application of foreign law in situations like this does not mean that the choice-of-law rules are superseded. On the contrary the party autonomy exists primarily in situations where there is expressed support for party

[21] The Swedish Code of Judicial Procedure, Chapter 35, Section 2.

[22] Förordning (1931: 429) om vissa internationella rättsförhållanden rörande äktenskap, adoption och förmyndarskap [Ordinance (1931: 429) on Some International Marriage, Adoption and Guardianship Relationships].

[23] See further Bogdan 2014, pp. 161–162.

autonomy in the applied choice-of-law rule, something that is quite common, both in national (autonomous) Swedish choice-of-law rules and in the EU instruments.

As to the question to what extent the conflict-of-law rules are applied *ex officio* by the judge, even if this runs counter to the wishes of the parties there is, of course, an initial difference between mandatory and non-mandatory issues. Party autonomy exists normally within the frames of proceedings dealing with non-mandatory issues. Even in relation to this group it may be stated that the application of the relevant choice-of-law rule is mandatory and that it may prove to be impossible to reach agreements referring to the application of foreign law which is not in line with the choice-of-law rule. There are examples from Swedish case law which supports this idea.[24] In general most Swedish scholars seem to agree that it is more likely that a court will consider the parties choice-of-law agreement, if they manage to reach such an agreement during the procedure.[25] An agreement reached before the procedure would probably not be regarded as binding, without the expressed support by the applicable choice-of-law rule.

C. Ascertainment of Foreign Law

General Aspects

When it is established that foreign law is applicable to a dispute, the general perception is that the judges have a duty to know the rules of law that they are bound to apply. As stated above, the legal principle *jura novit curia* is recognized in Sweden and expressed in the Swedish Code of Judicial Procedure where it is stated that proof of legal rules is not required.[26]

The principle of *jura novit curia* applies in principle also in relation to foreign law, but there is a possibility for the judges to request the parties' assistance as to present proof regarding the contents of foreign law.[27]

In other words, it is not possible to oblige the parties to provide evidence as to the content of foreign law, but a court may call upon the parties to do so, and take into account whether they comply with the request. In line with this the parties' allegations regarding the content of the foreign law are not binding on the court, but rather regarded as evidence to be evaluated freely in the same way as other kinds of evidence.

---

[24] See e.g. NJA 1973 p. 57 in which the Swedish Supreme Court, in a primarily non-mandatory case, choose to apply German Law, notwithstanding the fact that there was an agreement that Swedish law was to be applied. In this case the Swedish Supreme Court paid attention to the fact that the parties, at the time of the proceedings, no longer agreed as to the applicable law.

[25] Bogdan 2014, p 41; Jänterä-Jareborg 1997, pp 133–134, 146–148; Jänterä-Jareborg 2003 pp 336–355 and Pålsson, L., "Svensk rättspraxis i internationella familje- och arvstvister [Swedish Case-law Regarding International Family and Inheritance Law]", Norstedts Juridik 2006 (cit. Pålsson 2006), p 41.

[26] Swedish Code of Judicial Procedure, 35:2 subsection 2.

[27] Swedish Code of Judicial Procedure, 35:2 subsection 2, second sentence.

As stated above, the principle rule is that the court is supposed to know the contents of the applicable law and in line with this it may be proposed that the burden of proof, also in relation to foreign law, lies with the judge. In the process of ascertaining the content of foreign law there are no specified regulated procedural means to be considered. The judges are authorized to use their personal knowledge and they may undertake any personal research in order to determine foreign law. After evaluating everything that has occurred in accordance with the dictates of its conscience, the court shall determine what has been proved in the case.[28] This includes proof of foreign law. It may also be stressed that courts, in cases dealing with non-mandatory issues, is to regard the fact that a party admits a certain circumstance as full proof.[29] This general principle is relevant also in relation to proof of foreign law and in relation to proof of the existence of foreign elements in the case.

A court may also obtain an opinion on a certain issue (i.e. the content of foreign law) from an external legal expert.

There are no legal restrictions on the admissibility of specific means of proof of foreign law (e.g. only documentary means of proof, or only documentary means of proof corroborated by oral testimony of an expert, or only documentary means of proof duly certified by a foreign authority, or other limitations) and the Swedish procedural law admits documentary proof for determination of foreign law, even if it is not corroborated by oral testimony of an expert.

However, the court may choose to reject proof, if it finds that a circumstance that a party offers to prove is without importance in the case, or if the evidence offered is unnecessary or evidently without effect. This is a rule on evidence in general that also applies in relation to proof of foreign law.[30]

The Use of Judicial Networks

As indicated above, the quest of ascertaining foreign law may be a burden for a court. With the aim of providing guidance in this matter there are established networks that may be used to provide information about foreign law. In this regard Sweden is part to the European Convention on Information on Foreign Law signed in London 7 June 1968[31] and its Additional Protocol, signed in Strasbourg 15 March 1978[32] (the London rules). From a Swedish point of view the London rules are administered by the Ministry of Justice and potential requests as to the content of foreign law in line with the provisions in the Convention are to be directed to the

[28] Swedish Code of Judicial Procedure, 35:1 subsection 1.

[29] Swedish Code of Judicial Procedure, 35:3.

[30] Swedish Code of Judicial Procedure, 35:7. See further Ekelöf, P.O., Edelstam, H. and Heuman, L. "Rättegång IV [Judicial Procedure IV]", Norstedts Juridik 2009, pp. 37–41.

[31] See further, http://conventions.coe.int/Treaty/Commun/QueVoulezVous.asp?NT=062&CM=8&DF=21/11/2014&CL=ENG

[32] See further, http://conventions.coe.int/Treaty/Commun/QueVoulezVous.asp?NT=097&CM=8&DF=21/11/2014&CL=ENG

Ministry of Justice.[33] It is also the Ministry of Justice that, from the Swedish point of view, is the contact point for the European Judicial Network.[34]

Tasks in connection with international judicial cooperation, including among other things judicial cooperation in civil and commercial matters, are designated to a Central Authority, which is organised as a division of the Ministry of Justice. In other words it is the Central Authority that provides information about the contents of Swedish and foreign law.

Swedish authorities, but not private enterprises or individuals, may turn to the Central Authority for information about foreign law, in both criminal and civil matters.

An inquiry concerning foreign law is to be sent in writing (by post, fax or email) to the Central Authority. The Central Authority answers the inquiry directly if information is available or can be easily obtained. If a more thorough analysis is required the Central Authority arranges for the translation of the inquiry and forwards it to the Central Authority in the state in question or to the Swedish Embassy or mission there.

The reply is dispatched by using the same channels as applied when the inquiry was sent to the Central Authority (if not otherwise agreed) and the ambition is that this is done with priority. If a translation of the answer is necessary this is to be handled by the inquirer.

There are no available statistics in relation to the above mentioned instruments. Consequently, it is not possible to state to what extent and on what occasions and how frequently the authorities in Sweden resort to the European Convention on Information on Foreign Law. One general observation is that the Convention is mainly used in the fields of family law and that Swedish courts seldom apply it as a means of obtaining information.[35]

Neither are there any statistics available as to how frequently the authorities in Sweden resort to the European Judicial Network for the purposes of determination of foreign law.

As to the question how the concerned authorities assess the efficiency of each of the aforementioned mechanisms it is a question for the court to investigate *in casu*.

Costs for Ascertainment of Foreign Law

There are no costs involved in relation to neither the London rules nor the European Judicial Network, but it may bring forth a delay of the procedure. Furthermore, it may be difficult for the judges to assess the quality of the information provided by

[33] The European Convention on Information on Foreign Law is implemented in the Swedish legal system by Förordning (1981: 366) om rätt att i visa fall begära upplysningar om innehållet i utländsk rätt [Ordinance (1981: 366) Concerning the Right in Certain Cases to Request Information as to the Contents of Foreign Law].

[34] As to the investigation on foreign law conducted by the Ministry of Justice (the Central Authority) see further http://www.government.se/information-material/2014/05/international-judicial-co-operation--the-role-of-the-central-authority/. See also Ordinance (1981: 366) on the Right in Certain Cases to Request Information on Foreign Law.

[35] See further Jänterä-Jareborg 1997, pp. 274–291 and Jänterä-Jareborg 2003, pp. 314–321.

the above mentioned instruments and my impression is that Swedish courts to a large extent prefer obtaining the necessary knowledge by asking external experts of their own choice. This may provide a better possibility to guarantee quality and a possibility to ensure control of the timeframe of the procedure.

Distribution of costs in relation to procedures in Sweden is governed by the principle rule that the losing party shall reimburse the opposing party all the litigation costs unless otherwise provided by law.[36] As long as it is the parties that have incurred costs in connection with the collection of evidence as to the content of foreign law, it is possible for the winning party to get reimbursement.

As to the possibility for the parties to obtain legal aid, there are certain statutory rules.[37] The possibility to obtain legal aid is to a large extent made dependent on the existence of legal assistance insurances. In Sweden, such insurances are usually included in household insurances and consequently there are few situations in which the act on legal aid will apply. However, if aid is provided for, it will cover cost in relation to the collection of evidence, including evidence as to the content of foreign law.

Usually it is the court that collects evidence as to the content of foreign law and in such situation the costs will be borne by the Court/State. There is no special budget for this in Swedish courts and no statistical information available as to the costs generated.

D. Interpretation and Application of Foreign Law

When foreign law is applicable the general principle is that this law is to be applied loyally (i.e. in conformity with how the law is applied in the country of origin). If a gap in foreign law is identified there are several suggestions as to how such a gap is to be filled. Similar models are suggested as a cure when it turns out that the court fails in establishing the foreign law that is to be applied (see below).

A gap may be solved by subsidiary application of the law of the forum, by application of another law with a content that is regarded as being close to the law that should have been applied or by the application of another law alternatively designated by the conflict of law rule.[38]

[36] Swedish Code of Judicial Procedure, section 18:1.

[37] Rättshjälpslag (1996: 1619) [Act (1996: 1619) on Legal Aid].

[38] See further Bogdan 2014, pp. 47–49; Jänterä-Jareborg 1997, pp. 332–359 and Jänterä-Jareborg 2003, pp. 307–335.

E. Failure to Establish the Content of Foreign Law

There are no specific remedies available in Sweden in relation to the failure to determine the content of foreign law. A decision may be appealed, as will be developed below in section IV, and there might be (although unlikely) possibilities to challenge a decision by way of using the rules regarding extraordinary measures, but there is no explicit regulation in relation to failure to determine the content of foreign law. As a matter of fact it is an open question how to handle this situation and there are not much case-law to draw conclusions from.[39]

Most scholars would agree that the question as to how a failure to determine the content of foreign law is to be solved depends upon the nature of the case. A failure may be solved by subsidiary application of the law of the forum, by application of another law with a content that is regarded as being close to the law that should have been applied or by the application of another law alternatively designated by the conflict of law rule. A failure to determine the content of foreign law may also, in certain situations, be solved by a dismissal of the claim that should have been governed by the foreign law.[40]

There are no explicit statutory sanctions for the failure to determine the content of foreign law. However, if a party, as explained above, refuses to comply with a judicial request to provide evidence as to the content of foreign law that may have consequences when the court decides on what law to apply.

IV. Judicial Review

In Sweden an issue related to application of foreign law may be invoked as a ground for appeal and there is a legally established possibility of appeal against a judicial decision before a superior jurisdiction on the grounds of incorrect application of law, national as well as foreign. There are no restrictions as to the possible (admissible) grounds of appeal. However, before civil cases may be adjudicated the appeal court will have to grant a leave to appeal. In relation to an appeal from a district court (tingsrätt) to the Appeal Court (hovrätten), a leave to appeal can only be granted if:

1. there are reasons to doubt the correctness of the appealed judgment, or
2. it is not possible, without leave of appeal, to review the correctness of the judgment from the district court, or it is of importance for guidance in the application of the law that a court of appeal decides on the case, or
3. if there are extraordinary causes (procedural errors or the case is of importance for many similar cases etc.) that motivate a review.[41]

---

[39] See further Jänterä-Jareborg, 1997, pp. 332–359.

[40] See further Jänterä-Jareborg 1997, pp. 337–348 and Jänterä-Jareborg 2003, pp. 324–335.

[41] Swedish Code of Judicial Procedure, section 49: 14.

Leave to appeal is required also for the Supreme Court to review a judgment from the court of appeal. In this situation leave to appeal may be granted only if:

1. it is of importance for the guidance of the application of law that the Supreme Court considers appeal; or
2. there are extraordinary reasons for such a determination, such as that grounds exist for relief for substantial defects or that a grave procedural error has occurred or that the result in the court of appeal is obviously due to gross oversight or to gross mistake.[42]

Furthermore, a Swedish judgment may be challenged after a judgment's final entry into force, on the basis of certain rules regarding extraordinary remedies in the Code of Judicial Procedure.[43] After a judgment in a civil case has entered into force, relief for a substantive defect may be granted for the benefit of any of the parties in certain situations. In relation to a situation in which courts have omitted the application of foreign law Chapter 58, Section 1, subsection 4 of the Code of Judicial Procedure might be applicable. This rule states that ground for relief may be if the application of law forming the basis of the judgment is manifestly inconsistent with statutory provisions. This rule applies in extraordinary situations and it is not likely that it will be applied merely due to the fact that foreign law is omitted. There has to be further arguments pointing in the direction that this means that the judgment is manifestly inconsistent.[44]

Another possibility is to argue that it is a grave procedural error not to apply foreign law in a certain case. The questions whether or not this might be a possible argument relates to the definition of the conduct. Is the fact that a court does not apply foreign law to be regarded as a procedural error or is it to be regarded as an error in the application of law? The answer depends on the situation. Obvious examples of procedural errors are lack of jurisdiction and if there exist exclusive jurisdictional rules that should have been regarded *ex officio*. However, it is not likely that an error in the application of foreign law may be defined as a procedural error. Consequently, it can be concluded that there is little relevance in analyzing the applicability of the rules regarding extraordinary remedies further, due to the fact that it is highly unlikely that the rules will come into play in relation to lack of application of foreign law.[45]

[42] Swedish Code of Judicial Procedure, section 54: 10.

[43] Swedish Code of Judicial Procedure, section 58: 1.

[44] See further Welamsson, L., "Rättegång VI [Judicial Procedure VI]", Norstedts Juridik 2004, pp. 208–241.

[45] See further Welamsson, L., "Rättegång VI [Judicial Procedure VI]", Norstedts Juridik 2004, pp. 242–253.

V. Foreign Law in Other Instances

In Sweden, by tradition, there is no sharp distinction between judicial and non-judicial authorities. In general Swedish authorities are independent and they apply law, in relation to cases where law is to be applied, under similar conditions as courts. Another observation of relevance in relation to the situation in Sweden is that notaries have a less salient position than in most other countries. It is therefore not particularly relevant to discuss application of foreign law in relation to notaries from a Swedish point of view.[46]

Partly due to the independent position of many Swedish public authorities it is quite common that non-judicial authorities are confronted with situations in which foreign law has to be taken into consideration, but it is not as common that foreign law is actually applied.[47] Nonetheless, the necessity to resort to foreign law occurs in a large number of situations, and there are relevant practical problems in relation to foreign law. One examples of a situation in which foreign law matters is cases of family reunification and another example is when local Swedish Social Boards are to consider a foreign decision on parenthood or when the Swedish Enforcement Authority are confronted with foreign law applied to maintenance obligations. An additional example is when the Migration Board[48] considers applications from people who want to visit, live in or seeks asylum in Sweden, or who want to become Swedish citizens.

One further example is the Swedish Tax Agency that also acts as Swedish Authority for the population registry.[49] The information in the population registry is important as to the "status" of people living in Sweden (e.g. regarding marriage and parenthood) and it is frequently used as evidence, although it is not binding on courts.

As responsible for the population registry the Tax Agency will have to take account of foreign law in a number of situations, e.g. whether or not a foreign marriage is valid in Sweden and whether or not a foreign declaration of parenthood is supposed to be recognized. The Tax Agency is also confronted with foreign law when it performs its obligation to issue certificates of no impediment to marriages when none of the future spouses are Swedish citizens. In those rare and special situation both Swedish law and the law of the country in which the future spouses are citizens are to be applied.[50]

---

[46] In 2008 the Directorate General for Internal Policies of the Union conducted a study in which, among other things, the Swedish view on authentic systems is presented. It is quite apparent from the Study that notaries are not common to the Swedish system. See further "Comparative study on Authentic Instruments National Provisions of Private Law, Circulation, Mutual Recognition and Enforcement, Possible Legislative Initiative by the European Union", November 2008, document no. PE 408.329. The study is available at: http://www.pedz.uni-mannheim.de/daten/edz-ma/ep/08/EST23673.pdf

[47] See further Jänterä-Jareborg 1997, pp. 228–234.

[48] See further: http://www.migrationsverket.se/English/Private-individuals.html

[49] As to information regarding the Population Registration in Sweden there are information available at the homepage of the Swedish Tax Agency, www.skatteverket.se. Information in English is available at: http://www.skatteverket.se/privat/sjalvservice/blanketterbroschyrer/broschyrer/info/717b.4.39f16f103821c58f680008017.html

[50] Lag (1904: 26) om vissa internationella rättsförhållanden rörande äktenskap och förmynderskap [Act (1904: 26) on Certain International Marriage and Guardianship Relationships], section 1:1, subsection 2.

Regarding the question of access to foreign law the situation is similar to the one described above (section III). There is no formal provision preventing non-judicial authorities from using the same possibilities that exists for courts, although it must be stated that the parties' possibilities of providing proof of the contents of foreign law are normally less adapted to the issues that non-judicial authorities are to handle. Another practical problem is the fact that the officials, at the non-judicial authorities that have to deal with the foreign law issues, may be without education in law, which in practice may imply difficulties in understanding the foreign law at hand.

In relation to the validity and recognition of foreign status decisions there exists a possibility to get advice from the Tax Agency and as to the specific question of fatherhood there exists a possibility for a non-judicial authority to approach the relevant District Court to receive a decision as to whether or not a foreign decision regarding fatherhood is to be recognised in Sweden.[51]

As regards whether or not the decisions of non-judicial authorities are subject to appeal it is impossible to draw general applicable conclusions due to the fact that there are so many complex situations in which foreign law may have to be regarded and not all of these situations amount to decisions subject to appeal. However, in situations where the authorities are actually deciding an issue, such decisions are subject to appeal to the Swedish Administrative Courts.[52] In such situations it is possible to raise questions as to the application of foreign law in a similar way as it is when a civil case is appealed.

VI. Concluding Remarks

A general conclusion is that there is a lack of sufficient statistical data in Sweden in relation to the issues at hand. One important contribution in advancing the possibilities to apply foreign law and to encourage the building of knowledge in this area would be to establish a system that provides more comprehensive and accurate statistical data on the number of cases necessitating application of foreign law.

Another conclusion is that "personal" networks are of crucial importance. Most practitioners, lawyers as well as judges, seem to prefer a direct contact with a colleague in the country of origin to obtain information as to the content of the applicable foreign law. Consequently it is likely that a more developed system, through which judges will be able to contact colleagues in other countries, would be appreciated. However, for such a system to work it is necessary to bridge potential language problems.

---

[51] See Lag (1985: 367) om internationella faderskapsfrågor [Act (1985: 367) on International Questions on Paternity], section 9 subsection 1.

[52] In the Swedish legal system there is a general right to appeal decisions from Authorities to Administrative Courts. The rule, that is found in section 22a of the Förvaltningslag (1986: 223) [Act (1986: 223) on Administration] has few exceptions. See also section 3, subsection 2, in which it is stated that article 6(1) of the European Convention on Human Rights is to be respected in relation to the possibility to appeal decisions from Authorities.

United Kingdom: The Traditional Approach to Foreign Law in Civil Litigation in the Legal Systems of the United Kingdom

Verónica Ruiz Abou-Nigm

Abstract The legal systems in the United Kingdom adopt an adversarial approach to judicial proceedings and consider the application and proof of foreign law as depending upon the rules of civil procedure and the law of evidence. In principle, it is for the parties to disclose the international character of a particular dispute that leads to the application of conflict-of-law rules, and in turn, to plead, and, if disputed, prove, the foreign law that may be applicable following such conflict-of-laws rules. This chapter examines the application of foreign law in the courts of the United Kingdom from a theoretical and a practical perspective. It argues that the positioning of foreign law is crucial to the adjudication of a dispute in international civil and commercial litigation and as such a core aspect of Private International Law (Conflict of Laws) methodology. It submits de lege ferenda that in certain circumstances the ability to take judicial notice of foreign law could provide the courts in the United Kingdom with 'another tool in the case management toolbox' if done with regard to the functional differences between the pleading and proof of foreign law by the parties, and applying foreign law ex officio. Such a possibility – even if used only in exceptional cases- could further enable the courts to provide a more efficient, cost-effective and fair case management.

Introduction

There are three different jurisdictions in the United Kingdom, England and Wales,[1] Scotland, and Northern Ireland. Each jurisdiction has its own legal system; English law, Scots law, and the law of Northern Ireland, respectively. These three legal systems adopt an adversarial approach to judicial proceedings and consider the proof

[1] England and Wales share a single legal jurisdiction.

V. Ruiz Abou-Nigm (✉)
Senior Lecturer in International Private Law, Edinburg of Law School, University of Edinburgh, Old College, South Bridge, Edinburgh EH8 9YL, UK
e-mail: v.ruiz.abou-nigm@ed.ac.uk

Y. Nishitani (ed.), *Treatment of Foreign Law - Dynamics towards Convergence?*,
Ius Comparatum – Global Studies in Comparative Law 26,
DOI 10.1007/978-3-319-56574-3_17

of foreign law as depending upon the rules of civil procedure and the law of evidence. In principle, it is for the parties to provide information regarding the international character of a particular dispute that lead to the application of conflict-of-law rules, and in turn, to plead, and, if disputed, prove, the foreign law that may be applicable following such conflict-of-laws rules. Furthermore, as foreign law needs to be pleaded and proved as a question of fact by the parties to the satisfaction of the court,[2] in many cases, the dispute may not effectively be adjudicated according to the law designated by the conflict-of-law rules if the latter is a foreign law and the parties have not fulfilled these procedural requirements.

In English law, it is a general principle of procedure that in the pleadings, *i.e.*, the documents stating the positions of claimant and defendant and identifying the issues in dispute, the parties plead only facts and not law.[3] It is for the court, once the facts have been asserted, to apply the law that the court knows, *i.e.*, English law. If either party wishes the court to apply foreign law, it must say so in the pleadings.[4] Hence, the voluntary nature of the pleading of foreign law is related to its characterization as a fact, and subject only to a few exceptions, the court has no power to refer to foreign law *ex officio*.

This contribution examines the application of foreign law in the courts of the United Kingdom from a theoretical and a practical perspective. It argues that the positioning of foreign law is crucial to the adjudication of a dispute in international civil and commercial litigation and as such a core aspect of Private International Law (Conflict of Laws) methodology. It submits *de lege ferenda* that in certain circumstances the ability to take judicial notice of foreign law could provide the courts in the United Kingdom with 'another tool in the case management toolbox' if done with regard to the functional differences between the pleading and proof of foreign law by the parties, and applying foreign law *ex officio*. Such a possibility – even if used only in exceptional cases- could further enable the courts to provide a more efficient, cost-effective and fair case management. To that effect this chapter discusses foreign law in principle (Part I) and foreign law in practice (Part II) followed by further examination of the blurry line between facts and law in the interpretation and application of foreign law in the United Kingdom (Part III). It concludes emphasizing the importance of the treatment of foreign law for Private International Law (Conflict of Laws) methodology.

---

[2] See R. Fentiman, *Foreign Law in English Courts*, Oxford University Press, Oxford, 1998, 2–3.

[3] D. McClean and V. Ruiz Abou-Nigm, *Morris, The Conflict of Laws*, 9th edn Sweet & Maxwell, London, 2016, para 1–009.

[4] The origins of this rule are early: *Fremoult v Dedire* (1718) 1 P.Wms. 429; see further D. McClean and V. Ruiz Abou-Nigm, *Morris, The Conflict of Laws*, 9th edn Sweet & Maxwell, London, 2016, para 1–009.

I. Foreign Law in Principle

The Ambiguity of the Underpinnings of the Approach to Foreign Law in the United Kingdom

In the courts of the United Kingdom foreign law is considered as a matter of fact,[5] although it must be understood that 'this is a question of fact of a peculiar kind'.[6] In relation to English law, *Fentiman* indicated more than 20 years ago that 'there is more to explaining the English conceptual assumptions in this area than pointing to English law's factual treatment of foreign law'.[7] The traditional English approach[8] is that issues of foreign law are issues of fact; and one of the main consequences of that proposition is that the courts are therefore prevented from taking judicial notice of foreign law, as they cannot generally take judicial notice of facts.

Although initially treated by the courts as a matter of fact, when the content of that law becomes the subject of an appeal to a higher court, it is then treated not merely as a question of fact, but reviewed in much the same way as if it was an issue of law.[9] In England, Scotland and Northern Ireland, an appellate court is always reluctant to interfere with trial court's findings of fact; however, in appeals on a point of foreign law, appellate courts are able to weigh the evidence and examine the question again.[10] Furthermore, unlike the usual treatment of facts, the court's previous findings as to foreign law can be considered as evidence of that foreign law if the judgment is in a citable form, *e.g.*, reported in an approved series of law reports.

The legal nature of foreign law is generally not based on specific statutory provisions but derives mainly from case law. However, there are certain statutory provisions that need to be taken into consideration, the most important of which in English law is s4 of the Civil Evidence Act 1972.[11] Pursuant to this rule, any finding

---

[5] *Mostyn v. Fabrigas* (1774)1 Cowp 161, 174 (per Lord Mansfield); *Bumper Development Corpn. V. Comr. of Police* [1991] 1 WLR 1362, 1368 (CA). Scotland: *Stuart v Potter, Choate and Prentice* [1911] 1 SLT 377.

[6] *Parkasho v Singh* [1968] P 233 per Cairns J at 250. See also *Dalmia Dairy Industries Ltd. v National Bank of Pakistan* [1978] 2 Lloyds Rep 223 per Megaw LJ at 286.

[7] R Fentiman, 'Foreign Law in English Courts', [1992] LQR 142, 143. See Fentiman latest work on this topic in R Fentiman, *International Commercial Litigation* (2nd edn, OUP, 2015) Ch. 20, 666–706.

[8] *Bumper Development Corp Ltd. v Metropolitan Commissioner of Police* [1991] 1 WLR 1362, 1367 et seq.

[9] *Macmillan Inc. v Bishopsgate Investment Trust Plc (No 4)* [1999] CLC 417. See R. Fentiman, *Foreign Law in English Courts*, Oxford University Press, Oxford, 1998, 201–202.

[10] Parkasho v. Singh [1968] P. 233, 250 (per Sir Jocclyn Simon P.); Dalmia Dairy Industries Ltd. v. National Bank of Pakistan [1978] 2 Lloyds Rep. 223, 286 (CA); Grupo Torras SA v Al Sabah [1996] 1 Lloyd's Rep 7, 18 (CA); Bumper Development Corpn. V. Comr. of Police [1991] 1 WLR 1362, 1368 (CA); The Saudi Prince [1988] 1 Lloyd's Rep 1, 3 (CA); A-G of New Zealand v Ortiz [1984] AC 1. See S Geeroms, Foreign Law in Civil Litigation, Oxford University Press, Oxford, 2004 at 4.49-4.54 and 5.68-5.87.

[11] "4. Evidence of foreign law.

or decision as to the content of foreign law that has been made in the High Court or Crown Court, or during any appeal thereof, may be submitted as evidence in another case for the purpose of proving that foreign law, unless the contrary is proved. This provision has been criticised since it allows parties to rely upon a prior interpretation of a foreign rule, which may have been out-dated or even become obsolete because of further developments in the foreign country.[12]

(1) It is hereby declared that in civil proceedings a person who is suitably qualified to do so on account of his knowledge or experience is competent to give expert evidence as to the law of any country or territory outside the United Kingdom, or of any part of the United Kingdom other than England and Wales, irrespective of whether he has acted of is entitled to act as a legal practitioner there. (2) Where any question as to the law of any country or territory outside the United Kingdom, or of any part of the United Kingdom other than England and Wales, with respect to any matter has been determined (whether before or after the passing of this Act) in any such proceedings as are mentioned in subsection (4) below, then in any civil proceedings (not being proceedings before a court which can take judicial notice of the law of that country, territory or part with respect to that matter)-(a) any finding made or decision given on that question in the first-mentioned proceedings shall, if reported or recorded in citable form, be admissible in evidence for the purpose of proving the law of that country, territory or part with respect to that matter; and (b) if that finding or decision, as so reported or recorded, is adduced for that purpose, the law of that country, territory or part with respect to that matter shall be taken to be in accordance with that finding or decision unless the contrary is proved: Provided that paragraph (b) above shall not apply in the case of a finding or decision which conflicts with another finding or decision on the same question adduced by virtue of this subsection in the same proceedings.(3) Except with the leave of the court, a party to any civil proceedings shall not be permitted to adduce any such finding or decision as is mentioned in subsection (2) above by virtue of that subsection unless he has in accordance with rules of court given to every other party to the proceedings notice that he intends to do so. (4) The proceedings referred to in subsection (2) above are the following, whether civil or criminal, namely-(a) proceedings at first instance in any of the following courts, namely the High Court, the Crown Court, a court of quarter sessions, the Court of Chancery of the county palatine of Lancaster and the Court of Chancery of the county palatine of Durham; (b) appeals arising out of any such proceedings as are mentioned in paragraph (a) above; (c) proceedings before the Judicial Committee of the Privy Council on appeal (whether to Her Majesty in Council or to the Judicial Committee as such) from any decision of any court outside the United Kingdom. (5) For the purposes of this section a finding or decision on any such question as is mentioned in subsection (2) above shall be taken to be reported or recorded in citable form if, but only if, it is reported or recorded in writing in a report, transcript or other document which, if that question had been a question as to the law of England and Wales, could be cited as an authority in legal proceedings in England and Wales". See also Practice Direction (Foreign Law Affidavit) [1972] 1 WLR 1433 and Non-Contentious Probate Rules 1987, r.19.

[12] K J Hood, 'Drawing Inspiration? Reconsidering the Procedural Treatment of Foreign Law' [2006] JPIL 181,185.

Does this Traditional Approach Defeat the Purpose of Conflict-of-Law Rules?

Theoretically one of the most contested issues in this sphere is whether this traditional approach to the treatment of foreign law in civil and commercial litigation in the courts of the United Kingdom impairs the purpose of conflict-of-law rules. This issue has raised academic discussion[13] and it has received judicial attention.[14] In fact, the treatment of foreign law as a question of fact to be pleaded and proved by the parties implies that the applicability of the foreign law and the efficiency of the choice of law solutions provided by conflict-of-laws rules, depend ultimately on the rules of procedure and evidence. This has the potential to dramatically undermine the importance of choice of law rules.

However, and despite the difficulty from a private international law perspective in accepting this traditional approach in principle, if the adversarial nature of legal proceedings in the courts of the United Kingdom and the paradigmatic pragmatism of the common law judicial style are to be fully acknowledged, it is necessary to admit that the results may well be less significant in practice. The nature of the dispute is likely to be such that the application of foreign law would be to the advantage of at least one of the parties, who in that case would plead it and prove it.[15] Otherwise, if it has no advantage to the parties, and therefore no one pleads it, an implied choice of the law of the forum by the parties to the dispute is being made.[16] Bearing in mind that the trend towards enhancing party autonomy in choice of law issues is well established, this could be seen just as a particular way of exercising that autonomy.[17]

II. Foreign Law in Practice

> English lawyers...are inclined to view the legal process as a means of resolving particular disputes, as opposed to a vehicle for excavating legal truth.[18]

As far as the treatment of foreign law is concerned the court's role is understood as being predictive rather than normative[19]; that is, in the words of Fentiman, 'the

[13] See R Fentiman, *International Commercial Litigation* (2nd edn, OUP, 2015) 666–706; K J Hood, 'Drawing Inspiration? Reconsidering the Procedural Treatment of Foreign Law' [2006] JPIL 181,185.

[14] Neilson v Overseas Projects Corporation of Victoria Ltd. [2005] HCA 54.

[15] See D. McClean and V. Ruiz Abou-Nigm, *Morris, The Conflict of Laws*, 9th edn Sweet & Maxwell, London, 2016, para 1–009.

[16] See T C Hartley, 'Pleading and Proof of Foreign Law: The Major European Systems Compared', (1996) 45 ICLQ 271, at 290–1. See also R Fentiman, 'Foreign Law in English Courts', [1992] LQR 142, 150–152.

[17] However, this has been criticised, especially in relation tostatus cases. See eg RD Leslie, 'Domestic Law Rules?' (1990) 35 Journal of the Law Society of Scotland 475.

[18] R. Fentiman, *Foreign Law in English Courts*, Oxford University Press, Oxford, 1998, 282.

[19] R Fentiman, *International Commercial Litigation* (2nd edn, OUP, 2015) 672.

judge's role is not to determine what foreign law is, but to decide what a foreign court would be likely to conclude if the matter came before it.'[20]

The Adversarial Nature of the Proceedings

To fully understand the assumptions underlying this approach it is necessary to bear in mind that in the courts of the United Kingdom the proceedings are adversarial rather than inquisitorial. That is to say that '...the court will have nothing to do with making enquiries to find things out for itself. It is not there to inquire, or to do anything of its own motion, but to hear and determine between parties according to the proofs which the parties can bring forward'.[21] In other words, the courts have neither the power nor the duty to obtain such evidence.

There are, however, exceptions to this principle. Foreign law need not be proved: (a) where a particular piece of legislation provides that the court shall take judicial notice of foreign law[22]; (b) when the foreign law is so notorious that the judge is entitled to take judicial notice of it; a commonly given example is the fact that roulette is not unlawful in Monte Carlo[23]; (c) the Supreme Court of the United Kingdom, when hearing an English or Northern Irish appeal, takes judicial notice of Scots law[24]; and conversely, when hearing a Scottish appeal, the Court takes judicial notice of English or Northern Irish law[25]; (d) Furthermore, it is not necessary to prove the foreign law if the parties agree on its content (admission).[26] In a few cases,

---

[20] Ibid, referring to *Re Duke of Wellington* [1947] 1 Ch 506, at 515; *Blue Sky One Ltd. v Mahan Air* [2010] EWHC 631 (Comm) at [88]; *First Nationwide v Revenue and Customs Commissioners* [2011] UKUT 174 (TCC) at [62].

[21] Pollock, Expansion of the Common Law (1904, Stevens & Sons, London) 33–34.

[22] Eg Maintenance Orders Act 1950, s. 22 (2). See also Art. 14 of the Convention on the Civil Aspects of International Child Abduction 1980 ('Hague Child Abduction Convention') as in force in the United Kingdom pursuant to Pt I of the Child Abduction and Custody Act 1985. Art. 14 establishes that 'In ascertaining whether there has been a wrongful removal or retention within the meaning of Article 3, the judicial or administrative authorities of the requested State *may take notice directly of the law of, and of judicial or administrative decisions, formally recognised or not in the State of the habitual residence of the child, without recourse to the specific procedures for the proof of that law* or for the recognition of foreign decisions which would otherwise be applicable' (emphasis added).

[23] *Saxby v Fulton* [1909] 2 KB 208, 211.

[24] *Elliot v Joicey* [1935] A.C. 209, 236; *MacShannon v Rockware Glass Ltd.* [1978] A.C. 795, 815, 821. Although these cases are from the House of Lords, the UK Supreme Court has stated that it will follow the same practice. See Perry v Serious Organised Crime Agency [2013] 1 AC 182, para 101. See also G Maher, 'Judicial notice and statute law', (2001) 117 *LQR* 71.

[25] *Douglas v Brown* (1831) 2 Dow. & Cl. 171 (HL); *Cooper v Cooper* (1888) 13 App. Cas. 88. Although these cases are from the House of Lords, the UK Supreme Court has stated that it will follow the same practice.

[26] *Beatty v Beatty* [1924] 1 KB 807.

the courts have determined questions of foreign law, particularly colonial law,[27] without proof.[28]

As previously stated, the pleading of foreign is in most cases voluntary in civil and commercial litigation in the courts of the United Kingdom. The parties may be inclined to plead foreign law if the particular foreign law applicable to the case following the relevant conflict of law rules is more advantageous than the law of the forum or where the law of the forum offer no equivalent cause of action or defence[29]; and exceptionally, where the pleading of foreign law is provided for as mandatory in the relevant conflict-of-law rule.[30]

No Judicial Notice of Foreign Law as a Means to Acquire Ad Hoc Judicial Knowledge of Foreign Law

The positioning of foreign law as a fact implies in practice that the parties ought to supply evidence of foreign law and that the court is limited to that evidence provided and prevented from engaging in their own enquiries as to the contents of foreign law.[31] Therefore, it is clear that the principle of *iura novit curia* is not applicable in the case of foreign law.

The courts in principle do not take judicial notice of foreign laws; the judge is treated as neither knowing, nor being able to know of his own volition, the content of the foreign law to be applied, and cannot apply foreign law *ex officio*.[32] Therefore, where foreign law applies, its content needs to be pleaded and proved to the court as a matter of fact by one or both of the parties to the dispute. If the foreign law is not pleaded and proved to the courts' satisfaction, then the court will not have judicial knowledge of the foreign law and will treat the case as a purely domestic one.[33] In this way, the treating and proving of foreign law as a question of fact allows the court to acquire judicial knowledge of the content of that law in order to apply it to the case at hand.[34]

---

[27] See Dicey, Morris and Collins, *The Conflict of Laws*, 15th edn, Sweet & Maxwell, London, 2012, para 9-009 at 322 and the jurisprudence referred therein.

[28] *Re Cohn* [1945] Ch. 5 (German Civil Code).

[29] See, inter alia, R Fentiman, *International Commercial Litigation* (2nd edn, OUP, 2015) 700–702.

[30] For example, in cases involving immovable property, registered interests, or the consequences of incorporation (see R Fentiman, *International Commercial Litigation* (2nd edn, OUP, 2015) 666).

[31] Di Sora v Phillipps (1863) HLC 624; Bumper Development Corpn. V. Comr. of Police [1991] 1 WLR 1362, 1369 (CA).

[32] Although the United Kingdom Supreme Court, when dealing with the law of another part of the United Kingdom, does have judicial notice of that law.

[33] Bumper Development Corp v Commissioner of Police of the Metropolis [1991] 1 WLR 1362, 1369.

[34] As Lord Mansfield said in *Mostyn v Fabrigas* 'the way of knowing foreign laws is by admitting them as facts' (1774) 1 Cowp 161, 174. See R. Fentiman, *Foreign Law in English Courts*, Oxford University Press, Oxford, 1998, 66.

It is conceptually important to distinguish between the following two principles; foreign law must be pleaded, and foreign law must be proved. There is a statutory exception to the former. If a case is governed by the law of a Commonwealth country, the court may order that law to be ascertained under the British Law Ascertainment Act 1859 when it regards it necessary or expedient to do so; orders for the ascertainment of a foreign law under this Act have been made at the court's volition despite the lack of pleading of foreign law by the parties.[35] There are several exceptions to the latter principle. This conceptual distinction is common to English and Scots law, albeit with the use of different legal terminology. In Scots law, foreign law needs to be relevantly averred, *i.e.,* setting out in the pleadings the substance of the foreign provision, how it becomes applicable and its effects in relation to the facts of the case before the court[36] (first principle). If relevantly averred, it must be established as a fact in the case[37] (second principle).

It is a matter for the party seeking to rely on the foreign law to adduce evidence of its applicability. If foreign law is not pleaded by at least one of the parties, or if the judge is not persuaded by the proof adduced, the court will apply domestic law[38] since, as already noted, the judge does not have the power to apply foreign law *ex officio*.[39]

Ascertainment of Foreign Law: The Pre-eminent Role of Expert Evidence

In English law the content of the foreign law must be proved, generally, by expert evidence.[40] Section 4(1) of the Civil Evidence Act 1972 states: '… a person who is suitably qualified to do so on account of his knowledge or experience is competent to give expert evidence as to the law of any country or territory outside the United Kingdom… irrespective of whether he has acted or is entitled to act as a legal practitioner there.' If the other party to the action disagrees with the content of the foreign law pleaded by the first party, then he too must produce expert evidence. Where two experts disagree as to the content or application of the foreign law, the judge will look at all the evidence put forward and decide which he believes to be the correct view; but he is not entitled to reject the evidence of expert witnesses if they agree and conduct his own research into the effect of that law.[41]

---

[35] Duke of Portland v Topham (1864) 11 H.L.C. 32.

[36] See P. R. Beaumont and and P.E. McEleavy, *A.E. ANTON, Private International Law*, 3rd edn W. Green, Edinburgh, 2011, para 27.174 and the jurisprudence cited therein.

[37] *Sanderson v Armour*, 1922 S.C. (HL) 117, 127.

[38] Macmillan Inc. v Bishopsgate Investment Trust Plc (No 4) [1999] CLC 417.

[39] Re Parana Plantations Ltd. [1946] 2 All ER 214; Szechter v Szechter [1971] P 286; Concord Trust v Law debenture Trust Corp Plc [2005] UKHL 27.

[40] Ganer v Lanesborough (1790) Peake 25; Bumper Development Corpn. V. Comr. of Police [1991] 1 WLR 1368 (CA).

[41] Bumper Development Corp v Commissioner of Police for the Metropolis [1991] WLR 1362.

The functions of the expert witness were summarised in *Macmillan v Bishopsgate*[42] as follows: '(1) to inform the court of the relevant contents of the foreign law; identifying statutes or other legislation and explaining where necessary the foreign court's approach to their construction; (2) to identify judgments or other authorities, explaining what status they have as sources of the foreign law; and (3) where there is no authority directly in point, to assist the English judge in making a finding as to what the foreign court's ruling would be if the issue was to arise for decision there.'

There are also three statutes and one international convention providing for the establishment of foreign law by other means. Section 4 of the Civil Evidence Act 1972 has already been noted. Additionally, the British Law Ascertainment Act 1859 permits the court to refer questions of foreign law to the superior courts of British colonies and some Commonwealth countries. The Evidence (Colonial Statutes) Act 1907 provides for courts in the United Kingdom to accept copies of government-printed legislation from countries under 'British possession', *i.e.,* 'any part of [Her] Majesty's dominions exclusive of the United Kingdom'[43] as evidence without proof having to be given that they were so printed. The text of such laws can be proved without expert evidence; nonetheless, the court may require expert evidence to show that the alleged law is still in force. The Act continues to apply to the legislation of many Commonwealth countries that are no longer part of Her Majesty's dominions.[44]

In England, the Civil Procedure Rules[45] allow the court to direct that only one expert witness should give evidence on behalf of both parties, even though that is not common practice in relation to proof of foreign law. Where foreign law is being pleaded in a case involving a judge and jury, the question as to the effect of the evidence of the foreign law is purely a matter for the judge and not the jury.[46]

In Scotland, foreign law is established as a fact in the case either by remit of consent to a foreign lawyer; by expert evidence; or by admission.[47] The British Law Ascertainment Act 1859 referred to above also applies. A remit made of consent to a foreign lawyer is used if the parties admit that a point is to be regulated by the law of a foreign country and refer it to the opinion of a person versed in that law. In that case, they can neither argue afterwards that the foreign law is inapplicable, nor that the opinion of the foreign lawyer is erroneous.[48] As is the case in England, foreign

---

[42] [1999] CLC 417, 424.

[43] Evidence (Colonial Statutes) Act 1907, s. 1(3).

[44] This is pursuant to UK statutory provisions to that effect: *Jasiewicz v Jasiewicz* [1962] 1 W.L.R. 1426. See Dicey, Morris and Collins, *The Conflict of Laws*, 15th edn, Sweet & Maxwell, London, 2012, para 9-022 at 330.

[45] Civil Procedure Rules, SI 1998/3132, rule 35.7.

[46] Administration of Justice Act 1920, s.15. In England and Wales, for the High Court see Senior Courts Act 1981, s. 69 (5).

[47] *Studd v Cook* (1880) 8 R. 249 at 252; see P. R. Beaumont and and P.E. McEleavy, *A.E. ANTON, Private International Law*, 3rd edn W. Green, Edinburgh, 2011, para 27.178 and the jurisprudence cited therein.

[48] *Welsh v Milne* (1844) 7 D. 213; see P. R. Beaumont and and P.E. McEleavy, *A.E. ANTON, Private International Law*, 3rd edn W. Green, Edinburgh, 2011, para 27.178 and the jurisprudence cited therein.

law is generally proved by expert evidence of lawyers familiar with it.[49] In uncontested petitions, affidavits as to the effects of foreign law are usually accepted, but they will not normally be received in contested cases.[50] Because the rule that foreign law must be proved as a matter of fact applies to English law like any other foreign law, it is usual to provide the evidence by two English law experts.[51]

As far as the qualifications of experts are concerned, section 4(1) of the Civil Evidence Act 1972 of England, as explained above, contains the rules as to who may be an expert witness; and *Macmillan v Bishopsgate*[52] summarises the functions of the expert witness. As for Scotland, there are no established rules as to what qualifies a witness to give evidence as to foreign law.[53]

The expert's report needs to be objective and coherent. 'The witness, however expert in the foreign law, cannot prevent the Court using its common sense; and the Court can reject his evidence if he says something patently absurd, or something inconsistent with the rest of his evidence'.[54] If the evidence of foreign law is clear and unambiguous, the court will treat it as conclusive and will not consider any other authorities that may be available to the court on that point.[55]

If both parties to the action agree and admit the content and application of foreign law, then the court will consider this as sufficient to apply the foreign law as they agree. If the application of foreign law is contested between the parties the judge will adjudicate the dispute as to the most persuasive version of the applicable law in the same way as he would decide upon any other fact of the case. He will consider the evidence put forward by the expert witness pondering their coherence and supporting documentation. He is not allowed to consider any other documentary evidence than the one produced by the expert.[56]

The usual practice in commercial litigation is for each party to submit expert evidence. The costs involved in pleading and proving foreign law in this traditional fashion are significant, but it has been considered that no other approach offers the parties such evidential opportunities, particularly the control over the presentation of their case and the opportunity to challenge that of the other party.[57] This process of each party proving foreign law by the production of normally expert

[49] *Mortimer v Nicol* (1835) 14 S. 94.

[50] P. R. Beaumont and and P.E. McEleavy, *A.E. ANTON, Private International Law*, 3rd edn W. Green, Edinburgh, 2011, para 27.178 and the jurisprudence cited therein.

[51] *Parnell v Walter* (1889) 16 R. 917.

[52] [1999] CLC 417, 424.

[53] P. R. Beaumont and and P.E. McEleavy, *A.E. ANTON, Private International Law*, 3rd edn W. Green, Edinburgh, 2011, para 27.184.

[54] A/S Tallinna Laevauhisus v Estonian State Steamship Line (1947) 80 Lloyd's Rep 99, 108 (CA).

[55] Duchess of Buckingham v Winterbottom (1851) 13 D. 1129 at 1146; cf. Baird v Mitchell (1854) 16 D. 1088 and Higgins v Ewing's Trustees 1925 S.C. 440 at 449.

[56] *Nelson v Bridport* (1845) 8 Beav 527, 541; *Concha v Murietta* (1889) 40 Ch D 543 (CA); *Lazard Bros v Midland Bank Ltd.* [1933] AC 289, 298 (HL).

[57] See R Fentiman, *International Commercial Litigation* (2nd edn, OUP, 2015) 683.

oral evidence also increases the duration of the proceedings, thereby increasing the overall costs of litigation.

In English law, the courts are allowed to direct each party's experts to give evidence concurrently, as an alternative to the traditional method of examination and cross-examination.[58] The general starting point for allocation of costs is that the unsuccessful party to judicial proceedings will be ordered to pay the costs incurred by the successful party in seeking or defending those proceedings. However, judges may depart from this starting point within the limits of their discretionary powers to make an order about costs.[59] In this respect, the aim of the Civil Procedure Rules is to accord flexibility and to encourage cost-efficiency in litigation.

The costs of obtaining expert evidence are normally recoverable by the successful party as part of the costs awarded to him or her.[60] The amount of recovery is in most cases limited to 'proportionate' costs. Proportionality is to be considered in relation to the value of payments or property which may be in dispute, and also in relation to 'the importance of the matter to all the parties'; 'the particular complexity of the matter or the difficulty or novelty of the questions raised'; and the 'skill, effort, specialised knowledge and responsibility' demanded of the expert witness.[61]

Intra U.K. Cases

The rules about proof of foreign law and its positioning as a question of fact applies to the law of the other jurisdictions of the United Kingdom, as well as to any other foreign law. This is particularly artificial and unnecessary when a rule is enacted in the same terms but in different statutes in England and Scotland. In these cases, it strikes as against cost-efficiency to require proof of the contents of the 'foreign' law. As recognised in the leading Scottish commentary on Private International Law, it is particularly artificial considering that 'the judges in either country will, in interpreting that rule in a domestic question, have regard to and interpret for themselves the relevant judicial decisions in the other'.[62]

[58] Practice Direction 35, para. 11. This practice is not yet developed in England.

[59] Civil Procedure Rules, Pt 44, rule 44.3 (4) and (5).

[60] Civil Procedure Rules, rule 34.4 (4) (party's expert's fees and expenses).

[61] Civil Procedure Rules, rule 44.5 (3).

[62] P. R. Beaumont and and P.E. McEleavy, *A.E. ANTON, Private International Law*, 3rd edn W. Green, Edinburgh, 2011, para 27.180.

III. Interpretation and Application of Foreign Law: The Blurry Line Between Fact and Law

In these legal systems the application of foreign law is to be done on the basis of the evidence adduced by the parties. The court is not permitted to look for additional sources of the foreign law or to supplement the evidence provided in any way. The role of the court in the process of determining the contents of foreign law is more significant when both parties to the litigation have produced evidence as to the relevant rules of foreign law and that evidence is contradictory. In these circumstances, the court needs to choose the more convincing submissions; it is possible to construe the contents of foreign law from the combined evidence produced. In other words, the court is entitled to take aspects from all the evidence presented by the opponent parties considered together.[63]

Ideally, the expert witness should include evidence as to the contents *and* the interpretation of the foreign law. However, when there is no expert evidence as to the interpretation of the foreign law, the courts are allowed to construe the foreign provisions as they would construe their domestic law, acting on the assumption that the foreign rules of interpretation are the same as those of their own law.[64] The function of the expert witness in relation to the interpretation of foreign statutes needs to be distinguished from the construction of foreign documents. In relation to the former, the expert witness explains to the court what the foreign provisions mean, if necessary, by reference to foreign rules of interpretation/construction. In relation to foreign documents, it is the court, in the light of the rules of interpretation/construction evidenced by the witness, and not the expert witness, who determines the meaning of the document.[65]

Consistently with the nature of foreign law as a matter of fact, and with the need to plead and prove the contents of foreign law, the court should not examine texts that have not been relied on by the expert or counsel.[66] That is to say, neither in England nor in Scotland or Northern Ireland, the court conducts its own research into foreign law. If it is a matter of construction, and no evidence is provided as to that effect, the court would apply the rules of construction of its own legal system, as explained above.

---

[63] See Dubai Bank Ltd. (No. 5) v Galadari, 1990 cited by M Sychold in the United Kingdom report prepared by the Swiss Institute of Comparative Law, The Application of Foreign Law in Civil Matters in the EU Member States and its Perspectives for the Future (available at http://ec.europa.eu/justice/civil/files/foreign_law_en.pdf).

[64] See Dicey, Morris and Collins, *The Conflict of Laws*, 15th edn, Sweet & Maxwell, London, 2012, para 9-018 at 328 and the jurisprudence referred therein.

[65] Ibid para 9-019 at 329.

[66] Ibid. Bumper Development Corpn Ltd. v Metropolitan Police Comr [1991] 1 WLR 1362.

Failure to Establish Foreign Law

The effect of pleading foreign law is to bring to the attention of the parties and the court the fact that foreign law may be relevant to the case. However, before the court applies foreign law, it must either be admitted as fact by both of the parties to the case, or proved to the satisfaction of the judge by one or other of the parties. The burden of proof of asserting foreign law lies on the party or parties relying on that law. If one party fails to prove the foreign law to the court's satisfaction, but the other party does, the court will apply the version of foreign law that it considers adequately proved. If neither party proves the foreign law to the court's satisfaction, then the court will apply its own domestic law. This solution is not entirely without difficulties. The default application of the *lex fori* may, in some cases, prove problematic, inappropriate or wholly artificial. In those cases, the courts in England and Wales may simply regard a party who has pleaded, but failed to prove foreign law, as having failed to establish his case without regard to the corresponding principles of English law.[67]

This reference to the *lex fori* in England and Wales, Scotland or Northern Ireland is based upon different considerations. In Scots law, there is a rebuttable presumption that foreign law is not different from Scots law.[68] It follows that, if this presumption cannot be rebutted by evidence, the court will apply Scots law on the basis that the contents of foreign law do not differ from it. This is also how the courts state the matter in English law.[69] However, as recognised by the leading commentary in English law, 'this mode of expression [the presumption of similarity] has given rise to uneasiness in certain cases'.[70] Put simply, where foreign law is not proved, the court applies English law by default.

Final Remarks

> ...[W]e hope that the time may not be far off then it will be permissible for the English courts to take judicial notice of decisions of foreign courts, including those in the European Union, (and perhaps academic writing) in deciding what the relevant foreign law is in cases of this kind[71]

---

[67] Dicey, Morris and Collins, *The Conflict of Laws*, 15th edn, Sweet & Maxwell, London, 2012, para 9-030 at 334 and the jurisprudence referred therein.

[68] P. R. Beaumont and and P.E. McEleavy, *A.E. ANTON, Private International Law*, 3rd edn W. Green, Edinburgh, 2011, para 27.171; cf. *Wilmington Trust Co. v Rolls Royce Plc*, [2010] CSOH 157 at [20].

[69] Conceptually the existence of a presumption of similarity has been questioned by Fentiman. See R. Fentiman, *Foreign Law in English Courts*, Oxford University Press, Oxford, 1998, 147.

[70] Dicey, Morris and Collins, *The Conflict of Laws*, 15th edn, Sweet & Maxwell, London, 2012, para 9-025 at 332 and the jurisprudence referred therein.

[71] *Morgan Grenfell & Co Ltd. v SACE* [2001] EWCA Civ 1932 at [53].

The positioning of foreign law is at the crux of Private International Law (Conflict of Laws) methodology, and it may become determinant in the adjudication of a dispute in international civil and commercial litigation. The traditional approach to this issue in the courts of the United Kingdom, although consistent with the adversarial nature of the proceedings, may at times result too limiting in relation to the possibilities of the courts in asserting and assessing the contents of foreign law. In England and Wales the Court of Appeal has supported a move towards judicial notice of foreign law[72] to allow more powers to the court in this regard. In certain circumstances the ability to take judicial notice of foreign law could provide the courts in the United Kingdom with 'another tool in the case management toolbox' if done with regard to the functional differences between the pleading and proof of foreign law by the parties, and applying foreign law *ex officio*. Such a possibility – even if used only in exceptional cases- could further enable the courts to provide a more efficient, cost-effective and fair case management.

It is suggested that at the current stage of the development of Private International Law in the legal systems of the United Kingdom (mostly known as Conflict of Laws in England and Wales, and Northern Ireland, and at times referred to as International Private Law in Scotland) a conceptual enhancement is needed as a necessary corollary to any change in this field *de lege ferenda*: that is, to envisage the treatment of foreign law as pertaining to the substance of Private International Law in the United Kingdom legal systems rather than an issue to be left to the rules on procedure and evidence. Undoubtedly, the continuum[73] between 'law' and 'fact' may not be necessarily the only way to look at this issue. And the traditional label of 'procedural' to the categorization of these issues may undermine the full effect that conflict-of-laws rules of the forum should produce. But before these issues can be fully analyzed and discussed, changes proposed, and ways forward suggested, it is for us, private international lawyers, to consider the treatment of foreign law as a core aspect of Private International Law. Failing to engage with its relevancy implies that the current developments towards harmonization of conflict-of-laws rules are, particularly in the sphere of choice of law, much less significant than they could be if the issue was approached as being essential to the choice of law methodology.

---

[72] *Morgan Grenfell & Co Ltd. v SACE* [2001] EWCA Civ 1932 at [53], see R Fentiman, *International Commercial Litigation* (2nd edn, OUP, 2015) 674.

[73] See R Fentiman, *International Commercial Litigation* (2nd edn, OUP, 2015) 704.

Switzerland: The Principle *Iura Aliena Novit Curia* and the Role of Foreign Law Advisory Services in Swiss Judicial Practice

Ilaria Pretelli and Shaheeza Lalani

Abstract The first part of the report aims at defining the content and limits of the principle *iura novit curia* whenever the courts needs to apply *iura aliena*. After assessing in which circumstances and on which grounds foreign law is applied in Switzerland, the report argues that the principle *iura novit curia*, when it comes to foreign law, needs to be nuanced proportionally to the linguistic and cultural accessibility of the foreign law applicable in the *forum*. Based on an analysis of case law, the first part concludes stating that foreign law is viewed as "law" in Switzerland and, as such, it cannot be proved by the parties, although they may be helpful to assess it.

The second part of the report describes the nature of the Swiss conflict of law rules and the frequency with which the application of these rules leads to the application of foreign law. It explains when foreign law may be applied ex officio and when parties may enter an agreement regarding their choice of law. It also explains the role of the courts and parties in ascertaining the content of foreign law; the nature of legal information on foreign law; and, the means used by Swiss judicial authorities to ascertain foreign law. Lastly, this part of the report evaluates whether there is a need to modify either the conflict of law rules or the treatment of foreign law in Switzerland.

I. Pretelli (✉)
Legal Adviser, Swiss Institute of Comparative Law, Lausanne, Switzerland
e-mail: ilaria.pretelli@isdc-dfjp.unil.ch

S. Lalani
Senior Researcher, University of Paris 1 – Panthéon-Sorbonne, Paris, France
e-mail: shaheeza_lalani@hotmail.com

Y. Nishitani (ed.), *Treatment of Foreign Law - Dynamics towards Convergence?*,
Ius Comparatum – Global Studies in Comparative Law 26,
DOI 10.1007/978-3-319-56574-3_18

Part I – The Principle *Iura Aliena Novit Curia*

Ilaria Pretelli

1. Application of Foreign Law in Switzerland

The Swiss legal system commands to Swiss authorities to give effect to foreign rules, under the conditions set by private international law rules in force.[1]

The Private International Law Act of 1987 (Federal Law on Private International Law of 18 December 1987, hereinafter PILA) introduced in the Swiss legal system the principle *iura aliena novit curia.* Article 16 PILA prescribes the application of foreign law *ex officio.* In addition, according to article 19 PILA, Swiss authorities need to apply mandatory provisions of a foreign law if the circumstances of the case require it.[2]

Other rules that prescribe the application of foreign law may be found in special subject-matter legislation (namely on banks and insurance contracts)[3] and in international treaties ratified by Switzerland.[4] Among these are multilateral and bilateral treaties, sometimes longstanding as the treaty with the United States of America of 1850 and the one with Italy of 1868.[5]

The primacy of international law over national law derives, at the international level, from the rule *pacta sunt servanda* and from basic principles of public interna-

[1] Before the enactment of the PILA (Bundesgesetz über das Internationale Privatrecht (IPRG) vom 18. Dezember 1987 RS 291) the provisions of private international law were in the «Bundes Gesetz vom 25. Juni 1891 betreffend die zivilrechtlichen Verhältnisse der Niedergelassenen und Aufenthalter» (SR 211.435.1) and in two prior federal acts on civil capacity and marriage of 1881 and 1874. These provisions are no longer applied, with some notable exceptions, as *e.g.* ATF 119 II 281, 284, a decision of April 22nd,1993. On the problem of intertemporal law in private international law, see the Resolution of the International Law Institute, Dijon Session of 1981, *The Problem of Choice of Time in Private International Law*. On the doubts on the mandatory character of the PILA – recalled by Sh. Lalani, part II - Access to Foreign Law in Practice and in Perspective, par. 1, see Schwander, I., *Einführung in das Internationale Privatrecht*, Allgemeiner Teil, 2. A. St. Gallen 2000, n° 385.

[2] See Bucher, A., Art. 19, in Bucher A. (ed.), *Loi sur le droit international privé: Convention de Lugano, Commentaire romand*, Basel 2011, n° 1 ss., Mächler-Erne, M. & Wolf-Mettier, S., Art. 19, in H. Honsell et al. (eds.), *Basler Kommentar – Internationales Privatrecht*, 3 A., Basel 2013, n° 1 s., Vischer, F., Art. 19, in D. Girsberger et al. (eds.), *Zürcher Kommentar zum IPRG*, 2nd edition, Zürich 2004, n° 1 ss.

[3] Some conflict-of-laws rules may be found outside the PILA, in other federal legislation: See Art. 101a–c of the Federal Act on Insurance contracts of 2.4.1908 RS. 221.229.1, and Arts. 37f and 37 g of the Federal Act on Banks of 3.10.2003 RS952.0. For an exhaustive list see Bucher, A., Introduction, in Bucher A. (ed.), *Loi sur le droit international privé: Convention de Lugano, Commentaire romand*, Basel 2011, n° 4, p.16.

[4] Corboz, B., Art. 96, in B. Corboz et al. (eds.), *Commentaire de la LTF*, Bern 2014, n° 9, observes that failure to apply the PILA is censorable under Art. 95 FSCA (RS 173.110), whereas failure to apply rules included in ratified international conventions is censorable under Art. 96 FSCA.

[5] See, *e multis*, the decision of the Swiss Federal Court, 26.07.2010, 4A_421/2009 and Ballarino, T. & Pretelli, I., Una disciplina ultracentenaria delle successioni, *Rivista di Diritto Ticinese*, I-2014, p. 889–921.

tional law;[6] at the internal level it is recognised by Art. 1–2 PILA, stating explicitly: "This act does not affect international treaties".

The application of foreign law may also be demanded by private persons wishing to settle their private affairs in conformity to identified legal rules.[7] Party autonomy is widely recognized in Switzerland within the limits set by the *ordre public* clause (Art. 17 PILA) and mandatory rules (both Swiss and foreign: see Art. 18 and 19 PILA). For instance, Art. 116 on contracts, Art. 132 on torts, and Art. 52 on matrimonial property regimes allow the parties to enter into an agreement prescribing the application of a certain law; Art. 90 II and Art. 91 II on successions allow the *professio iuris.*

In connection with Art. 1 PILA, for Swiss private international law to be applied the presence of «international elements» need to be verified. As it may easily be observed, however, the importance of this condition can be treated in relative terms, since the PILA always limits the applicability of Swiss law in respect to a given foreign law *connected to the case*. The condition will thus always be verified since the PILA aims at solving a conflict between Swiss law and a competing foreign law. After all, in the absence of a foreign element, there would be no need to apply a foreign law and, even in that case, application of the PILA would designate Swiss law. It is figure out how the suppression of this condition could possibly influence the operation of the PILA in practice. As a matter of fact, each single PILA rule has its own scope of application in which the international element is either explicitated - as in art. 88 PILA - or irrelevant - as in the case of art. 95 PILA. In this respect, it can be observed that art. 95 I PILA contributes to define the scope of application of Swiss substantial rules on inheritance agreements - *i.e.* arts. 468 and 469 of the civil code - stating that those rules apply whenever the disposing party is domiciled in Switzerland *regardless of any other national or international element*. Art. 95 II, instead, supposes an international element for its own functioning, since it states that the aformentioned Swiss civil code rules also apply when the disposing party is a Swiss citizen, domiciled abroad, that makes a valid *optio legis* in favor of Swiss law.In light of the above, it seems redundant to repeat that the whole PILA needs an international element to become applicable, as if its rules needed a particular justification for their application because of a somehow different and peculiar *status* in respect of other rules, included in other pieces of legislation[8]

[6] See Brownlie, I., *Principles of public international law*, Oxford 2008, p. 4 et seq. 31 et seq.

[7] See Brulhart V., *Le choix de la loi applicable - questions choisies*, Berne 2004; Egeler S., *Konsensprobleme im internationalen Schuldvertragsrecht*, St-Gall 1994; Knapp B., Le droit suisse est. applicable au présent contrat, in *Etudes de droit international en l'honneur de Pierre Lalive*, Bâle/Francfort s/Main 1993, pp. 81–96; von Overbeck A. E, *L'irrésistible extension de l'autonomie en droit international privé, in* Nouveaux itinéraires en droit, Hommage à François Rigaux, Bruxelles 1993, p. 619–636; Siehr K., *Die Parteiautonomie im Internationalen Privatrecht, in* Festschrift Max Keller, Zurich 1989, pp. 489–510.

[8] See ATF 133 III 37, 39: "*La cause revêt des aspects internationaux, de sorte que le Tribunal fédéral, saisi d'un recours en réforme, doit vérifier d'office et avec un plein pouvoir d'examen le droit applicable*"; ATF 133 III 323, 327: «*La présente cause comporte des aspects internationaux [...]. Il faut donc contrôler d'office la question du droit applicable au litige, cela sur la base du droit international privé suisse en tant que lex fori*». Reference to the international aspects is always very broad and no particular elements are precisely identified or explicitely mentioned by the Supreme Court.

At any rate, it is important to note that Article 16 PILA prescribes to Swiss authorities to ascertain foreign law in their own motion.[9] Literally, the Act states that: «The contents of foreign law shall be established by the authority on its own motion».[10]

2. *The Principle* Iura Novit Curia *When It Comes to Foreign Law*

The intensity of the principle *iura aliena novit curia* varies in proportion to the capacity of the *curia* to access, interpret and apply the competent foreign law. In this respect, Swiss case law reveals that the more a foreign rule is accessible to the Swiss judge, the more the principle *iura novit curia* is of strict application. Conversely, the less accessible the foreign rule is, the more its determination will involve issues of proof and expert opinions, potentially affecting the right to be heard of each party.

Case law confirms that the ability of Swiss authorities to give legal effects to the foreign applicable law varies according to the characteristics of the law they are asked to apply. The accessibility of a foreign rule is not merely determined by its availability, for example on national public databases and websites,[11] but essentially by two main cultural factors.

The first being the language in which the foreign rule is written and the second one being the gap existing between the legal order of the *forum* and the foreign one, as regards to the «family» and tradition to which each of them belong.[12]

In this respect, a decision of the *Kassationsgericht des Kantons Zürich*[13] held that Art. 16 PILA allows the Swiss judge to take its decision on the basis of the foreign applicable law, without necessarily hearing the parties over its applicability and its content. This view, contested by one of the parties, was confirmed by the Swiss Federal Court.[14]

---

[9] RS 291. See the Message of the Federal Council on the Swiss Federal Law on International Private Law of 10th November 1982, FF 1983 I p. 301: "*l'article [16] oblige le juge à établir d'office le contenu du droit étranger. Le principe iura novit curia joue ainsi également pour l'application du droit étranger*". Likewise, ATF 121 III 436, 438: «*L'art. 16 LDIP consacre donc l'obligation pour le juge cantonal d'établir d'office le droit étranger*». See Keller, M. & Girsberger, D., Art. 16, in D. Girsberger et al. (eds.), *Zürcher Kommentar zum IPRG*, 2nd ed., Zürich 2004, ad art. 16, n° 16.

[10] English translation by Bucher, A., Art. 16, in Bucher A. (ed.), *Loi sur le droit international privé: Convention de Lugano, Commentaire romand*, Basel 2011, n° 1 s.

[11] See, *infra*, part II, par. 2.1. and 2.2.

[12] See Schlesinger, R. et al., *Schlesinger's Comparative Law*, 7th ed., London 2009, *passim*. See also Bussani, M. & Mattei, U., *The Cambridge Companion to Comparative Law*, Cambridge 2012, *passim*, arguing that each country's legal culture as a whole influences its positive legal order.

[13] Kassationsgericht des Kantons Zürich, Beschluss vom 4. September 1995, ZR 95/1996 S. 7, 9.

[14] Swiss Federal Court, 28.10.2004, 1P_390/2004 (not published), c. 2.2.: "s'agissant du droit de pays voisins, le juge ne doit pas solliciter systématiquement l'avis d'un expert judiciaire, car l'application du droit étranger aux cas concrets rentre dans ses attributions et non pas dans celles de l'expert".

Had the Court been in front of a Finnish rule, written in the Finnish language, the conclusion might have been different. This is confirmed by two more recent decisions.[15] In a case connected with the legal order of Saudi Arabia, the Swiss Federal Supreme Court took the (apparently) opposite view that the judge *a quo* had violated the right to be heard of the parties ex Art. 29,2 of the Swiss Federal Constitution, by founding its decision on Saudi Arabian rules, ascertained on its own motion, without hearing the arguments of the parties over the content, interpretation and application of Saudi Arabian law in the circumstances of the case.

At first glance, one would see a patent dyscrasy between the two decisions. However, it seems possible to solve the apparent antinomy, when considering that the principle *iura novit curia* enjoys different possible gradations: the need to proof, ascertain and argument on the content of foreign law being proportional to the distance between the foreign and the domestic legal system. Also, the need to allow *inter partes* debates on the content of foreign law depends on and varies according to the accessibility of the foreign law that needs to be applied by virtue of PILA rules. In turn, the accessibility of foreign law depends on the understanding of the language expressing it as well as on the knowledge of the legal order to which it belongs.

Accessibility is not an absolute factor, it depends on the gap existing *in concreto* between the foreign culture and the domestic legal context demanding the rule. If a Swiss judge is asked to apply Chinese contract law and, for personal reasons, he is at ease with the Chinese language and also happens to have studied Chinese contract law – *e.g.*, throughout the elaboration of a Ph.D. thesis comparing contract law in China and Switzerland – he will be less likely to appoint an expert in order to ascertain the content of Chinese law and may even apply Chinese law *ex officio,* in the same manner as the *Kassationsgericht des Kantons Zürich* did with German law.

Beyond these exceptional circumstances, Swiss judges have a comparatively easy access to German, Austrian, French and Italian law, given that three of the official languages spoken in Switzerland are also the official languages of these countries. The linguistic factors are connected to historical ones: the legal systems of the neighboring countries have common roots in Roman law and have permitted scientific exchanges and legal transplants through centuries within their territories.

Because of the importance of immigrated population well integrated in Switzerland, Swiss authorities may also be bilingual or simply familiar with foreign languages other than the official ones, as English, Portuguese and Spanish. A circumstance widening their capacity to deal with materials and documentation coming from countries where those languages are the official ones.

Regardless of individual skills and studies, the importance of judicial training – to be extended to legal training to all authorities applying legal rules – is now recognized as a key element in order to improve the application of foreign law in the *forum.*[16]

[15] ATF 118 II 188, 193 and 4A_364/2015 du 13 avril 2016 (arrêt non publié).

[16] See the improvements studied at the EU level to promote the knowledge of foreign legal systems through judicial training, especially with a view to improving mutual trust: Raffaelli, R. & Bux, U. (eds.), *Workshop The Training of Legal Practitioners: Teaching EU Law and Judgecraft,*

2.1. Interpretation and Application of Foreign Law

Swiss Courts interpret and apply foreign law in the same manner and to the same extent they presume that the law would be interpreted and applied in the foreign legal order that produced it.[17]

If the foreign law is applicable, for instance, in order to determine if a contractual obligation was fulfilled or not, all circumstances – as the existance of *force majeure* – need to be evaluated according to such law.[18] Likewise, Swiss courts may not exercise powers they normally exercise whenever these are considered exorbitant by the foreign legal system.[19]

Doubts may appear whenever the foreign rule is being applied and interpreted in contradictory ways within the legal order that produced it. The parties may take advantage of the uncertain content of the foreign rule, each of them – respectively – favoring the interpretation more suitable to win the case. In these circumstances, the Swiss Federal Court has adopted the pragmatic view of prescribing to Swiss Courts to give relevance to the most recent opinion of the foreign country's highest Court.[20] In certain countries, however, when there is a contradiction between recent legal doctrine and an ancient ruling of the highest Court, *in loco* tribunals may depart from the former ruling of the highest Court.[21] This circumstance confirms that the goal of law certainty can never be fully achieved for good. Thus, all in all, the Swiss approach seems to be the most appropriate one, since in most legal orders the ruling of the highest Court is considered at least as persuasive authority.

The necessity to refer to the ruling of the supreme foreign authority is clearly revealing that whenever foreign law is ascertained, Swiss Courts are not merely looking for a technical solution to a problem as if the foreign solution were perfectly equivalent to the national one. Rather they are looking for a legal settelment of the rights of the parties. Swiss authorities do not use a «*copy-paste*» technique in order to integrate the foreign rule within their national legal system. Rather, foreign law is applied as such not to disregard the legitimate expectations of the parties involved; the expectations generated under the empire of the competent foreign legal order.[22]

Compilation of briefing notes, PE 493.022 and PE 493.023 as well as Coughlan, J./Opravil, J./ Heusel, W., *ERA - Academy of European Law, Judicial Training in the European Union Member States*, PE 453.198. See also Pretelli I., Language as a Bridge Between Legal Cultures and Universal Justice: *Linguae Alienae Novit Curia*? in Martin Schauer and Bea Verschraegen (Eds), *General Reports of the XIXth Congress of the International Academy of Comparative Law*, Ius Comparatum, vol. 24, Springer, 2017, at 607 ff.

[17] ATF 126 III 492 c.3 c/aa.

[18] ATF 127 III 123, c. 2e.

[19] 4A_336/2008, c.5.1.

[20] Bucher, A., Art. 16, in Bucher A. (ed.), *Loi sur le droit international privé: Convention de Lugano, Commentaire romand*, Basel 2011, n° 7, referring to decision of 04.07.2003, 4P.137/2002, c. 7.2.1. *RSDIE* 2005, p. 134 and of 31.03.2009, 4A_428/2008, c.3.1., Elektrim, *ASA* 2010, p. 104.

[21] In many continental countries – for instance in Italy – courts are not strictly bound by the ruling of the highest Court, *e.g.* when they consider a ruling outdated in light of new legal principles or norms.

[22] On the concept of "legitimate expectations" see Quadri, R. Lezioni di diritto internazionale, Napoli 1969, p. 147 et seq.

Accordingly, Swiss courts should not apply foreign rules outside of their territorial scope of application. Therefore, when the foreign legal order (the one having shaped the rule that comes into play) does not apply its internal rules but commands to use foreign ones, Swiss authorities also follow the indication in most cases. Therefore, Art. 14 PILA, commands to take into account references to Swiss law made by foreign private international law rules (*«Rückverweisung»* / *«renvoi»*) under certain circumstances.

Art. 14 and other relevant rules of the PILA prescribe, in this respect, to refer to the foreign legal system as a whole: *i.e.* to apply foreign rules together with foreign conflict of laws rules, whenever these have to be taken into account according to the circumstances of the case.[23] Therefore the foreign rule is not picked out of the context in which it normally lives. Obviously, the judge determines *ex officio* the content of both foreign rules and foreign conflict of laws rules, whenever it is possible for him to do so.[24]

There is a unanimous agreement that the purpose of *renvoi* is to ensure that the outcome of litigation is the same, regardless of the *forum* in which it takes place.[25] Indeed, *renvoi* is a mechanism elaborated to achieve a uniform settlement of a given transnational case, regardless of the differences existing in the substantive rules of the legal orders connected with it. However, *Rückverweisung*, as a unilateral mechanism may only guarantee a uniform settlement if, and only if, the other legal order concerned does not have such a mechanism. It must be pointed out, in addition, that the mechanism of *Rückverweisung* is grounded also on additional relevant considerations, different from the principle of international harmony of solutions. These are: the principles of the *Gleichlauf* between *forum* and *ius*; the respect of the *Näherberechtigung*; the need to preserve the coherence of the national legal order within its borders.[26] It may also be observed that it ultimately aims at applying the *lex fori* instead of the foreign law.[27]

[23] Dutoit, B., *Droit international privé suisse, Commentaire*, 4th edition, Basel 2005, p. 58, n°4, Bucher, A., Art. 14, in Bucher A. (ed.), *Loi sur le droit international privé: Convention de Lugano, Commentaire romand*, Basel 2011, n° 206 s., Mächler-Erne, M. & Wolf-Mettier, S., Art. 14, in H. Honsell et al. (eds.), *Basler Kommentar Internationales Privatrecht*, 3rd edition, Basel 2013, n° 1 et seq., Heini, A., Art. 14, in D. Girsberger et al. (eds.), *Zürcher Kommentar zum IPRG*, 2nd edition, Zürich 2004, n° 1 et seq.

[24] Keller, M. & Girsberger, D., Art. 16, in D. Girsberger et al. (eds.), *Zürcher Kommentar zum IPRG*, 2nd ed., Zürich 2004, n°17; Siehr, K., Private international law at the end of the twentieth century: progress or regress?, in *Swiss reports presented at the XV International Congress of Comparative Law: Bristol, 27 juillet au 1 août 1998*, Zürich 1998, p. 431 et seq.

[25] Siehr, K., Private international law at the end of the twentieth century: progress or regress?, in Swiss reports presented at the XV International Congress of Comparative Law: Bristol, 27 juillet au 1 août 1998, Zürich 1998, p. 415 and note 31.

[26] On these principles see the synthesis offered by Najm, M.-C., *Principes directeurs du droit international privé et conflit de civilisations*, Paris 2005, p. 82 et seq., in French. See also Pretelli, I., *Garanzie del credito e conflitti di leggi*, Napoli 2010, pp. 297–302, and *passim* in Italian.

[27] See Francescakis, Ph., *La théorie du renvoi et les conflits de systèmes en droit international privé*, Paris 1958 and, in Switzerland, *e multis*, Aubert, J.-F., Une révision du droit international privé: La "Théorie du renvoi" de M. Francescakis, in *Annuaire suisse de droit international*,

2.2. Judicial Review

In the full exercise of its review authority, the Swiss Federal Court can assess whether the conflict of law rules were applied correctly, meaning whether the applicable law was correctly selected. Since a conflict of laws rule contains a vector for identifying the foreign law to be applied in order to solve a legal problem, the failure to identify the proper law or the circumstance that the foreign applicable law was ignored by a Swiss court, amount to violations of the PILA. Such violations, as any other violation of Swiss or international law, are subject to judicial review by the Swiss Federal Court.[28]

As the Swiss Federal Court verifies that conflict of laws rules have been properly applied by the inferior Courts,[29] it is, in certain cases, also empowered to review whether the foreign law so identified was properly applied.[30]

Art. 96 of the Swiss Federal Supreme Court Act (FSCA) addresses both issues by stating that – in the case of foreign law – a petition for review by the Federal Supreme Court may be founded on the non-application of a foreign law in violation of Swiss Private International Law[31]*or* – provided that the issue relates to non-pecuniary matters – on the inaccurate application of foreign law.[32]

In short, the Swiss Federal Supreme Court may give the proper interpretation of foreign law without sending the case back to the inferior court, provided that two conditions are met. The first is that the legal question must concern *a civil non-pecuniary matter*; the second is that *foreign law was indeed applied*, although erroneously.[33]

15(1958), p. 187–214; Reichart, P. A., *Der Renvoi im schweizerischen IPR: Funktion und Bedeutung*, Zürich 1996; Schnitzer, A. F., *Der Renvoi: Rück- und Weiterverweisung im Internationalen Privatrecht in Schweizerische Juristen-Zeitung*, Zürich 1973; Schwander, I., Einige Gedanken zum Renvoi, in *Liber amicorum Adolf F. Schnitzer*, Genève 1979, p. 411 *et seq.*,Sonnentag, M., *Der Renvoi im Internationalen Privatrecht*, Tübingen 2001; Romano, G. P., *Le renvoi en droit international privé – Thèse, antithèse et la recherche d'une synthèse*, Collection genevoise, Droit international, Zürich 2014.

[28] See Art.72 ss. and Art. 95 let. a) and b) of the Swiss Federal Supreme Court Act (FSCA) (RS 173.110). ATF 127 III 123, c. 2e., ATF 126 III 492: "*Der Rügegrund von Art. 43a Abs. 1 lit. a OG ist gegeben, wenn das massgebende ausländische Recht nicht in dem vom schweizerischen Kollisionsrecht geforderten Umfang (Art. 16 IPRG) angewendet wurde* (E. 3)", ATF 118 II 83, 85: "*Il appartient à la juridiction de réforme de contrôler d'office que le juge cantonal a appliqué le droit désigné par le droit international privé suisse*".

[29] ATF 118 II 83 c. 2b.

[30] ATF 127 III 123, c. 2e. and *supra* par. 1.2.

[31] ATF 119 II 93 c. 2c.

[32] Art. 96 let. a) and b) of the FSCA (RS 173.110), see Donzallaz, Y., Art. 96 *Droit étranger*, in *Loi sur le Tribunal fédéral – Commentaire*, Bern 2008, n° 3566 et seq; Corboz, B., Art. 96, in B. Corboz et al. (eds.), *Commentaire de la LTF*, Bern 2014, n° 14 et seq. The notion of pecuniary matter is given by Art. 74 al. 1 LTF fixing a minimal amount for submitting an appeal to the Swiss Federal Supreme Court.

[33] Swiss Federal Court, 07.04.1995, Dame X. c. X. (VS), *RVJ* 1996 p. 161; ATF 121 III 248.

In this respect, it is worth recalling that the notion of non-pecuniary matters is large; *e.g.* maintenance obligations in connection with family law cannot be qualified pecuniary matters, since their aim is not purely of economic character.[34] In pecuniary matters, an appeal may be lodged to censure the wrong interpretation of foreign law only in case of violation of Art. 9 of the Swiss Constitution – on the prohibition of arbitrary decisions – *and* provided that the amount in dispute is at least equivalent to 30.000 CHF. In this case, the party needs to prove that the decision based on foreign law is indubitably in contrast with the provisions of foreign law.[35]

3. Two Reasons Why Foreign Law Cannot Be "Proved"

The first reason lies in the difference between technical opinions by experts in non-legal fields and legal opinions on the content of foreign law. A well-established principle states that Courts may not depart without valid reason from the first kind of expert opinions, when they decide technical issues.[36]

Objective difficulties to determine the command given by a foreign rule may also lead to the appointment of an expert by the Court, despite the principle *iura novit curia*. In this case, however, even though judicial authorities will frequently rely on the expert opinion, in no case will they be bound by it.

The Federal Court has explicitly stated that interpretation and application of foreign law is a task inherent to the judicial function and may not be attributed to an expert.[37]

The second reason concerns the right of each party to be heard on the content of foreign law, which must be respected, as seen above[38] although Swiss Courts are not bound by the legal information displayed by the parties, even if these would hypothetically agree on the content of foreign law.[39]

[34] Von Overbeck, A.E., Die Ermittlung, Anwendung und Überprüfung der richtigen Anwendung des anwendbaren Rechts, in Hangartner Y., *Die allgemeinen Bestimmungen des Bundesgesetzes über das internationale Privatrecht*, St. Gallen, 1988, p. 103. Schwander, I., *Einführung in das Internationale Privatrecht*, Allgemeiner Teil, 2. A. St. Gallen 2000, n° 391. In respect of the distinction between pecuniary and non-pecuniary matters see Corboz, B., Art. 74, in B. Corboz et al. (eds.), *Commentaire de la LTF*, Bern 2014, n° 12–16.

[35] Swiss Federal Court, 23.02.2009, 5A_437/2008 at 2.1. See Corboz, B., Art. 96, in B. Corboz et al. (eds.), *Commentaire de la LTF*, Bern 2014, n° 16.

[36] ATF 130 I 337, c. 5.4.2.

[37] See the aforementioned decision of 28.10.2004, 1P.390/2004, at c.2.2. and *infra* par. 4.2. and note 81: "*[l'art. 16] consacre l'obligation, pour le juge, d'établir d'office le droit étranger [...] car l'application du droit étranger aux cas concrets rentre dans ses attributions et non pas dans celles de l'expert*".

[38] ATF 118 II 188, 193 on which see *supra*, par. 1.1.

[39] As regards to the legal opinions of the Swiss Institute of Comparative Law, the Federal Court stated explicitly: "*les avis de droit rendus par cet organisme [ne sont] pas assimilables à des rapports d'experts*" see Swiss Federal Court, 28.10.2004, 1P.390/2004, c. 2.

Swiss Courts are aware that ascertaining the content of a law is different from taking evidence over the existence of a fact,[40] since the aforementioned rule prescribing to the judge to rely on the expert opinion, as well as general evidence rules do not apply here.

Indeed, the Swiss Supreme Federal Court takes the view that Art. 16 § 1 PILA creates an obligation upon the judges to establish the content of Foreign Law *ex officio*.

4. Solutions in Cases of Failure to Establish Foreign Law

Legal information on the content of foreign law may not be sufficient to settle the dispute, for instance, when the principle given by the foreign rule is clear but the rules necessary to address the dispute in front of the Swiss courts are not known in detail. In these hypotheses, legal doctrine and case law admit that Swiss court may integrate the foreign rule with Swiss solutions or through comparative analysis.[41]

Integration of the content of foreign law through Swiss rules is only possible when the content of foreign law is comparable or at least compatible to that of Swiss law.[42] In addition, Swiss legal rules may not merely integrate but even substitute foreign applicable rules, when their content is not easily accessible. According to § 2 of Article 16 PILA, Swiss law applies if the contents of the foreign law cannot be established. For Swiss law to apply, the judge must have serious doubts about the results of the undertaken research of the content of foreign law.[43] Swiss law cannot apply as long as all available sources and means to ascertain the content of foreign law have been taken into account.[44] Among these, special attention is given to the

---

[40] See Swiss Federal Court, 27.05.2013, 5A_60/2013, c. 3.2.1.1.: "*L'emploi du terme "preuve" est. donc impropre, dans la mesure où il ne s'agit pas d'une preuve au sens strict, la norme étrangère étant une règle de droit*". The proof of foreign law, in particular, is not equivalent to giving to a party the "*fardeau objectif de la preuve, entraînant le cas échéant la perte du droit invoqué*"; See also: ATF 138 III 232, 237: "*Wie dargelegt hat fremdes Recht, das im Inland angewendet werden soll, jedoch nicht Tatsachen-, sondern Normcharakter, weshalb Art. 16 Abs. 1 IPRG vom "Nachweis" und nicht vom "Beweis" des ausländischen Rechts spricht*". See Schwander, I., *Einführung in das Internationale Privatrecht*, Allgemeiner Teil, 2. A. St. Gallen 2000, n° 388.

[41] Bucher, A., Art. 16, in Bucher A. (ed.), *Loi sur le droit international privé: Convention de Lugano, Commentaire romand*, Basel 2011, n° 7 with reference to ATF 126 III 495 and Swiss Federal Court decision of 02.09.2008, 4A_336/2008, c. 5.3.2. Bucher, A. & Bonomi, A., *Droit international privé*, 3rd edition, Basel 2013, p. 129 § 473.

[42] See the Swiss Federal Court judgments of 12.01.2006, 5C_222/2005, c. 2.5.

[43] ATF 128 III 346, 351 «*Nur wenn die erwähnten Bemühungen zu keinem zuverlässigen Ergebnis führen, ist ersatzweise Schweizer Recht anzuwenden. Dies ist auch dann der Fall, wenn ernsthafte Zweifel am Ergebnis aufkommen*».

[44] The Federal Council, Message concernant la révision totale de l'organisation judiciaire fédérale du 28 février 2001 (FF 2001, 4135), observes that a Court violates Art. 16 § 2 PILA if it applies Swiss law on the wrong assumption that the content of foreign law could not be established. The violation falls under Art. 90, al.1, let a) and Art. 95 FSCA (RS 173.110).

London Convention[45] and to the cooperation of the parties. In this respect, recourse to Swiss law is considered an *extrema ratio, i.e.* an exceptional remedy to the failure of establishing the content of foreign law.[46]

It is, however, admitted that the effort to establish the content of foreign law must be proportional to its objective: the solution of the legal issue decisive for the outcome of litigation. Concerns about costs, length and energies required to ascertain foreign law may justify the application of Swiss law, especially when the legal issue to solve through application of foreign law is not crucial or central as regards to the object of litigation.[47] That is particularly the case when the judge has to apply foreign law when deciding on *interim* or provisional measures.[48]

On the contrary, and quite obviously in light of the above, it is not possible to integrate foreign decisions or documents lacking essential elements, through the application of the Swiss rules that would have been applied in Switzerland by the authority that would have emitted the document, if it had been competent.[49]

5. Conclusion of Part I

On the whole, Swiss authorities have the duty and power to apply foreign law on their own motion even when the parties involved did not request its application.[50] However, as incidentally observed by the Swiss Federal Supreme Court, the principle *iura novit curia* does not apply to national rules and to foreign rules in the same manner. In particular, the Court recalls that national rules belong to a legal order that needs to be «known, applied and enforced by the authorities in charge of implementing it»; whereas foreign rules do not lead to the «implementation» of the foreign legal order as such, for the simple reason that the foreign legal order is not even truly known, in most cases, by the domestic Court giving effect to some of its legal rules.[51]

---

[45] European Convention of 7 June 1968 on Information on Foreign Law (RS 0.274.161). See Bucher, A., Art. 16, in Bucher A. (ed.), *Loi sur le droit international privé: Convention de Lugano, Commentaire romand*, Basel 2011, n° 10–13.

[46] Swiss Federal Court, 30.04.2008, 5A_50/2008, c. 4.

[47] ATF 128 III 346, 352. Dutoit, B., Supplément à la 4e édition du Commentaire de la loi fédérale du 18 décembre 1987, Basel 2011, p. 39, n°5.

[48] Swiss Federal Court, 08.11.2006, 5P_355/2006, c. 4.2.: «*Für den Arrest im Besonderen wird die Ansicht vertreten, dass der Gläubiger den Inhalt des anwendbaren fremden Rechts glaubhaft zu machen habe. Danach findet Art. 16 Abs. 1 IPRG im summarischen Verfahren keine Anwendung*».

[49] See Swiss Federal Court, 30.04.2008, 5A_50/2008, c. 4.3, as regards to a Brazilian decision determining the amount of maintenance to be paid, without the indication of the *dies a quo*.

[50] See Dutoit, B., *Droit international privé suisse, Commentaire*, 4th edition, Basel 2005, p. 57, n° 3 also on the difference of the Swiss approach from the French one.

[51] ATF 124, I, 49, 53 explicitly refers to Volken, P., *Die Internationale Rechtshilfe in Zivilsachen*, Zürich 1996, p. 139–140.

To put it differently, when national law is at stake, a public authority is enforcing its own legal order; the one that empowered it with the capacity of *ius dicere.* When foreign law is at stake, the vector to the foreign legal order provided by the PILA rule does not seem to integrate a technique for «copy-pasting» the content of the foreign rule in order to add it to the national legal system. Rather, the foreign rule is used as the best available legal parameter for guaranteeing transnational justice in the settlement of the specific cross-border case at stake.[52]

In Switzerland the nature of foreign legal rules is debated even though it seems difficult to deny that foreign rules are applied as any other legal norm, *i.e.* a norm having the ontological characteristics of positive law. In this respect, foreign law is not regarded by Swiss authorities as a mere factual *datum*, as if no legal system other than the Swiss one had the power to produce a text of "law". The legal character of foreign rules cannot be denied on the ground that for a rule to be characterized as "legal", in the Swiss perspective, it needs to be adopted through the procedures established by the Federal Constitution of the Swiss Confederation.[53]

Of course, the sources of the binding character of foreign legal rules differ from those of internal laws. Clearly, the binding character of a law within the legal system that produced it derives from that system's rules and principles: *e.g.* in Switzerland from the Federal Constitution. By contrast, when applied outside national borders, the same rule derives its binding character, if any, from a combination of internal and foreign sources. After all, the commandment to enforce a rule – no matter if internal or foreign – may only be given by the legal system exercising sovereignty on the authorities called upon to enforce that commandment. Thus, regardless of the paramount difference between the sources of the binding character of foreign and internal rules, both kind of rules are regarded as legal rules, provided that they were characterized as such by their respective authors. In other words, in order to qualify a foreign law as «law», the latter has to have the characteristic of a law in its own legal order. As a consequence, the application of rules of simple customary character – that are not binding legal rules within the legal order that produced them – will receive in Switzerland the same characterization and application as in their country of origin.

In systems adhering to legal positivism as Switzerland, Private International Law rules aim at permitting to foreign rules to produce effects within domestic boundaries, in the pursuit of a harmonious – though heuristic – justice for the individuals.[54] In this respect, the foreign rule remains a *foreign* and *legal* rule and does not need to be apprehended by the national legal system. It doesn't need to be, so to say, «nationalized» in order to be implemented abroad and to produce its typical effects *extra territorium.*

[52] *Supra* par. 2.1.

[53] See Art. 164 ff. of the Federal Constitution of the Swiss Confederation and in particular Art. 164–1: "All significant provisions that establish binding legal rules must be enacted in the form of a Federal Act". The English non official version is available here: https://www.admin.ch/ch/e/rs/1/101.en.pdf

[54] On the effects of the application of foreign law see Wengler, W., *Die Funktion der richterlichen Entscheidung über internationale Rechtsverhältnisse*, in RabelsZ 1951, pp. 1–31, p. 1–31.

Part II – Access to Foreign Law in Practice and in Perspective

Shaheeza Lalani

1. Conflict of Laws Rules

There is no provision in the Swiss Federal Private International Law Act[55] stipulating that the application of the conflict of law rules is mandatory. However, the predominant view, according to Swiss doctrinal sources[56] and case law,[57] is that these rules are mandatory.

The Swiss Federal Department of Justice's response to a questionnaire disseminated in 2007 by the Permanent Bureau of the Hague Conference on Private International Law,[58] provides an indication as to the frequency with which the Swiss conflict of laws rules lead to the application of foreign law. The response indicates that an average of 2% of the civil and commercial cases brought before the Swiss judicial authorities in 2006 required the application of a foreign law. Although the response provides no indication as to whether or not this percentage is likely to increase, it indicates that States whose laws are most frequently applied or invoked before judicial authorities in Switzerland include Germany, Italy, France, Austria, the United States and the Former Yugoslavia.

The most recent (2015) Annual Report of the Swiss Institute of Comparative Law (SICL)[59] also provides some indication as to the foreign laws most frequently applied or invoked before Swiss judicial authorities and indicates that requests addressed to the SICL are most often for information on the laws of Continental Europe. According to the same report, in 2015, 16 requests for information were

[55] SR 291.

[56] See for example, Dutoit, B., Droit international privé suisse: Commentaire de la loi fédérale du 18 décembre 1987, 4th ed., Basel, 2005, p. 57, n° 3. See also Bucher, A., ed., Loi sur le droit international privé: Convention de Lugano, Commentaire romande, Basel, 2011, ad. Art. 16, p. 226.

[57] ATF 118 II 83, 85 and ATF 133 III 323, 327.

[58] See the Swiss Response to Permanent Bureau of The Hague Conference on Private International Law, Feasibility Study on the Treatment of Foreign Law – Questionnaire, Preliminary Document No 25 of October 2007, available at http://www.hcch.net/upload/wop/genaff_pd09ch.pdf (11.01.2014) [hereinafter the "Hague Conference Questionnaire"].

[59] The SICL is an agency of the Swiss Federal Department of Justice, which is designated as the receiving and transmitting agency for requests regarding foreign law under Article 11 of the Federal Private International Law Act. It is also designated as such under Article 2 of the European Convention of 7 June 1968 on Information on Foreign Law (the "London Convention"). See Council of Europe Treaty Office, List of declarations made with respect to treaty No. 062, available at http://conventions.coe.int/Treaty/Commun/ListeDeclarations.asp?NT=062&CM=8&DF=24/02/2014&CL=ENG&VL=1 (24.02.2014). See also SR 0.274.161.

made by the Swiss federal authorities and 25 requests for information were made by the Swiss cantonal authorities.[60]

2. *Foreign Law Before Judicial Authorities*

2.1. Application of Foreign Law[61]

Foreign law may be applied before judicial authorities in Switzerland either *ex officio* or at a party's request. The application of the conflict of laws rules is widely regarded as mandatory in Switzerland,[62] and foreign law may be applied *ex officio* by virtue of conflict of laws rules in ratified international conventions[63] or the Federal Private International Law Act. If foreign law is designated as the applicable law under a provision of the Federal Private International Law Act, a Swiss court is required to apply the foreign law on its own motion, *i.e. ex officio*, without the parties calling for its application.

Where the Swiss rules of Private International Law give the parties the right to choose the governing law, parties may enter an agreement regarding their choice of law. This is, for instance, the case in relation to contracts (with the exception of consumer contracts),[64] including marriage contracts and contracts regarding the patrimonial consequences of a registered partnership.[65] The choice must either be express or clearly determinable from the terms of the agreement or the circumstances,[66] and the court must ensure that the choice is valid.[67]

[60] See Institut suisse de droit compare, *Rapport Annuel 2015*, available at http://www.isdc.ch/media/1236/rapport-annuel-2015_website.pdf (23.09.2016).

[61] Swiss courts will not apply foreign law that violates Swiss public policy or a mandatory provision of Swiss law: see Articles 17 and 18 of the Federal Private International Law Act.

[62] Dutoit, B., Droit international privé suisse, p. 57, n° 3.The *ex officio* application of the conflict of laws rules has been confirmed in the following decisions of the Swiss Supreme Court: ATF 130 III 417, cons. 2; ATF 130 III 462, cons. 4.1; ATF 131 III 153, cons. 3; ATF 131 III 511, cons. 2; ATF 132 III 626, cons. 3; ATF 132 III 609, cons. 4; ATF 132 III 661, cons. 2; ATF 136 III 142, cons. 3.2. All of these cases are cited in Dutoit, B., Droit international privé suisse: Commentaire de la loi fédérale du 18 décembre 1987, Supplément à la 4e édition, Basel, 2011, p. 39, n° 1. See also Bucher, A., ed., Loi sur le droit international privé, p. 226, n° 1–2.

[63] These are directly implemented in Switzerland, as Switzerland is a monist State: see Auer, A., Malinverni, G., and Hottelier, M., Droit constitutionnel suisse, vol. I, Berne, 2013, p. 456, n° 1344, citing ATF 130 I 312, 326. See also Bucher, A., Droit international privé, vol. 1/2, Basel / Frankfurt am Main, 1992, p. 152, n° 381.

[64] See Article 120, paragraph 2 of the Federal Private International Law Act.

[65] See respectively Articles 116, para. 1; 52; and 65c, para. 2 of the Federal Private International Law Act. Other provisions of the Federal Private International Law Act that give the parties the right to choose a foreign law as the governing law include Articles 90, paragraph 2; 104, paragraph 1; 105, paragraph 1; 119, paragraph 2; 122, paragraph 1; 135; 139; 163c, paragraph 2; and 187.

[66] See respectively Articles 116, para. 2; 53; and 65a of the Federal Private International Law Act.

[67] Dutoit, B., Droit international privé suisse, p. 57, n° 3.

2.2. Ascertainment of Foreign Law

In Switzerland, the "*iura novit curia*" principle applies and courts must ascertain the content of foreign law.[68] The court may also request assistance from the parties in the ascertainment of foreign law: the parties generally have better access than the judge to relevant information on the applicable foreign law.[69]

An important 'exception' to the *ex officio* ascertainment of foreign law exists for pecuniary matters, *i.e.* matters in which parties have a financial interest.[70] In these cases, the court may[71] shift the burden of ascertaining the content of foreign law[72] to (one of) the parties.[73] The court should not, however, place the burden of establishing the content of foreign law solely on the parties if the applicable conflict of laws rules do not give the parties the right to choose the *lex fori* and Swiss law is not applicable in the absence of a choice.[74]

A Swiss court may use legal texts, commentaries, case reports, journals and other scholarly works to ascertain the content of foreign law. Courts may also refer to experts: within Switzerland, the court may make inquiries to the Swiss Federal Department of Justice or the SICL; outside of Switzerland, the court may refer to foreign institutions or private persons, including law professors; foreign experts, through the London Convention; or Swiss or foreign diplomatic services.[75] However, the courts will generally rely on the information provided by the parties and the documents at the closest library; they will not consult the opinion of an expert unless this is produced or suggested by the parties.[76]

---

[68] See Article 16 of the Federal Private International Law Act. See also Bucher, A., ed., Loi sur le droit international privé, p. 225–26, n° 1.

[69] Bucher, A., Droit international privé, p. 148, n° 374.

[70] See Article 16 of the Federal Private International Law Act. The idea behind this exception was to place the financial burden of ascertaining foreign law on the parties rather than on the State, though this argument is not entirely convincing, as the court can still make the losing party bear the cost of research on foreign law: see Bucher, A., Droit international privé, p. 150, n° 375.

[71] Note that the court need not rely on the parties in this regard, particularly when the court has sufficient knowledge of the applicable foreign law: see 1P_390/2004 of 28 October 2004. See also Bucher, A., Droit international privé, p. 151, n° 378–79.

[72] This exception does not apply to foreign conflict of laws rules, which the court must ascertain *ex officio*. See Bucher, A., Droit international privé, p. 150, n° 376.

[73] See also Bucher, A. and Bonomi, A., Droit international privé, 3rd ed., Basel, 2013, p. 128, n° 467. See also Bucher, A., Droit international privé, p. 152, n° 381. In ATF 128 III 346, 352, the defendant, which had its registered office in the foreign State, was expected, based on its relationship to the foreign State, to produce information regarding the content of the foreign State's law.

[74] Bucher, A., Droit international privé, p. 153, n° 385. This could otherwise have the effect of circumventing the mandatory conflict of laws rules through the application of Article 16, paragraph 2 of the Federal Private International Law Act. Moreover, it could result in the imposition of an excessive burden on a weak party, such as a maintenance creditor.

[75] ATF 124 I 49, 52. Budgetary and human resource constraints make it illusory to solicit information from the Swiss Federal Department of Justice or foreign / Swiss embassies: see Bucher, A., ed., Loi sur le droit international privé, ad. Art. 16, p. 226, n° 5.

[76] Bucher, A., ed., Loi sur le droit international privé, ad. Art. 16, p. 226, n° 5.

In response to the Hague Conference Questionnaire, Switzerland indicated local specialized institutes and local private experts as being the main sources of expertise used to ascertain the content of foreign law.[77] The SICL is a specialized institute that was specifically created by federal law[78] in 1978 to provide information and legal opinions to tribunals, administrative bodies, lawyers and other interested persons on foreign law. Swiss federal law describes the SICL as the holder of a specialized library and a collection of documents on foreign legislation and international law. Indeed, the SICL, with over 700,000 bibliographic records in Swiss and foreign laws, and a legal staff trained in foreign countries, is a precious resource for ascertaining not only the content of foreign law, but also the practical application of relevant provisions.[79]

Although jurists at the SICL are not required have a bar admission or courtroom/trial experience,[80] they must have legal training and skills allowing them to address issues of international law, as well as the national laws of their countries of origin.[81] Other individuals providing legal information on foreign laws in Switzerland do not necessarily have to fulfil specific qualifications. A member of the Section of Foreign Lawyers of the Geneva *Ordre des avocats* (the OdA), to which membership is not mandatory, must be engaged in the independent practice of law; be admitted to, and in good standing with the Bar of a Member State of the EU or the EFTA; be practicing in Geneva under his or her title of origin and be registered under this title in the cantonal registry maintained by the Bar Commission.[82]

Legal information on foreign laws is not binding on Swiss judicial authorities[83] and it is significant that the Swiss Supreme Court, while noting that the independence and impartiality of the SICL are *a priori* guaranteed, has not made any presumptions regarding the validity or accuracy of legal opinions emanating from the SICL. In its view, this would negate any claims of judicial impartiality or

---

[77] See Permanent Bureau of The Hague Conference on Private International Law, Preliminary Document No 9A of March 2008; Feasibility Study on the Treatment of Foreign Law: Summary of the Responses to the Questionnaire, available at http://www.hcch.net/upload/wop/genaff_pd09ae2008.pdf (26.07.2008).

[78] SR 425.1.

[79] See Bucher, A., Droit international privé, p. 148, n° 368.

[80] In response to a questionnaire sent in 2010 to the SICL, Dr. Lukas Heckendorn, Head of the Scientific Division, indicated that only 7 out of the 12 jurists employed at the time by the SICL had bar admissions or experience in courtroom / trial representation: see Lalani, S., Doubt Develops where Certainty Ceases: Foreign Law in Domestic Courts, Ph.D. Dissertation, University of Lausanne, 2011.

[81] See the website of the SICL, available at www.isdc.ch (25.01.2014).

[82] See Article 36 of the Statutes of the OdA and Article 27 of the Swiss Federal Law on the Free Movement of Lawyers, 2000, SR 935.61. Note that if the member is admitted to and in good standing with the Bar of another State in which he or she continues to be under regulatory supervision, the admission is subject to the discretion of the Council of the OdA having regard *inter alia* that the professional activity is conducted concretely and preponderantly in Geneva, the duration of this activity, as well as the private domicile of the lawyer in the Canton.

[83] SR 272, Articles 150 and 157.

objectivity.[84] If the legal information is provided by the SICL, then it is verified by a senior legal staff member and the Director of the SICL.[85] Once the provided legal information has been verified through internal mechanisms, judicial authorities have an opportunity to examine the reliability of the provided legal information.[86] It should be noted that judicial authorities must place significant weight on the legal information provided by experts: a decision that disregards or diverges from the information provided by the experts must be justified.[87]

Although the unsuccessful party generally bears the overall costs of legal proceedings,[88] the party requesting information on foreign law may bear the cost of its ascertainment. Parties requesting information on foreign law from the SICL can pay between 150 and 400 Swiss Francs per hour, but no more than 700 Swiss francs per hour for a legal opinion.[89] The SICL charges reduced rates to federal and cantonal authorities unless services are rendered in relation to legal proceedings and costs borne by the parties. The SICL's rates are regulated by federal law.

3. Access to Foreign Law: Status Quo

Switzerland provides legal information through an official government website: www.admin.ch. In addition, all decisions of the cantonal tribunals are published online on official cantonal websites. The Hague Judicial Network and the European

[84] In the Swiss Supreme Court case, 1P_390/2004 of 28 October 2004, the Court stated that its freedom to take advice on the content of foreign law does not exempt it from acting in accordance with fundamental principles of procedure and from choosing an impartial and independent officer though that person may be related to one of the parties such that he or she does not appear objectively impartial and independent.

[85] In 1P_390/2004 of 28 October 2004, the court recognised the SICL as an autonomous institution funded by the federal government to provide legal information on foreign law to administrative and judicial authorities, as well as to lawyers and other interested persons (see Message du Conseil fédéral sur la création d'un Institut suisse de droit comparé, FF 1976 I 813). The court went on to describe the legal opinions emanating from the SICL as always being in writing, mentioning only the relevant and applicable rules of foreign law, leaving conclusions for the requesting body to draw from the legal information provided. The court specified that the scientific staff of the SICL does not offer legal advice and cannot be compared to lawyers or legal advisors appointed under the rules of private law to give legal advice to fee-paying clients.

[86] This was the case, for instance, in ATF 135 III 92 and ATF 126 III 327. In these cases, the Swiss Supreme Court assessed the reliability of legal information provided by the SICL respectively on the law of Bosnia & Herzegovina and Lebanon. The Court found the information to be accurate and reliable. Similarly, in ATF 114 V 258, the Swiss Supreme Court favourably cited the legal information provided by the SICL on the question of insurance law in European countries.

[87] ATF 130 I 337, c. 5.4.2. See also Bohnet, F. et al. Code de procédure civile commenté, Bâle, 2011, p. 633, n° 19.

[88] SR 272, Articles 106–108. See also Bohnet, F. et al., Code de procédure civile commenté, p. 412, n° 12.

[89] See Facturation des expertises on the website of the SICL, available at http://www.isdc.ch/fr/expertises-juridiques.asp/4-0-13490-5-4-0/ (24.01.2014).

Judicial Network (EJN) are available in Switzerland, and the statistics of the Swiss Federal Department of Justice indicate the number of requests made for information on Swiss Law and foreign law through the EJN.[90]

Other frameworks exist between Switzerland and other countries on the basis of the Hague Conventions of 15 November 1965 on the Service Abroad of Judicial and Extrajudicial Documents in Civil or Commercial Matters, 18 March 1970 on the Taking of Evidence Abroad in Civil or Commercial Matters, and 25 October 1980 on International Access to Justice.[91] In addition, Switzerland is a State Party to the London Convention, which it signed on June 23, 1969, but the Convention is not frequently used in practice.[92]

Switzerland is a State Party to the Hague Convention of 1 March 1954 on Civil Procedure, and relevant bilateral treaties relating to civil procedure.[93] Switzerland is also a Party to bilateral treaties relating to the transmission of judicial and/ or extra-judicial acts.[94] In addition, Switzerland is active in the European Union's Judicial Cooperation Unit (EUROJUST),[95] the International Criminal Court, as well as the UN Tribunals and Fact-Finding Commission. International/regional instruments appear to work well to facilitate access to Swiss law; access to foreign law in Switzerland is facilitated by the existence of the SICL.

4. Access to Foreign Law: Further Developments

In Switzerland, access to foreign law is apparently most needed, according to the 2015 Annual Report of the SICL, in matters of private international law, successions and family law.[96] With the existence of the SICL, there is no pressing need to improve access to foreign law in Switzerland. There is, however, a need to improve

[90] "Statistique," Federal Department of Justice, International Mutual Legal Assistance, available at https://www.bj.admin.ch/dam/data/bj/sicherheit/rechtshilfe/rhf-statistik-d.pdf (23.09.2016).

[91] See SR 0.274.131, SR 0.274.132 and SR 0.274.133. These countries include Austria, Belgium, France, Germany, Italy and Luxembourg.

[92] See Bucher, A., Droit international privé, p. 149, n° 373. See also Desch, E., *Best Practices Survey of the European Convention on Information on Foreign Law*, CDCJ (2002) 15 (Strasbourg: CDCJ, 30 April 2002) and Rodger, B.J. & Van Doorn, J., Proof of Foreign Law: The Impact of the London Convention *International and Comparative Law Quarterly* (1997) 46, pp. 151–173.

[93] For example with Austria, the Bahamas, the Dominican Republic, Estonia, Fiji, Great Britain, Kenya, Netherlands, Nauru Republic, Poland, Swaziland, Tanzania, Tonga, and Uganda. See SR 0.274.12.

[94] For example, with Belgium, the Czech Republic, France, Germany, Greece, Hungary, Italy, Luxembourg, Monaco, Pakistan, Slovakia and Turkey.

[95] EUROJUST, available at http://eurojust.europa.eu/Pages/home.aspx (15.01.2014). See also Swiss Federal Department of Justice, Statistics, available (only in German) at https://www.bj.admin.ch/dam/data/bj/sicherheit/rechtshilfe/rhf-statistik-d.pdf

[96] Institut suisse de droit compare, *Rapport Annuel 2015*.

external communication regarding the services and resources of the SICL,[97] particularly for matters of family law and successions, which affect private parties, including those who often cannot afford costly measures or are simply unaware that foreign law may be applicable to their disputes. There is perhaps also a need for improved coordination between foreign law experts and non-judicial authorities in Switzerland.

In our view, the Swiss conflict of laws rules need not be modified *de lege ferenda* to reduce the number of cases in which foreign law is applied. We neither believe that the treatment of foreign law in Switzerland should be changed *de lege ferenda,* nor do we believe that international or regional instruments which unify the treatment of foreign law would be useful.[98] Translations of Swiss legislation and judicial decisions (in other languages, including English) could, however, be useful to facilitate access to Swiss law.[99]

---

[97] See Meier, A., Substantive Law Applied by Arbitrators and Courts: Is It the Same?, in C. Müller et al. (eds.), *New Developments in International Commercial Arbitration 2015,* Zurich, Basel, Geneva, 2015.

[98] See Bachand, F., The Proof of Foreign Normative Facts Which Influence Domestic Rules, *Osgoode Hall Law Journal* (2005) 43, pp. 270–287. See also Sommerlad, K. & Schrey, J., Establishing the Substance of Foreign Law in Civil Proceedings, *The Comparative Law Yearbook of International Business* (1992), pp. 145–165; Graveson, R.H., Comparative Aspects of the General Principles of Private International Law (1963) 109 *Recueil des cours,* pp. 1–164; Lalani, S., Establishing the Content of Foreign Law: A Comparative Study, *Maastricht Journal of European and Comparative Law* (2013) 20, pp. 75–112; Lalani, S., A Proposed Model to Facilitate Access to Foreign Law, in A. Bonomi & G.P. Romano (eds.), *Yearbook of Private International Law,* Vol. XIII, Munich 2011, pp. 299–313. Contrast Esplugues, C. et al., eds., *Application of Foreign Law,* Munich, 2011.

[99] This would, for instance, have been useful in *Mastercard International Inc. v. Fédération Internationale de Football Association,* 464 F. Supp. 2d 246 (2006), *vacated in part,* 239 Fed. Appx. 625 (2d. Cir. 2007), where a United States District Court had to weigh expert evidence on Swiss contract law. See also the remarks of Judge Posner in *Bodum USA, Inc. v. La Cafetière, Inc.,* 621 F. 3d 624 (7th Cir. 2010), as they relate to the usefulness of legal materials published in English.

Part III
National Reports II – North and South America

The United States: The Use and Determination of Foreign Law in Civil Litigation in the United States

Peter Hay

Abstract In the United States, federal and state courts do not consider the possible applicability of foreign law ex officio: unless a party raises the applicability of foreign law and proves its content, forum law applies. This article details the statutory and case law as well as the evolution to a solution that retains the initial burden on the parties but provides for cooperation between court and parties for the determination of the content of the foreign law and makes the court's decision thereon appealable. Tables contain references to the law of each of the states of the United States.

Private International Law ("Conflicts Law") is mainly the law of the individual states in the United States; there is no uniform rule or approach as to when foreign law applies. When foreign law is applicable, the determination of its content is a question of procedure, governed by each state's procedural law and by a Federal Rule of Civil Procedure when the case is pending in a federal court. State procedural rules differ and even the uniform federal rule has received different interpretations in the Federal Circuits. The common-law heritage and structure of American law explain two aspects shared by all procedural rules for the determination of the content of foreign law: the court does not make the determination ex officio; instead, the parties must raise the issue that foreign law may be applicable and then assist the court in determining its content. Furthermore, the adversarial character of American litigation requires notice to the opponent, an opportunity for the opponent to rebut, and perhaps even a limitation on the court to appoint experts or masters. This article discusses the scope and application of the Federal Rule and the divergent approaches in state courts, as well as current attempts in some states to adopt legislation limiting or proscribing recourse to foreign law. An appendix provides references to all state statutes and to principal state decisions.

L.Q.C. Lamar Professor of Law Emeritus, Emory University; Alumni Distinguished Professor of Law Emeritus, University of Illinois; Universitätsprofessor emeritus, TU Dresden, Germany. The superb research of Daniel J. Levin, J.D. is gratefully acknowledged. This report was first published as an article in 62 Am.J.Comp.L. 213 (2014) and is reprinted here by permission of the Journal and the American Society of Comparative Law.

P. Hay (✉)
Professor, Emory University School of Law, Atlanta, GA 30322-2770, USA
e-mail: PHAY@emory.edu

Y. Nishitani (ed.), *Treatment of Foreign Law - Dynamics towards Convergence?*,
Ius Comparatum – Global Studies in Comparative Law 26,
DOI 10.1007/978-3-319-56574-3_19

I. Introduction

A. The Topic

How the content of foreign law is determined in civil litigation involves a number of questions that are relevant for all legal systems. Initial questions concern the extent to which a legal system refers to foreign law in the first place, and if it does, whether determination of the applicable foreign law is mandatory or occurs only when invoked by a party (thereby seeking to displace the otherwise applicable *lex fori*). It is only at this point that the manner of determining foreign law becomes relevant, whether done by the court *ex officio*, with the aid of expert testimony commissioned by the court or by a party, or by recourse to other sources of information. Once the foreign rule has been ascertained, the question arises how much consideration and weight the forum court should give to the interpretation and application of the foreign rule by that system's courts. Finally, is the forum court's determination subject to review by appellate tribunals?

Many legal systems provide rather clear answers to the fundamental questions of when foreign law is relevant and should be considered and applied, who determines its content and how, and whether the determination is appealable. In the United States, the answers are multifaceted, can therefore be difficult even in American practice, and are certainly baffling for foreign observers. This is so because the question of how to determine foreign law may arise in a variety of different settings and therefore be subject to different rules, with perhaps different results.

B. The American Setting

The United States does not present a unitary legal system in private law, in private international law, or for civil procedure. How to prove foreign law in civil litigation – its content and application in foreign practice – is therefore difficult to describe and makes it necessary to recall the essential structural characteristics of the American civil law system.

Private law is predominantly[1] the law of the individual states and other legislative jurisdictions[2] of the United States. Even when federal law-making authority exists,

[1] Peter Hay, Law of the United States, at vii, 8 n.18 (3d ed. 2010).

[2] Guam, Puerto Rico, Virgin Islands, Native American Reservations ("Indian country"), Northern Mariana Islands, American Samoa.

it might not be exercised[3] or courts may be directed to defer to state law.[4] Similarly, rules of conflicts law (private international law) are state law. In combination, these two factors mean that "foreign" cases may involve a foreign country, but also another American state (interstate conflicts cases)[5]; whether a law other than the *lex fori* will be applied also depends on the particular state's conflicts rules. While approaches to conflicts law (just as rules of substantive private law) are often similar, differences do exist.[6]

Civil cases may also be brought in federal court when the litigants are of different state citizenship or nationality and the amount in controversy exceeds $75,000. Since private law and conflicts law are state law, in these cases, federal courts must apply the law of the state in which they sit.[7] However, they apply their own (federal) rules of procedure; these, in turn, contain rules for proving foreign law that may differ from those used by the state courts of the same state.

Because of the commercial prominence of New York, many international cases are brought in federal court there, particularly in the District Court for the Southern District, which includes New York City. Appeals from the lower New York federal courts are decided by the Court of Appeals for the Second Circuit. For these reasons, this article draws heavily on cases decided by those courts.

---

[3] *See, e.g.*, Bank of Am.Nat'l Trust &Sav.Ass'n v. Parnell, 352 U.S. 29 (1956); Jackson v. Johns-Manville Sales Corp., 750 F.2d 1314, 1327 (5th Cir. 1985); O'Melveny & Myers v. FDIC, 512 U.S. 79, 87 (1994) (few areas – only those in which there is a significant conflict between federal and state policies – are appropriate for federal common law), *applied in* Eli Lilly do Brasil, Ltda. v. Fed. Express Corp., 502 F.3d 78, 84 (2d Cir. 2007) (air carrier's liability for lost or damaged freight).

[4] *See, e.g.*, Federal Tort Claims Act, 28 U.S.C.§ 1346(b)(1); Foreign Sovereign Immunities Act, 28 U.S.C. §§ 1330, 1603, 1605 (district court will use the law of the state in which it sits to resolve all issues except questions of jurisdiction); Sosa v. Alvarez-Machain, 542 U.S. 692, 759 n.6 (2004) (Ginsburg, J. joined by Breyer, J. concurring); Richard v. United States, 369 U.S. 1, 12–13 (1962); Rayonier v. United States, 352 U.S. 315 (1957); EM Ltd. v. Republic of Arg., 389 F. App'x 38 (2d Cir. 2010), *cert. denied*, 131 S.Ct. 1474 (2011); Gould Elec., Inc. v. United States, 220 F.3d 169 (3d Cir. 2000). *See also* Gary Born, *A New Generation of International Adjudication*, 61 Duke L.J. 775, 823–24 (2012) ("[I]t is likely that some one thousand cases involving claims against foreign states are pending in national courts at any given time and that some 250 new cases are filed each year.").

[5] In an early decision, the U.S. Supreme Court invoked "comity" as the basis for giving (extraterritorial) effect to the law of foreign countries and sister-states alike. Bank of Augusta v. Earle, 38 U.S. 519, 589 (1839).*See also*, Fisher v. Fielding, 34 A. 714, 715 (Conn. 1895) (the states of the United States are "independent and foreign sovereignties").

[6] Professor Symeon C. Symeonides prepares an annual survey of conflicts cases in American courts, with some commentary. This detailed survey appears in the American Journal of Comparative Law. *See, e.g.*, Symeon C. Symeonides, *Choice of Law in the American Courts: Twenty-Sixth Annual Survey*, 61 Am. J. Comp. L. 217 (2013).

[7] Klaxon Co. v. Stentor Elec.Mfg. Co., Inc., 313 U.S. 487 (1941); Day & Zimmerman, Inc. v. Challoner, 423 U.S. 3 (1975).

II. Determining the Relevance of Foreign Law

It is not the judge (the court) who directs the course of the proceedings in American civil litigation; it is the parties through their counsel (the "adversarial system"). Foreign law therefore must be invoked – raised by at least one of the parties – otherwise, its possible applicability is not in issue and the case will proceed on the basis of forum law.[8] This result follows directly from the common law's historic view of foreign law as "fact," rather than "law" (since the latter could issue only from the court's own sovereign).[9] Even with the fact approach greatly modified in modern law, the court does not, as a rule, apply foreign law *ex officio* on the basis of the forum's conflicts law.[10] When foreign law is not before the court, the *lex fori* necessarily applies. In fact, judicial decisions refer to a presumption in favor of forum law.[11] From this also follows that gaps in foreign law are resolved by reference to forum law, and not on the basis of principles underlying the foreign law or by analogy to other principles or concepts of the foreign legal system.[12]

---

[8] Carey v. Bahama Cruise Lines, 864 F.2d 201, 205 (1st Cir. 1988). *See also* Trenwick Am. Reinsurance Corp. v. IRC, Inc., 764 F.Supp.2d 274, 302–03 (D. Mass. 2011); Leser v. U.S. Bank Nat'l Ass'n, 2012 U.S. Dist. LEXIS 139493, at *16–17, 2012 WL 4472025, at *5–6 (E.D.N.Y. Sept. 25, 2012) (court disregarded choice-of-law clause and applied N.Y. conflicts law when parties relied only on N.Y. law during the proceedings; moreover, one party later claimed not to have assented to the clause).

[9] Peter Hay, Patrick J. Borchers, Symeon C. Symeonides, Conflict of Laws § 12.15 (5th ed. 2010) [hereinafter *Hornbook*]. A classic historical and comparative overview is Arthur Nussbaum, *The Problem of Proving Foreign Law*, 50 Yale L.J. 1018 (1941). For other early comments, see Peter Hay, *Die Anwendung ausländischen Rechts im internationalen Privatrecht – Vereinigte Staaten von Amerika [Use of Foreign Law in Private International Law – United States of America]*, 10 Materialien zum ausländischen und internationalen Privatrecht [Materials on Conflict of Laws] 102 (1968); Stephen L. Sass, *Foreign Law in Civil Litigation: A Comparative Survey*, 16 Am. J. Comp. L. 332 (1968). *Cf.* Pan. Processes S.A. v. Cities Serv. Co., 796 P.2d 276, 294 n.82 (Okla. 1990). *See generally* Imre Zajtay, *Die Lehre vom Tatsachencharakter und die Revisibilität ausländischen Rechts [The Doctrine of Foreign Law as Fact and Its Reviewability on Appeal]*, 10 Materialien zum ausländischen und internationalen Privatrecht 193 (Max-Planck-Institut, Hamburg, 1968). For a modern review of English law in comparison with Continental civil law, see Rainer Hausmann, *Pleading and Proving Foreign Law – A Comparative Analysis*, 2008 Eur. Legal F. I-1.

[10] *But see infra* note 41, with respect to the court's freedom (and perhaps readiness) to undertake independent research, thereby going beyond the information offered by the parties.

[11] *See, e.g.*, Curley v. AMR Corp., 153 F.3d 5, 14 (2d Cir. 1998); *Carey*, 864 F.2d at 205–06; Bresnahan v. Stride, 2012 Neb. App. LEXIS 227, at *14 (Neb. Ct. App. 2012); C.I.T. Corp. v. Edwards, 418 P.2d 685, 689 (Okla. 1966); Cherokee Pub.Serv. Co. v. Harby Cragin Lumber Co., 49 P.2d 723, 726 (Okla. 1935).For early comment, see Nussbaum, *supra* note 9, at 1036 *et seq. See also* Restatement (Second) of Conflict of Laws § 136 cmt. h (1971); Larry Kramer, *Interest Analysis and the Presumption of Forum Law*, 56 U. Chi. L. Rev. 1301, 1303 (1989); Michael Steven Green, *Horizontal* Erie *and the Presumption of Forum Law*, 109 Mich. L. Rev. 1237, 1260 n.110 (2011).

[12] The result may be quite different when proof of the foreign law, determined to be applicable, fails altogether. *See infra* notes 17, 62.

When a party does invoke foreign law, it will do so on the basis of the local state's conflicts law.[13] Since conflicts rules – decisional or statutory[14] – are "law," the choice-of-law decision is one for the court to make, and not for the jury, which decides questions of fact.[15] Once the court decides, on the basis of forum conflicts law, that foreign law is applicable, the *content* of that law historically presented a *question of fact*. Modern approaches, to be discussed below, now consider this issue to be a question of "law," also to be decided by the court (with the assistance of the parties), and therefore appealable. But, to repeat, characterizing the choice-of-law decision and the determination of the content of foreign law as "questions of law" (or similar thereto) does not affect the initial point that all of this does not occur *ex officio*, except in a few isolated cases,[16] but only upon party initiative. It is then another question what happens when proof, the determination of the content of foreign law, fails.[17]

While most of the American states follow traditional, territorially-oriented choice-of-law rules for succession and family law, fewer than a dozen continue to

---

[13] This is so regardless of whether the suit is pending in state court or in a federal court exercising diversity jurisdiction. *See, e.g.*, Grupo Televisa, S.A. v. Telemundo Commc'ns Grp., 485 F.3d 1233 (11th Cir. 2007). In that decision, both parties had raised the conflicts issue. It therefore overstates to say, in a general fashion, that "domestic conflict of laws rules may require the application of foreign law." Matthew J. Wilson, *Improving the Process: Transnational Litigation and the Application of Private Foreign Law*, 45 N.Y.U. J. Int'l L. & Pol. 1111, 1119 n. 26 (2013). See *also supra* note 7 and *infra* note 16. For exceptions, see *supra* note 3.

[14] With respect to the statutory law of Louisiana and Oregon, see *infra* note 19.

[15] To the extent that factual issues determine the choice-of-law decision, their resolution is also a matter for the court. *In re* Vitamin C Antitrust Litig., 810 F.Supp.2d 522, 562 (E.D.N.Y. 2011) (citing Nautilus Ins. Co. v. Reuter, 537 F.3d 733, 742–43 (7th Cir. 2008)).

[16] See, e.g., Druck Corp. v. Marco Fund Ltd., 290 F. App'x 441 (2d Cir. 2008); Aon Fin. Prods., Inc. v. Société Générale, 476 F.3d 90 (2d Cir. 2007); Jinro Am.Inc. v. Secure Invs., Inc., 266 F.3d 993 (9th Cir. 2001) (court determined foreign law with respect to some issues after parties failed to comply with court's request for assistance); Pittway Corp. v. United States, 88 F.3d 501 (7th Cir. 1996) (translations of French law provided by parties did not match, so the court, based on its own research, cited to "the authoritative French version"). Louise Ellen Teitz, Determining and Applying Foreign Law: The Increasing Need for Cross-Border Cooperation, 45 N.Y.U. J. Int'l L. & Pol. 1081, 1091–92 (2013) criticizes courts for "defaulting to U.S. law." The criticism may be well taken when foreign law is in issue in the first place and courts resort too readily to forum law, thereby avoiding a genuine conflicts analysis. However, raising the applicability of foreign law rests initially with the parties, as Federal Rule 44.1 itself makes clear. See supra at notes 10 and 11: raising the applicability of foreign law and determining its content are two different matters.

[17] In the older law, following the fact approach (*supra* note 9), the claim would be dismissed. *See* Walton v. Arabian Am. Oil Co., 233 F.2d 541 (2d Cir.), *cert. denied*, 352 U.S. 872 (1956). *See also infra* note 65. In modern cases, courts may still write that a claimed aspect of foreign law has not been "proved," or that the party has failed to convince the court, but may also often reach the same result (non-acceptance of the asserted meaning of a foreign norm) after extensive analysis of their own. *See, e.g.*, Nana Osei Bonsu v. Holder, 646 F.Supp.2d 273, 276 (D. Conn. 2009) (citing *Walton*, but reaching a result with respect to Ghanaian law contrary to the government's position on the basis of its own review). For discussion of *Walton*, see William L. Reynolds, *What Happens When Parties Fail to Prove Foreign Law?*, 48 Mercer L. Rev. 775 (1997). For further discussion, see *infra* note 65.

adhere to them strictly in contract and tort. Instead, most states apply modern approaches to determine, for instance, the law of the state of the "most significant relationship" (the approach of the Second Restatement). A state using the Second Restatement approach is instructed to make that determination with respect to particular *issues*, rather than to the whole case (that is, to engage in *dépeçage*), and to use the "principles" of the Second Restatement's Section 6. As shown elsewhere,[18] these principles give courts wide leeway in emphasizing internationality or, in contrast, forum interests. In fact, American cases do show a far greater "homeward" trend than does the statutory or decisional law of other (especially civil law) jurisdictions. Even the first two state codifications of portions of conflicts law are far more forum-oriented than newer codifications elsewhere.[19]

Legislative initiatives in a number of states – 33 states in 2010 by one account[20] – seek to bar courts in their respective states from some or even all resort to foreign law. Implementation of a constitutional amendment in one state, specifically targeting Sharia-based law, was enjoined by a federal court on federal constitutional grounds.[21] These efforts, of course, display a regrettably insular orientation. Even Greek and Roman law excluded foreign law only in litigation between local citizens; "The 'personality principle' applied, not the 'territoriality principle'".[22] Today's counterpart – the common-domicile rule in tort[23]– similarly performs a practical function (and also reflects possible party expectations), but it is broader

[18] Peter Hay, *Flexibility versus Predictability and Uniformity in Choice of Law*, Hague Academy, 226 Recueil des cours [Collected Courses] 281, 350–385 (1991-I) [hereinafter *Flexibility*]; Hay, *supra* note 1, at 105–08 (nos. 238–44). For a sampling of the case law employing the new approaches, not a comprehensive survey, see Peter Hay, Russell J. Weintraub, Patrick J. Borchers, Conflict of Laws – Cases and Materials 540–612 (14th ed. 2013) [hereinafter *Casebook*].

[19] *See* La. Rev. Stat. Ann. § 9:6001 (2010); Symeon C. Symeonides, *The Conflicts Book of the Louisiana Civil Code*, 83 Tul. L. Rev. 1041(2009); Or. Rev. Stat. §§ 81-100 – 81-135 (2002) (contracts); *id.* §§ 31-850 – 31-890 (torts). Both codifications contain mandatory rules providing for the application of forum law. *See Hornbook, supra* note 9, at § 2.25 nn.40 (contracts) and 49 (torts). For bibliographies on the Louisiana and Oregon codifications, *see* Symeon C. Symeonides, *Codifying Choice of Law Around the World* 366 and 369 (2014).

[20] David L. Nersessian, *How Legislative Bans on Foreign and International Law Obstruct the Practice and Regulation of American Lawyers*, 44 Ariz. St. L.J. 1647, 1653 *et seq.* (2012). For additional discussion, see *infra* note 104.

[21] Awad v. Ziriax, 670 F.3d 1111 (10th Cir. 2012). Like many other such efforts, the Oklahoma amendment was intended, at least in major part, to guard against any influence of Sharia law. *See* Sarah M. Fallon, *Justice for All: American Muslims, Sharia Law, and Maintaining Comity Within American Jurisprudence*, 36 B.C. Int'l & Comp. L. Rev. 153 (2013).

[22] Harold J. Berman, *Is Conflict-of-Laws Becoming Passé? in* Balancing of Interests – Liber Amicorum Peter Hay 43, 47 n.15 (Hans-Eric Rasmussen-Bonne et al., eds. 2005), with further references. *See also* Mario Bretone, Geschichte des römischen Rechts [History of Roman Law] 397 (German translation by Galsterer 1992).

[23] For a survey of American case law, see *Hornbook, supra* note 9, §§ 17.39, 17.40 (to p. 898). Precursors to the European Union's common-domicile rule ("Rome II" Regulation 864/2007, art. 4(2), 2007 J.O. (L 199/40) (EC)) can be found in a number of earlier European statutes. *See Flexibility, supra* note 18, at 366–67; *Casebook, supra* note 18, at 1143.

and not forum-focused. It gives litigants with a common foreign domicile the benefit of their home law.

The legislative initiatives mentioned above would bar the use of all non-forum law (generally or in specified instances), other than federal law benefitting from the federal Constitution's Supremacy Clause (the Constitution itself, federal law, and treaties). In this context, it is important to emphasize that contrary to earlier Supreme Court decisional law,[24] (general) public international law is not part of federal law[25]; only self-executing provisions of treaties ratified by the United States are.[26]

Even though most of the legislative initiatives have not been enacted, they reflect an extremely insular view of significant parts of the country. This attitude necessarily will find reflection in choice-of-law decisions that are based on the evaluation of contacts and the balancing of local as against foreign interests.[27] If some of these initiatives are enacted, current practice with respect to choice-of-law clauses could be affected.[28] Within limits,[29] American courts now honor choice-of-law clauses,[30] but what if local law forbids recourse to foreign law?

Except in commercial centers of the United States and their courts, foreign law – whether by a choice-of-law clause or by choice-of-law decisions that seek the most

---

[24] *See* The Paquete Habana, 175 U.S. 677, 700 (1900) (still cited by Justice O'Connor in her dissent in Roper v. Simmons, 543 U.S. 551, 604 (2005)).

[25] Ghaleb Nassar Al-Bihani v. Barack Obama, 619 F.3d 1, 16 (D.C. Cir. 2010) (en banc). *See also* Sosa v. Alvarez-Machain, 542 U.S. 692, 715, 720 (2004) (even when a statute – in this case the Alien Tort Statute (28 U.S.C.A. § 1350) – refers to the "law of nations," this is but a "modest" incorporation of international law, limited in the main to offenses recognized in 1789). *But see* Filartiga v. Pena-Irala, 630 F.2d 876, 887 (2d Cir. 1980) ("federal [subject matter] jurisdiction over cases involving international law is clear" (in this case, however, the federal Alien Tort Statute expressly referred to the law of nations)); Nersessian, *supra* note 20, at 1654 n.23 ("international law is federal law"). In view of the cases cited above, both of the foregoing assertions overstate. In the view of critics, the "'idea that law must emanate from the power of a sovereign state' ... neglects the fact that transnational commercial contracts, for example, are usually governed by supranational customary law, the law merchant ..." Berman, *supra* note 22, at 43 (citing Friedrich K. Juenger, *American Conflicts Scholarship and the New Law Merchant*, 28 Vand. J. Transnat'l L. 487, 490, 493 *et seq.* (1995). But see the case law cited above and Emily Kadens, *The Myth of the Customary Law Merchant*, 90 Tex. L. Rev. 1153 (2012).

[26] *Ex parte* Medellín, 223 S.W.3d 315 (Tex. Crim. App. 2006), *aff'd sub nom.* Medellín v. Texas, 552 U.S. 1491 (2008).

[27] It must be remembered that in more than half of American states, judges are not civil servants, but are elected and must stand for re-election or confirmation. *See* Hay, *supra* note 1, at 59 (no. 117A).

[28] The Kansas blocking statute already expressly extends to choice-of-law clauses. Kan. Stat. Ann. § 60-5104 (West 2012). For further discussion, *see infra* note 104.

[29] Both the Uniform Commercial Code (§ 1-301)(1) and the Restatement (Second) of Conflict of Laws (§ 187(2)) require that the chosen law bear a reasonable relation to the transaction, with the Restatement section also contemplating another "reasonable basis." An attempt to revise the UCC to permit the choice of an unrelated law in international transactions was abandoned in 2007.

[30] For a survey, see Peter Hay, *Forum-Selection and Choice-of-Law Clauses in American Conflicts Law*, *in* Gedächtnisschrift für Michael Gruson [Legal Essays in Memory of Michael Gruson] 195 (Theodor Baums and Stephan Hutter, eds. 2009).

closely connected law in an objective fashion –plays a far lesser role in the United States than in systems that couple fixed rules with a mandate for courts to determine the applicable law *ex officio*. To be sure, the bulk of litigation of international cases does take place in the commercial centers. Here as well, there may be differences in approach because of state/state and state-court/federal-court divergences. As in all matters relating to civil litigation in the United States, there is no "American rule."

III. Determining the Content of Foreign Law

In the absence of an overriding mandatory norm of forum law[31] and when foreign law seems relevant on the basis of forum conflicts law or a valid and acceptable choice-of-law agreement,[32] the issue then becomes how to determine what that foreign law provides. The common law's "fact approach" required parties to plead and prove the foreign law like any other fact. To soften the impact of the possible failure to meet that burden (e.g., dismissal), several presumptions were employed that could lead to forum law. They included that the foreign law was the same as forum law or that the foreign state had no law – that it was "uncivilized." The identity presumption was obviously of little value when the foreign law was that of an entirely different legal system.[33] Similarly, courts were loath to consider and call another country "uncivilized."[34]

[31] In contrast to European conflicts law (*see, e.g.*, "Rome I" Regulation 593/2008, art. 9, 2008 O.J. (L 177/6) (EC) (Contractual Obligations); "Rome II" Regulation, *supra* note 23, at art. 16 (Non-Contractual Obligations)), American cases and commentators do not use the concept of (overriding) mandatory norms. Nonetheless, many cases can be explained on that basis. A good example is Lilienthal v. Kaufman, 395 P.2d 543 (Or. 1964) (with both California, the place of making and performance of the contract, and Oregon, the domicile of the defendant, favoring a *pacta sunt servanda*-policy, Oregon law, allowing trustees of people declared incompetent to avoid contracts, prevailed). A mandatory norm of forum law expresses an overriding local public policy that obviates any further inquiry into what law might (otherwise) apply. The traditional "public policy" exception provides a corrective mechanism *after* a choice of law has been made and the result proved unpalatable. *See* Peter Hay, *Comments on Public Policy in Current American Conflicts Law*, *in* Die richtige Ordnung– Festschrift für Kropholler [The Right Order – Festschrift for Kropholler] 89, 100–02 (Dietmar Baetge et al., eds. 2008).

[32] *See, e.g.*, *supra* note 28.

[33] *See* Leary v. Gledhill, 84 A.2d 725 (N.J.1951); Sonnesen v. Pan.Transp. Co., 82 N.E.2d 569, 571 (N.Y. 1948); Pa. Life Ins. Co. v. Simoni, 641 N.W.2d 807, 811 (Iowa 2002) (a recent statement of the identity presumption). For a recent affirmation of the doctrine in Scotland, see Royal Bank of Scotland Plc v. Davidson, 2010 S.L.T. 92 at ¶ 17 (Court of Session, Outer House, 2009).

[34] Walton v. Arabian Am. Oil Co., 233 F.2d 541 (2d Cir.), *cert. denied*, 352 U.S. 872 (1956) illustrates both points: while, in a prior case (Siegelman v. Cunard White Star Ltd., 221 F.2d 189, 196 (2d Cir. 1955)), the court had taken judicial notice of English law, it would be an "abuse of discretion" to do so, in the case of foreign law as unknown and perhaps different from American law as that of Saudi Arabia, without proof by the party relying on it. Likewise, without proof by the parties that Saudi Arabia was "uncivilized," the court was not prepared to presume this to be the case. *See* Reynolds, *supra* note 17. For the role of presumptions in the post common-law era, see Edwin

In modern practice – whether under the Federal Rules of Procedure in federal court or under state statutes in state courts[35]– the parties must still invoke foreign law. A number of state court decisions still regard foreign law as "fact," to be pleaded and proved like any other fact,[36] but "proof" usually takes the form of sufficiently "assisting" the court (whatever that means) so that it can make the determination. The court, as it were, becomes the trier of fact. With respect to sister-state law, courts will take "judicial notice" of its content. Some state statutes extend this method – only a partial adaptation of the civil law's maxim of *iura novit curia* (see below at IV(A)(1)) – to foreign-country law. But even when authorized to do so, courts will rarely utilize this method when foreign country law is involved, and if they do, then only with respect to other common law jurisdictions, such as England. Overwhelmingly, the determination of the content of foreign law therefore proceeds as previously outlined.[37]

What sources does the court consider – is it limited by what the parties present or with respect to the kind of sources it may consult, or is it free to go beyond material offered by the parties? Since it is usually the parties who assert the applicability of foreign law in the first place, they will obviously support their assertions with references to foreign law, statutory and decisional,[38] citation to commentaries, and, foremost, with expert opinions, which in turn reference and rely on the foregoing sources. Experts thus are designated by the parties, and hardly ever by the court.[39] An expert need not meet specific conditions to qualify as such (e.g., be qualified to practice law in the foreign jurisdiction); he or she may be a foreign lawyer or academic, but also a domestic practitioner or academic who, on the basis of education, professional engagement, and experience, is acceptable to the court. Since nothing adduced by an expert binds the court,[40] the level of expertise demonstrated by a party's expert has little influence on the party's ability to introduce the expert's opinion, but rather goes to the acceptance of his or her views as persuasive.

P. Carpenter, *Presumptions as to Foreign Law: How They Are Affected by Federal Rule of Civil Procedure 44.1*, 10 Washburn L.J. 296 (1970–71).

[35] *Infra* notes 66 and 51 *et seq.*, respectively.

[36] *See, e.g.*, Ramsey Cnty.v. Yee Lee, 770 N.W.2d 572, 577 (Minn. Ct.App. 2009); Haltom v. Haltom, 2012 Neb.App.LEXIS 102, 2012 WL 1537839 (Neb.Ct.App. 2012).

[37] Illinois seems to adhere to the common law fact approach, while Iowa follows a mixed approach. An Illinois appellate court stated as recently as 2002 that "in Illinois, the laws of foreign countries must be pled and proven as any other fact." Bianchi v. Savino Del Bene Int'l Freight Forwarders, Inc., 770 N.E.2d 684, 695 (Ill.App. Ct. 2002). The Iowa Supreme Court noted that, while foreign statutory law may be judicially noticed, foreign decisional law must be pled and proved, i.e. "introduc[ed] into evidence." Pa. Life Ins. Co. v. Simoni, 641 N.W.2d 807, 810–11 (Iowa 2002).

[38] *See, e.g.*, Roberts v. Locke, 304 P.3d 116, 121 (Wyo. 2013) (party to furnish texts of foreign statutes, if necessary in English translation, and to prove decisional law by means of presenting the books containing the decisions or by parol evidence).

[39] *But see infra* note 86.

[40] See Karaha Bodas Co., L.L.C. v. Perusahaan Pertambangan Minyak Dan Gas Bumi Negara ("Pertamina"), 313 F.3d 70, 92 (2d Cir. 2002) (even foreign ministry's *amicus* brief was only "entitled to substantial deference, but would not be taken as conclusive evidence").

"American judges view foreign law through an American lens … For example, the premise that judicial opinions serve the same function in the French legal system as they do in the American legal system is false."[41] Expert opinions therefore are helpful, often perhaps essential. On the other hand, expert opinions are usually proffered by a party in support of its position, so it may be necessary for the court to make allowances and to discount the expert's "adversary spin."[42] For this reason, and since the Federal Rule establishes no hierarchy of sources for the determination of foreign law, it has been suggested that courts should do more on their own, such as engage in independent research or seek the assistance of others.[43] The latter might take the form of a court-appointed "master," himself or herself perhaps an expert in the foreign law, who will neutrally reach an opinion on the content of the foreign law and so advise the court.[44]A court's independent research to determine the content of foreign law resembles the *ex officio* determination by a civil-law court,[45] but it is not the same: the American court may (or may not) actively participate in

[41] Philip D. Stacey, *Foreign Law: Rule 44.1,* Bodum USA v. La Cafetiere, *and the Challenge of Determining Foreign Law*, 6 Seventh Circuit Rev. 472, 494 (2011), *at* http://www.kentlaw.edu/7cr/v6-2/stacey.pdf. *See also* Michael L. Wells, *French and American Judicial Opinions,* 19 Yale J. Int'l L. 81 (1994). Of course, the same can be true in reverse as well, for instance, when a civil law court concludes that reciprocity in judgment recognition is not assured because the common law jurisdiction has no statute to that effect, but only case law. For an example of the latter, see the 1909 decision of the German *Reichsgericht*: RGZ 70, 434 (1909).

[42] Bodum USA, Inc. v. La Cafetiere, Inc., 621 F.3d 624, 629, 632 (7th Cir. 2010) (Posner, J., concurring).

[43] *Id.* For further detail, see *infra* at notes 75–78. For discussion of the decision, see Stacey, *supra* note 41; Frederick Gaston Hall, Note, *Not Everything is as Easy as a French Press: The Dangerous Reasoning of the Seventh Circuit on Proof of Foreign Law and a Possible Solution*, 43 Geo. J. Int'l L. 1457 (2012). For the view that courts need not undertake an independent investigation, see Baker v. Booz Allen Hamilton, Inc., 358 F. App'x 476 (4th Cir. 2009). It is probably true that the Federal Rule (*infra* section IV(B)) does not require the court to undertake an independent investigation. The Rule establishes no "hierarchy" (*see Bodum*, 621 F.3d at 638 (Wood, J. concurring)), but gives courts "substantial discretion" (*see In re* Vitamin C Antitrust Litig., 810 F.Supp.2d 522, 561 (E.D.N.Y. 2011)). Hence, it does not require one form of evidence or method of procuring it or another. By like token, it does not preclude what Judge Posner advocates in *Bodum*. *See also infra* note 76. For a view, not representative of the majority approach, that a court may have an obligation to determine the content of foreign law on its own, see Aurora Bewicke, *The Court's Duty to Conduct Independent Research Into Chinese Law: A Look At Federal Rule of Civil Procedure 44.1 And Beyond,* 1 Chinese L.& Pol'y Rev. 97 (2005). For the view that the trial court may not conduct its own research, because inconsistent with the adversarial system, see Bianchi v. Savino Del Bene Int'l Freight Forwarders, Inc., 770 N.E.2d 684, 698–99 (Ill.App. Ct. 2002).

[44] See Matthew J. Wilson, *Demystifying the Determination of Foreign Law in U.S. Courts: Opening the Door to a Greater Global Understanding*, 46 Wake Forest L. Rev. 887, 932–933 (2011). With respect to court-appointed experts, see also *id.* at 927 *et seq.*; *infra* note 86.

[45] For Germany, see Reinhold Geimer, Internationales Prozessrecht [International Civil Procedure] no. 2577 et seq. (6th ed. 2009); Reinhold Geimer, Zöller –Zivilprozessordnung [Civil Procedure] § 293, at no. 14 *et seq.* (Reinhold Geimer, et al. eds., 30th ed. 2014). Even here, the parties can be expected to assist the court even though they do not carry a "burden of proof" with attendant negative consequences for not meeting it. *Id.* at no. 2588 and § 293 no. 16, respectively.

determining the content of foreign law, but it is the parties who make the issue relevant in the first place (see above).

American courts have no recourse to formal channels – through conventions, intergovernmental cooperation, or otherwise – for the determination of the content of foreign-country law. An exception is the 2010 Memorandum of Understanding between the chief justice of the Supreme Court of New South Wales and the chief judge of the Court of Appeals of New York on "References of Questions of Law" from one court to the other.[46] On the American side, answering a reference from a foreign court may constitute rendering an advisory opinion and therefore present constitutional problems, both on the state and federal levels.[47] The New York-New South Wales arrangement therefore contemplates a panel, consisting of a member of the Court of Appeals and of each of the four Appellate Divisions (New York's intermediary appellate courts), which functions in an unofficial capacity in answering questions referred to it.

IV. Modern Statutory Practice

A. *State Law*

1. "Judicial Notice" and *iura novit curia*

At common law, foreign law needed to be pleaded and proved by the party invoking it. If the "foreign law" was that of an American sister state, courts might take "judicial notice" of it; individual state statutes and later, a Uniform Act (below) required this.[48] The same practice might have applied if foreign country law was involved and that law was based on the common-law tradition.[49]

---

[46] The Memorandum of Understanding can be found at http://www.lawlink.nws.gov.au/practice_notes/nswes_pc.nfs/pages/538. For brief description, see J. J. Spigelman, *Proof of Foreign Law by Reference to the Foreign Court*, 127 L.Q.R. 208, 215 (2011).The text of the Memorandum does *not* require "the litigants' consent," as Matthew J. Wilson suggests: *supra* note 13, at 1137. The memorandum establishes a mechanism for the courts to inform themselves, once the parties have put the applicability of foreign law in issue. *See supra* at notes 10–17.

[47] Spigelman, *supra* note 46, at 216. This issue has also arisen under the American Interstate Uniform Certification of Law Act, with state court decisions taking conflicting positions. *See id.*at 214 n.46.

[48] *See* Uniform Judicial Notice of Foreign Law Act, 9 U.L.A. 399 (1951) (withdrawn 1966), Commissioners' Prefatory Note, at 399–400. Section 1 of the Uniform Act, *id.* at 401, provided, "Every court of this state shall take judicial notice of the common law and statutes of every state, territory and other jurisdiction of the United States."

[49] For such a provision in current law, *see, e.g.*, Md.Code Ann., Cts. & Jud. Proc. § 10–501 (West 1974) ("Every court of this State shall take judicial notice of the common law and statutes of every state, territory, and other jurisdiction of the United States, and of every other jurisdiction having a system of law based on the common law of England.").

What does "judicial notice" mean – then and now? Judicial notice does *not* mean – some exceptional cases apart – that the court determines on its own *what law* applies (Section II above) and then proceeds to determine the *content* of the foreign law that it found to be applicable (Section III above). As detailed earlier,[50] the party intending to rely on it must put foreign law in issue. "Judicial notice" then deals with the *manner* of determining the content of applicable foreign law. It is the court, not the fact-finding jury, that makes the determination; the court is free – perhaps obliged – to inform itself, and the ruling is then treated as one on a question of law.[51] A requirement to take "judicial notice" is thus considerably narrower than the civil law's standard of *iura novit curia*.

2. Uniform Acts[52]

Two uniform acts, since withdrawn, are reflected in some form in the statutory law of most states. The first, the *Uniform Judicial Notice of Foreign Law Act* (1936),[53] sought to assure judicial notice – in the sense discussed above – of sister state law within the United States. Its § 5 expressly excepted foreign-country law from the judicial-notice provision of § 2, but provided that it was to be "an issue for the court." Since even sister-state law had to be put in issue by the party invoking it, the difference in determining its content and that of foreign-country law was mainly a matter of degree: the court had to be convinced, and the burden for that was on the proponent.

The successor statute, the *Uniform Interstate and International Procedure Act* (1962), drops both the reference to "judicial notice" and the distinction between sister-state and foreign-country law of its predecessor. Formal "pleading" was the historic common-law method of putting facts (and any non-local law) in issue,[54] and while not specifically mentioned in the prior uniform law, it was implicit. But then statutory changes occurred, "eliminate[ing] much of the hyper technicality of

[50] See *supra* note 8. A 1942 New Jersey statutory formulation makes this very clear: "Whenever … law of any State … is pleaded in an action …, the court shall take judicial notice thereof. In the absence of such pleading, it shall be presumed that the common law of such State … is the same as the common law as interpreted by the courts of this State." N.J. Stat. Ann. § 2:98-28 (1942). *See also* Nussbaum, *supra* note 9, at 1021.

[51] *See* Uniform Act, *supra* note 48, §§ 2–3. For a (not very helpful) definition of "judicial notice," see City of Aztec v. Gurule, 228 P.3d 477, 480 (N.M. 2010).

[52] So-called "uniform acts" are proposed for country-wide adoption by The National Conference of Commissioners on Uniform State Laws [http://www.uniformlaws.org/], but are adopted as individual statutes, with or without changes, by participating states. Interpretation and application of a uniform act by the various individual state supreme courts may therefore diverge. *See* Hay, *supra* note 1 at 9 (no. 18).

[53] *Supra* note 48.

[54] An insufficient statement of the applicable law could be a ground for dismissal. *See, e.g.*, Int'l Film Distribution Establishment v. Paramount Pictures Corp., 155 N.Y.S.2d 767 (N.Y. Sup.Ct. 1956).

pleading and time-consuming motion practice."[55] In place of formal pleading (including details concerning the foreign law sought to be applied), the new uniform act required that a "party who intends to raise an issue concerning the law of any jurisdiction ... outside this state shall give notice in his pleadings *or other reasonable written notice*" (§ 4.01, emphasis added). The objective was to "avoid unfair surprise" to the opponent, while recognizing that "to force a party to set forth the substance of the foreign law at the pleading stage may be an onerous burden [since development of] the operative facts [might still be at an] embryonic stage. ... [Thus] any reasonable written notice will suffice.".[56]

Some state laws seem to go even further. For example, Connecticut law provides that even "reports of the judicial decisions of other states and countries may be judicially noticed ... as evidence of the common law of such states or countries and of the judicial construction of the statutes and other laws thereof."[57] But a look at Connecticut's case law shows that the provision has been applied only in sister-state (not foreign-country) cases and, moreover, that a court need not accord judicial notice "unless authoritative sources ... are made available to the court."[58] New York similarly provides for judicial notice of foreign law, but conditions this on a party's request to that effect and on the party "furnish[ing] the court with sufficient information to comply with the request" as well as on the party's giving notice to its adversary "of its intention to request" judicial notice.[59] And in Texas, a party who intends to raise an issue of foreign country law, in addition to giving notice, must furnish copies of "any written materials or sources that the party intends to use as proof of the foreign law" to all other parties at least 30 days before trial.[60]Absent sufficient evidence,[61] the court will apply forum law.[62]

---

[55] *See* Uniform Interstate and International Procedure Act, 13 U.L.A. 459 (1980) (withdrawn in 1977), Commissioners' Comments to § 4.01, at 495–96. On pleading as the "passive approach" for the court's determination, see also Shaheeza Lalani, *Establishing the Content of Foreign Law: A Comparative Study,* 20 Maastricht Journal of European and Comparative Law 75 (2013). *But see supra* note 37 for Illinois and Iowa.

[56] Commissioners' Comment, *supra* note 55. The rule is the same in federal courts. *See, e.g.*, DP Aviation v. Smiths Indus. Aerospace & Def. Sys.Ltd., 268 F.3d 829, 846 (9th Cir. 2001).

[57] Conn. Gen. Stat, § 52–164 (2013).

[58] Reardon v. Zoning Bd. of Appeals of Darien, 2012 Conn. Super.LEXIS 523, at *16, 2012 WL 802121, at *4 (Conn. Super.Ct. 2012). *See also* Pagliaro v. Jones, 817 A.2d 756 (Conn. App. 2003); *Paramount Pictures*, *supra* note 54.

[59] N.Y. C.P.L.R. 4511(b) (Consol. 2013). *See* Butler v. Stagecoach Grp., PLC, 900 N.Y.S.2d 541, 543 (N.Y. App. Div. 2010).

[60] Tex. R. Evid. 203. *See also supra* note 37.

[61] *See, e.g.*,PennWell Corp. v. Ken Assocs., 123 S.W.3d 756 (Tex. App. 2003), *reh'g denied*, 2004 Tex. LEXIS 836 (Tex. Sept. 10, 2004) (notice was proper, but evidence was sufficient for only one of two issues of foreign law; even though the court could have conducted its own research, it applied Texas law to the foreign law issue for lack of sufficient evidence from the propounding party). *See also* San Pedro Impulsora De Inmuebles Especiales, S.A. de C.V. v. Villarreal, 330 S.W.3d 27, 35 (Tex. Ct. App. 2010).

[62] The Appendix provides information about state law on a state-by-state basis.

B. Federal Law

Federal courts exercising diversity jurisdiction[63] apply state substantive law, which includes state conflicts law.[64] However, just as in conflicts law generally, courts apply their own procedure. Thus, each state will have its own – though often quite similar – rules of procedure for raising and determining issues of foreign law. So do federal courts, in the form of the (nationally uniform) Federal Rules of Civil Procedure, which may differ from the state law rules of the state in which the federal court sits. Earlier, mention was made of attempts in some states to limit or preclude recourse to foreign law by their courts.[65] If successful, such legislation would indirectly bind federal courts, in the sense that it would affect or change state conflicts law itself, which contrary to procedural rules, the federal court must apply.

Federal Rule 44.1, promulgated in 1966 and amended since then, applies to the raising and determining of foreign law in federal practice. It provides:

> A party who intends to raise an issue about a foreign country's law must give notice by a pleading or other writing. In determining foreign law, the court may consider any relevant material or source, including testimony, whether or not submitted by a party or admissible under the Federal Rules of Evidence. The court's determination must be treated as a ruling on a question of law.

The language is clear and straightforward: formal pleading – as under the historic fact approach – is no longer required (only written[66] "notice" is[67]), the court is

---

[63] See *supra* notes 2–3.

[64] *Supra* note 7.

[65] *Supra* note 20. For further discussion, see *infra* note 102 *et seq.*

[66] Fed. R. Civ. P. 44.1.

[67] Decisions differ as to how late a party may still give notice. The Ninth Circuit has permitted notice to be given after entry of a summary judgment when the issue related to attorneys' fees, but not when the issue concerned prejudgment interest. *Compare* APL Co. Pte.Ltd. v. UK Aerosols Ltd., 582 F.3d 947, 957 (9th Cir. 2009) *with* DP Aviation v. Smiths Indus. Aerospace & Def. Sys. Ltd., 268 F.3d 829, 849 (9th Cir. 2001), both critically noted by Mark T. Cramer, *Conquering Legal Xenophobia: Tips for Presenting and Proving the Laws of Foreign Countries in Federal Courts,* 1 Bloomberg Law Reports – Litigation No. 1 (2011). A suggested rule-of-thumb may be to say that notice of intent to invoke foreign law must be raised when the issue first arises (e.g., attorneys' fees after judgment has been recovered), although opinions may differ on when the issue "first arises," could have been expected to be raised, or becomes relevant. *See* Cramer, *supra*. Alternative pleading of the choice-of-law issue satisfies the notice requirement of Fed. R Civ. P. 44.1. Rationis Enters. Inc. of Pan.v. Hyundai Mipo Dockyard Co., 426 F.3d 580 (2d Cir. 2005). For another liberal view of the notice requirement, see *In re* Griffin Trading Co., 683 F.3d 819 (7th Cir.), *reh'g denied*, 2012 U.S. App. LEXIS 17019 (2012) (numerous and known foreign contacts were enough to suggest implication of foreign law), cited with approval in SEC v. Jackson, 908 F.Supp.2d 834, 858 n.15 (S.D. Tex. 2012).

An unusual approach was taken in Priyanto v. M/S Amsterdam, 2009 U.S. Dist. LEXIS 40873 (C.D. Cal. 2009). Neither party had given notice of foreign law, but foreign law issues were raised in a motion for partial summary judgment. The court noted the presumption that when foreign law is not raised, parties are taken to have waived their right to application of any law but forum law. *Id.* at 2057. *See also supra* note 8. When a party moving for summary judgment has not sustained

free to stay within or go beyond the material submitted by the parties, without being bound by the formal Rules of Evidence, and its ruling, "treated as a ruling on a question of law," is appealable, as discussed further below. Foreign law has become "a mixture of fact and law. Indeed foreign law is a *tertium genus*, a third category, between fact and law."[68]To illustrate further: even though treated as a ruling on "law" and therefore appealable, the court's foreign-law determination is generally considered not to have precedential value.[69] Given the leeway the Rule permits, federal practice has not been uniform in how courts reach a decision on the foreign law issue.[70]

Before adoption of the Federal Rule, some federal courts followed the practice of the state courts of their state under old Federal Rule 43(a), including, when appropriate, those courts' willingness to take "judicial notice" of foreign law.[71] Others followed another state approach, exemplified by decisions like *Walton*,[72]which required proof when judicial notice was not indicated, or perhaps when presumptions

its burden, the litigation should ordinarily be resolved in favor of the non-moving party. *Ibid.* But under what law? The obvious answer, in light of the foregoing, would have been under forum law. However, the court declined to resolve the issue "until and unless the lawyers do their jobs." *Id.* at 2058. It dismissed the motion without prejudice, thereby affording the moving party (and its opponent) the opportunity to comply with Rule 44.1. *See also In re* Tyson, 433 B.R. 68, 78–79 (S.D.N.Y. 2010) (on appeal from bankruptcy court, reviewed *de novo* conclusions concerning English law, as well as submissions of the parties on appeal, when the parties had made no prior submissions nor offered information on applicable foreign law).

[68] Stephen L. Sass, *Foreign Law in Federal Courts*, 29 Am. J. Comp. L. 97, 98 (1981), as quoted by Roger M. Michalski, *Pleading and Proving Foreign Law in the Age of Plausibility Pleading,* 59 Buff. L. Rev. 1207, 1211 n.20 (2011). For an extensive bibliography, see *id.*at 1208 n.7. For earlier comment, see also Arthur R. Miller, *Federal Rule 44.1 and the "Fact" Approach to Determining Foreign Law: Death Knell for a Die-Hard Doctrine*, 65 Mich. L. Rev. 613 (1967); Zatjay, *supra* note 9, at 197–201; Wolfgang Lauterbach, *Diskussion,* 10 Materialien zum ausländischen und internationalen Privatrecht 214 (1968) (foreign law as "a procedural tertium genus," author's translation); John G. Sparkling & George R. Lanyi, *Pleading and Proof of Foreign Law in American Courts,*19 Stan. J. Int'l L. 3 (1983); John R. Brown, *44.1 Ways to Prove Foreign Law*, 9 Tul. Mar.L.J. 179 (1984).

[69] Sparkling & Lanyi, *supra* note 68, at 63. With regard to state law practice, they cite four California decisions that arrived at inconsistent conclusions as to whether Americans could inherit under German law for purposes of the requirement of reciprocity under California law. *Id.* at n.376. The decisions are reviewed and analyzed in an Oregon Supreme Court decision – *In re* Estate of Krachler, 263 P.2d 769 (Or. 1953) – which states that, apparently, California superior courts can "independently" rule with respect to these issues, *id.* at 472–73 and 780, respectively, so that the binding effect of California Supreme Court decisions (in the cases cited) perhaps was not in issue.

[70] *Supra* at Section II. *See also* Committee on International Commercial Dispute Resolution, *Proof of Foreign Law after Four Decades with Rule 44.1 FRCP and CPLR 4511,* 61 The Record of the Association of the Bar of the City of N.Y. 49 (2006); Cramer, *supra* note 67; Charles R. Richey & Jerry E. Smith, *Federal Rules of Civil Procedure, Rule 44.1, Determining Foreign Law, in* 9 Moore's Federal Practice, § 44.1 (Matthew Bender 3d ed. 2013).

[71] *See In re* Petrol Shipping Corp., 37 F.R.D. 437 (1965), *aff'd*, 360 F.2d 103, *cert. denied*, 385 U.S. 931 (1966); *Hornbook, supra*note 9, at 119–21. For the narrow definition of "judicial notice" in this context, see *supra* note 51.

[72] Walton v. Arabian Am. Oil Co., 233 F.2d 541 (2d Cir.), *cert. denied*, 352 U.S. 872 (1956).

could help. However, this led to failure of the proponent's case when proof or presumption failed, basically mirroring the common-law approach. Federal Rule 44.1 introduced an independent procedure, even though it mirrors (in material respects) the parallel procedures introduced on the state level by the two Uniform Acts discussed above. The important difference is that in the interpretation and application of Rule 44.1, federal courts orient themselves by reference to federal practice – not state practice.

The parties, having indicated their intention to invoke foreign law (the question of whether foreign law may be relevant at all),[73] will offer material as to its content, most usually by way of expert testimony, which, "accompanied by extracts from foreign legal materials[,] has been and will likely continue to be the basic mode of proving foreign law."[74] But there are also countervailing considerations and dissenting voices.

The Seventh Circuit has shown great reluctance to use, let alone rely upon, expert opinions. In 2010, Judge Richard A. Posner wrote in *Sunstar* (and repeated these sentiments the same year in his concurrence in *Bodum*[75]) that, "relying on paid witnesses to spoon feed judges is justifiable only when the foreign law is the law of a country with such an obscure or poorly developed legal system that there are no secondary materials to which the judge could turn."[76] A less categorical, more "holistic" approach that has the court consider all sources, rather than to "reject expert testimony too readily," seems indeed preferable,[77] and is more in step with the non-hierarchical structure of Rule 44.1.[78]

Moreover, courts that do consider expert testimony do not accept and follow it blindly. Increasingly, courts find that experts are not qualified or their testimony is unhelpful or irrelevant. Even though "expert opinion has been and will likely

[73] *See supra* Section II.

[74] Jinro Am. Inc. v. Secure Invs., Inc., 266 F.3d 993, 1000 (9th Cir. 2001); Charles Alan Wright & Arthur R. Miller, Federal Practice & Procedure § 2446 (3d ed. 2011). For an earlier statement, see Milton Pollack, *Proof of Foreign Law,* 26 Am. J. Comp. L. 470, 471 (1978).

[75] Bodum USA, Inc. v. La Cafetiere, Inc., 621F.3d 624 (7th Cir. 2010).

[76] Sunstar, Inc. v. Alberto Culver Co., 586 F.3d 487, 496 (7th Cir.), *cert. denied,* 130 S.Ct. 3287 (2010).

[77] Stacey, *supra* note 41, at 501. Circuit Judge Wood expressed the same view in her separate concurring opinion in *Bodum*, 621 F.3d at 639.

[78] *Bodum, id.* (Wood, J. concurring). Stacey, *supra* note 41, at 500 n.168, also points to Federal Rule of Civil Procedure 1 in support of his criticism. That Rule mandates construction and administration of the Federal Rules in a manner designed to achieve their underlying purpose, namely, to bring about a "just, speedy, and inexpensive determination of disputes." "[R]elying nearly exclusively on written sources … [may not] lead to accurate and consistent decisions in foreign law cases." Stacey at 501. It may be too easy to say "it is not necessary for courts to master foreign law. In this area of global commerce, it is not incredibly difficult for federal courts to apply foreign law. In fact, it is much easier now than ever before given the fact of expert witnesses as well as burgeoning print and electronic materials." Wilson, *supra* note 44, at 894. The availability of (party-designated) expert witnesses does not solve all problems and the availability of print and electronic materials does not automatically make them understandable from an American perspective. *See supra* note 41. With respect to the possible use of special masters, see *infra* note 85.

continue to be the basic mode of proving foreign law," the 9th Circuit held in the *Jinro* case that the trial court did not commit error in not using the Korean expert's opinion in framing instructions to the jury.[79] The decision has been followed by a court in the Sixth Circuit.[80]

The last two decisions mentioned involve the extent and the manner in which the trial court's determination is reviewable on appeal. On the one hand, Rule 44.1 confers discretion on the court as to what it may consider, thus seemingly excluding a duty to undertake independent research.[81] On the other hand, the trial court's determination is treated as one on a "question of law." The latter means that a party's objection to the applicability or content of foreign law does not raise an issue of "material fact," precluding summary judgment,[82] and by like token, that the trial court's determination is reviewable on appeal. The review is *de novo*, so that the appellate court may now consider the same, additional, or other sources to arrive at its own determination. However, the cases do not yield easy answers to the question of what constitutes reversible error on the part of the trial court. In the *Jinro* case, mentioned above, the appellate court acknowledged that the trial court had considerable leeway, thereby softening an earlier stand in which it had considered rejection of unrebutted expert testimony to be reversible error in the absence of independent research by the court.[83] In yet a third case, the appellate court acknowledged that unrebutted expert conclusions may be rejected on the basis of the court's own research. In the last case, the appellate court asserted to have undertaken, but did not elaborate upon, its own independent review on appeal.[84]An example of an extraordinarily detailed review and evaluation of foreign law is the federal appellate court's decision in *Saldana Iracheta v. Holder*, in which the court had to determine the petitioner's U.S. citizenship, a question which in turn depended on whether he had the same filial rights with respect to his American father under Mexican law as does a legitimated child.[85]

---

[79] Jinro Am., Inc. v. Secure Invs., Inc., 266 F.3d 993, 1001–09 (9th Cir. 2001). This decision was followed in United States v. Boyajian, 2013 U.S. Dist. LEXIS 116492, at *44, 2013 WL 4189649, at *15 (C.D. Cal. 2013) (expert unqualified to comment on Vietnamese culture).

[80] Yeazel v. Baxter Healthcare Corp., 2011 U.S. Dist. LEXIS 36299, at *26 (N.D. Ohio 2011) (expert unqualified to give opinion on Chinese law).

[81] *See supra* note 43.

[82] *See, e.g.*, Banco de Credito Industrial, S.A. v. Tesoreria General de la Seguridad Social de España, 990 F.2d 827, 838 (5th Cir. 1993), *cert. denied*, 510 U.S. 1071 (1994); Inmobilaria Axial, S.A. de C.V. v. Robles Int'l Servs., Inc., 2010 U.S. Dist. LEXIS 74042, at *10–11, 2010 WL 2900991, at * 3–4 (W.D. Tex. July 21, 2010).

[83] Universe Sales Co., Ltd. v. Silver Castle, Ltd., 182 F.3d 1036, 1038 (9th Cir. 1999).

[84] Pazcoguin v. Radcliffe, 292 F.3d 1209, 1216 (9th Cir. 2001) ("Here, we have reviewed the Philippine statute at issue and have conducted our own research into Philippine law. Having considered these sources, we are satisfied that …"). For the main proposition (i.e., rejection of unrebutted expert conclusions on the basis of the court's independent research), see Access Telecom, Inc. v. MCI Telecomms. Corp., 197 F.3d 694, 713 (5th Cir.), *cert. denied*, 531 U.S. 917 (2000).

[85] 730 F.3d 419 (5th Cir. 2013). The case involved an appeal from an adverse decision of the Department of Homeland Security (DHS), i.e. not a matter to which Rule 44.1 technically applies, and the court did not refer to the Rule. However, as in *Paszcoguin*, *supra* note 84 (whether the use

One way to avoid party-biased expert testimony, and at the same time aid judges who lack the necessary background or expertise themselves, is the use of court-appointed experts[86] and "special masters," with the latter reviewing the case throughout the pretrial stage and submitting an analysis and recommendation to the court.[87] However, the use of court-appointed experts or special masters for the determination of issues of foreign law remains low, indeed rather exceptional. They are used in the main in complex litigation cases, such as multistate torts.[88]

---

of marihuana constituted a criminal offense under foreign law), the court undertook the same *de novo* review of the question of foreign law as under the Rule, noting (as a single distinguishing feature) that it owed no (or less) deference to the administrative agency (the DNS) than it would to a lower court, citing to its own decision in Bustamenta-Barrera v. Gonzales, 447 F.3d 388, 393 (5th Cir. 2006). The court undertook a detailed analysis of the civil code of Tamaulipas, Mexico, considered Library of Congress reports on legitimacy law of Tamaulipas and of Mexican paternity law in general, and assigned controlling importance to the effect under Mexican law – for instance, for purposes of inheritance – of acknowledgment and registration of a child's birth in the official local register in Mexico. The "filial rights" under Mexican law were decisive. "[I]t is the substance that matters, not the legal label. ... [T]here is no legal or logical basis for a holding that a mere textual distinction between 'acknowledgment' and 'legitimation' in the foreign law should be controlling, when the rights granted to the children are the same. ... No immigration purpose is advanced through such a distinction." *Saldana Iracheta*, 730 F.3d at 426.

[86] *See* Sparkling & Lanyi, *supra* note 68, at 55–57. Federal Rule of Evidence 706 provides the authority for such appointments. *But see* Douglas H. Ginsburg, *Appellate Courts and Independent Experts*, 60 Case W. Res. L. Rev. 303, 314 (2010) (considering appointment of independent experts by the court to be "antithetical to the adversary process of our common law legal system").

[87] *See* Sparkling & Lanyi, *supra* note 68, at 73–75. A classic example is Corporacion Salvaderena de Calzado, S.A. v. Injection Footwear Corp., 533 F.Supp. 290 (S.D.Fla. 1982), noting, however, that the appointment of special masters is an exceptional practice. *Id.* at 293. In this case, the court followed the special master's recommendation, that a judgment of El Salvador be denied recognition because of lack of reciprocity on the part of that country. The authority for the appointment of special masters is Federal Rule of Civil Procedure 53, which the U.S. Supreme Court defined in the leading decision of La Buy v. Howes Leather Co., 352 U.S. 249, *reh'g denied*, 352 U.S. 1019 (1957), emphasizing that the master is not to replace the court. 352 U.S. at 256. Rule 53 was revised and liberalized in 2003, no longer requiring exceptional circumstances to justify the appointment of a special master to perform any function if the parties consent. See Shira A. Scheindlin & Jonathan M. Redgrave, *Special Masters and E-Discovery: The Intersection of Two Recent Revisions to the Federal Rules of Civil Procedure*, 30 Cardozo L. Rev. 347 (2008). For historical discussion, see Linda J. Silberman, *Masters and Magistrates, Parts I and II*, 50 N.Y.U. L. Rev. 1071 and 1297, respectively (1975). For discussion of the *La Buy* decision, see Silberman II at 1354. For a very early decision using a special master, see Heiberg v. Hasler, 45 F.Supp. 638 (E.D.N.Y. 1942) (French workers' compensation law), decided before the Supreme Court's decision in *La Buy*, and before the revision of Rule 53.

[88] *See, e.g.*, Margaret G. Farrell, *The Function and Legitimacy of Special Masters: Administrative Agencies for the Courts*, 2 Wid. L. Symp. J. 235 (1997). For the view of a state court, that involvement in the determination of foreign law by the court itself (and, by definition, of experts or masters appointed by it) is incompatible with the American adversarial system of litigation, see Bianchi v. Savino Del Bene Int'l Freight Forwarders, Inc., 770 N.E.2d 684, 698–99 (Ill.App. Ct. 2002). It is important to note, however, that Illinois still follows the fact approach. *See supra* note 22.

V. Non-use or Rejection of Foreign Law

A. Choosing Forum Law

The content of foreign law only needs to be determined after it has been found to be applicable.[89] Choice-of-law analysis may well lead a court (state or federal[90]) to conclude that forum law applies, even when foreign law has been properly put in issue. In the absence of statutory conflicts rules,[91] the court's analysis will be guided by the contemporary American approaches to choice of law. Modern American choice-of-law analysis inquires whether there exists a "true conflict" between two potentially applicable laws, in the present context, between the *lex fori* and a foreign law.[92] When, on the basis of textual or policy ("governmental interest") analysis, the court concludes that the case presents a "false conflict," it will apply forum law.[93] Further detailed analysis of the content of the foreign law thus becomes unnecessary. In cases of "true conflicts," modern approaches emphasize the law with the "most significant relationship" to the claim, the transaction's "center of gravity," or the "governmental interests" of the respective states in having their law applied. How a court weighs contacts and interests can make the applicability of foreign law uncertain; a weighing of interests may also well lead to forum law.[94]

B. Dismissing Foreign Law Cases on Forum Non Conveniens *Grounds*

If the court finds that a case may call for application of foreign law, this fact may weigh substantially in its decision to grant a motion for dismissal in favor of the foreign jurisdiction on the ground of *forum non conveniens*.[95] Thus, in *Palacios v.*

---

[89] *Supra* note 32.

[90] *Supra* notes 2–3, 7.

[91] *But see supra*note 19.

[92] *See, e.g.*, Curley v. AMR Corp., 153 F.3d 5, 12 (2d Cir. 1998); Nat'l Oil Well Maint. Co. v. Fortune Oil & Gas Co., 2005 U.S. Dist. LEXIS 8896, 2005 WL 1123735 (S.D.N.Y. 2005). *See also* Abdelhamid v. Altria Grp., Inc., 2007 U.S. Dist. LEXIS 33938, 2007 WL 1346657 (S.D.N.Y. 2007); *In re* Refco Inc. Secs. Litig., 892 F.Supp.2d 534 (S.D.N.Y. 2012) (true conflict with regard to Bermuda law; court considered parties' filings, testimony of Bermuda law experts, and reviewed Bermuda case law).

[93] *E.g.*, Darby v. Societe des Hotels Meridien, 1999 U.S. Dist. LEXIS 9744, 1999 WL 459816 (S.D.N.Y. 1999).

[94] *See, e.g.*, Eli Lilly do BrasilLTDA v. Fed. Express Corp., 502 F.3d 78 (2d Cir. 2007) (deciding an international shipping contract case under federal common law, the court determined that New York had a greater interest than Brazil in the application of its law because the latter's validation principle would better comport with party expectations).

[95] For discussion of the *forum non conveniens* doctrine, see *Hornbook*, *supra* note 9, at §§ 11.8–11.13.

Coca-Cola Co.,[96] the court stated that the probable applicability of Panamanian law weighed in favor of dismissal. As the U.S. Supreme Court has pointed out, the lower court's discretion is not affected or limited by the possibility that the plaintiff will not enjoy the same procedural or remedial advantages in the foreign court that litigation in the United States would have provided.[97] The only, but necessary, predicate for a *forum non conveniens* dismissal is the availability of another forum.[98]

C. Public Policy

"'[I]nterests' ... drive both the choice and the rejection of a law as applicable to a case ..."[99] and, one should now add, may also play a role in the *forum non conveniens* decision. When foreign law is clearly applicable, the traditional public policy (*ordre public*) defense may still present a bar to its use. Courts and commentators agree: recourse to the public policy objection should be limited to instances in which the applicable foreign law (or a foreign judgment presented for recognition) violates "fundamental notions of justice or prevailing concepts of good morals."[100] Nonetheless, "interest" considerations underlie not only the determination of the applicability of foreign law in the first place, but also the potential decision to displace it on public policy grounds. The decision in *EM Ltd. v. Republic of Argentina* may serve as an example: the court held that Argentine law, applicable under the choice-of-law clause, and permitting a self-administered trust to shield assets against creditors, even when the settlor retained substantial control, violated New York's public policy.[101] One wonders whether the court would have reached the same conclusion if the trust had been validly created under the law of an American sister-state.

[96] 757 F.Supp.2d 347 (S.D.N.Y. 2010). *See also* Langsam v. Vallarta Gardens, 2009 U.S. Dist. LEXIS 52597, 2009 WL 8631353 (S.D.NY. 2009) (Mexican law); *In re* Air Crash near Peixoto de Azeveda, Brazil, 574 F.Supp.2d 272 (S.D.N.Y. 2008) (Brazilian law); BlackRock, Inc. v. Schroders PLC, 2007 U.S.Dist. LEXIS 39279, 2007 WL 1573933 (S.D.NY. 2007) (Brazilian law). For true conflict cases in which the court undertook a foreign-law analysis, see also Pegasus Aviation IV, Inc. v. Aerolineas Austral Chile, S.A., 2012 U.S. Dist. LEXIS 39319, 2012 WL 967301 (S.D.N.Y. 2012) (Argentine law).

[97] Piper Aircraft Co. v. Reyno, 454 U.S. 235 (1981), *reh'g denied*, 455 U.S. 928 (1982).

[98] *See, e.g.*, Yao-Wen Chang v. Baxter Healthcare Corp., 599 F.3d 728, 736 (7th Cir. 2010). For discussion, see *Hornbook*, *supra* note 9, at § 11.10.

[99] Peter Hay, *supra* note 31, at 102–03. *See also* Peter Hay, *Favoring Local Interests, in* Festschrift von Hoffmann 634, 642–45 (Herbert Kronke and Karsten Thorn, eds. 2011); Peter Hay, *Reviewing Foreign Judgments in American Practice – Conclusiveness, Public Policy, and* révision au fond, *in* Festschrift für Kaissis 365 (Reinhold Geimer & Rolf A. Schütze, eds. 2012).

[100] Greek Orthodox Patriarchate of Jerusalem v. Christie's, Inc., 1999 U.S. Dist. LEXIS 13257, at *15, 1999 WL 673347, at *5 (S.D.N.Y. 1999) (quoting Curley v. AMR Corp., 153 F.3d 5, 12 (2d Cir. 1998)) (no violation found), distinguished in Bakalar v. Vavra, 619 F.3d 136, 143–45 (2d Cir. 2010). For another decision finding no violation of forum public policy, see Wultz v. Bank of China, Ltd., 811 F.Supp.2d 841, 852–853 (S.D.N.Y. 2011).

[101] 389 Fed.App'x38 (2d Cir. 2010). For an American interstate decision that mixes together interest analysis for choice of law, mandatory norms of forum law, and public policy, see Brenner v. Oppenheimer & Co., Inc., 44 P.3d 364 (Kan. 2006), discussed in Hay, *supra* note 31, at 100–02.

Jurisdiction	Can court determine foreign law *sua sponte*?	Law or fact	Based on U.L.A.	Parallels F.R.C.P.44.1	Statute(s)	Is there a blocking statute?	Recent relevant judicial decisions
Alabama	No	Law	No	Yes	Ala. R. Civ. P. 44.1	Yes	Brotherhood's Relief & Compensation Fund v. Rafferty, 91 So. 3d 693 (Ala. 2011) (sister-state law).
Alaska	Yes	Law	No	No	Alaska R. Evid. 202	No	No recent info.
Arizona	Yes	Law	No	Yes	Az. R. Civ. P. 44.1	Yes	Kadota v. Hosogai, 608 P.2d 68 (Ariz. 1980).
Arkansas	No	Law	No	Yes	Ark. R. Civ. P. 44.1	No	Greene v. State, 977 S.W.2d 192 (Ark. 1998).
California	Yes	Law[a]	No	No	Cal. Evid. Code § 450*et seq.* (West 2013)[b]	No	*In re* Marriage of Nurie, 98 Cal. Rptr.3d 200 (Cal. Ct. App. 2009).
Colorado	No recent info.	Law	Yes	Yes	Colo. R. Civ. P. 44.1	No	No recent info.
Connecticut	Yes	Law	Yes	Yes	Conn. Gen. Stat. Ann. § 52-163a (West 2013), Conn. Evid. Code § 2-2	No	Ritcher v. Childers, 478 A.2d 613 (Conn. App. Ct. 1984).
Delaware	No	Law	No	Yes	Del. R. Civ. P. 44.1 Del. R. Evid. 202(e)	No	Vichi v. Koninklijke PhilipsElecs. N.V., 62 A.3d 26 (Del. Ch. 2012); Saudi Basic Indus. Corp. v. Mobil Yanbu Petrochem. Co., Inc., 866 A.2d 1 (Del. 2005), *cert. denied*, 546 U.S. 936 (Oct. 11, 2005).

(continued)

Jurisdiction	Can court determine foreign law *sua sponte*?	Law or fact	Based on U.L.A.	Parallels F.R.C.P.44.1	Statute(s)	Is there a blocking statute?	Recent relevant judicial decisions
District of Columbia	No	Law	No	Yes	D.C. R. Civ. P. 44.1	No	Oparaugo v. Watts, 884 A.2d 63 (D.C. 2003).
Florida	Yes[c]	Law	Yes	No	Fla. Stat. Ann. § 90.202 (4)	Yes	Transportes Aereos Nacionales, S.A. v. De Brenes, 625 So.2d 4 (Fla. Dist. Ct. App. 1993); Mills v. Barker, 664 So.2d 1054 (Fla. Dist. Ct. App. 1995).
Georgia	No	Law	No	Yes	Ga. Code Ann. § 9-11-43 (West 2013)	No	Kensington Partners, LLC v. Beal Bank Nevada, 715 S.E.2d 491 (Ga. Ct. App. 2011) (sister-state law).
Guam	No recent info.	Law	No	Yes	Guam R. Civ. P. 44.1	No	No recent info.
Hawaii	No	Law	No	Yes	Haw. R. Civ. P. 44.1 Haw. R. Evid. 202	No	Roxas v. Marcos, 969 P.2d 1209 (Haw. 1998).
Idaho	No	Law	No	No	Idaho R. Civ. P. 44(d)	No	Barrett v. Barrett, 232 P.3d 799 (Idaho 2010).
Illinois	No	Hybrid[d]	Yes	No	735 Ill. Comp. Stat. Ann. 5/8-1007 (West 2013)	No	Bianchi v. Savino Del Bene Int'l Freight Forwarders, 329 Ill. App. 3d 908 (Ill. Ct. App. 2002).[e]
Indiana	No	Fact[d]	Yes	Yes	In. St. Trial P. R. 44.1 Ind. Code § 34-38-4 *et seq.*	No	Suyemasa v. Myers, 420 N.E.2d 1334 (Ind. Ct. App. 1981).
Iowa	No	Fact[d]	No	No	Iowa Code §§ 622.59, 622.61	No	Doan Thi Hoang Anh v. Nelson, 245 N.W.2d 511 (Iowa 1976).

Kansas	No	Law	No	No	Kan. Stat. Ann. § 60-5101 *et seq.* (West 2012)	Yes	No recent info.
Kentucky	No recent information.						
Louisiana	Yes	Law	No	No	La. Code. Evid. Ann. art. 202 (2012)	Yes	Ghassemi v. Ghassemi, 998 So.2d 731 (La. Ct. App. 2008).
Maine	No	Law	Yes	Yes	Me. R. Civ. P. 44A	No	*In re* Estate of Wright, 637 A.2d 106 (Me. 1994).
					Me. Rev. Stat. Ann. tit. 16, § 401 *et seq.* (2013)		
Maryland	Yes	Law	Yes	No	Md. Code Ann., Cts. & Jud. Proc. § 10-501 *et seq.* (West 2013)	No	Moustafa v. Moustafa, 888 A.2d 1230 (Md. Ct. Spec. App. 2005).
Massachusetts	Yes	Law	No	Yes	Mass. Gen Laws Ann.ch. 233, § 70 (West 2013)	No	Berman v. Alexander, 782 N.E.2d 14 (Mass. App. Ct. 2003).
					Mass. R. Civ. P. 44.1		
Michigan	Yes	Law	No	Yes	Mich. R. Evid. 202	No	*In re* Estate of Crane, 2010 WL 935651, 2010 Mich. App. LEXIS 503 (Mich. Ct. App. 2010).
					Mich. Comp. Laws Ann.§ 600.2114a (West 2013)		
Minnesota	No	Law	Yes	No	2013 Minn. Stat. Ann.§§ 599.01, 599.02, 599.08, 599.11 (West)	No	Ramsey Cnty. V. Yee Lee, 770 N.W.2d 572 (Minn. Ct. App. 2009).[f]

(continued)

Jurisdiction	Can court determine foreign law *sua sponte*?	Law or fact	Based on U.L.A.	Parallels F.R.C.P.44.1	Statute(s)	Is there a blocking statute?	Recent relevant judicial decisions
Mississippi	Yes	Law	No	No	Miss. Code Ann. § 13-1-149 (West 2013)	No	Kountouris v. Varvaris, 476 So.2d 599 (Miss. 1985); Matter of Estate of Varvaris, 528 So.2d 800 (Miss. 1988).
Missouri	No	Law	Yes	No	Mo. Ann. Stat.§ 490.120 (West 2013)	No	James v. James, 45 S.W.3d 458 (Mo. Ct. App. 2001).
Montana	Yes	Law	Yes	Yes	Mont. R. Civ. P. 44.1 Mont. R. Evid. 202(b)(8)	No	No recent info.
Nebraska	No	Law	Yes	No	Neb. Rev. Stat. § 25-12, 101 *et seq*. (2012)	No	Haltom v. Haltom, 2012 WL 1537839, 2012 Neb. App. LEXIS 102 (Neb. Ct. App. 2012).[f]
Nevada	Yes	Law	No	Yes	Nev. R. Civ. P. 44.1 Nev. Rev. Stat. Ann.§ 47.140 *et seq*. (West 2012)	No	Dahya v. Second Judicial Dist. Court ex rel. Cnty.of Washoe, 19 P.3d 239 (Nev. 2001).
New Hampshire	Yes	Law	No	No	N.H. Rev. Stat. Ann.§ 519:32 (2013) N.H. R. Evid. 201	No	Brentwood Volunteer Fireman's Ass'n v. Musso, 986 A.2d 588 (N.H. 2009).
New Jersey	Yes	Law	No	No	N.J. R. Evid. 201	No	Fitzgerald v. Fitzgerald, 168 A.2d 851 (N.J. Super. Ct. Ch. Div. 1961).
New Mexico	No	Law	No	Yes	N.M. R. Civ. P. 1-044	No	Bayer v. Bayer, 800 P.2d 216 (N.M. Ct. App. 1990).

New York	Yes	Law	No	No	N.Y. C.P.L.R. 3016, 4511 (McKinney 2013)	No	Ponnambalam v. Ponnambalam, 35 A.D.3d 571 (N.Y. App. Div. 2006); Warin v. Wildenstein & Co., Inc., 746 N.Y.S.2d 282 (N.Y. App. Div. 2002).
North Carolina	Yes	Law	No	Yes	N.C. R. Civ. P. 44.1 N.C. Gen. Stat. Ann. § 8-4 (2013)	Yes	Speedway Motorsports Int'l, Ltd. v. Bronwen Energy Trading, Ltd., 2009 NCBC 3, 2009 NCBC LEXIS 17 (N.C. Super. Ct. 2009), *aff'd*, 706 S.E.2d 262 (N.C. Ct. App. 2009), *review denied*, 720 S.E.2d 668 (N.C. 2012).
North Dakota	No	Law	No	Yes	N.D. R. Civ. P. 44.1 N.D. Cent. Code. Ann.§ 31-10-04 *et seq.* (West 2011)	No	Haggard v. First Nat'l Bank of Mandan, 8 N.W.2d 5 (N.D. 1942).
Ohio	No	Law	No	Yes	Ohio R. Civ. P. 44.1	No	EnQuip Techs. Grp. Inc. v. TyconTechnoglassS.R.l, 986 N.E.2d 469 (Ohio Ct. App. 2012); Verma v. Verma, 903 N.E.2d 343 (Ohio Ct. App. 2008).
Oklahoma	No	Law	Yes	No	12 Okla. Stat. Ann. tit. 12, § 2201 *et seq.* (West 2013)	No	Panama Processes, S.A. v. Cities Serv. Co., 796 P.2d 276 (Okla. 1990).[g]
Oregon	Yes	Law	Yes	No	Or. Rev. Stat. Ann.§ 40.060 *et seq.* (West 2013)	No	Elliott v. Oregon Int'l Mining Co., 654 P.2d 663 (Or. Ct. App. 1982).

(continued)

Jurisdiction	Can court determine foreign law *sua sponte*?	Law or fact	Based on U.L.A.	Parallels F.R.C.P.44.1	Statute(s)	Is there a blocking statute?	Recent relevant judicial decisions
Pennsylvania	No	Law	Yes	No	42 Pa. Cons. Stat. Ann.§ 5327 (West 2013)	No	Maya v. Benefit Risk Mgt., 2013 WL 663158 (Pa. Com. Pl. 2013) (Trial Order).
Puerto Rico	No	Law	No	No	P.R. Laws Ann. tit. 32, Ap. IV, Rule 11 (2010)	No	Marrero Reyes v. Garcia Ramirez, 105 D.P.R. 90 (P.R. 1976).
Rhode Island	No	Law	Yes	Yes	R.I. R. Civ. P. 44.1 R.I. Gen. Laws Ann.§ 9-19-3 *et seq.* (West 2013)	No	Harodite Indus., Inc. v. Warren Elec. Corp., 24 A.3d 514 (R.I. 2011); Barger v. Pratt & Whitney, 2006 WL 2988458, 2006 R.I. Super. LEXIS 138 (R.I. Super. Ct. 2006).
South Carolina	No	Law	Yes	Yes	S.C. R. Civ. P. 44.1 S.C. Code Ann. § 19-3-110 (2012)	No	No recent info.
South Dakota	No	Law	Yes	Yes	S.D. Codified Laws §§ 15-6-44.1, 19-8-1 *et seq.* (2012)	Yes	Varga v. Woods, 381 N.W.2d 247 (S.D. 1986).
Tennessee	No	Law	Yes	No	Tenn. Code Ann. § 20-15-101 *et seq.* (West 2013)	Yes	No recent info.
Texas	No	Law	No	No	Tex. R. Evid. 203	No	Gerdes v. Kennamer, 155 S.W.3d 541 (Tex. App. 2004).
Utah	No	Law	No	No	Utah R. Civ. P. 44	No	Lamberth v. Lamberth, 550 P.2d 200 (Utah 1976).

Vermont	No	Law	No	Yes	Vt. R. Civ. P. 44.1	No	Fishbein v. Guerra, 309 A.2d 922 (Vt. 1973) (sister-state law).
Virgin Islands	No	Law	Yes	Yes	V.I. Code Ann. tit. 5, § 4926 (2012)	No	Fabrica de Tejidos La Bellota S.A. v. M/V MAR, 799 F. Supp. 546(V.I. Dist. Ct. 1992).
Virginia	Yes	No recent info.	No	No	Va. Code Ann. § 8.01-386 (West 2013)	No	No recent info.
Washington	No	Law	Yes	Yes	Wa. R. Super. Ct. Civ. R. 9(k), 44.1	No	Mulcahy v. Farmers Ins. Co. of Washington, 95 P.3d 313 (Wash. 2004).
West Virginia	Yes	Law	No	Yes	W.V. R. Civ. P. 44.1 W.V. R. Evid. 202	No	No recent info.
Wisconsin	No	Law	Yes	No	Wis. Stat. Ann. § 902.02 (West 2013)	No	Griffin v. Mark Travel Corp., 724 N.W.2d 900 (Wis. Ct. App. 2006).
Wyoming	No	Law	Yes	Yes	Wyo. R. Civ. P. 44.1 Wyo. Stat. Ann. § 1-12-301 *et seq.* (West 2013)	No	Roberts v. Locke, 304 P.3d 116 (Wyo. 2013).[h]

[a]*See* Cal. Evid. Code § 310 (West 2013)
[b]Especially see § 452(f)
[c]*See* Fla. Stat. Ann.§ 90.204 (1)
[d]*But see supra* section III, at 8-9
[e]*See supra* notes 37, 43, 88
[f]*See supra* note 36
[g]*See supra* note 9
[h]*See supra* note 38

Canada: The Status and the Proof of Foreign Law in Québec

Gérald Goldstein

Abstract In Québec, the designation of foreign law will depend on the application of choice of laws rules by judges. However their application depends on the parties invoking them and the content of foreign law is considered as a fact that must be pleaded and proven by the parties. A judge cannot apply it ex officio. The "burden" of establishing its content belong to the parties but the judge may use her own knowledge of the applicable foreign law. The usual means of ascertaining foreign law are oral proof by expert witness and written proof by certificate of a "jurisconsult". Information on foreign law provided to Québec authorities is not binding upon them and is subjet to their evaluation in terms of probative force. However, some foreign documents, including a decision issued by a competent foreign public officer, will have a special probative force. The party pleading a foreign law has to bear the costs of ascertaining it, but Québec judges have a discretionary power to apportion them between the parties. Gaps in foreign law will be filled with Québec law as well as complete failure to establish its content and the lex fori will apply as a default solution. There is no judicial review of the application of foreign law except if there was a fundamental error of law made by the lower court. Foreign law could also be applied before administrative or other non-judicial authorities, as well as in alternative dispute resolution method. Access to foreign law is facilitated by the fact that legal information is provided through governmental websites and some Canadians judges belong to the Hague Judicial Network, even if Canada is not a party to international or regional instruments on proof and information on foreign law. Nevertheless, the Hague Conventions on the protection of children apply in Québec and facilitate access to foreign law. In order to improve the situation, it would be useful to modify the rule which imposes a prerequisite that parties invoke the application of foreign law in order to ascertain its content. However, the adoption of international instruments unifying the treatment of foreign law does not seem to be required in order to improve its the status in Québec. In order to facilitate access to foreign law, Canada should become a member to the European Convention

G. Goldstein (✉)
Professor, Faculté de Droit, Université de Montréal, Pavillon Maximilien-Caron,
3101 Chemin de la Tour Case Postale 6128, succ. Centre-ville,
Montréal, QC H3C 3J7, Canada
e-mail: gerald.goldstein@umontreal.ca

Y. Nishitani (ed.), *Treatment of Foreign Law - Dynamics towards Convergence?*,
Ius Comparatum – Global Studies in Comparative Law 26,
DOI 10.1007/978-3-319-56574-3_20

of 7 June 1968 on Information on Foreign Law and work towards the adoption of a Hague convention based on the same model.

Introduction

In Québec as elsewhere, the application of foreign law is an immediate result of the reasoning striving to respect established principles relating to the resolution of conflict of laws in relation to cross-border situations. Such principles include respecting the parties' expectations, as well as attaining justice and applying the law that has objectively the closest connection to the dispute. However, the last stage of such a process of regulating cross-border cases could be entirely disrupted if it is impossible to know how the applicable foreign law would deal with the issues concerned.

In practice, therefore, questions relating to the proof and ascertainment of the content of foreign law are highly important. The underlying chapter will tackle these questions in relation to Québec by focusing on the following points:

I. Foreign law: Result of the Application of Québec Choice of Laws Rules
II. Foreign law before the Judicial Authorities of Québec
III. Judicial Review relating to the Application of Foreign Law in Québec
IV. Foreign Law in Instances Involving Non Judicial Authorities in Québec
V. Access to Foreign Law in Québec: Status Quo
VI. Access to Foreign Law in Québec: Improvement Needed

I. Foreign Law: Result of the Application of Québec Choice of Law Rules

In Québec law as in every other legal system, the application of foreign law theoretically depends on the application of an intervening rule, usually choice of law rules, whose status in court proceedings, *i.e.*, whether they are applied *ex officio* or not, ought to be explained below (A).[1] Such choice of law rules could easily lead to a foreign law because of the bilateral nature of most of the choice of law rules in

[1] See on Quebec Private international Law and proof of foreign law: G. GOLDSTEIN et E. GROFFIER, *Traité de droit civil. Droit international privé*, vol. 1, *Théorie générale*, Y. Blais, 1998, n° 93.1–109; C. EMANUELLI, *Droit international privé québécois*, Montréal, Wilson et Lafleur, 3ème éd. 2011, n° 443–453; H.P. GLENN, "Droit international privé", dans *La réforme du Code civil*, t. 3, Presses de l'université Laval, 1993, n° 12, p. 684; J.A. TALPIS et J.-G. CASTEL, "Le Code civil du Québec: Interprétation des règles du droit international privé", dans *La réforme du Code civil*, t. 3, Presses de l'université Laval, 1993, p. 801, n° 107–128; S. SCHERRER, "La loi étrangère devant le tribual québécois", fasc. 7, in *JurisClasseur Québec*, vol. *Droit international privé*, LexisNexis, 2012.

Québec law (B). In practice, these rules mostly lead to the law of a few specific states (C).

A. The Ambiguous Nature of the Application of Choice of Law Rules in Québec

Under Québec law the status of the application of choice of law rules is ambiguous.[2] As a part of domestic law, choice of law rules have a binding force on judges or parties. Moreover, Article 2807 of the Civil Code of Québec[3] [*hereinafter* C.c.Q.] states:

> Judicial notice shall be taken of the law in force in Québec.

Hence, there is no need for the parties to prove the content of such a choice of law rule in court proceedings. However, Article 2809 C.c.Q. states:

> Judicial notice may be taken of the law of other provinces or territories of Canada and of that of a foreign state, provided it has been pleaded.

Even if the judge understands that a choice of law rule could apply to the case at hand, it is up to the parties to plead its application. 'Without the party' pleading, the judge is not allowed to apply the choice of law rule on his own will (*ex officio*), even if he knows the content of foreign law. As a result, it can occur that both parties, although they know that foreign law governs the case at hand, agree to abstain from pleading its application, with a view to mutually avoiding the costs of proving it. According to Article 2809 C.c.Q., whenever a foreign law has not been pleaded, Québec law applies as the *lex fori*.

However, insofar as the judge understands that a choice of law rule is involved in the dispute, he has discretionary power to exercise his authority and ask the parties to provide him with more information on that point.[4] It may be that one party will then try to take advantage of this alternative reasoning. Both parties could nevertheless decide not to plead any foreign law and have Québec law applied instead. Such a tacit agreement does not need to fulfil any formal requirement and could be orally decided between the lawyers of both parties.

Indeed, it would be hard to find a case where a Québec judge decided to use his power to push the parties to invoke the applicable foreign law. Moreover it might be pointless, because, if the parties do not want to spend the money to ascertain the content of foreign law, they could plead it but not provide its content. As a result, a

---

[2] See J.A. TALPIS et J.-G. CASTEL, "Le Code civil du Québec: Interprétation des règles du droit international privé", dans *La réforme du Code civil*, t. 3, Presses de l'Université Laval, 1993, p. 801, n° 108–109.

[3] *Civil Code of Québec*, LRQ, c C-1991, http://www.canlii.org/en/qc/laws/stat/lrq-c-c-1991/latest/lrq-c-c-1991.html

[4] *Miller* v. *R*., [1997] R.J.Q. 3054 (C.S.); J.A. TALPIS et J.-G. CASTEL, "Le Code civil du Québec: Interprétation des règles du droit international privé", dans *La réforme du Code civil*, t. 3, Presses de l'Université Laval, 1993, p. 801, n° 111.

Québec judge would still be applying Québec law, the one he or she knows best. Why would she bother to ask the party to plead foreign law?

So, even if Québec choice of law rules have a binding force on a judge, he or she cannot apply them *ex officio* to refer to the applicable foreign law when none of the parties would plead it.[5] This ambiguity stems from the fact that, although one could somehow say that the application of our choice of law rules is *mandatory for the judge*, since the Civil Code states so in the particular case, however, he cannot apply it in order to lead to the designation of a foreign law *ex officio*. The parties can avoid such result, which seems to mean that, *for the parties*, the application of a choice of law rule is only *dispositive* or *optional*.

Such an ambiguous solution avoids difficult questions relating to the choice of a variable, which allows a distinction between mandatory and dispositive issues (whether the application of a choice of law rule is required as to mandatory matters or matters relating to public policy). However, allowing such a distinction might also be an incentive towards forum shopping in Québec.

B. The Frequency of the Application of Foreign Law in Québec

Most choice of law rules in the Civil Code of Québec are bilateral, so that there is no preference for the *lex fori*. Therefore, the choice of law rules could frequently lead to foreign law. However, such foreign law is not necessarily pleaded by the parties, so that it does not apply. Practically speaking, the frequency of the application of foreign law depends on the parties' specific interests in each specific case. In addition, a few choice of law rules included in specific statutes beside the Civil Code of Québec are unilateral rules, which lead to the application of Québec law. However, whenever the case at hand does not fall within the categories of legal relationships subject to the *lex fori* pursuant to these exceptional rules, general bilateral choice of law rules apply. Thus, the case might very well be governed by foreign law.

Obviously, like any other jurisdictions, foreign law is applied less frequently than the *lex fori* in Québec, since choice of law cases are less frequent than domestic cases.

C. Foreign Laws That Are Frequently Applied or Invoked Before Judicial Authorities in Québec

It is inevitable result that the law of states that have socio-economic links with Québec are most frequently applied or invoked in Québec. The most intimate links are provided with Ontario or New Brunswick, two neighbouring sister provinces. One could say that those laws are somewhat mostly applied in Québec courts. However, French law and various laws of the U.S.A. (State of New York, Vermont,

[5] See for instance: *Ahsan* v. *Second cup Ltd.*, J.E. 2003–736 (C.A.).

etc.) are also often applied, due to the fact that these jurisdictions reflect the traditional flow of international relationships with Québec.

II. Foreign Law Before the Judicial Authorities of Québec

The status of foreign law in Québec is best explained by its nature under the legal system of such province (A). Its nature is reflected in the conditions leading to the application of foreign law (B), in the means of ascertaining the content of foreign law (C) and in the solution given to a problem relating to the interpretation or the application of foreign law (D). Finally, whenever the content of foreign law cannot be ascertained, the *lex fori* applies (E).

A. Nature of Foreign Law in Québec

In Québec, foreign law or the law of another province of Canada, or more precisely the *content* of such a law, is simply considered as a fact, to be proven by any means as any other facts. As a result, Québec judges are never obliged to accept the experts' interpretation of foreign law. In addition, since the content of foreign law is supposed to be a question of fact, there is no possibility to go to an appellate court to challenge the fact. Therefore, there is no equal treatment of domestic and foreign law under Québec law.

B. Application of Foreign Law in Québec

In order to apply foreign law in Québec: 1° a private international law rule must be involved, which depends on proving foreign elements of the case; 2° such choice of law rule (either a classical choice of law rule or a mandatory rule under Art. 3079 C.c.Q.) must designate a foreign law; 3° such a law must be *pleaded by the parties* and 4° its *content* must be *proven*.

So, first, foreign law will apply in Québec whenever a choice of law rule will lead to it. However, in order to use such a conflict of law rule, it must be proven that the situation involves a foreign element leading to the application of such a specific rule. Exceptionally, when contractual relationships are concerned, parties can choose foreign law even if the contract has no foreign element under Article 3111 C.c.Q.

Québec judges have neither a duty, nor the power to discover a foreign element that might require the application of foreign law on their own motion. Court proceedings have an adversarial nature under Québec law, so the parties ought to provide the judge with factual elements themselves, in order that the court can decide on them.

Even when a choice of law rule points to foreign law, it is never applied *ex officio* in Québec, but the party who wishes to invoke it has to plead it. According to Article 2809 C.c.Q.:

> Judicial notice may be taken of the law of other provinces or territories of Canada and of that of a foreign state, provided it has been pleaded. The court may also require that proof be made of such law; this may be done, among other means, by expert testimony or by the production of a certificate drawn up by a jurisconsult.

One might conclude that there is no principle that favours an effective application of foreign law in Québec. However, pursuant to Québec private international law, foreign law could be applied either by employing a bilateral choice of law rule or by referring to Article 3079 C.c.Q. (relating to mandatory rules or «laws of immediate application»), which states:

> Where legitimate and manifestly preponderant interests so require, effect may be given to a mandatory provision of the law of another country with which the situation is closely connected. In deciding whether to do so, consideration is given to the purpose of the provision and the consequences of its application.

In such a case, the overriding mandatory nature of the foreign law will be a decisive factor to apply it. However, there is not a single instance in Québec where foreign law has benefited from such a preferential treatment.

Beside general choice of law rules or to Article 3079 C.c.Q., also foreign law that has a closer connection with the case at hand than the applicable *lex fori* may exceptionally be applied, since Québec law has adopted a general escape clause (Art. 3082 C.c.Q.):

> Exceptionally, the law designated by this Book is not applicable if, in the light of all attendant circumstances, it is clear that the situation is only remotely connected with that law and is much more closely connected with the law of another country.

C. Ascertainment of Foreign Law

The ascertainment of foreign law in Québec include issues as to which party has to ascertain it (1), which means can be used (2), which conditions individuals or institutions providing legal information have to fulfil (3), whether information on foreign law has binding force upon judicial authorities of Québec (4), whether the reliability of the obtained information on foreign law can be tested (5), and who bears the costs of ascertaining foreign law (6).

1. The Burden to Ascertain the Content of Foreign Law in Québec

In Québec, the parties have to prove the content of foreign law when they plead it in principle.[6] However, the "burden" of proof, or task of establishing the content of foreign law, does not belong *exclusively* to the parties. This is because also the judge

[6] See Montana c. Développement du Saguenay, [1977] 1 R.C.S. 32.

is authorized to use his or her own knowledge of the applicable foreign law[7] under Article 2809 C.c.Q.:

> Judicial notice may be taken of the law of other provinces or territories of Canada and of that of a foreign state, provided it has been pleaded. The court may also require that proof be made of such law [...].

As a result, whenever a judge uses his or her own knowledge of the applicable foreign law, the parties do not have the burden to prove its content. However, the judge does not have any duty to do so, since it would be too time consuming.

Exceptionally, when international child abduction cases are involved, Article 28 of the *Act Respecting the Civil Aspects of International and Interprovincial Abduction*,[8] states more specifically:

> In ascertaining whether there has been a wrongful removal or retention, the Superior Court may take notice directly of the law of, and of judicial or administrative decisions, formally recognized or not in the designated State in which the child is habitually resident, without recourse to the specific procedures for the proof of that law or for the recognition of foreign decisions which would otherwise be applicable.

So judges may take judicial notice of foreign laws in such a context, although they still have no obligation to do so.

2. Means Used in Québec to Ascertain Foreign Law

Article 2809 C.c.Q. states:

> The court may also require that proof be made of such law; this may be done, among other means, by expert testimony or by the production of a certificate drawn up by a jurisconsult.

The most usual means of ascertaining foreign law are expert witness, or oral proof, and certificate of a "jurisconsult", or written proof. Such certificate does not have to respect any specific formality.[9] A proper witness or a jurisconsult might be a lawyer or anybody having some knowledge of the specific foreign law involved. However any other means could be used such as an inquiry to an expert institute. If it is clear and precise, a written admission of the content of the foreign law signed by both parties will also suffice.[10]

---

[7] See for instance: *Yassin* v. *Green Park International*, 2010 QCCA 1455, EYB 2010-177634 (C.A.).

[8] R.S.Q., chapter A-23.1, http://www.canlii.org/en/qc/laws/stat/rsq-c-a-23.01/latest/rsq-c-a-23.01.html

[9] C. EMANUELLI, *Droit international privé québécois*, Montréal, Wilson et Lafleur, 3ème éd. 2011, n° 444, p. 273.

[10] See for instance: *H.O.* v. *C.B.*, [2001] R.D.F. 692 (C.A.); G. GOLDSTEIN et E. GROFFIER, *Traité de droit civil. Droit international privé*, vol. 1, *Théorie générale*, Y. Blais, 1998, n° 103; C. EMANUELLI, *Droit international privé québécois*, Montréal, Wilson et Lafleur, 3ème éd. 2011, n° 444, p. 275.

Québec judges do not usually maintain direct communication with foreign judges. However they could do so since they are allowed to use their own knowledge of foreign law. So they could ask direct questions to fellow judges they might know although there is no general formal frame for such communications.

3. Specific Qualifications for Individuals or Institutions to Provide Information on Foreign Law in Québec

In Québec, each expert must prove his or her expertise on the content of foreign law by establishing his or her credentials. Such credentials include a convincing explanation about how such expert has been in contact with the relevant foreign law and how deep such expert has had to deal with that law before. It would be ideal if the expert is either a practising lawyer in the foreign country[11] or a foreign law professor. However, an expert could also be a local researcher or professor from Québec, who has expertise in the relevant foreign law.

However, Article 2822 and 2823 C.c.Q. state:

> Article 2822. An act purporting to be issued by a competent foreign public officer makes proof of its content against all persons and neither the quality nor the signature of the officer need be proved.
>
> Article 2823. A power of attorney under a private writing made outside Québec also makes proof against all persons where it is certified by a competent public officer who has verified the identity and signature of the mandator.

As a result, for instance, a foreign judgment can serve as a proof of foreign law. The only condition would be that it originates from a *competent* foreign public officer, like a court registry officer. In such a case, the only proof required is that such an officer is deemed competent in the originating State. The relevant foreign law will determine which qualification the officer has to fulfil.

Along the same lines, whenever legal information is proven through a certificate drawn by someone working in or for a foreign Consulate which bears its official stamp, such a certificate will be sufficient to be considered as a reliable source of the content of the foreign law. Needless to say, foreign consulates normally require the expert who issues the certificate to have a specific legal background.

4. The Binding Force Upon Judicial Authorities of Québec of the Provided Legal Information

In principle, legal information on foreign law provided to Québec judicial authorities are not binding upon them. This is because foreign laws are considered as facts to be proven before the court and the probative force of an oral or written document of proof is evaluated by the judicial authorities.

[11] See for instance: *Yassin* v. *Green Park International*, 2010 QCCA 1455, EYB 2010-177634 (C.A.); *Deschênes* v. *Nurun inc.*, [2003] R.J.Q. 1824 (C.S.).

However, when dealing with international adoptions under the 1993 Hague Convention, information relating to the foreign law given by the corresponding foreign administrative authorities are binding on Québec authorities.

In addition, some foreign legal documents will have a special probative force under Québec law. Article 2822 C.c.Q. states:

> An act purporting to be issued by a competent foreign public officer makes proof of its content against all persons and neither the quality nor the signature of the officer need be proved.

As a result, any foreign document, including a decision, issued by a competent foreign public officer will be sufficient to prove its content in Québec and will be binding. Indirectly, such a rule could be helpful to prove the content of foreign statutes or case law, if the content of such a law is explained in the document.

However, such documents have only a presumptive probative force and it is possible to contest it since Article 2825 C.c.Q. states:

> Where an act or copy issued by a foreign public officer or a power of attorney certified by a foreign public officer has been contested, the person invoking it has the burden of proving that it is authentic.

As a result, it is possible to rebut this presumption and, in such a case, the content of the document will not have any binding force in Québec.

5. Mechanism to Examine the Reliability of the Provided Legal Information in Québec

Although there is no *specific* mechanism in Québec to examine the reliability of the provided information on foreign law, the judge will use all the available means to establish the probative force of the means of proving the foreign law. For instance, if an expert has been called to prove the content of a foreign law before the court, such witness might be cross-examined by the lawyer of the other party and the judge might directly ask him questions.[12] As previously stated, each expert must prove his or her expertise by establishing his or her credentials.

6. The Burden of the Costs of Ascertaining Foreign Law in Québec

The party pleading a foreign law has to bear the costs of ascertaining it in Québec. Expert fees, costs relating to translation and so on are qualified as litigation costs. Québec judges have a discretionary power to decide upon the litigation costs and to apportion them between the parties.

Québec law also has a scheme of legal aid based on the income of the party concerned, which could cover the costs of ascertaining foreign law. However, legal aid

[12] G. GOLDSTEIN et E. GROFFIER, *Traité de droit civil. Droit international privé*, vol. 1, *Théorie générale*, Y. Blais, 1998, n° 101; C. EMANUELLI, *Droit international privé québécois*, Montréal, Wilson et Lafleur, 3ème éd. 2011, n° 444, p. 272.

may be refused or withdrawn where the judgment would not be able to be executed subsequently.[13] This may be the case with international disputes, for example, when an immovable situated abroad is concerned and the foreign authority would assume an exclusive jurisdiction over the matter.

As for international child abduction cases, Article 36 of the Québec law that implements the 1980 Hague Convention[14] provides that no document pertinent to the application of this act needs any legalization or similar formality. As a result, the costs of proving a foreign law will be lower.

D. Interpretation and Application of Foreign Law in Québec

Foreign law might need to be interpreted in order for the judge to understand how it would influence the result of the case (1) or it might require a gap-filling (2).

1. Interpretation and Application of Foreign Law in Québec

As a starting point, Québec authorities do not deliver an interpretation of foreign law. When the content of foreign law is not clear enough, they will apply Québec law according to Article 2809 C.c.Q., considering that its content has not been established.

However, when very minor points of interpretation are involved, Québec authorities use the interpretation rules of the foreign law, as duly proven, or, if not, they simply apply Québec principles of interpretation.

2. Filling a Gap in Foreign Law in Québec

Gaps in foreign law could be filled with Québec law under Article 2809 C.c.Q., which states:

> Where such [foreign] law has not been pleaded or its content has not been established, the court applies the law in force in Québec.

If the gaps are too broad, Québec authorities will not apply the designated foreign law at all, since its content is not established. They will not try to fill those gaps with another foreign law which might be more closely related with the case than the *lex fori*, since such other foreign law has not been designated by the appropriate choice of law rule.

---

[13] See, s. 4.11, *An Act respecting Legal Aid and the provision of certain other legal services*, R.S.Q. chapter A-14, http://www.canlii.org/en/qc/laws/stat/rsq-c-a-14/latest/rsq-c-a-14.html

[14] *An Act Respecting the Civil Aspects of International and Interprovincial Abduction*, R.S.Q., chapter A-23.1, http://www.canlii.org/en/qc/laws/stat/rsq-c-a-23.01/latest/rsq-c-a-23.01.html

E. Failure to Establish Foreign Law in Québec

Whenever a party invoking the application of a foreign law fails to bring a convincing proof of the content of foreign law, the *lex fori* applies[15] in Québec courts according to Article 2809 C.c.Q., which states:

> Where such [foreign] law has not been pleaded or its content has not been established, the court applies the law in force in Québec.

The policy consideration behind such a solution has evolved. Before the reform of the Civil Code of Québec, foreign law was supposed to be the same as Québec law, so long as it is not proven. There was a "presumption of similarity" between the foreign law and the *lex fori*.

However such an absurd assumption has duly been criticized, so the new Civil Code did not adopt it. Nowadays, the reference to the *lex fori* is mainly justified by the fact that judges have a duty to render a decision in a due timeframe, so they cannot stop on the ground that they do not know the content of foreign law once they are seized with a dispute. Thus, judges are allowed to apply the law which they know the best, *i.e.*, the *lex fori*. The *lex fori* applies as a second-best solution in order to avoid a denial of justice. Judges in Québec will not look for the content of another foreign law that would be more closely related with the designated foreign law.

III. Judicial Review

Judicial review questions could be raised as to the meaning of the choice of law rule leading to the foreign law (A), or to the content of the foreign law itself (B).

A. Judicial Review Relating to the Meaning of Choice of Law Rules in Québec

A judge of a lower Québec court may have erroneously applied a choice of law rule, for instance, by misunderstanding the notion of domicile or habitual residence as a connecting factor of the relevant choice of law rule.[16] In such a case, an appeal to the higher courts is permissible up to the Supreme Court of Canada, since it would be an error in law and the upper courts ought to correct such errors. The prerequisite

[15] See for instance: *Issenman* v. *Nacos*, 2008 QCCS 4319, EYB 2008-147676 (C.S.); *Juljulian* v. *Juljulian*, 2007 QCCS 4588, EYB 2007-125371 (C.S.).

[16] See *Rees* v. *Convergia*, 2005 QCCA 353, J.E. 2005-738 (the lower court had taken into account the intention of a person in order to decide where he was habitually resident; however our Court of Appeal decided that such intention should not be taken into account since, in general, such factor should only be based on material facts).

would be the normal procedural conditions of an appeal, relating to, *inter alia,* the capacity of the party, time limit (within 30 days from the lower court judgment in principle, Art. 360 of the New Québec Code of Civil Procedure [*hereinafter* C.P.C.]), notices and service of proceedings. However, each level of courts has a procedure to refuse such appeals for various reasons (for instance, if such appeal is dilatory.).

The background policy consideration is that conflict of law rules constitute a part of the local law. As such, they must be respected and rightly applied by the judges. A more specific idea is that judges must respect the legislator's intent to locate the legal relationship in an appropriate legal system in cross-border cases. Most of Québec conflict of rules are based on the so-called "principle of proximity", according to which judges ought to apply the law that has objectively the closest connection with the legal relationship concerned. Some others rules, framed within a multifactorial choice of law rule, have a more substantive objective, such as Article 3109 C.c.Q. which designates the law that favours the formal validity of a juristic act.[17] Québec judges must respect these underlying considerations or principles. If they fail to do so, then an appellate judge has to intervene.

B. Judicial Review Relating to the Foreign Law Applied in Québec

When foreign law has erroneously been applied, in principle, since the lower courts have to deal with the facts, and since the content of foreign law is considered as a fact in Québec, appeal courts should not accept any appeal on such motive, unless the Court of Appeal is seized of a new fact that was not available in the lower court.[18] However, if a judge from a lower court unduly fails to apply a foreign rule whose content has been clearly proven, one could plead that there was a *fundamental error of law,* justifying an appeal to the higher court. Yet, such an appeal is seldom made in practice.[19]

The background policy consideration is that lower courts have to respect the objectives embedded in our choice of law rules. If they don't, the appellate courts must intervene. For instance, if a lower court erroneously decides that Québec law applies to a situation having no objective connection with Québec or disregarding the connecting factor included in the relevant choice of law rule, the superior judge must

[17] Art. 3109 C.c.Q. states: "The form of a juridical act is governed by the law of the place where it is made. A juridical act is nevertheless valid if it is made in the form prescribed by the law applicable to the content of the act, by the law of the place where the property which is the object of the act is situated when it is made or by the law of the domicile of one of the parties when the act is made. A testamentary disposition may be made in the form prescribed by the law of the domicile or nationality of the testator either at the time of the disposition or at the time of his death", http://www.canlii.org/en/qc/laws/stat/lrq-c-c-1991/latest/lrq-c-c-1991.html

[18] See C. EMANUELLI, *Droit international privé québécois*, Montréal, Wilson et Lafleur, 3ème éd. 2011, n° 44, p. 272.

[19] See also: *Yassin* v. *Green Park International*, 2010 QCCA 1455, EYB 2010-177634 (C.A.).

correct the judgment, since it would run counter to the notion of fair trial or amount to an injustice to the parties involved not to apply the appropriate foreign law.

IV. Foreign Law in Other Instances in Québec

In Québec, foreign law could also be applied before administrative or other non-judicial authorities (A), as well as in arbitration, mediation or any alternative dispute resolution method (B). Foreign law may also need to be ascertained in the advisory work of attorneys, advocates and other practitioners (C).

A. Application and Ascertainment of Foreign Law by Administrative or Other Non-judicial Authorities in Québec

1. Administrative Authorities of Québec

Whenever administrative authorities apply the law of a foreign state or another Canadian province, a specific cooperation scheme will be used, as in the case of the extra-provincial maintenance orders or the cooperation under the 1993 Hague Adoption Convention. This scheme is used relatively frequently, because these instruments duly respond to practical needs.

2. Québec Notaries

As far as Québec *notaries* are concerned, they are qualified as public authorities, while enjoying a comparable status as judges. However they bear more responsibility than judges in ascertaining the content of foreign law, since, as private legal advisors, they have to give advice to the parties and inform them of the legal situations. They are supposed to apply choice of law rules whenever the situation includes a sufficient foreign element. In addition, they have a duty toward the parties to ascertain the content of the applicable law. If they fail to do so, parties could sue them for civil liability for not adequately fulfilling their duties as notaries. The notaries incur civil liability on the ground of their fault or negligence. Such obligation to ascertain the content of the foreign applicable law is only considered as an *obligation de moyen* and not an *obligation de resultat*, although they have an *absolute* obligation to understand and inform the parties that a foreign element potentially implies a situation that prompts the application of choice of law. In order to ascertain the content of foreign law, notaries use the same means as courts would do.

3. Public Registry Officers in Québec

Although they are considered as public authorities, *public registry officers* in Québec have no duty to consult or establish the content of foreign law. For instance, when public registry officers are confronted with the registration of a marriage celebrated abroad or any other foreign document issued outside Québec, such as a birth certificate or death certificate, they enter the act in the registry as if it were an act done in Québec,[20] unless they have doubt about the authenticity or validity of the document.[21] Once the public officer refuses to enter the act in the registry, the claiming party ought to obtain a judicial declaration that the act is valid and eligible to be registered.

When the public officer ought to celebrate a marriage in Québec, the officer asks the future spouses to indicate where they are domiciled as a matter of simple formality without giving any consequence to this information. When they are domiciled abroad, the officer will still celebrate the marriage or civil union according to Québec and Canadian law, which accepts same-sex marriages and same-sex civil unions, without taking into account the foreign laws of those persons which might forbid such unions. As a result, those unions could be considered null abroad where the choice of law rules still submit marriage to the law of the spouses' domicile. However, under a Federal bill,[22] the validity of such unions performed in Canada will be recognized without having regard to the law of the foreign domicile of the spouses.

B. Application and Ascertainment of Foreign Law in Arbitration, Mediation or Other Alternative Dispute Resolution Schemes in Québec

The question of applying foreign law is raised in international arbitration involving commercial interests of business people. Due to the confidentiality principle, there is little way of knowing whether and how far the arbitrators decide to apply foreign law, even when the venue of arbitration is Québec. These arbitrators are not bound to the Québec judicial system, so they have no duty to apply Québec choice of law rules. However, pursuant to an arbitration clause that is valid in the eyes of arbitrators, the parties may have chosen Québec law when the arbitration proceedings take place in Québec. Such a choice is also valid under Québec law, since Article 3133 C.c.Q. states:

> Arbitration proceedings are governed by the law of the country where arbitration takes place unless either the law of another country or an institutional or special arbitration procedure has been designated by the parties.

---

[20] See s. 137 C.c.Q., http://www.canlii.org/en/qc/laws/stat/lrq-c-c-1991/latest/lrq-c-c-1991.html; http://canlii.ca/t/51v0v

[21] See s. 138 C.c.Q., http://www.canlii.org/en/qc/laws/stat/lrq-c-c-1991/latest/lrq-c-c-1991.html; http://canlii.ca/t/51v0v

[22] Bill C-32, *Civil Marriage of Non-residents Act*, First Session, 41 st Parliament, 60–61 Eliz. II, 2011–2012.

Alternatively, under this rule, if no choice has been made, an arbitrator seized of a dispute in Québec might decide that Québec substantive law will apply, especially if the arbitrator wants to have his arbitral award duly registered in Québec. In either of those circumstances, the arbitrator will have to respect Article 620 C.P. C., which states:

> Arbitration is the submission of a dispute to an arbitrator for a decision in accordance with the rules of law and, if appropriate, for a determination of damages. The arbitrator may act as amiable compositeur if the parties have so agreed. In all instances, the arbitrator decides the dispute in accordance with the stipulations of the contract between the parties and takes into account any applicable usages.

Consequently, foreign law is applied to the dispute either because parties haven chosen foreign law, or because the arbitrator decides in the absence of a choice of law that foreign law governs the dispute. In the latter case, Québec law relating to arbitration does *not* require them to use *any* system of conflict of laws rules, since they simply will apply "the rules of law which they consider appropriate". In other words, Québec law provides for the so-called "*voie directe*" methods to determine the applicable law. The arbitrators might simply decide that the law of state A should apply in accordance with the parties' alleged expectations. However, there is no qualified information available on this point.

Dealing with the question relating to the ascertainment of foreign law, Article 632 C.P.C., states that arbitrators "have all the necessary powers to exercise their jurisdiction, including [...] the power to appoint an expert".

C. Ascertainment of Foreign Law in Advisory Work by Attorneys, Notaries and Others in Québec

Notaries or lawyers usually ascertain the content of foreign law by a written document issued by an expert or foreign notary. One should mention that Article 2822 C.c.Q. states:

> An act purporting to be issued by a competent foreign public officer makes proof of its content against all persons and neither the quality nor the signature of the officer need be proved.

As a result, a notarized document that indicates the content of foreign law will have a strong probative force in Québec. Such a force will be sufficient for the practitioner to incur professional liability. Opinions written by foreign lawyers or professors are also often used by attorneys or notaries in contentious or non-contentious matters. They may also consult data banks through Internet, but they tend to prefer oral or written advice from a specialist, usually a conflict of law professor or a lawyer working at the foreign Consulate. Such practices are common in international or interprovincial cases.

Finally, the ascertainment of foreign law could also be required for research purposes at the provincial or federal level of government, in order to improve the quality of Canadian law through a comparative analysis.

V. Access to Foreign Law in Québec: Status Quo

Access to foreign law in Québec is facilitated by the fact that legal information is provided through governmental websites (A) and some Canadians judges belong to the Hague Judicial Network (B), even if Canada is not a party to international or regional instruments on proof and information on foreign law (C). Nevertheless, the main Hague Conventions on the protection of children apply in Québec and facilitate access to foreign law (D).

A. *Legal Information Provided Through Official Website in Québec*

All the federal laws and regulations of Canada are available free of charge at the official website.[23] The provincial laws and regulations of Québec are also available at the official site of the *Gazette officielle du Québec*.[24] Canadian judgments can be retrieved on the official websites.[25] Furthermore, there are some unofficial websites that provide information on statutes, regulations and judgments.[26]

B. *The Hague Judicial Network in Quebec*

Some Canadian judges including in Québec are members of the international network of judges created for the implementation of the 1980 Hague Child Abduction Convention.[27] Thus, judges in Québec are able to inquire foreign judges via network judges. Since Québec judges are allowed to use their own knowledge of foreign law

[23] http://laws-lois.justice.gc.ca/eng/acts/

[24] http://www3.publicationsduQuebec.gouv.qc.ca/gazetteofficielle.fr.html

[25] For instance, the following websites can be consulted: Judgments of the Supreme Court of Canada are available at http://scc.lexum.org/decisia-scc-csc/scc-csc/scc-csc/en/2013/nav_date.do; judgments of the Federal Court of Appeal are available at http://decisions.fca-caf.gc.ca/en/index.html; Judgments of the Québec Court of Appeal since 1987 are available at www.jugements.qc.ca (for its judgments since 1963 upon subscription: www.azimut.soquij.qc.ca); judgments of the Superior Court since 2000 are available at www.jugements.qc.ca (for its judgments since 1963 upon subscription: www.azimut.soquij.qc.ca).

[26] Visit, for example, at http://www.canlii.org/en/qc/index.html>. This website of the Canadian Legal Information Institute provides a link to foreign Legal Information Institute and other foreign legal sites such as <Droit.org>, Global Legal Information Network, etc.

[27] http://www.hcch.net/index_en.php?act=text.display&tid=21 See *The Judges' Newsletter on International Child protection*, 2009, vol. XV, special focus, theme 2, by P. Lortie (http://www.hcch.net/index_en.php?act=text.display&tid=60).

in the court proceedings, it makes sense for them to participate in this international network. Except for some other limited frameworks relating to interprovincial disputes as in the case of maintenance orders, Québec judges do not take part in any comparable scheme to directly communicate with foreign judges, but can only informally contact foreign authorities.

One should also note that the Canadian bankruptcy law[28] (which is federal law and not provincial law) creates an obligation to cooperate with foreign authorities. Article 275 of the *Bankruptcy Act* states:

(1) If an order recognizing a foreign proceeding is made, the court shall cooperate, to the maximum extent possible, with the foreign representative and the foreign court involved in the foreign proceeding.
(2) If any proceedings under this Act have been commenced in respect of a debtor and an order recognizing a foreign proceeding is made in respect of the debtor, every person who exercises any powers or performs duties and functions in any proceedings under this Act shall cooperate, to the maximum extent possible, with the foreign representative and the foreign court involved in the foreign proceeding.
(3) For the purpose of this section, cooperation may be provided by any appropriate means, including (*a*) the appointment of a person to act at the direction of the court; (*b*) the communication of information by any means considered appropriate by the court; (*c*) the coordination of the administration and supervision of the debtor's assets and affairs; (*d*) the approval or implementation by courts of agreements concerning the coordination of proceedings; and (*e*) the coordination of concurrent proceedings regarding the same debtor.

As a result, since this cooperation could take the form of "the communication of information by any means considered appropriate by the court", Article 275 allows direct communication of legal information with a foreign judge in bankruptcy proceedings.

C. International or Regional Instruments on Proof of and/or Information on Foreign Law

There is no multilateral of bilateral treaty involving Canada or Québec concerning the proof of and exchange of information on foreign law. Canada is not a party to any of the following international instruments: the European Convention of 7 June 1968 on Information on Foreign Law, Inter-American Convention of 8 May 1979 on Proof of and Information on Foreign Law or Convention of 22 January 1993 on Legal Assistance and Legal Relations in Civil, Family and Criminal Matters.

[28] *Bankruptcy and Insolvency Act*, R.S.C., 1985, c. B-3, http://www.canlii.org/en/ca/laws/stat/rsc-1985-c-b-3/latest/rsc-1985-c-b-3.html

D. Access to Foreign Law in Québec Through the Hague Convention Mechanisms

1. International Adoption

Québec has implemented the rules relating to the administrative collaboration organized by the 1993 Hague Adoption Convention.[29] As a result, the Québec Minister of Health and Social Services has to fulfill the duties of the Central Authority for Québec for the purpose of the Convention. The duties include the exchange of information as to the laws of Québec concerning adoption according to Article 7(2) (a) of the Hague Adoption Convention and the exchange of reports and certificates ascertaining that the rules of the Convention and the laws of the respective competent authorities, notably, relating to consent, have been complied with. In addition, Québec, as every State, has an obligation to provide documents to the depository of the Convention relating to its laws, notably concerning the functions of its administrative authorities.

2. International Child Abduction

Québec law has also implemented the 1980 Hague Child Abduction Convention.[30] According to Article 7 of the *Act Respecting the Civil Aspects of International and Interprovincial Abduction*, the Minister of justice of Québec ought to take any appropriate measures to exchange information relating to the social background of the child and, more specifically, "to provide information of a general character as to the law of Québec in connection with the application of this Act".

The legislation relating to cooperation in respect to international adoption and international child abduction are rather frequently used, since people in Québec often refer to international adoption. Moreover, international child abduction cases happen frequently. Each year, the average court decisions relating to international child abduction in Québec amount to 8–10, while the average court decisions relating to international adoption amount to 5. However, most cases are duly processed through administrative means without having recourse to the courts. According to the statistics, between 1990 and 2012, 686 international adoption cases have been processed each year in Québec (for a total of 15,779). Around a third of these are related to the adoption of Chinese children. However, they tend to diminish since 2006 because the new Québec rules respecting the 1993 Convention are stricter than the previous ones. There are presently no public data on the actual consequences of these instruments on the facilitation of access to foreign law.

---

[29] See *An Act to implement the Convention on Protection of Children and Co-operation in Respect of Intercountry Adoption*, RSQ, c M-35.1.3 (enforced since Feb. 1st, 2006), http://www.canlii.org/en/qc/laws/stat/rsq-c-m-35.1.3/latest/rsq-c-m-35.1.3.html

[30] *An Act Respecting the Civil Aspects of International and Interprovincial Abduction*, R.S.Q., chapter A-23.1, http://www.canlii.org/en/qc/laws/stat/rsq-c-a-23.01/latest/rsq-c-a-23.01.html

VI. Access to Foreign Law: Improvement Needed

Possible improvements relating to the access to foreign law in Québec could concern practically any person dealing with foreign legal relationships, although weaker parties such as consumers need more help (A). Some aspects of the treatment of foreign law in Québec could be improved (B), so as to broaden the methods of facilitating access to foreign law (C).

A. Practical Needs to Access Foreign Law in Québec

Like in other jurisdictions, there is need to improve access to foreign law in Québec for all categories of persons involved in international legal matters, such as judicial and administrative authorities, attorneys, notaries, arbitrators and so on.

There has been such a need to improve access to legal information on other Canadian jurisdictions as well, and all the more so when the civil law system of Québec was concerned. Such need has been felt in security transactions dealing with movables or in alimony and guardianship matters. However such access to information within Canada is much easier nowadays since several websites will give it for free and are regularly updated.

In terms of legal areas, the only difference stems from the means of the parties who need information on foreign law. In that perspective, family law, including succession matters, would be a favored topic since the parties have less means to ascertain foreign laws. In addition, weaker parties such as consumers do need to have access to foreign contract law and tort law, since they are often confronted with choice of law clauses imposed by the business, which does not help the weaker parties to clearly understand the content of the chosen law. Even if the business gives information, a huge amount of information written in a very complex manner is often provided, only to discourage the weaker parties to understand.

It seems that different levels of information need to be provided. In general, information on securities, commercial or corporate law could be easily explored in technical legal terms, since the actors are usually well-paid law firms. However, less detailed and abstract information should also be provided for clients who have less means.

B. Improvement Needed in Québec in the Resolution of Conflict of Laws

Technically, it would be useful to modify the rule in Québec which imposes a prerequisite that parties invoke the application of foreign law in order to ascertain its content (1). However, the adoption of international or regional instruments unifying the treatment of foreign law does not seem to be required to improve the status of foreign law in Québec (2).

1. Ascertainment of the Content of Foreign Law

Québec law should be modified so as to allow a judge to ask the parties to ascertain the content of foreign law even if the parties do not plead such foreign law, when a judge knows that, according to Québec conflict of laws rules, a foreign law should be applied instead of the domestic law. The actual law allows a Québec judge to ascertain himself the content of such foreign law, as long as a party pleaded that such law be applied.

It seems that such a future rule might be too cost-consuming for non-commercial parties and especially in extra-patrimonial family matters. However, it might be socially important to fully understand the context of a foreign family relationship, when dealing with parentage, guardianship, conditions and effects of marriage, divorce, and so on. Moreover, our judges are very reasonable and know when to intervene to support a weak party. Obviously, the creation of foreign data banks would be very helpful in the context of family matters.

2. International or Regional Instruments on the Treatment of Foreign Law

It is not clear that international or regional instruments which unify the treatment of foreign law would be helpful or useful, as opposed to providing data banks. However such unification might indirectly help the creation of data banks since those banks should use uniform ways of indicating the content of foreign law with uniform methods of citations.

C. Methods of Facilitating Access to Foreign Law

Since, obviously, international or regional instruments that establish administrative and/or judicial cooperation to exchange information on Member States' law are useful tools to facilitate access to foreign law, Canada should become a member to the *European Convention of 7 June 1968 on Information on Foreign Law* ("London Convention"),[31] which seems very helpful. Maybe a Hague convention based on the same model may well improve the current situation.

Such a convention should be open to all clients (1), would request some measures of filtering through a centralized authority of the requesting state in a private context (2), and the information provided should be binding on the requesting party (3). The services provided should be free if they are of general character, but not if they relate directly to the facts of a specific case (4). Finally, it should be noted that access to Canadian law is quite easy and established networks of Canadian lawyers are very active to facilitate interprovincial legal communication (5).

---

[31] See G. GOLDSTEIN et E. GROFFIER, *Traité de droit civil. Droit international privé*, vol. 1, *Théorie générale*, Y. Blais, 1998, n° 104 et 109.

1. Access to Such Instrument

Such an international instrument should be open to individuals and other authorities, like arbitrators, notaries and so on. In principle, legal information should be accessible to the public as much as possible. It might avoid a number of disputes over facts or provoke justified ones. In principle, the basic framework proposed by the Note of the Permanent Bureau of the Hague Conference on Private international Law in its Preliminary document n. 11 A (March 2009)[32] should be followed:

1. Facilitating *free access to online legal information* on foreign law, mainly dealing with legislation and case law, open for everybody.
2. Cross-border *administrative and judicial co-operation* dealing with specific requests on concrete situations by those judicial bodies, not already available via the Internet. Those services would probably be free as well for these bodies but not offered to individuals.
3. Finally, organising and *providing a global network of institutions and experts* for even more complex or more specific requests, by administrative or judicial bodies or even available to answer questions raised by individuals, based on a fee.

2. Direct Requests or Transmissions by the Central Authority of the Requesting State

It seems that such an issue relates more directly to access to foreign law by individuals, since the administrative or judicial cooperation has to pass through the competent authority of the requesting State. In other words, the problem does not really relate to a "public" but to a "private" context.

In such a "private" context, it seems that there should be direct access without requiring any help from the local competent authority of the requesting State, since adding any intermediary could make the system slower and more costly. However, such a local authority might be very useful to sort out the inappropriate requests coming from individuals or specific groups of people (some might be frivolous or too burdensome and some might have been asked already) and exercise some restraint on, or classification of, the content of the questions asked. In the end, such "filter" authority in the originating State would probably improve the efficiency of the system since it would classify the requests and send them to the appropriate corresponding foreign authority.

As a result, if the request happens within a "public" context (administrative or judicial), the process should be simplified since such requests are supposed to be "serious" (not frivolous or vexatious) and clearly stated. However, within a "pri-

---

[32] *Acessing the Content of Foreign Law and the Need for a Development of a Global Instrument in this Area*, Preliminary document n. 11 A (March 2009), Hague Conference on Private International law, The Hague, p. 6.

vate" context, there should be a centralized agency in the requesting place in order to sort out and filter the requests.

3. The Binding Character of the Answer

The answer provided by the foreign authority or body should be binding if the information comes directly from the authority in charge of the administration of the legislations since they are in a better position to know the content of foreign law. Moreover, this foreign authority would be neutral and would not try to influence in one way or another the foreign authority asking for the information.

Incidentally, it should also be clear which data banks on foreign law are official and which are not, since too much false information is circulating over the Internet and getting wrong legal information or advice have serious consequences.

4. The Costs of the Services on Legal Information

General legal information should be provided without costs as it is now through some data banks. However, legal services relating to the facts of a specific case cannot be provided without costs, since it requires specific research and therefore means which the authorities in charge of providing legal information to the public do not possess.

5. Facilitating Access to Legal Information Within Canada

Access to legal information within Canada is rather easy and well organized notably through Internet access.[33] Moreover, law firms have established networks and the Canadian Bar Association (CBA),[34] a voluntary organization formed in 1896. The CBA has been incorporated by a Special Act of Parliament on 15 April 1921 and represents today 37,000 lawyers, judges, notaries, law professors and law students from across Canada. Approximately two-thirds of all practising lawyers in Canada belong to the CBA. It is a very well organized and dynamic association, which meets regularly in various provinces and has provincial branches all over Canada. Creating lists of Canadian experts could be helpful for foreign lawyers. On the other hand, it is easy to find experts in interprovincial cases.

---

33 See http://www.canlii.org/en/qc/index.html (website of the Canadian Legal Information Institute).

34 See http://www.cba.org/

Conclusion

Proving and ascertaining the content of the foreign applicable law designated by the appropriate choice of law rule constitutes an integral part of the reasoning to point to the law that has objectively the closest connection with the dispute and, thereby, attain justice in an international context. Efforts should thus be continued to improve access to foreign law. Reaching such a goal should be less difficult in light of the means available nowadays through the Internet, which also prompted a revolution in communication, resulting in a remarkable increase in cross-border legal relationships and numerous conflicts of laws.

Argentina: The Changing Character of Foreign Law in Argentinian Legal System

Diego P. Fernández Arroyo and Paula María All

Abstract Application of foreign law has been controversial in Argentina because of the existence of a rule in the Article 13 of the 1869 Civil Code that qualified foreign law as a fact. However, both scholars and courts used some theories to justify the ex officio application of foreign law. Such theories were useless when the conflict rule was contained in a treaty because in those cases the second paragraph of the same Article expressly provided for the ex officio application of foreign law, unless otherwise ordered by the treaty. Furthermore, essential treaties in force in Argentina have established the principle of the ex officio application of foreign law, either explicitly (1889 and 1940 Montevideo Treaties) or implicitly (1979 Inter-American Convention on General Rules of Private International Law, Article 2). In addition, the erga omnes character of the latter provoked the repeal of the Article 13 of the Code Civil. Ultimately, the 2014 Civil and Commercial Code seems to follow the same principle of the Montevideo Convention on the matter (Article 2595)

---

*The authors wish to thank Kendra Wergin (from the University of Virginia School of Law) for her help in preparing the English version of the original report, elaborated long time before the XIX Congress of the Academy held in Vienna in July 2014, and published in the volume of National Reports prepared by the Argentinian Association of Comparative Law. At the moment of editing this new version (May 2015) Argentina has enacted a Civil and Commercial Code, approved by Act N° 26994 of 1st October 2014, which contains the internal dimension of Argentinian Private International Law (hereinafter PIL). See D.P. Fernández Arroyo, "A New Autonomous Dimension for the Argentinian Private International Law", *YBPIL* XVI (2014/2015) 217-231. According to Act N° 27077 of 16 December 2014, the Code entered into force on 1st August 2015. By consequence, this version of our contribution is necessarily different from the previous one because, although case law adopted in application of the old rules is essentially the same, the new internal dimension of Argentinian system of PIL has dramatically changed. Furthermore, due to editorial requirements, this version is shorter than the original one. In this contribution following abbreviations of Argentinian legal reviews are used: *DeCITA* (*Derecho del comercio internacional – Temas y actualidades*); *ED* (*El Derecho*); *JA* (*Jurisprudencia Argentina*); *LL* (*La Ley*); *RDCO* (*Revista de derecho comercial y de las obligaciones*).

D.P. Fernández Arroyo (✉)
Professor, Sciences Po Law School, 27 rue Saint Guillaume, 75005 Paris, France
e-mail: diego.fernandezarroyo@sciencespo.fr

P.M. All
Professor, Faculty of Law and Social Sciences, National University of Littoral, Cándido Pujato, 2751 Santa Fe, Argentina
e-mail: paulamariaall@hotmail.com

Y. Nishitani (ed.), *Treatment of Foreign Law - Dynamics towards Convergence?*,
Ius Comparatum – Global Studies in Comparative Law 26,
DOI 10.1007/978-3-319-56574-3_21

although, in any event, the Inter-American Convention shall prevail, not only because of its character but also due to the constitutional principle of primacy of international law.

I. Character of Conflict of Laws Rules

Within Private International Law (PIL) in Argentina, no regulation currently exists that expressly establishes that courts must apply conflict of law rules. That is, however, the notion unanimously accepted by doctrine and generally applied by courts.

Indeed, the mandatory character of the rules of conflict in the Argentinian system, both for their internal dimension and for their international dimension,[1] is beyond doubt. Judges cannot avoid applying conflict rules whenever a legal relationship falls in the scope of application of one of the rules. This should not be confused with the admission of the right to choose the applicable law in certain topics, clearly, regarding international contracts (with few exceptions). The fact that the parties have the right to choose the applicable law to govern certain legal relationships does not mean that conflict rules stop being mandatory. This mandatory character refers to the obligatory nature of the rules for judges, not for parties.[2] In this sense, if the parties do not make use of their right to select the applicable law to their contract, the judge will have to determine the applicable law according to what is expected in the corresponding rules (which in the internal dimension of the Argentinian system of PIL are contained in Article 2651 of the new Civil and Commercial Code). Further, when the parties exercise this right to choice of law, the mandatory nature is demonstrated in the unavoidable obligation of Argentinian judges to apply the law chosen by the parties, which they have been doing for longtime notwithstanding the absence of a specific rule in this sense.[3]

In this way, the National Commercial Court of Appeal, Panel E, in *"Deutsche Reiseburo, G.M. c. Speter, Armando,"* of 27 February 1984,[4] held that

> the burden of invocation of foreign law does not necessarily prevent Argentinian judges from applying a foreign law when the rules of conflict referred to impose them in this way. Otherwise, the application of irrevocable rules of conflict would remain subjected to the discretion of the parties, who would have the power to invoke or not invoke the foreign law indicated by Argentinian rules of conflict.

---

[1] By "internal dimension" of Argentinian system of PIL, we mean the subsystem composed by the rules of PIL adopted by Argentinian legislator. "International dimension" of Argentinian system of PIL, refers to the rules of PIL contained in the international instruments in force in Argentina.

[2] This confusion is found, for example, in A. Boggiano, *Derecho internacional privado*, 6th ed. (Abeledo Perrot, 2011) 152.

[3] Indeed, until the adoption of the Civil and Commercial Code in 2014 (see supra note *) the acceptation of parties' right to choice the law applicable to international contracts was based on courts' reasoning. No rule established that right.

[4] *LL*, 1984-D-563, *ED*, 108-232.

The number of cases in which the Argentinian courts have applied or taken into consideration foreign law is enormous. Evidently, cases also exist in which the courts have ignored the international nature of the case or have given doubtful interpretations that favor the application of Argentinian law.[5] It also happens that in various matters the criteria utilized as a connecting factor in the rule of conflict coincides with the forum chosen by the corresponding rule of jurisdiction. Actually, the Montevideo Treaty on International Civil Law (in its two versions from 1889 and 1940),[6] which is frequently applied, establishes the criteria of *parallelism* according to which if the law of a country is applicable the judges of that country have jurisdiction. It is obvious that when this overlap between the *forum* and the *ius* takes place, the hypothesis of the application of the foreign law disappears.

With these exceptions, it is difficult to establish a matter in which the application of foreign law would be more habitual than in others. The laws invoked or applied depend on each particular case. No concrete evidence or statistical study exists that shows if the law of one country or another is applied more often, or one convention more than another. It depends on the issue and the concrete case. As an example, during the period in force of Act 2393 of Civil Matrimony (that was in force for almost a century), divorce was prohibited, and marriage could only be dissolved by the death of one of the spouses. Against that backdrop, many people wishing to give some sense of legitimacy to their subsequent unions celebrated a second marriage abroad (often in Paraguay) that was absolutely void in Argentina. When in 1985 Act 23515 finally introduced divorce into Argentinian legal system, many cases about the validity of marriages involved the application of Paraguayan law.[7]

II. Foreign Law Before Judicial Authorities

A. Nature and Application of Foreign Law

1. General Overview of the Argentinian System of PIL

The Argentinian Constitution, in its version stemming from the constitutional reform of 1994, grants instruments of international law a higher hierarchy than domestic laws while incorporating international human rights standards at a constitutional level (Article 75.22).[8] The importance of the supremacy of treaties is rein-

[5] This happens particularly (but not exclusively) in labor cases. See *infra* paragraph 23.

[6] The 1889 version is in force in Argentina, Bolivia, Colombia, Paraguay, Peru and Uruguay. In Argentina, Paraguay and Uruguay the amended version of 1940 applies.

[7] See, for instance, Argentinian Supreme Court, 10 October 2000, "*R. L., M. v. D. A.*," *LL*, 2001-C-697; see S.L. Feldstein de Cárdenas, "Jurisdicción internacional y aplicación del derecho en materia de nulidad del matrimonio celebrado en el extranjero: cuestiones ni teóricas ni sutiles," in S.L. Feldstein de Cárdenas (ed.), *Derecho internacional privado y de la integración - Colección de análisis jurisprudencial* (La Ley, 2004) 79-85.

[8] N.P. Sagüés, "Los tratados internacionales en la reforma constitucional argentina de 1994," *LL*, 1994-E-1036. Actually, the primacy of international treaties in Argentinian legal order had already

forced by two facts: first, this supremacy covers all sectors of PIL and, second, there are many international treaties in force in Argentina.[9] Further, it should be noted that in the absence of specific rules to regulate a particular case, Argentinian courts generally construct their responses by way of an analogy referring to international treaties ratified by Argentina even though they may not be applicable to the case in question.[10] All of this suggests that the Argentinian system of PIL has a marked international character.[11]

In regard specifically to PIL, Argentina had already established the primacy of international treaties by means of the ratification in 1983 of the Inter-American Convention on General Rules of Private International Law (CIDIP II, Montevideo, 1979),[12] whose Article 1 establishes:

> Choice of the applicable rule of law governing facts connected with foreign law shall be subject to the provisions of this Convention and other bilateral or multilateral conventions that have been signed or may be signed in the future by the States Parties.
>
> In the absence of an international rule, the States Parties shall apply the conflict rules of their domestic law.

The second paragraph is especially significant, considering that it establishes the residual nature of the domestic rules of PIL.

Identical solution has been incorporated in the Chapter on PIL of the new Civil and Commercial Code. This Chapter, which contains a large part (although not the entirety) of the internal dimension of the new Argentinian system of PIL, establishes in its first provision (Article 2594):

> The legal rules applicable to situations linked with various national legal systems are determined by treaties and international conventions in force and applicable to the case and, in the absence of rules of international origin, Argentinian rules of private international law of domestic origin shall apply.[13]

---

been consacred by the Supreme Court, particularly in its decision of 7 July 1992 "*Ekmekdjian c. Sofovich*" (*ED*, 148-338).

[9] This is easy to realize by taking a look at the list of instruments collected in A. Dreyzin de Klor & D.P. Fernández Arroyo, *Derecho internacional privado argentino – tratados en vigor y otros textos relevantes* (Zavalía, 2009).

[10] For a clear expression of that, see National Civil Court of Appeal, Panel I, "*S., B.I. c/ C., V. y otro*," 21 November 2002 (*ED*, 201-153).

[11] See "Estudio preliminar," in the book mentioned in note 9.

[12] See T.B. de Maekelt, "General Rules of Private International Law in the Americas. New Approach," *Recueil des cours*, 177 (1982) 193-279. This Convention was approved in Argentina by Act n° 22921.

[13] Although it is clearly unnecessary, the same principle is specifically reiterated when dealing with international jurisdiction (Article 2601), international cooperation in general (Articles 2611 and 2612), and international cooperation related to legal kidnapping (Articles 2614 and 2642). Such a reiteration reinforces the primordial significance of the hierarchy of international instruments.

2. Nature of Foreign Law in the International Dimension of the Argentinian System of PIL

It is in this context that international instruments in force that refer in some way to the character of the rules of conflict and to the nature of foreign law should be analyzed. In this sense, it is fundamentally necessary to mention Article 2 of the Inter-American Convention on General Rules of PIL, which states:

> Judges and authorities of the States Parties shall enforce the foreign law in the same way as it would be enforced by the judges of the State whose law is applicable, without prejudice to the parties' being able to plead and prove the existence and content of the foreign law invoked.

It is beyond doubt that the intention of the framers of the Convention was to go beyond the solution that was already clearly established in the Montevideo Treaties. This is validated by the writings of the delegates who actively participated in the development of the Convention,[14] in the opinion of almost all of the leading books in Latin America,[15] and, *a contrario*, in the wording of the reservation made by Mexico at the time of signing the Convention.[16] In effect, the Convention on General Rules of Private International Law does not exclusively state that a judge must apply foreign law *ex officio*.[17] Additionally, the judge must investigate how the judge of the State whose law becomes applicable applies this law.

But, in reality, when Argentina ratified the Inter-American Convention on General Rules of Private International Law, the *ex officio* application of foreign law had already been present in the country for a long time. This is because, as it has already been mentioned, Argentina is party to the Montevideo Treaties of 1889 and 1940, and both expressly establish this solution.[18] Indeed, both versions include an Additional Protocol that establishes that the application of foreign law.

---

[14] See W. Goldschmidt, "Un logro americano en el campo convencional del derecho internacional privado," *ED*, 83–833; T.B. de Maekelt, *Teoría general del derecho internacional privado* (Academia de Ciencias Políticas y Sociales, 2005) 270–271; R. Silva Alonso, *Derecho internacional privado*, 9th ed. (Intercontinental, 2009) 154–155; G. Parra-Aranguren, "La Convención interamericana sobre normas generales de derecho internacional privado. Montevideo, 1979," *Anuario Jurídico Interamericano* (1979) 157–186; etc.

[15] R. Ruiz Díaz Labrano, *Derecho internacional privado* (La Ley, 2010) 289–290; E. Tellechea Bergmann, *Derecho internacional privado* (La Ley, 2010) 174–176; C. Fresnedo de Aguirre in D.P. Fernández Arroyo (ed.), *Derecho internacional privado de los Estados del Mercosur* (Zavalía, 2003) 316–318; etc.

[16] "Mexico interprets Article 2 to mean that it creates an obligation only when the existence of the foreign law has been proved before the judge or authority or its provisions are made known to them in some other way."

[17] Quite surprisingly, Panel A of the National Commercial Court of Appeal, based on a inaccurate narrow interpretation of Article 2 of the Convention, has denied that this rule establishes *ex officio* application of foreign law. See, for example, its decisions in "*BKS Developers SA le pide la quiebra BII Creditanstalt International Ltd.*", 28 October 2008, and "*Scrugli, Carlos Antonio c. HSBC Bank Argentina S.A.*", 16 October 2013. This isolated interpretation has been coined by Judge Uzal.

[18] See R.A. Ramayo, "Aplicación del derecho extranjero en el ámbito de los Tratados de Montevideo de derecho privado," *ED*, 167–152.

> shall be made *ex officio* by the judge of the case, notwithstanding that the parties can plead and prove the existence and content of the law invoked (Article 2).

If the Montevideo Treaties are applicable, therefore, the principle of the application of foreign law is manifested unequivocally. Thus one can clearly appreciate the ruling of the Supreme Court of the Province of Buenos Aires, "*Soto c/Exxe*," of 28 April 2004.[19] In that case, revoking a decision that had rejected a demand for dismissal based on the lack of invocation and proof of the applicability of Peruvian law,[20] Judge Hitters, *inter alia*, noted:

> In the impugned judgment the lower Court has confused –in my view– two issues that, because of their similarity, can be difficult to distinguish. The first is that relating to the imperative nature or unavailability of the connecting rules that determine the law applicable to the controversial legal relationship. The second is related to the proof of the foreign law. [...] From the premise of the imperative nature of the rule of conflict, the a quo has resulted incorrectly in the necessity of invocation and proof of non-domestic legislation for the litigants. The issues are different: although it is maintained that the parties can agree neither expressly nor tacitly on the criterion of connection distinct from that provided by our international private law, this does not necessarily mean that they must prove the existence and content of the foreign law.

Not much different is what Judge Fermé affirmed in the judgment of the National Civil Court of Appeal, Panel I, 14 April 1998, "*Rivas Cordero c/ Natanson*,"[21]

> Once the jurisdiction has been determined, in that which concerns the applicable law, it is necessary to consult, in the first instance, the sources of conventional Private International Law, since by opening the discussion about the terms relating to the existence of responsibility and reparation, it is incumbent on the judge to apply the pertinent law. The issue is not changed because of the fact that the parties had made their submissions with regard to civil Argentinian law and had consented to the decision that applied such law, inasmuch as not being able to choose the law applicable to the illicit facts, nor would it be possible to make reference to the tacit choice resulting from an invocation or consent matching that which occurred. A concluding procedural agreement is not viable on this point. The Court is obliged to apply ex officio the foreign law indicated by the rules of Private International Law.

In case one needs anything further, Argentina also signed the Convention with Uruguay on the Application and Information About Foreign Law of 1981[22] in which, obviously, the thesis of the *ex officio* application of foreign law is followed.

---

[19] LLBA, 2004-973.

[20] It is important to point out that Peru is party to the Montevideo Treaties of 1889, its Additional Protocol, and the Inter-American Convention on General Rules of 1979.

[21] *ED*, 182-753.

[22] Approved by Act n° 22.411.

3. Nature of Foreign Law in the Internal Dimension of the Argentinian System of PIL

a. The Background

Before the adoption of the new internal dimension of the Argentinian System of PIL, the position favorable to the *ex officio* application of foreign law was present in several previous projects on the matter.

Thus, in the 1998 Draft Civil and Commercial Code, Book VIII contained three articles dealing with the application of foreign law. The position in favor of the *ex officio* application could not have been clearer:

> Article 2533 (Application of foreign law). Judges shall apply *ex officio* foreign law designated by the conflict rule. In order for the application of foreign law to proceed, the foreign elements of the case are required to be clear or to have been demonstrated in the lawsuit.
> Article 2534 (Proof of foreign law). Judges shall establish *ex officio* the content of the foreign law, notwithstanding that the parties may plead and prove its existence and content.
> Article 2535 (Foreign law). Foreign law is understood to mean the decision with the greatest probability of being applied by the judges of that country.

In the same vein, the 2003 Draft Code of PIL 2003, elaborated by a commission created by the Ministry of Justice, included the following rule in its Article 11:

> Courts shall apply *ex officio* the foreign law designated by the rules of conflict, notwithstanding that the parties may plead and prove its existence and content. Foreign law is understood to mean the decision with the greatest probability of being applied by the judges of that country. The information and the proof of the foreign law shall be produced by the following means, among others: a) reports of courts and authorities of the country in question, when possible; b) opinions of experts on that law; c) legal texts and case law with indication of their validity, obtained in an irrefutable manner. It will not be possible to reject the demand because of lack of proof of content of the foreign law that should apply.

b. The New Rule

Article 2595 of the new Civil and Commercial Code establishes that:
When a foreign law becomes applicable:

> a) the judge establishes its content, and is obligated to interpret it as would the judges of the State to which that law pertains, notwithstanding that the parties may plead and prove the existence of the law invoked. If the content of the foreign law cannot be established, Argentinian law shall apply;
> b) …

While the formula is less clear than its precedents (inexplicably the authors have not wanted to use the right words, that is to say, "application *ex officio*"), both its content and the sources cited by the drafters (Article 2 of the Additional Protocol of the Montevideo Treaties of 1889 and 1940, and Articles 2 and 9 of the Inter-American Convention on General Rules of Private International Law) make clear that the idea must be the same. In any event, whatever the rule in question says, the primacy of treaties enshrined in the Argentinian Constitution will require that the applicable general rule be that of Article 2 of the mentioned Inter-American Convention.

The explanation is easy: the Inter-American Convention on General Rules of Private International Law is of "universal" character, which is to say, that its applicability does not depend on the connection of the case with other contracting States. As it happens with all "universal" international conventions, the Convention on the General Rules automatically replaces the domestic PIL rules of the States Parties with respect to all the issues that fall within its scope of application. This character, then, imposes the obligation to apply the foreign law *ex officio* in all the contracting States[23] in all cases.

With this understanding, which is the correct one, even the various theories advanced in another age by doctrine (and collected in various cases by jurisprudence) in order to justify the *ex officio* application of foreign law, despite the opposite disposition in the first paragraph of Article 13 of the repealed Civil Code,[24] had become outdated and useless.[25] Actually, that Article –that was understandable a century and a half ago when the application of foreign law seemed like something fairly exceptional, very difficult to realize in practice– was repealed at the very moment in which the Convention on General Rules entered into force.[26] Even before that date, the second paragraph of Article 13 could not be ignored. Indeed, the general rule that considered foreign law as a fact, did not apply when foreign law became applicable by virtue of a conflict rule contained in an international treaty. In this case, the application had to be made *ex officio*, unless otherwise stated by the

[23] Argentina, Brazil, Colombia, Equator, Guatemala, Paraguay, Peru, Uruguay and Venezuela. Mexico, notwithstanding its reservation to Article 2 of the Convention (see *supra* note 16), has introduced the principle of *ex officio* application of the foreign law in the article 14(I) of the Federal Civil Code, which provides that foreign law "shall apply in the same way as it would be applied by the respective foreign judge; in doing so, the judge may get information about the text, the binding character, the meaning and the legal scope of such law."

[24] Article 13 of 1869 Civil Code established: "The application of foreign laws, in the cases authorized by this Code, will never take place except at the soliciting of the interested party, who will have the burden of proving the existence of such laws. Foreign laws that become obligatory in the Republic by diplomatic conventions, or in virtue of special law, are exempted."

[25] This does not detract from the efforts to "actualize" an evidently outdated rule. See, particularly, W. Goldschmidt, *Derecho internacional privado*, 2nd ed. (Depalma, 1974) 470. In the opinion of this author, "foreign law constitutes a 'notorious fact', which does not mean a fact that all the world is aware of but a fact about which all the world can learn in an authentic way. The judge can informally keep such a notorious fact in mind, notwithstanding that the parties plead it and bring all the evidence that they feel necessary." See also A. Perugini, "Aplicación del derecho extranjero de oficio y calificaciones en el derecho internacional privado argentino. La apariencia de la cuestión previa", *LL*, 1984-D-560; M. Feuillade, "Aplicación procesal del derecho extranjero, con especial referencia a las posturas jurisprudenciales actuales en el derecho argentino", in *Derecho procesal transnacional. Homenaje al Profesor Doctor Gualberto Lucas Sosa* (Ábaco, 2013) 33.

[26] In this sense, W. Goldschmidt, "El derecho extranjero en el proceso. Los tres enfoques argentinos", *ED*, 115–802; E.L. Fermé, "Convención Interamericana sobre Normas Generales," in *Enciclopedia Jurídica Omeba*" (1987) 210–211.

treaty.[27] The importance of the exception is heightened if one takes into consideration the large number of international treaties in force in Argentina. Furthermore, the exception permitted the *ex officio* application based on a special provision.

Another important datum, before the ratification of the Inter-American Convention by Argentina, was the existence of Article 377 of the Federal Code on Civil and Commercial Procedure.[28] This article, which agrees with the general criteria of Article 13 of the former Civil Code, permits the judge to order investigation of the existence of the foreign law and to apply it in the case of inactivity of the parties. This is not an obligation, it is true, but the lack of proof of foreign law by the parties was no longer an obstacle to its application.

c. Case Law

Despite the fact that Article 13 of the Civil Code (and, in particular, its first sentence) had become inapplicable since the entry into force of the Inter-American Convention on General Rules of Private International Law, a considerable number of judicial decisions continued applying that disposition literally, in open ignorance of the provisions of the Argentinian system of PIL. The majority of those decisions come from labor jurisprudence and support, in different ways, that if the interested party does not plead and prove the foreign law, its application becomes impossible. It is not difficult to realize that, in general, this was a simple trick to justify the application of Argentinian law. Among others, the following decisions of the National Labor Court of Appeal can be cited:

- Panel V, 27 October 1998, "*Sarmiento, César Manuel c. Editorial Perfil S.A.*;"[29]
- Panel VIII, 18 April 1991, "*Savignon Belgrano, Carlos H. c. Editorial Abril S.A.*;"[30]
- Panel VI, 7 December 1994, "*Lema, René Eduardo c. Techint Compañía Técnica Internacional SA s. accidente ley 9688*;"[31]
- Panel VI, 25 March 1996, "*Antoñanzas, Eduardo Lucero c. ICI Duperial S.A. s. despido*;"[32]
- Panel II, 17 August 2000, "*Sánchez, Raúl c. Lichtenstein, Mario*;"[33]
- Panel II, 20 June 2001, "*Krautmann de Portaro, Berta c. Instituto Goethe Buenos Aires*;"[34]

---

[27] Given the fact that treaties on conflict of laws are made to unify the choice-of-law criteria, they normally contains mandatory conflict rules. The fact that some of them allow party autonomy does not change that mandatory character as we have already said (see *supra* paragraph 2).

[28] Modified by Act N° 22434 of 1981.

[29] *Derecho del Trabajo* XLVIII-B-1770 and http://fallos.diprargentina.com/2010/09/sarmiento-cesar-manuel-c-editorial.html

[30] *DJ*, 199-2-879.

[31] Judgment n° 41595.

[32] *ED*, 172–167.

[33] *JA*, 2001-IV-211.

[34] http://fallos.diprargentina.com/2010/10/krautmann-de-portaro-berta-c-instituto.html

- Panel X, 17 July 2007, "*Coelho, Germán Luis c. Enviro Control Ar S.R.L. y otros s. despido;*"[35]
- Panel VII, 28 November 2008, "*Castro, Fabián Alejandro c. Roura Cevasa Argentina S.A. s. despido.*"[36]

As an exception to this trend, there is at least a case in which the National Labor Court of Appeal opted to not violate Argentinian law. Indeed, Panel II in the case "*Benítez, María del Carmen c. Editorial Atlántida s. despido*", 6 November 2002,[37] made a correct interpretation of the rules in force (namely, Article 2 of the Inter-American Convention on General Rules of PIL and Article 377 of the Federal Code on Civil and Commercial Procedure), applying Spanish law *ex officio* to a labor relationship.

Conversely, several times it is the judges of other forums that have been the inattentive ones by not applying foreign law when they were obligated to do so. Thus, on this "sinner list," one can mention:

- National Civil and Commercial Court of Appeal, Panel II, 20 May 1994, "*Mundex S.A. v. Ilimex S.A. y otro s/ varios propiedad industrial e intelectual;*"[38]
- National Commercial Court of Appeal, Panel A, 4 May 2006, "*Multicanal S.A. s. acuerdo preventivo extrajudicial;*"[39]
- Same Court, same Panel, 28 October 2008, "*BKS Developers SA le pide la quiebra BII Creditanstalt International Ltd.;*"[40]
- National Commercial Court of Appeal, Panel D, 9 November 2009, "*Banco Holandés Unido c. González de Domínguez, Elisa E. y otros;*"[41]
- Civil, Commercial, Mining and Tax Court of Appeal of Mendoza, Panel 5, 7 February 2012, "*Aldeco, Juan Carlos s. Sucesión.*"[42]
- San Isidro Civil and Commercial Court of Appeal, Panel A, 28 February 2014, "*B.B. G.S. s/Sucesión testamentaria.*"[43]

In spite of these more or less isolated "blemishes," the most relevant and abundant jurisprudence advocates for the application of foreign law *ex officio*, although this is not always done correctly. Even before the entry into force of the Convention on General Rules and the modification of Article 277 of the Federal Code on Civil and Commercial Procedure, various Argentinian judges and courts had applied foreign law *ex officio*, with different arguments. See, for instance:

---

[35] www.semanariojuridico.info/jurisprudencia/tribunal/view/33/category

[36] http://fallos.diprargentina.com/2009/07/castro-fabian-alejandro-c-roura-cevasa.html

[37] http://fallos.diprargentina.com/2010/02/benitez-maria-del-carmen-c-editorial.html. See also the report made by C.D. Iud on http://asadip.files.wordpress.com/2009/11/informe-preliminar-sobre-la-aplicacion-de-las-convenciones-interamericanas-de-derecho-internacional-privado-por-los-tribunales-argen.pdf

[38] *Lexis Nexis* n° 7/2743.

[39] http://fallos.diprargentina.com/2009/10/multicanal-sa-s-acuerdo-preventivo.html

[40] *Supra*, note 17.

[41] http://fallos.diprargentina.com/2010/02/banco-holandes-unido-c-gonzalez-de_09.html

[42] http://fallos.diprargentina.com/2013/06/aldeco-juan-carlos-s-sucesion.html

[43] *ElDial.com* (A-1273-4).

- Civil Court of Appeal of the Federal Capital (Buenos Aires), 27 June 1941, "*R. de A.B.V.A.F.*;"[44]
- Same Court, Panel B, 8 May 1953, "*P.L. de G.R.R.F.*;"[45]
- Civil and Commercial Federal Court of Buenos Aires, 3 December 1958, "*Etablissement de Constructions Mécaniques de Vendeuvre c. Artimsa S.A.*;"[46]
- Nacional Court of Appeal "de Paz", Panel III, 22 December 1959[47];
- National Civil Judge of Frist Instance n° 30, 27 August 1973, "*Oreiro Miñones, José, s. sucesión*;"[48]
- National Commercial Judge of First Instance n° 13, 12 April 1976, "*Ocerín, José Pascual, c. Talleres Auxiliares de la Industria Minera S.A. (TAIM S.A.)*;"[49]
- National Civil Court of Appeal, Panel A, 14 March 1977, "*Kogan v. Quintana*;"[50]
- National Civil Court of Appeal, Panel D, 29 May 1981, "*Del Caño, Osvaldo c. Ramón C. Vita S.A. y otro.*"[51]

In the last 30 years, that is to say, since the regulatory changes indicated in the preceding paragraph, jurisprudence favorable to the *ex officio* application of foreign law is overwhelming. The reasons invoked can be different, but the most convincing is that relating to the repeal of Article 13 of the Civil Code by virtue of the entry into force of the Convention on General Rules. The judgment of the National Commercial Judge of First Instance n° 7, 21 October 1986, "*Banco do Brasil S.A. c. Astilleros Corrientes S.A.*,"[52] expresses that clearly, in the following terms:

> Foreign law should be applied ex officio by the judge, although the parties may not have claimed or proved how national jurisprudential doctrine has peacefully supported it (...), either through the different interpretations that have been given of Article 13 of the Civil Code (...), or through exercising the authority conferred to the Court by Article 377 of the Procedural Code, as of the reform of la 22434, or by virtue of the implied repeal of Article 13 of the Civil Code, at the adoption of the Inter-American Convention on General Rules of Private International Law.

Among the many judgments that apply foreign law *ex officio*, it is fitting to cite the following:

- National Commercial Court of Appeal, Panel E, 27 February 1984, "*Deutsche Reiseburo, G.M. c. Speter, Armando*;"[53]
- National Civil Court of Appeal, Panel F, 4 August 1988, "*Paleo de Rochi, Mariana*;"[54]

---

[44] "Either by a mandate to the parties or by the own judges' effort, the research about the existence of foreign law must be done."

[45] *LL*, 70-597 (application of Paraguayan law as a "notorious fact").

[46] *LL*, 97-25 (application of French law, stating that when a foreign law is easily knowable its proof is unnecessary).

[47] *LL*, 99-70.

[48] http://fallos.diprargentina.com/2009/08/oreiro-minones-jose-s-sucesion.html

[49] http://fallos.diprargentina.com/2008_04_01_archive.html

[50] *ED*, 76-455.

[51] *ED*, 95-441.

[52] http://fallos.diprargentina.com/2010/04/banco-do-brasil-c-astilleros-corrientes.html

[53] *Supra*, note 4.

[54] *LL*, 1989-B-18, *DJ*, 1989-1-792.

- National Commercial Court of Appeal, Panel E, 11 October 1988, "*Rhodia Argentina S.A. y otro c/Polisecki, Jorge B.*;"[55]
- National Commercial Judge of First Instance n° 7, 4 May 1988, "*Tavobe S.A. c. Cullen, Iván s. ejecutivo*;"[56]
- National Commercial Judge of First Instance n° 10, 30 June 1993, "*Casa Piano S.A. c. Dieffenbacher, Jorge y otro s. ejecutivo*;"[57]
- Same Judge, 19 December 1994, "*Seibel, Alberto c. Trachter, Daniel s. Ejecutivo*[58];
- National Civil Court of Appeal, Panel I, 9 March 1990, "*Frederick Parker Limited c. Villa, o Villa y Egea*;"[59]
- National Commercial Judge of First Instance n° 4, 23 December 1993, "*Mayer y Cía. c. Ciepsa S.A. y otros s. ordinario*;"[60]
- National Commercial Judge of First Instance n° 10, September 1994, "*Hydrosa Trading Ltd. c. Pinal Pharma S.A.C.I.F. s. ejecutivo*;"[61]
- National Civil Court of Appeal, Panel I, 14 April 1998, "*Rivas Cordero, Santiago c. Natanson, Jorge Gustavo o Gustavo Jorge Osvaldo s. daños y perjuicios*;"[62]
- Federal Supreme Court, 7 March 2000, "*Moka S.A. c. Graiver, David*;"[63]
- Nacional Commercial Court of Appeal, Panel A, 20 March 2007, "*Raij Kruchik, Abraham c. Banco Hipotecario S.A.*;"[64]
- Civil and Commercial Court of Appeal of Bahia Blanca, Panel II, 20 May 2008, "*Banco de la Provincia de Buenos Aires c. Melendi, Omar Darío y otra s. cobro ejecutivo*;"[65]
- National Commercial Court, Panel A, 4 September 2008, "*Biocrom S.A. s. concurso preventivo s. incidente de revisión por Chemline Healthcare Amaral & Co.*;"[66]
- National Commercial Court of Appeal, Panel C, 26 September 2008, "*Banco de Galicia (Cayman) Ltda. V. Rosarios, Diego s/ ejecutivo*;"[67]
- Same Court, Panel A, 28 October 2008, "*BKS Developers SA le pide la quiebra BII Creditanstalt International Ltd.*;"[68]
- National Federal Civil and Commercial Court, Panel II, 31 October 2008, "*Bradesco Seguros S.A. c. FJW S.A. de transporte s. faltante y/o avería de carga transporte terrestre*;"[69]

Possibly, the most commented (and fairly celebrated) decision on this issue is the judgment of the Supreme Court of Mendoza, 28 April 2005, "*Sabaté Sas S.A. c.*

[55] *ED*, 132-115.

[56] See M.B. Noodt Taquela, *Derecho Internacional Privado - Libro de casos*, 2nd ed. (La Ley, 2006) 344–348; http://fallos.diprargentina.com/2007/08/tavobe-c-cullen.html

[57] http://fallos.diprargentina.com/2007/08/casa-piano-c-dieffenbacher.html

[58] http://fallos.diprargentina.com/2006/12/seibel-c-trachter-s-ejecutivo.html

[59] See M.B. Noodt Taquela (note 56) 90–98; http://fallos.diprargentina.com/2007/08/frederick-parker-limited-c-villa.html

[60] http://fallos.diprargentina.com/2007/08/mayer-y-cie-c-ciepsa-1-instancia.html

[61] http://fallos.diprargentina.com/2008/06/hydrosa-trading-ltd-c-pinal-pharma.html

[62] *ED*, 182-752.

[63] *ED*, 195-523.

[64] http://fallos.diprargentina.com/2009/05/raij-kruchik-abraham-c-banco.html

[65] *El Dial*, 22 May 2009.

[66] http://ar.vlex.com/vid/biocrom-promovido-healthcare-amaral-57775467

[67] http://fallos.diprargentina.com/2009/05/banco-de-galicia-cayman-ltda-c-rosarios.html

[68] http://fallos.diprargentina.com/2009/03/bks-developers-le-pide-la-quiebra-bii.html

[69] http://ar.vlex.com/vid/bradesco-fjw-averia-transp-terrestre-57687445

Covisan S.A. s/Concurso Preventivo s/verificación tardía s/ inc. Casación."[70] The combination of correct reasoning and pedagogy in the explanation is surely what has placed this judgment in the podium of the "great decisions" of Argentinian PIL. In the decision, Judge Kemelmajer de Carlucci, after affirming the impact of the Convention on General Rules on the former Article 13 of the Civil Code, held:

> I have the conviction that the trustee was able to (…), and the judge should have, based on the principle of iuria novit curia, verified the legal system of French law. (…) As supported by doctrine, the principal aim in this discipline is to find a just solution within the bankruptcy liabilities of the named foreign creditors (…) it seems very far from that objective to deny the right to a creditor who is legitimated to be paid, from the time when the merchandise was delivered and which was never paid, only because the law of France (a country with which Argentina has a common legal history, that does not discriminate against creditors, and to whose legislation the judge can know, even by means of electronic means) was not proved. (…) I do not have doubts, then, that the appealed judgment suffers from a manifest excess of ritual rigor in the assessment of the burden of proof, and from disregard of the law at having closed their eyes to the French legislation.

B. Ascertainment of Foreign Law

1. Means Used to Ascertain Foreign Law

Argentina is a contracting State of the Brasilia Convention on Information in Legal Matters about the Law in Force and its Application (1972),[71] of the Inter-American Convention on Proof of and Information on Foreign Law (OAS, CIDIP II, Montevideo, 1979),[72] of the Convention with Uruguay on the Application of and Information on Foreign Law (already mentioned) and, within the context of MERCOSUR, of the Las Leñas Protocol on Cooperation and Jurisdictional Assistance on Civil, Commercial, Labor and Administrative Matters.[73] Furthermore, rules about the obligation to provide for information on the written law and on the case law are included in other bilateral conventions on judicial cooperation.[74] Although they are different, all these instruments establish the duty to collaborate with other Contracting States in ascertaining foreign law. An organ that centralizes information and helps to implement these instruments ("central authority") is fundamental in all of them.

---

[70] *LLGranCuyo*, 6/2005-495, comm. M.E. Uzal; *LL*, 2005-D-707, comm. G. Salort de Orchansky; *JA* 2005-IV-143; *SJA* 21 December 2005, comm. M. Barreiro & J. Boidman; *ED*, 214-373, comm. A.M. Soto,; *RDCO*, 2005-B-869, comm. C.E. Moro; comm. J.C. Córdoba, *DeCITA* 5/6 (2006) 453.

[71] Approved by Act n° 21447.

[72] Approved by Act n° 23506.

[73] Approved by Act n° 24578.

[74] Namely, Conventions with: Italy, approved by Act n° 23720, article 8; France, approved by Act n° 24107, article 9; Brazil, approved by Act n° 24108, articles 24–26.

As to the internal dimension of Argentinian PIL, the new Civil and Commercial Code contains some general indications about the way to practice international cooperation but it fails to provide for a clear rule about the means to ascertain foreign law. Indeed, Article 2612 says that without prejudice of the applicable international instruments, Argentinian courts shall ask foreign authorities for cooperation by means of letters rogatory. This has been the traditional way to implement international cooperation in Argentina and Article 132 of the Federal Code of Civil and Commercial Procedure already ordered it. More innovative, the codifier adds in Article 2612 that when the situation so requires, Argentinian courts may establish "direct communication" with judges from countries in which this practice is authorized, provided that due process is respected.

Nevertheless, no rule indicates what concrete means may be used to identify and prove foreign law before Argentinian courts. Different positions exist to this respect. For one restrictive position, the evidence would be the informational (from diplomatic delegations or authorities of the State whose law needs to be proven), documentary (legal texts, publications of doctrine or jurisprudence) and expert (opinions of professors or experts of foreign law). From a broad position (which is what has been imposed in practice[75]), in order that the judge is able to determine and apply the foreign law (although no positive rule establishes this), it would be possible to make use of as many means as considered necessary. Thus the judge can use documents, Internet sources, making use of the assistance of the parties, consultations or opinions of experts, works of foreign treatise writers, jurisprudence, etc. Consular reports, certifications of institutions, direct communications between judges and others can all be contributed. There already exists old jurisprudence that supports the possibility of contributing consular reports.[76] With respect to the admissibility of testimonial proof, see, for example Civil and Commercial Court of Appeal of Junín, 6 June 1982, "*A. H.M. c/I., M.M. y otros.*".[77]

No qualification or special characteristics are required for the people or institutions that provide legal information. In any case the courts, as lawyers in Argentina do increasingly more often, have resorted to the assistance of professors of PIL, whose reports have been expressly allowed as evidence.[78]

When Argentinian judges are asked to cooperate by foreign authorities, this cooperation shall be "large" according to Article 2611 of the new Civil and Commercial Code. Consequently, they must answer all demand of information about Argentinian law immediately except if the demand violates Argentinian public policy (Article 2612).

---

[75] See "Scrugli, Carlos Antonio c. HSBC Bank Argentina S.A.", supra, nota 17.

[76] See the list in M. Feuillade (*supra*, note 25) 331.

[77] *JA*, 1983-II-117.

[78] See, for example, "Frederick Parker Limited c. Villa, o Villa y Egea," supra, note 59.

2. Character and Cost of Legal Information

In the internal dimension of the system of PIL no express rule exists that establishes that the information provided is binding. In the international dimension, on the other hand, some of the mentioned instruments in force are inclined to believe that the sent information is not binding on the authorities. In this way, Article 5 of the Convention of Brasilia on Information in Legal Matters in Respect to Law in Force and its Application establishes that the response of the receiving body will not have binding force. In the same line, the Protocol of Las Leñas put forth by MERCOSUR states in its Article 30 that "the State that provides reports on the meaning and legal reach of its law will not be responsible for the opinion emitted nor is it obligated to apply its law according to the response given. The State that receives these reports will neither be obligated to apply nor to make apply the foreign law according to the content of the response received."

With respect to the cost of the information provided, in general it has been considered that such information should be provided for free except for specific situations such as, for example, the intervention of experts. In the international dimension, the Brasilia Convention establishes in Article 7.2 that "the response will be free, and in no case may result in the collection of fees or expenses of any nature." However, Article 2612 of Civil and Commercial Code expressly provides that Argentinian judges may fix an amount to be paid whenever the particular assistance asked costs money.

C. Interpretation and Application of Foreign Law

1. Interpretation and Application of Foreign Law: Imitation of the Foreign Judge

The formula, aforementioned in this Chapter, contained in Article 2 of the Convention on General Norms of PIL ("judges and authorities of the States Parties shall enforce the foreign law in the same way as it would be enforced by the judges of the State whose law is applicable"), enshrines the theory of "legal use," under the intellectual influence of W. Goldschmidt, president of the Argentinian delegation before the CIDIP II.[79] The same formula is present in Article 2595 of the new Civil and Commercial Code previously discussed.[80]

[79] W. Goldschmidt, a German scholar who had spent a long time in Spain, came to Argentina in the fifties and here remained until his death in 1987. An exceptionally gifted legal researcher as well as a pedagogic professor, he was the most influent author ever of Argentinian PIL and, without any doubt, one of the most outstanding scholars of Latin-American PIL. See M.J.A. Oyarzábal, "Das Internationale Privatrecht von Werner Goldschmidt. In Memoriam", *RabelsZ* (2008) 601. In order to circumvallate the characterization of Article 13 of the repealed Civil Code (according to which foreign law is a fact), Goldschmidt treated foreign law as a fact but of a "notorious" character, that is to say, a fact about which everybody can get information in an authentic way. *Supra*, note 25.

[80] *Supra*, paragraphs 18–22.

Obviously, utilizing this parameter of "imitation" of the foreign judge does not alter the responsibility of the judge that must decide the case. In the opinion of Feldstein de Cárdenas, "*in the interpretation of the foreign law, to the question of if the judges are bound by the opinions issued in the country of the legislation under discussion, it is necessary to respond in the negative. Although judges may base the totality of the decision on a foreign piece of legislation, they do not thereby stop being those who administer justice in the name and under the responsibility of the State to which they belong. It is up to them, then, to penetrate the meaning of the foreign law; they will keep in mind, obviously, the dominant jurisprudential opinions in the foreign country, but these opinions will not be binding on them.*"[81] In addition to this, it should be kept in mind that the provision in question contains a mandate for the judge that will not always be able to realize in optimal conditions. However, for a large quantity of cases, related to countries with which Argentina has long maintained fluid relations, that work will be relatively easy for the judge. The jurisprudence previously identified demonstrates this fairly well.

2. Failure to Establish Foreign Law

In the absence of a specific rule that indicates what the judge must do when foreign law cannot be ascertained, Argentinian courts had habitually resorted to the easiest solution, that is, applying Argentinian law, without further explanations. The last sentence of Article 2595(a) of the 2014 Civil and Commercial Code confirms this tendency, stating that:

> If the content of the foreign law cannot be established, Argentinian law will be applied.

The solution included in the new Argentinian PIL is regrettable. Before resorting directly to Argentinian law by default, it should be established that the legislation that presents the closest links with the case would be applied and, in the last circumstance, Argentinian law. The solution of resorting directly to Argentinian law does not have any logical explanation, above all if one considers that two articles later, in Article 2597, it is clearly shown that the Argentinian system of PIL is based on the principle of proximity corrected by public policy and imperative norms when pertinent. One plausible explanation would be that the most influential contributors to the new Code are judges and as such they do not want to see themselves obligated to carry out work that they suppose to be arduous. But such a position would not have much support given that not only have the same authors developed the exception clause of Article 2597, but also that in many cases the determination of the State most closely linked with the legal relationship constitutes a relatively easy task.

---

[81] S.L Feldstein de Cárdenas, "El control de constitucionalidad del derecho extranjero", in *Homenaje al Profesor Doctor Gualberto Lucas Sosa* (*supra*, nota 25) 315.

III. Judicial Review in Case of Error About Foreign Law

Article 4 of the Inter-American Convention on General Rules of Private International Law establishes that

> All the appeals provided for in the procedural law of the place where the proceedings are held shall also be admissible for cases in which the law of any of the other States Parties is applicable.

The norm thus provides that in the cases in which it is possible to attack a decision by erroneous interpretation of local law, either through ordinary or extraordinary means, it will also be possible to do so if the law that has been misinterpreted is foreign.

When the discussion refers to the application of a rule on the basis of an international treaty, extraordinary recourse is always appropriate.[82] This confirms what we said previously about the importance given to the priority implementation of treaties in Argentinian law. Moreover, the lack of consideration of an applicable treaty does not only enable extraordinary recourse before the Supreme Court but also suffices to qualify a judicial decision as arbitrary. That and nothing else is what the Court said in "*Banco de Italia y Río de la Plata S.A. c/ Banco Pan de Azúcar S.A. s/ diligencia preliminar*,"[83] 9 November 2004:

> This Court shares the opinion of the Prosecutor, as it considers that the Chamber has disregarded the study of the applicability to the case of different international treaties. That is sufficient to disqualify the extraordinary decision for arbitrariness.

Some years ago, in a case about the invalidity of a marriage celebrated in Paraguay ("*R.L., M. c/D.A.*", 10 October 2000[84]), the Supreme Court declared an extraordinary recourse appropriate against the judgment of the Court of Appeal for having ignored the applicable judicial framework that was none other than that of the Treaty of Montevideo of International Civil Law of 1940.

IV. Foreign Law in Other Instances

It does not occur very frequently that foreign law is applied or ascertained before the administrative or other non-judicial authorities. However, foreign law is applied in certain customs cases on the part of the customs agents and also for the notaries, in such cases as powers granted abroad, documents completed by foreign notaries or problems related to the validity of a business when a law requires a specific

---

[82] Federal Supreme Court, 10 April 2007, "*U., A. s/suc.*," *DJ*, 2007-II-247.

[83] LL, 17 June 2005, 7.

[84] *LL*, 2001-C-697. See comment of S.L. Feldstein de Cárdenas (*supra*, note 7) 79–85.

form with constitutive character and other law involved in the matter does not require this.[85]

Due to the archaic nature of Argentinian law of arbitration,[86] the number and the importance of international arbitrations taking place in Argentina has not been very significant. However, when this happens, the application of foreign law does not present any problem. In the vast majority of arbitrations, that application takes place by virtue of the express choice of the parties, a choice constituting a very powerful obligation for the arbitrators that they rarely fail to carry out. However, the specific determination of the applicable law usually takes place in a relatively flexible manner and without particular formalities, keeping in mind, in particular, all of its relevant uses (as ordered by all of the rules of the arbitration).

V. Access to Foreign Law: Status Quo

A. General Information on Argentinian Law

Argentina has a specific governmental website that contains all of the legislative information of the Argentinian legal system, at both the federal and state/provincial level. Curiously, it is part of the website of the Ministry of Economy and Public Finance (infoleg.mecom.gov.ar). In addition, on the specific theme of international protection of minors the site http://menores.gov.ar (developed in the framework of the Ministry of External Relations and Worship) contains abundant legislation and information, although it focuses more on being a site with international information for Argentinians than vice-versa. The jurisprudence of the Supreme Court of Justice is very easily accessible at www.csjn.gov.ar. Regrettably, the regulatory information and Argentinian jurisprudence contained in these sites is only available in Spanish.

The Central Authorities in matters of returning children (Ministry of External Relations and Worship) and in legal cooperation in general including maintenance obligations (Ministry of Justice and Human Rights) generally work satisfactorily and offer information in these areas for free. The requests for information received through Argentinian embassies or directly from individuals are channeled to the respective Central Authorities in each one of those ministries. The themes of these consultations are: nationality, falsification of public documents, prosecution of

[85] See R.J. Saucedo, "Visión panorámica de los documentos notariales extranjeros desde la República Argentina, con especial referencia a su fuerza probatoria,", in N.D. Lamber (ed.), *Consejo Federal del Notariado Argentino- Ponencia y fundamentos presentados: Circulación e inscripción de documentos provenientes del extranjero, Jornada Notarial Iberoamericana* (2006) 27–68.

[86] The 2014 Civil and Commercial Code includes a chapter on the so-called "arbitration contract" which intended to modernize Argentinian arbitral law. However, due to some last-minute changes in this chapter doubts about the success of the new rules have arisen. See D.P. Fernández Arroyo & E.H. Vetulli, "The New Argentinian Arbitration Law: A Train in an Unknown Direction?", *Arbitration International* 32 (2016) 349–372.

members of the judiciary and/or of armed forces, donations to philanthropic entities, operation of charities, possession of weapons by accredited embassy security personnel, penalties of community service, family law, procedures for accreditors in bankruptcy, reciprocity, jurisdictional immunity, etc.

B. Judicial Networks

Argentina has a Judge who is part of the International Hague Network of Judges that can provide information about Argentinian law in maters of family and youth.[87] There is a network of national judges and a liaison judge within the framework of the 1980 Hague Convention on International Child Abduction. The network of national judges keeps in contact with other judges of the network and with other networks of judges of foreign countries with the goal of understanding the functioning of the Convention in each country and how foreign law is applied there.

The Iberian-American Network of International Legal Cooperation (IberRed)[88] is a structure formed by Central Authorities and by points of contact proceeding from the Ministries of Justice and other judiciary authorities of the 22 countries that make up the Iberian-American Community of Nations, as well as by the Supreme Court of Puerto Rico. IberRed is dedicated to optimizing tools of civil and criminal judicial assistance, and to strengthening of the bonds of cooperation among the countries. IberRed was founded in October 2004 and is characterized as a purely Iberian-American forum with representatives of all the authorities with competence in matters of judicial cooperation. The Points of Contact are people designated by the Ministries of Justice, Public Prosecution and by the judicial organs of Iberian-American Countries. These designated persons (judges, prosecutors, and employees of the Ministry of Justice) are those that put into effect the operative actions of the Network.

In criminal matters, it is worth mentioning, within the Inter-American sphere, the Hemispheric Network of Criminal Cooperation of the Organization of American States (OAS) that connects predetermined points of contact using a secured, encrypted email system called GROOVE that permits the exchange of information.

Inspired by this latest initiative, the Network of Hemispheric Legal Cooperation in Matters of Family and Youth Law of the OAS[89] is also operating and using this same GROOVE email system. This Network is framed within the context of the Meetings of Ministers of Justice of the Americas (REMJA). Based on four inter-American conventions on international family law concluded by the OAS and with special emphasis on the rights of children, the Network facilitates access to the inter-American system of protection of the family and youth and promotes international cooperation in that area. The Network is made up of three components: a public website, a private website, and a system of secure electronic communications.

---

[87] See www.hcch.net/upload/haguenetwork.pdf

[88] See www.iberred.org

[89] See http://www.oas.org/dil/esp/derecho_de_familia.htm

VI. Access to Foreign Law: Further Developments

Mechanisms of access and application of foreign law can always be improved to benefit the legal and administrative authorities but also for all of their users, professionals or not. The creation, for example, of databases that systematize access to foreign legislation in a flexible and orderly way, as well as standardized forms, would facilitate the work of the operators who work directly or indirectly with these rules and who are confronted daily with the challenge of resolving situations with foreign elements. An instrument with these characteristics would facilitate the understanding of foreign law and would provide suitable channels to make the processing of international cooperation simpler. The information could be provided by organs or authorities with competence in the matters about which the information is solicited. Going beyond that, the basic elements established by The Hague Conference on PIL for the development of an instrument of access to foreign law becomes, in our opinion, totally relevant. The conventions in force are applied (some more than others) but are conceived for a world very different from the present. The communications revolution and the exponential growth of exchanges call for another type of response.

As for that relating to our country, the possibility of providing access to Argentinian legislation and jurisprudence in other languages (at least in English) would be very valuable. In this sense, translations of the new Civil and Commercial Code into English and into French are being prepared.

Uruguay: Proof of and Information About Foreign Law in Uruguay

Cecilia Fresnedo de Aguirre

Abstract This national report covers the following topics: First, the nature of conflict of laws rules and its mandatory application in court proceedings are analysed in light of the statutory rules and conventions that are in force in Uruguay. Second, treatment of foreign law before judicial authorities is addressed, which comprises an analysis of the nature of foreign law, the ascertainment of foreign law, as well as the interpretation and application of foreign law including the case of non-ascertainment of foreign law. Third, the judicial review as to the application of conflicts rules and foreign law is examined. Fourth, treatment of foreign law in other instances is scrutinized as to the administrative authorities and other non-judicial instances including arbitration, mediation and other alternative dispute resolution, as well as in attorneys and other professional's work. Fifth, the status quo on access to foreign law is analysed in view of information on foreign law available in Uruguay, as well as the mechanism of the international and regional instruments on proof of and information of foreign law in force in Uruguay and the international and regional settings to facilitate access to foreign law. Sixth, further developments in access to foreign law are envisaged by indicating practical needs and addressing conflict of laws solutions and methods of facilitating access to foreign law.

I. Conflict of Laws Rules

In Uruguay the application of conflict of laws rules is mandatory under Article 23 of the Constitution, which states that judges are liable for not applying what the law states. This is a general provision that includes all legal rules, including conflict of

The author wants to thank her colleagues Professors Eduardo Tellechea Bergman, Adriana Fernández Pereiro and Daniel Trecca, from the Uruguayan Central Authority, for some information they kindly provided me to complete this national report, and Professor Laura Capalbo for having read the whole paper before I handle it.

C. Fresnedo de Aguirre (✉)
Professor, University of the Republic, Montevideo, Uruguay
e-mail: ceciliafresnedo@gmail.com

Y. Nishitani (ed.), *Treatment of Foreign Law - Dynamics towards Convergence?*,
Ius Comparatum – Global Studies in Comparative Law 26,
DOI 10.1007/978-3-319-56574-3_22

laws rules. Article 524 of the Uruguayan General Code of Procedure states that in the absence of treaties or conventions, the Uruguayan courts shall apply the rules in Title X –International Procedural Rules- of this Code. This solution was taken from Article 1.1 of the 1979 Inter-American Convention on General Rules of Private international Law,[1] which states that "In the absence of an international rule, the States Parties shall apply the conflict rules of their domestic law". Uruguay is also a State Party to both, 1969 and 1986 Vienna Conventions on the Law of Treaties, whose Articles 27 state that "A party may not invoke the provisions of its internal law as justification for its failure to perform a treaty".

Uruguayan conflict of laws rules lead to the application of foreign law relatively frequently. The general basis of international jurisdiction is the so called Asser criterion, which states that the judges of the State whose law governs international juridical relationships are competent to hear matters arising out of those relationships (Art. 2401 of the Uruguayan Civil Code and Art. 56.1 of both, 1889 and 1940 Montevideo Treaties on International Civil Law, among others). Thus, whenever this is the basis of jurisdiction, the judge will apply his own law. However, there are other bases of jurisdiction, like that of the defendant's domicile, at the plaintiff's choice, when the action is of a personal-patrimonial nature (Art. 2401*in fine* of the Uruguayan Civil Code). When the latter is the basis of jurisdiction, the law applicable can be a foreign law if the conflict of laws rule so indicates.

In practice, the law of the following States is often applied before Uruguayan courts: Argentina, Brazil, Paraguay, Chile, Bolivia, Peru, Mexico, United States, Canada, Germany, Spain, Italy, France, Switzerland, and China. Exceptionally, Turkey, Namibia, India.

II. Foreign Law Before Judicial Authorities

A. *Nature of Foreign Law*

As far as the nature of foreign law is concerned, it has always been considered as "law" in Uruguay. Article 2 of the Additional Protocol to the 1889 Montevideo Treaties states that the application of foreign law must be made *ex officio* by the judge, without prejudice of the parties' being able to plead and prove the existence and content of the law invoked. That formula was kept identically in Article 2 of the Additional Protocol to the 1940 Montevideo Treaties. Article 2 of the 1979 Inter-American Convention on General Rules of Private International Law states that "Judges and authorities of the States Parties shall enforce the foreign law in the same way as it would be enforced by the judges of the State whose law is applicable, without prejudice to the parties' being able to plead and prove the existence and content of the foreign law invoked." The same latter formula was enshrined in the

[1] CIDIP-II, Montevideo. It was approved in Uruguay by Act N° 14.953, December 18, 1979.

1980 Bilateral Uruguayan-Argentinean Convention on Application and Information of Foreign Law.[2] Article 525.3 of the Uruguayan General Code of Procedure states basically the same as the two latter aforementioned rules.

As a consequence of the nature of foreign law as "law" in Uruguay, where it is considered as "law", it is applied *ex officio* since 1889. This is stated by the national and international private international law rules enumerated in the previous paragraph. However, parties must base their claims on the applicable law, and when that law is a foreign law, they usually invoke it. If they do not, the judge must apply it anyway and therefore find it out.

B. Ascertainment of Foreign Law

As for the ascertainment of Foreign Law, the parties are entitled to prove the content of foreign law, but they are not obliged to. The judge must apply foreign law when conflict of laws rules state so, no matter what the parties' attitude is. Even when the parties invoke and prove foreign law, the judge is free to find out by himself or through the mechanisms provided to him all about foreign law, its text, the validity, meaning and legal scope. The "*iura novit curia*" principle applies but with a different scope that regarding domestic law: it is *a posteriori* and specifically referred to the issues of the case. In other words, it is not supposed that the judge knows the content of all foreign laws but that he finds out about it in the given case and only regarding the specific issues of the case.

As for the method of the ascertainment of foreign law, documents and Internet sources are used. Assistance of the parties and expert witnesses may be used in Uruguay to ascertain foreign law. Furthermore, inquiry to an expert or expert institute, domestic or foreign judicial and/or non-judicial authorities, via bilateral or multilateral treaties for access to legal information, as well as direct communication of judges is used as well. Article 3 of the 1979 Inter-American Convention on proof and information on foreign law specifically admit "any of the suitable means of proof contemplated in both the law of the State of origin and the law of the State of destination". It adds that "For the purpose of this Convention, suitable means shall include the following: (a) Documentary proof consisting of certified copies of legal texts together with an indication of their validity, or judicial precedents; (b) Expert testimony, consisting of opinions of attorneys of experts on the matter; (c) The reports of the State of destination on the text, validity, meaning and scope of its law on specific points". As for "direct communication of judges", it is considered that judges are experts on their own law, so this means is included in item (b) of Article 3 of the Convention. Besides, the list in Article 3 is not strict but merely enumerative. The individuals or institutions that provide legal information must be experts, no matter whether they are public authorities, like judges or legal advisors at the Central Authority, or private experts, like professors or specialized practitioners.

[2]Approved in Uruguay by Act N° 15.109, 17/03/1981.

As for Uruguayan case-law, in "*La Mannheim v. C.O.S.C.O*" (Xiang –Cheng vessel)[3] the Uruguayan courts had international jurisdiction on the defendant's domicile basis (Art. 2401 of the Civil Code), but the law applicable was that of China –place of performance of the contract- under Article 2399 of the Civil Code. Under Article 525.3 of the General Procedure Code, the courts shall enforce the foreign law in the same way as it would be enforced by the judges of the State to which the referred rule of law belongs. Chinese law was ascertained using authenticated legal documents and experts opinions, and other documents and informations provided by the parties.[4] Neither the judge nor the court of appeals asked the Central Authority for information on Chinese law. It must be said that this was not the first case on the matter. In "*La Mannheim v. Uniglory Marine Corp.*" (Uniforward vessel)[5] the case was similar to the aforementioned: the Uruguayan courts had international jurisdiction on the defendant's domicile basis (Art. 2401 of the Civil Code), but the law applicable was that of China – place of performance of the contract- under Article 2399 of the Civil Code. The 1993 Chinese Maritime Law Code was applicable. The Uruguayan court considered that the clause stating limits of liability included in the printed general conditions on the back of the bill of lading was null under the referred Chinese Code, which states minimum limits of liability that cannot be reduced by ship-owners through printed stipulations included in bills of lading. Those low limits were even lower than those in the Paramount clause referring to the 1924 Brussels Convention.

There are several other cases where the Uruguayan judges apply a foreign law because it is the law of the place of performance of the maritime carriage of goods contract (Art. 2399 of the Civil Code): in "*Royal Insurance Int. Ltd. v. Flota Mercante del Estado*" *(Río Negro vessel)*, the Juzgado Letrado de Primera Instancia en lo Civil 14° (First Instance Civil Law Court), judgment N° 21, 26/02/92 (Salvo), *Revista de Transporte y Seguros* N° 11, case 192, the applicable law was that of Paraguay, under Article 26 of the 1940 Montevideo Treaty on International Commercial Navigation Law (law of the place of unloading). In "*SAFE Namibia v. Hermosa Trading y otros*" *(Pescatero Vessel)*, the Juzgado Letrado de Primera Instancia en lo Civil 10° (First Instance Civil Law Court), judgment N° 38, 27/05/03 (Alonso Flumini), consented, *Revista de Transporte y Seguros* N° 17, case 355, the applicable law was that of Namibia, particularly its Admiralty Law N° 105 (Art.

---

[3] Juzgado Letrado de Primera Instancia en lo Civil 17° (First Instance Civil Law Court), judgment N° 42, 24/10/94 (Sosa), confirmed by the Tribunal de Apelaciones Civil 3° (Civil Court of Appeals), judgment N° 8, 12/2/96 (Peri Valdez, Chalar, Ruibal Pino), *Revista de Transporte y Seguros* N° 10, case 186.

[4] The case was much more complicated because the contract contained a choice of law clause choosing the 1924 Brussels Convention on Bills of Lading as the applicable law. This clause was validated by Uruguayan judges under Chinese law.

[5] Juzgado Letrado de Primera Instancia en lo Civil 1° (First Instance Civil Law Court), judgment N° 8, 4/04/97 (Simón), revoked by the Tribunal de Apelaciones Civil 3° (Civil Court of Appeals), judgment N° 171, 15/09/99 (Minvielle, Klett, Chalar), *Revista de Transporte y Seguros* N° 13, case 257.

1.m, s and ee), of September 8, 1983, amended by the Law of Amendment of Admiralty Jurisdiction N° 87, 1992, Law of Amendment of General Law N° 129, 1992, and Law N1 94, 1996, of Shipwreck and Rescue. In "*Guardian Royal Exchange Assurance v. Zim Israel Navigation Co." (Zim Brasil Vessel)*, the Juzgado Letrado de Primera Instancia en lo Civil 10° (First Instance Civil Law Court), judgment N° 1256, 06/06/96 (Morales), confirmed by the Tribunal de Apelaciones Civil 3° (Civil Court of Appeals), judgment N° 81, 11/06/97 (Bossio, Olagüe, Hounie) *Revista de Transporte y Seguros* N° 11, case 191, the State of the place of performance was Turkey and therefore its law was applicable under Article 2399 of the Civil Code. In "*Pramsur S.A. y otro v. Transporte Fluvial Paraguayo S.A. y otro – Daños y Perjuicios – Casación*", the Uruguayan Supreme Court of Justice, judgment N° 281, 26/06/09, *Revista de Transporte y Seguros* N° 23, case 490, the applicable law was that of Paraguay under Articles 25–27 of the Montevideo Treaty on International Commercial Navigation Law (law of the place of unloading).

In "*Sun Alliance Insurance Uruguay S.A. v. Nedlloyd Lines*" (Nedlloyd Cristóbal Vessel), the Juzgado Letrado de Primera Instancia en lo Civil 2° (First Instance Civil Law Court), judgment N° 23, 11/09/98 (Castro), confirmed by the Tribunal de Apelaciones Civil 5° (Civil Court of Appeals), judgment N° 175, 03/09/99 (Van Rompaey, Rochón, Harriague), *Revista de Transporte y Seguros* N° 13, case 241, the applicable law was that of Mexico under Article 2399 of the Civil Code (law of the place of performance). The judge and the court of appeals considered that the Hague-Visby Rules (1924 Brussels Convention and the 1968 Visby Protocol) were applicable and not the domestic Mexican rules (Mexican Navigation Law of December 23, 1993), because of the international character of the relationship (an international carriage of goods contract). The Hague-Visby Rules were in force in Mexico since August 25, 1994, and these were the specific rules on the matter.

In "*Empress International Ltd. c/Latinka S.A y otros*",[6] the Uruguayan Supreme Court of Justice accepted as sufficient, within an *exequatur* process, the affidavit of the plaintiff's lawyer in the USA, duly notarized, stating that the defendants were duly notified under the laws of the State where the verdict was issued, that the due defence of the parties was guaranteed and that the verdicts could not be appealed under the law of the State of New York because there was *res judicata*. The Court based its decision on the fact that the plaintiff proved that it was impossible for him to obtain documentary proof from the USA court stating the *res judicata* because under their law they cannot issue such a document. In "*Fisher c/Consulado General del Uruguay*",[7] in "*ABN AMRO BANK N.V. (n. York) c/Wishaw Trading S.A.*"[8] and in "*Agrenco Madeira Comercio Internacional Ltda. c/Fuentesauco S.A y otro,*

[6] Supreme Court of Justice, judgment N° 610/2008, 18/08/2008, www.bjn.poderjudicial.gub.uy/BJNPUBLICA/hojaInsumo2.seam?cid=18733

[7] Supreme Court of Justice, judgment N° 369/2012, 15/02/2012, http://bjn.poderjudicial.gub.uy/BJNPUBLICA/seam/docstore/document.seam?docId=9&cid=7

[8] Supreme Court of Justice, judgment N° 136/2006, 21/08/2006, http://bjn.poderjudicial.gub.uy/BJNPUBLICA/hojaInsumo2.seam?cid=7

Exequatur de Laudo Arbitral",[9] the Supreme Court also accepted an affidavit to prove foreign law.

In "*Corazzi c/Jaspe*",[10] the Uruguayan Court of Appeals reaffirmed that the *iura novit curia* principle was in force both for domestic and foreign law under Articles 198, 143 and 525.3 of the Uruguayan General Procedure Code.[11] That is why the judge must investigate the applicable law no matter whether the parties have invoked it or not. In this case, the applicable law was the Italian one, specifically Article 2946 of the Italian Civil Code. The Court stated that the judge is not obliged to follow any special legal procedure to find out foreign law. Therefore, any means to do that is valid and acceptable.

In "*Royal Sun Aliance c/Costa Containers*",[12] the Uruguayan Court of Appeals accepted the information on foreign law filed by the parties. The applicable law was that of Mexico. In this and other maritime cases the parties usually file a printed version of the information on foreign law in the website of well-known sites, like that of the International Maritime Committee (CMI) and the Ibero-American Institute of Maritime Law (IIDM), and judges accept it. They can always check by themselves in the website to corroborate the information provided by the parties.

In "Fiscalía *Letrada Nacional en lo Civil de 3° Turno c/Ministerio de Educación y Cultura, Acción de Inconstitucionalidad*", the Supreme Court of Justice stated that applicable law –either domestic or foreign- does not require proof; on the contrary, both the court and the parties can make use of any legitimate procedure to evidence it.[13]

As far as the effects of the provided legal information are concerned, it is not binding upon judges, who maintain their technical independence to decide which information is more accurate. This is expressly stated in Article 6.3 of the 1979 Inter-American Convention on proof and information on foreign law: "The State that receives the reports referred to in Article 3.c. shall not be required to apply the law, or cause it to be applied, in accordance with the content of the reply received." The judge must evaluate the information received by all means of proof and information and decide according to his technical and independent criterion.

There is no mechanism to examine the reliability of the provided legal information. When the information is provided by the Central Authority, it is official and signed by the law professional in charge of the Central Authority and his law profes-

[9] Supreme Court of Justice, judgment N° 791/2012, 07/09/2012, http://bjn.poderjudicial.gub.uy/BJNPUBLICA/hojaInsumo2.seam?cid=21

[10] Civil Court of Appeals 6° (Tribunal de Apelaciones en lo Civil de 6° Turno), judgment N° 99/2008, 30/04/2008, www.bjn.poderjudicial.gub.uy/BJNPUBLICA/hojaInsumo2.seam?cid=18733

[11] www.parlamento.gub.uy

[12] Civil Court of Appeals 6° (Tribunal de Apelaciones en lo Civil de 6° Turno), judgment N° 297/2009, 02/11/2009, www.bjn.poderjudicial.gub.uy/BJNPUBLICA/hojaInsumo2.seam?cid=18733

[13] Supreme Court of Justice, judgment N° 1520/2013, 21/08/2013, http://bjn.poderjudicial.gub.uy/BJNPUBLICA/hojaInsumo2.seam?cid=21

sional assistants. This makes the information reliable, at least in principle. The judge or a non-judicial authority requiring the information can check it through other means of information, like internet or libraries.

In Uruguay it is the State that bears the costs of ascertaining foreign law, through the Central Authority and the law professionals that are in charge of that public organism. When necessary, the Central Authority asks for collaboration to the universities –either public or private ones- and the professors produce reports in that connection. They do it for free, or better, as part of their tasks at the university. Under Uruguayan law[14] the Central Authority bears among its commitments to answer questions coming from foreign competent organisms about Uruguayan domestic or private international law, as well as those coming from national public organisms about Uruguayan private international law of a foreign law.

However, only judicial or some non-judicial authorities have direct access to the Central Authority to ask for information on foreign law. Private parties, lawyers, notary publics and other legal operators have no direct access in that connection. In these latter cases the only means available to ascertain foreign law are private ones, which usually have a cost that must be borne by the interested private parties. Private parties can only ask the Central Authority indirectly, through judges, but that is possible only within a process in course, not when negotiating a contract or any other non-judicial context.

The access to foreign law is sometimes difficult in family law cases, particularly when there is no procedure yet and private parties have no economic means to afford alternatives to the Central Authority in finding information on foreign law.

The Inter-American Convention on Proof of and Information on Foreign Law works well when Central Authorities are well organized and count on technically good prepared employees, but it is not enough, mainly because of its regional character. A universal instrument of the kind would be very useful.

It would be very important to make use of new technologies to facilitate access to foreign law, like for example, providing such information in the web site of serious and recognized institution like the Hague Conference on Private International Law, at the global level, and the Organization of American States, at the regional one. Each country should provide information on its law and update it when necessary, through their Central Authorities, Ministries of Foreign Affairs, Universities, Bar Associations, or others.

It would help to facilitate access to foreign law, both in judicial and non-judicial scenarios, to have a specialized on line directory[15] of free access providing information on foreign legal professionals, experts and specialized institutions which can provide information on foreign law in a secure and controlled way.

[14] Decree 95/96 of March 12, 1996, amending Decree 407/1985, article 4.a)

[15] This was proposed in the Questionnaire sent by Ignacio Goicoechea regarding the subjects of the future works of the Hague Conference on Private International Law (HCCH), to be discussed in the ASADIP Meeting of November 24 and 25, 2011, in San José, Costa Rica.

C. Interpretation and Application of Foreign Law

In Uruguay, under Article 2 of the 1979 Inter-American Convention on General Rules of Private International Law, "Judges and authorities of the States Parties shall enforce the foreign law in the same way as it would be enforced by the judges of the State whose law is applicable, without prejudice to the parties' being able to plead and prove the existence and content of the foreign law invoked." The same latter formula can be found in the 1980 Bilateral Uruguayan-Argentinean Convention on Application and Information of Foreign Law and in Article 525.3 of the Uruguayan General Code of Procedure, which states basically the same as the two latter aforementioned rules. What before 1979 was a possibility for the judge becomes an obligation for him with the inclusion of the expression "in the same way as it would be enforced by the judges of the State whose law is applicable". This is not casual, but aims at a very specific target: that the judge does not change the foreign law indicated by the conflict of laws rule. It reduces the margin of manoeuvring of the judge, though without transforming him in an automaton that must apply foreign law in a mechanical way. As it was said before, Article 6.3 of the 1979 Inter-American Convention on Proof and Information of Foreign Law safeguards his independence.

All the aforementioned rules imply the obligation for the judge to take into account not only the text of the foreign law, but also the case law showing how it is applied in the State of origin. The judge must interpret foreign law under the principles of the legal system to which it belongs, and not to those of the forum.

However, this rule of interpretation has not an absolute character, since when in the State of origin there is more than one interpretation, the judge may choose the one he considers more adequate. Another example of relaxation of the general rule could be when there is an evident mistake in the foreign case-law.

Though there is no specific rule in Uruguay –neither conventional nor national- on the way to fill up gaps in foreign law, certain criteria stated in national and conventional rules must be followed. The main one is that judges "shall enforce the foreign law in the same way as it would be enforced by the judges of the State whose law is applicable". Thus, they should find out how these latter judges would fill the gap and do the same. It would be part of the information they will have to obtain about foreign law.

D. Failure to Establish Foreign Law

In Uruguay, cases when foreign law cannot be ascertained are quite exceptional. When that occurs, the most frequent solution is the application of the *lex fori*.

Under Article 15 of Uruguayan Civil Code the judge cannot stop rendering a judgment because of the silence, obscurity or insufficiency of the law. Therefore, he must find a solution, and though not perfect, the most practical solution is to apply his *lex fori*. Its main advantage is to ensure a uniform and foreseeable procedure in cases where foreign law cannot be ascertained. Its disadvantage is that it disobeys the mandate of the conflict of laws rule. However, the later disadvantage is common to all the other possibilities, like rejecting the claim for lack of proof of the foreign law, the application of another foreign law or the application of those legal principles that are common to civilized countries.[16]

III. Judicial Review

The parties can appeal to all courts including the Supreme Court if they consider that the judge has wrongly interpreted or applied any law, no matter whether it is a domestic law, a conflict of laws rule –either national or international- or a foreign law indicated by the latter. This is stated in Article 3 of both 1889 and 1940 Additional Protocols to the Montevideo Treaties, in Article 4 of the 1979 Inter-American Convention on General Rules of Private International Law, in Article 2 of the Bilateral Argentinean-Uruguayan Convention on Application and Information of Foreign Law and in Article 525.4 of the Uruguayan General Code of Procedure.

The conditions of access to the courts are those established in the procedural law of the State of the forum, since they are generic for any infraction to a rule of law, no matter its national or foreign character.[17]

The background ideas and policy considerations of this solution is to uniform and ensure a correct application of the law, which cannot be limited to domestic law but must include all rules of law, even foreign ones, which must be not only applied but applied correctly.

IV. Foreign Law in Other Instances

A. Administrative and Other Non-judicial Authorities

In Uruguay it occurs quite frequently that non-judicial authorities must apply foreign law. For example, the public officers of the Registry of Legal Statute apply foreign law to control divorce foreign judgments when a person who has obtained his divorce abroad wants to get married in Uruguay. He must file the foreign judgment in due form to prove his legal statute and thus be able to marry again. It is the public officers of the Registry of Legal Statue or its director who must control the foreign judgment under the foreign law. They can ask for information on the latter to the Central Authority (Decree N° 454/1996).

[16] ZAJTAY, Imre, "Le traitement du droit étranger dans le procès civil. Étude de droit comparé", *Rivista di diritto internazionale privato e processuale*, 1968, N° 2, pp. 269–270.

[17] See articles 241 to 292 of the Uruguayan General Code of Procedure.

Other non-judicial public authorities, like the Uruguayan Mortgage Bank (*Banco Hipotecario del Uruguay*) must ascertain the patrimonial legal regime of a married couple with their first matrimonial domicile abroad when the latter applies for a loan. They can ask for information on foreign law to the Central Authority (Decree N° 95–96/1996, amending Decree 407/1985).

Notary publics also apply foreign law to ascertain the patrimonial legal regime of a married couple with their first matrimonial domicile abroad, or the validity of a power of attorney issued abroad, or other documents, for different purposes.

In addition to the grounds mentioned above, non-judicial authorities are entitled to ask through the Central Authorities information on foreign law by means of documentary proof and expert testimony, under Article 3 (a) and (b), though not by means of (c), which is reserved to judges and courts (Art. 4), of the 1979 Inter-American Convention on Proof and Information of Foreign Law.

Notary publics, as well as lawyers and other interested individuals must find out for themselves the text, validity, meaning and legal scope of the applicable foreign law. However, if they are acting in the judicial sphere, they can ask the judge of the case to ask the Central Authority for information on foreign law. They can always resort to all available private means to get the necessary information on foreign law.

B. Foreign Law in Arbitration, Mediation and Other Alternative Dispute Resolution

In arbitration it is the arbitral tribunal or single arbiter who ascertains foreign law, with or without the parties' help, as any individual who is a law professional would do.

C. Foreign Law in Attorneys and Other Law Professional's Work

As it was said before, it is the professional who finds out the information regarding foreign law. He does it through internet, libraries, correspondents in the State whose law they must ascertain, among other means available. It occurs even more frequently that in the judicial sphere. The same occurs in some academic studies and research projects where the ascertainment of foreign law is needed.

V. Access to Foreign Law: Status Quo

A. Information on Foreign Law Available in Uruguay

There are some official web sites which offer free information on Uruguayan law, mainly that one of the Uruguayan Parliament: www.parlamento.gub.uy, and www.impo.com.uy

Uruguayan case-law can be found, for free, in www.bjn.poderjudicial.gub.uy

The Hague Judicial Network is available in Uruguay for the judge to directly communicate with a foreign judge to obtain legal information at http://www.hcch.net/index_en.php?act=text.display&tid=21. The Hague 1996 Convention on Jurisdiction, Applicable Law, Recognition, Enforcement and Cooperation in Respect of Parental Responsibility and Measures for the Protection of Children has recently entered into force in Uruguay and we can foresee that judicial communications may be probably developed regarding this Convention as well.

B. International and Regional Instruments on Proof of and Information of Foreign Law in Force in Uruguay

Uruguay is a State Party to the Inter-American Convention of 8 May 1979 on Proof of and Information on Foreign Law ("Montevideo Convention")which was approved by Act N° 14.953 of November 12, 1979; to the Additional Protocol to the 1889 Montevideo Treaties, approved by Act N° 2.207 of October 3, 1892 (Art. 2, 3 and 5); to the Additional Protocol to the 1940 Montevideo Treaties, approved by Act N° 10.272 of November 12, 1942 (Art. 2, 3 and 6); to the United Nations Convention on the recovery abroad of maintenance of June 20, 1956, approved by Act N° 16.477 of May 4, 1994 (Art. 4); to the Inter-American Convention on General Rules of Private International Law, Montevideo, CIDIP-II, 1979, approved by Act N° 14.953 of November 12, 1979 (Art. 2); to the Inter-American Convention on the International Return of Children, Montevideo, CIDIP-IV, 1989, approved by Act N° 17.335 of May 17, 2001 (Art. 9.1.c); to the Mercosur Protocol on Jurisdictional Cooperation and Assistance in Civil, Commercial, Labor and Administrative Matters, Decision CMC 05/1992, approved by Act 16.971 of June 5, 1998 (Art. 28–30); to the Bilateral Convention on Judicial Cooperation in Civil and Commercial Matters between the Oriental Republic of Uruguay and the French Republic, approved by Act N° 17.110 of May 12, 1999 (Art. 25) and to the Bilateral Convention on Legal Cooperation between the Oriental Republic of Uruguay and the Kingdom of Spain, approved by Act. 16.864 of September 10, 1997 (Art. 27).

There are also two bilateral agreements, with the Republic of Argentina and with the Federal Republic of Brazil, but they have been substituted by the Inter-American and Mercosur Conventions.

Uruguay is not a State Party neither to the European Convention of 7 June 1968 on Information on Foreign Law ("London Convention") or to the Convention of 22 January 1993 on Legal Assistance and Legal Relations in Civil, Family and Criminal Matters ("Minsk Convention).

C. International and Regional Settings to Facilitate Access to Foreign Law in Uruguay

In Uruguay there is the Ibero-American Web –IBERRED-, which includes Ministries of Justice or equivalents, Justice Departments or Attorneys General Offices and Judiciaries of Ibero-American countries. Each country designates a contact in each one of those organisms, differentiated by subject. Informal requests have been handled by this way, which enabled access to foreign law.

There is also the web site of the Organization of American States, where access to different areas of the laws of its Member States is available: for criminal law: http://www.oas.org/juridico/mla/sp/index.html; for family law: http://www.oas.org/dil/esp/derecho_de_familia.htm.

In fact and as surprising as it may be, these international/regional instruments are seldom used. There are no statistics.

However, when they are used they work reasonably well.

VI. Access to Foreign Law: Further Developments

A. Practical Need

Although, as I stated before, things work reasonably well in Uruguay, they can always been improved, mainly regarding private legal operators, like arbitrators, attorneys, notaries, and parties, particularly when the amount of the case does not enable to hire a foreign legal correspondent. This is due to the fact that, as it was said before, private legal operators and private parties have no direct access to the Central Authority. Moreover, outside the judicial sphere, they have no access at all to it.

Access to foreign law is needed in Uruguay in the context of international relocation, before doing business abroad, when it comes to the execution of a will, to contractual negotiations and also in the course of both arbitration and litigation.

I dare say that in family law is most needed in Uruguay, because there are many cases in this area where people and their lawyers cannot afford paying for a foreign correspondent to issue a report on the applicable foreign law. However, as it was explained before, when the process is already installed, they can ask the judge to request information on the foreign law to the Central Authority, and that is for free, because it is the State that covers the expenses of the Central Authority's functioning.

B. Conflict of Laws Solutions

I think that Uruguayan conflict of laws rules must be modified and updated in some aspects, but not to reduce the number of cases in which foreign law is applicable. Uruguayan courts have traditionally –since 1889- applied foreign law when their conflict of laws rules so indicate and this has caused no big trouble.

Uruguayan conflict of laws rules are mainly systematized in the Appendix of the Civil Code (Art. 2393 to 2404). There is a Draft General Act of Private International Law which is not yet in force, updating several solutions but not tending to reduce the number of cases in which foreign law is applied.

In my view, the treatment of foreign law in Uruguay should not be changed, and this is the general position of Uruguayan experts. This dates back to the nineteenth century, as above indicated. Doctrinal support can be found in: Opertti Badán, Didier, "*Exhortos y embargos de bienes en el extranjero*", Montevideo, Amalio Fernández, 1976; Opertti Badán, Didier, *Actas y Documentos, Segunda Conferencia Especializada Interamericana sobre Derecho Internacional Privado*, OEA, 1979; Ramírez, Gonzalo, *Proyecto de Código de Derecho Internacional Privado y su Comentario*, Buenos Aires, Ed. Félix Lajouane, 1888; Solari Barrandeguy, Marcelo, "El derecho extranjero y su tratamiento procesal en el sistema de derecho internacional privado uruguayo", *Revista Uruguaya de Derecho Internacional* N° 4, 1975–1976, pp. 285–305; Tellechea Bergman, Eduardo, "*Aplicación, tratamiento e información del derecho extranjero y su regulación en nuestro derecho internacional privado de fuente convencional y nacional*", en Derecho Internacional Privado y Derecho Procesal Internacional, Ed. Amalio M. Fernández, 1982; Tellechea Bergman, Eduardo, "Aplicación e información del derecho extranjero a nivel interamericano y especialmente uruguayo", *Derecho internacional privado – derecho de la libertad y el respeto mutuo – Biblioteca de derecho de la globalización*, CEDEP/ASADIP, Asunción, 2010, pp. 269–299; Tellechea Bergman, Eduardo, *Derecho Internacional Privado. Cooperación jurisdiccional internacional, Litigante ajeno al foro, Documentación extranjera, Aplicación del Derecho Extranjero, Proceso y prueba*, Montevideo, La Ley Uruguay, 2010, pp. 167–202; Fresnedo de Aguirre, Cecilia, *Curso de Derecho Internacional Privado*, T. I, Parte General, 2ª ed., Montevideo, FCU, 2004.

Without prejudice to the Uruguayan situation in this connection, I think a universal instrument, which does not exist, would be useful to overcome the inconveniences derived from the lack of a linking instrument with several non-regional States. From the regional and Uruguayan point of view, I think we have enough instruments. Notwithstanding, perhaps some aspects of them could be improved or complemented.

C. Methods of Facilitating Access to Foreign Law

In my opinion, international and regional instruments that establish administrative and judicial cooperation to exchange information on participating States' law are very useful tools to facilitate access to foreign law. If such international instruments were open not only to judicial authorities but also to individuals and any other authorities, that would be an improvement in comparison with the existing instruments.

In my view, the Uruguayan Central Authority works very well and is a guarantee for those who use their services. However, every possibility to enable access to foreign law should be encouraged; therefore, direct communication between authorities could be admitted and considered an improvement.

The risk of these direct communications could be the lack of uniformity of the information rendered by each authority. To minimize those risks, a new regulation could create "Legal Information Banks" and organize its bringing into operation by the States. The information could be obtained through direct legal communications or Central Authorities.

The answer provided by the requested State should not be binding, as it was stated in Article 6 of the Inter-American Convention on proof of and information on foreign law, because otherwise the technical independence of judges would be in jeopardy.

Regarding the advisability of providing services on legal information with or without costs, I think that it depends on what kind of services it is about. There are always private means of getting information on foreign law which have costs, but public services for judicial and non-judicial authorities should remain being provided by Central Authorities without costs, as it is now in Uruguay. The costs of the Central Authority are supported by the State, which means by all of us through taxes.

It would be very useful if each State could have a web site with free and public information on its laws and case-law available for everyone.

In addition, there could be other feasible methods of facilitating access to foreign law worldwide and to everybody, like enhancing direct communication of judges; establishing networks for other legal professionals (*e.g.*, law firms); identifying qualified experts or expert institutes (*e.g.*, creating a list of experts); and providing information on national laws on the Internet.

As for direct communication between judicial authorities, it should be taken into account that they are usually overburden with work, which makes unlikely that they could have time to answer requests of information from their foreign colleagues. Therefore, in my opinion it would be better to enhance, improve and facilitate the official system of information through Central Authorities. The Legal Information Banks could be useful instruments in that connection.

Venezuela: Finding Foreign Law in Venezuela. General Overview

Eugenio Hernández-Bretón and Claudia Madrid Martínez

Abstract In Venezuela, foreign law is determined and applied ex officio. This is the rule contained in international treaties in force (i.e., Bustamante Code and in Inter American treaties) and in domestic law. In practice, however, parties do much of the work. Courts and litigants research foreign law on the Internet, but courts are not bound by their findings or the parties' submissions on foreign law. Affidavits on foreign law are also common practice. The incorrect application of foreign law is subject to appeal even before the Supreme Court of Justice. There is no reported experience of courts or parties requesting international cooperation for obtaining information on foreign law. Costs incurred in finding foreign law are to be borne by the interested party, with the expectation of recovery of judicial costs if successful in litigation. Costs incurred by the courts in such a process are not borne by the litigants. Venezuelan courts are now more aware of their duties when applying foreign law and this is likely to lead to a more effective ways of finding foreign law.

I. Conflict of Laws Rules

In Venezuela, the application of conflict of laws rules is mandatory. Article 1 of the Statute on Private International Law mandates the determination of the applicable law, *inter alia*, through conflict of laws rules in cases related to foreign legal systems.[1] In Venezuela, all rules of law, including, conflict of laws rules, are applied *ex officio* pursuant to the principle of *iura novit curia*.[2] Their application is thus

[1] Published in Official Gazette Nr. 35.511 of 6 August 1998.

[2] Articles 12, 19, 243.4 and 274 of the Code of Civil Procedure, Article 2 of the Civil Code.

E. Hernández-Bretón (✉)
Professor, School of Law, University of Monteávila, Caracas, Venezuela
e-mail: Eugenio.Hernandez-Breton@bakermckenzie.com

C. Madrid Martínez
Professor, School of Law, Central University of Venezuela, Caracas, Venezuela

School of Law, Andrés Bello Catholic University, Caracas, Venezuela
e-mail: ccmm26@hotmail.com; cmadridmartinez@yahoo.es

Y. Nishitani (ed.), *Treatment of Foreign Law - Dynamics towards Convergence?*,
Ius Comparatum – Global Studies in Comparative Law 26,
DOI 10.1007/978-3-319-56574-3_23

mandatory for courts and other public officials. The parties are not required to invoke or prove them. This is also the opinion of commentators.[3]

Generally, conflict of laws rules, as embodied in the Statute on Private International Law, are of a bilateral nature, and as such could lead to the application of either the local law or the foreign law, indistinctly, and depending on the facts of the case at stake.

Although court decisions on these issues are limited, the majority of cases concern the application of the laws of the states of Florida and New York, United States of America, and of some Latin American states, like Chile and Colombia.

The Venezuelan conflicts of laws rules are basically comprised in the Statute on Private International Law. According to its Article 1, the sources of norms for dealing with cases connected with foreign legal systems are (i) the norms of Public International Law on the matter, especially those contained in international treaties in force in Venezuela; (ii) the domestic norms on Private International Law; (iii) the analogy; and (iv) the generally accepted principles of Private International Law. Additionally, for international contracts the *lex mercatoria* plays a very important role.[4]

Among the treaties in force in Venezuela, it is worth mentioning Articles 408 et seq. of the Bustamante Code; Articles 2 and 4 of the Inter American Convention on General Rules of Private International Law ("GRPIL Convention")[5]; Inter American Convention on Proof of and Information on Foreign Law ("Montevideo Convention").[6] In addition, Articles 2, 60 and 61 of the Statute on Private International Law regulate the proof and application of foreign law. From among the foregoing, we are of the opinion that the Statute on Private International Law is the main and most important source of all.

However, it is worth mentioning that Venezuelan courts are much more prone to the analysis of procedural rather than substantive law issues, which in turn is reflected in the relatively scarce amount of decisions on the merits applying foreign laws.

---

[3] Claudia Madrid Martínez, *La norma de derecho internacional privado*, Caracas, Universidad Central de Venezuela, 2004, at p. 55 et seq.

[4] Article 31 of the Statute on Private International Law.

[5] Approbatory law published in Official Gazette Nr. 33.252 of 26 June 1985, deposit of the instrument of ratification on 16 May 1985.

[6] Approbatory law published in Official Gazette Nr. 33.170 of 22 February 1985, deposit of the instrument of ratification on 16 May 1985.

II. Foreign Law Before Judicial Authorities

A. *Nature of Foreign Law*

As far as the nature of foreign law is concerned, it is considered as law in Venezuela (Article 408 of the Bustamante Code; Article 2 of the GRPIL Convention; Article 1 of the Montevideo Convention; Article 60 of the Statute on Private International Law). This is also the view of commentators and case law.[7]

B. *Application of Foreign Law*

Concerning the application of foreign law before judicial authorities, they are bound to apply foreign law *ex officio*.[8] Nonetheless, the parties may provide information as to the applicable foreign law, and the courts and authorities may order steps to be taken in order to acquire greater knowledge of the same (Article 408 of the Bustamante Code; Article 2 of the GRPIL Convention; Article 1 of the Montevideo Convention; Article 60 of the Statute on Private International Law).

As it will be explained more fully below, although in theory the courts and authorities are obliged to ascertain and apply foreign law *ex officio*, in practice "a party wishing to rely on foreign law is well advised to present evidence of it."[9]

---

[7] See Tatiana B. de Maekelt, Tratamiento procesal del derecho extranjero, Artículo 60, Tatiana B. de Maekelt et al. (Coordinación), *Ley de Derecho Internacional Privado Comentada*, Tomo II, Caracas, Universidad Central de Venezuela, 2005, at p. 1225 et seq.; Nicole Monleón, *Das internationale Privatrecht von Venezuela*, Max-Planck-Institut fuer auslaendisches und internationales Privatrecht, Studien zum auslaendischen und internationalen Privatrecht Nr. 204, Tuebingen, Mohr Siebeck, 2008, at p. 219 et seq.; Haydée Barrios and Zhandra Marín, "Información, aplicación y tratamiento procesal del derecho extranjero", (Tatiana B. de Maekelt et al., Coordinadores), *Derecho Procesal Civil Internacional*, Caracas, Academia de Ciencias Políticas y Sociales, Serie Estudios Nr. 88, 2010, p. 619 et seq.

[8] See, among others, File 000871, Foreign Credit Insurance Association v. Naviera Rassi C.A. et al., 20 December 2001, http://www.tsj.gov.ve/decisiones/scc/Diciembre/RC-0451-201201-00871.html; File 2012-0532, Export-Import Bank of the United States of America v. Supercable Alk Internacional, S.A., 9 May 2012, http://www.tsj.gov.ve/decisiones/spa/mayo/00499-9512-2012-2012-0532.html

[9] Richard S. Lombard, *American-Venezuelan Private International Law*, Bilateral Studies in Private International Law Nr. 14, Parker School of Foreign and Comparative Law, Columbia University in the City of New York, Dobbs Ferry, New York, Oceana Publications, 1965, at p. 95.

C. Ascertainment of Foreign Law

1. General Remarks

With regard to the way how judicial authorities ascertain foreign law, they are required to ascertain it *ex officio*. In this sense, the *iura novit curia* principle is equally applicable to domestic and foreign law. In order to fulfill their duty, the courts and other authorities may issue procedural orders requesting more information on foreign laws as they deem it necessary. The parties have the option, but not the burden, to provide information as to the applicable foreign law. This is a consequence of the formal requirement established in Article 340.5 of the Code of Civil Procedure, which mandates the plaintiff to make express reference in the relevant pleadings to the legal basis of his/her complaint. However, the judge is not bound by any such legal characterization.

As far as the means to ascertain foreign law is concerned (cf. *infra* V), still today, there is no statutory rule of Venezuelan law for the method of presentation of evidence of foreign law. The determination of the means used to ascertain foreign law is largely left to the parties and the courts preferences. The Bustamante Code and the Montevideo Convention allow for several options in order to provide information on foreign laws, including, but not limited to, international judicial cooperation. The Statute on Private International Law does not restrict or limit the means for the ascertainment of foreign law.

2. Methods Used in Venezuela

a. Documents

It is not uncommon for practitioners, courts and authorities to rely on documents and books when researching foreign legal texts, commentaries and case law, and to produce such materials as evidence of the applicable foreign law. However, due to the limited availability of those materials in Venezuelan libraries, either public or private, the interested parties prefer to opt for other alternatives. In the case of materials obtained abroad or locally which are drafted in a foreign language, parties are required to submit those materials translated into Spanish by a public interpreter admitted to act as such in Venezuela.

b. Internet Sources

Currently more and more judicial authorities and practitioners are resorting to Internet sources for researching foreign laws. This practice has been followed even by the Civil Cassation Chamber of the Supreme Court of Justice when faced with the difficulties of obtaining *ex officio* information about Swedish family law.[10] In this case the Venezuelan court acknowledged the scarcity of information available in Spanish in respect of parental guardianship, and thus resorted to the official webpage of the European Commission, European Judicial Network on Civil and Commercial Matters,[11] and also to the official webpage of the Swedish government,[12] where it found a Spanish translation of the applicable Swedish law on parental guardianship. This is also the approach favored by Venezuelan authors.[13]

c. Assistance of the Parties

As commented before, "a party wishing to rely on foreign law is well advised to present evidence of it".[14] In almost all cases where foreign law was at stake, parties provided information on foreign law in the widest variety of forms. Very rarely parties let judicial authorities alone with the task to research the contents, interpretation and force of applicable foreign law. In addition, one could even say that the courts expect that the interested parties devote considerable efforts and time in the process of providing the necessary foreign legal information.

d. Expert Witnesses

In Venezuela, the taking of the testimony of an expert witness on foreign law is gaining prominence among the methods for providing information on foreign law. The testimony is often recorded in an affidavit of law, in which the expert witness explains his/her opinions supported by case law, statutes and quotations from treatises, and not very differently from the usual way in which such affidavits are made in international arbitral practice.[15] In most cases the testimony is sworn before a

---

[10] File AA20-C-2009-000464, María Julia Méndez Casal v. Domingo Jose Rodríguez Polanco, 18 February 2011, http://www.tsj.gob.ve/decisiones/scc/febrero/EXE.000065-18211-2011-09-464.HTML

[11] http://ec.europa.eu/civiljustice/parental_resp/parental_resp_swe_es.htm

[12] http://www.sweden.gov.se/sb/d/3288/a/19570, with a link to http://www.spaininformation.org/sp_Legaliseringar.html

[13] Kumeyi Torres Yonekura, *La información sobre derecho extranjero obtenida a través de Internet: Su validez ante el juez en el sistema venezolano de Derecho Internacional Privado*, Thesis submitted for the Degree of Master on Private International Law and Comparative Law, Universidad Central de Venezuela, Caracas, 2004; see an abridged and updated version of the foregoing research paper in Víctor Hugo Guerra et al. (Coordinadores), *Estudios de Derecho Internacional Privado. Homenaje a Tatiana Maekelt: Contribución de sus alumnos*, Caracas, Escovar León, Universidad Católica Andrés Bello, 2012, p. 363 et seq.

[14] Richard S. Lombard, op. cit., at p. 95.

[15] Eugenio Hernández-Bretón, "La participación de 'testigos expertos' en el procedimiento arbitral internacional", *Boletín de la Academia de Ciencias Políticas y Sociales*, Nr. 150, Caracas, 2011, p. 203 et seq.

notary public or similar official, and subsequently legalized or apostilled as applicable. A commentator recommends, "it would be advisable for the notary to state that the affiants are known to him to be lawyers admitted to practice and practicing in the state concerned. The affidavit should state that the affiants are familiar with the law of the state and country concerned."[16] This will follow the provision of Article 409 of the Bustamante Code as explained herein below. It is worth mentioning, however, that contrary to international practice, it is unfamiliar in Venezuela to have the expert witnesses cross-examined by the opposing counsel. It is unclear whether an expert witness written testimony is subject to personal ratification by the witness before Venezuelan courts.[17]

e. Inquiry to Expert Bodies or Institutions

Venezuelan judicial practice is not inclined to the use of court appointed experts or expert institutes. It would be unusual if a court asks or appoints an independent expert or an expert institute, such as the very well known Max-Planck-Institute, to request his/her/its views on a given foreign legal issue, no matter how well his/her/its reputation may be.

As far as the inquiry to domestic judicial or non-judicial authorities is concerned, it is an unknown method for the ascertainment of foreign legal information in Venezuelan practice, and in our experience, Venezuelan courts and authorities have never used it. Theoretically, an inquiry to foreign judicial (or non-judicial) authorities would be available via multilateral treaties. However, in practice Venezuelan judicial authorities never use it.

Although Venezuela is a party to multilateral treaties (i.e., the Bustamante Code and the Montevideo Convention) providing for mechanisms to facilitate access to information on foreign law, including international judicial cooperation, we are not aware of a single reported case where Venezuelan courts have requested such legal information via bilateral or multilateral treaties.

In our experience, Venezuelan judicial authorities are reluctant to enter into direct communications with foreign judges in order to obtain information on foreign law.

f. Other Methods

The most usual methods for providing information on foreign laws are expert witnesses and the Internet. The former works fore mostly for the parties and the latter equally for both parties and judicial authorities.

---

[16] Richard S. Lombard, op. cit., at p. 95.

[17] File AA60-S-2008-00309, Michael Sterling Little v. Chevrontexaco Global Technology Services Company, 2 June 2009, http://www.tsj.gov.ve/decisiones/scs/Junio/0894-1609-2009-08-309.html

3. Qualification of Individuals or Institutions

As far as the qualification of individuals or institutions to provide legal information is concerned, there is no precise statutory requirement. However, in practice judicial authorities and litigators rely on Article 409 of the Bustamante Code as a generally accepted principle of Private International Law, and demand that two lawyers practicing in the jurisdiction concerned certify evidence on foreign laws. However, as pointed out before, in some instances courts are satisfied even with the sworn declaration of a single lawyer practicing in the relevant jurisdiction. No further qualifications are required although other academic and professional merits are certainly taken into account when examining the evidentiary value of the legal information provided.

4. Effects of the Provided Legal Information

The provided legal information clearly does not have binding effects. Judicial authorities are not bound by the information that is provided to them. They are free to evaluate the information received according to their sound judgment and understanding, as it is acknowledged in the last paragraph of Article 6 of the Montevideo Convention.

Furthermore, there is no statutory and precise mechanism to examine the reliability of the provided legal information. Judicial authorities have ample discretionary powers to determine the accuracy of the provided legal information. Once again, courts and judges are left to their sound judgment in order to evaluate information on foreign law.

5. Costs

In Venezuela, access to the courts is free of charge (Article 26 of the Constitution),[18] and judicial authorities cannot demand payment whatsoever for their services (Article 254 of the Constitution). Thus, if judicial authorities engage in the research of foreign law the Venezuelan State will bear the costs, but if the parties assume the task then each of them will bear the corresponding costs and expenses associated therewith, provided, however, that they may recover such costs and expenses if successful in the litigation (Article 274 of the Code of Civil Procedure).

[18] Published in Special Official Gazette Nr. 5.908 of 19 February 2009.

6. Other Issues

As the number of cases with foreign elements grows, Venezuelan courts have become more familiarized with issues of Private International Law. Awareness of the complexities of these type of situations, and of the needs of the parties involved have caused Venezuelan courts to be more willing to meet their duties and thus research and apply foreign laws *ex officio*. However, parties, to the extent possible, in practice assume the task of providing proof on foreign laws as if they were under the burden to do so.

D. Interpretation and Application of Foreign Law

Foreign law must be interpreted and applied as it would be applied in the country of origin (Article 2 of the GRPIL Convention). This means, among other things, that it would be applied in accordance with the principles in force in the country of origin. However, the application of foreign law must be made in such a way as to realize the objectives pursued by the Venezuelan rules of Private International Law (Article 2 of the Statute on Private International Law). This latter provision has been interpreted as establishing a basic rule for the characterization of foreign laws under a functional approach, within the framework provided by the Venezuelan conflict of laws rules, and as a basic rule to determine the scope of reference to a foreign law, in order to permit a *renvoi* of first or second degree under Article 4 of the Statute on Private International Law.[19]

According to the foregoing, a gap in foreign law must be filled up using the rules and principles on construction and interpretation of laws as they are applied in the relevant foreign law, and this irrespective of how dissimilar such rules and principles may be from those of Venezuelan law.

[19] Eugenio Hernández-Bretón, "An attempt to regulate the problem of 'characterization' in private international law", *Festschrift für Erik Jayme*, Band I, Heinz-Peter Mansel et al. (Editors), Muenchen, Sellier European Law Publishers, 2004, p. 332 et seq.; id., "Los objetivos de la normas venezolanas de conflicto", Jan Kleinheisterkamp/ Gonzalo A. Lorenzo Idiarte (Coordinadores), *Avances del Derecho Internacional Privado en América Latina. Liber Amicorum Juergen Samtleben*, Fundación de Cultura Universitaria, Montevideo, 2002, p. 169 et seq.; id., "En materia de calificaciones, reenvío y otros asuntos de Derecho Internacional Privado", *Cuadernos Unimetanos* Nr. 11/Septiembre 2007, Caracas, p. 227 et seq. See also Gonzalo Parra-Aranguren, *El régimen de los bienes en el matrimonio en el Derecho Internacional Privado venezolano,* Universidad Católica Andrés Bello, Cátedra Fundacional Caracciolo Parra León, Caracas, 2007, p. 192.

E. Failure to Establish Foreign Law

If the foreign law cannot be ascertained, the solution must be sought in an appropriate way. This is an unregulated area of law, and it is left to the discretion of the judicial authorities. In this connection, it should be borne in mind that courts have the duty to decide any case that is brought to their knowledge and are under the prohibition of *non-liquet* (Article 19 of the Code of Civil Procedure). Violation of this prohibition can lead to criminal liabilities (Article 206 of the Criminal Code, Article 86 of the Anticorruption Law).[20] We anticipate that the most likely position to be followed by Venezuelan judicial authorities in the case when foreign law cannot be ascertained would be to apply the relevant Venezuelan substantive rules.

It is a pragmatically simple approach. Because Venezuelan law would be applied, Venezuelan judicial authorities would feel more comfortable when deciding the issue at stake. Probably the underlying rationale would be that it is better to decide a case even under the wrong law than to leave it open and undecided. However, as it will be more fully discussed below, a decision rendered following the approach just described, may be subject to judicial review.

III. Judicial Review

A. Conflict of Laws Rules

When conflict of laws rules have erroneously been applied (i.e., the law of State A has been applied instead of the designated law of State B), the parties can appeal to higher courts including the Supreme Court. The application of conflict of laws rules is, as it is with any other Venezuelan laws, subject to appeal to higher courts including the Supreme Court. This is acknowledged in Article 4 of the GRPIL Convention, Article 412 of the Bustamante Code and in Article 61 of the Statute on Private International Law. Thus, the control of the correct application of Venezuelan conflict of laws rules will be allowed in the same cases and under the same circumstances as in respect of any other provisions of Venezuelan law. The control of the application of Venezuelan conflict of laws rules is a condition necessary to the control of foreign laws.[21]

The main driver of the Venezuelan solution appears to be the notion that conflict of laws rules are rules of law, and thus their correct application is subject to judicial control.

---

[20] Published in Special Official Gazette Nr. 6.195 of 19 November 2014.

[21] See File 000871, Foreign Credit Insurance Association v. Naviera Rassi C.A. et al., 20 December 2001, http://www.tsj.gov.ve/decisiones/scc/Diciembre/RC-0451-201201-00871.htm

B. Foreign Law

Exactly as in respect of the erroneous application of domestic conflict of laws rules, the erroneous application of foreign law is subject to appeals before higher courts, including before the Supreme Court of Venezuela. Thus, the control of the correct application of foreign laws will be allowed in the same cases and under the same circumstances as in respect of any provisions of Venezuelan law.

The main driver of the Venezuelan solution appears to be the principle of equality of procedural treatment of domestic and foreign laws.[22]

IV. Foreign Law in Other Instances

Administrative and other non-judicial authorities, including notaries, seldom apply and ascertain foreign law. It may be that such authorities consider that they are not bound to apply and ascertain foreign law. However, Article 2 of the GRPIL Convention and Article 2 of the Statute on Private International Law are clear enough as to impose a duty to apply foreign law *ex officio* on any and all Venezuelan authorities regardless of whether they are part of the judiciary. Probably tax authorities are better trained and, therefore, are better suit to research *ex officio* issues of foreign law, and in practice do apply it. However, we are not aware of situations where those authorities have relied on treaties on international judicial cooperation in order to obtain information on foreign law.

In international arbitration proceedings, parties relying on foreign law usually resort to expert witness testimony as a means to provide information on and/or proof of foreign law. Although arbitrators are subject to the duty of applying foreign law *ex officio*, they do very little research on their own regarding foreign law. They tend to expect that the parties provide the bulk of allegations and proof of applicable foreign law. The question about the ascertainment and proof of foreign law rarely or never arises in cases of mediation or other alternative dispute resolution mechanism. This is because in most, if not in all, arbitration cases in Venezuela, the merits of the dispute are subject to Venezuelan law.

In advisory work by attorneys, notaries, etc. in contractual negotiations, estate planning or family arrangements, the ascertainment of foreign law is a difficult task. Attorneys engaged in advisory work when faced with issues of foreign law commonly research those issues on the Internet. The results so obtained will provide a first conceptual approach that will help them in determining the necessary further steps in order to deepen a possible research of the issues. This assumes a certain command of the relevant languages and a prior understanding of the conflict of laws

[22] See Tatiana B. de Maekelt, "Recursos, Artículo 61", Tatiana B. de Maekelt et al. (Coordinación), *Ley de Derecho Internacional Privado Comentada*, Tomo II, Caracas, Universidad Central de Venezuela, 2005, at p. 1233 et seq.

queries that are relevant for the case at stake. Although this practice may sound as routine, it cannot be taken as determinative of the issues and may cause the Venezuelan attorney to face issues of professional responsibility, because he/she may not be sufficiently qualified to provide legal advice on those foreign law issues. In several instances after the Venezuelan lawyer has gained an insight of the particularities of the relevant foreign legal system it is that he/she then contacts lawyers admitted to practice in the relevant foreign jurisdiction for more formal advice. To this effect, legal networks provide a very useful tool.

Resorting to Comparative law, and thus to foreign law, is quite frequent in the drafting of laws and regulations by domestic authorities. The same applies to the preparation of research papers at the academic level.

V. Access to Foreign Law: Status Quo

Venezuelan State agencies do provide legal information through their official website.[23] However, the information found in those webpages is limited to the text of laws, decrees and regulations, in most of the cases taken directly from the Official Gazette, and not always timely updated. It is not frequent to find explanations on the law or guidance on Venezuelan law, because those webpages are not meant to provide any type of legal advice. It must be pointed out that the web page of the Supreme Court of Venezuela[24] is a repository of all the decisions rendered by the Court since the inception of the web page in 2000, and contains decisions of other lower courts.

As far as judicial network is concerned, Venezuelan courts, particularly the Supreme Court of Justice, have resorted directly to the information provided by the European Judicial Network in order to ascertain the contents of foreign laws, as mentioned above.[25] It may be reasonable to expect that other Venezuelan courts will research foreign laws in similar databases.

As mentioned, Venezuela is a party to the Montevideo Convention so that its mechanism can be used to collect information on foreign law. In addition, Venezuela is a party to the Bustamante Code, which also provides for mechanisms to facilitate access to foreign law among the contracting parties (Articles 410–411). There are no official figures available evidencing the application of either the Bustamante Code or the Montevideo Convention. In respect of the Montevideo Convention though, some commentators manifest certain satisfactory results,[26]

---

[23] See for example http://www.pgr.gob.ve/

[24] http://www.tsj.gob.ve

[25] See *supra* II(C)(2)(b).

[26] Eduardo Tellechea Bergman, "Aplicación e información del derecho extranjero en el actual ámbito interamericano y regional, con especial referencia al derecho uruguayo", Diego P. Fernández Arroyo/Nuria González Martín (Coordinadores), *Tendencias y Relaciones Derecho Internacional Privado Americano Actual (Jornadas de la ASADIP 2008)*, Mexico, Universidad Nacional Autónoma de México, Editorial Porrúa, ASADIP, 2010, p. 95 et seq., at p. 113.

while others consider it a failure similar to its European counterpart.[27] It is, thus, difficult to assess the practical results of the Montevideo Convention. Sarcastic as it can be, no one can say for sure whether or not the Montevideo Convention is "half dead".[28]

In our experience, these international instruments do not work well to ascertain foreign law. Several factors can be considered as impairing the success of the Montevideo Convention, namely (i) lack of knowledge of the Convention and its mechanisms, (ii) lack of well-provided law libraries and research centers, and (iii) lack of sensibility vis-à-vis the requests for information in light of petitions for international judicial cooperation among Latin American countries. In addition to the foregoing, time constraints and a heavy workload also influence the attitude of the judiciary to escape from the examination of issues of conflict of laws, and, accordingly, are determinative of their decision to avoid resorting to the mechanisms of international judicial cooperation for the gathering of information on foreign laws. Only teaching and State awareness of its international commitments will help to overcome the aforementioned deficit.

VI. Access to Foreign Law: Further Developments

A. *Practical Need*

Unquestionably, there is need to improve access to foreign law. It particularly applies to judicial authorities and other non-judicial authorities, which are faced with the largest amount of cases involving foreign laws.

As far as the circumstances in which access to foreign law is most needed, we believe that it is in the course of litigation. This does not mean that access to foreign law is not important for all remaining instances. In the latter cases, the parties may anticipate together with legal counsel a number of legal issues that may be consulted or verified with foreign counsel as appropriate. The same may be true for litigation matters. This would ease the tasks of judicial authorities and the parties.

Without hesitation, we consider that family law is the area where access to foreign law is more crucial, this is because parties involved in these situations are very rarely sophisticated and knowledgeable enough about legal issues, and may not have the financial resources to retain the services of competent legal counsel.

Access to foreign laws is a deficit of the Venezuelan system of Private International Law, which requires immediate correction. It would not be exaggerated to affirm

[27] Martin Nyota Lamm, *Die Interamerikanischen Spezialkonferenzen für Internationales Privatrecht*, Ergon Verlag, Würzburg, 2000, at p. 135.

[28] Christian von Bar and Peter Mankowski, *Internationales Privatrecht, Band I. Allgemeine Lehren*, Verlag C.H. Beck, Muenchen, 2003, at p. 375 referring to the European Convention on Information on Foreign Law: "*Sarkastisch, aber treffend ist die Bezeichnung des Übereinkommens als halbtot*".

that lack of easy and affordable access to foreign law is one of the main reasons that causes judicial authorities to refrain from ascertaining foreign laws, and which makes litigators reluctant to plead the applicability of choice of laws rules. The consequence of the foregoing is the scarce application of foreign laws by Venezuelan judicial authorities.

B. Conflict of Laws Solutions

The modification of Venezuelan conflict of laws rules does not appear as the most desirable way to solve the foregoing situation. We do not think that Venezuelan conflict of laws rules must be amended *de lege ferenda* to reduce the number of cases in which foreign law is applied. We believe that these rules are well balanced. The unsuccessful proposal (2014) to amend the Code of Civil Procedure ("Draft Code of Civil Procedure") did not contain any provision affecting current conflict of law rules.

Neither should the treatment of foreign law in Venezuela be changed *de lege ferenda*. We do not think that any changes are necessary in respect of the current status of Venezuelan laws regarding the treatment of foreign laws by judicial and non-judicial authorities. The *ex officio* application of foreign laws should be kept for all areas of law. The Draft Code of Civil Procedure does not change the foregoing.

Unfortunately, as explained above,[29] so far regional instruments in Latin America have proven unsuccessful.

C. Methods of Facilitating Access to Foreign Law

Theoretically, we think international or regional instruments that establish administrative and/or judicial cooperation to exchange information on participating States' law are useful tools to facilitate access to foreign law. However, in practice lack of commitment of the member states lead to very poor results.

Any instrument facilitating access to foreign law should be flexible enough to allow adaptations to future needs. It should also make affordable the access to the information and should not impose unnecessary formalities, such as legalizations or apostilles. The timing for answering the request should be kept to a minimum. Such international instruments should be open to not only judicial authorities, but also to individuals and/or any other authorities. However, the treatment of each case must be different, particularly in respect of costs.

Using intermediaries to send a request to foreign competent authorities or designated experts should be kept to a minimum. Transmission of the requests and the corresponding results should allowed by means similar to those allowed by The

---

[29] See *supra* V(5).

Hague Convention of 15 November 1965 on the Service Abroad of Judicial and Extrajudicial Documents in Civil or Commercial Matters.

The answer provided by the requested party should not be binding. The assessment of the information provided should be left to the authorities of the requesting state, otherwise, according to Venezuelan law, it could be understood that the authority to adjudicate the matter has been delegated to a third party in violation of the right to an ordinary judge or to a non-authorized official.

As far as the costs for the provision of services on legal information are concerned, a differentiated treatment should be given. In the situations where the judicial or non-judicial authorities request the information, the legal information should be provided without costs. On the contrary, if the interested parties request the information then they should bear the costs. In the case of Venezuela, the foregoing approaches would be consistent with constitutional and legal rules.[30]

It is to be noted that reliability and certainty of the information should be guaranteed at all times and in all cases.

Any method for accessing information on foreign laws would be a plus. We could think about enhancing direct communication of judges, establishing networks for other legal professionals (e.g., law firms), identifying qualified experts or expert institutes (e.g., creating a list of experts), or providing information on national laws on the Internet.

[30] See *supra* II(C)(6).

Part IV
National Reports III – Asia-Pacific Region and Africa

Australia: Foreign Law in Australian International Litigation: Developing the Common Law

Mary Keyes

Abstract The Australian courts are often required to consider the application of foreign law, especially in international civil litigation. The application of foreign law generally arises if one party relies on the foreign law, in which case that party bears the onus of proving the content and general interpretation of the foreign law. Most of the cases involve interlocutory applications. Foreign law is regarded as a question of fact, although one of a hybrid kind. Because of its characterisation as a question of fact, foreign law must be proven. At common law, this was usually done by expert evidence; legislation now facilitates the proof of documents which establish the foreign law. Often, both parties tender expert evidence as to the relevant foreign law. Sometimes, the evidence of experts conflicts, and sometimes it does not adequately establish the content of the foreign law. In the absence of proof, the court may apply a presumption that foreign law is the same as forum law, which justifies applying forum law to the issue, but Australian courts are becoming more reluctant simply to apply this presumption. There have been some recent and progressive innovations which facilitate the proof of foreign law, including the possibility of appointing a referee to determine the applicable foreign law, and the use of direct court-to-court communication in a small number of areas, including the Hague Judges Network. The Australian law requires further development, which seems more likely to occur if there were greater international cooperation in this area.

I. Australian Constitutional Structure and Sources of Law

Australia is a federal system of law, comprised of the federation (called the Commonwealth of Australia), six States and ten Territories. The Commonwealth, the States and the two most populous Territories have their own legislature and their

---

Thanks to Josh Keyes Liley for superb research assistance and insightful comments, and Professor Yuko Nishitani for helpful comments.

M. Keyes (✉)
Professor, Griffith Law School at Griffith University, 170 Kessels Road, Nathan, QLD 4111, Australia
e-mail: m.keyes@griffith.edu.au

Y. Nishitani (ed.), *Treatment of Foreign Law - Dynamics towards Convergence?*,
Ius Comparatum – Global Studies in Comparative Law 26,
DOI 10.1007/978-3-319-56574-3_24

own courts. Australia is a common law system, and most of the relevant Australian law in the area of the treatment of foreign law, as for many other areas relevant to private law and civil and commercial litigation, is common law derived from the English common law. The English common law remains an influential source of principle,[1] as supplemented and amended in all nine jurisdictions by legislation and case law relevant to the treatment of foreign law in international litigation. The laws of these nine different legal systems relevant to the treatment of foreign law are generally similar. The High Court of Australia, the ultimate appellate court for all the federal, State and Territory court systems, has a general supervisory jurisdiction, and therefore there is a single common law within Australia. There are few High Court decisions on foreign law. There are a number of influential decisions of intermediate appellate courts, particularly of the New South Wales Court of Appeal. Most cases about foreign law are first instance decisions, and many of these are decisions on preliminary questions that must be determined before trial, such as applications in which a defendant challenges the jurisdiction of the Australian court.

All nine jurisdictions have legislative provisions which facilitate proof of foreign law.[2] These provisions are not entirely identical, but they have the effect of modifying the common law rules relating to proof of foreign law in fairly similar ways. Australia also has several bilateral arrangements which facilitate various aspects of international litigation, including proof of foreign law.

Most areas of private law are within State and Territory competence, so conflicts of law are possible within the federation at least where the applicable laws are statutory.[3] The rules of jurisdiction and judgments applicable to intra-Australian litigation differ from those applicable in international litigation,[4] but the conflict of laws

---

[1] The Australian cases continue to cite English cases and English commentary, especially *Dicey, Morris & Collins on the Conflict of Laws* in its various editions. The leading treatise on Australian evidence law heavily references classic as well as recent English authorities in its discussion of the proof of foreign law: JD Heydon, *Cross on Evidence* (9th Australian ed, 2013, LexisNexis Butterworths), pp. 1383–1396.

[2] Each jurisdiction has its own Evidence Act, which contains rules which facilitate the proof of foreign law (see further below at III(C)(2)(a)). The Commonwealth, three states (New South Wales, Tasmania and Victoria) and both Territories (the Australian Capital Territory and the Northern Territory) have enacted uniform evidence legislation, which contains provisions relating to the proof of foreign law. The other three states (Queensland, South Australia and Western Australia) also have legislation which is in similar but not identical terms to the uniform evidence legislation. Other provisions of Australian legislation facilitate the proof of foreign law, for example, by permitting the Australian courts to take judicial notice of the legislation of foreign countries: Family Law (Child Abduction Convention) Regulations 1986 (Cth) (referred to below at n 42).

[3] There is 'but one common law' in Australia (*Kable v Director of Public Prosecutions for NSW* (1996) 189 CLR 51, 113), so there is no possibility of a conflict of laws if the relevant principles are derived from case law. Under the Constitution, if there is a conflict between Commonwealth law and the law of a State or Territory, the Commonwealth law prevails: Commonwealth of Australia Constitution Act 1901 ss 109, 122.

[4] Reid Mortensen, Richard Garnett and Mary Keyes, *Private International Law in Australia* (3rd ed, 2015, LexisNexis), chs 2 and 4 (dealing with jurisdictional principles) and ch 5 (dealing with judgments).

rules are generally the same, and may lead to the application of the law of another Australian jurisdiction. The Commonwealth Constitution requires Australian courts to give 'full faith and credit' to the legislation and public laws of other Australian jurisdictions[5]; a requirement that is obviously inapplicable to foreign laws. It is accepted that proof of foreign law is more onerous and difficult in international than in intranational cases.[6]

The primary sources of law in Australia can be accessed on official databases.[7] Some Australian legislation is freely available online in an authorised form, but the authoritative versions of case law are not freely available.[8] The law report series, which are the authoritative versions of case law, are commercially published. Most court decisions are published on the official court websites and other free databases. In this chapter, to facilitate access to the material, I have indicated medium neutral citations as well as citations to law reports.

Australia's historical relationship with Britain has important implications for the treatment and application of foreign law in cross-border litigation. Australia is a common law system which applies the adversarial model of civil procedure. Decisions of the English courts and the Privy Council were highly influential, if not directly binding, in Australia until recently[9]; Australian parliaments were constrained in their ability to legislate independently of Britain until the middle of the twentieth century[10]; and some British legislation continued to have direct application in Australia until the 1980s.[11] Australian courts and lawyers remain extremely familiar with the identification and application of relevant English laws, particularly case law. The similarity between Australian law and the law of other common law

---

[5] Commonwealth of Australia Constitution Act 1900, s 118.

[6] *Regie Nationale des Usines Renault SA v Zhang* (2002) 210 CLR 491, 517; [2002] HCA 10, [66] ('to undertake proof of foreign law is a different and more onerous task than, in the case of an intra-Australian tort, to establish the content of federal, State and Territory law'). See further below, at VII(A)(3).

[7] Every jurisdiction publishes its legislation on free databases. See for example https://www.legislation.gov.au/, which publishes Commonwealth legislation, and http://www.legislation.nsw.gov.au/, which publishes New South Wales legislation. Most courts publish their decisions on their official websites. See for example http://www.hcourt.gov.au/cases/cases-heard (recent decisions of the High Court of Australia). In some jurisdictions, the decisions of all the courts are published on official websites: http://www.caselaw.nsw.gov.au/ (decisions of the New South Wales courts). Australian court decisions are published on a number of other reputable websites, of which the longest established is the Australian Legal Information Institute (AustLII) which publishes a wide range of material, including legislation and case law, of all Australian jurisdictions: http://www.austlii.edu.au/

[8] Not every case is reported, and not every reported case is published in the authorised series of reports.

[9] Parties were able to appeal from the decisions of state superior courts to the Privy Council until 1986: Australia Act 1986 (Cth), and corresponding legislation of the same name enacted in the United Kingdom and all the Australian states.

[10] Statute of Westminster 1931 (UK); Colonial Laws Validity Act 1865 (UK).

[11] Now see the Imperial Acts Application Act 1969 (NSW) and similar legislation in the other states.

countries may be relevant in international disputes, in that Australian judges may be willing independently to interpret and apply the laws of common law countries without assistance, and may be more willing to apply a presumption in such a case that foreign law and forum law are similar.[12] Therefore, cases in which the foreign law is English, or that of some of the other Commonwealth countries, are likely to be resolved differently to those in which the foreign law is that of a non-common law legal system. The courts are especially confident in the interpretation and application of 'foreign' law where that is the law of another Australian jurisdiction.

II. Conflict of Laws Rules

A. *Nature of Conflict of Laws Rules*

The nature of conflict of laws rules[13] has attracted little attention in Australia. In the leading case on foreign law, the majority of the High Court of Australia noted that Australian courts were obliged to apply the tort choice of law rule in cases where the tort occurred outside the forum.[14]

Although choice of law rules ought to be given a mandatory effect, this may effectively be limited or avoided entirely by other factors. The parties have some ability to limit that effect by two litigation strategies. These strategies highlight the significance of the adversarial nature of litigation in Australia.

First, while the party whose case relies on foreign law has the burden of proving the content of that law,[15] if that party does not prove the content of the foreign law, the court may apply the presumption of similarity between foreign law and forum law.[16] This presumption, explained in detail below,[17] allows the courts to fill any gaps in the proof of foreign law by applying forum law. If the presumption of similarity is applied, the mandatory character of the choice of law rule may be defeated.[18]

---

[12] The presumption of familiarity between foreign law and forum law is discussed in detail below at III(D)(2).

[13] In Australia, 'conflict of laws' is taken to refer both to choice of law and also to the procedural issues of jurisdiction and the recognition and enforcement of foreign judgments. In this chapter, for the sake of consistency with the treatment of the issues in other chapters, I note where I am referring to jurisdictional issues rather than choice of law.

[14] *Neilson v Overseas Projects Corporation of Victoria Ltd.* (2005) 223 CLR 331, 342, 356, 357, 391, 395, 408, 415, 416; [2005] HCA 54, [15], [59], [64], [187], [200], [242], [261], [264]. See M Keyes, 'Foreign Law in Australian Courts' (2007) 15 Torts Law Journal 9, 27–28.

[15] *Regie Nationale des Usines Renault SA v Zhang* (2002) 210 CLR 491, 517–518; [2002] HCA 10, [68], [70].

[16] *Nicholls v Michael Wilson & Partners Ltd.* [2010] NSWCA 222, [323].

[17] At II(D)(2).

[18] Richard Fentiman, Foreign Law in English Courts (1998, OUP) p 148, cited with approval by Kirby J in *Neilson v Overseas Projects Corporation of Victoria Ltd.* (2005) 223 CLR 331, 396; [2005] HCA 54, [203]. In *Neilson v Overseas Projects Corporation of Victoria*, Gummow and Hayne JJ, who were in the majority, stated that because of the presumption of similarity, which

Second, the parties have the ability to accumulate actions, so where a party has multiple claims available to it based on the same facts and the same complaint, it may be possible to avoid the effect of an undesirable choice of law rule by a strategic choice of claim. This option is not always available but common law claims in contract and in tort are likely to be addressed separately, in which case the choice of law rule in tort has no bearing on the governing law for the related contract claim.[19] Australian courts sometimes apply forum legislation without regard to choice of law rules,[20] and if the plaintiff claims under forum legislation, the otherwise mandatory effect of choice of law rules may be avoided.

B. Application of Foreign Law in Practice

In most areas of law, the choice of law rules are internationalist and they often indicate that foreign law is the governing law. The main exceptions to this are in family law, in which the choice of law rule for most issues requires application only of forum law,[21] and in claims under forum legislation, in which case the courts may disregard choice of law considerations and simply apply that legislation. Most international litigation in Australia involves jurisdictional disputes. In jurisdictional disputes, one of the factors that the court takes into account in deciding whether to stay proceedings is whether the governing law is foreign.[22] Many recent decisions regarding choice of law, and the application of foreign law in particular, have arisen

they held was applicable in that case, 'Neither the absence of pleading the relevant content of foreign law, nor the absence of proof would be fatal to the case of the party relying on the relevant provision of foreign law': (2005) 223 CLR 331, 372; [2005] HCA 54, [125]. Some commentators take the view that accordingly Australian choice of law rules are not mandatory: Mortensen, Garnett and Keyes, above n 4, 242, James McComish 'Pleading and Proving Foreign Law in Australia' (2007) 31 Melbourne University Law Review 400, 408. Those arguments assume that courts will apply forum law according to the presumption of similarity, as both Mortensen et al. and McComish acknowledge. As noted below (at III(D)(2)), the Australian courts are becoming more likely not to apply the presumption of similarity, in which case the mandatory nature of choice of law rules becomes evident.

[19] *Busst v Lotsirb Nominees Pty Ltd.* [2003] 1 Qd R 477; [2002] QCA 296.

[20] *Akai Pty Ltd. v The People's Insurance Co Ltd.* (1996) 188 CLR 418.

[21] Foreign law is relevant to marriage validity, may be relevant to determining property entitlements, and the application of foreign law may be considered in jurisdictional disputes. There are a number of family cases in which reference is made to foreign law, including *In the Marriage of Khademollah* (2000) 26 Fam LR 686; [2000] FamCA 1045; *Murakami v Wiryadi* (2010) 268 ALR 377; [2010] NSWCA 7; *Chen v Tan* [2012] FamCA 225.

[22] *Voth v Manildra Flour Mills Pty Ltd.* (1990) 171 CLR 538, 565, adopting and applying the connecting factors identified by Lord Goff in *Spiliada Maritime Corporation v Cansulex Ltd.*, which include the governing law: [1987] AC 460, 477–478.

in this context.[23] Several cases also concern the effect of judgments in cross-border cases.[24]

There are no data systematically collected in Australia as to the foreign states whose laws are most frequently applied or invoked. The cases referred to in this chapter[25] concerned the laws of a wide range of countries, including Azerbaijan, the People's Republic of China, England, Germany, Iran, New Zealand, Norway, Singapore, Switzerland, Taiwan and the United States. Of those cases, United States law is most often relevant.[26]

III. Foreign Law Before Judicial Authorities

A. Nature of Foreign Law

In Australian law, foreign law is regarded as 'a question of fact of a peculiar kind'.[27] The 'existence, the nature and the scope' of foreign law is regarded as a question of fact, whereas the application of foreign law is a question of law.[28] The treatment of foreign law as a fact differs from other questions of fact in several respects. First, if an issue of foreign law arises in a case in which a jury is sitting,[29] the judge must decide the issue of foreign law,[30] whereas the jury would decide all other questions of fact. Second, an appeal court generally will not disturb findings of fact that have been made by trial judges, whereas an appeal court may reconsider the evidence before the trial judge on issues of foreign law and decide whether the trial judge's decision in relation to the content of that foreign law was justified.[31] Finally, an

---

[23] E.g. *Regie Nationale des Usines Renault SA v Zhang* (2002) 210 CLR 491, [2002] HCA 10. There are also a number of influential cases concerning the proof of foreign law which are applications for antisuit injunctions: *National Mutual Holdings Pty Ltd. v Sentry Corporation* (1989) 87 ALR 539; *TS Production LLC v Drew Pictures Pty Ltd.* (2008) 250 ALR 97; [2008] FCA 1110.

[24] E.g. *Boele v Norsemeter Holding AS* [2002] NSWCA 363.

[25] These are not comprehensive of all the Australian decisions involving the application of foreign law; nor is this designed as a representative sample.

[26] The cases referred to in McComish's thorough study of the Australian case law similarly involve the law of a wide range of foreign countries, amongst which US law is the most common: above n 18.

[27] *James Hardie & Co Pty Ltd. v Hall as Administrator of Estate of Putt* (1998) 43 NSWLR 554, 573, citing *Parkasho v Singh* [1968] P 233, 250.

[28] Heydon, above n 1, p 1383.

[29] That would be truly exceptional in Australia, where juries are hardly used in civil proceedings.

[30] Evidence Act 1995 (Cth) s 176, Evidence Act 1995 (NSW) s 176, Evidence (National Uniform Legislation) Act 2011 (NT) s 176, Evidence Act 2001 (Tas) s 176, Evidence Act 2008 (Vic) s 176, Evidence Act 2011 (ACT) s 176; Evidence Act 1929 (SA) s 63A; Supreme Court Act 1935 (WA) s 172.

[31] *James Hardie & Co Pty Ltd. v Hall as Administrator of Estate of Putt* (1998) 43 NSWLR 554, 573–574.

appeal court may permit further evidence of foreign law to be tendered,[32] whereas the tender of fresh evidence on other matters on appeal is only allowed in limited circumstances.

B. Application of Foreign Law

Foreign law is applied by courts almost always only at the instigation of the parties. This means that, generally, foreign law is applied only if at least one party has raised its potential application in litigation; naturally, the party which would benefit from the application of foreign law usually raises its application. The adversarial model of procedure is critical in the resolution of cross-border litigation in Australia. The parties have a great deal of freedom in the management of litigation, and their decisions as to how to plead their claims and defences, and what evidence to tender, are generally decisive. If at least one of the parties refers to foreign law, then the case will be decided by reference to the foreign law, unless there is some deficiency in the proof of foreign law.

The parties may expressly agree as to the content or meaning of the relevant foreign law, for example, by admitting allegations made in pleadings,[33] or by explicitly agreeing that the presumption of similarity between foreign and forum law[34] should be applied.[35] The parties may implicitly agree about the content of foreign law[36]; for example, by not disputing allegations made by the other party.[37] Consistently with the permissive nature of adversarial litigation, the courts will usually respect those agreements. Occasionally, the courts disregard the parties' agreements as to foreign law. In particular, the court may refuse to act on the parties' agreement that the foreign law is similar to forum law, if that appears to be actually unlikely. In *Damberg v Damberg*, the parties agreed that the German law relating to evasion of capital gains tax was the same as the Australian law. The New South Wales Court of Appeal took the view the German law on this issue should not be assumed to be the same as the Australian law and refused to respect the parties' agreement.[38]

---

[32] For example, *O'Driscoll v J Ray McDermott SA* [2006] WASCA 25, [14] (further evidence was permitted because the Australian choice of law rule had changed).

[33] *Damberg v Damberg* (2001) 52 NSWLR 492, 519; [2001] NSWCA 87, [154].

[34] See below, III(D)(2).

[35] *Damberg v Damberg* (2001) 52 NSWLR 492, 519; [2001] NSWCA 87, [154].

[36] *Mokbel v R* [2013] VSCA 118.

[37] *Damberg v Damberg* (2001) 52 NSWLR 492, 519; [2001] NSWCA 87, [154].

[38] *Damberg v Damberg* (2001) 52 NSWLR 492, 522; [2001] NSWCA 87, [162].

C. Ascertainment of Foreign Law

1. General Remarks

The party which relies on the foreign law has the burden of proving the content and meaning of that law.[39] The *iura novit curia* principle does not apply, rather, 'The courts of Australia are not presumed to have any knowledge of foreign law',[40] although if the content of a particular foreign law is so well known as to be 'notorious', the court may take judicial notice of it.[41] Legislation expressly permits the courts to do this in child abduction cases.[42] In litigation in which New Zealand law is applicable, the court may inform itself of the New Zealand law in 'any way that it considers appropriate'.[43]

As noted above, if the party which relies on the foreign law does not satisfactorily prove it, the presumption of similarity may be employed by the court to fill the gap in proof of the foreign law.

2. Means Used by the Australian Courts

The Australian courts use a variety of means to ascertain foreign law.[44] There are two principal means (namely, documentary and expert evidence) by which foreign law is ascertained, and a variety of other means which are used less frequently.

a. Documents

Legislation in every Australian jurisdiction enables the content of foreign law to be established by the production of documents containing the relevant foreign law.[45] This modifies the common law, according to which documentary evidence of foreign law would have to be introduced and proven by experts. A majority of jurisdictions have enacted uniform evidence legislation, which includes provisions relating to the proof of foreign law.[46] The three States which have not joined in the uniform

---

[39] *Regie Nationale des Usines Renault SA v Zhang* (2002) 210 CLR 491, 517–519, [2002] HCA 10, [68]–[72].

[40] *Neilson v Overseas Projects Corporation of Victoria Ltd.* (2005) 223 CLR 331, 370, 391, [2005] HCA 54, [115], [185].

[41] *Mokbel v R* [2013] VSCA 118, [26].

[42] Family Law (Child Abduction Convention) Regulations 1986 (Cth) reg 29(5).

[43] Trans-Tasman Proceedings Act 2010 (Cth) s 97(2).

[44] See also below at VI.

[45] It does not displace the ability of the parties to use expert evidence to prove the foreign law.

[46] This legislation applies in the Commonwealth, the Australian Capital Territory, New South Wales, the Northern Territory, Tasmania and Victoria: Evidence Act 1995 (Cth), Evidence Act 1995 (NSW), Evidence (National Uniform Legislation) Act 2011 (NT), Evidence Act 2001 (Tas),

scheme also have legislation that facilitates the proof of foreign law in slightly different terms.[47]

The uniform evidence legislation permits the proof of a foreign statute, proclamation, treaty or act of state by the production of:

a) a book or pamphlet, containing the statute, proclamation, treaty or act of state, that purports to have been printed by the government or official printer of the country or by authority of the government or administration of the country; or
b) a book or other publication, containing the statute, proclamation, treaty or act of state, that appears to the court to be a reliable source of information; or
c) a book or pamphlet that is or would be used in the courts of the country to inform the courts about, or to prove, the statute, proclamation, treaty or act of state; or
d) a copy of the statute, proclamation, treaty or act of state that is proved to be an examined copy.[48]

This evidence is normally produced by the parties, but courts may also rely on those provisions in identifying foreign legislation.[49] The uniform evidence legislation also provides that 'a book containing reports of judgments of the courts of the country' may be adduced as evidence of, in the first case, 'the unwritten or common law of the country',[50] and in the second case, the interpretation of that foreign legislation, 'if the book is or would be used in the courts of the country to inform the courts' on these matters.[51] The legislation in the other three states is similar, in that it enables the courts to consider primary sources of foreign law.[52] Legislation in two states also expressly permits reference to textbooks.[53]

These provisions are commonly referred to in cases involving the application of foreign law, but they do not apply exclusively, and the content of foreign laws may also be proven in expert evidence. The parties may also tender the relevant parts of the foreign law in translation if it is not written in English. The parties occasionally

---

Evidence Act 2008 (Vic), Evidence Act 2011 (ACT). The relevant provisions of the uniform Evidence Acts are ss 174–175.

[47] Evidence Act 1977 (Qld), s 68; Evidence Act 1929 (SA), s 63; Evidence Act 1906 (WA), ss 70–71.

[48] Section 174(1), Evidence Act 1995 (Cth), Evidence Act 1995 (NSW), Evidence (National Uniform Legislation) Act 2011 (NT), Evidence Act 2001 (Tas), Evidence Act 2008 (Vic), Evidence Act 2011 (ACT).

[49] *MindShare Communications Ltd. v Orleans Investments Pty Ltd.* [2000] FCA 521.

[50] Section 175(1), Evidence Act 1995 (Cth), Evidence Act 1995 (NSW), Evidence (National Uniform Legislation) Act 2011 (NT), Evidence Act 2001 (Tas), Evidence Act 2008 (Vic), Evidence Act 2011 (ACT).

[51] Section 175(2), Evidence Act 1995 (Cth), Evidence Act 1995 (NSW), Evidence (National Uniform Legislation) Act 2011 (NT), Evidence Act 2001 (Tas), Evidence Act 2008 (Vic), Evidence Act 2011 (ACT).

[52] Evidence Act 1977 (Qld) ss 68–69; Evidence Act 1929 (SA) s 63; Evidence Act 1906 (WA) s 70.

[53] Evidence Act 1929 (SA) s 63; Evidence Act 1906 (WA) s 71.

tender journal articles about the foreign law,[54] and sometimes expert witnesses refer to journal articles in their expert evidence.[55]

Internet sources are rarely referred to explicitly, but occasionally, judges locate foreign laws by Internet searches.[56]

b. Assistance of the Parties

The parties have the obligation to prove the content and general meaning of foreign law on which their claims or defences rely, which is done by the tender of documents or by expert evidence.

c. Expert Witnesses

In most cases, foreign law is proven by expert evidence. The expert's evidence is often given by way of witness statement or affidavit. Experts may also attend the hearing to give oral evidence, in which case the expert may be subject to cross-examination. The expert may refer in their evidence to foreign legal materials, and the court is then entitled to refer to those materials.[57]

An expert on foreign law must be qualified according to the normal rules relating to the qualification of experts. An expert must have specialised knowledge based on training, study or experience.[58] The opposing party may challenge the expert's qualifications, but this is rarely done. In most cases, the expert is a legal practitioner with extensive and recent experience in practising law in the foreign country. Some experts are academics,[59] some of whom also have practical experience,[60] and occasionally the experts are retired judges of the foreign legal system. In most cases, each party produces its own expert witness. It is not uncommon for the expert evidence to be incomplete, in terms of not comprehensively describing the content and general interpretation of the relevant foreign law, or inconsistent, in that each party often leads expert evidence that is different in some respects to the expert evidence led by the other party.

---

[54] This was noted by Gleeson CJ and Kirby J in *Neilson v Overseas Projects Corporation of Victoria Ltd.* (2005) 223 CLR 331, 339, 379, [2005] HCA 54, [3], [150].

[55] *TS Production LLC v Drew Pictures Pty Ltd.* (2008) 250 ALR 97, 107–108; [2008] FCA 1110, [53].

[56] *MindShare Communications Ltd. v Orleans Investments Pty Ltd.* [2000] FCA 521, [37].

[57] *TS Production LLC v Drew Pictures Pty Ltd.* (2008) 250 ALR 97, 106; [2008] FCA 1110, [48].

[58] Section 177(1)(b) Evidence Act 1995 (Cth), Evidence Act 1995 (NSW), Evidence (National Uniform Legislation) Act 2011 (NT), Evidence Act 2001 (Tas), Evidence Act 2008 (Vic), Evidence Act 2011 (ACT).

[59] In *Murakami v Wiryadi*, the expert was an Australian professor of Indonesian law: (2010) 268 ALR 377; [2010] NSWCA 7.

[60] In *Faxtech Pty Ltd. v Optronics Ltd.*, the expert was an English professor of private international law with practical experience: [2011] FCA 1320.

d. Inquiry to Expert Bodies or Institutions

The Supreme Court of New South Wales may, 'on the application of one or more parties or on its own motion, order that the question of foreign law be answered by a referee'.[61] Some of the other superior courts have general powers to refer matters for determination to referees, and could use that power to determine a question of foreign law.[62] Inquiry to expert institutes or domestic judicial and/or non-judicial authorities is not used in Australia.

Insofar as inquiry to foreign judicial and/or non-judicial authorities is concerned, in New South Wales, 'the Supreme Court may, on the application of one or more of the parties and with the consent of all the parties, order that proceedings be commenced in a foreign court in order to answer a question as to the principles of foreign law or as to their application.'[63] It is accepted that this method may be more expensive than using expert evidence, but it has been defended on the basis that it is quick and yields more accurate, certain and authoritative results.[64] This method is similar to that created by the British Law Ascertainment Act, an 1859 statute of the British parliament, which applied directly in Australia. This legislation allowed the courts of British dominions, including Australia, to remit questions of law directly to the courts of other British dominions, to provide an opinion to the requesting court on the application of its law to the facts of the case.[65] This procedure was rarely used and is no longer available in Australia.[66]

Inquiry via bilateral or multilateral treaties for access to legal information is available in Australia. Australia is party to bilateral treaties on Judicial Assistance in Civil and Commercial Matters with the Republic of Thailand and the Republic of Korea, which contain provisions relevant to the provision of information about laws. The treaties are broadly similar; both require the requested state, via its Central

[61] Uniform Civil Procedure Rules 2005 (NSW), r 6.44(2). This provision has only been used in one published case: *Marshall v Fleming* [2013] NSWSC 566 (reversed on appeal, *Marshall v Fleming* [2014] NSWCA 64).

[62] Federal Court of Australia Act 1976 (Cth), s 54A. The report of the referee is not binding on the court: s 54A(3). This provision has not been used in any published decision for the purposes of establishing the application foreign law.

[63] Uniform Civil Procedure Rules 2005 (NSW), r 6.44(1). This provision gives effect to Memoranda of Understanding entered into between the Supreme Court of New South Wales and the Supreme Court of Singapore, and with the New York Court of Appeals, which permit a court to make a request to the foreign court for its opinion on the application of its law to the facts of the case. See Memorandum of Understanding Between the Supreme Court of Singapore and the Supreme Court of New South Wales on References of Questions of Foreign Law 2010 and Memorandum of Understanding Between the Chief Justice of New South Wales and the Chief Judge of State of New York on References of Foreign Law 2010.

[64] *Marshall v Fleming* [2013] NSWSC 566, [21], citing JJ Spigelman, 'Proof of Foreign Law by Reference to the Foreign Court' (2011) 127 Law Quarterly Review 208, 213.

[65] British Law Ascertainment Act 1859 (Imp), s 1.

[66] It has been explicitly repealed in the Australian Capital Territory (Statute Law Amendment Act 2002 (ACT), Sch 4. See also Imperial Acts Application Act 1969 (NSW) s 8; Imperial Acts Application Act 1984 (Qld) s 7; Imperial Acts Application Act 1980 (Vic) s 5.

Authority, to provide the Central Authority of the requesting state with extracts from judicial records and legislation in cases in which nationals of the requesting state are involved.[67] In Australia, the Central Authority is the Commonwealth Attorney-General's Department.

Direct communication between local and foreign judges is also possible. Australian courts may in limited circumstances directly contact foreign courts to request information about foreign law. Under the UNCITRAL Model Law of Cross-border Insolvency, which Australia has adopted, an Australian court may directly request information from foreign courts.[68] Two judges of the Family Court of Australia are members of the Hague Judges Network. The court is only able to make a request for information directly to a foreign judge through the Hague Judges Network if both parties consent.[69]

3. Effects of the Provided Information

Generally, information provided about foreign law is not binding on the court, even if the expert evidence is uncontradicted.[70] However, the 'court should be reluctant to reject [expert evidence] unless it be patently absurd or inconsistent'.[71] The court should reject the evidence of a qualified expert as to the foreign law only rarely,[72] but it is permissible for Australian courts to do so in favour of their own conclusions.[73] This occurred in *Faxtech Pty Ltd. v ITL Optronics Ltd.*, in which Middleton

[67] Agreement on Judicial Assistance in Civil and Commercial Matters and Co-operation in Arbitration between Australia and the Kingdom of Thailand 1998 (Australian Treaty Series 1998, No 18), art.20; Treaty on Judicial Assistance in Civil and Commercial Matters between Australia and the Republic of Korea 2000 (Australian Treaty Series 2000, No 5) art.27. The treaty with Korea is not just limited to cases involving nationals of the requesting state; in addition, the requested state is obliged to provide 'information on its laws and regulations relating to a legal proceeding of the requesting Contracting Party': art.27(1).

[68] UNCITRAL Model Law on Cross-border Insolvency, art.25(2), which is adopted into Australian law by the Cross-Border Insolvency Act 2008 (Cth) s 6 (the Model Law is incorporated as Schedule 1 to the Act).

[69] The Honourable Justice Victoria Bennett, 'Improving the Operation of the 1980 Hague Convention: National and International Networking and New Approaches to Relocation', 6th World Congress on Family Law and Children's Rights, Sydney, Australia, 16–20 March 2013, [52].

[70] *Neilson v Overseas Projects Corporation of Victoria Ltd.* (2005) 223 CLR 331, 391, [2005] HCA 54, [185]; *James Hardie & Co Pty Ltd. v Hall as Administrator of Estate of Putt* (1998) 43 NSWLR 554, 573.

[71] *Sharif v Azard* [1967] QB 605, 616, approved in *Neilson v Overseas Projects Corporation of Victoria Ltd.* (2005) 223 CLR 331, 391, [2005] HCA 54, [185]; *James Hardie & Co Pty Ltd. v Hall as Administrator of Estate of Putt* (1998) 43 NSWLR 554, 573.

[72] *James Hardie & Co Pty Ltd. v Hall as Administrator of Estate of Putt* (1998) 43 NSWLR 554, 573. McComish found that uncontradicted expert evidence was 'frequently questioned, criticised or disregarded by Australian courts': above n 18, 430.

[73] *Neilson v Overseas Projects Corporation of Victoria Ltd.* (2005) 223 CLR 331, 391, [2005] HCA 54, [185]; *James Hardie & Co Pty Ltd. v Hall as Administrator of Estate of Putt* (1998) 43 NSWLR 554, 573.

J disregarded the expert opinion of an English academic as to whether the jurisdiction clause was exclusive according to English law.[74] Middleton J stated that, 'Using the cases and principles referred to by [the expert witness], I have brought my own legal reasoning to interpret the…agreement'.[75]

It is not uncommon for the court to be presented with conflicting expert evidence. In that case, the court must attempt to determine what the foreign law is, on the basis of the material put into evidence by the parties.[76]

Information about foreign law provided via the Hague Judges Network binds neither the parties nor the court; it provides propositions which the parties individually or mutually may or may not adopt and put into evidence.[77]

The reliability of the information about foreign law is mainly controlled by the rules relating to expert witnesses. Expert evidence about foreign law can be tested and challenged by the opposing party in cross-examination, by questions put to the expert by the judge. It may also be contradicted by other evidence, including expert testimony led by the opposing party.

4. Costs

The costs of ascertaining foreign law are usually borne by the parties. At the time of litigation, the party which seeks to rely on it must bear the costs associated with the proof of foreign law. Those costs may be partly recovered by the successful party at the conclusion of the case, because in Australian civil litigation the unsuccessful party bears the successful party's costs, although the successful party never recovers all of its costs.

5. Other Issues

There are significant issues associated with the use of experts in proving foreign law. Expert evidence is often contradictory or incomplete, which creates additional difficulties for the courts. Obtaining expert evidence is expensive, which particularly affects parties of limited means, who are especially likely to be involved in proceedings in the family jurisdiction. Australian law has been slow to recognise and respond to these difficulties but some of the innovations referred to above, particularly the use of referees and direct communication between courts, are promising.

---

74 [2011] FCA 1320, [8]–[14].

75 [2011] FCA 1320, [11].

76 *TS Production LLC v Drew Pictures Pty Ltd.* (2008) 250 ALR 97, 106; [2008] FCA 1110, [48].

77 Bennett, above n 69, [52].

D. Interpretation and Application of Foreign Law

1. General Remarks

Foreign law is interpreted and applied according to Australian law, 'by reference to' the law of the country of origin. The application of foreign law is done according to the Australian procedural rules on pleading and proof of foreign law. The Australian court 'derives the content of the rights and obligations of the parties by reference to the chosen foreign law'.[78]

Australian law distinguishes between the general interpretation of foreign law and the application of the foreign law to the facts of the case at hand. Evidence as to the general interpretation of the foreign law is admissible; indeed, it may be essential to assist the court in understanding what the foreign law is.[79] By contrast, the application of the foreign law to the facts of the case is always a question for the Australian court, and therefore evidence as to how the foreign law would be applied to the case is not admissible.[80] If the foreign law confers a discretion, evidence may be received about how the foreign court would exercise that discretion in general, 'with regard to any pattern of course of decision',[81] but evidence as to how the discretion would be applied in the particular case is not admissible.[82]

If the evidence as to the interpretation and general application of foreign law is held to be insufficient, then the Australian courts may apply Australian principles of interpretation, according to the presumption of similarity between foreign and forum law, which is discussed next.

2. Gaps in the Proof of Foreign Law

If the foreign law is not proven to the civil standard of proof (the balance of probabilities), then the court may apply the presumption of similarity between foreign and forum law, and forum law fills the gap.[83] This was done in the leading case on

[78] *Neilson v Overseas Projects Corporation of Victoria Ltd.* (2005) 223 CLR 331, 369; [2005] HCA 54, [113].

[79] *McHugh v Australian Jockey Club Ltd. (No 6)* [2011] FCA 1135, [5].

[80] *Neilson v Overseas Projects Corporation of Victoria Ltd.* (2005) 223 CLR 331, 371; [2005] HCA 54, [120]; *Allstate Life Insurance Co v Australia & New Zealand Banking Group Ltd. (No 6)* (1996) 64 FCR 79; *US Trust Co of New York v Australia and New Zealand Banking Group Ltd.* (1995) 37 NSWLR 131, 146; *Australian Competition and Consumer Commission v PT Garuda Indonesia Ltd. (No 8)* [2013] FCA 172; *Marshall v Fleming* [2014] NSWCA 64, [20].

[81] *Allstate Life Insurance Co v Australia & New Zealand Banking Group Ltd. (No 6)* (1996) 64 FCR 79, 82, cited with approval in *Neilson v Overseas Projects Corporation of Victoria Ltd.* (2005) 223 CLR 331, 371, [2005] HCA 54, [122].

[82] *Neilson v Overseas Projects Corporation of Victoria Ltd.* (2005) 223 CLR 331, 371, [2005] HCA 54, [120]–[122]; *Allstate Life Insurance Co v Australia & New Zealand Banking Group Ltd. (No 6)* (1996) 64 FCR 79.

[83] *Akai Pty Ltd. v The People's Insurance Company Ltd.* (1996) 188 CLR 418, 444.

proof of foreign law, *Neilson v Overseas Projects Corporation of Victoria Ltd.* ('*Neilson*').[84] In this case, a majority of the High Court of Australia held that the evidence as to the content of the applicable Chinese legislation was sufficient, but that the evidence as to how that law would be interpreted was insufficient.[85] The majority therefore applied the presumption of similarity, and on that basis applied Australian principles of statutory interpretation to determine if a discretion under Chinese law should be applied.

Recently, some Australian courts have not applied the presumption because the foreign and forum law are evidently dissimilar. This is likely if the foreign legal system is not a common law system,[86] if the foreign law is statutory[87] or procedural,[88] and if the relevant foreign law is not part of 'a field resting on great and broad principles likely to be part of any given legal system.'[89] On the other hand, a bare majority of the High Court in *Neilson*[90] held, without noting the differences between Chinese and Australian law, that the presumption of similarity should be applied, and on that basis used Australian principles of statutory construction to determine whether a discretion under Chinese legislation should be applied.[91] The minority in *Neilson* refused to apply the presumption of similarity, because of the apparent dissimilarity between the applicable Chinese law and its counterpart in Australian law,[92] and the general dissimilarity between the Chinese and Australian legal systems.

Recently, lower courts have become critical of the presumption of similarity, and do not always apply it. The New South Wales Court of Appeal refused to apply the presumption of similarity in several cases, particularly in cases in which the foreign

[84] (2005) 223 CLR 331, [2005] HCA 54.

[85] (2005) 223 CLR 331, [2005] HCA 54. Gummow and Hayne JJ held that it was not necessary to decide if the expert evidence was sufficient, because the result would have been the same in either event: 371–372, [124].

[86] *Damberg v Damberg* (2001) 52 NSWLR 492, 522; [2001] NSWCA 87, [162]. Cf. *Puttick v Tenon Ltd.* (2008) 238 CLR 265, 277–278, [2008] HCA 54, [31]. In *Neilson*, Kirby J noted that a presumption 'that a basic rule of the substantive law of England or some other common law country...is the same as Australia is one that might be justified in a particular case': *Neilson v Overseas Projects Corporation of Victoria Ltd.* (2005) 223 CLR 331, 343, 396, [2005] HCA 54, [203].

[87] *Damberg v Damberg* (2001) 52 NSWLR 492, 522; [2001] NSWCA 87, [162].

[88] *Boele v Norsemeter Holding AS* [2002] NSWCA 363, [40].

[89] *Damberg v Damberg* (2001) 52 NSWLR 492, 522; [2001] NSWCA 87, [162].

[90] *Neilson v Overseas Projects Corporation of Victoria Ltd.* (2005) 223 CLR 331; [2005] HCA 54.

[91] *Neilson v Overseas Projects Corporation of Victoria Ltd.* (2005) 223 CLR 331, 372, 411, 416, [2005] HCA 54, [126], [249], [267].

[92] *Neilson v Overseas Projects Corporation of Victoria Ltd.* (2005) 223 CLR 331, 343, 348, 396–397, [2005] HCA 54, [16], [36], [203]–[204]. The Chinese law gave a discretion to disapply the law of the place of the tort in favour of the law of the place of the parties' joint nationality, whereas Australian law does not permit any such exception. Kirby J also noted that 'it would be an absurd fiction to pretend that the elaborate principles of statutory construction developed by, or applicable to, Australian courts have exact equivalents in the courts of China, given the divergent historical and jurisprudential traditions of the two legal systems': 395, [198].

legal system was not a common law country.[93] In some first instance decisions, the courts have refused to apply the presumption.[94]

If the presumption of similarity is not applied, the issue on which proof of foreign law depends will be decided against the party who bears the onus of proof. This may lead to the claim being dismissed as not proven,[95] or the defence failing.

As noted above,[96] many cases involve the law of countries that are dissimilar to Australian law, and therefore the presumption of similarity is likely to become increasingly unhelpful in resolving lacunae in the proof of foreign law.

E. Failure to Establish Foreign Law

If the foreign law cannot be ascertained, forum law may be applied according to the presumption of similarity. As noted above, Australian judges are now likely to consider whether the foreign law should be assumed to be similar to forum law, and if not, to refuse to apply this presumption. The presumption is more likely to be applied to fill in incidental, rather than substantial, gaps in the evidence as to foreign law.[97] If the presumption is not applied, the issue would have to be decided against the party which has relied on the foreign law.

The policy behind the presumption of similarity is somewhat obscure. In a judgment that has been influential in later cases in which courts have refused to apply the presumption of similarity, Heydon JA suggested that it was never intended to apply to every situation, but rather that its application always depended on there being a high degree of similarity between the foreign law and forum law.[98]

In the adversarial system of procedure, the courts are required to determine the case on the basis of the submissions made, and the material presented, by the parties.

---

[93] *Damberg v Damberg* (2001) 52 NSWLR 492, 522; [2001] NSWCA 87, [162]; *Boele v Norsemeter Holding AS* [2002] NSWCA 363; *Severstal Export GmbH v Bhushan Steel Ltd.* [2013] NSWCA 102, [68]. On the other hand, in *Nicholls v Michael Wilson & Partners Ltd.*, Lindgren AJA held that claims of breach of contract, torts of inducing breach of contract and conspiracy to injure and claims of breach of fiduciary duty should be treated as fields 'resting on broad principles likely to be part of any given legal system', even though the foreign law in question was the law of Kazakhstan: [2010] NSWCA 222, [334].

[94] *PCH Offshore Pty Ltd. v Dunn (No 2)* (2010) 273 ALR 167, 182; [2010] FCA [112]. This may be so even where the foreign legal system is a common law system, if the foreign law is statutory: *McHugh v Australian Jockey Club Ltd. (No 6)* [2011] FCA 1135, [6] (in which the applicant had tendered the Competition Act 1998 (UK), the Treaty on European Union, the Treaty on the Functioning of the European Union, the Sherman Act (US) and the Commerce Act 1986 (NZ), but had led no evidence as to how those laws applied).

[95] *Neilson v Overseas Projects Corporation of Victoria Ltd.* (2005) 223 CLR 331, 348, [2005] HCA 54, [35].

[96] At I(3).

[97] McComish, above n 18, 438–439.

[98] *Damberg v Damberg* (2001) 52 NSWLR 492, 518; [2001] NSWCA 87, [144]–[146].

In *Neilson*, the plaintiff initially led no evidence as to the applicable Chinese law. Gleeson CJ noted that

> it was necessary for the trial judge to decide the issues raised by the parties on the evidence which they presented. This is adversarial litigation, and the outcome of such legislation is commonly influenced by the way in which the parties have chosen to conduct their respective cases.[99]

Two other members of the majority stated that 'Neither the absence of pleading the relevant content of the foreign law nor the absence of proof [of the foreign law] would be fatal to the case of the party relying on the relevant provision of foreign law'.[100] Members of the minority disagreed with this approach, insisting that if the party whose case relied on the foreign law had failed to prove it, their case should simply fail.[101]

It has been suggested that it is more accurate to say that the court applies its own law in default of proof of the foreign law, rather than that forum law applies because foreign law is presumed to resemble it.[102] The trend of the recent Australian cases – with the very significant exception of the High Court's decision in *Neilson* – is inconsistent with that suggestion. It may be permitted in some cases to presume similarity, and on that basis to apply Australian law if there is a gap in the proof of foreign law. But it cannot be assumed that this will be effective in all cases, and therefore, Australian law will not always be applied in default of proof of foreign law.

IV. Judicial Review

A. *Conflict of Laws Rules*

An error in the application of conflict of laws rules is an error of law from which the parties can appeal,[103] subject to the usual constraints on appeals.[104]

---

[99] *Neilson v Overseas Projects Corporation of Victoria Ltd.* (2005) 223 CLR 331, 338; [2005] HCA 54, [1].

[100] *Neilson v Overseas Projects Corporation of Victoria Ltd.* (2005) 223 CLR 331, 372; [2005] HCA 54, [125]. Gleeson CJ similarly noted that 'it was necessary for the trial judge to decide the issues raised by the parties on the evidence which they presented': ibid., 338, [1]. See similarly Adrian Briggs, 'The Meaning and Proof of Foreign Law' [2006] Lloyd's Maritime and Commercial Law Quarterly 1, 6.

[101] *Neilson v Overseas Projects Corporation of Victoria Ltd.* (2005) 223 CLR 331, 348; 397–398 [2005] HCA 54, [35], [206].

[102] Briggs, above n 100, 6.

[103] E.g. *Fleming v Marshall* [2011] NSWCA 86.

[104] There is no right to appeal to the High Court of Australia. The parties can only appeal with the special leave of the court: Judiciary Act 1903 (Cth) s 35A.

B. Foreign Law

When foreign law has erroneously been applied, the parties can appeal that decision. As noted above, foreign law is regarded as a question of fact, but one of a 'peculiar kind'.[105] One of the peculiarities of the factual characterisation of foreign law is that the parties may appeal from the decision of the primary judge on the basis that the primary judge misapplied the foreign law, although they cannot appeal against other decisions as to the facts. The appellate court is under a duty 'to examine the evidence of foreign law which was before the trial judge and to decide for itself whether that evidence justified the conclusion to which the trial judge came'.[106]

This solution was inherited from the English common law. It has been suggested that the availability of appeal on questions of foreign law may be an important protection for the parties, given that trial judges are often confronted by inconsistent expert evidence as to the foreign law, and also that it emphasises that evidence of foreign law is not purely factual, in the same way as other evidence as to facts.[107]

V. Foreign Law in Other Instances

A. Foreign Law in Administrative Decisions

Foreign law is often relevant in proceedings before administrative tribunals. This frequently occurs in the migration context, and particularly in the context of appeals from initial decisions of the Commonwealth Minister to the Administrative Appeals Tribunal, which is part of the executive government of the Commonwealth. In that context, foreign law is ascertained and applied in a similar way to its application in civil litigation, although the rules of evidence do not apply strictly to this tribunal.[108] Foreign law may also be relevant in taxation cases, some of which are also decided initially in administrative proceedings.

---

[105] *James Hardie & Co Pty Ltd. v Hall as Administrator of Estate of Putt* (1998) 43 NSWLR 554, 573, citing *Parkasho v Singh* [1968] P 233, 250; see above, II (A)(1).

[106] *James Hardie & Co Pty Ltd. v Hall as Administrator of Estate of Putt* (1998) 43 NSWLR 554, 573–4, citing *Parkasho v Singh* [1968] P 233, 250.

[107] Fentiman, above n 18, 201–202.

[108] Migration Act 1958 (Cth) ss 353(2)(a), 420(2)(a).

B. Foreign Law in Alternative Dispute Resolution

Foreign law is ascertained and applied in commercial arbitration in much the same way as in international litigation.[109] Expert witnesses provide evidence to the tribunal as to the foreign law,[110] and the parties may agree as to aspects of the applicable foreign law.[111] There is no information available as to the use that is made of foreign law in mediation and other forms of dispute resolution in Australia.

C. Foreign Law in Advisory Work by Lawyers

There is no information published on how lawyers identify relevant foreign law in advisory work. Private international law and comparative law are not required subjects in order to qualify for admission to practice in Australia, and in most law schools they are not compulsory. Some practising lawyers may be unfamiliar with the relevance and application of foreign law in cross-border transactions.

IV. Access to Foreign Law: Status Quo

A. Legal Information on Official Websites

Australian legislation and case law from all jurisdictions is published on official websites.[112] The official websites of the courts of each Australian jurisdiction provide some information about court processes. The Commonwealth Attorney-General's website provides information about applicable processes in international litigation. There are few formal means by which information about Australian law may be sought,[113] but Australian government departments and agencies, particularly the Commonwealth Attorney-General's Department, receive and respond to informal requests for information about Australian law from outside Australia.

---

[109] *BHP Billiton Ltd. v Oil Basins Ltd.* (2007) 18 VR 346; [2007] VSCA 255; *Re Independent State of Papua New Guinea (No 2)* [2001] 2 Qd R 162, 171.

[110] *BHP Billiton Ltd. v Oil Basins Ltd.* (2007) 18 VR 346; [2007] VSCA 255.

[111] *Re Independent State of Papua New Guinea (No 2)* [2001] 2 Qd R 162, 171.

[112] See above n 7.

[113] The main exceptions are the provisions of the bilateral treaties that Australia has with Thailand and the Republic of Korea: see above II(B)(1)(h).

B. Direct Communication Between Judges

Two judges of the Family Court of Australia are members of the Hague Judges Network[114]; direct court-to-court communication is permitted in cross-border insolvency cases[115]; and Australian courts may directly communicate with judges in Thailand and the Republic of Korea, under bilateral treaties with those countries.[116]

C. Bilateral Arrangements on Foreign Law

As noted above, Australia is party to two bilateral treaties on Judicial Assistance in Civil and Commercial Matters with the Republic of Thailand and the Republic of Korea, which contain provisions relevant to the provision of information about laws.[117]

In 2010, the Supreme Court of New South Wales entered into two Memoranda of Understanding to facilitate access to information about foreign law, one with the Supreme Court of Singapore and the other with the New York Court of Appeals.[118] These Memoranda are in slightly different terms, but generally permit each court to refer questions of foreign law to the other court. Subsequently, the New South Wales Uniform Civil Procedure Rules were amended to include specific provisions enabling the NSW courts to appoint a referee to answer a question of foreign law.[119] This is not limited to the foreign courts with which the Supreme Court of New South Wales has entered into Memoranda of Understanding.

The amendments were intended to give effect to the Memoranda of Understanding, but the New South Wales Court of Appeal held in March 2014 that the system envisaged in the Memoranda for resolving an issue of foreign law by a foreign court – which contemplates a reference from the Chief Justice of the NSW Supreme Court to the Chief Justice of the foreign court, and for the foreign Chief Justice to appoint the referee or referees – is incompatible with the system for appointment of a referee under the NSW rules of court, under which the NSW court must appoint the referee.[120]

[114] See above at II(C)(2)(i).

[115] See above at II(C)(2)(i).

[116] See above, II(B)(1)(h).

[117] See above II(B)(1)(h).

[118] See above, n 63.

[119] Uniform Civil Procedure Rules 2005 (NSW) r 6.44.

[120] *Marshall v Fleming* [2014] NSWCA 64. Both Uniform Civil Procedure Rules 2005 (NSW) rr 6.44(2) and 20.14 only empower the NSW Supreme Court to appoint a referee.

D. Other Regional Arrangements

Australia has a treaty with New Zealand to facilitate Trans-Tasman court proceedings and enforcement of judgments.[121] The treaty itself does not address the proof of foreign law, but the legislation which gives effect to it permits the Australian court to 'inform itself' about New Zealand legislation 'in any way that it considers appropriate'.[122]

E. Use and Effectiveness of Bilateral Arrangements to Facilitate Proof of Foreign Law

Legislation which facilitates proof of New Zealand law is sometimes used,[123] but the other bilateral arrangements are scarcely used. As at August 2016, the provisions relevant to the proof of foreign law of Australia's bilateral treaties with Thailand and the Republic of Korea had never been cited in Australian courts. As at August 2016, there was only one published decision in which a New South Wales court had ordered that a referee be appointed under the rules based on the Memoranda of Understanding entered into by the New South Wales Supreme Court.[124]

The similarity between the Australian and New Zealand legal systems means that problems with the proof and application of foreign law are minimized in litigation involving the application of New Zealand legislation. In litigation involving the application of the law of the Republic of Korea or Thailand,[125] the courts do not refer to the bilateral arrangement, perhaps suggesting a lack of awareness of the

[121] Agreement between the Government of Australia and the Government of New Zealand on Trans-Tasman Court Proceedings and Regulatory Enforcement [2013] Australian Treaty Series 13. The treaty was concluded in 2008 but did not come into effect until 2013.

[122] Trans-Tasman Proceedings Act 2010 (Cth) s 97. This legislation also facilitates the proof of other issues relevant to New Zealand law, including the proof of official instruments, acts of state and public documents: ss 98–102. These provisions repeat those of the Evidence and Procedure (New Zealand) Act 1994 (Cth) ss 40–45, which was repealed and ceased to have effect when the Trans-Tasman Proceedings Act 2010 (Cth) came into effect, in October 2013.

[123] The Trans-Tasman Proceedings Act 2010 (Cth) only came into effect in October 2013, and at the time of writing in August 2016, its provisions relating to the proof of New Zealand law had not been cited in any Australian cases. Its predecessor, the Evidence and Procedure (New Zealand) Act 1994 (Cth), has been used in Australian litigation.

[124] *Marshall v Fleming* [2013] NSWSC 566. This decision was overturned on appeal to the New South Wales Court of Appeal for several reasons. See *Marshall v Fleming* [2014] NSWCA 64, discussed below at text accompanying n 120.

[125] There is little commercial litigation involving these countries, but there have been several applications in the Family Court involving commercial surrogacy arrangements that were made in Thailand, and in several of these cases, Thai law relating to parental status is sometimes referred to. In those cases, Thai law is proven by expert evidence, rather than by reference to the bilateral treaty: see e.g. *Ellison & Karnchanit* [2012] FamCA 602, [23].

provisions of these treaties on the part of parties and courts. The mechanism under the New South Wales rules of court, allowing a court to order that proceedings be commenced in a foreign court to determine a question about foreign law, has only been recently established, and is likely to be regarded by parties and courts as relatively expensive and time-consuming. If the parties agree that the forum courts should exercise jurisdiction, or if the court determines that it should exercise jurisdiction, then it is difficult to justify the costs and inconvenience of requiring the parties separately to litigate a question of foreign law in a foreign court, even though there are obvious advantages in the foreign court determining the application of its own law to the facts.

VII. Access to Foreign Law: Further Developments

A. Practical Need to Improve Access to Foreign Law

1. General Comments

It is desirable to improve access to foreign law for courts and for the parties, especially those of limited financial means.[126] There are significant problems associated with the current system, particularly the costs associated with the identification, proof and application of foreign law, including the real prospects of the court being provided with no, insufficient, or conflicting evidence as to foreign law. The former Chief Justice of the Supreme Court of New South Wales noted that 'Experts are expensive, can be difficult to procure, are of varying expertise and ability and are frequently partisan.'[127] There has been little effort to directly resolve these problems.

Foreign law is often relevant in migration and refugee law, and improving access for the benefit of decision-makers, government departments, and applicants involving in migration decisions is also highly desirable.

2. Access to Foreign Law in Different Areas of Law

There are no differences in the need to access foreign law in different areas that arise as a matter of principle, but in practice, accessing and comprehending the application of foreign law is more challenging when the substance of the foreign law is highly complex or different to forum law. The costs and difficulty associated with the identification of relevant foreign law are likely to impact disproportionately on parties of limited financial means. Foreign law is rarely relevant in family litigation

[126] This is especially important in the family jurisdiction, particularly in child abduction cases: Bennett, above n 69, [53], [69].

[127] Spigelman, above n 64, 210.

in Australia, because the general choice of law rule requires only the application of the law of the forum, but where it is relevant – especially in child abduction cases – the costs to the parties of accessing expert evidence is often prohibitive,[128] and other solutions need to be identified.

3. Access to the Law of Other Australian Jurisdictions

The Commonwealth Constitution obliges the courts of Australian States to give 'full faith and credit…to the laws, public Acts and records, and the judicial proceedings of every State'.[129] It also provides that Commonwealth legislation is 'binding on the courts, judges and people of every State'.[130] Australian courts have little difficulty in accessing, interpreting and applying the laws of other Australian jurisdictions, and can transfer proceedings to other Australian courts if the proceedings are more appropriately determined in them.[131] There is no need to improve access to legal information within Australia.

B. Conflict of Laws Solutions

1. Changes to Relevant Principles of Law

The Australian choice of law rules should not be modified to minimize the number of cases in which foreign law is applicable; if anything, some choice of law rules should be reformed to minimize the reference to the lex fori per se. On the other hand, the Australian principles of jurisdiction have been widely criticised, on the basis that they are too broad and are likely to lead to the court exercising its jurisdiction in cases which would be more appropriately resolved in foreign courts, including in cases in which foreign law is the applicable law.[132] Reform to the jurisdictional

---

[128] See Bennett, above n 69, [53], [69].

[129] Commonwealth of Australia Constitution Act, s 118. The national uniform evidence legislation provides that 'All public acts, records and judicial proceedings of a State or Territory that are proved or authenticated in accordance with this Act are to be given in every court, and in every public office in Australia, such faith and credit as they have by law or usage in the courts and public offices of that State or Territory.' (section 185 Evidence Act 1995 (Cth), Evidence Act 1995 (NSW), Evidence (National Uniform Legislation) Act 2011 (NT), Evidence Act 2001 (Tas), Evidence Act 2008 (Vic), Evidence Act 2011 (ACT)).

[130] Commonwealth of Australia Constitution Act, s 5.

[131] Jurisdiction of Courts (Cross-Vesting) Act 1987 (Cth) s 5, and legislation of the same name in all Australian jurisdictions.

[132] This is particularly so since Australian courts insist that the fact that the governing law is foreign law will not necessarily justify staying proceedings on the basis of *forum non conveniens*: *Puttick v Tenon Ltd.* (2008) 238 CLR 265, 277–278; [2008] HCA 54, [31].

rules should therefore lead to a reduction in the number of cases in which the Australian courts are required to apply foreign law.

2. Changes to the Treatment of Foreign Law

Although there are some obvious problems with the Australian law, it would not be simple to change the treatment of foreign law. Within an adversarial system, it is controversial for the court to determine *ex officio* whether to consider foreign law, especially if that were inconsistent with the manner in which the parties pled and proved their claims and defences. However, it seems likely that the current trend, according to which the courts are less likely simply to assume similarity between Australian and foreign law, will continue. If the parties make no submissions as to the foreign law in such cases, rather than dismiss the claim or defence, the courts should perhaps consider whether it was possible to ascertain the foreign law without the parties' assistance, for example by making greater use of referees or court-appointed experts, or to invite the parties to make further submissions.

3. International and Regional Instruments

The development of international or regional instruments which facilitate access to, and proof of, foreign law would be very useful in terms of improving the treatment of foreign law in Australia. This would be particularly important from an Australian perspective when the foreign law is not from a common law system and is not written in English.

C. Methods of Facilitating Access to Foreign Law

1. Instruments Establishing Administrative and Judicial Cooperation

Instruments that establish cooperation for the exchange of information about law are useful and sensible tools to facilitate access to foreign law. In an adversarial legal system, it can be problematic that the proof of foreign law is entirely left to the parties. This is for two reasons: first, it creates an additional burden on the parties and therefore an additional barrier to parties of limited financial means. Second, it creates the very real possibility of a conflict in expert evidence. The methods that have been developed in Australia to establish foreign law, other than by reference to expert evidence, each provides a useful basis for considering how the treatment of foreign law might further be improved. The solution adopted in the New South Wales Memoranda of Understanding, and subsequently established in the New South Wales rules of court, which require separate proceedings to be conducted in the foreign system is unattractively expensive and undermines the parties' wishes to litigate in the forum pursuant to Australian jurisdictional principles, which do permit litigation to be commenced and continued in Australia even though foreign law is applicable.

2. Structure and Mechanisms of Instruments for Improved Cooperation

Instruments to improve cooperation for the exchange of information about foreign law should be open to judicial authorities and to government departments.

a. Direct Requests

It should be possible for a request to be sent directly to the competent authority of the foreign state. This method appears to work effectively in the Hague Judges Network, and in cross-border insolvency cases.

b. Effect of Response from Requested State

The answer provided by the requested state about its law should not be binding on the courts or on the parties.

c. Cost for Services on Legal Information

Services on legal information should be provided without cost by the requested state.

3. Other Methods of Facilitating Access to Foreign Law

Other methods should be considered in order to improve and facilitate access to foreign law. These include facilitating direct communication between judges, establishing networks of legal professionals, establishing lists of qualified experts and expert institutions, and providing relevant and accessible information via the Internet.

a. Direct Communication Between Judges

This appears to be effective in the context of the Hague Judges Network, although Justice Bennett, one of the Australian members of the Network, noted resistance from some Family Court judges to the use of direct court-to-court communication, on the basis that the parties should bear the onus of proving relevant foreign law.[133] This reflects the novelty of this model, and similar resistance may initially be expected in some other jurisdictions, too. The judges who have used court-to-court communication seem convinced of the utility of this method.

b. Networks for Legal Professionals

The establishment of networks for lawyers should be encouraged, particularly through the professional associations. A number of international law firms are now established in Australia, and this is likely to have a positive effect in increasing familiarity with and access to information about foreign law.

c. Qualified Experts and Expert Institutes

Identifying qualified experts or expert institutes, for example by creating a list of experts, would be novel in Australia but it is a sensible idea that is likely to avoid many of the problems in the current Australian system, particularly the problems relating to the quality of evidence, incomplete and conflicting evidence.

d. Information on National Laws on the Internet

The laws of many foreign systems are already available on the Internet, but accurately locating the relevant, current principles, interpreting and understanding the application of those principles poses many challenges for Australian judges, lawyers and laypeople.

4. Access to Legal Information Within Australia

Legal information within Australia is already freely and comprehensively available, but the complexity of the federal system of law in Australia makes it important to improve access to information to those outside Australia about how the federal system may affect the resolution of international litigation including Australia. Information about the adversarial nature of litigation in Australia and its implications, and the operation of the Australian common law, should also be provided.

[133] Bennett, above n 69, [69].

Japan: Proof of and Information About Foreign Law in Japan

Shunichiro Nakano

Abstract According to Japa3nese theory and practice, the application of conflict of laws rules is regarded as mandatory. Once designated by the conflict of laws rules, foreign law ought to be applied by the domestic courts in the same manner as is domestic law. Foreign law is considered "law" and the judicial authorities have a duty to apply it *ex officio*. Judges are obliged to interpret and apply governing foreign law in the same manner as judges in the country of origin do. If the content of applicable foreign law cannot be ascertained, the recent literature and the court practice supports the application of *lex fori*. The misapplication of the designated foreign law constitutes grounds for an appeal to the Supreme Court.

I. Introduction – Japanese Private International Law and Application of Foreign Law

The Japanese Code of Private International Law (AGRAL)[1] was enacted in 2006 and came into force on January 1, 2007. Before the former Code of Private International Law (*Horei*)[2] was revised in 1989, foreign law was quite frequently applied in Japan, as the old Law primarily designated the law of the husband's or father's home country for international family law issues.[3] In contrast, under the new Law, if it is common to both parties, nationality is used as a connecting factor for marriage, matrimonial property, divorce and parental rights (Articles 25, 26, 27 and 32 AGRAL).[4] In the area concerning the choice of law for tort liability, the

[1] *Ho no Tekiyo ni kansuru Tsusokuho* (Act of General Rules for Application of Laws [Act No. 78 of 2006]). English translation of this act is available at: [http://www.pilaj.jp/text/tsusokuho_e.html].

[2] *Horei* (Act on the Application of Laws [Act No. 10 of 1898]). English translation of this act is available at: [http://blog.hawaii.edu/aplpj/files/2011/11/APLPJ_03.1_okuda.pdf].

[3] Article 14, 15, 16 and 20 *Horei* [before revision of 1996].

[4] Article 25 AGRAL stipulates, the "effect of a marriage shall be governed by the national law of the husband and wife if their national law is identical", and this provision is applied *mutatis mutan-*

S. Nakano (✉)
Professor, Graduate School of Law, Kobe University, Rokkodai 2-1, Nada-Ku, Kobe-Shi, Kobe, Hyogo 657-8501, Japan
e-mail: snakano@kobe-u.ac.jp

Y. Nishitani (ed.), *Treatment of Foreign Law - Dynamics towards Convergence?*,
Ius Comparatum – Global Studies in Comparative Law 26,
DOI 10.1007/978-3-319-56574-3_25

stereotypical application of *lex loci delicti commissi* has been abandoned (Articles 17, 20 and 21 AGRAL).[5] These reforms have led to a considerable reduction in the number of cases in which foreign law is applied in Japan. However, as the law governing succession is as ever determined solely based on the nationality of the deceased (Article 36 AGRAL), and the proper law of contract is subject to the parties' autonomy (Article 7 AGRAL), the application of foreign law is by no means rare in practice.

Although no official statistics are available on the application of foreign law in Japan, South Korean laws seem to be applied quite often in international family law or succession law cases. The reason underlying this is the large percentage of Korean residents in Japan due to geographical and historical factors. For the same reason, North Korean laws, Chinese laws and Taiwanese laws are often applied by Japanese courts, along with the laws of other states including the Philippines, Vietnam, Brazil, the United States and England. Furthermore, in terms of *renvoi* (Article 41 AGRAL) and the reciprocity requirement for the recognition of foreign judgments (Article 118 no.4 of the Japanese Code of Civil Procedure),[6] foreign private international law and civil procedure law must often be applied in court proceedings.

Although Japanese private international law does not include any express provision on the nature of its conflict of laws rules, Japanese theory generally regards their application as mandatory,[7] a rule which also seems to be followed by court practice.[8] This interpretation is justified by the observation that the goal of conflict of laws rules – i.e., the transnational harmonization of judgments by designating the

dis to the marital property regime and divorce (Article 26 (1) and 27). According to Article 32 AGRAL, the "legal relationship between parents and their child shall be governed by the child's national law if it is the same as the national law of either the father or mother".

[5] Although Article 17 AGRAL maintains *lex loci delicti commissi* principle, Article 20 AGRAL provides, "notwithstanding the provisions of the preceding three articles, the formation and effect of claims arising from a tort shall be governed by the law of the place which is manifestly more closely connected with the tort than the place determined pursuant to the preceding three articles, considering that the parties had their habitual residence in the same jurisdiction at the time when the tort occurs, the tort constitutes a breach of obligations under a contract between the parties, or other circumstances of the case."

[6] English translation of this act is available at: [http://www.japaneselawtranslation.go.jp/?re=02].

[7] Nishitani, The Global Need for Accessing the Content of Foreign Law – A Reality – A Perspective from Japan [http://www.hcch.net/upload/hidden/2012/foreignlaw_submissions.html], p. 2; Tameike, *Kokusaishiho Kogi* [Private International Law], 3rd ed., 2005, p. 19. The theory of "facultative conflict of laws rules" is often referred to in the literature, but is rarely supported. Maruoka,"*Flessner no Nin-i-teki Teishokuho Riron*" (Flessner's Theory of Facultative Conflict of Laws Rules) (1)–(4), *Okayama Hogaku* (Okayama University Law Review) vol.30 no.1 (1980) – 4 (1981); Sano, "*Nin-i-teki Teishokuho no Riron ni tuite*" (On the theory of Facultative Conflict of Laws Rules), *Okayama Hogaku* vol. 49 no. 3 = 4 (2000), p. 245.

[8] As an isolated exception, the Osaka District Court Decision of 12.4.1960, *Kaminshu* (Lower Court Decisions) vol. 11 no.4 p. 817, dismissed the claim by applying Japanese law, based on the fact that the claimant failed to submit and prove that foreign law was applicable.

appropriate governing law – cannot be achieved should their application depend on the parties' intention.[9]

II. Foreign Law Before Judicial Authorities

A. *Ex officio Application of Foreign Law*

Once designated by the conflict of laws rules, foreign law ought to be applied by the domestic courts in the same manner as is domestic law. In this sense, because there is basically no difference in their applicability, they must be dealt with equally. Moreover, the designated foreign law must be accurately applied, otherwise the goal of private international law could not be properly achieved. Given these perspectives, foreign law is considered "law" under prevailing conflict of laws theory in Japan.[10] As a consequence, the judicial authorities have a duty to apply foreign law *ex officio*.[11]

Nevertheless, civil procedure law academics occasionally voice differing opinions. According to Mikazuki, strict application of the *ex officio* principle in this context may impose an intolerable burden on Japanese judges, as they are not trained to apply foreign laws. Therefore, he denies that judges have a duty to apply foreign law *ex officio*, and suggests instead that a form of "intermediate treatment" lying somewhere between the *ex officio* principle and the adversarial principle be adopted, entitling judges to apply foreign law regardless of the parties' pleadings.[12] Sakai goes further by treating foreign law as "fact" and applying the adversarial principle in normal civil and commercial proceedings.[13] Were his idea to be followed, the judge would inevitably be bound by the agreement of the parties on particular foreign law content, regardless of whether it was correct.

Although these diverging opinions may make a partial contribution to alleviating the burden on judges in ascertaining and applying foreign law, they are hardly sup-

---

[9] Tameike, *supra* note 7, p. 19.

[10] Tameike, *supra* note 7, p. 245; Ikehara, *Kokusaishiho Soron* (General Theory of Private International Law), 1973, p. 231; Yamada, *Kokusaishiho* (Private International Law), 3rd ed., 2004, p. 130; Kawamata, "*Wagakuni Saibansho ni okeru Gaikokuho no Tekiyo*" (Application of foreign law in Japanese Court), *Hogaku Ronso* (Kyoto University Law Review) vol. 62 no. 5 (1956) p. 20.

[11] Tameike, *supra* note 7, p. 245; Ikehara, *supra* note 10, p. 231; Yamada, *supra* note 10, p. 130; Kawamata, *supra* note 10, p. 20; K.Yamamoto,"*Gaikokuho no Tekiyo*" (Application of Foreign Law), in: Sakurada = Dogauchi (eds.), *Chushaku Kokusaishiho* (Commentary on Private International Law), vol. 2 (2012), p. 254.

[12] Mikazuki, "*Gaikokuho no Tekiyo to Saibansho*" (Application of Foreign Law and Courts), in: Sawaki = Aoyama (eds.), *Kokusai Minji Soshoho no Riron* (Theory of International Civil Procedure Law), 1987, p. 263.

[13] Sakai, in: Honma = Nakano = Sakai, *Kokusai Minji Tetsuzukiho* (Law of International Civil Procedure), 2nd ed., 2012, p. 166.

ported by Japanese theory and practice, mainly because they are incompatible with the goal of designating the applicable law through conflict of laws rules.

B. Ascertainment of Foreign Law

In accordance with generally accepted legal doctrine in Japan, judges have a duty to ascertain the contents of foreign law *ex officio*. In other words, the "*iura novit curia*" principle also applies to foreign law.[14] On the other hand, in order to address the difficulties of ascertaining the contents of foreign law, judges may call for the assistance of the parties,[15] which helps to mitigate the difficulties judges must contend with in practice. Nevertheless, judges have both the right and the obligation to investigate the contents of foreign law, as they are not bound by the information provided by the parties.[16] The same applies to cases in which the parties agree upon the specific contents of foreign law.

Other than the assistance of the parties described above, Japanese judicial authorities usually use documents (relevant books,[17] journals, etc.) and Internet sources to ascertain the contents of foreign law. While expert witnesses, inquiries to an expert or expert institutes, are rarely used in this regard, reports written by party-appointed experts are occasionally submitted in court proceedings. In family court proceedings, judges sometimes refer to the Family Division of the General Secretariat of the Supreme Court. Inquiries to foreign judicial or non-judicial authorities and direct communication with foreign judges are not approaches used in Japan. Making requests via bilateral or multilateral treaties for access to legal information is not available as an option, as Japan has not ratified any of the relevant treaties (see *infra* V A).

---

[14] Nishitani, *supra* note 7, p. 3; Tameike, *supra* note 7, p. 245; Yamada, *supra* note 10, p. 130.

[15] For example, courts may urge parties to refer to the relevant foreign embassy in Japan for legal information on their home country. See Kato, *Shogai Kaji Jiken Seiri Noto* (Notes on International Family Law Cases), 2nd ed., 2008, pp. 66, 71.

[16] Until the 1926 revision, the Japanese Code of Civil Procedure provided as follows: "Regional customary laws, commercial customs, bylaws or foreign laws in force are to be proven. Courts may make necessary investigations *ex officio* whether or not the parties prove them." Although the current Code of Civil Procedure lacks such a provision, the same interpretation is generally employed in both theory and practice. Tameike, *supra* note 7, p. 245; Yamada, *supra* note 10, p. 130.

[17] As useful tools, reference is often made to Kimura et al. (eds.), *Shogai Koseki no tameno Kakkoku Horitsu to Yoken* (Laws and Requirements of Foreign States for the Practice of International Family Registration), 2007 and *Shogai Mibunkankei Senrei Hanrei Soran* (Decisions and Precedents on Personal Status with Foreign Elements) (Looseleaf/CD-ROM). Japanese translations of important statutes of neighbouring countries such as China, South Korea and the Philippines can also be found in *Koseki Roppo* (Codes and Regulations of Family Registration) and *Koseki Jitsumu Roppo* (Codes and Regulations for the Practice of Family Registration), which are practice "companions".

Individuals and institutions that provide legal information in Japan do not have to hold any specific qualifications. The legal information provided is not binding upon the judicial authorities. Instead, they are obliged to investigate and assess the reliability of the information submitted *ex officio*, although there is no particular mechanism by which the reliability of the legal information provided is examined.

While the cost of a party-appointed expert report related to ascertaining the contents of foreign law is borne by the requesting party, the cost of a court-appointed expert must be borne by the party against whom costs are awarded.

C. Interpretation and Application of Foreign Law

In accordance with prevailing conflict of laws theory in Japan, judges are obliged to interpret and apply governing foreign law in the same manner as do judges in the country of origin.[18] The same applies to cases in which the applicable foreign law does not cover a certain point related to the issue submitted to the Japanese courts. In any such case, the Japanese judge is obliged to fill the void as if he were a judge of the governing law state.[19]

D. Failure to Establish Foreign Law

Judges in some lower court decisions have made presumptions concerning uncertainties in the foreign law applicable to the case based on the law of the other state with the law "most similar" to the applicable foreign law. For example, South Korean family law has been employed as a reference in order to address family law issues related to North Korean nationals, in circumstances where the Japanese courts had no knowledge of North Korean family law.[20] This solution is supported by much of the conflict of laws literature as it is well-suited to the most appropriate application of governing law.[21] Yet it still requires scrutiny. If the contents of applicable foreign law can be presumed with sufficient clarity from the law of the state with the "most similar" law, they should be regarded more accurately as having

[18] Tameike, *supra* note 7, p. 244; Yamada, *supra* note 10, p. 133; Fukuoka High Court Decision of 10.2.2009, *Hanrei Jiho* (Law Case Reports) no. 2043 p. 89.

[19] Tameike, *supra* note 7, p. 250; Ikehara, *supra* note 10, p. 240; Yamada, *supra* note 10, p. 134; Osaka High Court Decision of 22.4.2003, *Kasai Geppo* (Family Court Reports) vol.56 no.5 p.124.

[20] Fukuoka District Court Decision of 14.1.1958, *Kaminshu* vol. 9 no. 1 p. 15; Osaka Family Court Decision of 22.8.1962, *Kasai Geppo* vol. 15 no. 2 p. 163; Kyoto Family Court Decision of 13.6.1963, *Kasai Geppo* vol. 15 no. 10 p. 153.

[21] Tameike, *supra* note 7, p. 249; Ikehara, *supra* note 10, p. 243; Yamada, *supra* note 10, p. 136; Kawamata, *supra* note 10, p. 28.

been "ascertained". In other words, this solution is better classified as a method by which to ascertain the relevant contents of applicable foreign law.[22]

Another solution proposed by some academics is to resort to the supplementary or "second-best" connection: for example, if the relevant content of a party's national law cannot be ascertained following due investigation, the law of that party's habitual residence is applied.[23] This idea is aimed at achieving the goal of private international law, i.e., application of the law of the most closely connected state to the issue at hand. However, the merit of this approach is not without question, as such a supplementary connection almost always results in the application of *lex fori*.

Thus, much of the recent literature supports the direct application of *lex fori* if the content of the applicable foreign law cannot be ascertained.[24] This solution has also been favoured in many court decisions due to its clarity and practicability.[25]

E. Judicial Review

As conflict of laws rules are regarded as part of the Japanese legal system, their misapplication constitutes grounds for an appeal.[26] While the Supreme Court may only grant leave for an appeal where "the judgment in the prior instance is found to involve material matters concerning the construction of laws and regulations" (Article 318(1) Code of Civil Procedure), the Supreme Court has regarded the erroneous application of conflict of laws rules as "material" within the meaning of this Article.[27]

Although restrictive interpretations are suggested from time to time,[28] prevailing Japanese theory[29] and practice[30] have consistently acknowledged that misapplying

---

[22] Kanzaki,"*Junkyo Gaikokuho no Fumei o megutte*" (On the Unclear Contents of Applicable Foreign Law), *Hogaku Kyokai Zasshi* (Journal of the Jurisprudence Association) vol. 107 no. 6 (1990) p. 1039; K.Yamamoto, *supra* note 11, p. 362.

[23] Kanzaki, *supra* note 22, p. 1039; K.Yamamoto, *supra* note 11, p. 364.

[24] Mikazuki, *supra* note 12, p. 267; Sawaki-Dogauchi, *Kokusaishiho Nyumon* (Introduction to Private International Law), 7th ed., 2012, p. 54; Yokoyama, *Kokusaishiho* (Private International Law), 2012, p. 89.

[25] Nagano Family Court Decision of 12.3.1982, *Kasai Geppo* vol. 35 no. 1 p. 105; Osaka District Court Decision of 27.9.1985, *Hanrei Jiho* no. 1179 p. 94; Kyoto District Court Decision of 30.9.1987, *Hanrei Jiho* no. 1275 p. 107.

[26] Nishitani, *supra* note 7, p. 5.

[27] Supreme Court Decision of 26.9.2002, *Minshu* (Supreme Court Decisions of Civil Cases) vol. 56 no. 7 p. 1551; Supreme Court Decision of 29.10.2002, *Minshu* vol. 56 no. 8 p. 1964.

[28] Mikazuki, *supra* note 12, p. 276; Sakai, *supra* note 13, p. 172.

[29] Tameike, *supra* note 7, p. 251; Yamada, *supra* note 10, p. 139; Nishitani, "*Gaikokuho no Tekiyo Ihai to Jokoku*" (Misapplication of Foreign Law and Appeal to the Supreme Court), in: Sakurada = Dogauchi (eds.), *Kokusaishiho Hanrei Hyakusen* (Court Cases on Private International Law), 2nd ed., 2012, p. 239.

[30] Supreme Court Decision of 2.7.1981, *Minshu* vol. 35 no. 5 p. 881; Supreme Court Decision of 25.2.1997, *Kasai Geppo* vol. 49 no. 7 p. 56; Supreme Court Decision of 18.3.2008, *Hanrei Jiho* no. 2006 p. 77.

the designated foreign law constitutes legitimate grounds for an appeal to the Supreme Court. This solution is not only a logical consequence of giving applicable foreign law the status of "law" (see *supra* II 1), but is also based on policy considerations including the following: (i) so far as foreign law is designated as the applicable law by conflict of laws rules, its interpretation in domestic courts must also be consistent; (ii) the Supreme Court is responsible for ensuring proper adjudication through the correct application of law; (iii) with its personnel and material resources, the Supreme Court is better equipped to investigate the contents of foreign law than is any other court.[31]

III. Foreign Law in Other Instances

A. Administrative Authorities

Japanese law requires Japanese nationals to report marriages, divorces, acknowledgements of paternity, adoptions, etc., to the local authority, which compiles such items of personal information in a family register (*Koseki*). In cases involving foreign elements, officials of the local authority responsible must assess the legal validity of such juridical acts under the respective governing laws before accepting notifications. The acquisition of Japanese nationality may also depend upon the validity of certain juridical acts such as an acknowledgement of paternity,[32] which often requires the application of foreign law. Although the number of cases to which foreign laws are applicable arguably fell dramatically after private international law was revised in 1989 (see *supra* I), the application of foreign laws by local authorities is by no means rare.

Where a foreign law is to be applied by the administrative authorities, reference is usually made to the relevant literature in Japanese.[33] If sufficient information cannot be collected from available sources, the local authority will eventually turn to the Civil Affairs Bureau of the Ministry of Justice.

---

[31] K.Yamamoto, *supra* note 11, p. 366.

[32] Article 3 (1) Nationality Act provides: "In cases where a child acknowledged by the father or mother is under 20 years of age and the acknowledging father or mother was a Japanese citizen at the time of the birth of the child, Japanese nationality may be acquired through notification to the Minister of Justice if that father or mother is currently a Japanese citizen or was so at the time of death."

[33] See *supra* note 17.

B. Court-Connected Mediation

Many family law or succession law disputes are settled through the court-connected mediation procedure (*Chotei*) in Japan.[34] Where the case involves foreign elements, family court mediators and clerical officers are first required to ascertain the governing law, as some foreign legal systems do not allow for the resolution of family law disputes (*inter alia* divorce) by mediation. In order to facilitate the mediation procedure, mutual comprehension of the applicable law often plays a significant role. In succession disputes, the content of the applicable foreign law – such as the statutory share rules in inheritance cases – is usually decisive. In cases in which the applicable foreign law should be ascertained, mediators usually resort to the Japanese literature.[35] If the mediator has sufficient foreign language skills, the Internet and other foreign language resources are relied upon, although this is not a normal procedure.

C. Arbitration

Foreign law must frequently be applied in international commercial arbitration.[36] The way in which foreign law is ascertained under international arbitration procedure seems different from the method employed in Japanese court litigation. Like judges in the common law jurisdictions, arbitrators usually urge the parties to submit information relating to the contents of the applicable law. Even the applicable law determination – i.e., the contents of applicable conflict of laws rules – often depends on the parties' submissions. In order to prove the contents of the applicable substantive law or private international law, the parties need to obtain expert reports from time to time.

---

[34] For example, as Japanese law allows for divorce by agreement (*Kyogi Rikon*), only 10% of divorce disputes are handled by the courts. Among these cases, 80% are settled by mediation in family courts. [http://www.mhlw.go.jp/toukei/saikin/hw/jinkou/tokusyu/rikon10/03.html].

[35] See *supra* note 17.

[36] Accordint to Article 36 (1) *Chusai Ho* (Arbitration Act), the "arbitral tribunal shall decide the dispute in accordance with such rules of law as are agreed by the parties as applicable to the substance of the dispute". Failing such agreement, "the arbitral tribunal shall apply the substantive law of the State with which the civil dispute subject to the arbitral proceedings is most closely connected" (Article 36 (2)).

D. Lawyers and Other Practitioners

Access to foreign law is frequently required in the course of an attorney's advisory work, such as in divorce counselling or succession cases, or in negotiating or drafting contracts, etc. Most notaries seldom come across cases requiring reference to foreign laws, but they sometimes do, for example in notarizing wills of foreign nationals. How they clarify the contents of foreign law varies, depending on their expertise. Lawyers specializing in international legal affairs use a whole range of literature and Internet resources, including those written in foreign languages. Transnational law firm networks are also frequently relied upon. Major law firms even employ registered foreign lawyers (*Gaikokuho Jimu Bengoshi*), who are qualified to provide foreign law-related legal services in Japan.[37] Most lawyers and notaries specializing in domestic legal affairs will refer to widely available literature.

In addition to the professionals noted above, patent agents (*Benrishi*) specializing in foreign affairs often need to ascertain the details of foreign laws in order to support their clients in preparing for patent applications in foreign states. Tax accountants (*Zeirishi*) working for clients doing business abroad may be required to inquire into foreign tax regulations. Judicial scriveners (*Shiho Shoshi*)[38] also frequently encounter cases involving the application of foreign laws in producing legal documents concerning foreign national succession.

IV. Access to Japanese Law

The Administrative Management Bureau of the Ministry of Internal Affairs and Communications provides information on Japanese laws in Japanese through its official website.[39] English translations of the main Japanese codes are provided by the Ministry of Justice.[40] In addition, each ministry usually responds to written or oral English language requests for information on Japanese law for which the ministry is responsible without charge.[41]

[37] See Art 3 Act on Special Measures concerning the Handling of Legal Services by Foreign Lawyers (Act No. 66 of 1986).

[38] Judicial scriveners are authorized to represent clients in real estate registrations, commercial registrations, the preparation of legal documents, etc. Judicial scriveners may also represent clients in some types of court and mediation proceedings. See [http://www.shiho-shoshi.or.jp/english/index.html].

[39] [http://law.e-gov.go.jp/cgi-bin/idxsearch.cgi]

[40] [http://www.japaneselawtranslation.go.jp/?re=02]

[41] Response to the 2008 Questionnaire of Hague Conference on the Treatment of Foreign Law from Japan (*hereinafter* "2008 Response of Japan") (http://www.hcch.net/upload/wop/genaff_pd09jp.pdf), no. 10–12.

The Supreme Court provides information on Japanese court decisions in Japanese through its website.[42] English translations of recent Supreme Court judgments are also available.[43]

V. Access to Foreign Law

A. Status Quo and Call for Improvement

Japan has not concluded any bilateral or multilateral treaties on proof or information of foreign law[44] to date. Neither the Hague Judicial Network,[45] the European Judicial Network,[46] nor any other comparable framework is available. There are no other international or regional settings designed to facilitate access to foreign law.

Consequently, the current foreign law access situation in Japan is far from satisfactory. The process of ascertaining the contents of foreign law is not only time-consuming and costly, but also has unpredictable results. Many judges, local authority officials and mediators have no choice but to resort to Japanese literature, as they have not received sufficient training to enable them to use foreign language literature and Internet resources. There are not yet sufficient trustworthy Japanese language sources of information on foreign laws. Japanese translations of foreign statutes do not always reflect up-to-date legislative information. Parties required to use party-appointed expert reports face high costs they must bear themselves.

Thus, judicial and administrative authorities must be given a more efficient and easy-to-use mechanism enabling them to explore the detailed contents of applicable foreign law. In particular, easier access to foreign law is needed in the course of court-connected mediation and litigation in family and succession law cases.

---

[42] [http://www.courts.go.jp/search/jhsp0010?hanreiSrchKbn=01].

[43] [http://www.courts.go.jp/english/judgments/index.html].

[44] European Convention of 7 June 1968 on Information on Foreign Law ("London Convention") [http://conventions.coe.int/Treaty/en/Treaties/Html/062.htm], Inter-American Convention of 8 May 1979 on Proof of and Information on Foreign Law ("Montevideo Convention") [http://www.oas.org/juridico/english/treaties/b-43.html], Convention of 22 January 1993 on Legal Assistance and Legal Relations in Civil, Family and Criminal Matters ("Minsk Convention") [http://www.unhcr.org/4de4edc69.html]. Ratification of these treaties is not on the agenda. See 2008 Response of Japan no. 2.

[45] [http://www.ejtn.net/PageFiles/6333/International_Hague_Network_of_%20Judges_EN.pdf].

[46] [http://www.ejn-crimjust.europa.eu/ejn/].

B. Towards International Cooperation

In light of the above analysis, international or regional instruments related to foreign law proof and information would be highly useful tools facilitating access to foreign law in Japan. Such international instruments should be open not only to the judicial authorities, but also to individuals and other authorities. A request for legal information should be sent directly to the competent authority or designated expert body of the foreign state, instead of being transmitted by the competent authority of the requesting state, which usually takes time.

On the other hand, considering the established procedural treatment of foreign law in Japan (see *supra* II A, B), the answer provided by the requested state should not be binding on the requesting authority. To give individuals easier access to foreign law, legal information services should be provided free of charge. Further, to make such international instruments workable, due regard must be had in order not to place too great a burden on participating states. For example, the languages used in communications must be restricted to the language of the requested state and English.[47]

In addition to such international instruments, enhancing direct communication among judges, establishing networks for other legal professional organizations such as law firms, identifying qualified experts and expert institutes, and providing information on national laws on the Internet are all considered feasible ways to facilitate access to foreign law.

C. Need for Conflict of Laws Reform

The prevailing view is that Japanese judges must ascertain and apply foreign law *ex officio*. At the same time, in order to mitigate their workload, judges may request that the parties assist in this respect (see *supra* II A, B). There seems to be no real need to change this treatment of foreign law *de lege ferenda*, as it has generally functioned well to date. As the procedural treatment of foreign law is usually deeply rooted in the procedural law and conflict of laws system of each state, its unification through international or regional instruments would be too bold, costly and time-consuming, even if it would not be without merit.

Although there is not sufficient clarity on this point, in the context of international commercial arbitration, arbitrators seem to depart from the *ex officio* principle and rely on the common law approach, even if the place of arbitration is located in Japan (see *supra* III C). This vague tendency suggests that strict application of the traditional *ex officio* principle may also be doubtful in the international commercial

[47] 2008 Response of Japan no. 32 states, "It is burdensome for the States whose official language is not English of French to provide legal information both in English and in French. It is preferable not to burden the States with mandatory obligation to provide in both languages."

litigation context. In contract and tort cases, as legal counsel generally engage more actively in defense activities, the *ex officio* principle does not seem to be indispensable. In contrast, in many family law and succession law cases, in which the parties are not represented by attorneys, adoption of the common law approach would be inappropriate.

On the other hand, as far as Japanese private international law is concerned, Article 36 of the AGRAL[48] – according to which succession shall be governed solely by the national law of the decedent – should be promptly revised. The rigidity and inadequacy of this provision is obvious, in that it pays no regard to the will of the deceased or their last habitual residence. Under this provision, many succession cases involving foreign nationals should be governed by foreign laws even if the deceased was born in Japan and had never visited their home country, and the successors were all Japanese and residing in Japan. Such an outcome is hardly justifiable.

At the same time, the skills of Japanese legal professionals in seeking and finding relevant legal information in a foreign language must be enhanced, which requires drastic changes in law school educational strategy. However, the reform of legal education is a daunting task for the Japanese Legal Society in view of the present turmoil over law schools and the bar exam system.[49]

[48] Article 36 AGRAL: "Inheritance shall be governed by the national law of the decedent."

[49] Since Japanese legal education was reformed in 2004, an unexpectedly high number (74 as of 2013) of law schools have been founded. The average success rate for the new bar exam was expected to be 60–70%, but turned out to be only 25–30% in reality. Even if law school graduates pass the bar exam, finding sufficient jobs in law firms is becoming increasingly difficult. All of these realities have made law schools unattractive, leading to a decline in student numbers, worsening the financial situation and prompting changes to high-minded educational policy at many law schools in Japan.

Macau: Proof and Information About Foreign Law in Macau

Guangjian Tu

Abstract Macau is a jurisdiction of civil law tradition. Although the application of conflict of laws rules is theoretically mandatory, it has been difficult to find a case where a foreign law has been actually applied, either because of lex fori favouritism or some other reasons, since Macau established its own conflict of laws system in December 1999. In Macau, foreign law has a hybrid nature and it is considered as something between "law" and "fact" but more is the former and less is the latter; both the judicial authority and the parties may have the burden to prove the content of foreign law. Although there are many ways to ascertain a foreign law, given the convenience of our digital era, it is submitted that inter-governmental cooperation by online would be the most desirable way to resolve the problem of access to foreign law.

Introduction

Macau is a Special Administrative Region (SAR) within the People's Republic of China (PRC).[1] Although it is very small, with an area of 29.2 km^2 and a population of only 591,900,[2] it enjoys a high degree of autonomy according to the Basic Law of the Macau Special Administrative Region of the People's Republic of China (Macau Basic Law), in which the relationship between the Central Government and the SAR was set.[3] The SAR has the power of administration, legislation and final

[1] There is another SAR established on 1 July 1997 within China, namely Hong Kong, which has a very similar political status to and enjoys the same degree of autonomy as Macau under the policy of "One Country, Two Systems" advocated by the late leader, Deng Xiaoping.

[2] These figures were released by the Statistics & Census Bureau of Macau and they can be found at http://www.dsec.gov.mo/Statistic.aspx?NodeGUID=58449a77-0f33-432f-918f-df2af8b4ea67 and http://www.dsec.gov.mo/Statistic.aspx?NodeGuid=7bb8808e-8fd3-4d6b-904a-34fe4b302883 (last visited 10 October 2013).

[3] The Macau Basic Law can be found at http://bo.io.gov.mo/bo/i/1999/leibasica/index_uk.asp (last visited 10 October 2013).

G. Tu (✉)
Professor, Faculty of Law (FLL), University of Macau, Room 3019, E32, Avenida da Universidade, Taipa, Macau, China
e-mail: gjtu@umac.mo

Y. Nishitani (ed.), *Treatment of Foreign Law - Dynamics towards Convergence?*,
Ius Comparatum – Global Studies in Comparative Law 26,
DOI 10.1007/978-3-319-56574-3_26

adjudication.[4] Only very few laws, mainly those related to national security and sovereignty, made by the Central Government as Attachment III to the Macau Basic Law, are applicable to the territory of Macau. Macau itself can make all other laws, including public and private ones.[5] Due to the fact that Macau can have its own private laws independent of and different from those in the mainland China, Macau is therefore an independent "country" in the sense of Private International Law (PIL).[6]

Owing to the historical reason that Macau was previously a colony of Portugal before its return to the motherland, the current legal system of Macau has been mainly based on its colonizer's and most Macau codes reflect the features of their Portuguese counterparts.[7] As far as the issue of proof of and information about foreign law is concerned, Macau also has its own system and rules that are independent of those in the Mainland China but essentially based on the Portuguese ones. This report will provide as detailed information as possible for this aspect of PIL in Macau.

I. Conflict of Laws Rules

Macau Civil Code, which is the most important source for conflict of laws rules, was derived from the 1966 Portuguese Civil Code.[8] Although the "localisation" of laws in Macau provided a good chance for Macau to update, modernise and adapt such laws as were previously applicable in Macau so that they could follow contemporary trends and be more compatible with the ethnic, cultural and historic reality

[4] See Arts 16, 17 and 19 of the Macau Basic Law.

[5] The power of the SAR is much broader than that of a province in China and it is also the author's view that the autonomy enjoyed by the SAR is more than that of a state in a federal country such as in the United States of America (USA), see Chapter Two of the Macau Basic Law.

[6] "The laws previously applicable in Macau will basically remain unchanged [after the handover]…". see Arts 8 and 18 of the Macau Basic Law. Hereinafter, the term "country" is, of course, used in the sense of PIL in this paper.

[7] Macau has gone through 4 distinct periods for its legal history including its PIL history: a period of mixed Chinese-Portuguese jurisdiction (1557–1849), a colonial period (1849–1974), a transitional period (1974–1999) and the period currently as a SAR within China, generally see Guangjian Tu, *Private International Law in Macau*, Beijing, China Social Science Academic Press, 2013, pp. 44–50.

[8] Macau Civil Code came into force on 1 October 1999. The choice of law rules are detailed in Chapter III, Title I of Book 1. This law can be found at http://bo.io.gov.mo/bo/i/99/31/codcivpt/default.asp (visited 10 October 2013). All the laws of Macau mentioned in this paper can be found at this website; it will not be quoted again. The laws in Macau usually only have Portuguese and Chinese versions unless indicated otherwise in this report. While the Macau Civil Code has partially been translated into English, choice of law rules have been left almost untouched. For the partial translation of the Macau Civil Code, see http://papers.ssrn.com/sol3/papers.cfm?abstract_id=1280595 (visited 10 October 2013).

of Macau,[9] not many changes had been made for the new Macau Civil Code in general, nor for the provisions on the issues of choice of law in that code in particular. More concretely, one author said: "After the process of localisation, the Macau Civil Code retains almost 90 per cent of the content of the original Portuguese Civil Code of 1966".[10]

As its colonizer, Portugal, Macau is a jurisdiction of civil law tradition and the application of conflict of laws rules is mandatory in Macau. Theoretically, the judges must apply the rules *ex officio*. Although most conflicts rules in the Macau Civil Code are neutral, even-handed and can frequently lead to the application of foreign laws, in practice, either because of *lex fori* favouritism or judicial convenience or some other reasons, it has been difficult to find a case where a foreign law has been actually applied since Macau returned to the motherland and established its own independent conflict of laws system.[11]

II. Foreign Law Before Judicial Authorities

A. *The Nature, Application and Ascertainment of Foreign Law*

In Macau, foreign law has a hybrid nature and it is considered as something between "law" and "fact" but more is the former and less is the latter.[12] Accordingly, a foreign law can be applied by judicial authorities either *ex officio* or at the request of the party, which can be seen from Article 341 of Macau Civil Code.[13] From the same Article, one can also see that both the judicial authority (under the "*iura novit curia*"

---

[9] See Gaolong Liu & Guoqiang Zhao, *New Commentaries on Macau Laws*, Macau, Macau Foundation, 2005, pp. 7–9, 18–21.

[10] See Xiaoqin Tang, *Macau Contract Law*, Netherlands, Kluwer Law International, 2009, p 21.

[11] See Guangjian Tu, "the Conflict of Laws System in Macau" (2010) 40 *Hong Kong Law Journal* p. 85.

[12] See Tu, *supra* note 7, 168–69; Jin Huang & Huacheng Guo, General Part of Macau Private International Law, Macau, Macau Foundation, 1996, p. 86.

[13] See Article 341 of Macau Civil Code (Customary Law or Law outside the territory of Macau), which says:

1. A party who invokes a customary law or a law outside the territory of Macau shall prove the existence and content of that law. The court, however, shall also ascertain that law *ex officio*.
2. If a court must decide the case according to a customary law or a foreign law, the court shall also ascertain that law *ex officio* where both of the parties did not invoke that law or even where no objection is raised to the invocation of that law.
3. Failing to determine the contents of the applicable law, the court shall resort to the general principles of Macau law.

principle) and the parties can have the burden to prove the content of foreign law in a case.[14]

There are many ways to ascertain a foreign law. Theoretically, all the means including documents, internet sources, assistance of the parties, expert witnesses, inquiry to an expert or expert institute, inquiry to domestic judicial and/or non-judicial authorities, inquiry to foreign judicial and/or non-judicial authorities, inquiry via bilateral or multilateral treaties for access to legal information and direct communication of judges can be utilized to ascertain a foreign law in Macau.

According to the general practice in Macau, the individuals or institutions which provide legal information should have to fulfil some specific qualifications. Once it is confirmed that the concerned individuals or institutions are qualified to do the job, the legal information provided by them shall be regarded as valid and is binding upon judicial authorities. Yet, it is not clear whether there is any further mechanism to examine the reliability of the provided legal information and who will bear the costs of ascertaining foreign law.

B. Interpretation and Application of Foreign Law

Basically, in Macau, foreign law shall be interpreted in the same way as what it is in the country of origin, which can be seen from Paragraph 1, Article 22 of Macau Civil Code.[15] If there is a gap in the applicable foreign law, the gap shall, in the first place, be filled up according to the available case law and scholarly doctrines in the country of origin, failing which local standards can come to fill in the gap.

C. Failure to Establish Foreign Law

Due to the feature of internationalism of PIL in Macau, local law shall come into play only if it has to when there is a failure to establish the applicable foreign law. Therefore, if the applicable foreign law is a special law in the country of origin and unascertainable, the relevant general law or general principles in that country will be resorted to; failing which, the most similar law in another country could be applied. Only after all these laws are unascertainable, Macau local law can be

[14] *Ibid.*

[15] See Paragraph 1, Article 22 of Macau Civil Code (Interpretation and Ascertainment of the Applicable law), which says:

> The applicable law shall be interpreted in the same way as how it should have been done in the jurisdiction to which it belongs.

applied. This is the view of Portuguese scholarly doctrines[16] and one can also see in Article 341 and Paragraph 2, Article 22 of Macau Civil Code.[17]

III. Judicial Review

A. Conflict of Laws Rules

Based on the idea that the mistake of applying a local conflicts rule is a mistake of applying the local law, where a conflict of laws rule has erroneously been applied, the parties can appeal to the higher court, even to the Court of Final Appeal in Macau if other common conditions for appeal can be satisfied. There is no extra specific requirement that must be met for the parties to appeal in such a case.[18]

B. Foreign Law

Based on the idea that a mistake must be given the chance to be corrected whether foreign law is regarded as an issue of fact or law, it is agreed that where a foreign substantive law has erroneously been applied, the parties can appeal to the higher court including the Court of Final Appeal if other common conditions for appeal can be satisfied.[19]

IV. Foreign Law in Other Instances

Actually, in Macau, it is rarely seen that a foreign law is applied and ascertained before an administrative or any other non-judicial authorities and very hard to find such a reported case. And it is also rarely seen that a foreign law is applied and ascertained in arbitration, mediation or any other alternative dispute resolution (ADR) mechanism because ADRs are extremely under-developed in Macau. The same applies to advisory work by attorneys, notaries, etc.

---

[16] See Tu, *supra* note 7, p. 169.

[17] See Article 341; Paragraph 2, Article 22 of Macau Civil Code (Interpretation and Ascertainment of the Applicable Law), which says:

> Where it is impossible to ascertain the content of the applicable law, the supplementary alternative applicable law shall be applied…

[18] See Article 639 of Macau Civil Procedure Code (the Basis for Appeal), which says:

> Violation or misapplication of any substantive or procedural law … can be appealed to the Court of Final Appeal …

[19] *Ibid*; Huang & Guo, *supra* note 12 at 90.

V. Access to Foreign Law: Status Quo

Although there is a specific website designed by the Government Printing Bureau of Macao to provide legal information for local laws and international (-regional) treaties (-agreements) that Macau has joined/ratified,[20] there is, unfortunately, no such corresponding official website to provide legal information for foreign laws.

Both the Hague Judicial Network and European Judicial Net-work (EJN) are not concerned with Macau and there is no any other comparable framework available in Macau, either for Macau judges to be able to directly communicate with a foreign judge to obtain legal information on foreign law.

The fact that Macau has not joined/ratified any multi-(bi-) lateral treaty or agreement that can specifically regulate the proof of and/or information on foreign law, however, does not prevent Macau from acceding to some inter-national (-regional) instrument which may have some provisions to that effect. For Example:

(A) Article 23 of the Arrangement between Macau SAR and mainland China regarding Service of Documents and Taking of Evidence says "At the request of the requesting court, the requested court can research and provide the relevant laws in its territory"[21];
(B) Article 7 of the Agreement on Juridical and Mutual Judicial Assistance between the Macao Special Administrative Region of the People's Republic of China and the Democratic Republic of Timor Leste says "The present Contracting Parties promise the undertaking to each other that they will swap, without any charge, legal documentations, legal works, especially official gazettes, as well as other law reports and legal journals published by the relevant public entities"[22];
(C) Article 8 of the Agreement on Juridical and Mutual Judicial Assistance between the Macao Special Administrative Region of the People's Republic of China and the Republic of Portugal says "The present Contracting Parties also agree that legal documentations and legal works shall be exchanged without any charge, especially the official gazettes, law reports and legal journals published by the public entities".[23]

---

[20] Normally, there are 3 different versions of the provided legal instruments on this website i.e. Chinese version http://cn.io.gov.mo/; English version http://en.io.gov.mo/; and Portuguese version http://pt.io.gov.mo/

[21] This Arrangement was singed on 15 August 2001 and came into force on 15 September 2001. For a Chinese version, see http://bo.io.gov.mo/bo/ii/2001/35/aviso39_cn.asp (last visited on 17 October 2013); for a Portuguese version, see http://bo.io.gov.mo/bo/ii/2001/35/aviso39.asp (last visited on 17 October 2013).

[22] This Agreement was signed on 21 November 2008. For a Chinese version, see http://bo.io.gov.mo/bo/i/2008/50/aviso31_cn.asp (last visited on 17 October 2013); for a Portuguese version, see http://bo.io.gov.mo/bo/i/2008/50/aviso31.asp#31(last visited on 17 October 2013).

[23] This Agreement was signed on 17 January 2001. For a Chinese version, see http://bo.io.gov.mo/bo/ii/2001/06/aviso10_cn.asp (last visited on 17 October 2013); for a Portuguese version, see http://bo.io.gov.mo/bo/ii/2001/35/aviso39.asp (last visited on 17 October 2013).

Nevertheless, there is no available statistics that can indicate how frequent these international treaties are used in practice and whether these treaties have actually facilitated access to foreign law or not. According to the current reporter, there is no any other international or inter-regional setting to facilitate access to foreign law. All these might be attributable to the reason that foreign law is seldom applied in Macau and *vice versa*.

VI. Access to Foreign Law: Further Developments

A. *Practical Need*

In the view of the current reporter, there is an absolute need to improve access to foreign law, particularly for judicial authorities, administrative and other non-judicial authorities and parties, especially those who cannot afford costly measures because foreign law is more likely to be concerned with them in their job or daily life. There are many circumstances where access to foreign law is acutely needed in Macau, in particular before doing business abroad, in the course of contractual negotiations and litigation. Meanwhile, commercial contract law, family law and succession law are probably the three areas where access to foreign law is mostly needed because many Macanese people are doing business in mainland China and/or Hong Kong and there are many cross-border marriage and succession cases among the three regions. Given this situation, there is, of course, a need to improve the access to legal information of other jurisdictions within the same country i.e. mainland China and Hong Kong.

B. Conflict of Laws Solutions

In the reporter's opinion, neither should the conflict of laws rules in Macau be modified *de lege ferenda* to reduce the number of cases in which foreign law is applied, nor should the treatment of foreign law in Macau be changed *de lege ferenda.*

An inter-national (-regional) instrument which unifies the treatment of foreign law could surely be helpful but it is the current reporter's estimation that they might only be limitedly useful in practice.

C. Methods of Facilitating Access to Foreign Law

The current reporter agrees that an inter-national (-regional) instrument that establishes administrative and/or judicial cooperation to exchange information on participating States' laws is definitely a useful tool to facilitate access to foreign law. And such an international instrument should be open not only to judicial authorities, but also to individuals and/or any other authorities who might need the access to foreign law. Meanwhile, under that instrument, there would be more efficiency if a request on foreign law could be directly sent to the competent authority or designated expert body of the foreign state, instead of being transmitted by the competent authority of the requesting state. Moreover, the answer provided by the requested state normally should be binding unless there is a fraud and without any costs if possible.

Given this digital era, the current reporter thinks that providing information on national laws through the internet is probably the best method of facilitating access to foreign law and the easiest and cheapest way for the concerned party to access foreign law if one can ensure that the legal information is provided with accuracy on an official website. As said, China is a multi-jurisdiction country including Macau SAR, Hong Kong SAR and mainland China (probably also Taiwan). To facilitate access to legal information in other jurisdictions, a common framework joined by all should definitely be useful.

Turkey: The Treatment of Foreign Law in Turkey

Zeynep Derya Tarman

Abstract This paper deals with the treatment of foreign law under Turkish private international law. The paper initially explains the legal history in this area of law by introducing the preceding legislative acts and the law currently in force entitled "Private International Law and International Civil Procedure Law" ("PILA"). After presenting PILA's scope of application, the paper examines the application of foreign law before Turkish courts in light of certain articles of PILA and Turkish civil law. Accordingly, where the conflicts of laws rules indicate so, it is the judge's duty to accurately apply foreign law to disputes with a foreign element ex officio. In connection with this duty, parties' limited role in determining the applicable law, the judge's obligation to obtain information to ascertain the content of foreign law and the examination by the court of cassation are explained. The paper then details the means and legal sources provided to judges for access to foreign law. Nevertheless, it is stated that in practice judges are reluctant to apply foreign law for constraints in time and knowledge.

I. Introduction

A. History

With the rapid growth in both the production and consumption of goods and services, Turkey has become one of the fastest growing economies of the world. This growth, coupled with incentives,[1] has attracted foreign investors to Turkey, and ultimately leading to an increase in transactions with a foreign element. Turkish private

[1] Law no. 4875 on Direct Foreign Investments has been enacted in 2003 with the aim of providing incentives for direct foreign investments in Turkey. This law replaced a former equivalent: "Law no. 6224 concerning the Encouragement of Foreign Capital" (Official Gazette, 18.1.1954-8615).

Z.D. Tarman (✉)
Associate Professor, Department of Private International Law, Koc University Law School, Rumeli Feneri yolu, 34450 Sariyer/Istanbul, Turkey
e-mail: ztarman@ku.edu.tr

Y. Nishitani (ed.), *Treatment of Foreign Law - Dynamics towards Convergence?*,
Ius Comparatum – Global Studies in Comparative Law 26,
DOI 10.1007/978-3-319-56574-3_27

international law, the area of law addressing such transactions, has therefore gained further significance in recent years.

The original primary source of Turkish private international law was the 'Provisional Law on the Rights and Duties of Foreign Residents in Turkey', which originated from fourteenth Century laws of the Ottoman Empire.[2] This law contained only one article (Art.4) addressing conflict of law rules. Although incapable of providing suitable solutions for cases, the provisional law remained in force for approximately 67 years after the formation of the Republic of Turkey. Subsequently, the Private International Law and International Civil Procedure Act (hereafter: "PILA 1982") entered into force.[3] This Act, however, also failed to respond to necessary practical demands over time.[4] Following the enactment of PILA 1982, Turkey became party to many international conventions. Contradictions emerged between the international conventions and the existing provisions of PILA 1982. For example, under the Hague Convention on the Law Applicable to Maintenance Obligations, dated 2 October 1973,[5] maintenance obligations are governed by the domestic law of the habitual residence of the maintenance creditor, whereas Article 21 of PILA 1982 determines the debtor's national law as the connecting factor. Besides, there was only one conflict of law rule (Art.24) applicable to all fields of contract law. For instance, PILA 1982 did not provide any special conflict of law provisions for consumer contracts, employment contracts, contracts relating to intellectual property rights, and contracts relating to the carriage of goods. Finally, with the entry into force of the new Turkish Civil Code[6] in 2001, updated principles were introduced – especially in family law matters concerning marriage and child custody. These amendments, however, could not be taken into consideration when applying PILA 1982. In response to this issue, the Ministry of Justice established a commission for the preparation of a new code. At the drafting stage of the Private International Law and International Civil Procedure Law (hereafter: "PILA")[7] new views, improvements and international treaties in the area of private international law were taken into consideration.[8] The commission aimed to include provisions which accorded with the main principles accepted in international conventions and European legislation. Furthermore, the scope of the new code reflected the observa-

[2] TEKINALP, G., Milletlerarası Özel Hukuk Bağlama Kuralları (*Private International Law Conflict of Law Rules*), 11.Edition, Istanbul, 2011, 2.

[3] Law no. 2675 and dated 20.5.1982 (Official Gazette. 22.6.1982-17701).

[4] TEKINALP, G., 4;. CELIKEL, A./ERDEM, B., Milletlerarası Özel Hukuk (*International Private Law*), 12. Edition, Istanbul, 2012, 41.

[5] Official Gazette. 6.2.1983-17951.

[6] Turkish Civil Code no. 4721 (Official Gazette. 8.12.2001-24607).

[7] Law no. 5718 and dated 27.11.2007 (Official Gazette. 12.12.2007-26728). For an English translation see 'Texts, Materials and Recent Developments. Turkey: The 2007 Turkish Code on Private International Law and International Civil Procedure', *Yearbook of Private International Law* (9) 2007, 583–604. For a German translation of the Code, see KRÜGER, H. and ERTAN N.F., 'Neues Internationales Privatrecht in der Türkei', *IPRax* 2008, 283–290.

[8] Preamble No. 18 of the PILA.

tions and amendment proposals of the legal doctrine during the practical application of PILA 1982.[9]

B. Structure of the PILA

Enacted in 2007, PILA is almost identical to its predecessor insofar that both govern three main issues: 1) determining the applicable state law in private matters having cross-border implications (a foreign element); 2) determining the relevant state court that has jurisdiction in such matters; and 3) determining the conditions under which a foreign decision may be recognised and enforced in Turkey.[10] The foreign element, although a prerequisite for the application of this Act, is not defined in PILA. Rather, it is broadly defined by legal doctrine and case law. Accordingly, 'foreign elements' are understood to be the facts of the case, and that may suggest the dispute is governed by foreign law. Usually, such facts correspond to a connecting factor of the relevant conflict of law rule (*e.g.* nationality of the parties; place of habitual residence; place where the damage is occurred; place where the contract is performed).[11]

The PILA has two main parts: Conflict of Laws, and International Civil Procedural Law. The first main part has two subchapters named: General Provisions (Art.1–8), and Conflict of Laws Rules (Art.9–39).[12] The International Civil Procedural Law regulates the international jurisdiction of the Turkish courts and the recognition and enforcement of foreign court decisions and arbitral awards in Turkey.[13]

---

[9] TEKINALP, G., 5.

[10] In Article 1 of PILA, the scope of the application is indicated as: "The law applicable to transactions and relations pertaining to private law that involve a foreign element, the international jurisdiction of Turkish courts, the recognition and enforcement of foreign judgments are stipulated by this Act."

[11] TEKINALP, G., 22.

[12] It must be noted that beside PILA, the Turkish Commercial Code contains provisions regarding conflict of law rules. For example, Articles 766 and 767 of the Commercial Code are applied to foreign exchange transactions containing a foreign element.

[13] For more information on Turkish private international law, see TEKINALP, G., 'The 2007 Turkish Code Concerning Private International Law and International Civil Procedure', *Yearbook of Private International Law* 2007, 313–341; TEKINALP, G., NOMER, E. and ODMAN, A., in: B. Verschraegen (ed.), *International Encyclopaedia for Private International Law*, Kluwer 2012, Chapter on Turkey; TARMAN, Z.D., Remarks on the General Principles of Turkish Private International Law, Honorary Volume for Professor Emeritus Sp. Vrellis 2014, 825–836; TARMAN, Z.D., The Applicable Law to Contractual and Non-contractual Obligations under Turkish Private International Law, Nederland Internationaal Privaatrecht (NIPR) 2009/1, 15–24; SURAL C./ TARMAN Z.D., Recognition and Enforcement of Foreign Court Decisions in Turkey, *Yearbook of Private International Law*, Volume 15 (2013/2014), 485–508.

II. Foreign Law Before Judicial Authorities

A. General Information About PILA Article 2

Article 1 states that PILA should be applied to private law disputes involving a foreign element. The existence of a foreign element gives rise to the potential application of the rules of a foreign legal system. In private law relations containing a foreign element, the aim is to apply the law which has the closest relationship to the case.[14] In accordance with the relevant applicable connecting factor, the law of another legal system may have the closest relationship to the parties or dispute and be appointed as the applicable law. For example, the national law of the person, or the common national law or the habitual residence of the parties might refer to a foreign law system.[15] If it is established that the domestic law of a foreign legal system has the closest relationship to a particular case, the judge shall apply the relevant law in accordance with PILA Article 2/I. Article 2 states: *"The judge shall ex officio apply the Turkish conflict of law rules and the applicable foreign law pursuant to these rules."* Since the application of the Turkish private international law/ conflict-of-law rules is mandatory, Turkish courts inevitably apply these rules *ex officio*. A judge's duty to apply conflict of law rules is justified by the fact that any rule of law must have binding force. The mandatory application of Turkey's conflict of law rules is thus situated within the general duty to apply the law of the forum. The mandatory conflict of law principle entails the judge's duty to apply the relevant conflict of law rule *ex officio*, even where it runs counter to the wishes of the parties. While the application of foreign law is mandatory, nonetheless, this does not mean that the foreign law is within the scope of national law. In other words, the applicable law in a dispute may be foreign law, but the competence to apply that foreign law is appointed to the judge by PILA, as a regulation of domestic law.[16]

In Turkish private international law, public policy may prevent the application of a foreign law pursuant to Article 5 PILA. Foreign law rules which must be applied according to the conflict of law rules, but are later understood as violating Turkish public policy, shall not be applied.[17] The main principal is to apply the foreign law to a dispute if it is indicated by PILA. If, however, the application of foreign law is clearly contrary to the fundamental principles of Turkish law, human rights, and the ethics of Turkish society, in other words, contrary to public policy, the judge does not apply the foreign law by reason of public policy (PILA Article 5). The limits of the public policy concept are neither clear nor defined in Turkish law. Therefore, a judge's discretion plays a very important role in the assessment of whether the

---

[14] NOMER, E., Devletler Hususi Hukuku (*International Private Law*), 20. Edition, Istanbul, 2011, 20.

[15] NOMER, E., 109.

[16] NOMER, E., 186; SANLI, C./ESEN E./ATAMAN F.I., Milletlerarası Özel Hukuk (*Private International Law*), 2.Edition, Istanbul, 2014, 62.

[17] NOMER, E., 161.

application of the foreign law will result in violation of Turkish public policy. Notwithstanding judges' discretion, a contradiction to public policy must be "manifest" in order to assure its strict application in practice by the judges.[18]

B. Nature of Foreign Law

The nature of foreign law is a disputed matter. It changes depending on the various legal systems involved. No common view exists whereby foreign law is accepted as a law or as a fact. Rule 18 of Dicey and Morris[19] describes the English position on proof of foreign law which breaks the subject down into the following principles: (1) Foreign law is a fact, so that (i) foreign law must be pleaded, and (ii) proved, unless otherwise accepted; (2) to the satisfaction of the judge; (3) in general, foreign law must be proved by (i) expert evidence (usually by foreign practitioners), while (ii) the court will not conduct its own research; and (4) the burden of proof lies on the party who bases his claim or defence on it, and if this party fails, the court will apply English law. None of the above applies under Turkish law; foreign law is treated as law.[20] Turkish courts must apply foreign law once the PILA points to a foreign law, regardless of what the parties plead. The Turkish courts must establish foreign law *ex officio*. However, it is accepted that the judge cannot know foreign law and if it is needed the judge is free to accept assistance from the parties. Since the nature of foreign law is not a fact, the judge is not bound by the information rendered by the parties. Courts will frequently conduct their own research. In taking evidence, courts are not limited to the use of court experts, and there are no defined limits on what can be used as evidence of foreign law. It is observed that Turkish courts appoint experts on foreign law and tend to favour Turkish academics over foreign practitioners.[21]

In cases where Turkish conflict of law rules point to the application of foreign law, the court must disclose this inference to the parties, where they were previously unaware of this fact. If both parties plead under Turkish law, however, the courts will regularly construe this as a choice of Turkish law by the parties, even if they were seemingly unaware of the possibility that foreign law might apply to their case. However, such agreements are valid only to the extent that Turkish private international law allows parties to choose the applicable law, which is generally the case in contract and tort law disputes. On the other hand, matters relating to, in particular, property, family, and inheritance law may not be subject to a choice of law by the parties under Turkish private international law rules. Article 14 of PILA states that the grounds for and the effects of divorce and separation shall be governed

---

[18] CELIKEL, A./ERDEM, B., 149.

[19] DICEY A. V./MORRIS J.H.C., The Conflict of Laws, 12th ed. by Lawrence Collins with specialist editors, 2011, 226.

[20] CELIKEL, A./ERDEM, B., 172–173; NOMER, E., 186.

[21] TEKINALP, G., 57; SANLI, C./ESEN E./ATAMAN F.I., 68.

by the common national law of the parties. Where both spouses have the same foreign citizenship, then the law of the state of their common citizenship is applicable. In other words, a Turkish court is required to apply foreign law on its own motion (*ex officio*). Therefore, the application of foreign law does not depend on the fact whether the parties have invoked its application.

In private international law various connection points are determined in order to find the law which establishes the closest relation with the case. For family and inheritance law in particular, citizenship is used as the main criterion for finding the applicable law and citizenship of the party should be claimed and proved by the parties (the Code of Civil Procedure Art.190). The judge cannot put forward and take facts into consideration on his/her own motion. If there is a dispute regarding the determination of the facts establishing the connection points, this dispute becomes an evidentiary issue.[22] The party who makes a claim is liable to prove that claim (Turkish Civil Code Art.6). The principle of preparation of the case by the parties in determining the facts, is enshrined in Article 25 of the Civil Procedural Code, and has limited legal exceptions. In determining the facts, the judge is bound by the information submitted by the parties. In cases where any fact proved by the claiming party refers to foreign law, the judge applies the foreign law on its own motion.

In conclusion, the judge firstly categorizes the case depending on the conflict of law rules, and according to that rule(s), the judge determines the applicable law. If the relevant rule(s) indicates the application of foreign law, the judge applies it on its own motion.[23] Accordingly, foreign law is applied as law under Turkish law.[24] Foreign law put forward by the parties is not a fact; therefore, a judge is not bound by the propounded information. The judge can benefit from many sources while determining the scope and content of the foreign law. Additionally, a judge's obligation to apply foreign law on its own motion supports the concept that foreign law is accepted as law, rather than fact.

C. Application of Foreign Law

Article 2 of PILA stipulates that the judge applies foreign law when PILA makes reference to it. As understood from the close interpretation of Article 2, the application of the foreign law shall not be necessarily put forward by the parties. However, where parties wish to put forward their choice of law, this must be brought to the attention of the judge. For instance, the parties are allowed to choose the applicable law in the field of contract law. In this case the parties will rely on the applicability of the chosen law.[25] However, the choice of law will not be taken into consideration

[22] NOMER, E., 188.

[23] TEKINALP, G., 57.

[24] CELIKEL, A. /ERDEM, B., 174.

[25] NOMER, E., 188.

in respect of a special legal relationship where the applicable law is proscribed by the lawmaker, and any choice of law by the parties will be disregarded at trial. In such cases the judge will apply the law to which PILA refers to, regardless of the choice of the parties. A court decision rendered in accordance with the law chosen by the parties will be reversed in this case.[26]

According to PILA, if the application of foreign law is sought, then the ascertainment of foreign law becomes an issue at hand to be resolved. Besides, the accuracy of the content of the foreign law is also of significance. A judge must apply the foreign law accurately and appropriately in order to ensure justice. Since the aim of expedient justice is prioritized, the foreign law must be ascertained using an accelerated procedure. However, delays are compounded by the difficulties judges encounter while determining the foreign law and striving to fully understand and appreciate its correct application. Decisions by the Court of Cassation have indicated that the judge undertakes the application of the foreign law.[27]

D. Ascertainment of Foreign Law

In Turkish law, there is a principle called *iura novit curia* ("the court knows the law") enshrined in Article 33 of the Civil Procedural Code. Furthermore, Article 2/I of PILA, which states that judges apply the foreign law on their own motion, is based on the principle of *iura novit curia.* However, this principle is not applicable in cases where foreign law is applied.[28] Since the judge is unable to know the content of the foreign law, the foreign law must be researched and analysed. The judge's obligation to carry out research and the option of seeking help is defined under Article 2/I PILA. It is an incorrect assumption to accept that the judge knows the foreign law.[29] Turkish courts are required to know only Turkish law (*iura novit curia*), including the Turkish conflict of law rules stipulated in PILA. Therefore,

---

[26] Civil Department no.2 of Court of Cassation (O.G. 20.9.1995-22410): This decision regarding a divorce case serves as a model: "*The parties have foreign nationalities. According to the rule in PILA, the divorce is not subject to Turkish law...It is not allowed to decide only according to the parties' will which says that Turkish law is to be applied". In Turkish law, the grounds for and the effects of divorce and separation shall be governed by the common national law of the parties. Where the parties have different nationalities, the law of common habitual residence, if this does not exist, Turkish law shall apply (PILA Article 14). The choice of law is not allowed* (www.kazanci.com)."

[27] Civil Department no.11 of Court of Cassation, E.1997/5344, K.1997/5910, 16.9.1997: "Pursuant to Turkish law the judge must make a decision ex officio (Code of Civil Procedure Art. 76) and the judge applies the conflict of law rules by its own motion (Law no.2675, Art.2/I). There is not any hesitation in the doctrine and in the practice of the courts. The application of foreign law should not be necessarily brought forward by the parties under Turkish procedural law. The judge ascertains the foreign law according to the private international law rules. This is judge's official duty" (www.kazanci.com).

[28] NOMER, E., 186. SANLI, C./ESEN E./ATAMAN F.I., 62.

[29] NOMER E., 187.

Turkish courts are not required to have knowledge of foreign law, which can thus be established by hearing evidence.

A judge can obtain assistance from the parties regarding the determination of foreign law's content, as indicated in PILA. Furthermore, PILA states that the judge applies the foreign law by its own motion. However, if the judge does not have sufficient knowledge about the foreign law, the judge may ask for assistance from the parties in this respect. At the first step, priority is given to determine the content of the foreign law in accordance with the judge's personal legal background and his own research. The judge should apply the foreign law in accordance with the provisions determined by him. Moreover, the judge is obliged to apply the foreign law as it is applied in the respective foreign country.[30] Besides the accurate application of foreign law, the effect of the provisions which are propounded by the parties to the judge must be discussed. The judge is not bound by the foreign law's provisions which are put forward by the parties.[31] This applies also in cases where the parties agreed on the content of the foreign law.[32] According to Article 2 of PILA, the parties undertake the obligation to help the judge. The judge also has the obligation of *ex officio* examination, and, in cases where foreign law is applied, may ask for help from the party who will benefit from the application of that foreign law. However, asking for help from the parties on foreign law does not amount to a burden of proof. Since the foreign law rules are not accepted as fact, the special procedural rules on evidential burdens regulated in the Civil Procedural Code do not apply in such cases.[33] The only goal of the judge is to obtain accurate and sufficient information about the content of the foreign law that he/she is going to apply in the specific case. The judge can take help from the parties present during the proceedings, but simultaneously, the judge is not bound by the claim of either one of the parties.[34] In other words, if a judge is uncertain about the information presented, he/she is at liberty to conduct his/her own research. Any court judgment rendered without asking for help or without applying the European Convention on Information on Foreign Law will be likely reversed by the Court of Cassation.[35]

[30] SANLI, C./ESEN E./ATAMAN F.I., 69.

[31] CELIKEL, A./ERDEM, B., 174; SANLI, C./ESEN E./ATAMAN F.I., 67.

[32] CELIKEL, A./ERDEM, B., 174.

[33] NOMER, E., 192.

[34] CELIKEL, A./ERDEM, B., 174.

[35] Civil Department no.2 of Court of Cassation, E.16427/K.54973, 4.2007: "…It is not safe to make a decision and ascertain the content of foreign law without asking the help of the parties, benefiting from the European Convention on Information on Foreign Law, applying ex officio the foreign law in light of this information (PILA Art.2/I)" In the same direction: Civil Department no.2 of Court of Cassation, E.2006/21951, K.2007/17742, 25.12.2007 and Civil Department no.2 of Court of Cassation, E.2008/13740, K.2008/14696, 6.11.2008 (www.kazanci.com).

E. Interpretation and Application of Foreign Law

Foreign law must generally be applied in the same way as it is applied by the courts in the country in question.[36] It is, therefore, generally insufficient to rely only on textbooks and translations of the statutes. This also implies that Turkish courts are required to review legislation and judgements to the same extent as the courts in the relevant country. If the question under consideration has not been decided by foreign courts, the Turkish courts are authorized to develop the law as the foreign court presumably would.

F. Failure to Establish Foreign Law

The application of a foreign law is inappropriate in the event of failure to find the content of that foreign law. Similarly, an action must not be dismissed on the grounds that foreign law could not be proved. A rule was introduced to Turkish law and regulated under Article 2/II PILA. According to this provision, if the content of the foreign law could not be found then the judge applies Turkish law to the case. The information and the law presented by the judge or the parties may sometimes be insufficient to resolve the case at bar. In such cases, jugdes may be hesitant to apply foreign law. Under these circumstances, the application of Turkish law to the case will be more convenient rather than the foreign law. In this situation, Turkish law and the foreign law are not afforded the same weight. Since the law which has the closest connection with the case does not provide the solution for the dispute, it is impossible to apply that law to the case. As a result, Turkish law provisions are applied in the absence of such provisions under the foreign law. Not dissimilar to the system under PILA 1982, in the event of failure to determine the content of the foreign law, a judge applies *lex fori,* Turkish law (Art. 2/II PILA). The application of the law of the forum as a substitution for foreign law is only a solution in cases where accessing information on foreign law is not possible.

G. Judicial Review

Similar to other first instance judgments, trial court judgments in cases where foreign law is applicable are, in principle, subject to review by superior courts. When trial court findings are challenged from the point of view of foreign law, a basic distinction is usually made between a failure to designate the law correctly according to the Turkish conflict of law rules, on the one hand, and materially incorrect application of the applicable foreign law, on the other.

---

[36] CELIKEL, A./ERDEM, B., 174; NOMER E., 193.

The Turkish Court of Cassation examines whether or not the determination of the applicable law is correctly in accordance with PILA. This examination scrutinizes the procedures used in ascertaining the applicable law. In other words, the court examines whether Turkish law (*lex fori*) or the law of another legal system is applicable to the case. This analysis is conducted in light of PILA's conflict of law rules. If national law rules are violated, any such violation is grounds for appeal to the Court of Cassation. Concerning the content of the foreign law, the Court of Cassation also has the authority to examine the accuracy of application of foreign law.[37] Since the Court of Cassation pursues a goal to serve justice based on the facts, the misapplication of foreign law can be a subject for review. Accordingly, the misapplication of the foreign law is also within the scope of the appeal court's examination.[38]

III. Access to Foreign Law

A. *European Convention on Information on Foreign Law*

Turkey became a party to The European Convention on Information on Foreign Law (known as 'the London Convention')[39] signed in London under the auspices of the Council of Europe[40] in order to facilitate the obtaining of information on the content of foreign law easier and faster. The convention aims to create facilities in gathering information on foreign law and make it for judges easier to solve disputes involving a foreign element. Article 2 of the present Convention obligates each Contracting Party to set up or appoint a receiving agency to carry out the functions set out in the Convention provisions. The receiving and transmitting agency of Turkey is, like in many other countries, the Ministry of Justice.

Although there are often references to this Convention especially in case law in Turkey,[41] in practice the information obtained from the agencies abroad is, in most cases, insufficient for a Turkish judge to resolve the case at bar. The information contains the translation of the relevant articles of the foreign law and is not always useful for the resolution of a case.

[37] NOMER, E., 194.

[38] CELIKEL, A./ERDEM, B., 179; SANLI, C./ESEN E./ATAMAN F.I.,70. In the same direction: Civil Department no.2 of Court of Cassation, E.6548, K.1610, 18.3.1969.

[39] http://conventions.coe.int, CETS No:062 (46 countries including Turkey ratified the convention status as of 20.10.2014).

[40] Official Gazette. 26.8.1975-15338. Turkey, at the same time, is also a party to the additional protocol of the convention. Official Gazette. 14.4.2004-25433.

[41] Civil Department no.2 of Court of Cassation, E.2006/16427, K.2007/5497, 3.4.2007; Civil Department no.2 of Court of Cassation, E.2006/21951, K.2007/17742, 25.12.2007 (www.kazanci.com).

B. Other Sources

It is the judge's duty to find the content of foreign law by utilising all available resources. Therefore, a judge, besides the convention, can use other sources to determine the content of the foreign law. Turkish law allows the judiciary to use personal knowledge and undertake personal research on the applicable law. Turkish courts are authorized and sometimes expected to conduct their own research on foreign law.[42] The courts often rely on legal literature on foreign laws in the Turkish language. For example, extensive and rather up-to-date documentation on foreign family and inheritance laws is available, so experts will usually be appointed only in complicated family or inheritance law cases. The judge may request help from the Ministry of Justice, Turkish embassies and consulates in foreign countries or foreign delegations in Turkey. Simultaneously, the judge may consult research institutes and faculty members at universities specialized in comparative and foreign law in order to obtain information about the subject matter. As indicated in the decision of the Court of Cassation,[43] in practice judges obtain the information mainly from two institutions within the structure of Istanbul University Faculty of Law, namely the Research Centre in International Law and International Relations and the Research Centre in Comparative Law. The judge does not consult these institutions in order to prove facts. On the contrary, the institutions provide the judge with knowledge on foreign law, and therefore, the expert reports as a means of evidence under the Turkish civil procedural law must be differentiated.[44] Article 2 PILA states that parties are free to put forward their own expert opinions on foreign law. If both parties agree to take a certain position on foreign law, courts may take this into account when establishing foreign law. This will reduce the court's duty to establish the foreign law as it is, but will not relieve the court entirely from this duty.[45] If the judge does not find the information provided by the parties to be satisfactory, he/she is at liberty to disregard this information and conduct his/her own research.

C. Article 2 of PILA in Practice

Turkey does not collect statistical data on the number of cases in which foreign law is applied or on costs generated by the application of foreign law. Further to this study, judges in Istanbul were interviewed directly to gather information on the application of foreign law. Turkish judges stated that the rate of the application of

[42] NOMER E., 192; SANLI, C./ESEN E./ATAMAN F.I., 66.

[43] Civil Department no.11 of Court of Cassation, E.1997/5344, K.1997/5910, 16.9.1997 (www.kazanci.com).

[44] NOMER, E., 192–193.

[45] NOMER, E., 193; SANLI, C./ESEN E./ATAMAN F.I., 67.

foreign law is less than the number of the disputes including a foreign element. In practice, the European Convention on Information on Foreign Law is known by the Turkish judges. According to the collected statements, however, besides the obligation of application of the foreign law *ex officio*, the judges frequently request assistance from the parties. Actually, in practice, the judges observe the foreign law as fact and accept that it is within the scope of the burden of proof, pursuant to Article 6 of the Turkish Civil Code. Accordingly, judges wait for the parties to produce the information on foreign law and apply it accordingly. The interviewed judges openly indicated that they avoid the application of foreign law in cases where the parties did not raise the application of foreign law. The main reason was the irregular access to foreign law. Other reasons given were the fear of delay in proceedings due to the bureaucratic obstacles in obtaining information on foreign law and the wish of the parties or counsel for Turkish law to be applied. Improving access to foreign law might therefore lead to an increased willingness by the Turkish judges to apply foreign law. Turkey did not join the European Judicial Network[46] on the grounds that it is too early to establish a judicial network between the judges or to become a member to them because of Turkey's substructure and the related workload burden.

IV. Conclusion

Turkey shares borders with eight other countries and has a reasonably internationally-minded Private International Law, which on a number of grounds leads to the application of foreign law. Regarding family and inheritance law in particular, citizenship (and not domicile) is used as the main criterion for determining the applicable law. As the number of foreigners residing in Turkey is increasing due to several factors, this implies that Turkish court proceedings involving foreign family or inheritance law are becoming increasingly more frequent. As a result of the development of international relations, the number of international commercial litigation cases to which foreign law applies increases as well. It often happens that, under a rule of conflict of laws, a court is called upon to apply a principle of foreign law, particularly in questions of family, inheritance or contract law. In this respect, prior to the application of foreign law, it is important to ascertain the content of foreign law and to examine the results of its application. According to Article 2 PILA, the parties may help the judge in order to obtain information about foreign law. Additionally, the procedural law of Turkey encourages judges to resort to international mechanisms for the purposes of ascertaining the foreign law. The judge can direct his information request in accordance with the London Convention via competent

[46] http://www.ejn-crimjust.europa.eu/ejn/

authorities to the country where the relevant foreign law is applied. In situations where foreign law is applied, methods for gathering information by the most efficient means without wasting time should be aspired to. Information gathering procedures should be relieved of bureaucratic obstacles. Providing a judge with informationon foreign law should not remain as a burden on any of the parties. Rather, it should be shared and the methods of information acquisition on foreign law should be facilitated and made easier. As a result, both the judge and the parties would benefit, leading to an increased willingness by Turkish judges to apply foreign law.

Israel: Proof of and Information About Foreign Law in Israel

Talia Einhorn

Abstract The application of foreign law by a national court, for whatever reason, is a challenging endeavor. The court is required to decide legal issues as if it were a court of the foreign state. Yet, a national judge can neither be expected nor required to be familiar with the foreign legal system as he is with his own. If the application of foreign law is not to be invariably frustrated, then such application should only be conditioned upon the judge acquiring reasonable understanding of the solution which that foreign system might have for the problem at hand.

The paper analyzes critically the rules prevailing in Israel at present, concluding that the present situation, concerning the ascertainment and proof of foreign law, is confusing and expensive, and hence burdensome to both the parties and the courts. It proposes a reform of the Israeli law rules, pointing out however that the only way to cope well with the ever growing need to apply foreign law requires a special kind of legal education. Top students should be encouraged to learn foreign languages and specialize in at least one major foreign legal system in that foreign country. Comparative law courses, in which the differences and similarities between the approaches of legal systems to the solution of similar problems are critically analyzed, should play an important role in legal education. In each country, at least one university library should hold foreign legal texts – statutes, commentaries and textbooks, in the respective foreign languages. Even if those are made available on electronic databases in the future, access to these databases will still require an investment of substantial resources. In the author's opinion there can be no substitution to expertise, earned through intensive hard work, in short a challenge for long distance runners.

T. Einhorn (✉)
Professor, Department of Economics and Business Administration,
Ariel University, Ariel, Israel

Visiting Senior Research Fellow, Faculty of Management, Tel-Aviv University,
Recanati Building, P.O. Box 39040, Ramat-Aviv, Tel-Aviv IL 6139001, Israel
e-mail: taliaeinhorn@gmail.com

Y. Nishitani (ed.), *Treatment of Foreign Law - Dynamics towards Convergence?*,
Ius Comparatum – Global Studies in Comparative Law 26,
DOI 10.1007/978-3-319-56574-3_28

I. Conflict of Laws Rules

A. The Application of Conflict Rules

The application of conflict rules is mandatory in Israel. There is no general rule allowing parties to designate in each matter a law of their choice to govern their relationship. Thus, the Supreme Court held that a person could not subject her estate to a law other than the law of her domicile at the time of her death (which is the conflict rule under the Israeli Succession Law, 5725-1965).[1] However, in some matters of civil and commercial law, party autonomy is respected, in line with the principle that *pacta sunt servanda* and the need to protect the parties' legitimate expectations. The courts will not respect the parties' choice if it is incompatible with Israeli external (or international) public policy.

Israeli PIL treats all foreign legal systems equally. In principle, Israeli conflict rules strive to apply the law of the state with the closest connection to the factual circumstances. In practice, however, foreign law is not always applied, even though the applicable PIL rule provides that it should be applied. Since the courts do not take judicial notice of foreign law, and the party that wishes to rely on foreign law has to prove it, it may happen that the case will be decided on the basis of Israeli law, rather than foreign law (cf. para. II (B) *infra*).

B. Foreign Laws Invoked in the Israeli Courts

In the Israeli courts, the laws of European states, e.g., Belgium, England, France, Germany, the Netherlands, Poland, Russian Federation, Switzerland, Ukraine; the laws of Canadian Provinces; various US States; India; New Zealand, have all been invoked in pertinent cases.

---

[1] *Attorney General – the Administrator General v. Plonit*, Application Family Appeal 594/04, 59(3) PD 297 (29 November 2004). In one case, *Nafisi v. Nafisi*, Further Hearing 1558/94, 50(3) PD 573 (25 August 1996), Justice Barak suggested that §15, Spouses (Property Relations) Law, 5733-1973, being a choice-of-law rule, is just a dispositive rule, which only applies if the parties did not make may an agreement that provides otherwise. This statement has been correctly criticized and cannot be taken as reflecting properly Israeli law. Celia Wasserstein Fassberg, "Law and Justice in Choice of Law: Matrimonial Property after *Nafisi v. Nafisi*", *Mishpatim* 31 (2000): 97 (in Hebrew); Rhona Schuz, "Choice of Law in Relation to Matrimonial Property: the Existing Law and Proposals for Reform", *Bar-Ilan Law Studies* 16 (2001): 425 (in Hebrew).

II. Foreign Law Before Judicial Authorities

A. Foreign Law as a Fact

In Israel, foreign law must be pleaded and proved as a fact. Admittedly, this qualification is flawed with respect to its underlying logic. Law, even foreign law, is a legal element in court proceedings, not a fact. However, the practical implications of this approach are attractive. It enables courts not to take judicial notice of foreign law, and leaves it to the parties to ascertain its contents to the extent that they wish to rely on it. For obvious reasons, this approach is particularly suitable in civil and commercial cases. The party that wishes to rely on the foreign law bears the costs of proving it. In matters affecting third parties, such as status, succession, or matrimonial property, a different approach may be necessary.

In one case, concerning a contract with a choice-of-law clause stipulating that German law applies, this qualification led both the Haifa District Court and the Israel Supreme Court to conclude that, if the plaintiff has not properly pleaded foreign law in his statement of claim, the claim could be dismissed.[2] Indeed, the qualification of foreign law as fact – if taken seriously – must lead to this result. Fortunately, in most cases, judges have not pursued this logic to its limits. Nevertheless, in a number of cases courts have required the parties to amend their pleadings and adduce expert evidence.[3] Only after being convinced that the parties are incapable of doing so, have the courts applied the *lex fori*. This procedure makes litigation unnecessarily expensive.

B. Application of Foreign Law

The Israeli pertinent legal rules can be summarized as follows:

(a) If foreign law applies to a case, it must be pleaded and proved as a fact.

---

[2] *Hess Form Licht Company v. Handasat Hashmal Kelalit*, Application Permission to Appeal 3924/01, tak-Supreme 2002(1), 268 (10 February 2002). Both the District Court and the Supreme Court held that, since the presumption of similarity of the foreign law and Israeli law could not hold in this case (a contract in which German law was stipulated as the applicable law chosen by the parties), the claim could be dismissed if the foreign law was not proved to the satisfaction of the Court. A similar decision was reached by the American Court in *Walton v. Arabian American Oil Co.*, 233 F. 2d 541 (2d Cir. 1956). That case is no longer a leading case, if it ever was. Although possible in theory, a court would rarely dismiss a claim because the applicable foreign law has not been proved.

[3] Cf. Shava, "The Presumption of Similarity of Laws", *Iyyunei Mishpat* 4 (1975): 583 (in Hebrew), at 588. To be sure, there are also cases in which the courts applied Israeli law as soon as the foreign law was not pleaded or proved with sufficient clarity by the parties – see, e.g., *Trade House Progress v. Kevutzat Hai-El Sachar Benleumi*, CC (Tel-Aviv) 103462/97, tak-Magistrate 2001(3), 870 (22 October 2001).

(b) If the contents of the foreign law have not been established, it may be presumed that the foreign law is identical to Israeli law, and Israeli law should be applied instead.
(c) The presumption concerning the identity of laws has been qualified by the following three cumulative preconditions[4]:

    (1) that there is no effective practical possibility of proving the contents of the foreign law and, consequently, unless the presumption is applied, the claim will be dismissed: and
    (2) that there is no reason to suspect the parties of having conspired not to produce evidence regarding the contents of the foreign law, in contravention of the public interest, or the interests of third parties, who could not appear in court and litigate the case; and
    (3) that the elementary notions of justice concerning the pertinent case are uniform and are likely to impose an obligation in all civilized countries.

(d) In most cases, the courts require that the foreign law be proved by expert evidence.[5]

These rules apply unless a different rule has been stipulated in a statute that deals with a specific type of case.[6]

The application of the existing rules is often difficult and cumbersome. The presumption regarding the identity of laws has given rise to much awkward and uneasy discussion in the case law. The rule could have stated that, if the foreign law is not proved, the court should instead apply its *lex fori*, not because of a presumption that it is identical to the law which should have applied, but simply because this is the only law of which the court has judicial notice.[7]

[4] Cf. Menashe Shava, ibid. Admittedly, Shava had in mind mainly questions of status when he suggested these three preconditions, ibid., 590. However, in practice, judges often cite these conditions indiscriminately, also in cases involving contracts, especially labour contracts, torts, property law, succession, etc.

[5] However, the court may rely on mere allegations made by the plaintiff in his statement of claim as to the contents of that law, as soon as those were not contradicted by the defendant – cf. *Rabintex v. Halima*, Case (Israel National Labour Court) 57/71–3, tak-National 98, 2463 (10 August 1998). The court stated that, in fact, there is no better proof of the foreign applicable law; In another case, the court accepted a decision made by an Italian court between the same parties as sufficient proof of the applicable Italian law – cf. *X v. Y*, Family Case (Tel-Aviv) 5062/97, tak-Family 97(1) 17, 23 (9 March 1997).

[6] For example, §14 of the Appendix to The Hague Convention (Return of Abducted Children) Law, 5791-1991, authorizes, in conformity with the wording of the Convention, the judicial and administrative authorities, in ascertaining whether there has been a wrongful removal or retention, to take notice directly of the law of, and of judicial or administrative decisions, formally recognized or not, in the State of the habitual residence of the child, without recourse to the specific procedures for the proof of that law or for the recognition of foreign decisions which would otherwise be applicable – cf. para. II(C) *infra*.

[7] Indeed, in a recent case, the Haifa District Court held that, since English law, which should have governed the contractual obligation that was the subject-matter of the dispute, has not been proved, it will apply Israeli law. The Court made no reference, it is submitted correctly, to the presumption

The preconditions attached to the presumption have contributed to the confusion. Why should parties who wish to save the cost of expert evidence, or have the *lex fori* apply for any other reason, nevertheless be required to demonstrate that there is no effective practical possibility of proving the contents of the foreign law? It is likewise difficult to see why the court should be interested in the parties' state of mind (conspiracy or not) regarding their avoidance to rely on the foreign law, unless the result reached is incompatible with the international (external) public policy of the forum state. Courts of law are perfectly capable of dealing with such problems,[8] and making this matter part of the issue of proving foreign law is confusing.

Finally, can Iranian, Iraqi, Indian or Jordanian law be seriously presumed to be identical to Israeli law? And why is it necessary to be able to assume uniformity among legal systems in order to apply the *lex fori*? Thus, in once case concerning succession, the Supreme Court concluded that, since the spouse could not prove to its satisfaction that Iranian law recognized the community of property between spouses in the matrimonial property that they had acquired, the Court could not fill the vacuum by applying Israeli law which would have entitled the spouse to receive one half of the matrimonial property included in the estate.[9]

In another case, the Court declared that the duty in principle of the father to support his minor children could be presumed to apply almost worldwide.[10] However, in yet another case, the Court refused to apply the presumption with respect to the duty to indemnify the former wife for the costs that she incurred in caring for the minor child.[11]

Another example of the difficulties is provided by the dispute surrounding the copyright in the deciphered Dead Sea Scrolls.[12] In the first instance, the Jerusalem District Court held that American law was applicable. Yet, it relied on the presumption of identity of laws to apply Israeli law for the following reasons: According to

---

of identity of laws – cf. *Vitol Energy SA v. Trans KA Tankers Management Co. Ltd.*, CC (District Court, Haifa) 197/07, Nevo electronic database (29 August 2011). Cf., similarly, *Sussman's Civil Procedure*, 7th ed. (Shlomo Levin [ed.]) (Jerusalem: Israeli Company for Professional Training, 1995) (in Hebrew), §112, who writes in his authoritative treatise that, if a party did not plead and prove the contents of the applicable foreign law, the judge will decide the case according to Israeli law. No reference is made to the presumption of identity of laws.

[8] On this point see further Peter Nygh, *Autonomy in International Contracts* (Oxford: Oxford University Press, 1999) 226, 232–233; and, in a general context, Kurt Siehr, "Die Parteiautonomie im Internationalen Privatrecht", in: *Festschrift für Max Keller* (Zürich, 1989) 485–510.

[9] *Nafisi v. Nafisi*, Further Hearing 1558/94, 50(3) PD 573 (25 August 1996), 584–585. In other cases, the court had no trouble in applying Israeli law to cases in matters of succession – see, for example, *Estate of Forugi and Kleinberg v. Estate of Koren and Eliahu Insurance Co.*, CC (Jerusalem) 1296/99, tak-District 2000 (4), 1304 (17 December 2000).

[10] *Chiadri v. Chiadri*, CC (Tel-Aviv) 713/92, tak-District 93(1), 346 (23 March 1993).

[11] *X and 4 minor children v. Y.*, Family Case (Tel-Aviv) 63880/98, tak-Family 2000(2), 286 (11 June 2000). Under Israeli law, Jewish law determines the duty to make such payments regarding the Jewish population. The court held that it cannot be presumed that such a rule applies also in legal systems other than Jewish law.

[12] Kimron v. Hershel Shanks, Eisenman, and the Biblical Archaeological Society, CC (Jerusalem) 41/92 [5753-1993(3)] PsM 10 (30 march 1993).

the Court, the presumption should apply in cases of contract or tort. In this case, the issue was copyright which, although part of property law, its violation nevertheless has the character of a claim in torts, thus justifying the application of the presumption to the content of copyright law. Furthermore, the Court presumed that the legal systems of all civilized states, including the US, were identical. Consequently, the Court concluded, with respect erroneously, that U.S. law, like Israeli law, recognized moral rights in copyright at that time.[13]

Furthermore, in one case the presumption has misled the court to rely on additional criteria to support the application of the *lex fori*. In that case,[14] the District Labor Court of Jerusalem decided that Israeli, rather than Jordanian, law should be applied to an employment contract made and performed in Judea for the following reasons:

(1) the contents of Jordanian law had not been sufficiently proved;
(2) Israeli law was presumed to be not only identical but superior to Jordanian law, mandating its application since, according to the Court, contract law requires that considerations of justice and public policy [i.e., Israeli public policy] be taken into account – especially in employment contracts.

C. Ascertainment of Foreign Law

1. General Remarks

The principle *iura novit curia* does not apply in Israel to foreign law. Courts have only judicial notice of Israeli law.

One important exception is, however, noteworthy. In principle, according to the Interpretation Ordinance, 1945, as well as its new version of 1954, and the Interpretation Law, 5741-1981, the religious laws (written or unwritten) of all recognized religious communities[15] are an integral part of Israeli law and, consequently, within the judicial notice of the court, without need to be proved, as is the case with foreign law. Israeli courts occasionally required that the religious laws be proved by the parties on the basis of expert opinions. This may be done on the basis of §8(c), Family Court Law, 5755-1995, and Rule 258L(1), CPR, which allows the Court to

[13] On appeal, the Supreme Court held that, according to the pertinent rules of Israeli private international law, Israeli law, rather than American law, applied – cf. *Eisenman, Robert E., Hershel Shanks and BAR (Biblical Archaeological Review) v. Kimron*, CA 2790/93, 54(3) PD 817 (30 August 2000).

[14] *Mahmud Hamis v. David Bernard*, Case (Jerusalem Labor Court) 51/570–3, tak-Labor 95(1), 16 (6 February 1995).

[15] Those include the Eastern (Orthodox), Latin (Catholic), Gregorian Armenian, Armenian (Catholic), Syrian (Catholic), Chaldean (Uniate), Greek-Catholic – Melkite, Maronite, Syrian (Orthodox), the Druze (since 1957), Episcopal Evangelical (since 1970) and Baha'i (since 1971). Other religious laws of which the Israeli Courts have judicial notice are Jewish Law (*halakha*) and Muslim Law (*shari'a*).

appoint an expert in family matters. Courts have accepted expert opinions as an *amicus curiae*, stating that they cannot be expected to have judicial notice of the religious laws of all religious communities.[16]

Israel has enacted laws which regulate certain aspects of personal matters on a secular, territorial basis, e.g., the Succession Law, 5725-1965, and the Spouses (Property Relations) Law, 5733-1973. In family matters which are not regulated by secular legislation, the civil courts (at present, the family court) must still apply, *ex officio*, religious law,[17] albeit under different rules of procedure and evidence (which may substantially affect the result achieved in the case). Even though the Israeli family courts have applied *ex officio* the religious laws of the various religious communities in numerous cases, it may none the less be doubted to what extent this application properly reflects religious law. With respect to the Christian Communities, the published cases seem to cite only the provisions of the applicable religious laws, without however any reference to commentary. So far, the laws of most religious communities, and any existing commentaries,[18] collections of cases decided by the

[16] Cf., e.g., *A.B. v. M.B.*, CC (Tel-Aviv) 778/50, 876/50, 3 PsM 263 (6 April 1951), at 287, per Judge Zeltner, and in *re Testament of the deceased Michael Polak and re Ginsburg v. Eugenia Polak and Leib Bulein*, Succession Case (Tel Aviv) 115/54, 12 PsM, 129 (31 May 1956); *Minor v. Ploni*, Family Case (Tel Aviv) 67250/00, tak-Family 2001(1), 112 (25 February 2001). Cf., also, the decision of President Landoi in *Dorit Bloch and Anton Wilhelm Bloch v. The Attorney General*, Application for Dissolution of Marriage 8/81, 35(4) PD 449 (5 October 1981) – in reaching a conclusion on the basis of Canon Law, President Landoi considered an expert opinion and finally accepted the expert's conclusions, after checking directly commentaries and literature on the subject, underlining that the Canon Law is within the Court's judicial notice; cf., Izhak Englard, *Religious law in the Israel Legal System* (Jerusalem: Sacher Institute, Hebrew University Faculty of Law, 1975) (in Hebrew) 88 ff.

[17] Cf., e.g., the application *ex officio* in maintenance cases of the Byzantine Family Law with respect to matters of the Eastern Orthodox Church by Israeli secular courts – *Estate of Asa'ad Kalil Ayub Al-Wil Za'athra*, Succession Case (District Court, Haifa) 178/55, Nevo electronic database (27 June 1968); *A.L. v. A.I.*, Various Civil Applications (Family Court, Krayot) 1417/08, Nevo electronic database (4 June 2008); *Plonit v. Ploni*, Family Case (Tel-Aviv) 35053/04, Nevo electronic database (3 March 2005). The Byzantine Family Law was also applied to members of the Copt Orthodox Church, *L. v. H.*, Family Case (Nazareth) 32231-01-10, Nevo electronic database (19 December 2010); The Eastern-Catholic Code was applied to Greek-Catholic maintenance claims by the Family Court *ex officio* in, e.g., *'A.K.S. v. 'A.V.N.*, Family Case (Nazareth) 10211/06, Nevo electronic database (10 January 2011), and *D.P. v. 'A.P.*, Family Case (Tiberias) 55922-10-10, Nevo electronic database (27 February 2011); The Druze Personal Status Law was applied *ex officio*, e.g., by the District Court in *Jamilla Sallah Shwach v. Nuaf Muhamad Halabi*, Maintenance Case (District Court, Haifa) 54/69, 73 PsM 58 (20 November 1970); the Personal Status Law of the Roman Catholic religion, published by the Latin Patriarch in Jerusalem, was applied by the District Court in *Lily Habra v. Anton Habra*, Personal Status Case (District Court, Tel-Aviv) 839/67, 63 PsM 183 (28 May 1968).

[18] A commentary that provides insight into the family laws of the various religions, including, among others, the Roman Catholic Church and the new *Codex Iuris Canonici*, in effect since 27 November 1983; the Eastern Catholic Churches (Greek Catholics – Melkites, Armenian (Catholic), Syrian (Catholic) included); and the various Orthodox denominations (including the Armenian Orthodox (Gregorian), Chaldean (Uniate), Copt Orthodox, Eastern Orthodox, Greek Orthodox), is to be found in Josef Prader, "Die religiösen Eherecte", in: Bergmann/ Ferid, *Internationales Ehe- und Kindschaftsrecht* (Frankfurt a.M.: Verlag für Standesamtswesen, looseleaf, contribution last updated 1992).

religious tribunals, and textbooks, are not readily available, not even in the university law libraries.

With respect to the Druze Community, the law itself has been published,[19] but the situation may be even more complicated, since the Druze religion is secret, and only a *Qadi Madhab* is competent to interpret and apply it.[20] In practice, all religious courts and tribunals apply their respective laws *ex officio*, in a manner which is very different from the Israeli civil courts. The latter, following the common law civil procedure, require the parties to argue all legal points. The judge is not expected, nor should he, raise legal arguments and apply legal rules at his own initiative. Even if the judge considers doing so expedient and necessary, such intervention should be done in a restrictive manner and the parties should be asked to present their positions with respect to those first.[21]

Another exception is provided by the Hague Convention on Civil Aspects of International Child Abduction, 1980 (the "Child Abduction Convention"). The Convention authorizes the judicial and administrative authorities, in ascertaining whether there has been a wrongful removal or retention, to take notice directly of the law of, and of judicial or administrative decisions, formally recognized or not in the State of habitual residence of the child, without recourse to the specific procedure for the proof of that law, or for the recognition of foreign decisions, which would otherwise be applicable (Art. 14). The Convention was implemented in Israeli law with the enactment of the Hague Convention (Return of Abducted Children) Law, 5751-1991. According to this Law, the Convention provisions have the same effect as Israeli statutes enacted by the *Knesset*. Art. 14 has been relied upon by the Israeli courts.[22]

[19] The Druze Personal Law has been reproduced in Arabic and in Hebrew in Nissim Dana (ed.), *The Druze* (Ramat Gan: Bar-Ilan University Press, 1998) (in Hebrew), Annex A, pp. 225–277. The law is essentially based on the Lebanese Druze Personal Status Law, with a couple of important changes introduced by the Druze Community in Israel.

[20] Cf., e.g., the Protocol of the *Knesset* Constitution, Law and Justice Committee, regarding amendment No. 18 (concerning the competence of a *Qadi Madhab*) of the Druze Religious Courts Law (Protocol No. 352, Committee session of 28 February 2011), in which the secrecy of the Druze religion is discussed. As it turns out, even lawyers who appear before the Druze Religious Court do not know the law, as interpreted by the Druze Religious Courts, since they have no access to all of its sources, and cannot rely on such sources – ibid.
<http://www.knesset.gov.il/protocols/heb_search.aspx?ComId=6>

[21] *Sussman's Civil Procedure*, *supra* n. 7, §268; cf. further references in this matter, Talia Einhorn, *Private International Law in Israel*, 2nd ed. (Kluwer Law International 2012), para. 536, fn 537.

[22] Cf., e.g., *Ploni v. Almonit*, Family Case (District Court, Tel Aviv) 5062/97, Nevo electronic database (9 March 1997), per Judge Gaifman; *Almonit v. Ploni*, Family Court Case (Tel Aviv) 57489-07-13, Nevo electronic database (2 April 2012), per Judge Schneller; cf. Gali (Pollack) Ron, *Family Courts in Light of Case Law* (Tel Aviv: Israel Bar Association, 2009) (in Hebrew), pp. 287 f., with further references to case law.

2. Methods of Ascertaining Foreign Law

Israeli civil procedure is based on the English traditional civil procedure rules. Consequently, foreign law has to be pleaded by the party that wishes to rely upon it in its statement of claim, or statement of defence, as the case may be, making proper reference also to the foreign applicable legal rules upon which the party wishes to rely.[23] In principle, foreign law has to be proved by expert evidence. However, the court may rely on mere allegations made by the plaintiff in his statement of claim as the contents of that law, if those were not contradicted by the defendant.[24] In one case, the court accepted a decision made by an Italian court in a dispute that had arisen between the same parties as sufficient proof of the applicable Italian law.[25]

In principle, the burden of proof should be discharged by the party that wishes to rely on the foreign law.[26] In one case, the District Court required both parties to amend their pleadings and produce expert evidence concerning the contents of German law. On appeal, the Supreme Court reversed this part of the District Court's decision, stating that in this case, in which both the District and the Supreme Court were of the opinion that the presumption regarding identity of laws did not apply, it was the duty of the plaintiff alone to prove the foreign law.[27] Should the plaintiff fail to do so, the District Court was instructed to re-consider the defendant's application to have the claim summarily dismissed.[28]

Israeli law does not provide a conclusive definition of who may be recognized an expert on foreign law.[29] According to established case law, a lawyer or a jurist who engages, whether in practice or as an academic or in some other way, in the legal system that needs to be proved, may serve as an expert witness who may prove the applicable foreign law. Their degree of expertise and the weight to be given to such testimony are left at the court's discretion.[30] Consequently, a proper expert opinion will provide the court with information substantiating the expertise of the witness, as well as the foreign sources and legal materials on which the expert opinion is based.[31] If such materials are not provided, the court will not give much weight, if

[23] *Sussman's Civil Procedure*, *supra* n. 7, §112, at p. 137 and §302, at p. 377, with further references to Israeli case law.

[24] Cf. *Rabintex v. Halima*, Case (Israel National Labor Court) 57/71-3, tak-National 98, 2463 (10 August 1998). The Court stated that, in fact, there is no better proof of the foreign applicable law.

[25] Cf. *X v. Y*, Family Case (Tel Aviv) 5062/97, tak-Family 97(1) 17, 23.

[26] Sussman's Civil Procedure, *supra* n. 7, §112, at p. 137.

[27] *Hess Form Licht Company v. Handasat Hashmal Kelalit*, Application Permission to Appeal 3924/01, tak-Supreme 2002(1), 268 (10 February 2002).

[28] Cf. the criticism of such dismissal in para. II(A) *supra*.

[29] Uri Goren, *Issues in Civil Procedure*, 12th ed. (Tel Aviv: Syaga, 2015) (in Hebrew), p. 448 f.

[30] Cf., e.g., Berg Yaakov & Sons Ltd. v. Berg East Imports, CA 6796/97, 54(1) PD 687.

[31] Cf., e.g., Stanislava Stolovich v. The Organization for the Implementation of the Social Security Treaty Israel – West Germany, CA (District Court, Tel Aviv) 3203/02, Nevo electronic database (10 July 2005).

any, to that opinion.[32] The weight that a court gives to an opinion, in which the expert did not refer to a pertinent legal provision of the foreign law, and only dealt with it in response to his cross-examination, will be diminished.[33] Likewise, if the expert is affiliated with the party, the weight of his evidence will be considerably diminished.[34]

Even though the onus of proof regarding the contents of the foreign law has to be discharged by the party that wishes to rely upon that law, it often happens that both parties submit expert opinions, but there is no need to do that. A party may cross-examine the expert of the other party, and such cross-examination, if carried out properly, may refute the expert opinion.[35]

If the court cannot decide which of the conflicting expert opinions presented by the parties is the correct one, it may, without being obliged to do so, appoint an expert, with or without the parties' consent.[36]

The costs of ascertaining foreign law are born initially by the party that seeks to prove the foreign law and rely upon it. However, the other party may incur costs, too, in its efforts to refute the expert witness brought by the first party. At the end of the trial, the successful party is entitled to a refund of its costs, including the sum that it had to spend with respect to the expert opinion. It is noteworthy that courts do not necessarily award the successful party full compensation for its expenses.

One obstacle that deserves special mention concerns the little use made of video conferences, which could have contributed to lower the costs. In a decision of 2007 in this matter, the Supreme Court held, by majority opinion, that despite technological developments, a video conference should still be allowed only in rare cases, especially if the witness has a good reason for being unable to appear in court, and that this matter should be clearly regulated by the legislature.[37] None the less, in a recent decision, the Family Court in Tel-Aviv allowed an expert on Hong-Kong law to be cross-examined via video conference.[38]

---

[32] Cf., e.g., *Hannah Nava v. Talia and Chaim Sardes*, CA (District Court, Tel Aviv) 3203/02, Nevo electronic database (31 March 2010).

[33] *Hannah Nava v. Talia and Chaim Sardes*, ibid.

[34] Cf., e.g., *Warner Bros. International Television Distribution, a Division of Time Warner Entertainment Co., LP v. Zvi Yochman, CPA, as trustee, and Tevel Ltd.*, Insolvency Proceedings (District Court, Tel Aviv) 1361/02, Various Civil Applications 3896/04, Nevo electronic database (1 September 2004).

[35] Cf., e.g., *Gazprom Transgaz Ukhta Ltd. v. Double Kay Petroleum Products 1996 Ltd.*, Originating Summons (District Court, Tel Aviv) 30752-05-11, Nevo electronic database (19 March 2012).

[36] Cf., e.g., *Richard Virus v. Nicole Libuton*, Civil Appeal (District Court , Central District) 51367-05-12, Nevo electronic database (28 October 2012).

[37] *Dori & Tschaikowsky v. Shamai Goldstein*, Application Permission to Appeal 3810/06, tak-Supreme 2007(3), 4667 (24 September 2007). Cf., further, regarding the reasons given for this decision, as well as other ones, Einhorn, *Private International Law in Israel*, *supra* n. 21, paras. 1229 f.; cf. also Goren, *Issues in Civil Procedure*, *supra* n. 29, pp. 557 f.

[38] *Ploni v. Almonit*, Family Case (Tel-Aviv) 45419-05-10, Nevo electronic database (27 March 2012), per Judge Naftali Shilo.

A special method of ascertaining foreign law has been devised by the Israel Supreme Court. Justices of the Israeli Supreme Court solicit individuals trained in the American and Commonwealth legal traditions, as well as European legal systems, to work as foreign clerks. Each foreign clerk is assigned to a specific Justice and is expected to conduct legal research and draft memoranda regarding legal questions that pertain to pending cases. When applicable, such studies are taken into consideration in opinions rendered by the Court.[39]

The quality of the research and memoranda prepared under this method may be questioned.[40] The foreign clerks have usually just graduated from law school. According to the webpage, "there is a clear preference to candidates who finished their 2nd year of law school (at least)". They are not always qualified lawyers, and have not yet gained sufficient experience and expertise in their respective home country legal systems. They are required to carry out research in a large variety of legal areas, including public international law, constitutional law, criminal law, tort law, contract law, corporate law, civil procedure, private international law, etc. Their access to the legal materials of their home country is limited, to the extent that those are not available in Lexis. This limitation is of special importance in the case of Civilian legal systems, that are mostly not available in English. So far, the Supreme Court library does not provide access to databases that are not in English, and access to European civilian legal texts, commentaries and textbooks in foreign languages (other than English) is rather limited.

D. Interpretation and Application of Foreign Law

Under Israeli law, foreign law has to be interpreted and applied in the same way that it is interpreted and applied in the country of origin. This can be demonstrated in numerous cases. The parties strive to prove to the judge how the legal rules would fare in their country of origin. A gap (*lacuna*) should be filled in a similar manner. The court needs to ask itself what a court in the state of origin would have done in the circumstances. Naturally, the interpretation and application of foreign law cannot be as complete and good as the understanding of local law. That would never

---

[39] More information regarding this procedure is available on the Supreme Court webpage http://elyon1.court.gov.il/eng/Clerking_opportunities/index.html

[40] Cf. Adam M. Dodek, "The Charter…in the Holy Land?" *FORUM Constitutionnel* (1996) 8:1, critically analyzing the application of the Canadian Charter of Rights and Freedoms by the Israeli Supreme Court; Philipp Stricharz, "Foreign Clerks at the Supreme Court of Israel", *JA [Juristische Arbeisblätter]* 2004/6, pp. IV-VI; regarding the problematic application of foreign law, and comparative legal research, carried out in the fields of private international law and unjustified enrichment, cf., e.g., Einhorn, *Private International Law in Israel, supra* n. 21, paras. 269–280 (rejection by the Supreme Court of the common domicile exception in traffic accidents); Talia Einhorn, "The Expansion of Israeli Unjust Enrichment Law: the Mixed Blessings of a Mixed Legal System", in: *Aufbruch nach Europa: 75 Jahre Max Planck Institut für Privatrecht* (Basedow et al. [eds.]) (Mohr Siebeck 2011), pp. 905–922.

happen. The judge should use the documents, materials and evidence available and make the most of them.

E. Failure to Establish Foreign Law

If the foreign law cannot be ascertained, Israeli law will apply. However, since the aim of the Israeli court should be to apply the foreign law, as far as possible, in the same way that the foreign court would have applied it, it is submitted that the Israeli court may first apply the rules of another legal system which is similar to the applicable foreign law. This is especially suitable where the applicable foreign law provides no clear-cut answer to the problem at hand, but a similar legal system does.

III. Judicial Review

A. Conflict of Laws Rules

If conflict of law rules have been applied erroneously, this is a matter of law, and the unsuccessful party may appeal the decision to higher courts, including the Supreme Court.

It should be noted that in the Israeli legal system, there is a right of appeal from a district court judgment[41] to the Supreme Court, if the district court was the trial court of first instance. If the case was heard by a magistrate court, then there is a right of appeal from its judgment to the district court, sitting as an appellate court in such cases. A further appeal from the district court to the Supreme Court requires the granting of leave to appeal, either in the judgment itself, or by the Supreme Court. In appropriate cases the Supreme Court may order a further hearing of the case – i.e., a special procedure whereby the appeal is heard again by an enlarged panel of at least five Justices of the Supreme Court, reserved for cases that raise a problem which is significant, difficult or new.[42] Other judicial decisions of the

---

[41] In this context, a judgment means a court decision that ends the court proceedings with respect to a certain issue, even if it is only a partial judgment of the case, which does not settle all matters definitively, and even if it only brings a formal end to the proceedings without deciding the rights and obligations of either party, e.g., a decision to dismiss a case without prejudice.

[42] Cf., e.g., *Skaler v. Yuviner*, Further Hearing 4655/09, tak-Supreme 2011(4), 647 (25 October 2011). The case concerned two Israelis, one of whom drove a car and the other – a passenger in that car, who had a traffic accident in New Zealand. In its further hearing, the Supreme Court held, by a majority of 5 to 2, that the common domicile exception did not apply in Israel, and that the law of New Zealand should apply to that case. Cf., further, on this case, Einhorn, *Private International Law in Israel*, *supra* n. 21, paras. 269–280; The conflict rules regarding marital property were also the subject-matter of a further hearing – *Victoria Nafisi v. Simantov Nafisi*, Further Hearing 1558/94, 50(3) PD 573 (25 August 1996). Cf. Einhorn, ibid., para. 699.

magistrate courts and the district courts, such as those concerning interim relief or the admissibility of evidence, may be appealed only if leave to appeal is granted by the respective appellate court, i.e., the district court or the Supreme Court, as the case may be.

B. Foreign Law

Foreign law is a fact. Consequently, if it has been applied erroneously, an appellate court will not intervene in the findings of the lower court, unless the lower court has disregarded the pertinent evidence presented to it, or if the mistake is evident on the face of the erroneous judgment. However, extraordinarily, an appellate court may grant a party leave to present additional evidence, usually subject to costs that need to be paid to the other party. It has happened that a party, whose claim had been dismissed *in limine* by the trial court, was granted leave by the Supreme Court to submit an expert opinion regarding the applicable foreign law, according to which the trial court erred in deciding that, under that foreign law, there was no case to answer.[43] The Supreme Court allowed the appeal and ordered the District Court to accept the expert opinion, hear the case and decide it on its merits.

IV. Foreign Law in Other Instances

A. Administrative Authorities

There is no available information regarding the application of foreign law by administrative authorities.

B. Arbitration

In arbitration proceedings that have their seat in Israel, arbitrators are not necessarily bound to decide the dispute according to law.[44] However, to the extent that an arbitral tribunal, has to decide the dispute according to law, Israeli law provides no rules regarding the law applicable to the decision on the merits. An arbitral award

[43] *Sussman's Civil Procedure*, *supra* n. 7, §316, at p. 393, referring to *Compagnie française de participation v. Shmuel Flatto Sharon*, CA 556, 557/84, 40(2) PD 298. In this case, the claim was dismissed *in limine* by the District Court. However, according to an expert opinion, that was first presented on appeal to the Supreme Court, the claim should not have been dismissed under the foreign applicable law.

[44] Cf. Rule 14, Israeli Arbitration Rules, included in Annex II, Arbitration Law, 5728-1968.

may however be set aside if "the arbitrator did not make the award in accordance with the law though the arbitration agreement required him to do so" (§24(7), Arbitration Law).[45]

It is submitted that the following rules will apply[46]: The arbitral tribunal has to decide the dispute according to the rules of law chosen by the parties, which may be the laws of a given state (which may mean its substantive law or, alternatively, the whole of its law, including its choice of law rules),[47] or rules such as the UNIDROIT Principles of International Commercial Contracts,[48] or the Lando Principles of European Contract Law (PECL),[49] or general principles of the *lex mercatoria*. Failing such a choice or, to the extent that the rules chosen do not cover the whole of the dispute, the arbitral tribunal will decide the dispute according to the rules of law with which the case has the closest connection.[50]

Another question may concern the application of foreign mandatory rules of law. Courts in major arbitration centers agree that parties are generally entitled to submit all their disputes to arbitration, including those that may raise questions of foreign mandatory rules of law, such as competition law issues, securities statutes and regulations, etc.[51] In Israeli law there are no rules or precedents regarding the application of mandatory rules in international commercial arbitration. As a matter of fact, Israeli law is unclear even with respect to the application, in arbitration proceedings, of Israeli mandatory rules, such as competition law, in purely domestic cases. It is submitted that arbitrators should not ignore mandatory rules, even in purely domestic cases, and that arbitral awards made without consideration given to such matters should be subject to review in this respect. Disregard of foreign mandatory rules may later on affect adversely the enforceability of the arbitral award.[52]

The party that seeks to rely on foreign law in the arbitration process, will have to discharge the onus of proof regarding the contents of the foreign law, by pleading it and providing expert evidence regarding its contents.

The situation is entirely different with mediation and other means of non-binding mechanisms of alternative dispute resolution. Whereas arbitration often seeks to

---

[45] There is no international treaty harmonizing the grounds for setting aside arbitral awards (Art. 1, New York Convention, harmonizes only the grounds for challenging recognition and enforcement of foreign arbitral awards). None the less, in most states today, setting aside implies a limited review – cf. Tibor Várady et al., *International Commercial Arbitration – A Transnational Perspective*, 6th ed. (West, 2015), p. 954, and pp. 985 ff.

[46] Cf. Einhorn, *Private International Law in Israel, supra* n. 21, paras. 1422–1427.

[47] If not stated clearly, or not clear in the circumstances, this will be a matter of interpretation.

[48] Cf. UNIDROIT Principles of International Commercial Contracts (Rome: UNIDROIT 2010) http://www.unidroit.org/english/principles/contracts/principles2010/integralversionprinciples2010-e.pdf

[49] Cf. Ole Lando and Hugh Beale (eds.), *Principles of European Contract Law*, revised ed. (The Hague: Kluwer Law International 2000–2003).

[50] Such a rule conforms to Israeli law principles governing choice of law rules in general.

[51] Cf., in general, Giuditta Cordero Moss, *International Commercial Arbitration – Party Autonomy and Mandatory Rules* (Oslo: Tano Aschehoug 1999).

[52] Cf., further, Einhorn, *Private International Law in Israel, supra* n. 21, paras. 1428 ff.

settle a dispute according to legal rules, mediation is usually used for the settlement of disputes by focusing on the parties' common interests. Consequently, it may be expected that there will usually be little need for the proof of foreign law.

C. The Ascertainment of Foreign Law in Advisory Work by Attorneys

Attorneys may have to ascertain foreign law, to the extent required by the advisory work that they perform. In certain cases, ignoring foreign law may amount to professional negligence. Especially nowadays, there is ever more need to ascertain foreign law if the case has transnational aspects. Determining and ascertaining foreign law will be done by seeking advice from foreign experts, often by colleagues overseas who are also called to deal with the issues at hand.

V. Access to Foreign Law: Status Quo

A. Official (Government) Website

Israel does not provide legal information through an official (government) website.

B. The Hague Judicial Network[53]

To enhance the smooth operation of the 1980 Hague Child Abduction Convention, Israel has appointed a member in the Hague Judicial Network – previously Justice Neal Hendel (when he was a Judge at the District Court of Jerusalem, until his appointment to the Israel Supreme Court), and at present Judge Ben-Tzion Greenberger, of the District Court in Jerusalem. This network was established in order to facilitate the return of abducted children, by helping to secure the safe return of the children to their country of domicile just prior to the abduction, to ensure that the abducting parent would be able to conduct proceedings regarding the custody of the abducted child without being threatened with arrest for having kidnapped the child, to assist in expediting the hearing of the case in the requesting country, as well as contribute to the uniform interpretation of the Convention.

According to Justice Hendel,[54] Israeli judges have not asked to communicate directly with foreign liaison judges to obtain legal information. One does not find

---

[53] *See* list of Network members at <https://assets.hcch.net/docs/18eb8d6c-593b-4996-9c5c-19e4590ac66d.pdf>. In 2013, the Hague Conference published a brochure, entitled *Direct Judicial Communications - Emerging Guidance regarding the development of the International Hague Network of Judges and General Principles for Judicial Communications*, accessible at <https://www.hcch.net/en/publications-and-studies/details4/?pid=6024&dtid=3>

[54] On 3 December 2013 Justice Hendel kindly answered the author's questions regarding his role as liaison judge.

Israeli cases in which information has been sought from the international liaison judge in a foreign country. There have not been direct communications between Israeli judges and foreign judges seized by the same parties with a case, similar to the Canadian case *Hoole v. Hoole*, in which a joint hearing was conducted by Justice Donna Martinson, the Network Judge for British Columbia at that time, who had found it appropriate for the Supreme Court of British Columbia to communicate directly with the Circuit Court in the State of Oregon and participate in a joint hearing held in open court in both Oregon and British Columbia, with counsel present.[55]

In his role as international liaison judge, Justice Hendel received questions from judges in foreign countries regarding Israeli civil procedure rules applicable to such cases – when is there a right of appeal, and when is there need to apply for leave to appeal, whether a certain rule applies in Israel, the duration of such proceedings in Israel (appeals included), how the Israeli courts apply certain Convention provisions. The answers provided were general in character, not relating to the specific case. Justice Hendel was of the opinion that trial judges should not be approached by him directly, so they would not feel pressured by the circumstances but be able to decide the case independently. Justice Hendel added that taking part in liaison judges conferences was a very important aspect of the Hague Judicial Network, since it provided judges with the opportunity to discuss the interpretation and application of the Convention in their respective jurisdictions, and thus contribute to its harmonious interpretation and application.

The Hague Judicial Network seems to provide a fine collaboration among judges from different countries. Yet, its scope of application is limited to the Hague Child Abduction Convention, which calls for such cooperation. Even though the specific circumstances of each case may be complex from a personal point of view, the legal issues are usually not very difficult, and it is an asset to be able to use modern means of telecommunications in order to assist parents and children to overcome the problems of relocation, expedited hearing, and related issues. However, it is not always possible to make effective use of the Network.[56]

---

[55] *Hoole v. Hoole*, [2008] BCSC 1248. In British Columbia there were guidelines applicable to court to court communications in cross-border cases, approved by BC Supreme Court, regarding the conduct of such joint hearings, that ensured fair hearing to all parties involved; cf. the comments and further references to the use made of the Hague Judicial Network, by the Honorable Justice Robyn Moglove Diamond, of the Court of Queen's Bench, Family Division, Winnipeg, Manitoba, Canada, at the conference on "International Judicial Initiatives Dealing with Cross Border Child Protection", 6th World Congress on Family Law and Children's Rights, Sydney, Australia (March 17–20, 2013), paper dated December 2012.

[56] Cf. the pertinent criticism of *Re E (Children)*, [2011] UKSC 27, by Schuz, *The Hague Child Abduction Convention*, ibid., at pp. 296–298. In that case, the English judge at the court of first instance sought information from the Norwegian international liaison judge. The Norwegian judge provided only a partial answer, and the English judge noted that it was fairly clear that the Norwegian judge did not understand his question. Thorpe, LJ, in charge of international judicial communications in the UK, was not prepared to seek clarification from "a no doubt very busy judge". Schuz considers the failure to seek such clarification as indicating the limits to the usefulness of this mechanism, since partial information may be misleading or even worse than no information at all.

It is submitted that such a network cannot be extended to other fields of law that involve more complex legal questions. It is highly unlikely that a foreign judge will be able, on the basis of communications from a colleague in another country, to come up with an opinion relating to the exact factual situation. Given the number of national cases that judges have to cope with, it can hardly be foreseen that, on top of those, they would have the time to study foreign cases just as thoroughly and provide the necessary legal advice regarding cases that are heard in foreign countries.

C. International or Regional Instruments Regarding Information on Foreign Law

Israel is not a state party to any international or regional agreement regarding information on foreign law, nor are there international or regional settings to facilitate access to foreign law.

D. The Shortcomings and Drawbacks in International and Regional Instruments

Preparing a memorandum that explains how any given case would be solved under foreign law requires, first, a careful analysis of the factual situation, followed by an analysis of its treatment under the foreign legal system. Finally, the analysis has to be stated in terms that will be understood by a jurist who operates in the Israeli legal system. It often happens that even identical terms may have a different meaning in the foreign and the Israeli system.[57] Hence, technical translations of texts would be

---

[57] In one Israeli case, *Ploni v. Almoni, Attorney at Law*, Originating Summons 4576-09-11, Nevo electronic database (14 May 2012), the Israeli District Court concluded that the plaintiff, who had signed a letter dismissing his Israeli attorney, was in bad faith, and consequently dismissed his claim, simply because the Court had misunderstood the difference between the competence of a person to whom a Betreuer, or custodian, had been appointed under German law, and the competence of a person to whom a guardian had been appointed under Israeli law. The appointment of a Betreuer does not render the person legally incompetent, as is the case when a guardian is appointed under Israeli law. It only means that henceforth his acts require his custodian's approval. Consequently, since the plaintiff had his custodian's consent, he could lawfully perform legal acts. Unfortunately, the parties and, consequently the Court, too, were not aware of this important difference between the legal systems; cf. also the example brought by Rhona Schuz, *The Hague Child Abduction Convention* (Hart, 2013), at p. 156, referring to a decision of the US District Court for the Eastern District of Michigan – *Tsimhoni v. Eibschitz-Tsimhoni* (Unreported, 26 March 2010), in which the US Court held that the children had not become "habitually resident" in Israel during their 3-month stay there, immediately before their removal from Israel. In doing so, the US Court gave no weight to the finding in the Israeli Court's declaration, made under Art. 15, Hague Child Abduction Convention, that they had done so – *Ts.L. v. E-Ts.M.*, Family Case (Kfar Saba) 29189-12-09, Nevo electronic database (23 December 2009). Schuz submits that Art. 15 declarations

misleading. All of these require a high degree of expertise in the pertinent legal field and are also time consuming.

Thus, for example, in Germany, when the opinion of experts at Max Planck Institute for Comparative and International Private Law in Hamburg (MPI) is sought by courts, the Institute receives the file itself so that the expert can become acquainted with the factual situation that the judge is faced with. The researchers are highly qualified jurists, who had already written their doctoral dissertations, they are very well acquainted with both the foreign language and its legal terminology as well as the German legal system.

VI. Access to Foreign Law: Further Developments

A. Improving Accessibility to Foreign Law

It is submitted that there is need to improve access to foreign law, in a variety of contexts, for judicial authorities, administrative and other non-judicial authorities, arbitrators, attorneys and parties. Such access is necessary not only in cases involving cross-border aspects, but also as a source of inspiration in domestic cases, for which Israeli law has not yet developed a proper solution, or that the domestic solution has become dated.

B. Conflict of Laws Solutions

In my opinion, it is not advisable to modify existing conflict rules for the sake of reducing the number of cases in which foreign law is applied. The application of foreign law in such cases promotes justice as well as the legitimate expectations of individuals and business organizations whose activities involve foreign elements. Since, in Israeli law, it is up to the party that wishes to rely on the foreign law, to plead and prove that law, there is no need to change the conflict rules.

---

should be considered binding, unless they are clearly out of line with the autonomous interpretation of the Convention, none the less concedes that the question of the child's habitual residence prior to removal has to be determined by the courts of the requested state, in this case the US court, not the Israeli court.

C. Suggestions for Reform

The present situation in Israel, concerning the ascertainment and proof of foreign law, is confusing and expensive, and hence burdensome to both the parties and the courts. Therefore, I would propose a reform along the following lines:

(a) Foreign law will be regarded as law, not fact;
(b) Courts will be deemed to have judicial notice of foreign law and be authorized to apply foreign law *ex officio*. The judge should use the documents, materials and evidence available and make the most of them. The judge should be authorized to appoint an expert to ascertain the contents of the pertinent foreign law;
(c) Rule (b) does not derogate from the parties' autonomy to agree to have cases litigated under Israeli law, if they may exercise such autonomy under private international law rules, as is the case, for example, in civil and commercial matters;
(d) If the foreign law cannot be ascertained, Israeli law will apply. However, since the aim of the Israeli court should be to apply the foreign law, as far as possible, in the same way that the foreign court would have applied it, the Israeli court may first apply the rules of another legal system which is similar to the applicable foreign law. This is especially suitable when the applicable foreign law provides no clear-cut answer to the problem at hand, but a similar legal system does.
(e) With the development of technology, the decisions limiting the use of video conferences should be reviewed. By now, video conferencing has gained acceptance in the whole common law world.[58] Even though a video conference may never be as good as physical presence in the courtroom, there may be room to relax the rigid approach prevailing at present. The English rules regarding this matter may serve as a good model.[59] In England, too, the court's permission is required, however the rules acknowledge the advantages of video conferences and their considerable savings in time and cost and do not confine them to rare cases.

D. Methods of Facilitating Access to Foreign Law

It is difficult to devise methods, or instruments, that would facilitate access to foreign law. Cases involving foreign elements are similar to domestic cases in so far as the specific factual situation of each must be looked at carefully. The foreign legal

[58] Cf. the comparative study in *B. v. Dentists' Disciplinary Tribunal*, [1994] NZLR 95 (High Court Auckland) (27 May 1993), noting the acceptance of video linking and conferencing in Australia, Canada, England and the US; cf. also *Cross and Tapper on Evidence*, 11th ed., Colin Tapper (ed.) (Oxford: Oxford University Press 2007), p. 61. Regarding the situation under Israeli law, cf. the criticism of Yehiel Shamir, "Taking Evidence via Video Conference in International Litigation", *Hamishpat* 8 (2003): 595 (in Hebrew).

[59] Cf. the English CPR, Practice Direction 32, para. 29.1, Annex 3.

rules must be applied to these facts, not to an abstract case that does not exist. Special care has to be taken with respect to translations, since every translation is an interpretation. Words in all languages have more than one connotation, and choosing the right one for a translation requires the skill of a person who is not only familiar with both languages and trained in both legal systems, but has also acquired full understanding of the particular legal field under consideration. Similar to the situation obtaining in domestic legal systems, no single lawyer can be an expert in all areas of the foreign law. Providing access to translations of statutes may be misleading. The attorney, or judge, may have the impression that he or she had understood the text, whereas in the foreign legal system it has been interpreted in an entirely different manner.

Most important is the awareness of the pitfalls and problems involved in ascertaining and applying foreign law. Such awareness will promote a more careful approach to this matter, as well as the understanding that easy, ready-made solutions, must be given up.

It is my opinion that the only way to cope well with the ever growing need to apply foreign law requires a special kind of legal education. Top students should be encouraged to learn foreign languages and specialize in at least one major foreign legal system in that foreign country. In a globalized world, comparative law courses, in which the differences and similarities between the approaches of legal systems to the solution of similar problems are critically analysed, should play an important role in legal education.[60] In each country, at least one university library should hold foreign legal texts – statutes, commentaries and textbooks, in the respective foreign languages. Even if those are made available on electronic databases in the future, access to these databases will still require an investment of substantial resources. There can be no shortcuts or substitution to expertise, earned through intensive hard work, in short a challenge for long distance runners.

[60] Cf. Kurt Siehr, "Teaching Comparative Law and Comparative Law Teaching", *Swiss Reports Presented at the XVth International Congress of Comparative Law* (2002): 139, 139–141.

Tunisia: Treatment of Foreign Law in Tunisia

Lotfi Chedly and Béligh Elbalti

Abstract This report outlines the status of foreign law in Tunisia. It explains that the application of conflicts rules in Tunisia is always mandatory for the judge. However, these rules are imperative for the parties to the extent that the object of the dispute is a category of rights that the parties cannot dispose of freely. Foreign law is treated as law and not fact; and Tunisian judges, without being obligated to, have the power to ascertain, with the assistance of the parties when necessary, the content of the foreign law. The application and the interpretation of the conflicts rules as well as foreign laws are subject to the control of the Tunisian *cour de cassation*. The Report also indicates that access to foreign law needs to be enhanced in order to ensure better resolution of private disputes involving foreign elements.

I. Introduction

In a system that is open to the world, the application of foreign law can often be inevitable. Rules of private international law make the recourse to foreign law possible to solve disputes with foreign elements. The application of foreign law is thus deemed "an object directed by consideration of justice, convenience [and] the necessity of international intercourse between individuals".[1] This report deals with the treatment of foreign law in Tunisia. In the absence of conventions dealing with

[1] International Court of Justice, judgment of 28 November 1958, *ICJ Report* 1958, p. 94.

L. Chedly
Professor, Faculty of Legal, Political and Social Sciences, The University of Carthage, Tunis, Tunisia
e-mail: Lotfi.Chedly@Fsjps.Rnu.Tn; chedlylotfi@yahoo.fr

B. Elbalti (✉)
Associate Professor, Graduate School of Law and Politics, Osaka University, Osaka, Japan
e-mail: benkei.tun@gmail.com

Y. Nishitani (ed.), *Treatment of Foreign Law - Dynamics towards Convergence?*,
Ius Comparatum – Global Studies in Comparative Law 26,
DOI 10.1007/978-3-319-56574-3_29

the issues of conflict of laws,[2] answers are essentially provided for by Tunisian domestic law.[3]

Prior to the promulgation of the Code of Private International Law (*hereinafter* "CPIL"), conflict of laws issues were mainly governed by a Beylical Decree (*décret beylical*),[4] whose scope of application was limited to issues of personal status.[5] The decree did not contain any rule relating to the procedural aspects of the application of foreign law. In the absence of legislative guidance, Tunisian case law had to fil the gap and constructed a regime for the application of foreign law.[6] According to the old regime, Tunisian substantive law, especially in matters relating to personal status, was deemed imperative (*d'ordre public*) as it was applied without recourse to choice of law rules when a Tunisian party was involved in the dispute.[7] However, when the issue concerned only foreigners, conflict of laws rules were considered mandatory for the parties in the sense that they did not have the right to renounce their application.[8] In any case, foreign laws were regarded as mere facts and, therefore, their application and interpretation were not subject to the control of the *Cour de cassation*.[9]

This state of affairs was strongly criticized by Tunisian scholars. They denounced the instauration of the so called "*privilège de nationalité*" as a hidden form of a

[2] Very few conventions concluded by Tunisia contain choice of law rules. For example, the bilateral convention concluded with France in 1957 (Convention of 9 March 1957) contains in its Article 2 a choice of law rule relating to personal status of French nationals. According to the said Article, the personal status – as defined under Tunisian law – of French nationals is governed by French law.

[3] Most of choice of law rules are included in the 1998 Code of Private International Law (Title V – Articles 26 to 76). Other conflicts rules can be found in different pieces of legislation. See for example, Law No. 1957-0003 of 1 August 1957 relating to the regulation of civil status (Article 31); Law No. 2000-93 of 3 November 2000 relating to the promulgation of the Code of Commercial Companies as subsequently modified (Article 10); Law No. 94-36 of 24 February 1994 as modified by the law No. 2009-33 of 23 June 2009 relating to Literary and Artistic Property (Articles 56 and 57). Interestingly, all these dispersed conflicts rules are of unilateral nature contrary to the rules included in the 1998 code, which are mainly bilateral conflicts rules.

[4] *Décret beylical* of 12 July 1956 as modified by the law n°57-40 of 27 September 1957. The Beylical decree of 1956 consisted only of 5 Articles. See *Revue Critique de droit international privé*, 1957, p. 752.

[5] The concept of "personal status" is widely understood to encompass issues of matrimonial property, will and succession as well as status or legal capacity of persons. See, K Meziou, "Tunisie – Droit International Privé", *JurisClasseur Droit Comparé*, Fasc. 60, 2012, n°12.

[6] See A Mezghani, *Droit international privé, États nouveaux et relations privées internationales – système de droit applicable et droit judiciaire international,* (CÉRES/CERP, 1991) *pp. 286ff*; M A Hachem, *Leçons de droit international privé, Livre II: Les conflits de lois (droit applicable à une relation transfrontière)*, (CPU, 1997) 38ff, 110.

[7] See for example, the decision of Tunis Court of Appeal, n°56468 of 25.12.1963 (*Zacco* case), *RJL*, 1964(4), pp. 66 ff. According to the Tunis Court of Appeal, "when a party to a dispute is a Tunisian and different laws enter into conflict, provisions relating to Tunisian personal status, which are imperative (*d'ordre public*), are applicable above other laws."

[8] Cass civ n°2994 of 2.4.1964, *Clunet*, 1968, p. 121, comm. M Charfi.

[9] See for example cass civ n°5934 of 21.3.1968, *Clunet*1974, p. 166, comm. M Charfi.

"*privilège de religion*".[10] They also attacked the assimilation of foreign law to simple facts and highlighted its incompatibility with considering conflict of laws rules as imperative.[11] To put an end to an era of incomplete legislation and inconsistent, much-criticized jurisprudence, the CPIL was enacted in 1998.[12] The code was deemed to be modern, progressive, liberal and consistent with the modern spirit of private international law.[13] With respect to the status of foreign law, the new code clarifies, in more or less detailed provisions, the regime applicable to foreign laws designated by conflict of laws rules.

The issues relating to the application of foreign law, subject of this report, will be dealt with as follow. Part II and III will analyze the application of conflict of laws rules and foreign laws before Tunisian judicial authorities. Part IV will address the issue of the available judicial review. Part V will briefly discuss the application of foreign law by other non-judicial instances. Finally, Part VI examines the questions of access to foreign law.

II. Conflict of Laws Rules

The CPIL lays down the approach Tunisian judges must follow each time they deal with a private international law issue. According to this approach, Tunisian judges must raise *ex officio* the issue of the application of the conflict rules included in the code when the facts of the dispute reveal a significant foreign element that connects the dispute to a foreign legal order. Then, depending on the nature of the category of rights at issue, the judge applies the relevant conflicts of rules. The discussion below will (1) identify the legal framework adopted by the Code and (2) assess the regime of choice of law rules.

---

[10] M Charfi, "Abolir les privilèges", *Revue Tunisienne de Droit*, 1972, pp. 11ff; K Meziou, "Le droit international privé tunisien en matière du statut personnel", *in* J-Y Carlier & M Verwilghen, *Le statut personnel des musulmans – Droit comparé et droit international privé*, (Bruylant, 1992) pp. 281 ff.

[11] A Mezghani, *supra n 6, pp. 286ff;* M A Hachem, *supra* n 6 pp. 38ff, 110–111.

[12] Law No 98-97 of 27 November 1998 relating to the promulgation of the Private International Law Code, Official Gazette No. 96 dated 1 December 1998, pp. 2332 ff.

[13] See K Meziou, "Introduction au code de droit international privé", in *Le code tunisien de droit international privé deux ans après: Première journée d'étude en droit international privé organisée par la Faculté des Sciences Juridiques, Politiques et Sociales (Tunis) le 19 avril 2001*, (CPU, 2003) pp. 1ff; M-L Niboyet, "Regard européen sur le nouveau droit international privé tunisien", in Le code tunisien de droit international privé deux ans après, ibid., pp. 147ff; A Mezghani, *Commentaires du Code de droit international privé*, (CPU, 1999) pp. 12 ff.

A. The Legal Framework

1. Solutions of the Code

According to Article 26 CPIL, "when the legal relationship is international, the judge *shall apply the rules set forth in the present code*; in the absence of rules, the judge shall identify the applicable law by an objective determination of the connecting legal category" (emphasis added). The concept of "international relationship" is defined in the Code itself. According to Article 2, "shall be considered international the legal relationship that is connected at least by one of its significant elements to one or more legal orders other than the Tunisian one." Therefore, the existence of a significant foreign element is the condition upon which conflicts rules are to be applied. In the absence of corresponding choice of law rule, Article 26 adopts what is called the traditional choice of law approach as conceptualized by *Savigny*. The applicable law has to be determined by categorizing the legal issue (relationship) and attaching to it an appropriate connecting factor in order to determine the law applicable to the case.[14] This neutral and objective approach guarantees, in principle, an equal treatment and the equivalence between domestic and foreign law.

Accordingly, Tunisian judges *have the obligation* to apply the conflict of laws rules included in the Code. They have to invoke their application *ex officio* even though the parties did not base their claim on the applicable foreign law. Put differently, the application of conflicts rules is *mandatory*. Tunisian judges cannot disregard the international nature of the dispute and pass over the application of conflicts rules when the facts of the dispute reveal a significant foreign element that connects the dispute to a foreign legal order.[15]

The mandatory nature of the conflicts rules is strengthened by Article 28 of the CPIL.[16] Considered by some scholars as the cornerstone of the Tunisian conflict of laws system,[17] Article 28 determines the authority of conflicts rules by drawing a fundamental distinction between two situations. On the one hand, when the object of the conflicts rule is a category of rights over which the parties have no free disposition, the conflicts rules are binding for the judges and imperative for the parties. This means that Tunisian judges have to raise *ex officio* the applicability of conflict rules *and* have the obligation to apply them regardless of how the parties present their case. On the other hand, when the object of the conflicts rule is a category of rights over which the parties have free disposition, judges are *still* required to apply

[14] A Mezghani, *supra* n 13, p. 37; M A Hachem, "Le Code tunisien de droit international privé", *Rev. crit. DIP,* 1999 at 237.

[15] A Mezghani, *supra* n 13, p. 61.

[16] According to Article 28, "the conflict of laws rule is *imperative* when its object is a category of rights over which the parties cannot dispose of freely (para.1). In other cases, the conflict of laws rule *is binding upon the judge unless the parties expressly manifest their willingness to preclude its application*. (Para.2)" (Emphasis added).

[17] L Chedly & M Ghazouani, *The Code of Private International Law* (Tunis, 2008) p. 402 (in Arabic).

conflicts rules *unless* the parties decide otherwise. Therefore, the authority of conflicts rules depends on the nature of rights involved in the proceedings, *i.e.* whether these rights are available or unavailable.[18] Tunisian scholars commonly categorize patrimonial rights (i.e. rights that can be evaluated in money, such as legal obligations and real rights) as available rights, and extra-patrimonial rights (i.e. rights that cannot be evaluated with money such as personality rights, family rights, succession etc.…) as unavailable rights.[19]

Although the CPIL adopts the classical distinction based on the nature of the right involved (available/unavailable), it does not adopt a mixed model according to which the application of foreign law is mandatory in some cases and discretionary in others. In fact, Tunisian judges enjoy no discretion over the application of conflicts rules. The available nature of the rights involved does not render the application of conflicts rules discretionary: their application is always mandatory for the judge.[20] This means that even if available rights are involved, Tunisian judges continue to be bound by the choice of law rule if the parties do not choose to evince its application. However, if the parties choose to exclude the application of the choice of law rule, then Tunisian judges are bound by the parties' choice. This is usually explicable on the grounds of procedural convenience not because the application of the foreign law is voluntary or discretionary. Tunisian scholars justify the solution adopted in the Code by explaining that conflict of laws rules are rules of law and, as such, always binding on the judge whose primary mission is to apply rules of law. Therefore, and according to the criterion of available and unavailable rights, choice of law rules are either imperative or optional only for the parties.[21] In other words, the application of conflict of laws rules is mandatory for the judges but, depending on the nature of the rights involved, the parties can choose by a common agreement to elude their application.

The agreement to set aside conflicts rules is commonly called "procedural agreement". In Tunisian law, this agreement has to be reached during the litigation, not before it starts. The validity of procedural agreements depends on the satisfaction of two conditions.[22] The first condition relates to the scope of the agreement. As

---

[18] For further analyses see, L. Chedly, L'office du juge et la règle de conflit (deux ans après l'entrée en vigueur du code de droit international privé), *in Le Code de droit international privé deux ans après*, *supra* n 13, pp. 97ff; S. Bostanji, "Foreign law before Tunisian judges", *in Table ronde sur le code de droit international privé (4 et 5 mai 2001)*, (Tunis, 2002) pp. 57ff (in Arabic). M Ben Moussa, "Foreign Law in the Tunisian Code of Private International Law", *The Arabian Journal of Academic and Jurisprudence*, 2005, pp. 165 ff (in Arabic).

[19] L Chedly & M Ghazouani, *supra* n 17, pp. 407 ff.

[20] Cf. K Meziou, *supra* n 5, n°19.

[21] See, L Chedly, *supra* n 18, p. 106; S. Bostanji, *supra* 18, p. 67.

[22] An additional condition can be found in Article 71 CPIL. According to Article 71, which relates to the choice of law in tort, "parties may, after the occurrence of the injurious act, agree on the application of the law of the forum as long as the case is pending before first instance courts." However, the scope of application of this additional condition is limited only to tort actions. It is also argued that the procedural agreement is only acceptable when its purpose is to set aside foreign law. See, A Mezghani, *supra* n 13, p. 62.

mentioned earlier, only available rights can be subject of such an agreement (Article 28 para.2). The second condition relates to the form of the agreement. According to Article 28 para.2, the agreement should be express. This means that the parties to the dispute should expressly declare their intention to preclude the application of the conflict of laws rule. Put differently, the mere fact that parties did not invoke the application of the choice of law rule cannot be regarded as procedural agreement. Therefore, the option given to the parties to preclude the application of conflicts rules is very limited; it can neither be presumed nor implied.[23]

2. Case Law

Tunisian case law, *in general*, follows the commands of the code. In many recent decisions, Tunisian courts, after detecting the foreign element that they deem significant, apply the relevant conflict of laws rule. However, this has not always been the case. In fact, there exists a number of decisions, where Tunisian courts did not comply with the solutions detailed above. Especially during the first years of application of the newly adopted provisions of the CPIL, Tunisian case law showed a certain degree of confusion.[24]

First, several court decisions did not clearly distinguish between the legal obligation of the judge to apply conflict of laws rules (even though the parties have not expressly relied on foreign law to support their claims), and the imperative nature these rules (the possibility acknowledged to the parties to renounce the application of the conflicts rules). In these decisions, lower courts (especially courts of first instance) considered that they had duty to apply conflict of laws rules *because* they were imperative i.e. involving unavailable rights. This position implies that if the case did not involve unavailable right, the judge would not have the duty to invoke *ex officio* the conflicts rules. These decisions ignore the fact that choice of law rules, as rules of law, are *always* binding for the judges irrespective to the nature of the rights involved in the dispute, and were criticized as such.[25]

Other lower court decisions are more controversial. In certain cases, even though the international character of the dispute (the foreign nationality of one of the parties, their foreign domicile etc.) was clearly revealed, lower courts ignored the application of the conflict rules. In these cases, Tunisian lower courts simply considered the dispute as purely domestic one and, without invoking CPIL, applied Tunisian substantive law to the case.[26] Even more controversial are certain lower courts' decisions that refused to consider the dispute in question international just because one or both parties were Tunisian nationals.[27]

---

[23] A Mezghani, *supra* n 13, p. 62; S Bostanji, *supra* n 18, pp. 70–71.

[24] For detailed analyses of this question, see L Chedly, *supra* n 18, p.97 ff.

[25] The nature of the rights involved has *only* impact on the parties' freedom to apply the conflict of laws rules. L. Chedly, *ibid.*, pp. 104–109.

[26] See examples cited by L Chedly, *ibid.*, pp. 100–103.

[27] See the decision of the Tribunal of First Instance of Tunis of 29.6.1999 in which the Tribunal of

However, several decisions of the *cour de cassation* show that the Tunisian Supreme Court is eager in ensuring that lower courts comply with the legislature's commands. With regard to the internationality of the dispute, the Tunisian *cour de cassation* clearly stated that the existence of a foreign element triggers the conflictual mechanism and that lower courts are bound by the approach provided for in the Code.[28] As to the authority of the conflict of laws rules, the Supreme Court, in a decision rendered on December 7, 2006, expressly referred to Article 28 as imposing an obligation on the judges to apply choice of law rules as these rules are mandatory in nature.[29] In another decision relating to contractual obligation (and therefore concerns a category of available rights) rendered in 2005, the Tunisian Supreme Court clearly stated that "according to the paragraph 2 of article 28 CPIL, the application of conflict of laws rules in order to determine the applicable law to the dispute is mandatory unless the parties expressly show their intention not to apply it."[30] The same can be said about a number of decisions rendered by lower

Tunis considered that "only Tunisian law is applicable in divorce matters when one of the parties to the dispute is Tunisian on the date of the conclusion of the marriage contract, and this in accordance with public policy." Case n°26-855, comm. S Ben Achour, *Revue trimestrielle de droit*, 2000, pp. 403 ff. See also the decision rendered by the Tunis Court of Appeal n°36946 of 4.11.2006 (unpublished), cited in L Chedly & M Ghazouani, *supra* n 17, p. 71. In this decision, the court of appeal considered that since the case involved a Tunisian couple who was married in Tunisia, and gave birth to a child holder of the Tunisian nationality, *the mere fact that the couple resided* abroad could not confer the legal relationship an international character. The court added that in the absence of a foreign element as in the case at hand, there were no rooms for the provisions of CPIL to be applied.

[28] It is worth to mention here the decision of the *cour de cassation* n°5128 of 9.3.2006 (a dispute related to the succession a deceased person who was a foreigner holder of both Swiss and Iranian nationalities) in which the Supreme Court held that the dispute was subject to articles 54 to 56 CPIL relating to choice of law in matter of succession after upholding the international character of the dispute. *Bulletin de la cour de cassation,* partie procédure civile et commerciale, 2006, p. 277 (in Arabic). In another decision, which was rendered in the occasion of a dispute relating to an international contract, the *cour de cassation* overruled the decision of the lower courts because they did not respect the approach prescribed by the Code. Cass civ No. 1875 of 21.9.2004, *Bulletin de la cour de cassation. Civ.* 2-2004, pp. 159ff (in Arabic). The court held that "article 26 CPIL provides that the judge shall apply the rules set forth in the present code when the legal relationship is international and, in the absence of rules, the judge shall identify the applicable law by an objective determination of the connecting legal category. The correct approach in the case at hand requires from the trial court to categorize correctly the disputed after it makes sure whether the contract is international or not and then designate the governing law by applying the choice of law rule. Since the appealed judgment and before it the judgment of first instance did not, in accordance to the provisions of CPIL, followed this mandatory approach [it violated the law] especially articles 26 and 28."

[29] Cass civ n° 2830 of 7.12.2006, *Bulletin de la cour de cassation. Civ.* 2006, pp. 283ff (in Arabic). In this decision, which was rendered in a matter related to succession, the court criticized the decision of a lower court that did not follow the approach prescribed in the code. According to the Supreme Court, "the approach of designating the applicable law in the Tunisian private international law is principally based on a conflictual approach which follows a logical reasoning. This consists in categorizing first the legal relationship in question according to the categories recognized in Tunisian law; then, applying the choice of law rules corresponding to the said category in order to determine the legislative competence of either the *lex fori* (Tunisian law) or the foreign law...".

[30] Cass civ n°7146 of 26.4.2005 (unpublished) cited in L Chedly & M Ghazouani, *supra* n 17, p. 426.

courts. In these decisions, even though the parties did not plead the application of the foreign law, lower courts complied with their duty to invoke conflict of laws rule as matter of legal obligation under article 28 in both cases involving unavailable right as well as cases involving available rights.[31]

B. Assessment

The Code adopts an objective approach in order to determine the law applicable to the case (Article 26). Therefore, it is logical to expect a high likelihood for foreign law to be designated and applied. Although there are no accurate statistics on how frequently a Tunisian court designates foreign law under a conflict of laws rule, the multilateral nature of the conflict of laws rules included in the Code naturally leads to the designation of foreign law. Given that Tunisia is part of the Arabic world and is geographically proximate to Europe, the courts are more likely to apply the law of Arabic and certain European countries with which Tunisia has close relationship, especially when issues relating to family matters are involved.[32] In contractual matters, the Code upholds the principle of party autonomy (Article 62).[33] This allows parties to choose foreign law and make Tunisian courts apply it to their disputes.[34]

The regime adopted for the application of conflict of laws rules laid down by the Code is fully satisfactory.[35] Conflict of laws rules are always mandatory for the judge regardless of their object or nature. Whether or not the parties plead the application of foreign law has no impact on the duty of the judge to raise the choice of law issue. However, as Tunisian scholars point out, even though the Code requires the application of the conflict of laws rules when the internationality of the dispute

[31] Chedly, *supra* n 18, pp. 109–111.

[32] According to the Office of Tunisian in Abroad, about 10% of the Tunisian population are emigrants living abroad. Europe is the first destination with 84.5% of Tunisian emigrants living in different European countries especially France (54.7%), Italy (15.5%), and Germany (7.1%). Emigration to other Arabic countries is estimated to 12.3%. http://www.ote.nat.tn/index.php?id=133. For analysis of emigration from private international law perspective, see K Meziou, "Migrations et relations familiales", *Collected Courses*, Vol. 345, 2009, pp. 9 ff.

[33] Article 62: "A contract shall be governed by the law chosen by the parties. To the extent that the applicable law has not been chosen by the parties, the contract shall be governed by the law of the by the law of the State where the party whose obligation is decisive for the characterization of the contract has his/her domicile, or, when the concluded contract falls within the scope of his/her professional or commercial activity, the law of his place of business."

[34] See cass civ No. 1875 *supra* n 28.

[35] Although, in practice, Tunisian courts do not sometimes strictly comply with its commands. For example, in a recent case involving a divorce between a Tunisian emigrant resident in Japan with a Japanese national (wife), the Court of First Instance of Tunis, without any reference to the CPIL, decided the case as if it were purely domestic and pronounced the divorce on the basis of Tunisian substantive law (Code of Personal Status) without any reference to choice of law rules included on the CPIL, although, in this case, Japanese law should have been applied in application of Article 49 CPIL. Tribunal of First Instance of Tunis, decision n°81855 of 13.12.2011 (unpublished).

is revealed, it says nothing about the obligation of the judge to investigate the existence of the foreign element when the parties fail to reveal — or actively conceal — the internationality of their dispute. Tunisian scholars agree that, since judges have the legal obligation to invoke *ex officio* conflict of laws rules, they should, *de lege feranda*, bear similar obligation to investigate the existence of the foreign element of the dispute.[36] This would ensures the effectiveness of the conflicts rules, because their application depends essentially on the existence of a significant foreign element.[37]

III. Foreign Law Before Judicial Authorities

A. *Nature and Application of Foreign Law*

As a general rule, Tunisian judges have to apply *ex officio* the designated foreign law irrespective of the parties' intentions, unless the parties expressly request otherwise when the issue concerns available rights. Accordingly, there are two conditions for the foreign law to be applied. First, the foreign law should be designated by the conflict of laws rule.[38] Second, there should be no express agreement of the parties to preclude its application.

As detailed more fully below, foreign laws are regarded as law in Tunisia and not mere fact. However, this does not mean that the principle of *iura novit curia* applies when the application of foreign law is in question.[39] In fact, due to its exteriority, foreign law is subject to a specific procedural regime under which the content of the applicable foreign law should be established, otherwise Tunisian law, as the law of

[36] Authors justify this solution by the logical connection that exists between invoking conflict of laws rules and invoking the foreign element of the dispute. They base their opinion on certain provisions of the Code of Civil and Commercial Procedures (CCCP) which allow the judge to take into consideration facts that the parties have not expressly invoked to the condition that the principle of *audi alteram partem* is respected. This is inferred from a combination of several articles of CCCP namely articles 4 and 86 CCCP. Article 4 provides that "every party shall have the right to consult the documents of the procedure and all other documents submitted by the other party." Article 86 states that "the judge can, if he deems it necessary, through a *juge rapporteur*, proceed to any measure of instruction…he deems helpful to reach the truth."

[37] See, L Chedly, *supra* n 18, pp. 112ff sp. 117; M. Ben Jemia, S. Ben Achour & M Bellamine, "L'ordre public en droit international privé tunisien de la famille", *in* N. Bernard-Maugiron & B. Dupret, *Ordre public et droit musulman de la famille en Europe et en Afrique du nord*, (Bruylant, 2012) p.200.

[38] In exceptional cases, however, foreign law can be applied without recourse to choice of law such as the application of foreign *lois de police*. According to Article 38 para.2 "a judge shall give effect to provisions of foreign law non designated by the conflict of laws rules, if it appears that the foreign law has close connection with the legal situation in question and that the application of the said provisions is essential having regards to their pursued purpose."

[39] S Bostanji, *supra* n 18, p. 75; A Mezghani, *supra* n 13, p. 70.

the forum, applies.[40] This means that when foreign law is sought to be applied, its content cannot be presumed to be known by the judges. Its content should be established for it to be applied.

B. Ascertainment of Foreign Law

The question of the ascertainment of foreign law designated by choice of law rules is governed by Article 32 CPIL,[41] which clarifies the role of the judge and the parties as to (1) the question of burden of proof and (2) the means that should be used to ascertain of the content of the foreign law.

1. The Role of the Judge and the Parties in the Ascertainment of Foreign Law

Article 32 para.1 states that Tunisian judges "may, within the limits of their knowledge and within a reasonable time limit, ascertain *ex officio* the content of the foreign law designated by the conflict of laws rule". No distinction here is made on the basis of the nature of choice of law rules, and thus, as far as the ascertainment of foreign law is concerned, the issue is governed by a single, uniform regime. When the judge takes the initiative to bring the proof of the content of the designated foreign law, the judge's endeavor, according to Article 32, is subject to two limits.[42] The first limit concerns the extent of the knowledge of the judge. Where the content of the foreign law is accessible, the judge can take all the necessary actions to establish the content of the law on its own motion. The second limit concerns the time within which the judge has to bring the proof of the foreign law. This means that the proof of foreign law should be brought within a reasonable time limit.

The wording of Article 32 suggests that judges are allowed — but not obliged — to establish the content of foreign law. Thus, as generally understood, the ascertainment of the content of foreign law is *not an obligation,* but only a *discretion* conferred on Tunisian judges. It is suggested that this discretion is generally limited to cases where conflict of laws rules are bilateral. However, when the conflicts rules pursue a certain substantive result (alternative choice of law rules), Tunisian judges

---

[40] According to Article 32 *in fine*, "if the content of the foreign law cannot be established, Tunisian law shall apply."

[41] Article 32 states as follow: "Judges may, within the limits of their knowledge and within a reasonable time limit, ascertain *ex officio* the content of a foreign law designated by the conflict of laws rule, and that with the assistance of the parties if necessary. In the other cases, the party whose claim is based on a foreign law shall establish its content. The proof shall be established in written including affidavits of law. If the content of the foreign law cannot be established, Tunisian law shall apply. In any case, adversarial principle shall be respected."

[42] S Bostanji, *supra* n 18, pp. 76 ff.

have no discretion in establishing the content of foreign law.[43] This is because the application of foreign law depends on a prior examination by judges of the content of all the eligible laws designated by alternative connecting factors, to choose the applicable law that fits the best the objectives and the policies pursued by the conflicts rule.[44]

As for the parties, Article 32 contemplates two situations. If the judge decides on its own motion to produce the proof of the foreign law, the judge can ask for the assistance of the parties if their assistance is deemed necessary (Article 32 para.1). Here, the parties play only a secondary role in proving foreign law. For example, the judge can ask the parties to make complementary investigation to shed light on how the foreign law is actually applied in the legal system to which it belongs. In other cases, the content of foreign law must be established by the party whose claim is based on foreign law (Article 32 para.2). Here, the parties play a principal role. In particular, when one party claims the application of foreign law, logically, that party must bring proof to support that claim. Article 32 seems to adopt a pragmatic approach. Parties cannot invoke the application of foreign law with the only purpose of delaying the outcome of the proceeding. In that case, they have to bear the cost and burden of bringing the proof of its content.[45]

In either case — whether the content of the foreign law is established by the court or by the parties — Tunisian judges have to respect the adversarial principle of the proceeding, according to Article 32 *in fine*.

2. Means of Proving Foreign Law

With respect to the means of proving the content of foreign law, Article 32 para.3 simply requires that "the proof shall be established in writing including affidavits of law". Article 32 does not require a specific means of proof. It can be any method provided that the formality of writing is respected. Accordingly, the testimony of

[43] See, L Chedly, *supra* n 18, p. 121 ff.

[44] The typical example given by Tunisian scholars are those of Articles 51 and 52 CPIL which concerns respectively choice of law rules in maintenance obligation and the establishment of parent-child relationship. According to Article 51, "Maintenance obligations shall be governed by the national law of the maintenance creditor, or the law of his/her domicile, otherwise, by the national law of the maintenance debtor or by the law of his/her domicile. The judge shall apply the most favourable law for the maintenance creditor (last para. omitted)" As for Article 52, it states that "The judge shall apply the most favourable law for the establishment of the parent-child relationship, between the national law of the defendant or the law of his/her domicile, or The national law of the child or the law of his/her domicile (last paragraph omitted)". See, L Chedly, "Structure de la règle de conflit et intérêt de l'enfant", *RJL*, 2002 n°spécial Famille, pp. 9 ff.

[45] For further developments, A Mezghani, *supra* n 13, pp. 72–74; M Ben Moussa, *supra* n 18, p. 175; L Chedly & M Ghazouani, *supra* n 17, pp. 455 ff. See for example the preparatory judgement of the Tribunal of First Instance of Tunis n°9901 of 13.10.1999 (unpublished) in which the tribunal required from the plaintiff who claimed the application of Swiss law to produce evidence of its content and the way it is interpreted in Switzerland according to academics and case law. Judgment quoted in L Chedly & M Ghazouani, *supra* n 17, p. 463–464.

expert witnesses (such as law professors, lawyers and consultants) is generally not acceptable, but their written opinions can be submitted to the court. Other alternative means of proof, such as direct communication of judges or inquiries are also conceivable; but, here again, the formality of writing should also be respected. The formality of writing binds not only parties, but also judges.[46]

This formality is justified by the adversarial principle guaranteed by Article 32 *in fine*. This entitles each party to reply to the allegations of the opponent and question the accuracy of the legal information submitted relating to the interpretation and application of foreign law. However, judges are not bound by the information provided by the parties.[47] In this respect, judges enjoy broad discretionary power to examine the accuracy of the provided information. They are also required to verify the reliability and impartiality of the submitted legal information, especially when it is no delivered by public authorities. In addition, when the parties submit contradictory information, judges can favor a set of information over the other.[48]

It is generally admitted that the written documents do not necessarily have to be official nor delivered by official institutions or public authorities. Therefore, in addition to affidavits of law mentioned in Article 32, law review or journals, academic books, copies of court decisions, including internet sources, can be accepted.[49] Moreover, individuals or institutions asked to provide information about foreign law need not demonstrate any specific qualification to do so. However, it is logical to require a certain level of legal expertise. In practice, it seems that Tunisian judges usually refer to foreign law compilations and codes when they are available, and with the proliferation of online sources, often consult official homepages (such *legifrance* for French law) or official governmental or ministerial portals, to the extent their knowledge of the foreign language allows them to do so.[50]

C. Interpretation and Application of Foreign law

According to Tunisian law, the designated foreign law in CPIL refers to foreign substantive law, not foreign conflict of laws rule, since *renvoi* has been excluded from the Code (Article 35).[51] The designated foreign law includes all the rules applicable in the foreign legal system according to its formal sources (Article 33)[52] — such as legal

[46] M Ben Moussa, *supra* n 18, p. 174.

[47] M. Ben Jemia, S. Ben Achour & M Bellamine, *supra* n 37, p. 203.

[48] A Mezghani, *supra* n 13, p. 74.

[49] M Ben Moussa, *supra* n 18, p. 173; S Bostanji, *supra* n 18, pp. 84.

[50] See, M. Ben Jemia, S. Ben Achour & M Bellamine, *supra* n 37, p. 203.

[51] Article 35 states that "unless otherwise provided by the law, *renvoi* shall not be admitted, whether it leads to the application of the Tunisian law or the law of a different country". For critics against the exclusion of *renvoi* see L Chedly, "Le rejet inopiné du renvoi par le Code de droit international privé", *in Mélanges offerts au Doyen Sadok Belaid,* (CPU, 2004) pp. 295 ff.

[52] Article 33 states that "the foreign law designated by conflict of laws rules includes all applicable rules in accordance with the formal sources of that law."

texts, case law and customs.[53] In case the designated applicable law changes, transitional provisions of the foreign law should be respected (Article 31).[54] However, this does not solve all the questions relating to the application of foreign law. This is because difficulties relating to the interpretation of foreign law are always likely to arise.

According to Article 34 CPIL, "the judge shall apply a foreign law as it is interpreted in the legal order where it belongs". Scholars argue that Tunisian judges should not give their own interpretation to a clear foreign law provision, nor try to correct the interpretation adopted in the foreign legal order.[55] Therefore, if the foreign law is not correctly applied in the legal order where it belongs, Tunisian judges should nevertheless apply it in the same way.[56] Certain court decisions require the parties claiming the application of foreign law to show how it is interpreted in the state of origin by both courts and academics.[57] This would facilitate for the judge a better understanding of how the foreign law is interpreted and actually applied in its country of origin. Where there is no consensus on the meaning of foreign law — such as where courts of different levels or different chambers of the same court of the state of origin apply different interpretations — the interpretation most widely adopted in the foreign legal order should apply. However, if there are different contradictory interpretations, and the judge is unable to decide which interpretation prevails, the content of the foreign law is then declared unclear. In this case, forum law should apply.[58]

D. Failure to Establish Foreign Law

When the judges or the parties fail to ascertain the content of the applicable foreign law, Tunisian law, as the law of the forum, applies. This is provided for by Article 32 para. 4 according to which "if the content of the foreign law cannot be established, Tunisian law shall apply." Tunisian scholars explain the subsidiary application of the *lex fori* by the necessity to avoid a denial of justice.[59]

Some scholars distinguish between two situations where foreign law cannot be ascertained. The first one is where the content of the foreign law could not objectively be established despite the efforts of the judges and/or the parties. In this case, the subsidiary application of the *lex fori* is plainly justified. However, and this is the

[53] M Ben Moussa, *supra* n 18, pp. 165 ff.

[54] Article 31 CPIL: "Shall be applicable the transitional provisions of a law designated by the conflict of laws rule."

[55] A Mezghani, *supra* n 13, p. 75; L Chedly & M Ghazouani, *supra* n 17, p. 469.

[56] L Chedly & M Ghazouani, *ibid.*

[57] For example, Tribunal of First Instance of Tunis n°9901 of 13.10.1999 *supra* n 45.

[58] L Chedly & M Ghazouani, *supra* n 17, p. 470

[59] L Chedly & M Ghazouani, *ibid.*, p. 459.

second situation, if failure of the proof of the designated foreign law is due to reluctance or delaying tactics of one party, the claim should be dismissed.[60] This solution is justified by the wording of Article 32 para.4 which accepts the subsidiary application of Tunisian law only if the content of the foreign law *could not* (objectively) be established.

E. Assessment

The majority of scholars explain that Article 32 only confers discretion on judges to prove foreign law, and that Tunisian judges are not required, but merely permitted, to establish the content of the designated foreign law.[61] Understood as such, Article 32 has attracted virulent criticism.[62] The argument is that the discretion in matters of proof of foreign law is inconsistent with the obligation of judges to raise and apply *ex officio* foreign law. This is because the mandatory nature of conflicts rules and the obligation placed on the judges to raise and apply *ex officio* foreign law would become illusory if a similar obligation is not imposed upon judges to ascertain *ex officio* the content of foreign law. This (supposed) discrepancy and incoherence between the Articles of the CPIL would render the application of foreign law unpredictable and dependent only on either the discretion of judges or the interest of the parties.[63] According to this view, Article 32 should, *de lege lata*, be modified, or *de lege ferenda*, interpreted in way that imposes an obligation to establish the content of foreign law.

---

[60] A Mezghani, *supra* n 13, p. 73; L Chedly & M Ghazouani, *supra* n 17, p. 460.

[61] However, according to other opinions, Article 32 does not confer a mere discretion to the judge in the meaning that Tunisian judges are not free to decide whether or not bring proof of foreign law. See M Ben Moussa, *Commentaries on The Code of Private International Law*, (Tunis, 2003) pp. 303, 306–307 (in Arabic); *idem*, "Foreign Law in the Tunisian Code of Private International Law", *The Arabian Journal of Academic and Jurisprudence*, Vol. 32, 2005, pp. 165 ff (in Arabic); M A Hachem, "Foreign Law and International Public Order", *in Colloque sur le code tunisien de droit international privé (12 mars 1999)*, (CEJJ, 2000), pp.81ff (in Arabic), *idem*, *supra* n 12, p. 239. According to this opinion, Article 32 simply tries not to impose an unrealistic and absolute obligation on the judges since in certain cases it is very difficult to ascertain the content of foreign law.

[62] See, L Chedly, *supra* n 18, p. 125; S Bostanji, *supra* n 18, pp. 80ff; M. Ben Jemia, S. Ben Achour & M Bellamine, *supra* n 37, p. 201; A Mezghani, *supra* n 13, pp. 71–72; L Chedly & M Ghazouani, *supra* n 17, p. 453 ff.

[63] S Bostanji, *supra* n 18, pp. 80–81.

IV. Judicial Review

A. *Conflict of Laws Rules*

The correct application of conflict rules by lower courts is subject to the control of the *Cour de Cassation*. This control is not only limited to cases where lower courts fail to apply choice of law rules, but also when these rules are not correctly applied.[64] This is explained by the fact that conflicts rules are rules of law, and, as such, their application and interpretation are always subject to the control of the *Cour de Cassation*.[65]

B. *Foreign Law*

According to Article 34 para.2, "the interpretation of foreign laws shall be subject to the control of the Court of Cassation." Thus, the *Cour de Cassation* controls the application and interpretation of foreign law whenever there are apparent errors. The *Cour de Cassation* has confirmed this in several decisions, declaring that the application and interpretation of foreign law by lower courts is subject to its control.[66]

V. Foreign Law in Other Instances

Foreign law is often called on to be applied outside of any judicial proceeding or dispute. The question of application of foreign law before non-juridical authorities has not attracted the attention of scholars in Tunisia. One question that scholars have discussed is the application of conflict of laws rules relating to marriage by civil registrars or notaries, especially on question of polygamous marriage.[67] As a general rule, the authorities in charge of celebrating marriages have no discretion as to the question of foreign law. In case of marriage between a

[64] Cass civ n°5128 of 9.3.2006, *supra* n 28; Cass civ n°1875 of 21.9.2004, *supra* n 28; Cass civ n° 2830 of 7.12.2006, *supra* n 29.

[65] According to Article 175(1) of the Code of Civil and Commercial Procedure, "Appeal against judgments of last resort is possible in the following cases: (1) when the judgement contains a violation, a misapplication or misinterpretation of the law".

[66] For exemple, cass. civ. n° 7146 of 26.5.2005, (unpublished) quoted in L Chedly & M Ghazouani, *supra* n 17, p. 472; cass. civ. n°2830 of 7.12.2006, *supra* n 29. Comp. with *supra* n 9.

[67] See for example, K Meziou, "Le principe de monogamie et la formation du mariage", *in Polygamie et répudiation dans les relations internationales – Actes de ma table ronde organisée à Tunis le 16 avril 2004*, Editions ABConsulting, 2006, pp.9ff; *idem*, "Migrations et relations familiales", *supra* n 32.

national and a foreigner in Tunisia, civil registrars and notaries have to comply with the provisions of the CPIL relating to marriage (Article 45 and 46).[68] It is then for the spouses to prove foreign law by providing certificates of matrimonial eligibility or certificates of celibacy, if necessary.[69]

The issue of ascertaining foreign law in arbitral tribunals is not addressed in the Tunisian Arbitration Code of 1993 (TAC).[70] Generally speaking, arbitration is only available for matters the parties can settle freely.[71] Since these are contractual matters and since parties enjoy a degree of freedom to decide the way their dispute will be settled, arbitrators are bound by the agreements of the parties. In the absence of agreement, it is the role of arbitrators to both determine and apply foreign law. Arbitrators should be able to take all the necessary measures to establish the content of foreign law. As for other alternative dispute resolution mechanisms, such as conciliation and mediation, it should be noted that there are no established legal frameworks for their implementation in Tunisia.[72]

[68] In addition to CPIL, there is a special law that regulates issues of civil status. See for example, the law n°57-3 of 1 August 1957 regulating Civil Status, published in the Official Gazette of 30 July and 2 August 1957. As for regulations, there are several notices (*circulaires*) of the Ministries of Interior and Justice which govern the activities of official registrars and notaries.

[69] Article 46 para. 2 requires from civil status officer or public notary to not "conclude the marriage only upon the presentation of an official certificate which attests that the concerned future spouse is free from any other marital union".

[70] The only provision which relates to the application of foreign law is Article 73 TAC. According to this Article, "(1) the arbitral Tribunal shall decide the dispute in accordance with the law agreed upon by the parties; (2) in the absence of designation by the parties, the arbitral tribunal shall apply the most appropriate law to the dispute; (3) the arbitral tribunal may decide *ex aequo et bono* if the parties have expressly authorized to do so; (4) In any case, the tribunal shall decide in accordance with the terms of the contracts and shall take into account the usages of commerce applicable to the transaction".

[71] Article 7 TAC states as follow: "No arbitration is permitted in (1) matters regarding law and order; (2) disputes related to nationality; (3) disputes concerning personal status except for financial that ensue there from; (4) matter where no arbitration is permitted; (5) disputes involving the State, public administrative authorities and local communities, with the exception of disputes arising from international economic, commercial or financial relationship, regulated by chapter three of the present Code (i.e. international arbitration)."

[72] It should however be mentioned that conciliation is mandatory before courts of first instance in Tunisia in matters relating to labor and family affairs. However, there are no specific ADR provisions except for Arbitration.

VI. Access to Foreign Law

A. Status Quo

Information about Tunisian law is not easy to access for non-Arabic and non-French speakers. A notable exception is the field of foreign investment. Here, English translation of legal texts and overviews of the legal framework of investment are available. This can be explained by the importance of foreign investment for the development of the Tunisian economy and the importance the State places on attracting foreign investors. This endeavor should extend to cover all areas of law. It can be done by creating adequate frameworks that facilitate academic research (national and comparative). It should also cover both legal text and the development of case law.[73] Recently, however, Tunisia has created several official sites and governmental and ministerial portals to provide information about Tunisian in both French and Arabic.[74] In addition, in recent years, there are increasing efforts to publish legal texts (notably statutes and codes) in English. [75]

At the regional and international level, several conventions (both bilateral[76] and multilateral[77]) relating to legal and judicial assistance establish mechanisms of regular exchange of information between authorities of contracting states. One example is the Riyadh Arab Agreement for Judicial Cooperation concluded in 6 April 1983 (Riyadh Convention).[78] Tunisian judges can rely on the mechanism established by these con-

[73] Unfortunately, except for a certain number of decisions of the *Cour de Cassation*, which are usually reported in the Annual Bulletin of the *cour de cassation* (last published issue concerns decisions rendered in 2009), case law – especially lower court decisions – are not officially reported. It is therefore for researchers and scholars to use their personal network in order to obtain information about new decisions and make them available for the public. Still, the number of these (officially unreported) decisions that can be found in Tunisian law reviews is far from being sufficient.

[74] As examples, it is possible to mention here the portal of the Ministry of Justice (www.e-justice.tn) which provides information about Tunisian legal system and, most importantly, includes a database of the published decisions of the Tunisian *Cour de cassation* (but only in Arabic) since 1959 (last visited, September 2014). There is also the official homepage of the Tunisian Official Gazette (www.iort.gov.tn) in which all recent legal texts are regularly published in Arabic, French and English. See also the National Portal of Legal information, which also provides different legal information in Arabic, French and English (http://www.legislation.tn/en). Other sites also provide information about Tunisian law (in French), for example www.juristetunisie.com.

[75] See, for example, the Centre of Judicial and Legal Research which has recently published some commentaries on several Tunisian codes including English translation of their provisions.

[76] For example, the Convention of legal and judicial assistance concluded with Algeria (26 July 1963, Article 1), China (4 May 1999, Article 27), Emirates (7 February 1975, Article 1), Pologne (22 March 1985, Article 8), Russia (26 June 1984, Article 43), Argentine (16 May 2006, Articles 8–10), Spain (24 September 2001, Article 26).

[77] For example Convention of Ras Lanouf of 9 and 10 March 1991 concluded between Countries of Arab Maghreb Union ratified by Tunisia by virtue of the law n°93-91 of 29 November 1991 (but has not entered into force yet).

[78] The Riyadh Convention was ratified by Tunisia by the law n°85-69 of 12 July 1985 (Official Gazette n°54 of 16 July 1985). According to the first Article of the Riyadh Convention (entitled Exchange of information), "ministries of justice of the contracting parties shall regularly exchange

ventions (which usually require contracting state to request the necessary information through diplomatic channels) to obtain information about foreign law. With certain countries (especially Arabic countries), the cooperation is even enhanced with the creation of a legal entity whose purpose is to facilitate access to national law.[79]

However, these settings established by international conventions do not really facilitate access to foreign law. This can be explained by the lack of qualified personal and material resources.[80] Moreover, there is a lack of clear evidence whether judges or practitioners make use of these services. Many of them may not even be aware of their existence. Due to the insufficiency of the information, law firms and lawyers commonly use their own personal networks to obtain the information they need.

B. Further Developments

In practice, there are significant limitations to applying foreign law in Tunisia. The insufficiency of academic publications is a key cause, knowing that there is no expert institutes specializing in comparative law in Tunisia. The weakness of current comparative law scholarship is even aggravated by the fact that it is limited to either French law (or other francophone European countries) or other Arabic countries and basically relies on the scholarly publications made thereof. In addition, most of the studies dealing with private international law issues are limited to family law at the detriment of other fields of law. In practice, Tunisia has sought to improve the status of comparative law, for example by creating masters' courses in comparative law (especially the common law). However, the situation is unlikely to improve since comparative law publications are paltry and next generation of scholars are not actively encouraged to pursue the field.

Therefore, there is an imminent need to widen access to foreign law for all actors involved in the Tunisian legal process. Moreover, the information-sharing mechanism established by the conventions should be strengthened. With Tunisia joining the Hague Conference club, Tunisia's accessibility to foreign law is likely to improve either by concluding the Hague conventions or by accessing already established juridical and administrative cooperation mechanisms.[81]

---

the text of legislations in force, legal and judicial publications, pamphlets and studies containing legal statutes and judgments, as well as information pertaining judicial regulations."

[79] For example, Article 2 of the Riyadh convention requires from contracting parties to "lend material and moral support, as well as qualified scientific personnel, to the Arabic Centre of Legal and Judicial Research, to fully undertake its role in the documentation and development of Arab cooperation in the legal and judicial fields." A homepage was set up in order to facilitate exchange of information. Legal information about member countries of the Arab League can be found at the homepage of the League of Arab States (http://www.lasportal.org) under "legal network of Arab". This site provides information about domestic law, case law, international conventions…etc. (in Arabic).

[80] This information is based on personal correspondence.

[81] Tunisia has recently joined the Hague Conference on Private International Law and became on 4 October 2014 the 78th Member of the Conference See, https://www.hcch.net/en/news-archive/details/?varevent=387

Commonwealth Africa: Foreign Law in Commonwealth African Courts

Richard Frimpong Oppong

Abstract This paper examines how foreign law is treated in the courts of Commonwealth African countries within the context of private international law. It examines the treatment of foreign law as a fact and the attendant consequences. The paper also examines the important issue of access to legal information and how that can be assessed.

I. Introduction

The focus of this paper is on Commonwealth African countries.[1] Private international law rules in Commonwealth Africa are embodied mainly in legislation and case law (common law). These are considered sources of law in the countries under study. Thus, to the extent that it is pleaded – because as is noted below foreign law is treated as fact, which must be pleaded and proved – the courts in those countries are bound to apply the relevant conflict of law rules to decide a case involving a foreign element. This does not mean that foreign law will be automatically applied when found by the relevant choice of law rule as the applicable law. The application of foreign law is subject to exclusionary rules.[2]

Ascertainment and application of foreign law occurs mainly before courts. Although arbitration is well promoted, national legislation on arbitration do not address the issue of how foreign law is ascertained and applied. However, it is likely that subject to minor modifications to suit the arbitration context, arbitrators will follow the same rules as the courts.

---

[1] These are: Botswana, the Gambia, Ghana, Kenya, Lesotho, Malawi, Namibia, Nigeria, Sierra Leone, South Africa, Swaziland, Tanzania, Uganda, Zambia and Zimbabwe (hereafter, the countries under study). Cameroon, Mauritius, Mozambique, Rwanda, Seychelles are also part of the Commonwealth but are not examined in this paper. Gambia and Zimbabwe are currently not members of the Commonwealth but are included in this study.

[2] Richard Frimpong Oppong, *Private International Law in Commonwealth Africa* (Cambridge: Cambridge University Press 2013) at 23–26.

R.F. Oppong (✉)
Associate Professor, Faculty of Law, Thompson Rivers University, 900 McGill Road, Kamloops, BC V2C 0C8, Canada
e-mail: roppong@tru.ca

Y. Nishitani (ed.), *Treatment of Foreign Law - Dynamics towards Convergence?*,
Ius Comparatum – Global Studies in Comparative Law 26,
DOI 10.1007/978-3-319-56574-3_30

II. Foreign Law Before the Courts

An important private international law issue to which there are varying responses from legal systems across the world is the nature and proof of foreign law. This section outlines the law in the countries under study in the form of brief country reports. The next section provides a comparative assessment of the existing laws.

In Botswana, foreign law is a fact that must be proved by expert evidence.[3] The courts do not take judicial notice of foreign law. Like other factual averments in a case, it requires evidence given by an expert witness, who could be a lawyer practising in the respective foreign country. In applying these principles, it is immaterial whether the foreign country shares the same legal tradition as Botswana, especially in cases where the court is dealing with a foreign statute.[4] In addition to proof from expert evidence, and subject to the existence of a convention between the two countries, a Botswana court may make reference to a superior court in a foreign country in order to ascertain the law applicable to the facts of a case pending before it.[5]

In Gambia, whenever a court has to decide a point of foreign law, the opinions of especially skilled persons (experts) in the foreign law are deemed relevant facts. Such opinions are admissible evidence. The experts may also produce books which they consider works of authority on the foreign law. After receiving books on foreign law and expert opinion thereon, the court is entitled to construe them for itself. In other words, the court is not bound by expert opinion or pronouncements in books tendered in evidence.[6]

In Ghana, although the concept of foreign law is not defined in any statute, it can be inferred from the Evidence Act 1975 that it encompasses the law of 'an organisation of states to the extent that such law is not part of the law of Ghana' and the laws of foreign states or their sub-divisions.[7] In other words, both unincorporated international laws and foreign state laws are treated as foreign law.[8] Foreign law is treated as fact.[9] A person who relies on foreign law must prove it with evidence. Although it is a question of fact, the jury does not determine it; the determination of foreign law is for the court.[10] An expert witness must provide proof of foreign law.[11]

---

[3] *Mtui* v. *Mtui* 2000 (1) BLR 406 at 413; *Garmroudi* v. *The State* 1987 BLR 409. See generally Evidence (Commonwealth Statutes) Act 1923; Evidence (Commonwealth and Foreign Acts of State and Judgments) Act 1910.

[4] *Point Trading (Pty) Ltd.* v. *The Attorney General* 2004 (1) BLR 75.

[5] Commonwealth and Foreign Law Ascertainment Act 1910.

[6] Evidence Act 1994, ss. 57 and 58.

[7] Evidence Act 1974, s. 1(2).

[8] Customary international law is part of Ghanaian law. See *Republic* v. *High Court, Ex Parte Attorney General, NML Capital Ltd.*, Civil Motion No.J5/10/2013 (Supreme Court of Ghana, 2013). Accordingly, one need not prove customary international law with expert evidence.

[9] *Davis* v. *Randall* [1962] 1 GLR 1; *In re Canfor (Deceased); Canfor* v. *Kpodo* [1968] GLR 177; Evidence Act 1974, s. 1(2).

[10] Evidence Act 1974, s. 1(2).

[11] Godka Group of Companies v. PS International Ltd. [1999–2000] 1 GLR 409.

The competence of an expert witness is a question of law for the judge.[12] A local counsel who has never practised in Indiana, USA before is not a competent expert on Indiana law.[13] On the other hand, a priest of the Maronite Roman Catholic Church could be regarded as an expert witness on the matrimonial laws of Lebanon.[14] Merely presenting a judge with the text of a foreign law, and leaving him to draw his own conclusions does not satisfy the requirements of proof by evidence.[15] Where a party fails to meet the requisite standard of proof, which is proof on the balance of probabilities, the court will apply the presumption that the foreign law is the same as Ghana law.[16]

In Kenya, when a Kenyan court has to determine a point of foreign law, opinions upon that point are admissible if given by persons especially skilled in such foreign law.[17] In the field of the administration of estates, the Probate and Administration Rules provide that, where evidence of foreign law is required on an application for a grant, the affidavit of any person who practises, or has practised, as a barrister, solicitor, advocate or other legal practitioner in that country and who is conversant with its law, may be accepted by the court. The court may dispense with this rule in special circumstances if it is satisfied that a person who does not possess similar qualifications, sufficiently possesses knowledge of the foreign law.[18]

In Lesotho, courts do not ordinarily take judicial notice of foreign law. It must be proved by the evidence of an expert witness, who may be either a professional lawyer or the holder of an office that requires legal knowledge or at any rate gives him special opportunities to become acquainted with the law.[19] In the absence of such proof, foreign law is presumed to be the same as the *lex fori*.[20] However, in appropriate cases, a Lesotho judge may take judicial notice of foreign law – in this instance, South African law.[21]

In Malawi, foreign law is treated as a fact and must be proved by expert evidence.[22] This principle extends to customary laws of other African countries.[23] And, for that purpose, a person who has lived in Rhodesia (now Zimbabwe) and studied

[12] *Huzaifeh* v. *Saba* [1939] 5 WACA 181.

[13] Godka Group of Companies v. PS International Ltd. [1999–2000] 1 GLR 409.

[14] *Khoury* v. *Khoury* [1958] 3 WALR 52.

[15] Godka Group of Companies v. PS International Ltd. [1999–2000] 1 GLR 409.

[16] Evidence Act 1974, s. 40; Moubarak v. Holland West Afrika Lijn [1953] 14 WACA 262; Godka Group of Companies v. PS International Ltd. [1999–2000] 1 GLR 409.

[17] Evidence Act 1963, s. 48.

[18] Probate and Administration Rules 1981, s. 30.

[19] *Serobanyane* v. *Serobanyane*, CIV\APN\290\91 (High Court, Lesotho, 1991).

[20] *Serobanyane* v. *Serobanyane*, CIV\APN\290\91 (High Court, Lesotho, 1991); *Weng* v. *Weng*, CIV/T/351/99 (High Court, Lesotho, 1999); *Ndlovu* v. *Employment Bureau of Africa Ltd.*, CIV/APN/142/98 (High Court, Lesotho, 2002); *Mutua* v. *Matholoane*, CIV/APN/183/94 High Court, Lesotho, 1994).

[21] *Mohapi* v. *Motleleng* [1985–1989] LAC 316.

[22] *Commissioner for Taxes* v. *A Ltd.* [1973–1974] 7 MLR 211.

[23] *Kamcaca* v. *Nkhota* [1966–1968] ALR Mal. 509 at 516.

customary law by attending court cases will be considered as an expert witness on Rhodesian customary law.[24] Similarly, a notary versed in Italian law,[25] and an advocate practising at Tete in Portuguese East Africa (now Mozambique)[26] have been held as qualified to give evidence on Italian and Portuguese law, respectively. The burden of proving foreign law lies with the party who bases a claim or defence on it. When foreign law is not proved, the court will apply the *lex fori*.[27]

In Namibia, courts treat foreign law as fact that must be proved by expert evidence.[28] A Namibian court cannot take judicial notice of foreign law (in this instance English law). It must be proven by the evidence of an expert witness – normally by lawyers practising in the courts of the country whose law our courts want to ascertain. Once proven by the evidence of duly qualified experts, the court is constrained to accept it as a correct statement of the foreign law and must apply it as such.[29] It has been held that a professor at the University of London who had already taught courses on the legal systems of the Commonwealth of Independent States, including the legal system of the Ukraine, with a few years of law practice experience in a law firm where he was responsible for practice in the Commonwealth of Independent States, and had frequently given evidence before English courts on aspects of Soviet law, including Ukrainian law, was qualified to give expert evidence on Ukrainian law. It was not necessary for his knowledge and experience to embrace specific branches of Ukrainian law.[30] When proving foreign law, there is no inflexible rule either regarding the production of foreign statutes, or the duty of the court itself to examine them. Both matters depend on the circumstances of a case – the governing factor is whether it is necessary to examine the foreign statutes in order to reach a satisfactory conclusion on them.[31] Where a party seeks to rely on foreign law the onus lies upon him to prove what the law is. Failing such proof the court must apply Namibian law, adopting the fiction that the foreign law is the same as the law of Namibia. This presumption does not only apply to the common law but also to law governed by a statute.[32]

In Nigeria, foreign law is a fact that must be pleaded and proved – if a party fails to do so, the court will apply Nigerian law.[33] This rule does not extend to laws of

[24] *Kamcaca* v. *Nkhota (No. 2)* [1966–1968] ALR Mal. 518 at 523.

[25] *In the Estate of Barretta* [1984–1986] 11 MLR 110.

[26] *Gouveia* v. *Gouveia* [1923–1960] ALR Mal. 239 at 241.

[27] *Maseko* v. *Maseko* [1973–1974] 7 MLR 310.

[28] Westdeutsche Landesbank Girozentrale (Landesbausparkasse) v. Horsch 1992 NR 313 at 314, 1993 (2) SA 342 at 344.

[29] Dowles Manor Properties Ltd. v. Bank of Namibia 2005 NR 59.

[30] MFV Kapitan Solyanik Ukrainian-Cyprus Insurance Co. v. Namack International (Pty) Ltd. 1999 (2) SA 926, 1997 NR 200.

[31] Ibid.

[32] Dorbly Vehicle Trading & Finance Company (Pty) Ltd. v. Nekwaya, Case No. A 191.98 (High Court, Namibia, 1998).

[33] *Murmansk State Steamship Line* v. *Kano Oil Millers Ltd.* [1974] (3) ALR Comm. 192; *Ogunro* v. *Ogedengbe* [1960] 5 FSC 137.

States within the Nigerian federation; statute compels Nigerian courts to take judicial notice of laws of states within the federation.[34] Under the Evidence Act 2011, when a court has to decide a point of foreign law, the opinions upon that point of persons especially skilled in such foreign law (experts) are considered relevant facts. The opinions of experts who are acquainted with such law in their profession are regarded as admissible evidence. Such an expert may produce before the court, books which they declare to be works of authority upon the foreign law in question. After receiving all necessary explanation from the expert, the court may construe the books for itself. The judge decides any question as to the effect of evidence given with respect to foreign law.[35] In determining whether a person is 'especially skilled', the test is always the knowledge and experience of the particular witness and whether the evidence justifies the conclusion that he or she is especially skilled. This means no more than special knowledge, training or experience in the matter in question.[36] In line with this, it was held that a Russian lawyer and head of the legal department of Sovfracht, a state-operated firm of Shipping Brokers in Russia, qualified as an expert on Russian law.[37]

In South Africa, each aspect of foreign law – the law of a state recognised by South Africa[38] – is a factual question and evidence on any aspect thereof should emanate from someone with the necessary expertise.[39] However, it is not a factual question whether foreign law applies – that is a question of law.[40] A senior consultant in a tax and legal unit of an accounting firm in Maputo who was legally qualified and possessed extensive experience of the Mozambican legal system, qualified as an expert witness.[41] The onus rests on the person who relies on foreign law to prove it.[42] Unless it is otherwise adequately proven to the satisfaction of the judge, the foreign law is presumed to be the same as South African law.[43] This presumption

---

[34] Evidence Act 2011, s. 122(2), *Peenok Ltd.* v. *Hotel Presidential Ltd.* (1982) 12 SC 1; *Benson* v. *Ashiru* [1967] 1 All NLR 184.

[35] Evidence Act 2011 ss. 68 and 69; *Melwani* v. *Chanhira Corporation* [1995] 6 NWLR 438; *Bhojwani* v. *Bhojwani* [1995] 7 NWLR 349.

[36] *Ajami* v. *The Comptroller of Customs* (1952–1955) 14 WACA 34; *Ajami* v. *The Comptroller of Customs* (1952–1955) 14 WACA 37.

[37] Murmansk State Steamship Line v. Kano Oil Millers Ltd. 1974 (3) ALR Comm. 192.

[38] Ocean Commodities Inc. v. Standard Bank of SA Ltd. 1978 (2) SA 367 at 376; Standard Bank of SA Ltd. v. Ocean Commodities Inc. 1980 (2) SA 175 at 181 and 183.

[39] *Schlesinger* v. *Commissioner of Inland Revenue* 1964 (3) SA 389 at 396; *Atlantic Harvesters of Namibia (Pty) Ltd.* v. *Unterweser Reederei Gmbh of Bremen* 1986 (4) SA 865. See generally, CF Forsyth, *Private International Law – The Modern Roman-Dutch Law Including the Jurisdiction of the High Courts*, 5th ed (Cape Town: Juta and Company Ltd., 2012) at 107–128.

[40] *Burchell* v. *Anglin* 2010 (3) SA 48 at 54–59.

[41] *Skilya Property Investments (Pty) Ltd.* v. *Lloyds of London Underwriting* 2002 (3) SA 765.

[42] *Anderson* v. *The Master* 1949 (4) SA 660.

[43] *Rogaly* v. *General Imports (Pty) Ltd.* 1948 (1) SA 1216; *Harnischfeger Corporation* v. *Appleton* 1993 (4) SA 479; *Estate H* v. *Estate H* 1952 (4) SA 168; *Bank of Lisbon* v. *Optichem Kunsmis (Edms) Bpk* 1970 (1) SA 447; *Deutsche Bank* v. *Moser* 1999 (4) SA 216.

is of general application; it applies to both statute and common law.[44] However, the courts have cautioned against its unthinking invocation.[45]

When proving foreign law, it is not enough for an expert merely to refer to the decision of a foreign court where an interpretation of the meaning and effect of a statute has been given. The expert should at least state the *ratio* of the decision on which he or she relies. The court is not bound to apply a foreign decision as evidence of foreign law if it is satisfied, on all the evidence, that the decision does not accurately represent the foreign law. Where the expert does not justify his or her interpretation of a foreign statute, the court is free to apply its own interpretation, or at least apply the presumption that the rules of interpretation under the foreign law would be the same as in South Africa.[46] Put more emphatically, a South African court is not bound by expert opinion on foreign law; it can look at the text of foreign law and make its own judgment as to its meaning.[47] Section 1(1) of the Law of Evidence Act 1988 empowers the court to take judicial notice of foreign law insofar as it can be 'ascertained readily and with sufficient certainty'.[48] Access to authoritative sources is an important consideration when applying this provision.[49] Relying on the provision, courts have taken judicial notice of the Family Law (Scotland) Act, 1985 as the law regulating the proprietary consequence of marriage in Scotland,[50] prescription in Greece,[51] as well as aspects of English and German civil procedure.[52]

In Swaziland, where foreign law governs a transaction, it must be proved as a fact by a practitioner duly admitted in that country.[53]

In Tanzania, foreign law is a matter of fact and cannot be invoked without pleading it.[54] Under the Evidence Act 1967, when a court has to determine a point of foreign law, the opinions of persons possessing special knowledge, skill, experience

---

[44] *Bank of Lisbon* v. *Optichem Kunsmis (Edms) Bpk* 1970 (1) SA 447; *Rogaly* v. *General Imports (Pty) Ltd.* 1948 (1) SA 1216.

[45] *ITT Continental Baking Co.* v. *Registrar of Trade Marks* 1980 (2) SA 127.

[46] *Continental Illinois National Bank* v. *Greek Seamen's Pension Fund* 1989 (2) SA 515 at 544.

[47] *Atlantic Harvesters of Namibia (Pty) Ltd.* v. *Unterweser Reederei Gmbh of Bremen* 1986 (4) SA 865 at 874; *Standard Bank of South Africa Ltd.* v. *Ocean Commodities Inc.* 1983 (1) SA 276 at 294.

[48] *Harnischfeger Corporation* v. *Appleton* 1993 (4) SA 479; *Hlophe* v. *Mahlalela* 1998 (1) SA 449; B.S.C. Martin, 'Judicial Notice of Foreign Law' (1998) 31 *Comparative and International Law Journal of Southern Africa* 60; Bernard Martin, 'The Ascertainment of Foreign Law by Means of Judicial Notice' (1997) 8 *Stellenbosch Law Review* 377; A. J. Kerr, 'Judicial Notice of Foreign and Customary Law' (1994) 111 *South African Law Journal* 577.

[49] Harnischfeger Corporation v. Appleton 1993 (4) SA 479.

[50] *Hassan* v. *Hassan* 1998 (2) SA 589.

[51] *Monokandilos* v. *Generale Des Carriers et Des Mines SA*, Case No. 11261/2001 (High Court, South Africa, 2010).

[52] *C Hoare & Co.* v. *Runewitsch* 1997 (1) SA 338; *Holz* v. *Harksen* 1995 (3) SA 521.

[53] *Bonham v. Master Hardware (Pty) Ltd.*, Civil Trial 294/08 (High Court, Swaziland, 2009); *Southern Textiles (Pty) Ltd.* v. *Taga Investments*, Civil Case No. 4223/2007 (High Court, Swaziland, 2009).

[54] *Auto Garage Ltd.* v. *Motokov* [1972] 1 ALR Comm. 17.

or training in such foreign law (experts) are taken as relevant facts.[55] It has been held that the 'German law' current in Tanzania prior to and/or during the occupation by British forces was not foreign law to be proved by expert evidence, but lay within judicial notice of the court. Under German law, the court referred to laws prevailing in Tanganyika (now Tanzania) at the time when Tanzania was under German administration.[56]

In Uganda, when a court has to decide a point of foreign law, opinions on that point are admissible if given by persons especially skilled in such foreign law.[57] As regards the law of England, the court may dispense with the need for proof by expert evidence, and instead rely on recognised treaties on English law such as the Halsbury's Law of England.[58]

In Zambia, in the case of *Mwiba* v. *Mwiba*,[59] the issue of the nature of a marriage fell to be decided by Rhodesian law. However, there was no proof of that law. The court embarked on its own research. It took judicial notice of the fact that marriages among indigenous Africans, particularly in Central Africa, do not resemble Christian marriages and are potentially polygamous.

In Zimbabwe, under Section 25 of the Civil Evidence Act 1992, a Zimbabwean court shall not take judicial notice of the law of any foreign country or territory,[60] nor shall it presume that such law is the same as Zimbabwean law.[61] Any person who, in the opinion of a court, is suitably qualified to do so on account of his knowledge or experience, shall be competent to give expert evidence as to the law of any foreign country or territory, whether or not he has acted, or is entitled to act, as a legal practitioner there. Thus, an affidavit from a certified family law specialist in California, USA, who is very familiar with the California laws pertaining to marital dissolutions and related actions, is admissible in terms of the Act in proof of those laws.[62] Section 25 does not render Zimbabwean courts incompetent to interpret foreign laws without resort to expert evidence. Accordingly, the Supreme Court of Zimbabwe is competent to interpret a New Zealand statute without the aid of an expert on New Zealand law.[63] Section 25 further provides that, in considering any issue as to the law of any foreign country or territory, a court may have regard to: any finding or

[55] Evidence Act 1967, s. 47(1).

[56] *Land Officer* v. *The Motor Mart and Exchange* [1953–1957] TLR 295.

[57] Evidence Act 1909, s. 43; *Amrit Goyal* v. *Hari Chand Goyal*, Misc.App.No.649 of 2001 (High Court, Uganda, 2003).

[58] *F.L. Kaderbhai* v. *Shamsherali Zaver Virji*, Civil Appeal No.10 of 2008 (Supreme Court, Uganda, 2010).

[59] [1980] ZR 175.

[60] Historically, the courts could take judicial notice of foreign law. See *Grauman* v. *Pers* 1970 (1) RLR 130 at 133 where the court took judicial notice of the South African Rules of Court.

[61] *Walker* v. *Industrial Equity Ltd.* 1995 (1) ZLR 87.

[62] *G* v. *G* 2003 (5) SA 396, 2002 (2) ZLR 408.

[63] *Registrar-General of Citizenship* v. *Todd* 2002 (2) ZLR 680. See also *G & P Ltd.* v. *Commissioner of Taxes* 1960 (4) SA 163 (the court interpreted U.K. tax legislation without expert evidence); *Mandimika* v. *Mandimika* 1997 (2) ZLR 352 (the court embarked on its own research on the nature of Ghanaian marriage).

decision purportedly made or given in any court of record in that country or territory where the finding or decision is reported or recorded in citable form,[64] any written law of that country or territory, and any decision given by the High Court or the Supreme Court of Zimbabwe as to the law of that country or territory.

III. Comparative Review of Existing National Laws

A comparative review of the laws in the countries under study reveals that the principle that foreign law is a fact is well entrenched.[65] From it are derived two other principles, namely that foreign law must be pleaded and proved by evidence.

Although foreign law has not been expressly defined in any statute, it is implicit in decided cases that it refers to the laws of other states. Ghana has gone beyond this definition to include the laws of 'an organisation of states to the extent that such law is not part of the law of Ghana'.[66] Treating international law in the same way as national law appears to be a departure from the English common law position – the position of the legal system on which the legal systems of Commonwealth African countries are founded.[67] Indeed, other than the statutory language, there is no decided case that supports the view that courts in Ghana (and indeed in any of the other countries) treat international law as a category of fact, which must be pleaded and proved by expert evidence. Indeed, in cases where international law has been invoked in Ghanaian courts, no expert witnesses have been called to prove it; it has always been a matter reserved for counsel.[68] This is a sound position the courts have taken. Unlike foreign law, judges learn international law as part of their legal education and international law is not country-specific. It cannot therefore be presumed that judges are not cognizant of principles of international law.

In recent times there has been much talk about the rise of non-state law. In Kenya it has been held the parties may choose 'transactional law (including general principles of law, international development law, the lex mercatoria, codified terms and practices and trade usages)'.[69] However, it remains to be decided into which category

---

[64] A finding or decision shall be taken to be reported or recorded in citable form only if it is reported or recorded in writing in a report, transcript or other document which, if it has been prepared in connection with legal proceedings in Zimbabwe, could be cited as an authority in legal proceedings in Zimbabwe.

[65] See also the Supreme Court of Somalia case of *Adan Deria Gedi* v. *Sheikh Salim El Amoudi* 1964 (1) ALR Comm. 385.

[66] Evidence Act 1974, s. 1(2).

[67] *Trendtex Trading Corp.* v. *Central Bank of Nigeria* [1977] 2 WLR 356 at 377; I. A. Hunter, 'Proving Foreign and International Law in the Courts of England and Wales' (1977–1978) 18 *Virginia Journal of International Law* 665.

[68] See e.g. *Republic* v. *High Court (Comm. Div. Accra, Ex parte Attorney General*, Civil Motion No J5/10/2013 (Supreme Court of Ghana, 20 June 2013).

[69] Nedermar Technology BV Ltd. v. Kenya Anti-corruption Commission [2008] KLR 476 at 499. But see Eagle Super Pack (Nigeria) Ltd. v. African Continental Bank Plc [2006] 19 NWLR 20 in

(fact or law) non-state laws, such as the *lex mercatoria* and other principles developed by private organisations, would be placed. Like foreign laws of states, non-state law is likely to be treated as fact, which must be pleaded and proved with evidence.

The fact that foreign law has to be pleaded implies a judge cannot of his own motion introduce foreign law, let alone embark on independent research to ascertain it. In other words, unless foreign law is pleaded, the courts will decide a case as a purely domestic one. An exception to this appears in Botswana. A Botswana court is given the discretion, wherever it considers it 'necessary or expedient for the proper disposal of any action', to remit the facts of the case for the opinion of the appropriate Commonwealth or foreign court.[70] However, there is no reported case in which this discretion has been exercised.

Expert evidence is required to prove foreign law in all the countries under study. It remains within the courts' power to determine who qualifies as an expert. However, neither the courts nor statutes have insisted on any special qualifications: academics, legal practitioners and persons with legal knowledge acquired through experience or observation have all been held to qualify as experts. This flexibility is appropriate because a court is not bound by expert opinion; it remains the ultimate judge of what constitutes foreign law. There is no limit on the scope of materials that could be relied on by experts when proving foreign law – statutes, judicial decisions, textbooks, journal articles and affidavits have all been held admissible, provided they meet the requisite national rules on admissibility.

There is a rebuttable presumption (codified by statute in Ghana) that foreign law is the same as the *lex fori*. This presumption has been criticised,[71] and in Zimbabwe, statutorily abrogated.[72] The presumption operates as the fall-back or gap-filling principle in cases where a party who relies on foreign law has been unable to satisfactorily prove it, that is, on the balance of probabilities, or where foreign law cannot be ascertained.[73] On the other hand, in appropriate cases, such as where the court is of the opinion that the application of a presumption would occasion injustice, or that it would be wholly artificial to apply the *lex fori*, it is open to the court to decide that the party on whom the burden of proof lies has failed to establish his case – a failure to prove foreign law is a failure to discharge the burden of proof. The background ideas or policy considerations that inform the adoption of this presumption have not been clearly articulated in legislation or case law. What is clear is that the rule was borrowed from the English common law. In general, it looks like a rule of convenience.

---

which it was held that in order for the Uniform Customs Practice for Documentary Credits to be applicable, it must be incorporated in a contract.

[70] Commonwealth and Foreign Law Ascertainment Act 1910.

[71] See e.g. Lord Collins of Mapesbury *et al.* (eds), *Dicey, Morris and Collins on the Conflict of Laws*, 15th ed. (London: Sweet & Maxwell, 2012), para 9-025. But see *Bank of Lisbon* v. *Optichem Kunsmis (Edms) Bpk.* 1970 (1) SA 447 at 451.

[72] Civil Evidence Act 1992, s. 25(1).

[73] Ellison Khan, 'What Happens in a Conflicts Case when the Governing Foreign Law is not proved?' (1970) 87 *South African Law Journal* 145; Charles Wesley, 'The Presumption that Foreign Law is the same as the Local Law: An Absolute Tradition Revised' (1996) 37 *Codicillus* 36.

There is division among the countries under study as to whether a court can take judicial notice of foreign law. Courts in South Africa are allowed by statute to do that, but Zimbabwe courts are statutorily prevented from doing so.[74] In Lesotho, there is judicial support for courts taking judicial notice of foreign law, or at least South African law, but the Botswana courts have cautioned against doing that, even in respect of South African law. There is merit in courts taking judicial notice of foreign laws, especially the laws of legal systems with which they have a lot in common.[75] Many aspects of South African law would be familiar to a Botswana judge because both countries share the Roman-Dutch legal tradition. Similarly, aspects of English common law will not be unfamiliar to a Ghanaian or Nigerian judge. Indeed, as was observed in *G & P Ltd.* v. *Commissioner of Taxes*, 'the reason for the rule requiring evidence to prove foreign law is the lack of familiarity of a local court with foreign law. The more familiar the local court is with the relevant topic of foreign law, so the need for evidence diminishes in inverse ratio.'[76]

However, law always displays its own unique domestic subtleties and nuances that are likely to be unfamiliar to an external observer. It may not always be appropriate for a judge to make authoritative pronouncements about foreign law and proceed to base a decision on it without recourse to the opinion of persons well-tutored in it, or until after an adversarial inquiry to test the soundness of such opinion. Indeed, even in South Africa where courts are allowed to take judicial notice of foreign law, this can only be done in instances where foreign law can be 'ascertained readily and with sufficient certainty'. Similarly, in *Mohapi* v. *Motleleng,*[77] Justice Schutz observed: 'I think it would be the height of unreality for judges sitting in Lesotho who ordinarily practise in South Africa not to take judicial notice of South African law. But I should not be taken as holding that Lesotho judges should at all times and in all circumstances take judicial notice of South African law'.

In the countries under study, cross-examination is the main means of testing the reliability of the information provided by the parties or their expert witnesses on foreign law. The courts do not embark on an independent investigation of the content of foreign law. They decide cases on the basis of the facts – including foreign law, which is treated as a fact – presented by the parties. The cost of ascertaining foreign law is borne by the parties, but a winning party may be able to recover such cost as part of legal costs ordered by the court to be paid by the losing party.

In the countries under study, when private international law rules or foreign law has been erroneously applied, the parties can appeal to an appropriate court within the statutorily defined judicial hierarchy. Although foreign law is treated as fact and, ordinarily, appeals on questions of fact as narrowly circumscribed,

[74] Historically, this position had judicial support in South Africa. See *Schlesinger* v. *Commissioner of Inland Revenue* 1964 (3) SA 389 at 396.

[75] Fui Tsikata, 'Proving Familiar Foreign Law' (1987–1988) *Review of Ghana Law* 249; Ellison Khan, 'Proving the Laws of our Friends and Neighbours' (1965) 82 *South African Law Journal* 133.

[76] 1960 (4) SA 163 at 168.

[77] [1985–1986] LAC 316 at 321–322.

foreign law is a special fact and the rules regarding the grounds one which one can appeal a question of fact have not been applied too rigidly to foreign law in any reported case.

IV. Access to Foreign Law

At present, access to legal information e.g. judgments of courts, statutes and academic commentary is provided through official or government and unofficial sources. Some of these sources are accessible through subscription; others provide free access to information. For example, as part of the Free Access to Law Movement, the South African Legal Information Institute, the Ugandan Legal Information Institute, National Council for Law Reporting in Kenya provide access to legal information in southern Africa, Uganda and Kenya respectively.

There is certainly the need for improved access to foreign law, especially the laws of other African countries. Judicial authorities, attorneys, arbitrators and academics stand to benefit from such improved access. At present, although there are a number of websites that provide access to such information, the information tends to be unstructured, un-indexed and difficult to search through.

It is not possible to precisely stipulate which areas of law access to foreign law are most needed in the countries under study. One can however assume that given the volumes of international commercial transactions as opposed to personal relationships that give rise to conflict of laws issues in the countries under study, the commercial law is the area most in need of access to foreign law.

Currently, none of the countries under study is party to any international or regional instrument on proof of and/or information on foreign law. Given the very similar nature of the laws in the countries under study on issues related to ascertainment of foreign law it is unlikely that a regional instrument that unify the treatment of foreign law would be useful to them. The position may be different in respect of a continental or international instrument since diversity becomes more poignant in such a context. Similarly, a regional or international instrument that establishes administrative or judicial cooperation to exchange information on foreign law would be useful to facilitate access to foreign law, especially in the context of litigation.

Part V
Hague Conference on Private International Law

The Evolution of Work on Access to Foreign Law at the Hague Conference on Private International Law

Philippe Lortie and Maja Groff

Abstract In 2006, the Permanent Bureau of the Hague Conference on Private International Law was requested to begin exploratory work on a possible new international Convention addressing the treatment of foreign law. At subsequent international experts' meetings convened by the Hague Conference, however, it was concluded that it would not be worthwhile to "attempt to comprehensively harmonise the different approaches to the treatment of foreign law, as there [was] no need or likelihood of any success for such harmonisation". Yet, the Experts agreed that there was "clearly a need to facilitate access to foreign law" and they "supported the Permanent Bureau's continued work in the area". This article provides an overview of preliminary work conducted to date by the Permanent Bureau on a potential new Hague Convention or other international co-operation mechanisms to facilitate access to foreign law at the global level, as well as noting international developments on this topic and offering prospective views.

Introduction to the Hague Conference on Private International Law and Its Work[1]

The Hague Conference on Private International Law (hereinafter the "Hague Conference" or the "Conference") is an Inter-Governmental Organisation whose origins date back to 1893. The purpose of the Organisation is to harmonise rules of private international law (a field also referred to as *conflict of laws*). This body of

[1] For more information on the Hague Conference, see <www.hcch.net>.

P. Lortie (✉)
First Secretary, Permanent Bureau of the Hague Conference on Private International Law, Churchillplein 6b, 2517 JW The Hague, The Netherlands
e-mail: pl@hcch.nl

M. Groff (✉)
Senior Legal Officer, Permanent Bureau of the Hague Conference on Private International Law, Churchillplein 6b, 2517 JW The Hague, The Netherlands
e-mail: mg@hcch.nl

Y. Nishitani (ed.), *Treatment of Foreign Law - Dynamics towards Convergence?*,
Ius Comparatum – Global Studies in Comparative Law 26,
DOI 10.1007/978-3-319-56574-3_31

law is relevant in a very broad range of *cross-border* situations involving individuals or commercial and other entities, which often implicate diverse legal systems. In this age of globalisation, such situations increasingly give rise to manifold complex legal questions and create an urgent need for co-ordination, communication and co-operation between legal systems.

The mission of the Hague Conference is to find internationally-agreed approaches and solutions to issues such as: *Which court is competent to deal with a dispute arising from a cross-border situation? Which law applies to such cross-border situations? How does a national court recognise and enforce foreign judgments? How is regular cross-border co-operation of administrative and judicial authorities ensured?*

The work of the Conference covers a wide range of areas, from commercial and finance law to international civil procedure and judicial co-operation, and from child protection to matters of marriage and personal status. The ultimate goal of the Organisation is to strive for a world in which, despite differences between legal systems, individuals as well as companies and other entities can enjoy a high degree of legal security.

The Hague Conference maintains close co-operation with the United Nations, including its subsidiary bodies (in particular UNCITRAL) and funds (in particular UNICEF), as well as many other global intergovernmental organisations (such as UNIDROIT) and regional intergovernmental organisation (such as the European Union, which is itself a Member of the Conference). The Hague Conference also engages in activities with various non-governmental organisations, such as professional and academic associations.

The primary method used by the Hague Conference to harmonise rules of private international law consists in preparing (including through extensive research), negotiating, drafting, monitoring and providing assistance with implementation of multilateral treaties, known as "Hague Conventions". Since the 1950s, the Hague Conference has adopted 38 such instruments. Examples include the Hague Conventions on:

- Facilitating the production abroad of public documents (such as birth certificates, notarial acts), through the use of Apostilles (incl. electronic Apostilles)
- International civil procedure: the service of documents abroad, the taking of evidence abroad, and international access to justice
- Choice of court agreements in international contracts
- Recognition and enforcement of judgments
- Contracts: international sales and agency
- Torts: international products liability and traffic accidents
- Trusts
- Securities held with an intermediary
- Recognition of marriages and divorces
- Marital property relations
- International child protection
- International child abduction
- Intercountry adoption

- International recovery of child and family support
- Protection of vulnerable adults
- International inheritance: form of wills, succession to the estates of deceased persons.

Many of these Conventions establish a framework for administrative and judicial co-operation among States – an additional reason why the Hague Conference is also referred to as the "World Organisation for Cross-Border Co-operation in Civil and Commercial Matters."

The Work of the Hague Conference on Foreign Law

Initial Mandate for a Feasibility Study

In April 2006, the Council on General Affairs and Policy of the Hague Conference ("the Council"; then the "Special Commission on General Affairs and Policy"), the governing body of the Organisation, invited the Permanent Bureau (the Secretariat of the Organisation) to prepare a feasibility study on the possible development of a new instrument providing for international co-operation on the treatment of foreign law.

2007 International Experts Meeting

Initially, the work of the Hague Conference concentrated on the feasibility of a new international instrument addressing the differences in *treatment* of foreign law in national courts. An Experts' Meeting held from 23–24 February 2007,[2] however, concluded that it would be pointless to "attempt to comprehensively harmonise the different approaches to the treatment of foreign law, as there [was] no need or likelihood of any success for such harmonisation". Yet, the Experts agreed that there was "clearly a need to facilitate access to foreign law" and they "supported the Permanent Bureau's continued work in the area". These conclusions were shared by the Council on General Affairs and Policy in 2007. Consequently, the focus of the feasibility study shifted from the *procedural treatment and legal status of foreign law*, in particular in civil and commercial proceedings, to the need for *cross-border administrative and legal co-operation* for the purpose of accessing the content of foreign law.

At its April 2007 meeting, the Council on General Affairs and Policy of the Conference invited the Permanent Bureau to develop a questionnaire with a view to identifying practical difficulties in accessing the content of foreign law and determining the areas of foreign law for which information is most often required.

[2] See Prel. Doc. No 21 A of March 2007, "Feasibility Study on the Treatment of Foreign Law: Report of the Meeting of 23–24 February 2007." This document is available on the Hague Conference website at <wwwlhcch.net>, under "Governance" then "Council on General Affairs and Policy" and "Meeting of April 2007".

This questionnaire also invited Members of the Hague Conference to comment on the models suggested in the feasibility study and their possible implementation.

2007–2008 Member Questionnaire Results

A Questionnaire was circulated to Members of the Organisation in October of 2007.[3] Responses were received from 31 Members[4] and a summary of the responses was prepared for the 2008 meeting of the Council on General Affairs and Policy of the Conference.[5]

As a preliminary matter, the Questionnaire asked a number of questions with regard to the status of implementation and operation of existing regional treaties on proof of or information on foreign law. In summary the responses received reflected that:

- A majority of reporting Member States were Party to the "London Convention".[6]
- Over half of reporting States were Party to one or more bilateral treaties that have provisions for the sharing of foreign legal information.
- States receive and send between 0 and 38 requests under bilateral or multilateral treaties on foreign law per year, with an average of nine requests.
- Delays to respond to or receive a response from a request under one of these treaties range from 1 week to 25 weeks, with an average response time of 12 weeks.
- A slight majority of States reported that they do not foresee an increase in incoming and outgoing requests in the future.

The Questionnaire went on to ask some questions with regard to the level of satisfaction with and shortcomings of present treaty/instruments relevant to proof of or information on foreign law. In summary the responses received seem to reflect that:

---

[3] See Prel. Doc. No 25 of October 2007, "Feasibility Study on the Treatment of Foreign Law" (hereinafter called "the Questionnaire"). This document is available on the Hague Conference website at <wwwlhcch.net>, under "Governance" then "Council on General Affairs and Policy" and "Meeting of April 2007".

[4] These Members included Argentina, Australia, Austria, China (Hong Kong SAR), Croatia, the Czech Republic, Denmark, Egypt, Estonia, the European Community (Part IV of the Questionnaire only), Finland, France, Germany, Hungary, Iceland, Italy, Japan, Latvia, Lithuania, Malaysia, Netherlands, New Zealand, Poland, Romania, Slovakia, Slovenia, Sweden, Switzerland, Turkey, the United Kingdom and the United States of America. All individual responses to the Questionnaire are posted on the Hague Conference website at the following address: <www.hcch.net> under "Governance" then "Council on General Affairs and Policy" then "Meeting of April 2008" and "Individual Responses to the Questionnaire on the Treatment of Foreign Law".

[5] See Prel. Doc. No 9A of March 2008, "Feasibility Study on the Treatment of Foreign Law – Summary of the Responses to the Questionnaire" (hereinafter called "Responses to the Questionnaire"). This document is available on the Hague Conference website at <wwwlhcch.net>, under "Governance" then "Council on General Affairs and Policy" and "Meeting of April 2008".

[6] The European Convention of 7 June 1968 on Information on Foreign Law (Council of Europe).

- Almost half of responding States were satisfied with their treaty obligations concerning foreign law, with particular praise for the London Convention.
- Almost half of responding States gave grounds for their dissatisfaction and suggestions for improvement of treaties, notably with regard to time delays when using the instruments and the use of the instruments in the context of complex litigation.

The Questionnaire also invited responses on a number of questions concerning free public access to legal information, touching upon issues such as: online access to legislation through official websites; policies of States in responding to general requests for information on the content or application of its law; availability of services to people in other States; costs for legal information services for individuals located abroad; and, foreseeable increases in the proportion of people in other States making general requests for information on the content or application of its law. In summary the responses received reflected that:

- The overwhelming majority of States provide online information on their legislation via an official government website, sometimes with this information in one or several non-official languages.
- Most States respond to written or oral requests for information on their laws at no cost and without distinguishing as to whether the request originates from within or from outside the State.
- A majority of States foresee an increase in demand for these services by persons outside their State in the coming years.

Several questions dealt with access to information on the content of foreign law at the litigation stage, such as: the percentage of cases requiring the application of foreign law; the most common areas of foreign law applied by or invoked before the State judicial authorities; and, the States whose laws are most frequently applied by or invoked before judicial authorities. In summary the responses received reflected that:

- Overall, a relatively small proportion of civil and commercial law cases in reporting States currently require the application of foreign law.
- The most common area of law where foreign law is applied is family law, including the international protection of children; it was reported that foreign law is applied more frequently in family law cases than in other civil cases and in commercial cases, but commercial law is reported also to be applied relatively frequently.
- Where foreign law is applied it is most often the law of a State with which the forum State has a regional, political, or historic tie.

The Questionnaire then addressed a number of practical issues, such as: ways in which judicial authorities ascertain foreign law and sources of foreign law consulted by these authorities; how sources of foreign law are verified or authenticated; how language barriers are overcome; the qualification of experts providing information on the content of foreign law; the costs of such expertise; the common characteristics of requests for information on foreign law; and, the transmission of requests for information directly sent to receiving agencies. In summary the responses received reflected that:

- Judicial authorities employ a diversity of methods by which to ascertain, verify, and translate the content of foreign law, following no uniform pattern according to legal tradition.
- The source and requirements of expertise regarding foreign law vary widely by State; reliance on judicial authority (local or foreign) is clearly an exception.
- A majority of States apply a principle whereby it is the party to litigation who raises the issue of foreign law or against whom costs are awarded that is responsible for paying for the consulted foreign law expert.
- The judicial authorities in States are generally not enabled, through conventional or treaty law or otherwise, to make direct requests for information on foreign law to the receiving agency in the State addressed.

At the end of the Questionnaire, Members were asked for their views on the future development of an instrument and/or mechanisms to access information on the content of foreign law. Twelve States[7] and the European Community (EC) submitted a response to the question as to whether the Hague Conference should develop a new global instrument or mechanisms to access information on the content of foreign law. Of these twelve responding States, seven answered affirmatively that they were "of the view that the Hague Conference should develop a global instrument and/or mechanisms to access information on the content of foreign law,"[8] while five of these States indicated that they were not.[9] Several States[10] that answered negatively went on to express their preferences in the case that such an instrument or mechanism were to be developed by the Hague Conference.

Members were also asked about specific components or features of a possible future instrument or mechanisms. Nine States[11] indicated that they were in favour of flexibility under an instrument or mechanism with respect to the availability of several channels through which information on foreign law could be sought and in relation to experts from whom information could be obtained.[12] Regarding flexibility in the use that could be made of each such channels to ascertain the content of foreign law, all nine responding States save one[13] reported that they would be in favour

[7] Argentina, Australia, China (Hong Kong SAR), Croatia, Egypt, Iceland, Japan, Malaysia, New Zealand, Switzerland, Turkey and the United States of America.

[8] Argentina, Croatia, Egypt, Malaysia, Switzerland, Turkey and the United States of America.

[9] Australia, China (Hong Kong SAR), Iceland, Japan and New Zealand.

[10] Australia, China (Hong Kong SAR), Japan and New Zealand.

[11] Argentina, Australia, Croatia, Egypt, Malaysia, New Zealand, Switzerland, Turkey and the United States of America.

[12] See Question 30(a)(i) of the Questionnaire.

[13] Turkey answered negatively to this question, citing the need for a quicker and simpler global mechanism to access foreign law. Argentina, Australia, Croatia, Egypt, Malaysia, New Zealand, Switzerland and the United States of America answered affirmatively.

of such flexibility.[14] Eight responding States[15] answered affirmatively that they supported the use of information technology to ensure the speedy processing of requests and the alleviation of language barriers in accessing foreign law.[16] Seven[17] of nine responding States indicated that they would be in favour of the provision of an objective and general description of the law of the foreign State (including references to relevant case law) rather than a specific answer concerning a given case, and two responding States[18] indicated that they would prefer a mechanism whereby both types of information could be requested.[19] Nine States responded that the information received on foreign law should not be binding on a receiving court.[20] Nine States indicated that such an instrument or mechanism should be of general scope in order to permit access to different areas of foreign law.[21] Five States[22] responded that such an instrument or mechanism should contain provisions on legal assistance to accommodate individuals with few or no resources, while three responding States suggested that it should not.[23] Five States[24] supported the extension of a potential instrument or mechanism to notaries or other professionals outside of the litigation context, while four States[25] did not support such an extension. Five States[26] indicated that they would be in favour of making information on the content of their law available online in a central database, while four States expressed doubts as to the overall gains of providing a centralized, comprehensive database of their law apart from what is already provided.[27] Finally, five States[28] reported that they would support combining an instrument or mechanism with a centralised internet-based scheme.[29]

[14] See Question 30(a)(ii) of the Questionnaire.

[15] Argentina, Australia, Croatia, Egypt, Malaysia, New Zealand, Switzerland and the United States of America.

[16] See Question 30(a)(iii) of the Questionnaire.

[17] Argentina, Australia, Croatia, Egypt, New Zealand, Switzerland and Turkey.

[18] Malaysia and the United States of America.

[19] See Question 30(a)(iii) of the Questionnaire.

[20] Argentina, Australia, Croatia, Egypt, Malaysia, New Zealand, Switzerland (100% of Cantons agreeing), Turkey and the United States of America. No other Member has responded to this Question.

[21] Argentina, Australia, Croatia, Egypt, Malaysia, New Zealand, Switzerland, Turkey and the United States of America. No other Member has responded to this Question.

[22] Argentina, Egypt, Malaysia, Switzerland and Turkey.

[23] Australia, New Zealand and the United States of America.

[24] Argentina, Croatia, Egypt, Malaysia and Switzerland.

[25] Australia, New Zealand, Turkey and the United States of America.

[26] Croatia, Egypt, Japan, Switzerland and Turkey.

[27] Australia, Malaysia, New Zealand and the United States of America.

[28] Argentina, Croatia, Egypt, Switzerland and Turkey.

[29] Australia, Japan, Malaysia and the United States of America answered negatively to this question.

At its April 2008 meeting, the Council invited the Permanent Bureau to continue to explore mechanisms to improve global access to information on the content of foreign law, including at the litigation stage. The Permanent Bureau was invited to report and, if possible, to make a recommendation as to future action to the Council in 2009. Further exploration of the topic revealed the increasing practical importance of *information on (foreign) law* available *online*.

2008 International Experts Meeting

In October 2008, a Group of experts met at the Permanent Bureau to discuss global co-operation on the provision of online legal information on national laws. As the Report[30]of this meeting demonstrates, the recent development worldwide of the online accessibility and digitisation of legal information – in particular of laws, legislative records (parliamentary debates and other explanatory materials), judicial decisions, and legal literature – and of rendering this material accessible, generally without costs to the public, has been truly astounding.

On the one hand, the increasing accessibility online of legal materials enables the resolution of certain – although by no means all – questions on the content of foreign law, thus reducing to a certain extent the need for traditional international legal co-operative machinery. On the other hand, this development poses in itself a number of important challenges, in particular in cross-border situations, which would benefit from tailored, supportive forms of international co-operation. Indeed, the October 2008 Experts' Meeting formulated some "Guiding principles to be considered in developing a future instrument" (hereinafter the "Guiding Principles of 2008″, included in Annex I to this document) concerning free access to legal materials in e-form, facilitating re-publication/re-use, integrity, identification of the origin, preservation, uniform citation, translations, knowledge-based systems, and support and co-operation, specific to online legal information in a cross-border context.[31]

The October 2008 Experts' Meeting was unanimous in its view that, no matter how perfected, the accessibility of online legal information could only provide a solution to certain needs for information. More particularly, there would always remain a need for "a photograph" of the law as applied at a certain time in a particular context. An effective mechanism allowing courts, in particular, to obtain such infor-

[30] See Permanent Bureau, "Report of the Meeting of Experts on Global Co-operation on the Provision of Online Legal Information on National Laws (19–21 October 2008)", Prel. Doc. No 11 B of March 2009 for the attention of the Council of March/April 2009 on General Affairs and Policy of the Conference. Available on the Hague Conference website at <www.hcch.net> under "Governance" then "Council on General Affairs and Policy" and "Meeting of March-April 2009".

[31] See Permanent Bureau, "Accessing the content of foreign law and the need for the development of a global instrument in this area – A possible way ahead", Prel. Doc. No 11 A of March 2009 for the attention of the Council of March/April 2009 on General Affairs and Policy of the Conference, Annex. Available on the Hague Conference website at <www.hcch.net> under "Work in Progress" then "General Affairs".

mation from abroad would remain essential. This finding confirmed the conclusions of the February 2007 meeting of experts,[32] but put the previous findings within the context of continuously increasing availability of online legal information.

2009 Three Part Proposal for the Development of a New Instrument

In the light of the work carried out between 2006 and 2009, the sketch of a new international instrument, in three parts, was proposed in order to assist discussion at the 2009 Council of the Hague Conference.[33]

Part I: Facilitating access to online legal information on foreign law. This part would focus on assuring the free accessibility of a country's or regional economic integration organisation's main legal materials, particularly legislation, case law and international agreements (and potentially doctrine that would be particularly important in civil law jurisdictions) for online publication and re-publication/ re-use; it could possibly provide some guidance on realistic quality standards or best practices for such free access and online publishing, and perhaps provide for a permanent body of experts to monitor the development of practical standards and/or best practices in these areas, also with a view to the compatibility or "interoperability" of global online publishing standards.

Part II: Cross-border administrative and/or judicial co-operation. This part would provide for the handling of requests for information in response to concrete questions on the application of foreign law in relation to a specific matter that arises in court proceedings (and possibly also in other contexts), and for which information available online is not sufficient.

Part III: A global network of institutions and experts for more complex questions. This part would address situations where there may be a need for accessing more in-depth information on complex legal questions in specific areas (*e.g.*, insolvency or inheritance), or in the course of complex litigation that involves the interface of multiple areas of foreign and/or local law(s). Here, one might think of a series of networks of qualified organisations (bar associations, comparative law institutes, organisations of notaries and other specialists, whose services would not be free) facilitated via the Permanent Bureau.

At its meeting of April 2009, the Council took note of the extensive exploratory work done by the Permanent Bureau. The Permanent Bureau was invited to convene

[32] See Permanent Bureau, "Feasibility Study on the Treatment of Foreign Law – Report on the meeting of 23–24 February 2007", Prel. Doc. No 21 A of March 2007 for the attention of the Council of April 2007 on General Affairs and Policy of the Conference, pp. 5–6, "Post-discussion proposed model". Available at <www.hcch.net> under "Governance" then "Council on General Affairs and Policy" and "Meeting of April 2007".

[33] See, *supra*, note 30, at pp. 5–6.

a Working Party consisting of experts from Members to explore further the feasibility of mechanisms described above with the understanding at this stage that this will not lead to the development of a binding instrument.

At its meeting of April 2010, the Council took note of the outcome of the consultations with stakeholders undertaken by the Permanent Bureau to solicit their views on the need for an instrument in this area. The Council noted that these consultations had not provided sufficient support to justify convening an expert meeting. The Council invited the Permanent Bureau to continue its work to facilitate access to, and exchange of information concerning, foreign law in the context of existing Hague Conventions. The Council decided to retain this item on its Agenda and to revisit the issue at its next meeting.

2010–2011 IBA and ABA Questionnaires and Commentary of Other Stakeholders

After the April 2010 Council Meeting, the International Bar Association (Arbitration Committee) and the American Bar Association (Section of International Law) expressed to the Permanent Bureau an interest in the access to foreign law project, and potentially assisting in contributing to the project. The Permanent Bureau worked with these two organisations to devise a short questionnaire addressed to their respective members on the need for an international instrument on access to foreign law. A compilation of responses to these questionnaires shows a majority (60–80%) of legal professionals responding considered there to be insufficient resources available to find and ascertain foreign law via the Internet or otherwise.

In addition, the Permanent Bureau has liaised with the American Association of Private International Law (ASADIP) and the Commonwealth Secretariat, which are both supportive of finding solutions to facilitate access to foreign law at a global level. A number of other international and regional organisations have also expressed interest in this topic.

A 2011 survey of 49 "stakeholders" in India (including prominent judges, lawyers, and several legal academics), undertaken by an independent legal researcher, has also produced interesting results supportive of further global work on this topic.

At its April 2011 meeting, the Council noted the further work undertaken by the Permanent Bureau in this area. The Council decided that the Permanent Bureau should continue monitoring developments but not at this point take any further steps in this area, and to revisit the issue at its annual meetings. The Permanent Bureau monitored the topic from 2011, reporting to the Council on various developments annually.

Developments and Highlights Arising in the Course of On-Going Monitoring

Court to Court MOUs Pioneered by the Supreme Court of New South Wales

A number of common law jurisdictions have been particularly active in developing innovative mechanisms to facilitate access to foreign law in the context of cross-border civil and commercial litigation. An important development is the 2010 memoranda of understanding between the Supreme Court of New South Wales (Australia) and the Supreme Court of Singapore, and between the Chief Justices of the Supreme Court of New South Wales and of New York State, on references of questions of foreign law.[34] These arrangements provide interesting procedures for one court to request the foreign court or a panel of foreign judges to determine questions of their law which are at issue in proceedings before the first court. The Supreme Court of New South Wales has expressed its openness to applying this mechanism with other courts around the world.

2014 case law of the Court of Appeal of New South Wales addresses the utilisation of the MOU with New York State, providing useful clarification as to the operation of the court-to-court cooperation mechanisms set out in the MOUs.[35] The MOU system has also been cited favourably in subsequent academic literature in Singapore, the United States of America and Australia as presenting a model of a partial solution in this area.[36]

2012 International Joint Conference of the European Commission and the Hague Conference on Access to Foreign Law in Civil and Commercial Matters

From 15 to 17 February 2012, a conference on "Access to Foreign Law in Civil and Commercial Matters" was jointly organised in Brussels by the European Commission and the Hague Conference. Over 130 experts, including judges, lawyers, notaries,

[34] Both memoranda are available at: <http://www.supremecourt.lawlink.nsw.gov.au/supremecourt/sco2_internationaljudicialcooperation.html>.

[35] *Marshall v Fleming* [2014] NSWCA 64.

[36] See *e.g.*: Teo Guan Siew & Wong Huiwen Denise, "Referring Questions of Foreign Law to the Court of the Governing Law – No Longer 'Lost in Translation,'" 23 *Singapore Academy of Law Journal* 227 (March 2011); Matthew J. Wilson, "Demystifying the Determination of Foreign Law in U.S. Courts: Opening the Door to a Greater Global Understanding," Vol. 46 *Wake Forest Law Review* 887 (December 2011); and, James McComish, "Forum Non Conveniens and Foreign Law in Australia," published on Conflict of Laws .net, 26 April 2011 (available at: <http://conflictoflaws.net/2011/forum-non-conveniens-and-foreign-law-in-australia-2/>).

academics and public officials from all regions of the world attended this meeting.[37] In addition, representatives from the United Nations, the International Monetary Fund, the World Bank Group, the Commonwealth Secretariat, the *International Organisation of la Francophonie*, the League of Arab States, the European Parliament, the European Commission, the International Bar Association (Arbitration Committee), the International Union of Notaries, the American Association of Private International Law, the Council of the Notariats of the European Union, the European Group on Private International Law, the Uniform Law Commission, the American Bar Association Section of International Law, the Max Planck Institute for Comparative and International Private Law, the Swiss Institute of Comparative Law, the Free Access to Law Movement and the Permanent Bureau of the Hague Conference were in attendance.

The joint conference unanimously reached a number of conclusions and recommendations emphasising "the increasing need in practice to facilitate access to foreign law, in many areas of the law such as in family law, the law of succession and commercial law, as a result of, among other things, globalisation and the cross-border movement of persons, goods, services and investments."[38] The conference also emphasized the need for co-operation mechanisms to be developed at the global level, and underlined that work in this area has an "important component of access to justice, strengthens the rule of law, and is fundamental to the proper administration of justice."[39] (The full Conclusions and Recommendations of the conference are available in Annex II to this document.[40]).

Related Work at Other International/Regional Organisations or Institutions

The "UNESCO/UBC Vancouver Declaration" of September 2012 was promulgated at a conference convened by UNESCO's Director General, involving 500 participants from 110 countries, entitled "The Memory of the World in the Digital Age: Digitization and Preservation".[41] The conference produced a set of key principles on digital information, which clearly echo and support a number of the "Guiding

[37] Experts attended from Albania, Australia, Belgium, Canada, China, Croatia, Cyprus, the Czech Republic, Denmark, Finland, France, Germany, Greece, Hungary, India, Japan, Kenya, Latvia, Lithuania, Malta, Mexico, the Netherlands, Oman, Poland, Portugal, Romania, Slovakia, Slovenia, Spain, Sweden, Switzerland, Turkey, the United Kingdom, the United States of America and Venezuela, among others.

[38] See Annex II to this document, Conclusion and Recommendation No 1.

[39] Conclusion and Recommendations Nos 2 and 3, available *ibid.*

[40] Also available at: <http://www.hcch.net/index_en.php?act=events.details&year=2012&varevent=248>.

[41] See:<http://www.unesco.org/new/fileadmin/MULTIMEDIA/HQ/CI/CI/pdf/mow/unesco_ubc_vancouver_declaration_en.pdf>.

Principles of 2008" (see Annex I)[42] developed at the 2008 Hague Conference experts meeting on global online legal information.[43]

The International Federation of Library Associations and Institutions (IFLA), the leading international body representing the interests of library and information services and their users, recent Strategic Plan (2010–2015) has as a key goal and priority activities to ensure equitable and free access to information as a basic human right.[44] The IFLA Law Libraries section is, in harmony with this priority, promoting access to *free legal information* as a basic human right. The Law Libraries Section has contacted the Permanent Bureau, expressing interest in participating in work at the global level in this area at the Hague Conference, in particular "to encourage governments to make laws available for free, in an official, authenticated, and sustainable" form.[45]

At the regional level, a number of concrete endeavours continue to address and improve access to foreign legal information, both generally, and for judges and courts in the context of litigation.

Within the European Union work is ongoing in the context of the European Judicial Network, the "EJN".[46] The 2009 update to the Council Regulation establishing the EJN strengthened provisions regarding the network's duty to facilitate access to foreign law within the Union[47] (to also work in connection with the "London Convention"[48]) and added legal practitioner/bar associations to the network, to facilitate connection to expertise in foreign law.[49]

The third Annual European Legal e-Access Conference, with the theme "E-justice, improving legal access throughout the European Union", took place in Paris, in November 2012, as a partnership of many prominent French and European institutions, including the Swiss Institute of Comparative Law.[50]

---

[42] *E.g.*, principles bearing on integrity of digital documentary heritage and the accessibility, authenticity, reliability and historic preservation of digital materials (Principles 1 and 3), privacy protections in the digital environment (Principle 4), the promotion of international co-operation in this field (Recommendation to UNESCO k.), the development of laws that ensure citizen rights to relevant knowledge and the use of "open format" information (Recommendations to UNESCO Member State a. and e.), the use of recognised metadata standards (Recommendation to the private sector b.), among others.

[43] See *supra*, note 31 and "Accessing the Content of Foreign Law: Report of the Meeting of Experts on Global Co-operation on the Provision of Online Legal Information on national Laws (The Hague, 19–21 October 2008)," drawn up by the Permanent Bureau, Prel. Doc. No 11 B of March 2009 for the attention of the 2009 Council on General Affairs and Policy of the Conference, Annex I.

[44] Available at: <http://www.ifla.org/files/assets/hq/gb/strategic-plan/2010-2015.pdf>, at pp. 1 and 2.

[45] Official correspondence with the Permanent Bureau, 2012–2013.

[46] Council Decision 2001/470/EC establishing a European Judicial Network in civil and commercial matters (modified by Decision 568/2009/EC of the European Parliament and of the Council of 18 June 2009).

[47] *Ibid.*, Art. 5(2) *c)*.

[48] *Supra*, note 6.

[49] Art. 2 of the Decision establishing the EJN, *supra*, note 46.

[50] See: <http://www.legalaccess.eu/?lang=en> and <http://www.legalaccess.eu/?3rd-European-legal-e-access>.

With respect to developments within the Commonwealth, the Commonwealth Law Ministers at their 2011 meeting mandated the Commonwealth Secretariat "to develop a proposed Scheme on international civil legal co-operation for consideration at the next meeting of Senior Officials." This proposal, originally made by the Attorney General of Australia in 2011, includes the topic of access to information on foreign law, and was considered in Botswana in May of 2014 at the triennial meeting of Commonwealth Law Ministers. The Commonwealth Law Ministers' 2011 Meeting in Sydney recognised that "the increasing international mobility of people, assets, goods and services means that more businesses and individuals are involved in international civil and commercial transactions" and that "[t]he secure planning of such transactions would be served by better mechanisms for obtaining reliable and authoritative information about the laws and practices of other legal systems."[51] A former Australian Attorney General has stated that it is important to improve "access to reliable information for courts, government agencies, parties and citizens"; that "[t]he existing legal framework for resolving international civil litigation [...] is poorly co-ordinated, outdated and inefficient [and] imposes unnecessary costs on citizens, businesses and states [...]"; and, that further international work in this area within the Commonwealth "has the capacity to support trade and economic development, [and] improve access to justice."[52]

Additionally, a joint endeavour of UNIDROIT and the European Law Institute[53] is exploring the development of a model civil procedure code for Europe based on the 2004 Principles of Transnational Civil Procedure developed by UNIDROIT and the American Law Institute (ALI), which note that "foreign law is a particularly important subject in transnational litigation."[54] This new European project includes "Access to information and evidence" as the theme of one of the three main working groups (composed of academics, judges and practitioners) for the project.

Bilateral Agreements

The Permanent Bureau keeps a "passive" inventory[55] of bilateral treaties which provide for co-operation between States to facilitate access to foreign legal information. For example, in 2012–2013, several bilateral treaties between Australia and the Republic of Korea, and Australia and Thailand were brought to the attention of the Permanent

---

[51] See para. 14, available at: <http://www.secretariat.thecommonwealth.org/document/238332/clmm_2011.htm>.

[52] The Hon. Robert McClelland MP & Mary Keyes (2011): International civil legal co-operation, Commonwealth Law Bulletin, 37:4, 661–669, at pp. 666 and 661, respectively.

[53] See: <http://www.unidroit.org/work-in-progress-studies/current-studies/transnational-civil-procedure>.

[54] See para. 22 and comment P-22B, available at: <http://www.unidroit.org/instruments/transnational-civil-procedure>.

[55] *I.e.* bilateral treaties which have been shared by third parties or come to the attention of the Permanent Bureau in the course of conducting work in other areas of law.

Bureau.[56] Many countries in all regions of the world are party to bilateral treaties, often under the heading of judicial co-operation or under general co-operation in civil and commercial matters, which include specific provisions addressing the facilitation of access to foreign law.[57]

The "Guiding Principles of 2008"

The "Guiding Principles of 2008" (see Annex I) developed at the 2008 Hague Conference experts meeting on global online legal information[58] have proved to be influential at a number of venues.

The *Uniform Electronic Legal Material Act* (2011)[59] of the Uniform Law Commission of the United States of America has been introduced or enacted in 20 U.S. jurisdictions thus far.[60] The Act's official Commentary makes explicit reference to the 2008 Guiding Principles. Commentators describe the Hague Guiding Principles of 2008 as a "best practices document" which represented "important guidelines that were repeatedly consulted in the drafting process" of the 2011 Uniform Act.[61]

The "Guiding Principles of 2008" have also been influential at the preeminent global network of legal information institutes (LII's), which works with courts, governments and academia around the world to provide free access to reliable national and regional legal information, globally accessible via the Internet.[62] AustLII, a prominent LII that provides comprehensive free access to Australian law (case law and legislation), has received an Australian Research Council grant to research and develop methods by which courts can provide cases with guaranteed authority and integrity, in order to put relevant aspects of the Hague Guiding Principles of 2008 into practice at the national level.

---

[56] Treaty on Judicial Assistance in Civil and Commercial Matters between Australia and the Republic of Korea (Canberra, 17 September 1999), entry into force 16 January 2000, at Art. 27; Agreement on Judicial Assistance in Civil and Commercial Matters and Co-operation in Arbitration between Australia and the Kingdom of Thailand (Canberra, 2 October 1997), at Art. 20.

[57] See, for example, a description of China's many (36) bilateral treaties in this area in Yujun Guo, "Legislation and Practice on Proof of Foreign Law in China," *Yearbook of Private International Law*, Vol. 14 (2012/2013), at p. 301.

[58] See *supra*, notes 31 and 43.

[59] Commentary to the recent *Uniform Electronic Legal Material Act* (2011) of the National Conference of Commissioners on Uniform State Laws (the Uniform Law Commission) of the United States of America, at pp. 13 and 16 (available at: <http://www.uniformlaws.org/shared/docs/electronic%20legal%20material/uelma_final_2011.pdf>).

[60] See: <http://www.uniformlaws.org/LegislativeFactSheet.aspx?title=Electronic%20Legal%20Material%20Act> (last consulted October 2016).

[61] See G. Greenleaf, A. Mowbray, and P. Chung, "The Meaning of 'Free Access to Legal Information': A Twenty Year Evolution" (October 6, 2012), Law via Internet Conference, 2012 (available at SSRN: http://ssrn.com/abstract=2158868 or http://dx.doi.org/10.2139/ssrn.2158868), at p. 13.

[62] *Ibid.*

National Developments

Academic work in the United States of America cites past Hague Conference Preliminary Documents in this area, making a call for the further development of mechanisms to ascertain foreign law in U.S.-based trans-national litigation, which is on the increase, and noting the fundamental importance of the proper ascertainment of applicable foreign law, as, of course, it can be determinative of the outcome of a relevant case.[63]

In the Middle East/Gulf region, the Permanent Bureau has been informed that a new Omani civil law has been issued which guarantees access to foreign law in civil and commercial matters in Oman.[64]

On the African continent a considerable number of new Legal Information Institutes (or "LIIs") have been established in recent years, with institutes established, for example, in South Africa (2014), Zimbabwe (2014), Namibia (2013 and 2011), Sierra Leone (2012), Zambia (2012), among many others. LIIs work with courts, governments and academia around the world to provide free online access to reliable national and regional legal information, globally accessible via the Internet.[65]

Other Highlights

Hague Conference scientific work in this area has been favourably cited in a range of recent scholarly articles brought to the attention of the Permanent Bureau, for example, in the Yearbook of Private International Law.[66] An overview article was also published in the *Liber Amicorum* for retiring Hague Conference Secretary General Hans van Loon, sketching a range of international co-operation options as a result of the 2012 international Joint Conference of the European Commission and the Hague Conference on Access to Foreign Law in Civil and Commercial Matters.[67]

The 25-country survey on proof of and information on foreign law that has been conducted under the auspices of the International Academy for Comparative Law

---

[63] Wilson, *supra*, note 36.

[64] Royal Decree No. 29 of 2013.

[65] See G. Greenleaf, A. Mowbray, and P. Chung, *supra*, note 61.

[66] S. Lanlani, "A Proposed Model to Facilitate Access to Foreign Law," and C.E. Mota, "Harmonization of Private International Law in Europe and Application of Foreign Law: the 'Madrid Principles' of 2010," *Yearbook of Private International Law*, Vol. 13 (2011), pp. 299–313 and pp. 273–297, respectively. See also: S. Lalani, *Doubt Develops where Certainty Ceases: Foreign Law in Domestic Courts* (Doctoral Thesis: Lausanne, 2012); C.M. Germain, "Digitizing the World's Laws", *Cornell Law Faculty Working Papers* (2010: Paper 72); and, *ibid.*, among others.

[67] P. Lortie and M. Groff, "The Missing Link between Determining the Law Applicable and the Application of Foreign Law. Building on the Results of the Joint Conference on Access to Foreign Law in Civil and Commercial Matters (Brussels, 15–17 February 2012)" in *A Commitment to Private International Law: Essays in Honour of Hans van Loon*, Intersentia (2013).

will no doubt helpfully supplement previous Hague Conference scientific work already undertaken in this area. The Permanent Bureau will study with interest the results of this study shared at the 19th International Congress of Comparative Law in Vienna in July 2014.[68]

Conclusion

In sum, there remains a great deal of activity in this area at the regional and national levels, but still as of yet no modern international, multilateral co-operation instrument or mechanisms.

A range of provisions found in various existing Hague Conventions have addressed issues of foreign law or foreseen and provided for the need for administrative or judicial cooperation to better establish the content of foreign law. For instance, under Article 14 of the Hague 1980 Child Abduction Convention an authority concerned with a return application "may take notice directly of the law of, and of judicial or administrative decisions, formally recognised or not in the State of habitual residence of the child, without recourse to the specific procedures for the proof of that law or for the recognition of foreign decisions which would otherwise be applicable".[69] Furthermore, Country Profiles under the Hague 1980 Child Abduction and the Hague 2007 Child Support Conventions both provide non-binding information to the public and legal practitioners at no cost concerning the relevant national laws and procedures in relation to the operation and implementation of the relevant Convention.

Additionally, the 1996 Hague Child Protection Convention marks a new phase in the development of co-operation mechanisms within Hague Conventions, echoing the spirit of the recent bilateral court-to-court MOUs addressing questions of foreign law. In particular Articles 8 and 9 of the 1996 Child Protection Convention contain procedures whereby jurisdiction may be transferred from one Contracting State to another in circumstances where the judge normally exercises jurisdiction, *i.e.*, in the country of the child's habitual residence.[70] Similar mechanisms exist at

---

[68] See: <http://www.iuscomparatum.org/141_p_30597/vienna-congress-2014.html>.

[69] It is interesting to note that some States have adopted similar rules with regard to the approval of adoption decision in the context of Article 17 *b)* of the *Hague Convention of 29 May 1993 on Protection of Children and Co-operation in Respect of Intercountry Adoption*. See, for example, Article 574 and 3092 of the *Code civil du Québec*.

[70] For example, under Article 8 of the 1996 Hague Child Protection Convention, by way of exception, an authority having jurisdiction under Article 5 or 6, if it considers that the authority of another Contracting State would be better placed in a particular case to assess the best interests of the child, may either: (i) request that other authority, directly or with the assistance of the Central Authority of its State, to assume jurisdiction to take such measures of protection as it considers to be necessary, or (ii) suspend consideration of the case and invite the parties to introduce such a request before the authority of that other State. Article 9 of the 1996 Hague Child Protection

the national level, such as under the Uniform Canadian Transfer of Jurisdiction Act, which allows for transfer of part of a proceeding to *foreign* as well as other Canadian courts or the Uniform Certification of Questions of Law [Act] [Rule] (1995) from the Uniform Law Conference of the United States of America which provides for the option of referring a question of foreign law of Mexico or Canada to the courts of those States.

The question is now whether —and when— there is or will be a desire from the international community for broader and more general measures to address, in a systematic fashion, the facilitation of access to foreign law at the global level, rather than through heretofore piecemeal national or regional approaches. And, when the time is ripe for such efforts, what specific forms such facilitation should take. Consultations with stakeholders and recent academic writing on this topic have indeed revealed both its important economic/administration of justice dimensions (*i.e.*, the foreseeable, efficient, timely and reliable ascertainment of foreign law when it must be applied in national courts), and its important access to justice aspects across diverse legal systems, including both civil law and common law legal traditions. Given the reality of globalization and contemporary cross-border movement and activity of persons or companies, the laws of foreign States inevitably affect those implicated in cross-border circumstances, thus representing an increased burden and heightened uncertainty so long as reliable and accessible global mechanisms are not in place.

Annexes

Annex I

Guiding Principles to Be Considered in Developing a Future Instrument[71]

Free Access

1. State Parties shall ensure that their legal materials, in particular legislation, court and administrative tribunal decisions and international agreements, are available for free access in an electronic form by any persons, including those in foreign jurisdictions.

Convention sets a mirror scheme for the counterpart authorities identified in Article 8(2). The judicial co-operation system necessary to support these communications is laid out in Articles 30 and following of the Convention.

[71] Principles developed by the experts which met on 19–21 October 2008 at the invitation of the Permanent Bureau of the Hague Conference on Private International Law as part of its feasibility study on the "access to foreign law" project.

2. State Parties are also encouraged to make available for free access relevant historical materials, including preparatory work and legislation that has been amended or repealed, as well as relevant explanatory materials.

Reproducing and Re-use

3. State Parties are encouraged to permit and facilitate the reproduction and re-use of legal materials, as referred to in paragraphs 1 and 2, by other bodies, in particular for the purpose of securing free public access to the materials, and to remove any impediments to such reproduction and re-use.

Integrity and Authoritativeness

4. State Parties are encouraged to make available authoritative versions of their legal materials provided in electronic form.
5. State Parties are encouraged to take all reasonable measures available to them to ensure that authoritative legal materials can be reproduced or re-used by other bodies with clear indications of their origins and integrity (authoritativeness).
6. State Parties are encouraged to remove obstacles to the admissibility of these materials in their courts.

Preservation

7. State Parties are encouraged to ensure long-term preservation and accessibility of their legal materials referred to in paragraphs 1 and 2 above.

Open Formats, Metadata and Knowledge-Based Systems

8. State Parties are encouraged to make their legal materials available in open and re-usable formats and with such metadata as available.
9. States Parties are encouraged to cooperate in the development of common standards for metadata applicable to legal materials, particularly those intended to enable and encourage interchange.
10. Where State Parties provide knowledge-based systems assisting in the application or interpretation of their legal materials, they are encouraged to make such systems available for free public access, reproducing and re-use.

Protection of Personal Data

11. Online publication of court and administrative tribunal decisions and related material should be in accordance with protection of personal data laws of the State of origin. Where names of parties to decisions need to be protected, the texts of such decisions and related material can be anonymized in order to make them available for free access.

Citations

12. State Parties are encouraged to adopt neutral methods of citation of their legal materials, including methods that are medium-neutral, provider-neutral and internationally consistent.

Translations

13. State Parties are encouraged, where possible, to provide translations of their legislation and other materials, in other languages.
14. Where State Parties do provide such translations, they are encouraged to allow them to be reproduced or re-used by other parties, particularly for free public access.
15. State Parties are encouraged to develop multi-lingual access capacities and to co-operate in the development of such capacities.

Support and Co-operation

16. State Parties and re-publishers of their legal materials are encouraged to make those legal materials more accessible through various means of interoperability and networking.
17. State Parties are encouraged to assist in sustaining those organisations that fulfil the above objectives and to assist other State Parties in fulfilling their obligations.
18. State Parties are encouraged to co-operate in fulfilling these obligations.

Annex II

European Commission

HCCH
HAGUE CONFERENCE ON PRIVATE INTERNATIONAL LAW
CONFÉRENCE DE LA HAYE DE DROIT INTERNATIONAL PRIVÉ

Access to Foreign Law in Civil and Commercial Matters

Conclusions and Recommendations

From 15 to 17 February 2012, at a conference organised jointly by the European Commission and the Hague Conference on Private International Law, experts from Albania, Australia, Belgium, Canada, China, Croatia, Cyprus, the Czech Republic, Denmark, Finland, France, Germany, Greece, Hungary, India, Japan, Kenya, Latvia, Lithuania, Malta, Mexico, the Netherlands, Oman, Poland, Portugal, Romania, Slovakia, Slovenia, Spain, Sweden, Switzerland, Turkey, the United Kingdom, the United States of America, Venezuela, the United Nations, the International Monetary Fund, the World Bank Group, the Commonwealth Secretariat, the International Organisation of la Francophonie, the League of Arab States, the European Parliament, the European Commission, the International Bar Association – Arbitration Committee, the International Union of Notaries, the American Association of Private International Law, the Council of the Notariats of the European Union, the European Group on Private International Law, the Uniform Law Commission, the American Bar Association Section of International Law, the Max Planck Institute for Comparative and International Private Law, the Swiss Institute of Comparative Law, the Free Access to Law Movement, as well as the Permanent Bureau of the Hague Conference on Private International Law, met in Brussels, Belgium, to discuss access to foreign law in civil and commercial matters.

The joint conference unanimously reached the following conclusions and made the following recommendations:

1. The conference emphasises the increasing need in practice to facilitate access to foreign law, in many areas of the law such as in family law, the law of succession and commercial law, as a result of, among other things, globalisation and the cross-border movement of persons, goods, services and investments.

2. The conference stresses the need for, and the advantages of, co-operative mechanisms to be developed at the global level to facilitate access to foreign law.
3. The conference agrees that access to foreign law is an important component of access to justice, strengthens the rule of law, and is fundamental to the proper administration of justice.
4. The conference confirms that any global instrument in this field should focus on the facilitation of access to foreign law and should not attempt to harmonise the status of foreign law in national procedures.
5. Any future instrument in this field should not be exclusive in nature, but rather should be complementary to existing and future mechanisms that also facilitate access to and the treatment and application of foreign law.
6. Any future instrument should contemplate a range of mechanisms to cater to the needs of various actors of different means and resources who are seeking access to foreign law, including judges, legal practitioners, notaries, government officials and the general public, in a variety of circumstances, and should be operational in different legal systems and traditions, and address language barriers. Circumstances may include cross-border litigation and non-contentious matters such as contractual negotiations, estate planning, and family arrangements.
7. The conference recognises the opportunity offered by advances in information technology, with a view to providing effective, cost-efficient and prompt access to foreign law.
8. Mindful of the "Guiding Principles to be Considered in Developing a Future Instrument" (annexed hereto) proposed by the experts group convened by the Hague Conference on Private International Law in October 2008, the conference confirms that States should make available without cost to users legislation and relevant case law online. Such information should be authoritative, up-to-date, and also include access to law previously in force.
9. The conference recognises that additional mechanisms are needed to obtain tailored foreign legal information, for example, the application of the information to specific facts, which may require the interpretation of the relevant law by judges, government officials, foreign law experts or expert institutes.
10. The conference notes initiatives among courts of different States to facilitate the requesting and the receiving of opinions or decisions on foreign law in particular cases and encourages broad dissemination of the terms, the implementing procedures and actual experience with such initiatives.
11. The conference recognises that where in the context of adjudication involving foreign law, an opinion or a decision on the application of that law from a foreign court is requested, procedures should assure the due process rights of the parties.
12. The conference notes initiatives in different States and regions establishing and promoting networks for legal professionals, including judges, which facilitate co-operation and enhance access to foreign law.

13. The conference highlights the value of establishing or improving mechanisms to identify qualified experts or expert institutes to assist with accessing the content of and interpreting foreign law.
14. The conference recognises that tailored foreign legal information, for example, the application of the information to specific facts, which may require the interpretation of the relevant law by judges, government officials, foreign law experts or expert institutes, does not necessarily have to be provided without cost to users, and the provision of such services at a cost may enable better services.

Questionnaire on Proof of and Information About Foreign Law

I. Conflict of Laws Rules

1. Is the application of conflict of laws rules mandatory or facultative in your state?
2. Do conflict of laws rules of your state frequently lead to the application of foreign law?
3. Please identify, if possible, the states whose laws are most frequently applied or invoked before judicial authorities in your state.
4. Please feel free to comment further on I.

II. Foreign Law Before Judicial Authorities

(A) Nature of Foreign Law

1. What is the nature of foreign law in your state? Is it considered to be "law" or "fact", or of a hybrid nature?

(B) Application of Foreign Law

1. When, and under what conditions, is foreign law applied before judicial authorities in your state? *Ex officio*, at a party's request, or under any other conditions?
2. Please feel free to comment further on (B).

(C) Ascertainment of Foreign Law

1. How does a judicial authority ascertain foreign law in your state? Does the "*iura novit curia*" principle apply? Or do the parties have to prove the content of foreign law?
2. What kind of means are used to ascertain foreign law? (*cf. infra* V)

   a) documents;
   b) Internet sources;
   c) assistance of the parties;
   d) expert witnesses;

Y. Nishitani (ed.), *Treatment of Foreign Law - Dynamics towards Convergence?*,
Ius Comparatum – Global Studies in Comparative Law 26,
DOI 10.1007/978-3-319-56574-3

e) inquiry to an expert or expert institute;
f) inquiry to domestic judicial and/or non-judicial authorities;
g) inquiry to foreign judicial and/or non-judicial authorities;
h) inquiry via bilateral or multilateral treaties for access to legal information;
i) direct communication of judges; and/or
j) any other methods (please specify).

3. Do individuals or institutions that provide legal information have to have specific qualifications?
4. Is the legal information provided binding upon judicial authorities?
5. Is there a mechanism to examine the reliability of the legal information provided?
6. Who bears the costs of ascertaining foreign law?
7. Please feel free to comment further on (C).

(D) Interpretation and Application of Foreign Law

1. How is foreign law interpreted and applied in your state? Same as in the country of origin?
2. How is a gap in foreign law filled in your state?

(E) Failure to Establish Foreign Law

1. What is the solution in your state when foreign law cannot be ascertained?
2. What are the background ideas or policy considerations of this solution?

III. Judicial Review

(A) Conflict of Laws Rules

1. When conflict of laws rules have been applied erroneously (*i.e.,* the law of State A has been applied instead of the designated law of State B), can the parties appeal to higher courts including the supreme court? If yes, under what conditions?
2. What are the background ideas or policy considerations of this solution?

(B) Foreign Law

1. When foreign law has erroneously been applied, can the parties appeal to higher courts including the supreme court? If yes, under what conditions?
2. What are the background ideas or policy considerations of this solution?

IV. Foreign Law in Other Instances

1. How is foreign law applied and ascertained before administrative or any other non-judicial authorities? Does it frequently occur?
2. How is foreign law applied and ascertained in arbitration, mediation or any other alternative dispute resolution? Does it frequently occur?
3. How is foreign law ascertained in advisory work by attorneys, notaries, etc. (*e.g.*, in contractual negotiations, estate planning or family arrangements)? Does it frequently occur?
4. Please mention any other areas where foreign law may need to be ascertained.

V. Access to Foreign Law: Status Quo

1. Does your state provide legal information through an official (government) website?
2. Is the Hague Judicial Network (*see* "Judicial Communications" at http://www.hcch.net/index_en.php?act=text.display&tid=21), the European Judicial Network (EJN) (http://ec.europa.eu/civiljustice/index_en.htm) or any other comparable framework available in your state for judges to directly communicate with foreign judges to obtain legal information?
3. Is your state party to any international or regional instruments on proof of and/or information on foreign law, such as:

   a) European Convention of 7 June 1968 on Information on Foreign Law ("London Convention");
   b) Inter-American Convention of 8 May 1979 on Proof of and Information on Foreign Law ("Montevideo Convention");
   c) Convention of 22 January 1993 on Legal Assistance and Legal Relations in Civil, Family and Criminal Matters ("Minsk Convention"); and/or
   d) Any other bilateral or multilateral treaties? (Please specify and briefly explain.)

4. Are there any other international or regional settings to facilitate access to foreign law?
5. Are these international/regional instruments or settings frequently used? If available, please include statistical data.
6. Do these international/regional instruments or settings work well to facilitate access to foreign law?
7. If not, why? Are there shortcomings or drawbacks in the existing system (*e.g.*, time-consuming; lack of reliability; lack of tailored information; difficulties of translation)?
8. Please feel free to comment further on V.

VI. Access to Foreign Law: Further Developments

(A) Practical Need

1. In your opinion, is there a need to improve access to foreign law? If yes, for whom in particular:
   a) judicial authorities;
   b) administrative and other non-judicial authorities;
   c) arbitrators;
   d) attorneys;
   e) notaries;
   f) parties, especially those who cannot afford costly measures; and/or
   g) any other stake holders? (Please specify.)
2. In which circumstances is access to foreign law most needed in your state? If possible, please specify and describe:
   a) in the context of international relocation;
   b) before doing business abroad;
   c) execution of a will;
   d) contractual negotiations;
   e) in the course of arbitration;
   f) in the course of litigation; and/or
   g) any other circumstances (please describe).
3. In what areas of law is access to foreign law most needed in your state (*e.g.*, commercial law, family law, law of succession, etc.)? If possible, please specify and describe.
4. If your state consists of more than one legal system, has there been any need to improve access to legal information on other jurisdictions?
5. Please feel free to comment further on (A).

(B) Conflict of Laws Solutions

1. Do you think that the conflict of laws rules of your state should be modified *de lege ferenda* to reduce the number of cases in which foreign law is applied? If yes, how and why?
2. Do you think that the treatment of foreign law in your state (especially whether or not to apply it *ex officio*) should be changed *de lege ferenda*? If yes, how and why? Should it apply to the entire areas of law or only limited to some areas (*e.g.*, contracts)?
3. Do you think international or regional instruments that unify the treatment of foreign law would be useful?
4. Please feel free to comment further on (B).

(C) Methods of Facilitating Access to Foreign Law

1. Do you think international or regional instruments that establish administrative and/or judicial cooperation to exchange information on participating states' law are useful tools to facilitate access to foreign law?
2. If yes, what would be the appropriate structure and mechanisms of such instruments? (If applicable, please also consider your answer to V (5)–(7)).
   a) Should such international instruments be open not only to judicial authorities, but also to individuals and/or any other authorities?
   b) Should it be allowed that a request be directly sent to the competent authority or designated expert body of the foreign state, instead of being transmitted by the competent authority of the requesting state?
   c) Should the answer provided by the requested state not be binding?
   d) Should services on legal information be provided without costs?
   e) Are there any other factors to be taken into consideration? (Please specify.)
3. Are there any other feasible methods of facilitating access to foreign law? For example:
   a) enhancing direct communication between judges;
   b) establishing networks for other legal professionals (*e.g.*, law firms);
   c) identifying qualified experts or expert institutes (*e.g.*, creating a list of experts);
   d) providing information on national laws on the Internet; and/or
   e) any other methods (please specify).
4. If your state consists of more than one legal system, what kind of methods do you think would be useful to facilitate access to legal information on other jurisdictions?
5. Please feel free to deliver any other comments on (C).

Printed by Printforce, the Netherlands